China's Innovation Challe*

G000300559

The miracle growth of the Chinese economy has decreased from a compound annual growth rate of 10 percent to less than 7 percent by 2015. The two engines of growth – export on a scale never before witnessed and massive infrastructure investments – are reaching the point of diminishing returns. This poses the central question explored in this book – can China escape the middle-income trap? Assuming current political arrangements remain unchanged and that it does not or cannot adopt Western sociopolitical economic regimes, can China develop an indigenous growth model centered on innovation?

This compilation gathers leading Chinese and international scholars to consider the daunting challenges and complexities of building an innovation-driven Chinese growth model. Providing several comprehensive perspectives, it examines key areas such as the institutional system, technology, sociocultural forces, and national policy. The analyses and their conclusions range from strong optimism to deep pessimism about China's future.

ARIE Y. LEWIN is Professor Emeritus of Strategy and International Business at Duke University, and Editor-in-Chief of the journal *Management and Organization Review* as well as Distinguished Visiting Professor at Shanghai Jiao Tong University. His research focuses on organization adaption and renewal, co-evolution, and the globalization of innovation.

MARTIN KENNEY is a professor at the University of California, Davis, and Senior Project Director at the Berkeley Roundtable on the International Economy. His research focuses on entrepreneurship, venture capital, innovation, and university–industry relations in Silicon Valley and East Asia.

JOHANN PETER MURMANN is Professor of Strategic Management at the Australian Graduate School of Management, part of the UNSW Australia Business School. He is a senior editor of the journal *Management and Organization Review*. His research focuses on the role of innovation in the development of industries.

China's Innovation Challenge

Overcoming the Middle-Income Trap

Edited by

ARIE Y. LEWIN

MARTIN KENNEY

JOHANN PETER MURMANN

CAMBRIDGE
UNIVERSITY PRESS

CAMBRIDGE
UNIVERSITY PRESS

University Printing House, Cambridge CB2 8BS, United Kingdom

Cambridge University Press is part of the University of Cambridge.

It furthers the University's mission by disseminating knowledge in the pursuit of education, learning and research at the highest international levels of excellence.

www.cambridge.org
Information on this title: www.cambridge.org/9781107566293

© Cambridge University Press 2016

First published 2016

Printed in the United Kingdom by Clays, St Ives plc

A catalog record for this publication is available from the British Library

Library of Congress Cataloging in Publication data
Lewin, Arie Y., 1935– editor. | Kenney, Martin, editor. | Murmann, Johann Peter, 1967– editor.
China's innovation challenge : overcoming the middle-income trap / edited by Arie Y. Lewin, Martin Kenney, Johann Peter Murmann.
Cambridge, United Kingdom : Cambridge University Press, 2016.
LCCN 2015047143 | ISBN 9781107127128 (hardback)
LCSH: Technological innovations – Economic aspects – China. | Economic development – China. | China – Economic policy. | China – Economic conditions. | BISAC: BUSINESS & ECONOMICS / International / General.
LCC HC430.T4 C4637 2016 | DDC 338.951–dc23
LC record available at http://lccn.loc.gov/2015047143

ISBN 978-1-107-12712-8 Hardback
ISBN 978-1-107-56629-3 Paperback

Contents

List of figures	*page* vii
List of tables	ix
List of contributors	x
Preface	xvii
1	China's innovation challenge: an introduction	1
	ARIE Y. LEWIN, MARTIN KENNEY, AND JOHANN PETER MURMANN	
2	New structural economics: the future of the Chinese economy	32
	JUSTIN YIFU LIN	
3	Impact of China's invisible societal forces on its intended evolution	56
	GORDON REDDING	
4	The road ahead for China: implications from South Korean's experience	87
	MICHAEL A. WITT	
5	Innovation and technological specialization of Chinese industry	108
	KEUN LEE	
6	China's political economy: prospects for technological innovation-based growth	121
	DOUGLAS B. FULLER	
7	Transforming China's IP system to stimulate innovation	152
	MENITA LIU CHENG AND CAN HUANG	
8	Building the innovation capacity of SMEs in China	189
	JOHN CHILD	

9   Who benefits when MNEs partner with local enterprises in
    China?   219
    SIMON C. COLLINSON

10 Advantages and challenges for Chinese MNEs in global
    competition   248
    YVES DOZ AND KEELEY WILSON

11 Emerging trends in global sourcing of innovation   267
    SILVIA MASSINI, KEREN CASPIN-WAGNER, AND
    ELIZA CHILIMONIUK-PRZEZDZIECKA

12 Why is China failing to leapfrog India's IT outsourcing
    industry?   298
    WEIDONG XIA, MARY ANN VON GLINOW, AND
    YINGXIA LI

13 Barriers to organizational creativity in Chinese companies   339
    ZHI-XUE ZHANG AND WEIGUO ZHONG

14 Institutional and cultural contexts of creativity and
    innovation in China   368
    CHI-YUE CHIU, SHYHNAN LIOU, AND LETTY Y.-Y.
    KWAN

15 Reframing research for cross-cultural management   394
    ROSALIE L. TUNG

16 China's innovation challenge: concluding reflections   418
    ARIE Y. LEWIN, MARTIN KENNEY, AND JOHANN
    PETER MURMANN

Bibliography   426
Index   469

For further information on the project, please see:
http://chinas-innovation-challenge.news
https://www.facebook.com/china.innovation.challenge/

Figures

1.1 USPTO utility patents granted for selected countries
(1963–2014) *page* 7
1.2 Chinese government funding for R&D in universities
and research institutes (in billions of yuan) (2004–2013) 9
1.3 Domestic S&T papers by higher education, and Chinese
S&T papers published in international journals and
indexed by SCI and EI (in thousands of papers)
(2001–2013) 10
1.4 Bachelor's degrees awarded in natural sciences and
engineering in the United States and various countries
by year (2000–2010) (in thousands) 13
1.5 PhDs awarded in natural sciences and engineering in the
United States and various countries by year (2000–2010) 14
3.1 Summary of findings from the World Values Surveys
overlapped with development implications and religious
or other identifying heritages 65
4.1 Per capita GDP and institutional quality for 166
economies (2013) 88
4.2 Business system model 93
4.3 A simplified representation of the Chinese business
system 94
4.4 A simplified presentation of the Korean business system 97
4.5 Per capita GDP and democracy for 141 economies 100
5.1 Cycle time of technology shown in US patents by China
and Korea/Taiwan 116
7.1 Invention patent applications for country office statistics
(1995–2013) 155
7.2 Volume of patent applications (1995–2013) 169
7.3 Case volume of utility model patents examined by
China's patent reexamination board (2000–2013) 174

9.1 Recombinations of location-specific and firm-specific
assets leading to new ownership advantages 229
9.2 The respective innovation benefits for MNEs and their
local partners in China 232
11.1 Location of service providers, by region, (a) 2007 and (b)
2012 274
11.2 Locations of R&D processes (2012) (top 15 locations,
% of all locations) 274
11.3 Locations of engineering processes (2012) (top 15
locations, % of all locations) 275
11.4 Locations of product design (2012) (top 15 locations,
% of all locations) 275
11.5 Evolution of offshoring processes in (a) India
(1985–2012) and (b) China (1992–2012) 276
11.6 Number of researchers in selected countries
(2000–2013) 280
11.7 Gross domestic expenditure on R&D in total (PPP
dollars – current prices) 282
11.8 Gross domestic expenditure on R&D from foreign
business enterprises (PPP dollars – current prices) 282
11.9 R&D intensity (GERD as % GDP) (2003 and 2013) 283
11.10 Company and other nonfederal funds for industrial
R&D performed in China and India by majority-owned
US foreign affiliates (in million USD) 283
11.11 Technology creation in China and India: dependence on
developed economies 284
11.12 Patent applications filed under the Patent Cooperation
Treaty by Chinese and Indian residents and non-
residents (1990–2012) 285
11.13 Patent applications filed under the Patent Cooperation
Treaty by countries in selected technologies – change in
2011 compared to 2003 (2003 = 100) 286
13.1 Comparisons between Jiangsu and Guangdong on
innovation (patent application) 352
14.1 Four country clusters identified by the differences and
similarities of six types of innovation outputs 371
14.2 Differences among the four clusters of countries in their
performance on knowledge creation, knowledge impact,
and knowledge diffusion based on GII-2013 data 373

Tables

5.1 US patents granted to selected countries (1981–2010) *page* 113

7.1 China's gross national expenditure on R&D (GERD) and Government S&T Appropriation Fund Statistics (2004–2013) 160

7.2 Sources of university gross national expenditure on R&D (GERD) (2009–2013) (in CNY 100 million and percent) 161

7.3 Volume of university technology transfers (2003–2013) 162

7.4 Value of university technology transfers (2003–2013) 163

7.5 Statistics on patent invalidation (2008–2013) 172

7.6 Statistics on patent invalidation cases and resolution (2008–2011) 173

7.7 Utility model patent statistics on patent invalidation cases and distribution of outcomes (2000–2013) 174

9.1 Four types of firm-specific advantage 228

11.1 Sourcing models 269

11.2 Cooperation in innovation by enterprise manufacturing sector (average EU28) and company size (2010–2012) (in %) 272

11.3 Innovation systems and policies of India and China 278

11.4 Use of freelancers in China and India (data of one online marketplace for 2011–2013) 291

12.1 Evolution of global outsourcing 299

12.2 Model cities' three- to five-year goals and policies 309

13.1 Differences in factors related to entrepreneurial spirit across representative regions 350

13.2 Summary of Tencent and Huawei strategies aimed at developing innovation 361

Contributors

Keren Caspin-Wagner is a research associate at Duke University, USA, and Director of Research at ORN (Offshoring Research Network). Her research interests include open innovation and crowdsourcing, creativity and innovation, behavioral strategy, and entrepreneurship. Her current research is focused on the effects of online marketplaces for STEM (science, technology, engineering, and mathematics) talent on individuals, organizations, and society.

John Child is a professor of commerce at the Birmingham Business School, University of Birmingham, and is also a professor at Lingnan University College, Sun Yat-sen University, and the Plymouth Business School, University of Plymouth. He has been Editor-in-Chief of *Organization Studies* and a Senior Editor of *Management and Organization Studies*. His areas of research are organization studies and international business. He is currently working on the internationalization of small and medium-size enterprises (SMEs) and the negative social consequences of hierarchy.

Eliza Chilimoniuk-Przezdziecka is an assistant professor at the Institute of International Economics, Warsaw School of Economics, Poland. Her research is focused on foreign direct investment as well as offshoring, and their effects in home and host economies. She regularly teaches International Economics in Warsaw School of Economics, Poland, and Offshoring from Business Perspective in Trier University, Germany.

Chi-Yue Chiu is Choh-Ming Li Professor of Psychology and Dean of Social Science at the Chinese University of Hong Kong. His current research focuses on cultures as knowledge traditions and the social-cognitive processes and evolution of social consensus. He is also interested in the dynamic interactions of cultural identification and cultural knowledge traditions and the implications of such interactions on cultural competence and intercultural relations.

Simon C. Collinson is the Dean of Birmingham Business School and Professor of International Business and Innovation at the University of Birmingham. He is a council member of the UK ESRC and sits on the executive board of the Chartered Association of Business Schools. His research spans the fields of regional systems of innovation, China, organizational complexity, and international comparisons of multinational enterprises. Until recently, he was a visiting professor at Zhejiang University, China.

Yves Doz is the Solvay Chaired Professor at INSEAD and a professor of strategic management. He has researched and published widely on the strategy and organization of multinational companies. His books include *The Multinational Mission*, with C.K. Prahalad, *From Global to Metanational*, with Jose Santos and Peter Williamson, *Fast Strategy*, with Mikko Kosonen, and most recently *Managing Global Innovation*, with Keeley Wilson. He is a Fellow of the Academy of Management, of the Academy of International Business, and of the Strategic Management Society.

Douglas B. Fuller is a Zhejiang Province One Thousand Talents Program Professor in the Department of Business Administration of Zhejiang University's School of Management. His research interests include technology policy, technology strategy, comparative political economy, East Asian politics, and international business. He has a book (forthcoming) – *Paper Tigers, Hidden Dragons* – on how China's uneven institutional terrain shapes firm and national technological trajectories.

Can Huang is a professor and co-director of the Institute for Intellectual Property Management at the School of Management, Zhejiang University, China. His research interests include innovation management, intellectual property rights, and science and technology policy. He was a senior research fellow at the United Nations University-MERIT in Maastricht, the Netherlands, and holds a PhD in Industrial Management from the University of Aveiro, Portugal, an MS in Engineering, and a BA in Economics from Renmin University of China.

Martin Kenney is a professor in Community and Regional Development at the University of California, Davis, and a senior project director at the Berkeley Roundtable on the International Economy.

His interests are in entrepreneurship, venture capital, innovation, university–industry relations, and the evolution of Silicon Valley. His books include *Biotechnology: The University-Industrial Complex* (1986), *Breakthrough Illusion* (1990), *Beyond Mass Production* (1993), *Understanding Silicon Valley* (2000), *Locating Global Advantage* (2004), and *Public Universities and Regional Growth* (2014). He has been a visiting professor at Cambridge, Hitotsubashi, Kobe, Osaka City, Stanford, and Tokyo universities and the Copenhagen Business School.

Letty Y.-Y. Kwan is a research assistant professor in the Department of Psychology at the Chinese University of Hong Kong. Her research focuses on how individuals perceive their own and others' cultures and the psychological implications of such perceptions. Her research explicates the different social functions of culture, specifically on trust relations and creative processes.

Keun Lee is a professor of economics at the Seoul National University. He obtained PhD degree from the University of California, Berkeley. He has been awarded the 2014 Schumpeter Prize for his monograph on Schumpeterian Analysis of Economic Catch-up by the International Schumpeter Society. He is also the president-elect of this Society.

Arie Y. Lewin is Professor Emeritus Strategy and International Business Duke University. He has been a visiting scholar at Hitotsubashi, Rotterdam School of Management, Uppsala Business School, St. Gallen University, and University of Manchester Business School. He is a Fellow Academy of International Business and has received the Inaugural Academy of Management Trail Blazer Award, the Academy of Management Distinguished Service Award. He was the founding editor of *Organization Science* and the editor-in-chief of the *Journal of International Business Studies* and presently is the editor-in-chief of *Management Organization Review*. His research focuses on organization adaptation and renewal, co-evolution and the globalization of innovation.

Yingxia Li is an associate professor at Beijing Union University. Her research is focused on project management in outsourcing context. She is a member of the Expert Council of the Occupational Skill Testing Authority of the Chinese Ministry of Human Resources and Social Security.

Justin Yifu Lin is a professor and honorary dean at the National School of Development, Peking University. He was the chief economist of the World Bank, 2008–2012, and founding director of the China Center for Economic Research (CCER) at Peking University. He is a corresponding fellow of the British Academy and a fellow of the Academy of Sciences for the Developing World.

Shyhnan Liou is an associate professor at the Institute of Creative Industry Design, National Cheng Kung University, Taiwan. His research interests are innovation, entrepreneurship, and organizational behavior.

Menita Liu Cheng is a post-doctoral research fellow at Zhejiang University School of Management's Institute for Intellectual Property Management in China. Her research interests include national technology and innovation policies and their effects on corporate strategies. She holds a PhD in business strategy from Peking University and a bachelor's in science from Purdue University. She is recognized as a distinguished international scholar by the PRC Government and was awarded a full scholarship for her research on corporate entities in China during her doctorate career.

Silvia Massini is a professor of economics and management of innovation at the Alliance Manchester Business School, University of Manchester, and a director of the Manchester Institute of Innovation Research. Her research focuses on adoption, adaptation, and diffusion of technological, organizational, and management innovations; dynamics of innovators and imitators; absorptive capacity routines and capabilities; intellectual property strategies; and global sourcing of innovation. She has published her research in such journals as *Research Policy, Organization Science, Journal of International Business Studies, Organization Studies, Regional Studies, Academy of Management Perspectives, Industry and Innovation,* and *Small Business Economics.* She is a senior editor of the journal *Management and Organization Review.*

Johann Peter Murmann is a professor of strategic management at the Australian Graduate School of Management UNSW Australia Business School. Earlier he was on the faculty of Northwestern University's Kellogg School of Management and has held visiting scholar positions at many universities around the world, such as the Wharton School, University of Pennsylvania, Harvard Business School, and Fudan

University. He is a senior editor of the journal *Management and Organization Review*. A key focus area in his research is the role of innovation in the development of industries. His book *Knowledge and Competitive Advantage: The Coevolution of Firms, Technology and National Institutions* received the 2004 Joseph Schumpeter Prize.

Gordon Redding is based in London as Visiting Professorial Fellow at University College London and is former director of the University of Hong Kong Business School, the INSEAD Euro-Asia Centre, and the HEAD Foundation, Singapore. His work has been mainly on the comparison of systems of capitalism, with a special interest in those of the Chinese. He is now working on a general theory of the role of education in societal progress. His work is within socio-economics, with a bias toward the inclusion of cultural influences.

Rosalie L. Tung is the Ming and Stella Wong Professor of International Business at the Beedie School of Business, Simon Fraser University. She also held the Wisconsin Distinguished Professorship at the University of Wisconsin and was on the faculty at the Wharton School. She served as the 2003–2004 President of the Academy of Management and is the 2015–2016 President of the Academy of International Business. She has published widely on the subjects of international management and organizational theory and is the author or editor of eleven books.

Dr. Mary Ann Von Glinow is the Knight Ridder Eminent Scholar Chair in International Management at Florida International University. A former President of both the Academy of Management and the Academy of International Business, her research has ranged from *U.S.-China Technology Transfer* (1990, Prentice Hall), to her current work on China's outsourcing software development industry to cross-cultural contexts, or polycontextuality. A Fellow of the Academy of Management, the Academy of International Business, and the Pan Pacific Business Association, she also serves on several animal welfare boards, and is on the Advisory Board of Volvo-Geely.

Keeley Wilson is a consultant and senior researcher in the strategy area at INSEAD, Fontainebleau. Her field of expertise is innovation and her research on global innovation focuses on optimizing innovation footprints, managing collaborative innovation, leveraging dispersed knowledge, establishing and integrating sites in China and India, and innovation regime change.

Michael A. Witt is a professor of Asian Business and Comparative Management at INSEAD. His area of specialty is international business and, in particular, comparative institutional analysis (national business systems, varieties of capitalism) and the impact of institutional differences on firm behavior and outcomes. He is the lead editor of the *Oxford Handbook of Asian Business Systems* (2014) and the editor-in-chief of *Asian Business & Management*, a major journal in the field.

Weidong Xia is Knight Ridder Research Fellow and Director of PhD Program in Healthcare Management and Information Systems in the College of Business Administration, Florida International University. Prior to that, he was on the faculty of the Carlson School of Management at the University of Minnesota. One of his research interests relates to organizational transformation and internationalization.

Zhi-Xue Zhang is a professor of organization and strategy and the director of the Center for Research in Behavioral Science at Guanghua School of Management, Peking University. He received his PhD in social psychology from the University of Hong Kong. Dr. Zhang's research interests include Chinese leadership, team process, negotiation, and conflict management. He has published papers in leading English and Chinese journals. He got the National Natural Science Funds for Distinguished Young Scholar of China in 2009, and received the Best Micro Paper Award from the International Association of Chinese Management Research in 2012. He is currently the senior editor of *Management and Organization Review*.

Weiguo Zhong is an assistant professor of Organization and Strategy at the Guanghua School of Management, Peking University. He received his PhD in strategy and marketing from the City University of Hong Kong. Dr. Zhong's research interests include technology innovation, interorganizational relationships, top management team dynamics, and internationalization strategy of firms from emerging markets. His papers have been published in scholarly journals and won several international recognitions such as Best Paper Awards from the Academy of Management and Emerald/IACMR Chinese Management Research Fund Award.

Preface

Technological Innovation to Play Decisive Role in Driving China's Economic Transformation

> *Premier Li Keqiang, Seminar on Sixtieth Anniversary of the Establishment of the Academic Division of the Chinese Academy of Sciences, July 28, 2015*

The chapters in this volume originated at the Inaugural *Management and Organization Review* (MOR) Research Frontiers Conference held at the Hong Kong University of Science and Technology in December 2014. The guiding approach to this collection is the concern articulated eloquently by the World Bank and the Development Research Centers of the Chinese State Council in their joint 2013 report *China 2030*. The questions this book and its authors explore are whether China needs the massive social and political structural reforms that some authors believe are necessary or whether China can undertake a transition to continue its economic growth to become a wealthy nation using indigenous solutions that eschew reforms based on models adapted from developed countries. While there continues to be a debate about whether "middle-income traps" truly exist (Bulman, Eden, and Nguyen 2014), we accept the basic proposition that continuing significant economic growth represents a daunting challenge for China, as the portfolio of highly effective policies that created surplus labor in the rural economy that made China the manufacturing hub of the world, and created the resources for building infrastructure (roads, railroads, ports, airports, electric power, telecommunications, etc.), new cities, and massive residential housing projects, runs its course.

As China considers various combinations of policy options and reform initiatives, it is clear that it faces policy challenges at every level, from macroeconomics to invigorating new sources of innovation and growth, energizing technological upgrading of existing industrial and service sectors, exploiting and entering new industrial and service sectors, galvanizing a new culture of entrepreneurship and entrepreneurial startup companies, reforming higher education, decreasing debilitating institutional interdependencies, and dramatically lowering intra-economic transaction costs, while improving its quality of life and expanding social welfare and health care and environmental sustainability.

Policymakers and economists in China have been analyzing and evaluating lessons from earlier economic development experiences in Japan, Taiwan, Israel, and Korea and of the city-states of Singapore and Hong Kong. Although lessons can be learned, these experiences cannot be easily replicated by China. Founding conditions, history, sheer scale, and the government system raise serious questions as to their applicability in China. The chapters in this book explore the arguments as to why, why not, and how China might evolve a combination of economic development industrial and sociopolitical policies to continue and sustain its trajectory of development and avert the World Bank angst of not being able to escape the middle-income trap. What is unique about this book is its timely exploration of multifaceted elements of the China future economic development quandary. The book incorporates micro-organizational behavior, macro-organization and strategy, knowledge creation and innovation, and industrial policies, as well as the imprinting role of founding conditions and history.

The book frames a dialectic that contrasts two scenarios. The first, optimistic scenario argues that China can build ever-stronger innovation capability and catch up with the most advanced economies in the gross domestic product (GDP) per capita. The second, more pessimistic scenario makes the case that, without radical reforms, existing Chinese political and economic institutions will inexorably relegate China to the middle-income trap. These two scenarios structure the analyses and contributions in the book. It would be foolish to try to predict which of these scenarios will unfold in China over the next twenty years. The book, however, illuminates the hurdles China faces and what needs to be done to surmount them. We are certain that policymakers are acutely aware that the "new normal" of slower economic development presents complex and difficult challenges that demand new ideas and new directions for change that can take Chinese firms and society beyond incremental improvements in quality and efficiency.

References

Bulman, David, Eden, Maya, and Nguyen, Ha. 2014. Transitioning from low-income growth to high-income growth: Is there a middle-income trap? Policy Research Working Paper 7104. Washington, DC: World Bank.

World Bank & Development Research Center of the State Council, P. R. C. 2013. *China 2030: Building a Modern, Harmonious, and Creative Society*. Washington, DC: World Bank.

1 | China's innovation challenge
An introduction

ARIE Y. LEWIN, MARTIN KENNEY, AND
JOHANN PETER MURMANN

1.1 Why a book on China's innovation challenge?

Over the past four decades, China has evolved from being largely isolated and irrelevant to the world economy to having the world's second-largest economy, and it is widely expected to have the largest economy in the near future.[1] In the process, China went from having a largely agricultural economy, with over 80 percent of population in the countryside, to becoming a major industrial economy, with less than 30 percent of population working in agriculture. Without repeating well-known historical details, the economic liberalization that began in 1978 was accompanied by a national policy that created surplus labor in the rural economy and unleashed a migration to the free-trade economic zones, which became hubs of low-cost, labor-intensive manufacturing for exports. In this respect, China followed the strategy of Japan after World War II, of South Korea under President Park Chung Hee, and of Taiwan under the Kuomintang. Exports were the source of national income that financed massive investment in infrastructure (roads, railroads, electric power, hydro-power, flood control, nuclear power, airports, etc.), new cities, housing, and supporting supplier industries. China also attracted and encouraged unprecedented foreign direct investment (FDI) combined with policies that required sharing and transferring needed technologies. Even as exports increased, a new consumer society was being created that needed almost every imaginable amenity. As a result, it built a foundation for sophisticated industrial capabilities in mature industries that has given rise to globally competitive firms in areas such

---

[1] In October 2014, the International Monetary Fund (IMF) (2014) calculated that, in purchasing power parity terms, China had the world's largest economy.

as construction, high-speed rail, heavy engineering, shipbuilding, and steel making, to name a few important sectors.

Even as consumption increased, China also continued to benefit from very high savings rates. In 1981 (three years after the liberalization of the economy), the savings rate was about 20 percent of the gross domestic product (GDP). In 1988, it increased to 30 percent, and since 1988 it has averaged 40 percent. The high savings rate has been ascribed variously to the social, political, and financial uncertainties felt by households in China due to economic liberalization, the decreasing state ownership that reduced the government's participation in providing social welfare such as health care and pensions, and the one-child policy. Chinese people could no longer count on the government for social welfare, in particular retirement benefits. The need to save for retirement was also a direct consequence of the one-child policy, which places the burden of caring for aged parents on a single son or daughter. Chinese parents also were motivated to save so that their children could obtain a high-quality education, whether at home or abroad. A lack of certainty about property rights as well as the underdeveloped financial infrastructure and lack of investment options for building wealth also led Chinese to keep money in bank accounts.

Regardless of the reasons for the high savings rate, it enabled the Chinese government to underwrite enormous investments in infrastructure, housing, new cities, state-owned enterprises (SOEs), space programs, national defense, and the like. However, more recently the persistent high savings rate has prompted many economists to argue that it has slowed the growth of a consumer economy that would have the potential to shift the economic basis of the Chinese economy from an overreliance on exports and infrastructure investment to final consumption.

This breakneck growth has come at a very high human cost and includes the growth of a huge migrant population; family separation due to the need for parents to leave their children with grandparents so that they can pursue attractive jobs in regions other than the one of their residence; generations of families without access to social welfare, health care, or education;[2] and pollution of air, water, and soil on an

---

[2] Many migrants moving from the countryside to the cities or the new special economic zones were not legally entitled to social welfare, health care, and education benefits that, by statute, were only provided by the localities where

unimaginable scale. The scale of the economic transformation also resulted in the wasteful allocation of resources, manifested in over-building (roads that go to nowhere, new airports with little activity, idle factories, and empty buildings in new cities, etc.) as well as the arbitrary displacement of citizens from land by local and central governments – the last of which created an easy source of revenue as well as wide-spread corruption. Together or separately, all of these threaten the popular legitimacy of the Chinese Communist Party (CCP) and create an uncertainty that could affect continued economic growth and development.

Since 1978, China has also made enormous investments in educa-tion, including higher education. In 1991, China's R&D investment was RMB 15.08 billion ($2.83 billion), or approximately 0.7 percent of GDP; in 2013, R&D investment increased to RMB 1.185 trillion ($191.44 billion), or approximately 2.01 percent of GDP. The increase in the share of GDP overall was fueled not only by the expansion of resources devoted to research but also by an economic growth rate of more than 8 percent annually over the period (World Bank 2015). As a result, in purchasing power parity terms, China has become the second-largest spender on R&D in the world and may have even surpassed the United States (OECD 2014). This is a clear indica-tion of the Chinese government's commitment to increasing the econ-omy's innovative capacity (State Council 2006; World Bank 2013). The critical issue is whether the massive investment in R&D, 74 percent of which comes from the corporate sector (OECD 2014: 292), can be converted into innovations that can increase the value added and the productivity of the Chinese economy.

Although there can be little doubt that, until now, the bulk of Chinese research has not been truly world class, the rapidity of the improvement in breadth and depth is unprecedented (Fu 2015). In terms of technological achievements, China is the first developing country to have a manned space program (BBC 2003), to possess the ability to design and build supercomputers, and to give rise to world-class telecommunications firms, to name only a few.

Since the publication of the seminal paper by Robert Solow (1957), the role of innovation in economic growth has become widely accepted

they were registered as residents. Of course, legal migrants were registered in their new cities and thus were entitled to receive these social benefits.

(Aghion, David, and Foray 2009; Kim and Nelson 2000; Landau and Rosenberg 1986; Nelson and Romer 1996).[3] Recognizing the importance of imitation in the early days of a country's attempts to build an advanced economy (Westney 1987), Ashby's (1956) Law of Requisite Variety underlines the importance of enabling innovation through either the acquisition of new technology or its indigenous development in the new ecosystem. In the early stages, much depends on enabling processes of "imitation" to create the basis for new capabilities (for a discussion of this at the organizational level, see Ansari, Fiss, and Zajac 2010). China has been very effective at adopting and imitating technologies through various means, from FDI, technology licensing, and judicious acquisitions abroad to outright copying. Success at acquiring and assimilating more advanced technologies or entering into higher value-added technological fields is greatly contingent on building the institutions and social conditions that provide the requisite absorptive capacity (Cohen and Levinthal 1990; Lewin, Massini, and Peeters 2009). In reality, there are many instances in which the attempted transplantation of practices and even far simpler physical assets such as machinery to unprepared regions has utterly failed because the necessary absorptive capacity did not exist or because the technological gap was too great (Lee, Chapter 5, in this volume). Thus, the transformation of any economy that aspires to drive growth through knowledge creation and innovation depends on previous investments in building human, organizational, and infrastructural assets so that it can encourage and harness innovation as an engine of economic growth and development.

The choice of Xi Jinping as president of China coincides with a widespread recognition that the economic policies that undergirded China's rapid growth likely have reached their limits. Two pillars of the economic miracle have reached diminishing returns or are near exhaustion. First, the migration of surplus labor from the rural economy to the cities and the industrial sectors is ending. Although less than 30 percent of the population still resides in rural areas, the bulk of this population cannot be mobilized due to age, poor health, and lack of education (see, e.g., Du, Park, and Wang 2005). Second, continuing the massive

---

[3] Of course, Karl Marx wrote extensively on the role of technology in the advance of the "productive forces," so it should be no surprise that the CCP advocates research. However, it is equally clear that before the liberalization begun by Deng Xiaoping in 1978, the Chinese innovation system was ineffective at best.

internal investment rate in infrastructure projects is not sustainable largely because the most productive projects have already been completed, resulting in diminishing returns (or even no returns at all). A case can be made that President Xi sees his mission as continuing and entrenching the hegemony of the CCP. This may be the key underlying reason for the sustained and intensive anti-corruption campaign being waged under the sole control of the CCP (with no involvement or participation by the public at large) and the urgency it feels to continue growth and avoid a "middle-income trap."

The dilemmas faced by Chinese policymakers are vexing. The CCP believes that its legitimacy depends, in large part, on delivering economic growth. For Xi, previously employed strategies to escape the "middle-income trap" entail a transition to more democratic institutions that would threaten the power of the CCP: in his view, the examples of such transitions in South Korea and Taiwan are unacceptable for China to follow.[4] Thus, since 1978, the adoption of market mechanisms for organizing economic activity has become acceptable particularly when integrated with government-driven economic or social initiatives, while political liberalization is viewed with much greater suspicion. Indeed, Justin Yifu Lin (Chapter 2 in this volume) advocates such a policy, combined with an emphasis on technological upgrading, which in combination are intended to increase the value-added output of Chinese industries. Similarly, the rise of companies such as Alibaba, Baidu, Netease, Sina, Sohu, Tencent, and Xiaomi have identified the digital service economy as a powerful new engine of economic growth.[5] Beijing, Hangzhou, Shanghai, and Shenzhen have vibrant startup ecosystems, indicating the possibility that China can

---

[4] Advocates of democratic forms of capitalism are reminded that throughout its more than 3,000 years of history and sixty-seven years of rule under the CCP, the Chinese people have only known and learned to survive centralized authority. A precipitous transition to a democratic form of social and political organization could be as chaotic as it was when the Communist Party of the Soviet Union collapsed in 1991 under Mikhail Gorbachev. The Chinese people have a long-term perspective and the fear of collapse and disunity is a motivating factor for supporting a strong central government.

[5] China has the most successful Internet startup ecosystem outside the United States. However, it is important to recognize that in many Internet-related industries, the Chinese government has closed its market to international competition.

succeed in building innovatory and entrepreneurial capabilities that could evolve into new powerful drivers of economic development.

It is clear that China aspires to – indeed, believes that it must – develop an innovative economy. Since 2005, China has aggressively increased its domestic expenditures on R&D at a compound annual growth rate of approximately 20 percent (from $55 billion in 2005 to $257.8 billion in 2013). However, as many people in the government recognize, China must eliminate the many institutional barriers to innovation and entrepreneurship that still exist, as well as transform its university-based science, technology, engineering, and mathematics (STEM) teaching and research (World Bank 2013).

1.2 Scholars differ in their views on China's prospects

Scholars, however, differ in their view of how easy or difficult it will be for China, with its one-party political system, to develop an indigenous model that will be successful in creating a knowledge- and innovation-based economy.

1.2.1 The optimistic view

The optimistic view is advanced in Chapter 2 by Lin. China has a rich history of invention, and there is no reason to believe that Chinese people inherently cannot be innovative. Before the rise of the West, China was the global leader in technology, having invented paper, printing, the compass, and gunpowder, among a plethora of other inventions, centuries earlier than they appeared in the West (Needham 1954). The admiration of European travelers such as Marco Polo for Chinese science and technology is evident from texts that circulated in the thirteenth, fourteenth, and fifteenth centuries (Adas 1989). However, as Gordon Redding (Chapter 3 in this volume) points out, these centuries of leadership were followed by many centuries of stagnation. Yet, as Lin argues, since the economic liberalization unleashed by Deng Xiaoping (the de facto leader, though without an official title as such) in 1978, the change has been dramatic. There is no doubt that China is capable of innovating (see, e.g., Breznitz and Murphree 2011). The question today is how innovative the Chinese can become, in contrast to the previous belief that China

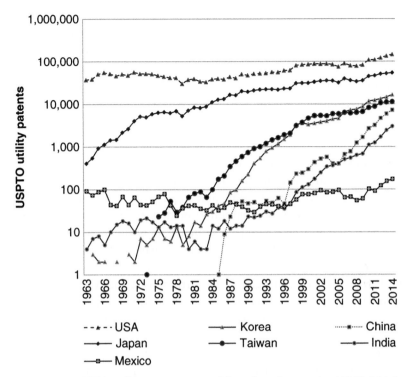

Figure 1.1 USPTO utility patents granted for selected countries (1963–2014)
Source: USPTO, various years.

could not possibly be innovative. To put it even more succinctly, how far can China go?

Innovativeness can be measured in a wide variety of ways. One of the most common measures is patenting (for a detailed discussion, see Cheng and Huang, Chapter 7, in this volume). As Figure 1.1 indicates, the number of Chinese patents registered with the United States Patent and Trademark Office (USPTO) has increased dramatically and is following a pattern similar to the one by Japan in the 1960s and Taiwan and Korea beginning in the 1980s. Whether this pattern will continue for China is uncertain, but it provides evidence for the optimists that China's innovative capacity is increasing dramatically.

China recognizes the imperative of developing and building a new growth model centered on innovation. Most recently, this national priority has been reaffirmed by Premier Li (2015), who has called for greater efforts to encourage innovation in science and technology, stating that innovation is the "golden key" to China's development. He stressed the need for breakthroughs in important technologies, for more people to start science and technology-based businesses to transform their talent into productivity, and for China to create a fair and open environment for these firms by removing "obstacles that hold back startups and innovation."

Upgrading of universities. The first modern Western-style universities were established in the 1890s. After 1911, when the Qing dynasty was overthrown, the new republican government under the Nationalist Party (Kuomintang) made scientific learning one of its priorities and sent Chinese students to both the United States and Japan (Hayhoe 1989). Yet, by any measure, Chinese universities were hopelessly behind the global frontier. In 1949, when the CCP won the civil war against the Nationalists, Chinese universities were in shambles. Immediately upon taking power, the CCP adopted the Common Program, which declared that natural science should be placed at the service of industrial, agricultural, and national defense construction (Hayhoe 1989) and, presumably, any technologies developed should be transferred to the productive sectors of the economy.

After it rose to power, the CCP adopted the Soviet model of economic development, with the Chinese Academy of Sciences specializing in basic research, while various research institutes were tasked with applied research and universities were relegated to teaching (Liu and White 2001). The Cultural Revolution of 1966–1976 disrupted education across the board, especially at Chinese universities and research institutions. As a number of chapters in this volume point out, in 1978, in the aftermath of the end of the Cultural Revolution two years earlier and China's opening up spearheaded by Deng, it was recognized that scientifically and technologically China badly lagged behind not only the United States, Europe, and Japan but, increasingly, some of its Asian neighbors, dubbed "the Asian Tigers." In the years that followed, a plethora of new policies were introduced to encourage "socialism with Chinese characteristics" (i.e., blending socialism with markets) and improve China's global scientific and technological standing.

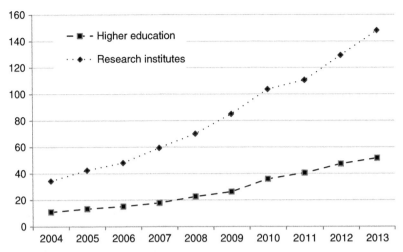

Figure 1.2 Chinese government funding for R&D in universities and research institutes (in billions of yuan) (2004–2013)
Sources: Chen, Patton, and Kenney, 2015; Ministry of Science and Technology of the People's Republic of China, 2005–2014.

In 1978, the third plenary session of the eleventh CCP Central Committee concluded that the connection between academic research and industrial needs was weak, and new policies were introduced to encourage Chinese research institutions to address social and economic development (Chen and Kenney 2007). In the early 1980s, because of a severe national budget crisis, university budgets were cut dramatically. However, in the 1990s, research funding for top universities increased dramatically, in the overall environment of expanding university and research institute R&D funding, particularly through the 985 Project, which began in 1998, and massively increased research funding for selected groups of universities, with the goal of moving them into the ranks of top-tier elite global research universities (on recent growth, see Figure 1.2).[6] This is also reflected in the pursuit of sixteen huge national science and engineering projects identified by the State Council in 2006. Each of them addresses major technologies deemed to be of strategic importance for the Chinese economy, national defense, and overall competitiveness. From 2004 to 2013,

[6] For a discussion of the impacts of the 985 Project on university research publications, see Zhang, Patton, and Kenney (2013).

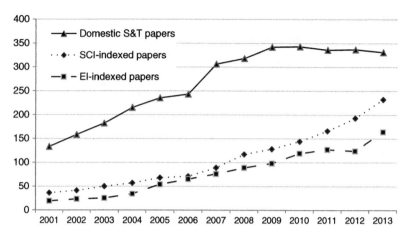

Figure 1.3 Domestic S&T papers by higher education, and Chinese S&T papers published in international journals and indexed by SCI and EI (in thousands of papers) (2001–2013)
Sources: Chen, Patton, and Kenney, 2015; Ministry of Science and Technology of the People's Republic of China, various years.

both university and research institute R&D expenditures increased at a compound annual rate of 18.9 percent and 20.55 percent, respectively – in nine years, R&D funding roughly quintupled.

The growth in research funding was reflected in an increase in Chinese academic publications. The growth in publications is documented in Figure 1.3. Domestic publications increased dramatically until 2009 but then leveled off, in large measure because the Chinese government changed policy to encourage publication in leading international journals. This can be seen in the fact that publications listed in the Science Citation Index (SCI) and Engineering Index (EI) continued to increase. On the assumption that international journals have a more rigorous peer-review process, this growth in citations is an indication that Chinese R&D capacity has increased in quantity and also in scientific relevance.

As Menita Liu Cheng and Can Huang show in Chapter 7, the number of university patents has increased dramatically. However, many of these patents have been criticized as being of little or no value. Much of the increased patenting activity is in response to government pressure for "results" and to incentives that reward volume, not scientific or technical significance. The weakness of university technology transfer has been diagnosed as a combination of weak and unclear intellectual property (IP) protection, lack of research of sufficiently high quality and commercial relevance, and lack of absorptive capacity by Chinese firms (Chen, Patton, and Kenney 2015). Of course, patents and licenses are only a small component of the overall contributions of research universities to creating an innovative economy. These observations suggest that, while Chinese university R&D has clearly improved in volume and quality, multiple obstacles remain to be surmounted before this research can contribute directly to increasing the innovative capacity of the Chinese economy. Yet, indirectly, the experience that students are gaining in world-quality research is providing a trained cadre of individuals with research skills that should be valuable for firms intent upon increasing their capabilities.

Improvements in venture capital funding. Since 2008, China has had the second-largest venture capital (VC) market in the world, and, since 2000, more VC-financed startups from China have been listed on US markets than those of any other country (see Jin, Patton, and Kenney 2015). Douglas Fuller (Chapter 6 in this volume) points out that domestic Chinese VC firms, in contrast to Western VC firms operating in China, are largely unwilling to invest in early-stage firms and concentrate on safer late-stage investments (see also Cheng and Huang, Chapter 7, in this volume, on cooperation between foreign and domestic venture capitalists). Despite the many obstacles, ably described by Fuller, China has been one of the most dynamic VC markets in the world with both domestic and leading global investors.

The dynamism of the local VC-financed ecosystem is due in no small measure to the fact that the Chinese government protects its telecommunications and many Internet industries from outside competition. The enormous electronic and Internet-obsessed Chinese market severely limits foreign competition, creating enormous market openings for indigenous firms. This protection has been positive in that it allowed the formation of a powerful entrepreneurial ecosystem. Yet, with the exception of a few makers of video games, Chinese Internet firms have had little success internationally. Thus, the Chinese VC industry, while large, remains autarchic, funding innovations that, though successful in the domestic market, have little impact outside China. Whether this internal focus will result in globally competitive

VC-financed technological developments or new business models in the future is uncertain, and the recent stock market disorder may not augur well for VC investing in the future.

China has many opportunities and advantages compared to almost every other country at a comparable level of development. We elaborate here on the most important ones.

Size of the market.   For previous global innovation leaders, domestic market size was of great importance. The race for colonies at the end of the nineteenth century was, in large measure, a race for markets (Hobson 1902; Lenin 1916).[7] Of course, overseas markets have been important, but the size of the Chinese consumer and producer markets is increasingly significant. In the case of China, exports grew from only 8.9 percent of GDP to an astonishing 35 percent in 2006, after which it began to gradually decline to 22.6 percent in 2014. It was not that the exports declined in absolute terms but that the domestic market was growing relatively more rapidly.

As Yves Doz and Keeley Wilson (Chapter 10 in this volume) point out, the size of the Chinese domestic market is staggering. Beginning in 2010, China had the highest level of automobile sales in the world, though sales have begun to decline in 2015. In 2013, 23 million automobiles were sold in China, the most ever for any country (Hirsch 2015). A similar situation holds in smartphones: even with a slowdown in sales, in 2014 Chinese consumers made nearly one-third of the entire world's purchases (Kharpal 2015). The patterns in automobiles and smartphones are repeated in nearly every sector of consumer goods and services, such as the Internet, computers, solar photovoltaics, household appliances, and producer goods such as machine tools and construction equipment. Even in industries such as pharmaceuticals, due to its aging population, China is viewed as a critical market.

As the domestic market grew, it also changed from one in which low-quality, unsophisticated products were acceptable into one where consumers began to demand higher quality and design (Doz and Wilson, Chapter 10, in this volume). For example, Apple's largest market

---

[7] Of course, China was a victim in this race for colonies or, at least, concessions, and this is one of the lingering touchpoints of animosity toward the previous colonists.

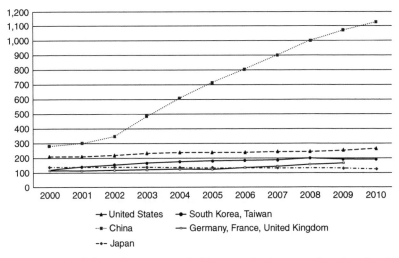

Figure 1.4 Bachelor's degrees awarded in natural sciences and engineering in the United States and various countries by year (2000–2010) (in thousands)
Source: Adapted from National Science Foundation, 2014.

outside the United States is now China (Popper 2015). This desire among many Chinese for quality extends to products ranging from electronics and makeup to food. This desire for enhanced quality and consumer choice offers Chinese manufacturers significant opportunity for upgrading and gaining market share. Thus, Chinese producers have enormous avenues for potential growth.

Science and technology workforce. The sheer size of the Chinese economy and education system and the emphasis on investing in human capital focused on science and technology by increasing the capacity of universities to educate scientists and engineers mean that China has built an enormous STEM workforce. As Figures 1.4 and 1.5 show, the number of STEM graduates is remarkable and has grown much more rapidly in China than in developed countries. As discussed in Chapter 11, debates continue over the quality of these STEM graduates at both the bachelor's and PhD levels. However, the willingness of US universities to admit a significant number of them for further study suggests that some are of high quality. This suggests that China is likely to be able to populate its industry with technical talent. However,

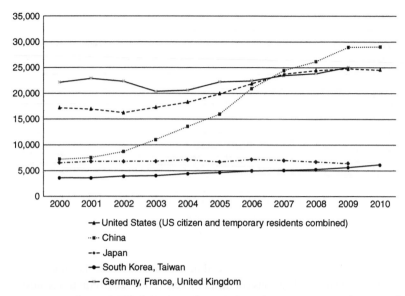

Figure 1.5 PhDs awarded in natural sciences and engineering in the United States and various countries by year (2000–2010)
Source: Adapted from National Science Foundation, 2014.

the obsession in policy circles with engineering talent leads us away from considering how innovative these engineers are and will be.

The overwhelming emphasis on technical talent may come at the expense of creating the innovative designers and artists that make products desired by consumers. In today's competitive, design-intensive world, producing incremental innovations and undifferentiated commodities for low-end consumers is unlikely to lead to the kind of higher value-added activities that characterize advanced economies. As China's economic evolution proceeds, transformational innovation and design creativity will be much more critical than graduating an ever-increasing number of traditionally trained engineers (see also the discussion in Chapter 14). Transforming the STEM postgraduate education system to nurture creativity, radical innovation, and design sensibility is recognized as a top-priority national goal. However, as discussed in Chapter 14, the challenges and complexities of unleashing and institutionalizing such a transformation in the ecology of Chinese higher education are unfortunately far more difficult than training more engineers.

1.2.2 The pessimistic view

Although China has improved its technological capabilities significantly in the past four decades, moving from a middle- to a high-income economy is qualitatively different and much more difficult than moving from a low- to a middle-income society. As Gordon Redding (Chapter 3 in this volume) articulates forcefully, the level of complexity of interactions required in a high-income country is orders of magnitude greater than in a middle-income country. To cope with this complexity – according to the chapters in this volume by Redding (Chapter 3), Michael Witt (Chapter 4), and Chi-Yue Chiu, Shyhnan Liou, and Letty Y.-Y. Kwan (Chapter 14) – China will require a decentralization of power based on self-organization and trust, a process that will be extremely challenging to implement in a system conditioned by history and culture to value centralization, which today is reinforced by the CCP's imperative of maintaining control. At this stage of China's evolution, it is difficult to imagine the new institutional regimes and mechanisms that would bring about an "innovation society." Even if the CCP were willing and able to relinquish its monopoly on power, the pessimistic view identifies important barriers in the existing configuration of Chinese society that will make it difficult to create a truly innovative country that will be able to catch up with high-income countries.

Governance challenges due to size.   The scale of China's population and geography, coupled with multilayered ethnic and cultural diversity, would make governance difficult under any system, but in a centralized system, it is even more challenging. However, since establishment of the Qin dynasty in 221 BCE, by Emperor Qin Shi Huang, China has only known centralized forms of government. Decisions made at the center must make their way down the bureaucracy and be translated into action in different local environments. As Douglas Fuller (Chapter 6 in this volume) notes, the mid-level government officials do this translation, and the outcomes are visible in the variation in the innovation ecosystems of Beijing, Shanghai, and Guangzhou (Breznitz and Murphree 2011; Crescenzi, Rodríguez-Pose, and Storper 2012).

China's size, diversity, and scale create enormous coordination difficulties for a command economy that can be expected to stymie change, particularly when it threatens the discretionary power and control over resources and policy implementation and even over enactment of local economic agendas of lower-level government functionaries. The same institutional configuration enables considerable policy experimentation – a flexibility noted by Lin (Chapter 2) and analyzed in detail with respect to the national initiative to leapfrog India in business services outsourcing, analyzed in Chapter 12. At the same time, China's huge scale gave it advantages in attracting FDI to build the automotive and other industries and global capacity in railroads, heavy engineering, and construction simply because of unprecedented investment in infrastructure as well as in science and technology. But it also has its drawbacks in terms of responsiveness and building shared interpretations of lessons learned.

System of intellectual property.   Many observers in China and elsewhere have noted that the weak Chinese IP regime is an important obstacle to gaining full advantage from knowledge creation and innovation, even though this very weakness has facilitated the imitative importation of technology that contributed to rapid Chinese industrial development. As many of the contributors to this book suggest, the weak protection for IP might now present an obstacle to domestic investment in R&D, as other domestic firms can easily copy their innovations. Cheng and Huang (Chapter 7 in this volume) outline the actions that the Chinese government has taken to solve important problems with IP protection and suggest that still more change can be expected. Chiu, Liou, and Kwan (Chapter 14 in this volume) go even further, arguing that this tendency toward imitation is deeply rooted in group cultural norms that make it difficult to give voice to ideas that are outside the in-group consensus. These cultural factors are further reinforced by an absence of institutional trust and top-down institutional and bureaucratic controls in the R&D resource allocation process.

Corruption.   China, like so many other developing countries, suffers from deep and endemic corruption. Apart from the qualms one might have about Western values-centric measures of transparency and corruption, even the Chinese government recognizes the seriousness of corruption for both the further development of the Chinese economy and its own legitimacy. This has led to serious anti-corruption campaigns with severe penalties for misdeeds. One unintended consequence may be that mid-level bureaucrats and business executives will refrain from creative activity for fear of being caught up in these anti-corruption campaigns. However, the more important question may be whether corruption can be controlled in the authoritarian environment and relatively opaque operations of the Chinese economy and political and regulatory systems.[8] Addressing corruption may be difficult, due to concern that unleashing social movements to expose it could lead to popular mobilization that might tarnish the image of the CCP or even threaten its hold on power. Thus, corruption creates a significant dilemma: escaping the middle-income trap almost certainly requires a dramatic decrease in corruption and the forces that generate it, but a concerted attack on corruption might call into question the CCP's legitimacy.

Environmental degradation. The chapters in this book do not directly address the impact of Chinese economic growth on the physical environment, both in China and globally, but, by any measure, this impact has been enormous and might be catastrophic, especially with respect to global climate change.[9] Rising global sea levels could inundate cities such as Shanghai and Hong Kong and have a damaging effect on global and Chinese agriculture. Moreover, pollution has already had and is likely to continue to have a devastating impact on China including a veritable epidemic of pollution-related illness and a despoliation of land and water resources. Chinese officials are taking these threats seriously as the potential for economic disruption from them have become manifest. As of 2015, China is a leader in producing and introducing green technologies (Mathews 2014). Whether these efforts will be sufficient to offset all the environmental effects of Chinese growth is uncertain. What is certain is that China faces an environmental crisis characterized by extraordinarily high levels of air, land, and water pollution and a rapidly growing environmental movement that might expand to the point of threatening the CCP's legitimacy. Addressing these multiple crises is sure to complicate China's continuing economic growth, even

---

[8] The authors are fully aware that apparently transparent countries such as the United States suffer from forms of "quasi-corruption," such as massive campaign contributions that influence policy and government decisions. However, in most everyday activities, developed nation citizens do not directly experience the necessity of bribing officials so that they will discharge their duties.

[9] It is clearly unfair to blame China entirely for this, as consumers in the developed countries are, on a per capita basis, far more responsible for global climate change than is the average Chinese.

as they offer ample opportunity for innovation (see, e.g., Economy 2011).

Increased global tensions.   Massive changes in global economic and political strength unfortunately have often been accompanied by conflict. For example, the rise to power of Germany, the United States, and Japan in the Pacific during the late nineteenth and first half of the twentieth centuries was accompanied by two global conflicts. Although the world is currently far from any such conflict, Chinese muscle flexing is causing regional tension, which could have unpredictable effects on China's further development and progress. Although possible geopolitical changes are outside the scope of this book, they could affect China's responses if economic stagnation occurs.

1.3 A preview of the chapters

This book explores the opportunities and barriers that China faces in building a more innovative economy at different levels of analysis. The authors of each chapter also present their perspective on a particular policy or research agenda at their level of analysis.

1.3.1 Socioeconomic and political analysis

Chapter 2, by Justin Yifu Lin, was mentioned above in our optimistic viewpoint on China's ability to continue to grow and escape the middle-income trap. In addition to having a distinguished career as an academic economist both in the United States and China, Lin served as the chief economist of the World Bank from 2008 to 2012 and has had close acquaintance with the problems in many developing countries as well as China. He argues that every economically backward country can grow 8 percent annually if it pursues industrial policies consistent with its level of development.

In the chapter, he offers a six-step framework for how developing countries can formulate effective policies for economic growth. He calls his theory "new structuralism" because, as in the development theories prominent in the 1950s and 1960s, he sees a central role for the state in selecting specific industries for development and building the physical and institutional infrastructure to allow entrepreneurs to establish firms that will drive growth in those sectors. The theory differs from the "old" structuralism by emphasizing that a country must choose industries in which the country has a latent comparative advantage – by this, he means those that are not too distant from its existing capabilities and in which it can exploit factor advantages such as inexpensive labor. New structuralism rejects the neoliberal "Washington Consensus" theories that, when adopted in countries such as Chile or Russia, failed to bring about sustained economic growth.

Reviewing world economic history over the past 300 years, Lin contends that all countries that successfully caught up with more advanced industrialized countries implemented policies that are consistent with his "new structuralism." Given that China's GDP is only a quarter of that of the United States and that other East Asian countries at China's current level of development grew for an additional two decades at a rate of around 8 percent before slowing down (e.g., Japan from 1951 to 1971 and South Korea from 1977 to 1997), Lin believes that China can continue to grow at around this rate to exceed a middle-income level. For this to happen, Lin contends, China needs to continue its policy of gradually upgrading its economy by targeting sectors slightly beyond its current capabilities and consistent with its comparative advantages and let the market gradually play an ever-larger role in the economy. Because, in some sectors of the economy, China is already approaching the technological frontier, Lin emphasizes that it will become increasingly important for it to become an innovator in these sectors, rather than relying on imported technology. From a larger perspective, Lin's contribution suggests that China is becoming sufficiently confident to propose a countermodel to the US-inspired Washington Consensus model.

Not all scholars are as optimistic as Lin that China will be able to escape the middle-income trap. Chapter 3, by Gordon Redding, provides a strong counterpoint to Lin's confidence. Redding is skeptical that the overall governance structures that allowed China to transition from a poor to almost a middle-income level will allow it to continue its growth trajectory and achieve the level of GDP per capita of high-income countries such as South Korea, Taiwan, or Japan. Although Redding welcomes Lin's call for policies tailored to the specific development stage of an economy, he suggests that scholars incorporate insights from history, sociology, and political science into an analysis of China's future challenges. He argues that even two countries at the

same state of development can differ substantially in societal organization and thus require different approaches to stimulate economic
growth. Japan had a very different social structure and history from
China's. Therefore, just because Japan grew at a rate of 8 percent for
twenty years after 1951, when it was at the same level of development
as China is today, it does not mean that the same will occur in China.

Redding contends that economic growth at low levels of development is qualitatively different than it is at higher levels of development.
Moving from a middle-income to a high-income economy, in his view,
increases the level of internal economic complexity at an exponential
rate. He is doubtful that China's hierarchical governance structure can
deal with this level of complexity. In his reading of economic history, all
existing examples of countries that have moved into the high GDP per
capita group have accomplished this through a decentralization of
decision-making and a devolution of power to a "middle level" that
can invent new forms of stable order that are beyond the reach of the
central authority. Aside from this devolution of power, Redding
believes that the ability to innovate and trust strangers are two other
societal characteristics that must develop in order for the wealth creation frontier to be reached. Redding does not believe that China can
achieve an advanced economy without fundamentally transforming
these key aspects of Chinese society.

These two chapters, expressing almost diametrically opposite positions, are the ends of the continuum on which the other chapters are
located. They all lie somewhere between Lin's optimism and Redding's
skepticism regarding the ability of China's economy to attain high
income.

While Lin drew his optimism regarding China's future in part from
the South Korean experience, Michael Witt, based upon a detailed
analysis of Korea in Chapter 4, is somewhat skeptical about China's
ability to reproduce the Korean experience in escaping the middle-
income trap. Witt observes that historically China has not had difficulty in inventing physical technologies but has found it challenging to
develop the institutions and social structures that can fully exploit
those technologies to upgrade its economy. He believes that, going
forward, China's root problem is not that it lacks the capacity for
developing physical technologies but, rather, that it does not have the
proper institutions to achieve a high-income economy. Drawing upon
the theory of national business systems, he observes that high-income

countries (e.g., the United States and Germany) can organize their economies very differently. Moreover, he notes that, over time, different national systems have not converged to adopt a single optimal model but, rather, have maintained their differences, thus suggesting that there is considerable path dependence in the development of each system. With this grounding, Witt finds strong similarities between the business systems in China today and those in South Korea around 1980. However, as it moved from having a middle- to a high-income economy, Korea responded by becoming much more democratic. In contrast, the CCP seems intent on continuing its monopoly on power in China. Witt concludes that if the CCP is successful in maintaining its control over all aspects of society, China will fall into the middle-income trap. If, for some reason, the CCP loses control over China's transformation process, the country could follow the same path as Korea and achieve a high-income economy.

Keun Lee has devoted much of his career to analyzing the reasons as to why some countries are successful in catching up economically while others are not. In Chapter 5, he notes that at least thirty countries have fallen into the middle-income trap and describes the various mechanisms by which this can happen. Lee's core argument is that catching-up by middle-income countries requires that they invest in sectors with short technology cycles. Cycle time here refers to the speed with which technologies change or become obsolete as well as the speed and frequency at which new technologies emerge. In sectors with a long cycle time, incumbent firms have a key advantage over new entrants. Hence, it is advantageous for middle-income countries to specialize in sectors with a short cycle time. His theory of catch-up bears striking similarities to Lin's, but he explains that his theory is particularly relevant for countries that are in the upper-middle-income bracket. Lee's first conclusion is that China has upgraded its education system sufficiently to develop the human resources needed for innovation. His second and more important conclusion is that China has specialized in industries with a short cycle time. For these reasons, he is confident that China will not fall into the middle-income trap for lack of innovative capability.

In Chapter 6, Douglas Fuller postulates that many of the very institutional arrangements that contributed to China's rapid development are now paradoxically becoming impediments to further development. He identifies three drivers of Chinese expansion – government gradualism, local incentives to local officials, and, the one he stresses most, financial repression – that are now obstacles to escaping the middle-income trap. "Financial repression" refers to government policies that keep interest rates lower than they would otherwise have been. This repression, he argues, has particularly benefited SOEs and led to a massive misallocation of capital. These obstacles are exacerbated by misguided government industrial policy and, ultimately, the Leninist party–state system. Even though these earlier policies were vital to China's success, he believes future success will depend on whether the government can overcome vested interests and reorganize the financial system and state–business relations sufficiently to allow continued economic growth.

Many observers and a number of chapters in this book single out China's system of IP protection as an obstacle to further economic growth. In Chapter 7, Menita Liu Cheng and Can Huang briefly outline the evolution of the system, identify a number of weaknesses, and discuss policy initiatives underway to address them. The Chinese IP system was imported from the West but has evolved to become uniquely Chinese, with a complicated governance system. For Western observers, the enforcement of IP protection is of greatest concern, and the authors suggest that this is gradually being addressed. The scale of patenting in China is remarkable, as today the State Intellectual Property Office processes 32 percent of the world's total, and this is accelerating at a breathtaking pace – from 2012 to 2013, it increased 26 percent. The authors show that this is driven by government policies. First, China has an intermediate patent category, utility patents with a lower standard of examination and uniqueness that encourages trivial patents. Second, the government offers generous incentives to defray patenting costs, making it essentially costless, and tax breaks that can even make it profitable to patent. The result of the government's intense pressure and the utility patent system is the filing of an enormous number of "junk patents" with little commercial value. Finally, they single out the university technology transfer system for reform. This chapter provides the reader with a deeper understanding of the current state of Chinese IP policies and its likely future directions.

1.3.2 Enterprise-level analysis

In Chapter 8, John Child places his discussion within the context of global interest in small and medium-size enterprises (SMEs), which are already an important component of the Chinese national innovation system. He believes that one of the ways to avoid the middle-income trap is for China to increase the innovatory capacity of its SMEs, which are already an enormous part of its economy. The competitive advantage of Chinese SMEs in the past was based on their ability to produce relatively mature products at low cost. However, their future success will depend increasingly on their ability to engage in product innovation. Child explores the situation of SMEs in China through the lens of four widely used management theories: the resource-based view, the institutional perspective, the network perspective, and the entrepreneurial perspective. Concurring with a number of the other chapter authors, Child argues that the SOEs are particularly problematic for SMEs in terms of competition, access to capital, and ability to recruit top-quality talent. Moreover, along with Redding, Child identifies lack of trust and overreliance on informal networks as blockages to increased SME innovation. As a result, even when Chinese SMEs are innovative, it is in only an incremental way, retarding their ability to advance to a stage in which they can introduce novel products and services. Given the importance of SMEs globally and in China, there is ample opportunity for empirical research that can contribute to theory testing and building in this area. We return to this point in the concluding chapter.

During the past two decades, China has benefited from more FDI than any country in the world except the United States (UNCTAD 2014). Moreover, this investment has gone toward commercial activities ranging from sales and marketing to manufacturing and R&D. From a national innovation systems' perspective, Simon Collinson, in Chapter 9, examines the relationships between local Chinese firms and their multinational enterprise (MNE) partners and the bidirectional learning that results. Technology transfer, learning, and spillover effects have long been recognized as key channels for enhancing the ability of firms, industrial sectors, and economies to innovate and compete. Collinson's chapter, based on survey data and personal interviews, explores the complex relationship between MNEs and their Chinese partners. He finds that Chinese firms gain access to assets, technology, resources, and capabilities, while MNEs benefit from local knowledge and connections. Both the success and the types of learning from these relationships vary widely by industry. Using an in-depth case study of the civilian aerospace sector, he finds that capabilities were not transferred but, rather, were reshaped to adapt to the local environment. He found that Chinese government intervention meant to spur technology transfer and promote indigenous innovation, while often successful, negatively affected the sustainability of those partnerships. This chapter provides unique and granular insights into the scale, in terms of numbers and depth, of interaction and knowledge transfer that occurs between local firms and MNEs. Collinson offers an important perspective on how this form of knowledge acquisition can be transformed into innovation as part of China's efforts to escape the middle-income trap.

It is only recently that Chinese MNEs have developed significant offshore operations instead of simply exporting to foreign markets. In Chapter 10, Yves Doz and Keeley Wilson explore this phenomenon. They note that, in contrast to MNEs from developed countries, Chinese MNEs did not enter the global economy by first exploiting home-based advantages and then advancing to capture and leverage host-country advantages. Instead, Chinese MNEs are pioneering a new model that leverages their enormous and somewhat protected domestic market, lagging home-based resources, rapid internationalization, and access to capital to acquire firms with superior technical capabilities in developed countries. This effort is part of China's quest for foreign assets, such as advanced technology, to upgrade current activities and capture higher value-added segments of the global value chain.

Doz and Wilson suggest that Chinese MNE acquisitions are often in fields with mature technologies and are used to learn, explore, and remedy disadvantages. In effect, acquisitions allow them to purchase the wide varieties of knowledge (technical, marketing, and organizational) that leading firms in developed countries have built. For Chinese firms, doing so offers another avenue for increasing the knowledge content of their products and contributes to escaping the middle-income trap. Doz and Wilson highlight the hurdles that Chinese firms face in building global innovation networks by integrating their acquisitions. They conclude by calling for more research on the new global innovation networks that leading Chinese firms are building.

1.3.3 Sectorial-level analysis

Chapter 11, by Silvia Massini, Keren Caspin-Wagner, and Eliza Chilimoniuk-Przezdziecka, directly addresses China's opportunity to develop a new growth model built on knowledge creation and innovation. It does so by comparing innovation systems and policies in India and China to gain a deeper understanding of whether China is overtaking India as the global source of innovation. This chapter complements and extends the contributions by Cheng and Huang (Chapter 7) and Fuller (Chapter 6) by describing a long-evolving trend that is driving companies in developed countries to seek external sources of service and innovation activities and disperse them across the globe. Companies in developed countries are increasingly sourcing innovations through market channels such as licensing, joint ventures, mergers and acquisitions, as well as through many forms of outsourcing.

The chapter also discusses new trends in which companies increasingly unbundle higher value-added activities, such as innovation projects and outsourcing specific projects to innovation providers, as well as a new trend of employing STEM freelancer talent located anywhere in the world on demand. The underlying drivers of these trends are advances in information and communications technologies, pressure to increase the productivity of product development and research activities, the desire to exploit knowledge clustered around the world, and the need to cope with a shortage of domestic STEM talent. These dynamics frame the opportunities for economies such as China's to participate in global knowledge creation and develop their domestic innovation capabilities to support new engines of economic growth.

The chapter concludes that China's STEM workers are discovering new opportunities by finding employment on demand as freelancers and that the best and brightest, who have pursued graduate education in the West (often with the support of nationally funded research grants), are increasingly finding ways to remain outside the country. Both trends benefit companies in the developed countries while increasing the brain drain in China.

Chapter 12, by Weidong Xia, Mary Ann Von Glinow, and Yingxia Li, is a detailed study of the complexities and challenges that China faces in implementing a specific national initiative consistent with the framework outlined by Lin (Chapter 2). The specific case involves upgrading the domestic business services outsourcing industry to compete globally. The Chinese government framed the initiative as "Leapfrogging India's IT Outsourcing Industry." It was the first central initiative intended to upgrade the domestic business services outsourcing industry as one strategy for moving beyond manufacturing exports.

The chapter describes the history of China's national strategy to "leapfrog" India in services outsourcing. By 2013, Indian business services outsourcing accounted for $86 billion (55 percent) of the global offshore outsourcing market, compared with China's $45 billion (28 percent). Dalian was considered the model city for entering the global market for business services outsourcing because it had already developed a specialty of providing business services outsourcing for Japanese and Korean companies and accounted for 13 percent of China's total in 2013.

The chapter serves as a reminder of institutional and contextual barriers involved in implementing central industrial policies and the limitations of creating competition between model cities when their prior experience has been in building and developing manufacturing export bases. Service and innovation industries have entirely different institutional requirements, as discussed in other chapters, and it will require more than trial-and-error competition between cities to build the capabilities for competing on the bases of knowledge creation and innovation.

1.3.4 Individual, organizational, and cultural analysis

Chapter 13, by Zhi-Xue Zhang and Weiguo Zhong, advances the argument that most Chinese companies are innovation handicapped. The authors contend that Chinese companies – whether state- or privately owned – do not have the mind-set or managerial and organizational capabilities to become innovative enterprises. The barriers that this chapter identifies are the absence of transparent rules for conducting business and the multilevel dependence of business owners and managers on personal relationships (*guanxi*) with government officials, CCP leaders, and other business people at various levels. Managers at SOEs perceive career advancement to be linked to satisfying government-set political and economic targets. Private business owners depend on maintaining "good relationships" with local officials and on delivering performance that is aligned with the goals of the local government. The lack of transparency in the conduct of business puts a high premium on managing the enterprise's dependence on its political and regulatory environment.

To understand the current conundrum, it is important to recognize that, after the economic liberalization in 1978, entrepreneurship grew apace, as firms in every sector could succeed just by satisfying pent-up demand. Firms only had to produce in quantity but did not have to upgrade product quality, have innovative designs, or develop new products – much less surpass competitors with disruptive products, technologies, or marketing strategies. This environment did not encourage innovation. However, several new companies founded in recent years can serve as models for innovation-based enterprises. The authors portray firms such as Tencent, Alibaba, and Huawei as examples of privately owned technology startups that are world class, although in each case success was facilitated by central government policies that excluded direct global competitors. The chapter also notes that certain regions of China, such as the provinces of Guangdong, Zhejiang, and Jiangsu, have historically been more entrepreneurial and can serve as the leading edge in China's efforts to achieve an innovation-driven economy.

Chapter 14, by Chi-Yue Chiu, Shyhnan Liou, and Letty Y.-Y. Kwan, makes the case that the huge investment by China to upgrade its STEM human capital (e.g., investment in university education and attraction of talented returnees) by itself will not create a new transformational innovation-based economy. The authors analyze in detail institutional challenges discussed by Redding (Chapter 3) and complement analyses by Fuller (Chapter 6) and by Zhang and Zhong (Chapter 13). They identify institutional and cultural constraints that hinder the creation of a vibrant national innovation system. Mirroring the analysis by Redding (Chapter 3) regarding the role of "personalism" and the lack of institutional trust, the chapter documents the dynamics of control mechanisms and the role of in-group identity as negatively affecting the adoption of innovative ideas. Even when the government makes special efforts to entice Chinese researchers to return to China with promises of "cultural leniency," in reality the system rewards loyalty and group consensus. Studies on Chinese STEM returnees and of science and technology also highlight the lack of transparency, which acts as a barrier to intellectual curiosity. To bring about more radical innovation, the authors call for institutional and cultural environments that protect individual rights, discourage group centrism, and encourage intercultural learning.

Rosalie L. Tung, in Chapter 15, explores the extent to which scholars of cross-cultural management recognize the increasing importance of China and Chinese firms in global trade. Since the economic reforms were introduced in 1978, China has received massive FDI and, as noted by Doz and Wilson in Chapter 10, has recently begun to engage in large FDI of its own. Analyzing the evolution of cross-cultural research and how it has dealt with the rise of East Asian economies, she finds that the existing cross-cultural theories have significant shortcomings because they (1) treat countries such as China as having a single homogenous population and culture, rather than recognizing the heterogeneity within one country; (2) posit that the cultural distance between any two agents leads to negative outcomes; (3) assume that the impact of cultural distance between two actors is not influenced by the firms in which the actors are embedded; and (4) bundle individual distance measures between agents into aggregates. She concludes that, to be helpful to MNEs operating in China and Chinese MNEs doing business in other countries, cross-cultural research should be reframed and focus on building more comprehensive models of comparative management that are better able to deal with the complexities of the contexts in which managers find themselves.

1.4 Some final thoughts

China is an outlier among emerging countries seeking to attain a high-income economy. Most recent examples of countries that have made this journey, such as Japan, Taiwan, Singapore, Hong Kong, and especially South Korea, can be instructive. But China's scale, long history of centralized authoritarian government, culture, complexities, and enormous contradictions, with tendencies and countertendencies, preclude any definitive attempt to prescribe how China could succeed in making innovation its "golden key" to development. Obviously, regardless of future developments and its ability to become an innovative economy, China is not going away as a global economic and political force. Even if its progress stopped, the entire world would have to continue to adjust to the changes already underway in China.

We hope we have whetted your appetite for reading many of the chapters. While we expect that many readers will want to read the chapters in order, others might wish to start with later chapters and then work their way backward. In our final chapter, we draw on all the chapters to offer some reflections on what we have learned.

References

Adas, M. 1989. *Machines as the Measure of Men: Science, Technology, and Ideologies of Western Dominance*. Ithaca: Cornell University Press.

Aghion, P., David, P. A., and Foray, D. 2009. Science, technology and innovation for economic growth: linking policy research and practice in "STIG Systems." *Research Policy* 38(4): 681–693.

Ansari, S. M., Fiss, P. C., and Zajac, E. J. 2010. Made to fit: how practices vary as they diffuse. *Academy of Management Review* 35(1): 67–92.

Ashby, W. R. 1956. *An Introduction to Cybernetics*. London: Chapman & Hall.

BBC. 2003. China puts its first man in space. October 15. http://news.bbc.co.uk/2/hi/asia-pacific/3192330.stm (accessed July 10, 2015).

Breznitz, D., and Murphree, M. 2011. *Run of the Red Queen: Government, Innovation, Globalization, and Economic Growth in China*. New Haven: Yale University Press.

Chen, A., Patton, D., and Kenney, M. 2015. Chinese university technology transfer: a literature review and taxonomy. Working Paper. University of California, Davis.

Chen, K., and Kenney, M. 2007. Universities/research institutes and regional innovation systems: the cases of Beijing and Shenzhen. *World Development* 35(6): 1056–1074.

Cohen, W. M., and Levinthal, D. A. 1990. Absorptive capacity: a new perspective on learning and innovation. *Administrative Science Quarterly* 35: 128–152.

Crescenzi, R., Rodríguez-Pose, A., and Storper, M. 2012. The territorial dynamics of innovation in China and India. *Journal of Economic Geography* 12(5): 1055–1085.

Du, Y., Park, A., and Wang, S. 2005. Migration and rural poverty in China. *Journal of Comparative Economics* 33(4): 688–709.

Economy, E. C. 2011. *The River Runs Black: The Environmental Challenge to China's Future*. Ithaca: Cornell University Press.

Fu, X. 2015. *China's Path to Innovation*. Cambridge University Press.

Hayhoe, R. 1989. China's universities and Western academic models. In *From Dependence to Autonomy: The Development of Asian Universities*, G. Philip and V. Selvaratnam (Eds.) pp. 25–61. Dordrecht: Springer.

Hirsch, J. 2015. Carmakers fret over China's slowing auto market. *Los Angeles Times*, September 2. www.latimes.com/business/autos/la-fi-0902-automakers-china-20150903-story.html (accessed September 14, 2015).

Hobson, J. A. 1902. *Imperialism: A Study*. New York: James Pott.

International Monetary Fund (IMF). 2014. World economic outlook: legacies, clouds, uncertainties. www.imf.org/external/pubs/ft/weo/2014/02/.

Jin, X., Patton, D., and Kenney, K. 2015. Signaling legitimacy to foreign investors: evidence from Chinese IPOs on U.S. markets. Berkeley Roundtable on the International Economy Working Paper 2015–4. www.brie.berkeley.edu/wp-content/uploads/2015/02/Signalling-Legitimacy-in-Chinese-IPOs-on-the-US-Market1.pdf.

Kharpal, A. 2015. Smartphone market is slowing massively . . . blame China. *CNBC*, August 26. www.cnbc.com/2015/08/26/smartphone-market-is-slowing-massivelyblame-china.html (accessed September 14, 2015).

Kim, L., and Nelson, R. R. 2000. *Technology, Learning, and Innovation: Experiences of Newly Industrializing Economies*. Cambridge University Press.

Landau, R., and Rosenberg, N. 1986. *The Positive Sum Strategy: Harnessing Technology for Economic Growth*. Washington, DC: National Academies Press.

Lenin, V. A. 1916. *Imperialism: The Highest Stage of Capitalism*. Moscow: Progress.

Lewin, A. Y., Massini, S., and Peeters, C. 2009. Why are companies offshoring innovation? The emerging global race for talent. *Journal of International Business Studies* 40(6): 901–925.

Li, K. Q. 2015. Symposium on science and technology strategy. *Xinhua News Service* Beijing, China, July 27. http://news.xinhuanet.com/english/2015-07/28/c_134455919.htm (accessed September 14, 2015).

Liu, X., and White, S. 2001. Comparing innovation systems: a framework and application to China's transitional context. *Research Policy* 30(7): 1091–1114.

Mathews, J. 2014. *Greening of Capitalism: How Asia Is Driving the Next Great Transformation*. Stanford University Press.

Ministry of Science and Technology, People's Republic of China. Various years. *China Science and Technology Statistics Data Book*. www.sts.org.cn.

National Science Foundation. 2014. Science and engineering indicators 2014 digest. www.nsf.gov/statistics/seind14/index.cfm/digest/stem.htm.

Needham, J. 1954. *Science and Civilization in China*. 7 vols. Cambridge University Press.

Nelson, R. R., and Romer, P. M. 1996. Science, economic growth, and public policy. *Challenge* 39(2): 9–21.

OECD. 2014. OECD science, technology and industry outlook 2014. www.keepeek.com/Digital-Asset-Management/oecd/science-and-technol ogy/oecd-science-technology-and-industry-outlook-2014_sti_outlook-201 4-en#page1/.

Popper, B. 2015. Apple's second biggest market is now China, not Europe. *The Verge*, April 27. www.theverge.com/2015/4/27/8505063/china-is-now-apples-second-biggest-market/ (accessed September 13, 2015).

Solow, R. M. 1957. Technical change and the aggregate production function. *Review of Economics and Statistics* 39: 312–320.

State Council, People's Republic of China. 2006. The national medium- and long-term program for science and technology development: an outline. University of Sydney. http://jpm.li/46/.

UNCTAD (United Nations Conference on Trade and Development). 2014. World Investment Report 2014. http://unctad.org/en/PublicationsLibrary/ wir2014_en.pdf (accessed August 30, 2015).

United States Patent and Trademark Office (USPTO). Various years. Calendar Year Patent Statistics. www.uspto.gov/web/offices/ac/ido/oeip/ taf/reports.htm.

Westney, D. E. 1987. *Imitation and Innovation: The Transfer of Western Organizational Patterns in Meiji Japan.* Cambridge: Harvard University Press.

World Bank. 2015. GDP growth (annual percent). http://data.worldbank.org/ indicator/NY.GDP.MKTP.KD.ZG/ (accessed September 15, 2015).

World Bank & Development Research Center of the State Council, P. R. C. 2013. *China 2030: Building a Modern, Harmonious, and Creative Society.* Washington, DC: World Bank.

Zhang, H., Patton, D., and Kenney, M. 2013. Building global-class universities: assessing the impact of the 985 Project. *Research Policy* 42 (3): 765–775.

2 | New structural economics
The future of the Chinese economy
JUSTIN YIFU LIN

2.1 Why we need to rethink development economics

Economic theories help us understand the underlying causalities of observed economic phenomena. More than logic exercises, theories have practical relevance: economic agents – governments, firms, households, and individuals – use them to guide their decisions so as to achieve the desired results. If existing theories fail to help us understand the underlying causalities of the observed phenomena or if decisions based on these theories fail to achieve their intended goals, we have to rethink them. Development economics is in need of rethinking.

Development economics is a young field in modern economics. It emerged after the World War II to guide the reconstruction of war-ravaged countries and the nation-building of newly independent former colonies.

2.1.1 Structuralism, the first wave of development thinking, comes up short

The first wave of development thinking was structuralism. It posited that if a developing country wanted to catch up with developed countries in terms of income and power, it needed to build the modern, capital- and technology-intensive industries that dominated the developed countries. However, developing countries could not manage this transformation. Why not? Economists blamed market failures arising from structural rigidities for blocking such industries from developing spontaneously and prospering (Rosenstein-Rodan 1943).

This chapter is based on the keynote speech delivered at the Inaugural Management and Organization Review (MOR) Research Frontiers Conference held at Hong Kong University of Science and Technology on December 4, 2014.
The chapter represents a synthesis of my most recent views and draws on earlier work such as Lin (2013a).

Structuralism recommended that governments overcome market failures by mobilizing and allocating resources to build directly large-scale modern industries through import-substitution strategies (Prebisch 1950).

The intentions of structuralism were noble, and the underlying theory was coherent. But countries that adopted import-substitution strategies typically fell into a pattern of rapid growth driven by large-scale investments, followed by economic crises and long periods of stagnation. An example was China's campaign in the 1950s to "Overtake Britain in 10 years and catch up with the United States in 15 years." Capitalist countries as well as socialist countries followed the strategies advocated by structuralism (Chenery 1961). The results were universal failure (Krueger and Tuncer 1982; Lal 1994; Pack and Saggi 2006).

2.1.2 So does neoliberalism, the second wave of development thinking

The failure of structuralism to narrow the income gaps between developing and developed countries led to the emergence of the second wave of development thinking in the 1980s: neoliberalism. At that time, national government intervention was pervasive in developing country economies, leading to rent-seeking, bribery, and embezzlement; multiple economic distortions; inefficient resource allocation; and weak overall performance. The contrast with developed economies, with their well-functioning markets and hands-off governments, was stark. Economists attributed the weak economic performance in developing countries to government failures. To improve economic performance and bridge the gap between the developed and developing countries, the latter were advised to build a well-functioning market economy by implementing the measures referred to collectively as the "Washington Consensus": privatization, marketization, and liberalization (Williamson 1990).

Again, the logic seemed sound. But countries that applied this shock therapy often experienced economic collapse, stagnation, and frequent crises, and thus the gap between developing and developed countries widened (Cardoso and Helwege 1995). Growth rates were lower and economic crises became more frequent under Washington Consensus policies in the 1980s and 1990s than under the structuralist policies of the 1960s and 1970s. Some economists referred to this period as the "lost decades" for developing countries (Easterly 2001; Easterly, Loayza, and Montiel 1997).

2.1.3 A third wave emerges: the new structural economics

During this time, some economies in East Asia were pursuing an entirely different economic model. In the 1950s and 1960s, Japan and the four Asian tigers – Korea, Taiwan, Singapore, and Hong Kong – were quietly catching up with developed countries. These newly industrializing economies grew rapidly from the 1950s to the 1970s by following an export-oriented development strategy based initially on labor-intensive, small-scale industries and gradually climbing the industrial ladder to larger, more capital-intensive industries (Amsden 1989; Chang 2003; Wade 1990). However, the prevailing economic theory of structuralism, which advocated import substitution to build up big heavy industries directly, labeled these policies as off the mark.

In the 1980s and 1990s, under the sway of the Washington Consensus, economists branded state-led economies as less efficient than market economies and called for transforming them into market economies through shock therapy: removing all economic distortions by ending government interventions and by leaping in a single bound from a state-led economy to a market economy. They theorized that separating the transition into two or three steps, as China was doing, would lead only to failure. China's dual-track reform continued to protect and subsidize nonviable state-owned firms in the old prioritized capital-intensive industries while liberalizing the market for labor-intensive industries, which had been repressed. Many economists predicted rampant rent-seeking and deteriorating resource allocation. In reality, however, economies that experienced stability and rapid growth, like Cambodia, China, and Vietnam, all followed the dual-track reform approach. Their governments encouraged a market economy or transition to a market economy, as emphasized by neoliberalism, while also intervening actively in the economy, as emphasized by structuralism.

These successes suggest the need for a third wave of development thinking. Policies based on structuralism and neoliberalism failed not only to achieve their goals and but also to explain the rare economic development successes that did occur. The new structural economics that I propose as a third wave of development thinking can explain why the successful economies were all export-oriented and why their successes were predicated upon the notion that both the government and market would play key roles.

2.2 What is "new structural economics"?

When I started in 2009 to promote the new structural economics as the third wave of development thinking, I called for a return to Adam Smith, not to *The Wealth of Nations*, a short-hand way of referring to the results of Smith's research, but to the full title, *An Inquiry into the Nature and Causes of the Wealth of Nations*, which emphasizes Smith's methodology. I proposed following Smith in analyzing the nature and causes of economic development, asking what the nature of economic development is and what its causes are.

2.2.1 Technological innovation and industrial upgrading

Rapid, sustained economic growth is a modern phenomenon, emerging only in the eighteenth century. Before then, average annual growth of per capita income in Western Europe was just 0.05 percent; at that rate it would take an economy 1,400 years to double per capita income (Maddison 2006). From the eighteenth century to the mid-nineteenth century, annual growth in per capita income in Western European countries accelerated to 1 percent, enabling per capita income to double in just seventy years. From the mid-nineteenth century to the present, per capita income growth accelerated to 2 percent a year, shrinking the doubling time to thirty-five years. The impetus for accelerating growth was the Industrial Revolution of the mid-eighteenth century: continuous technological innovations and industrial upgrading made possible the acceleration of labor productivity and income growth that boosted per capita income.[1]

In other words, modern economic growth is a process of continuous technological innovation, which raises labor productivity, and

---

[1] The Industrial Revolution was still in its infancy when Adam Smith was writing *An Inquiry into the Nature and Causes of the Wealth of Nations*. Consequently, Smith paid little attention to technological innovation and industrial upgrading; rather, he focused on trade and specialization with given technologies and industries, i.e., the division of labor.

industrial upgrading, which moves an economy from low value-added industries to higher value-added ones. But taking advantage of the potential of technologies and new industries requires well-functioning hard infrastructure to get products into large domestic and foreign markets. As the scale of trade increases, market exchanges are at arm's length, thus requiring contracts and contract-enforcing legal systems. And as the scale and risk of investment increase with the upgrading of technology and industries, the financial structure must evolve. Thus the entire soft infrastructure of institutions needs to improve accordingly (Harrison and Rodriguez-Clare 2010; Kuznets 1966; Lin and Nugent 1995).

Therefore, while modern economic growth appears to be a process of rising labor productivity, it is actually a process of continuous structural changes in technologies, industries, and hard and soft infrastructure. The new structural economics uses a neoclassical approach to study why different countries have different structures in technologies, industries, soft and hard infrastructures, as well as what causes the structure in a country to change (Lin 2011).

Why do I use the term "new structural economics"? By convention, when we use the neoclassical approach to study economic structure, we call it "structural economics." We call it the "new" structural economics to distinguish it from the first wave of development thinking, which was called structuralism. This practice has precedents in modern economics. For example, Douglass North, who used the neoclassical approach to study institutions in the 1960s, referred to it as the "new institutional economics" to distinguish it from the "institutional school," which flourished in the United States in the early twentieth century.

2.2.2 Factor endowments as the starting point of inquiry

What is the core hypothesis of the new structural economics?

In brief, a country's economic structure at any given time is endogenous to its factor endowments – the amounts of capital, labor, and natural resources at that time. Countries at different development stages differ in the relative abundance of factor endowments. In developing countries, capital is generally relatively scarce, while labor and often natural resources are relatively abundant. In developed countries, capital is relatively abundant, while labor is relatively scarce. Though an economy's factor endowments are given at any particular time, they can change over time. The new structural economics posits an economy's factor endowments as the starting point for development analysis because they are an economy's total budget at that time. Furthermore, the structure of endowments determines the relative prices of factors: prices of relatively abundant factors are low, while prices of relatively scarce factors are high. That means that the relative prices of capital, labor, and natural resources differ in countries at different development stages.

Why is it important to note that an economy's endowments and endowment structure at any specific time determine its total budget constraint and the relative prices of factors? It is because relative factor prices determine a country's comparative advantage. Thus a prerequisite to achieving competitive advantage is for a country to develop its industries according to its comparative advantages (Porter 1990). For example, countries with relatively abundant labor and relatively scarce capital would have a comparative advantage in labor-intensive industries because production costs will be lower than in countries with relatively scarce and more expensive labor.

In developed countries, income and labor productivity are high because the countries' relative capital abundance means that their industries and technologies are capital intensive. If a developing country wants to catch up to the income and industrial structure of developed countries, it first needs to increase the relative abundance of capital in its factor endowment structure to the level in advanced countries. The ultimate goal of economic development is to raise a country's income, the intermediate goal is to develop capital-intensive industries, and the immediate goal should be to accumulate capital quickly so that the country's comparative advantages change to more capital-intensive industries. In other words, boosting a country's income requires industrial upgrading, and industrial upgrading requires changing a country's endowment structure (Ju, Lin, and Wang 2015).

How can a country accumulate capital quickly? Capital comes from saving economic surpluses. If a country's industries are all consistent with its comparative advantages, as determined by its endowment structure, the country will be competitive in both domestic and international markets and generate the largest possible surplus. If all investments are made in industries that are consistent with the comparative advantages determined by a country's endowment structure, the returns to investment will be maximized and the propensity to save will be at its highest. With the largest possible surplus and the highest incentives to save, capital will be accumulated in the fastest way possible. The changes in endowment structure and comparative advantages pave the way for changes in industrial structure and the accompanying hard and soft industrial infrastructure.

But comparative advantage is an economic concept. How is it translated into the choices of technologies and industries made by entrepreneurs? Entrepreneurs care about profits. They will invest in industries in which a country has a comparative advantage if relative factor prices reflect the relative scarcities of factors in the country's endowments (Lin 2009b; Lin and Chang 2009). If capital is relatively scarce, the price of capital will be relatively high; if labor is relatively scarce, the price of labor (wages) will be relatively high. Under an unfettered price system, profit-maximizing entrepreneurs will use a relatively inexpensive factor to substitute for a relatively expensive factor in their choice of production technologies, investing in industries that require more of a relatively inexpensive factor and less of a relatively expensive factor. A price system with these characteristics can arise only in a competitive market. And that is why successful economies are either market economies or on their way to becoming one.

2.2.3 The endogeneity of economic structure, sources of market failures, and government interventions

If markets are so important, what is the government's role in economic development? Economic development is a process of structural change with continuous technological innovations, industrial upgrading, and improvement in infrastructure and institutions. When the factor endowment structure changes, economies need first movers that are willing to enter new industries that are consistent with changing comparative advantages and that are eager to use the new technologies. The risks for first movers are high. If they fail, they bear all the losses, and if they succeed, other firms will immediately follow them into the industry. The resulting competition will eliminate any monopoly profits (Aghion 2009; Romer 1990). There is an asymmetry between the losses of failures and the gains of successes for the first movers (Hausmann and Rodrik 2003).

No matter whether the first movers succeed or fail, they provide society with useful information. The government should encourage first movers and compensate them for the information externality they generate. Otherwise, there will be little incentive for firms to be first movers in technological innovation and industrial upgrading (Harrison and Rodriguez-Clare 2010; Lin 2009b; Lin and Monga 2011; Rodrik 2004). In addition, the success or failure of first movers also depends on whether improved hard and soft infrastructure match the needs of the new industries. Improving infrastructure and institutions is beyond the capacities of individual firms. The government needs to either coordinate firms' efforts to improve infrastructure and institutions or provide those improvements itself. If spontaneous market forces are expected to achieve the transformation without the government taking a facilitating stand, the structural change will not happen at all or will happen very slowly.

The new structural economics helps in understanding why structuralism failed to recognize the endogeneity of economic structure and sources of market failures. The import-substitution catch-up strategy required governments to give priority to capital- and technology-intensive industries, thus defying developing countries' comparative advantages. Firms in those industries were not viable in open and competitive markets. Entrepreneurs would not voluntarily invest in those industries, which were doomed to fail in competitive markets, without government protection and subsidies. Structuralism mistakenly regarded market failures as the cause of developing countries' inability to develop advanced, capital-intensive industries and called on the government to protect and subsidize nonviable firms in comparative advantage-defying industries.

The new structural economics also helps in understanding why neoliberalism failed to recognize the endogeneity of government interventions and the need for the government to facilitate structural change. In developing countries, market distortions were endogenous to the government's need to protect and subsidize nonviable firms that had been promoted by the government's previous import-substitution strategies. Eliminating protections and subsidies would doom nonviable firms, resulting in large-scale unemployment, social and political unrest, and slow economic growth. To avoid those consequences and to continue to prop up nonviable capital-intensive industries that were still considered the cornerstone of modernization, governments often continued to protect them through new and less visible means after removing previous protections and subsidies in line with the precepts of the Washington Consensus.

The new protections and subsidies were usually less efficient than the old ones, especially in the transition economies of the former Soviet Union and Eastern Europe (World Bank 2002). In addition, neoliberalism threw the baby out with the bathwater, vehemently opposing any role for governments in facilitating structural change. Chile was a typical example. A model student of Washington Consensus reform, Chile diligently implemented the Washington Consensus reforms in the 1980s and then removed all government protections and subsidies. Chile ranks high among developing countries on the World Bank's Doing Business Index, based on indicators of the ease of doing business and investing. However, Chile has not seen dynamic structural change for more than thirty years, and as a result unemployment is high, income gaps have widened, and Chile remains mired in "the middle-income trap."

The new structural economics also justifies the gradual, dual-track approach to reform that conventional economic thought labeled the wrong approach to transition. Dual-tracking calls for maintaining stability during the transition and stimulating dynamic and sustainable economic growth by continuing transitory protection of the nonviable firms in the old priority sectors while removing restrictions to entry and facilitating the development of previously repressed industries that are consistent with the country's comparative advantages. The dynamic growth of sectors consistent with comparative advantages helps the economy rapidly accumulate capital and changes the factor endowment structure. That makes some formerly nonviable firms in capital-intensive industries viable and creates jobs for workers who were unemployed because of the shutdown of nonviable firms. Once firms in the new sectors are viable, the transitory protection and subsidies can be eliminated, bringing the transition to a market economy to a smooth end (Lau, Qian, and Roland 2000; Lin 2009b, 2012; Naughton 1995; Subramanian and Roy 2003).

2.3 Growth identification and facilitation: an application of new structural economics

Economic theories are intended to help people understand and change the world. How can the government in a developing country apply the new structural economics to achieve dynamic structural change and economic growth? To leverage the government's limited resources for the largest possible impact on structural change and economic growth, the government needs to know which new industries are consistent with the country's changing endowment structure and which infrastructure and institutions require improvements to enable those new industries to thrive.

2.3.1 Why previous attempts at industrial policy failed

In other words, the new structural economics advocates the use of industrial policy to enable structural change. The government needs to identify priority industries first and then improve infrastructure and institutions to facilitate their growth. Theoretically, industrial policy should be a useful instrument for the government to achieve its facilitating role. In practice, industrial policies have largely failed in developing countries, tainting their reputation in mainstream economics. But if the government does not facilitate the development of industries in line with the country's comparative advantage, new industries are unlikely to emerge spontaneously, as Chile shows. Without new industries, countries cannot achieve robust economic growth, solve the employment challenge, and escape the low- or middle-income trap.

To reject all industrial policy because of past failures is to miss the opportunity of understanding why most industrial policies failed and improving them in the future. They failed because in many cases the governments, with all the best intentions, tried to be too ambitious in supporting advanced industries before the economy had the right endowment structure to support them. Not understanding that a country's industrial structure is endogenous to its endowment structure, governments often focused on industries that were inconsistent with the country's comparative advantages. That meant that the firms in priority industries were not viable in open and competitive markets, so governments had to protect and subsidize them, grant them monopoly rights, or provide low-price capital, raw material, and land. Such distortive interventions created economic rents that stimulated rent-seeking, embezzlement, and corruption (Krueger 1974; Krugman 1993). Haste made waste.

2.3.2 What's needed for a successful industrial policy?

A desirable industrial policy aims instead to facilitate the growth of industries with a latent comparative advantage, enabling them to become the country's competitive advantage in the market quickly. An industry with latent competitive advantages has the lowest factor costs of production for an industry of its kind in the world. This cost competitiveness comes from the comparative advantages determined by the factor endowments. But competitiveness in the market also requires low transaction costs, which depend on infrastructure and institutions. If these are not appropriate for the industry, high transaction costs will boost total costs. Comparative advantages will be latent only, even though the factor cost of production is low. A government that wants to facilitate economic development through industrial policies must help industries with latent comparative advantage ease the bottlenecks of infrastructure, the financial environment, the administrative red tape and the legal system to reduce transaction costs.

How can governments identify industries with latent comparative advantages? History offers many lessons of what to do and what to avoid.

Since the sixteenth and seventeenth centuries successful economies have shared a common feature: their industrial policies aimed to help firms enter industries that had flourished in dynamically growing countries that were slightly more developed than they were. They were able to exploit the latecomer's advantage. For example, the Netherlands was the most developed country in the world at the time in the sixteenth and seventeenth centuries, with a highly developed wool textile industry. The British wool textile industry was immature by comparison. The British government implemented policies to encourage imports of machinery and skilled workers from the Netherlands. Those policies worked. At that time per capita income in Great Britain was at 70 percent of the Dutch level. That meant that their endowments and comparative advantages were not too different.

Following the Industrial Revolution, Great Britain became the most advanced economy in the world. In the late nineteenth-century, France, Germany, and the United States used similar policies to catch up with Great Britain. Their per capita incomes at that time were already about 60–75 percent of the British level (Gerschenkron 1962). In Japan, the Meiji Restoration was also successful with its industrial policies.

Japan's industrial policy targeted industries in Prussia rather than Great Britain. Japan's per capita income was 40 percent of Prussia's but only about 20 percent of Great Britain's. In the 1950s and 1960s, Japan imitated industries in the United States at a time when its per capita income exceeded 40 percent of the US level. Later, the four Asian tigers (Korea, Taiwan, Singapore, and Hong Kong) succeeded by imitating Japan's industries. Their per capita incomes were about 30–40 percent of Japan's at the time (Akamatsu 1962; Chang 2003; Ito 1980; Kim 1988).

Other countries also targeted and tried to imitate industries in the United States after World War II but failed. One reason was that their income levels were less than 20 percent of the US level. For example, in the 1950s China targeted and tried to imitate US industries even though its per capita income was just 5 percent of the US level. With the government's efforts to build up advanced industries, China was able to test atomic and hydrogen bombs in the 1960s and launch satellites in the 1970s, the achievements came at a very high price to the economy. In 1979, when China began its transition to a market economy, its per capita income was less than one-third the average in sub-Saharan African countries.

2.3.3 A new two-track, six-step framework for industrial policy

Drawing on the experience of successful economies and the theory of comparative advantage, I propose a new growth identification and facilitation framework for industrial policy, this framework has two tracks and six steps (Lin and Monga 2011).

Step 1. Identifying tradable goods industries. When the government of a developing country seeks to facilitate industrial upgrading in nonresource manufacturing, it should identify the tradable goods industries in countries that have been growing dynamically for the previous twenty to thirty years and whose per capita income is about 100 percent or at most 200 percent higher than its own. Although experience suggests that 100 percent has been a successful reference point, a larger leap could be justified because technology and industrial upgrading change much faster today.

The tradable goods and services produced in the target countries have a good chance of being those in which the pursuing country has a latent comparative advantage. If a country has grown rapidly in the last twenty to thirty years, the industries in its tradable sectors must be consistent with its comparative advantage. But because of rapid capital accumulation and wage increases, the industries that were consistent with the comparative advantages of the targeted country's previous factor endowment structure will soon lose their comparative advantage. The fairly small difference in income level means that endowment structures and comparative advantages do not differ much between the countries. The sunset industries that are about to lose their comparative advantage in the targeted country will become the pursuing country's sunrise industries because of latent comparative advantage. A country's comparative advantages become clear in comparisons with a country's own experiences or those of other countries.

Step 2. Identifying obstacles.   Among the industries identified in Step 1, the government may give priority to those in which some domestic firms have already entered spontaneously and try to identify the obstacles impeding these firms from upgrading the quality of their products and the barriers that limit entry by other private firms. The usual barriers are related to high transaction costs. Is the primary impediment deficient infrastructure, poor logistics, inadequate financial support, or a limited pool of skilled workers? Obstacles can be identified using value-chain analysis or the growth diagnostic framework suggested by Hausmann, Rodrik, and Velasco (2005). The government can then take steps to ease those binding constraints, using randomized controlled experiments to test the effectiveness of these measures before scaling up policies at the national level (Duflo 2004).

Step 3. Encouraging firms in other, more advanced economies to relocate to the pursuing country.   Some of the industries identified in this way may be new to the country. The government could adopt measures to encourage firms in the targeted higher income countries to relocate, drawn by the prospect of lower labor costs. The government could also establish incubation programs to catalyze the entry of private domestic firms into these industries.

Step 4. Paying attention to successful businesses in new industries.

Technology changes fast, which means that there are likely to be industries today that did not exist twenty years ago. Some domestic entrepreneurs may discover new profitable opportunities that were not identified in Step 1. Consider information services in India in the 1980s. In the beginning, Indian firms outsourcing to US companies used satellite communication, which was extremely expensive. The Indian government built fiber-optic systems that greatly reduced communication costs, helping Indian information service companies gain a competitive advantage over other companies in the world. When new technology brings new opportunities and domestic private firms have already discovered them, the governments should pay close attention to their success and provide support to scale up those industries.

Step 5. Using special economic zones to attract domestic and foreign companies.

In developing countries with poor infrastructure and an unfriendly business environment, budget and capacity constraints prevent governments from making necessary improvements to benefit every industry in the country within a reasonable timeframe. Instead, the government can use industrial parks, export processing zones, or special economic zones to attract private domestic and foreign firms to invest in the targeted industries. Improvements in infrastructure and the business environment within these special areas can reduce transaction costs and facilitate the development of industries with latent comparative advantage. The special economic areas also have the advantage of encouraging industrial clustering, which can lower logistical costs.

Step 6. Compensating pioneering firms for the externalities they generate.

The government may provide limited incentives to pioneering domestic or foreign firms that invest in industries identified in Steps 1 and 4, to compensate them for the public knowledge created by their investments. The incentives should be limited in time and budget allocations because the targeted industries should have a latent comparative advantage that enables them to become competitive in domestic and foreign markets once transaction costs fall. The incentives may be in the form of a corporate income tax holiday for a limited number of years, priority access to credit (in countries with financial repression), or priority access to foreign reserves for importing key equipment (in countries with capital controls). To minimize the risk of rent-seeking and political capture, the incentives should not be in the form of monopoly rent, high tariffs, or other distortions. The government may reward firms in Step 4, which discovered successful new industries by themselves, with special recognition for their contributions to economic development.

This kind of compensation for externalities differs from the protections and subsidies of the old import-substitution strategy that aimed to help nonviable firms in priority industries stay in business. The firms encouraged in this new framework have low factor costs of production and are viable in the market, so their profitability can be raised by improving their management once soft and hard infrastructure are improved and transaction costs are lowered.

2.4 The new structural economics sheds light on other economic issues

The new structural economics approaches development from a different perspective and yields insights into many important questions in economic development beyond those related to the appropriate roles of the market and government in development. The key insight is that the structure of the real economy is different at different stages of development and that consequently the economic constraints faced by economic agents and the options available to them also differ, as does the most effective choice for governments, firms, and households. The same option may result in different outcomes for countries at different development stages.

Here, I'd like to highlight a few examples of how the perspective of the new structural economics sheds light on a few important economic issues.

2.4.1 *Need for a different financial structure for developing countries that are ready for takeoff*

The new structural economics argues for different financial structures for countries at different stages of development. Finance textbooks and journals call on developing countries to promote modern financial institutions – big banks, stock markets, and venture capital – like those in developed countries. These modern financial institutions developed spontaneously in the United States and other developed countries to meet the financial needs of firms in industries that are consistent with the comparative advantages in developed countries. Those countries are rich in capital endowment, and their technologies and industries are the most advanced and capital intensive in the world. Technological innovation and industrial upgrading depend on expensive and risky indigenous research and development. These countries need financial institutions that can mobilize large amounts of funds and spread risks. Big banks, stock markets, and venture capital firms meet these requirements.

These financial institutions are, however, ill-suited to the financing needs of firms in developing countries, where goods and services are produced by small household farms and micro, small, and medium-size companies in labor-intensive industries. The capital requirements for investment and operation are fairly small, the technologies applied are mature, and the markets are established and less risky. Thus the financial structure should consist mainly of small and medium-size regional financial institutions, which can better serve the financial needs of household farms and small businesses (Lin, Sun, and Jiang 2013).

2.4.2 The government's proper role in an economic crisis

The global financial and economic crises in 2008 depressed production in both developed and developing countries and forced firms to shed jobs. Keynesian economics recommended active fiscal policies in such circumstances, to boost demand and create jobs. However, many economists opposed such measures, fearing that budget deficits would soar. To finance soaring deficits, governments have to raise taxes explicitly or implicitly, and so firms and households expect future taxes to rise. To smooth consumption, taxpayers will save now to meet this future tax burden, thus offsetting rising government spending and debt by lowering private spending, leaving total demand almost unchanged. As a result, underproduction and unemployment do not budge, but government debt piles up and the business environment deteriorates. This situation is referred to as the Ricardian equivalence trap (Barro 1974). The debate between the two schools of thought has been endless.

The new structural economics sees countercyclical policy as a way to facilitate structural change. Physical infrastructure is a binding constraint to growth, especially in developing countries, and governments need to get involved in removing infrastructure bottlenecks to facilitate economic development. In this context, recessions are typically a good time to invest in infrastructure for three main reasons: investment costs are lower; infrastructure investments boost short-term demand and promote long-term growth; and the Ricardian equivalence trap can be avoided because the increase in future growth rates and fiscal revenues can compensate for the cost of these investments.

All macroeconomic theories, including Keynesianism, neoclassical synthesis, new Keynesian school, and the rational expectation school, focus on the problems in developed countries. Since economic growth is slow and the economic structure is fairly stable in developed countries, macroeconomic theories abstract structural change from business cycles. However, experience in developing countries provides an opportunity to study structural changes and business cycles simultaneously. For this analysis, I propose the theory of "Beyond Keynesianism" (Lin 2009a, 2013b).

2.4.3 Structural changes needed in agriculture and natural-resource-abundant countries

So far, the discussion of industrial upgrading has highlighted manufacturing. But structural change is also needed in agriculture. In most developing countries, 70 percent or more of the labor force works in agriculture. As in industry, structural changes in agriculture involve technological innovation and industrial upgrading to increase labor productivity. In an agrarian economy, agricultural households produce mainly grains for self-consumption. As agriculture and the economy develop, farmers gradually produce not only grains but also cash crops with higher value addition. The technology, infrastructure, and marketing required for cash crops are different from those required for grains. And agricultural development is impeded by externalities and coordination problems that are beyond the ability of individual farmers to resolve and thus require government help.

In addition, countries with abundant resource endowment, like many of those in sub-Saharan Africa, often have abundant labor as well as abundant natural resources. These countries should turn the rents from natural resources into capital to support the development of labor-intensive manufacturing industries that create jobs and begin to climb up the industrial ladder. Used appropriately, abundant natural resources are an advantage for economic development. The United States, a resource-rich country, owes its economic success not only to its advantages in extractive industries, but also to its development of manufacturing industries. The share of manufacturing in GDP is much larger than the share of extractive industries.

In resource-abundant countries, the new structural economics would recommend that a share of revenue from natural resources be invested in human capital, infrastructure, social capital, and compensation for first movers in new, nonresource industries to facilitate structural transformation. To be most effective, these resources should finance investment opportunities that remove binding constraints on industrial diversification and upgrading, especially in infrastructure and human capital. With the transparency and prudent management in resources management needed to prevent corruption, and an industrial policy that focuses on removing binding constraints for nonresource-based industries with latent comparative advantages, a country's resource abundance will be a blessing rather than a curse on development.

2.5 How long can China continue its miraculous growth?

No country in human history has ever grown so fast for so long as China did in the past three decades after its transition from a planned economy to a market economy in 1979. Its average annual growth was as high as 9.7 percent in the twenty-six years between 1979 and 2014. From the new structural economics perspective, looking forward, China still has the potential, based on the advantage of backwardness, to grow at around 8 percent annually for another twenty years:

1. In 2008, China's per capita income was 21 percent of US per capita income measured in purchasing power parity (Maddison 2010). The income gap between China and the United States indicates that there is still a large technological gap between China and the advanced industrialized countries. China can continue to enjoy the advantage of backwardness before closing up the gap.

2. Maddison's estimation also shows that China's current relative
   status to the United States is similar to Japan's in 1951,
   Singapore's in 1967, Korea's in 1977 and Taiwan, China's in
   1975. The annual growth rate of GDP reached 9.2 percent in
   Japan between 1951 and 1971, 8.6 percent in Singapore between
   1967 and 1987, 7.6 percent in Korea between 1977 and 1997, and
   8.3 percent in Taiwan between 1975 and 1995. China's development strategy after the reform in 1979 is similar to that of Japan,
   Korea, Singapore, and Taiwan, China. China has the potential to
   achieve another twenty years of 8 percent growth. After twenty
   years of dynamic growth, Japan's per capita income measured in
   purchasing power parity was 65.6 percent of that of the United
   States in 1971, Singapore's was 53.9 percent in 1987, Korea's was
   50.2 percent in 1997, and Taiwan's was 54.2 percent in 1995.
   If China maintains 8 percent growth in the coming two decades,
   by 2030 China's per capita income measured in purchasing power
   parity may reach about 50 percent of US per capita income.
   Measured by purchasing power parity, China's economic size may
   then be twice as large as the United States; and measured by the
   current market exchange rates, China may be about the same size as
   the United States.

How much the above potential can be realized depends on external
conditions, such as how quick the developed countries recovered from
the Great Recession as a result of the 2008 global financial crisis, and
internal conditions, such as the elimination of remaining distortions in
its dual-track, gradual transition to a well-functioning market economy
(Lin 2012). If realized, China will achieve the eighteenth Congress of
Chinese Communist Party's targets of doubling the per capita GDP and
household income on the basis of 2010 and becoming a high-income
country by 2020.

That said, China also needs to increasingly become an innovator in
its own right. As a middle-income country, in many sectors that China
has comparative advantage, other higher-income countries have grad-
uated, or are close to graduating, from those sectors – for example,
consumer electronics. If China wants to maintain leadership in those
sectors, China will need to develop the technology/product innovation
when it reaches the frontier. China can then become a global techno-
logical/industrial leader in those sectors. With foresight, China will be

able to gradually shift from absorbing the existing technology to become an indigenous innovator of new technology for driving its growth.

2.6 Concluding remarks

What I have discussed today is obviously preliminary. Acceptance of the new structural economics as a new wave of development thinking requires further theoretical and empirical work. The new structural economics offers a wealth of opportunities for research, and I invite you to join me. I hope this chapter will stimulate the audience to approach economic development along the lines I have elaborated today and bring the new structural economics into the mainstream of development economics.

The new structural economics offers real hope of a better future for developing countries. It makes clear that poverty is not destiny. Every developing country has the potential to grow dynamically for decades and to become a middle- or even a high-income country in one or two generations. But that can happen only as long as it implements the right industrial policies to facilitate development of the private sector along the lines of the country's comparative advantages and taps into the potential of the latecomer's advantage. Countries can grow at 7, 8, or 9 percent for several decades, as the Commission on Growth and Development (2008) found for thirteen high-performing developing economies and as China has demonstrated since the launch of its economic transition in 1979 (Lin 2012).

Achieving such results will require a change in mindset. In the first two waves of development thinking, economists used high-income countries as the reference. They examined what those countries had and could do well (capital-intensive industries, well-functioning market) and recommended that developing countries follow suit.

The new structural economics turns that model upside down. It recommends that developing countries look at what they can do well based on what they have and then create the conditions to scale up what they can do well. What they have is their abundant supply of labor or natural resources. What they can do well is revealed by industries that are consistent with the country's comparative advantages. Governments should create the conditions to facilitate the progression of those industries to a position of competitive advantage so that they can grow dynamically. Dynamic growth will create the foundation for sustained growth, income generation, and poverty reduction and begin to close the gap with high-income countries. Developing countries can do this by realizing the potential of the latecomer's advantage in technological innovation, industry upgrading, and other dimensions of structural change. By growing much faster than the high-income countries they can eliminate poverty and close the gap with advanced countries within one or two generations.

References

Aghion, P. 2009. *Some Thoughts on Industrial Policy and Growth*. Document de Travail 2009–09. Observatoire Français des conjonctures économiques. Paris: Sciences Po.

Akamatsu, K. 1962. A historical pattern of economic growth in developing countries. *Journal of Developing Economies* 1(1): 3–25.

Amsden, A. H. 1989. *Asia's Next Giant*. New York and Oxford: Oxford University Press.

Barro, R. J. 1974. Are government bonds net wealth? *Journal of Political Economy* 82(6): 1095–1117.

Cardoso, E., and Helwege, A. 1995. *Latin America's Economy*. Cambridge, MA: MIT Press.

Chang, H.-J. 2003. *Kicking Away the Ladder: Development Strategy in Historical Perspective*. London: Anthem Press.

Chenery, H. B. 1961. Comparative advantage and development policy. *American Economic Review* 51(1): 18–51.

Commission on Growth and Development. 2008. *The Growth Report: Strategies for Sustained Growth and Inclusive Development*. Washington, DC: World Bank.

Duflo, E. 2004. Scaling up and evaluation. In *Annual World Bank Conference on Development Economics 2004*, F. Bourguignon and B. Pleskovic (Eds.). Washington, DC: World Bank.

Easterly, W. 2001. *The Elusive Quest for Growth: Economists' Adventures and Misadventures in the Tropics*. Cambridge, MA: MIT Press.

Easterly, W., Loayza, N., and Montiel, P. J. 1997. *Has Latin America's Post-Reform Growth Been Disappointing?* World Bank Policy Research Paper 1708. Washington, DC: World Bank.

Gerschenkron, A. 1962. *Economic Backwardness in Historical Perspective: A Book of Essays.* Cambridge, MA: Belknap Press of Harvard University Press.

Harrison, A., and Rodríguez-Clare, A. 2010. Trade, foreign investment, and industrial policy for developing countries. In *Handbook of Economic Growth*, Vol. 5, D. Rodrik (Ed.). Amsterdam: North-Holland.

Hausmann, R., and Rodrik, D. 2003. Economic development as self-discovery. *Journal of Development Economics* 72 (December): 603–633.

Hausmann, R., Rodrik, D., and Velasco, A. 2005. Growth diagnostics. In *The Washington Consensus Reconsidered: Towards a New Global Governance*, J. Stiglitz and N. Serra (Eds.). Oxford: Oxford University Press.

Ito, T. 1980. Disequilibrium growth theory. *Journal of Economic Theory* 23(3): 380–409.

Ju, J., Lin, J. Y., and Wang, Y. 2015. Endowment structures, industrial dynamics, and economic growth. *Journal of Monetary Economics* 76: 244–263.

Kim, Y. H. 1988. *Higashi Ajia Kogyoka to Sekai Shihonshugi (Industrialisation of East Asia and the World Capitalism).* Tokyo: Toyo Keizai Shimpo-sha.

Krueger, A. 1974. The political economy of rent-seeking society. *American Economic Review* 64(3): 291–303.

Krueger, A., and Tuncer, B. 1982. An empirical test of the infant industry argument. *American Economic Review* 72(5): 1142–1152.

Krugman, P. 1993. Protection in developing countries. In *Policymaking in the Open Economy: Concepts and Case Studies in Economic Performance*, R. Dornbusch (Ed.). New York: Oxford University Press.

Kuznets, S. 1966. *Modern Economic Growth: Rate, Structure and Spread.* New Haven, CT: Yale University Press.

Lal, D. 1994. *Against Dirigisme: The Case for Unshackling Economic Markets.* San Francisco: International Center for Economic Growth, ICS Press.

Lau, L., Qian, J. Y., and Roland, G. 2000. Reform without losers: an interpretation of China's dual-track approach to transition. *Journal of Political Economy* 108(1): 120–143.

Lin, J. Y. 2009a. Beyond Keynesianism. *Harvard International Review* 31(2): 14–17.

Lin, J. Y. 2009b. *Economic Development and Transition: Thought, Strategy, and Viability.* Cambridge: Cambridge University Press.

Lin, J. Y. 2011. New structural economics: a framework for rethinking economic development. *World Bank Research Observer* 26(2): 193–221.

Lin, J. Y. 2012. *Demystifying the Chinese Economy.* Cambridge: Cambridge University Press.

Lin, J. Y. November 2013a. New structural economics: the third wave of development thinking. *Asia Pacific Economic Literature* 27(2): 1–13.

Lin, J. Y. 2013b. *Against the Consensus: Reflections on the Great Recession.* Cambridge: Cambridge University Press.

Lin, J. Y., and Chang, H. 2009. DPR debate: should industrial policy in developing countries conform to comparative advantage or defy it? *Development Policy Review* 27(5): 483–502.

Lin, J. Y., and Monga, C. 2011. DPR debate: growth identification and facilitation: the role of the state in the dynamics of structural change. *Development Policy Review* 29(3): 259–310.

Lin, J. Y., and Nugent, J. 1995. Institutions and economic development. In *Handbook of Development Economics*, Vol. 3, T. N. Srinivasan and J. Behrman (Eds.). Amsterdam: North Holland.

Lin, J. Y., Sun, X., and Jiang, Y. 2013. Endowment, industrial structure, and appropriate financial structure: a new structural economics perspective. *Journal of Economic Policy Reform* 16(2): 109–122.

Maddison, A. 2010. *Historical Statistics of the World Economy: 1-2008 AD.* www.ggdc.net/maddison/Historical_Statistics/horizontal-file_02-2010.xls

Naughton, B. 1995. *Growing Out of Plan: Chinese Economic Reform 1978–1993.* Cambridge: Cambridge University Press.

Pack, H., and Saggi, K. 2006. Is there a case for industrial policy? A critical survey. *World Bank Research Observer* 21(2): 267–297.

Porter, M. E. 1990. *The Competitive Advantage of Nations.* New York: Free Press.

Prebisch, R. 1950. *The Economic Development of Latin America and Its Principal Problems.* New York: United Nations. Reprinted in *Economic Bulletin for Latin America*, 7(1): February 1962, 1–22.

Rodrik, D. 2004. *Industrial Policy for the Twenty-First Century.* Cambridge, MA: Harvard University.

Romer, P. M. 1990. Endogenous technological change. *Journal of Political Economy* 98(5): S71–S102.

Rosenstein-Rodan, P. 1943. Problems of industrialization of eastern and southeastern Europe. *Economic Journal* 111(210–211): 202–211.

Subramanian, A., and Roy, D. 2003. Who can explain the Mauritian miracle? Mede, Romer, Sachs, or Rodrik? In *In Search of Prosperity: Analytic*

Narratives on Economic Growth, D. Rodrik (Ed.). Princeton, NJ: Princeton University Press.

Wade, R. 1990. *Governing the Market*. Princeton, NJ: Princeton University Press.

Williamson, J. 1990. What Washington means by policy reform. In *Latin American Adjustment: How Much Has Happened?*, J. Williamson (Ed.). Washington, DC: Institute for International Economics.

World Bank. 2002. *Transition, the First Ten Years: Analysis and Lessons for Eastern Europe and Former Soviet Union*. Washington, DC: World Bank.

World Bank. 2010. "Research for Development: A World Bank Perspective on Future Directions for Research." Policy Research Working Paper 5437. Washington, DC: World Bank.

3 | Impact of China's invisible societal forces on its intended evolution

GORDON REDDING

3.1 Introduction

The argument to be made in this chapter may be summarized as follows. Societies evolve in their own distinct ways and produce their own 'business systems'. These different ways derive largely from the societal heritage, because it shapes the institutions and norms. Such a heritage may stretch back far into pre-history. Societies may also evolve through change, although some contain more internal barriers than others. As complex adaptive systems, they may be seen as products of constant interplay between three main elements: political power, economic action, and cultural structures of meaning, all three penetrated by technology.

As economies progress toward greater wealth, their internal complexity increases exponentially. This new complexity requires adequate sophistication in its handling and such is only available when substantial devolution of power has taken place and when encouragement has been given for the spontaneous re-inventing of forms of stable order by societal actors dealing directly with the complexity. This is seen in this account as an active, responsive, responsible, and autonomous 'middle' within society. In the advanced economy case, it allows a society to go beyond the capacity of central government to respond effectively to the complexity.

To achieve economic coordination and control capable of matching world standards of competitive efficiency, a society needs – in addition to stable order – two strong capacities: *innovativeness* in the form of

An earlier version of this argument was presented at the Inaugural Research Frontiers Conference of *Management and Organization Review*, Hong Kong, December 7, 2014. The author wishes to thank Arie Lewin, Michael Witt, Christian Welzel, Martin Kenney, and Peter Murmann for discussions and inputs on the topic. He acknowledges also a large number of anonymous Chinese business people who have been helpful with their thoughts.

knowledge creation and innovation and *cooperativeness* in the form of being able to trust strangers. These rest on configurations of societal features that foster and support the capacities. The configurations are likely to be special to each society in the detail, but – when effective – will exhibit certain universal features. Most societies cannot handle the full complexity and intensity of a modern economy because they do not have enough of the two capacities. Some are likely to learn and progress more fully. China does not currently have enough of the two capacities and may or may not learn and progress fully. The reasons for this lack are generally not discussed or dealt with in policymaking, as they exist largely in the world of meanings and ideas, and they affect processes rather than tangibles. This does not mean that they can be ignored.

These challenges may be summarized in three questions: (i) Can large-scale industrial and business organization be achieved indigenously at world standards of efficiency by a fusion of *hierarchy* and *innovativeness*? In other words, can organizations engage their personnel in using their commitment and creativity at world competitive standards of intensity? (ii) Can social capital be built to a point where strangers can be trusted? (iii) Can conformity and order be achieved without resort to fear, so can a more benevolent form of domination evolve? Most analyses of China take a partial view and would benefit from a perspective that unites more the sociological, the economic, and the political, even though inevitably less specialized.

The position of the Chinese government remains experimental but moving toward a set of strong regional hubs with much devolved power, energized by competition for key resources controlled at the center, and with uncertainty restrained by the Party members holding all key positions. In these hubs, forms of alliance between public and private and outsiders are proliferating. The private sector remains the main dynamo and source of productivity. It could be argued that this formula achieves the simultaneous loose-tight properties of control necessary in handling great complexity and scale. But it could also be argued that other societies have gone beyond that design into forms of order that extend self-organization much further, and necessarily so.

The range of analyses about China is currently very wide and covers positions of optimism; advice – usually external – as to what is needed next; and pessimism about long-term prospects. Much commentary is colored by the introduction of criteria assumed to have universal applicability, despite it being known that business systems will contain much that is distinct to a particular society. The move toward a *new structural economics* that acknowledges the salience of local context is welcome but may benefit from the cross-fertilization possible with other disciplines.

The central question remains: As in most single-party states, can the government loosen control sufficiently to release the potential energy of an autonomous bourgeoisie or 'middle'? Or can it foster the emergence of a functional equivalent? Both questions are set against the ultimate challenge of retaining societal order under the onslaught of a massive increase in the complexity of transactions if, among other difficulties, the barrier of doing business with strangers can be surmounted. This test of capacity for progress is coming to be seen more widely as the middle-income trap, and most countries approaching it fail to get through. China will be approaching that trap about ten years from now (World Bank/China State Council 2013). How might it get through?

It is rare to find analyses that examine matters at the societal scale while at the same time taking account of the deeper subtle influences that work at the level of organizations. I have in mind here forces that have direct but obscured impact on the passing of the crucial test of productivity per capita. Such commentary has to be multi-disciplinary, historic, and systemic. This chapter takes the risks involved in such analytic adventurism, not because it permits sweeping statements, but because the subject deserves the respect of matching complexity on the ground with complexity in the account. This brief version of such an account is designed to ask harder-than-average questions of those who specialize in a single main discipline or perspective.[1] It aims to bring matters to the surface that are usually hidden and little researched. It rests on some of the research literature and on forty years of close interaction with China and its organizations.

3.2 The general problem of societal progress

Any analysis of a society's form of progress must take account of at least three main categories of influence: the *political* realm is where the structure and nature of authority are settled; the *economic* realm is

---

[1] Readers seeking a less brief treatment are referred to Redding and Witt (2007) and Witt and Redding (eds) (2014).

where the structure and nature of organizations are settled, where the society's chosen form or order is shaped by institutions, and where the society's resources are put to use; the *cultural* realm is where the mindsets of people become engaged in legitimizing the connections between the *political* and the *economic*. These three aspects of context are in constant reciprocal interaction and the total tends to evolve as the surrounding world imposes forces for change, as, for instance, with technology.

Historically, the transitions of the Agricultural, Industrial and currently the Information Revolutions have induced increasing densities and usages of invested capital, human capital, and social capital. A society's capacity to handle such transitions is an outcome of its accumulated capacity for transformation. Herein lies a tension between the relatively 'destructive' forces brought by innovation and the stabilizing forces brought by high levels of cooperativeness. For instance, can a business system survive the early riots about technical change when occupations are lost? Can a system invent new structures for wider exchange transactions? Political leadership, as it were, walks a tightrope holding these forces in dynamic balance, as each force needs the other if transformation is to succeed. It often takes political genius, or at least courage, to keep these forces in balance, while moving forward on an upward-sloping high wire. On the ground level, people may more simply be muddling through and working around obstacles.

In these transitions some societies move faster and further than others in achieving wealth. This relates to – especially in the transitions of the Industrial and Information Revolutions – an exponential rise in the complexity of how a society's economy works. Some societies evolve structures and institutions to handle this while remaining stable. Others are still struggling with the smooth linking of the political, economic, and cultural that is entailed. The score normally kept for this game is *productivity*: a measure of the efficiency with which the available resources are put to use. This in turn rests heavily on two processes: the rational and responsive sourcing and allocating of *financial capital* in pursuit of its most efficient use; and the motivations, commitments, creativity, confidence, and knowledge of the individuals doing the work in the organizations. High intensity of such contributions is only possible when the use of power in the society is seen as legitimate in its relations with the use of resources; in other words, the political, economic, and cultural realms are in adequate harmony. The essential challenge for many societies is that central control works only up to a point. After that the next level of complexity can only be handled by the diffusion of initiative into an educated population able to handle the new complexity while the total remains stable. Herein lies the essential Chinese puzzle. Autocracy will get you only so far.

An indicator that this is a very difficult game to play lies in the measured trajectories of countries making the attempt to handle the proliferating complexity of a modern economy. Most fail or at least plateau out at a level that leaves them aspirants rather than major players (in terms of performance quality, not size). At its simplest, the phenomenon is referred to as the 'middle-income trap' (Eichengreen, Park, and Shin 2011). The evidence is clear that countries tend to approach it from a 'developing' condition and move up to about US$ 15,000 per capita GDP and then level off. Few get past that invisible barrier. The advanced economies went through the barrier decades ago and have moved up historically to levels of around 40,000 plus. China is currently at about the 11,000 mark and will reach the 15,000 level in about a decade.[2] China's challenge, and the central question in this chapter, is whether its current system is adequate for handling the exponential increase in decision complexity induced by entering a modern – as opposed to a pre-modern – environment of economic coordination, control, and individually motivating legitimacy.

3.3 The basic rules for societal progress

Industrial revolutions at any time in history tend to unfold in ways that reflect two sources of influence. The first is a set of proclivities to behave in certain ways that are anchored in a particular society's inherited traditions for order, relationships, and action. So in the first Industrial Revolution, that of Britain in the eighteenth and nineteenth centuries, society was structured around ideals of individual freedom that had accreted over centuries and had become deeply embedded. In mainland

---

[2] Numbers used in such global comparisons are made problematic by an absence of standardization (related to regular new attempts to standardize) among the global bodies issuing them. The figures adopted here are those used commonly in the literature on the middle-income trap. For example, Eichengreen, Park, and Shin (2011) and World Bank/China State Council (2013).

Europe, the influence of the 'Protestant Ethic' in the northern countries, as fully understood, has arguably remained potent, as one of the legacies of the Reformation and the Enlightenment. In the Japanese equivalent during the late nineteenth century, the business organization became a transposition and re-interpretation of the traditional *ie* or *collective work unit*. According to Schmuel Eisenstadt,[3] it is possible to see Japan itself as an *ie* type of civilization, in which the major features are strong extended kinship, strong collective goals, functional hierarchy, and a very high degree of autonomy of the organizational units. The subsequent amplifying of that same social psychology produced the 'Japanese management' phenomenon that the global world of business learnt so much from, especially in such features as lean production, now the world standard.

Such societal forms of influence help to explain the variety of systems of capitalism and of national socio-economic structures more generally. It is visible in the case of China in features such as the continuing significance of familism, reliance on interpersonal trust but mistrust of strangers, and of dominant patrimonial government.[4]

The second influence on a society's evolved formula for progress comes from outside, in the form of examples to emulate, techniques to acquire, and ideas to consider. Japan in the late nineteenth century modernized in its own way but with extensive absorption of lessons deliberately sought elsewhere. The early evolution of Western Europe's economies was strongly supported by the use of Arab mathematics and numbering used in accounting, carried north in a Mediterranean civilizational heritage. Singapore deliberately courted multinationals as contributors to its industrialization in the late twentieth century. China is going along with the business systems standardized by the World Trade Organization (WTO). In fostering a fruitful connection with Hong Kong, it left itself open to outside methods and ideas, even while knowing that the opening of the window would bring in the flies.

Modernization is a response to the radically increasing complexity that is attached to any thriving economy working to reach the higher levels of GDP per capita. That complexity has several strands to it. There is firstly the potential rise in the number of exchange transactions

---

[3] Eisenstadt cites on this question Murakami (1984).

[4] *Oxford English Dictionary*: Patrimonial: 'a traditional type of social structure in which a (male) ruler maintains authority through officials, an army etc., retained by him and having loyalty to him personally.'

across the economy and across its borders. In a very high-level economy, anyone can do business with anyone else (within and because of
the usual constraints of compliance with the rules), so that the volume,
size, and range of possible transactions become very large indeed. But
this only works when the society has constructed reliable and efficient
institutions to underpin the risks of doing business with people who are
otherwise strangers. Such institutions include widely available trust-
worthy information, efficient protective commercial law, transparent
rules and rights, intermediaries such as trusted bankers, professions to
guarantee specialist conduct, and so on.

All of these institutions serve to empower individual actors and to
lessen their dependence on personalism as a prime guarantee of the
conduct of others. In the modern case, interpersonal trust is normally
enhanced by the addition of this 'system trust' as societies advance.
Interpersonal trust (as with *guanxi* in China) may well get the country
to the 15,000 barrier, but it is not likely to be enough for it to achieve
the 40,000 plus found elsewhere. Reliance on it (and by extension the
weakness of supporting institutions) is one of China's most significant
long-term handicaps. It is termed 'social capital' and is part of a cluster
of invisible requirements that provide a society with the transformative
capacity it needs. It is of course feasible for China to choose its own
development formula based on the retention of personalism as its
primary form of social capital in the economy. This would have predictable costs, as will be argued later.

Other aspects of the impending advance of complexity relate to the
outcomes of education: the tolerance of pluralism, the encouragement
of responsible autonomy and specialization, the flourishing of debate,
and the encouraging of creativity and risk-taking. All reflect the very
strong empowerment wave that has been growing globally in recent
decades and that is moved by the globalization and information revolutions, plus the economic and psychic benefits associated with democracy, and so clearly visible in Taiwan and South Korea.

If one seeks advice on the keys to successful societal transformation,
it is useful to derive them from the accounts of success so far but only so
long as the trajectories are seen as local interpretations of possible
general deeper determinants. How was it done in Western Europe,
North America, Japan, Korea, and Taiwan? Studies of these complex
and varied examples tend to confirm the presence of two major features
that – when achievable – allow the society to handle the transition to

the complex world of a modern economy. First, a balance must be achieved between the political, economic, and cultural, enough to retain stability in the socio-economy. Second, advantage must be taken of that balance to generate the dynamism to create wealth and foster its distribution. This dynamism may then challenge the stability of the balance.

As far as dynamic action is concerned, a highly significant institution in successful cases has been a large, influential, and autonomous middle class, or *bourgeoisie*. Such a body is normally made up of business owners and managers, professionals and white-collar workers, and public servants, all participants in capitalism. It is this body that has historically in successful cases taken the majority of the initiatives that deliver well-functioning order and the creation of wealth. This is normally achieved with government encouragement. So, civil society is permitted, and perhaps encouraged, to form institutions that enable order to stabilize. A stock exchange is regulated by a committee of members. A Press Council disciplines the press to remain civilized as well as open and so free from censorship bodies. This ensures that the new complexities are addressed by those dealing directly with them, such talent being both fertile and numerous, and societally responsible if their status is to be legitimate. The extensive work of Deidre McCloskey (2006, 2010) on this feature demonstrates its power. The warning of Marie-Claire Bergere (2007) that China is trying to produce a system of capitalism without capitalists (by coopting them into the Party) serves to raise a serious question about how political evolution is designed to proceed without such a major interest-group wielding influence. There has always been an instinctive acceptance of state dominance.

In addition to having the key actors and their having freedom to act is the question of what *processes* are associated with societal success. The answer lies in two key features, acting as catalysts: *innovativeness* and *cooperativeness*. Joel Mokyr's (2009) fine-grained study of the first Industrial Revolution identified them clearly, referring to them as (1) a game against Nature (technology) and (2) a game of interacting with other people (institutions). These two vital forces are arguably related to deep-seated instincts supporting species survival, as I will shortly discuss. As catalysts they need to be manifest at a high level of intensity, and they need to fit reciprocally with the surrounding system of which they would be outcomes. Their presence makes all the difference. But the way they work may well be influenced by very long evolutionary societal histories, and before treating them in more detail, it is necessary to make a brief excursion into new and still adventurous research about that evolution, because – if true – its main contention has significant implications for how any society will evolve. Is China already pre-shaped?

3.4 The evolutionary shaping of societal structures

We know from decades of research that there are two major cultural clusters into which societies tend to fit. One of them stresses hierarchy, compliance, and strong psychological dependence on membership of a specific collectivity like a family or a tribe. Power here is given much attention and comes to be finely divided. Acceptance produces stability. The other cluster stresses individual autonomy and equality as principles. This latter form tends to bring with it less rigidity of structure but also a higher sense of personal responsibility to the wider community. Authority here is resisted except when needed and merited. These two clusters were labeled by Geert Hofstede (1980) as either High Power Distance/Collectivism or Low Power Distance/Individualism.

More recent work by the World Values Surveys under Ronald Inglehart and a large team of global scholars has shown new aspects of the same two clusters, this time under a wider definition of the societal ideals being measured (see Figure 3.1). Here the main summary dimensions identified are (a) values along a range from 'survival' to 'self-expression' and (b) values along a range from 'traditional' to 'secular-rational'. These large-scale and continuous World Values Surveys have also revealed shifts in recent decades away from the survival/traditional pattern toward the self-expression/secular-rational as societies adjust their cultures in an overall global drift described by Christian Welzel (2013) as 'freedom rising' via empowerment.

Figure 3.1 illustrates the cultural clustering of such values. They appear to fit with long-term heritage, including religion. The clusters also fit with per capita wealth, showing relative poverty associated with survival/traditional values and relative wealth associated with secular/rational/self-expression ideals. This is underpinned by the co-evolution of certain core elements expressing freedom: over 129 countries, it is clear that these elements co-evolve, but with technological progress taking the lead. The culture zones account for most of the variation:

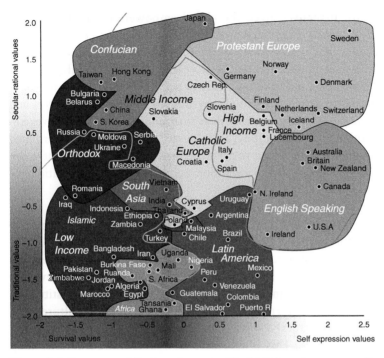

Figure 3.1 Summary of findings from the World Values Surveys overlapped with development implications and religious or other identifying heritages (Welzel 2014).

78 percent for technological progress, 79 percent for civic entitlement, and 72 percent for emancipative values. Such data are *prima facie* evidence of deep forces at work in societies and must be accounted for in assessing the likelihood of any society moving from the middle-income category to the high-income. How might we probe this issue?

All modern societies have in some way or other released the energy of their people by dismantling central autocracy and yet remaining stable. This has often taken centuries, as might prove to be the case for India, where at least according to Margaret Thatcher 'they have done the hard part first.' The most significant question relating to China's evolution is about the redistribution of power into society. It might be said that it is already being done, in which case the follow-up questions are: How does that work? And how might it continue? In order to assess those questions it is necessary to understand the continuing influence of China's heritage on its room for maneuver given the global empowerment trend revealed by the World Values Surveys.

A point that is now widely accepted is that forms of human society evolved over tens of thousands of years in ways that reflected their ecological context. Put simply, the way a set of people found a means of staying alive safely – essentially by finding food, water, shelter, and protection – was largely set by their surrounding conditions of vegetation, animal life, topography, and climate. Their responses determined how their societies came to be structured and organized. There are patterns in this aspect of evolution and a particular implication for China.

The first human societies were bands of hunter-gatherers, but at some point around 10,000 to 15,000 years ago there began to appear forms of settlement, based on the keeping of animals and the growing of crops. How these new larger social units came to be stabilized has since been imprinted on the societies that evolved from them. Such imprinting takes place when early institutions 'lock in' related forms of order, and the society's culture then legitimates the total evolving form and it keeps replicating and reinforcing itself. This is traceable now over extraordinarily long periods of time.

One new train of thought acknowledged only in brief here as fascinating but pending fuller development is the 'cool-water hypothesis' proposed and documented by Christian Welzel (2013). In this theory, societies evolved differently as their surrounding natural ecology shaped their options. The argument is essentially simple. When societies stabilized in conditions where there was reliable all-year rainfall, and where land was not limited, people could choose to settle without having to worry over the sharing of core essentials, especially water. They might well choose to collaborate for defense, but otherwise they could get on with their livelihoods without the constant close scrutiny or supervision by others. Their evolved individualism would come to support principles of equality, and their ideals stress trust in the probity of others in the community, against whom they were not competing. The outcome is summarized by Welzel and Inglehart (2013, 10) as follows:

Northwestern Europe and Japan pioneered the industrial take-off because their societies entered the pre-industrial age equipped with multiple autonomies and a pluralistic power structure. This was a distinctive advantage because plural autonomies are a prerequisite to unleash the ubiquitous inquisitive energies needed to feed the science and technology explosion of an industrial take-off. But the root cause why these two civilizations had this advantage is environmental: the Cool-Water condition harbours an existential root autonomy – from which derivative autonomies at more advanced stages of market development evolve.

Reciprocal altruism – a central building block for all human societies – in the conditions of autonomy took the form of following ideals of communal duty. The distribution of this type overlaps with the top-right quadrant of the World Values graph (Figure 3.1) and so encompasses northwest Europe, Japan, and the English-speaking countries (including many of their predictably influenced ex-colonies). The overlap of this cluster with societal prosperity begs many questions for future research.

The alternative societal formula evolved in different ecologies. Here water resources were relatively scarce or unpredictably threatening, as with floods, or required shared efforts to obtain, as with irrigation or in rice cultivation; climates were warmer than in the other case but more disease-inducing; land was more scarce and required control over access; resources were abundant but clustered together; everyone could know what everyone else was doing; and reciprocal altruism was exercised through clear norms of reciprocal exchange. Population densities could become high and, because of this, competition for scarce resources could threaten the community.

In this case, group survival came to be based on the acceptance of domination by a central authority figure, the 'big man' of much anthropology. Subjection to that order became instinctive and hierarchy became normal along with its attendant responses: the moral understandings in ideals such as paternalism and the institutions of patrimonialism. The early work of Carl Wittfogel (1957) on China's political economy made clear that China's centralized governments are traceable to the early need for the state to take control of access to water in the interests of population survival. The government was responding to the fact that the areas of greatest potential food production were also the areas of greatest potential loss of life from floods. Using corvee labor this produced a gigantic physical infrastructure of water control and transport canals. From the building of the 800-mile Imperial Canal at the end of the sixth century CE China eventually constructed approximately 200,000 miles of waterways over its areas of fertile land. It became a 'hydraulic civilization.' Once set, the system became path dependent and has not altered in its basic design since. The government remains essential for the macro-control of resources and is given the power in accordance with the dependence of the population on its administration. And water remains a national challenge that only government can handle because of the huge nature of the projects needed. So too for transport, and a modern-day reminder of the government assumption of this infrastructure burden is visible in its recent vast investments in the building of railways, roads, urban transport systems, and airports.

Another perspective on this same issue is offered by Lucian Pye (1990, 58), who suggests that 'China is not just a state in the family of nations. China is a civilization pretending to be a state ... Viewed from another perspective the miracle of China has been its astonishing unity.' This is in large measure attributable to the overpowering obligation of rulers to keep it unified and the resulting legitimation of that in cultural attitudes to power and authority. From that great hierarchical structure run two consequences on which he remarks: the inward-looking groupings and cellular structure of a society that 'existed only at the local level' (59); and the absence of national institutions of society, there being 'a taboo on the articulation of interests' (65).

The simple *possibility* is raised that China remains in essence a carry-forward of such a society, its character set around the civilizational ideal of central authority. If that is so, then northern Europe, North America, and Japan may equally be carrying forward a societal character set around more autonomous individuals, living in a different earlier ecology. Such patterns might well have evolved over 60,000 years.

Having said that, it is appropriate to examine the China/Japan contrast for what it may reveal about societal progress, and about the contrasting trajectories of near neighbors with subtle but significantly different ancient heritages, and with very different current levels of performance.

A final related point about the human heritage comes from research on innate human drives as they evolved from the progressing of the *homo sapiens* species. Survival in the early stages of human evolution depended on two primary drives wired into the limbic system: *to defend* and *to acquire*. As societies became more socially complex, two new drives were added to the earlier two acquired from primate ancestry. The new drives were *to bond* and *to learn* (Lawrence and Nohria 2002). Such drives are hard-wired into our species, as responses to increasing social complexity. It is perhaps not surprising to find them visible as transformative capacities in the present-day handling of complexity: what I refer to as *cooperativeness (to bond)* and *innovativeness (to learn)*.

3.5 Comparing China and Japan

Japan's GNI per capita stands at six times that of China. Its reformed industrial giants remain formidable forces in the global economy and display globally competitive efficiency in technology and organization. The politico-economic structures of the two economies remain very different. Can China ever match Japan in performance? If China is diffident about taking lessons from the West, might it take lessons from Japan, a country where cultural affinities are at first glance close?

A deep study of the contrast is available in Shmuel Eisenstadt's (1996) analysis of Japanese civilization, and in this he elaborates on the origins of perhaps the most significant contrast in social psychology between the two societies. In Japan, the primary unit of identity is the person's own community, or what the Japanese sociologist Chie Nakane (1971) calls a person's 'frame': a unit of society often defined around employment, and going well beyond the nuclear family. Identity within this social unit takes on magnetic significance, just as in China does membership of a family. From that starting point, the ways of organizing economic action use different structures and have different psychologies of both identity and motivation.

This feature in Japan's social nature is traceable to several aspects of early separation between the two civilizations. Despite a great deal of common cultural heritage, most notably Buddhism and Confucianism, Japan was never taken over by China politically or ideologically. Japan tended to absorb outside influences of many kinds over centuries by a process of re-formulating them to fit with deep Japanese understandings resting in Shinto. In simple terms, the Shinto world view celebrates the sociability of human beings and the significance of community in nature. Even though holding only symbolic influence, and being based in ritual rather than the exercise of direct power, it still today meets the spiritual needs, albeit informally, of about 80 percent of the population. It also exists as an extension of the peoples' identity with Japan itself and supports the continued legitimacy of the Emperor. It is perhaps for this reason, and reflecting on Chinese society diffracted into family units, that Sun Yat Sen, in designing the first of China's twentieth-century revolutions, is reputed to have observed that China is like a tray of loose sand, while Japan is like a piece of solid granite.

Going further into understanding the contrasts, Eisenstadt pointed to differences in conceptions of statehood and community. Thinking absorbed from China that supported the early form of Confucian-inspired hierarchy at the outset of the Tokugawa shogunate after 1600 was re-interpreted subsequently, not just by Tokugawa himself, but by a series of influential political philosophers such as Ogyu Sorai (Najita 1998). Put at its simplest, the central role of *li* (the rules of order) was redefined. This principle, so crucial in Chinese political philosophy, allowed for the imposition of conformity by stressing the *fusion* of the transcendental and the mundane. Life in reality should be conducted according to guidelines established in a version of heaven, the principles consequently being metaphysical. This philosophy was challenged by Japanese thinkers and the imposed heavenly conformity replaced by a more grounded ideal. This latter was based on saving other people in their real surroundings. The transcendant principle was no longer superior or prior. Ideals about order became more objective, more particular, seen more in context, and more realistic. Resting on Japanese ideals about the sociability of human beings, and the signifi-cance of community in nature, a re-affirmed Japanese societal philoso-phy emerged.

Significant outcomes of this flowed together as influences to decen-tralize power in Japanese society and to permit it to evolve toward meeting the challenges of new complexity in the late nineteenth cen-tury. Examples of such changes are the emergence of an autonomous bourgeoisie; the decentralization of most government administration into the 360 *han* or regions; the emergence of different autonomous societal realms, such as that of art and poetry, and so the encourage-ment of pluralism; the softening of hierarchy with consensus seeking; the professionalization of administration; and the widespread growth of education. Above the entire scene perhaps the most significant China–Japan difference came from the separation of powers at the top. The emperor who symbolized Japan was not charged with running the country. That duty fell to others who themselves were constrained by the imperial presence. China by contrast seemingly cannot function without a single dominant emperor or equivalent.

To summarize, these two societies work with quite different social material in crafting their economies, if material is understood in terms of its qualities in fostering innovativeness and cooperativeness, and in achieving a legitimate form of order. This difference lies in the degree of empowerment of the average individual: in Japan strongly so within the rules; in China strongly not so within the rules. The human heritage will have given people in each society the same innate drives to defend, acquire, bond, and learn. The expression of these drives is, however, shaped differently by the contrasting settings and what they mean.

3.6 The role of cooperativeness

In Eric Beinhocker's (2007) study of the origins of wealth, he points out the impact of increasing socio-economic complexity on the conduct of business and reaches the disarmingly straightforward conclusion that the battle between firms is essentially fought by *competing to cooperate*. His meaning is that a firm might well work out a strategy for market penetration but that putting it into practice needs to be done more efficiently than in other firms and that this rests on a range of social technologies and relationships. These include coordination with sources of finance to satisfy expectations; with customers to satisfy demands; with subcontractors for specialist needs; with government for aspects of compliance; with employees to engage their maximum levels of work efficiency, creativity, and commitment. It is in this arena of forms of cooperation that the most distinct efficiencies are reached and success and failure are established. It is here that the firm's response is worked out to the fact that competitive environments determine what 'fitness function' will best guarantee survival and growth. Business strategy is all about finding a formula that others will find difficult to replicate, therefore using forms of cooperativeness distinct to the firm, then replicating the successful form before others join the game. This is one of the reasons why the management of human resources can be used by firms as a way of establishing a corporate culture that is hard for other firms to copy.

Cooperativeness in a society works in two ways and these are determined by its dominant form of trust. One way is to use networks of personal reciprocal obligation, and these can extend sideways across an economy and also up and down in an organization, then up to a societal business system. In China, one of the strongest institutions is that of *guanxi*, a form of bonding with strong supportive norms about reciprocity. Vertically, a similar reciprocity is expressed in paternalism. In either case the glue is personalistic. The result is very strong bonding but very limited *extension* of cooperativeness. The general context is one in which you trust those with whom you are bonded but you are not in a position to trust strangers. This inhibition derives from two related conditions: the sense of others competing for scarce resources is heightened for those emerging from a legacy of deprivation and there is a vacuum in terms of duty to the community beyond family. Between the family and the state is an empty space, and it is an aspect of what I will argue is the hollow center. The World Values Survey (2009) reports that 89 percent of Chinese people do not trust strangers.

The institutions that fill that vacuum in high-intensity societies are what Lynne Zucker (1986) sees, in her studies of trust, as forms of insurance; they underwrite the risks of transacting with unknown people. Such institutions include reliable and protective law, open reliable information, professions that standardize and control the conduct of their members, fair regulations, and so on. But listing such institutions only gives half the story. The real contribution of such forms of system trust lies in their 'ownership' – and often their origin – lying with the members of society who interact most closely with the domains they cover. The interest of such responsible citizens must lie in persuading the average person that the institution provides order for the public good rather than private gain. This is how the process becomes legitimized on moral terms; its exponents are seen as decent people and come to be respected as such. The committee members of a Chamber of Commerce are usually unpaid, volunteer members of the local business community, helping to run an organization that represents and fosters commerce for the benefit of all.

3.7 China's challenge of cooperativeness

It is a core challenge for a totalitarian state to permit the transfer of influence into the body of society. Control remains essential. In China, the function of the Party is to permit this and it has worked to produce a great deal of decentralized economic decision-making power in the regional hubs and the major cities (Xu 2011). But just as control by the Party provides comfort at the center that order is not threatened, it also ensures that an autonomous body does not evolve to accumulate countervailing power. In effect the government is filling the hollow center with its own administrative system. That is, in a limited sense, a rational choice. But the question is open as to whether it matches the need for handling escalating complexity. Governments are not usually equipped to understand detailed matters on the ground. Nor do entrepreneurs usually need advice from state planners on their business strategies. And increasingly autonomous citizens are not motivated by proliferating administration.

The main question is whether it fosters cooperativeness at the level likely to be competitive by world standards. The answer is probably not. The evidence for this is presented in Christian Welzel's (2013) 'contagion thesis' in relation to the effects of emancipation as tracked globally. Once freedom is tasted, it tends to be more and more desired. Once acquired it fosters greater taking of opportunity. Once opportunities are being taken an economy can grow faster. This is a 'utility ladder'. The ladder stands on empowerment.

If one considers two main alternatives – having (a) an autonomous *bourgeoisie* or (b) a government-controlled form of strategy-making and assets allocation – then the evidence from China itself supporting the thriving 'middle' (reminiscent of the German Mittelstand) is overwhelming. Despite its still relatively dis-integrated nature, the private sector, as recently analyzed in detail by Nicholas Lardy, has become 'the major source of economic growth, the sole source of job creation, and the major contributor to China's still growing role as a global trader' (Lardy 2014, 2–3). Most markets are now competitive. Private firms produce about two-thirds of output. It is clear that some form of *bourgeoisie* exists, and that its members have produced so far an economic miracle, but in terms of influence on society's controlling structures and institutions it remains a weak form. It remains diffracted. Its weakness is attributable to several features: not having secure long-term property rights; control by the Party, including compliance under conditions of anxiety or fear; the weakening of traditional civilizational ideals about family as the centerpiece of moral order; and yet duty to family constraining communal spirit; the 'unnaturalness' of civil society in Chinese tradition other than via philanthropy; the weakness of system trust; central control of information; and restriction of pluralist debate. In comparison with high-intensity per capita societies this middle is hollow. The power within it is separated into small pieces, as with the tray of loose sand. Hovering above is the controlling force of state power.

Outcomes of this set of limitations amount to weaknesses in the deepening of cooperativeness across the economy. Civil society surveys score China at the same level as Russia, and well below advanced economies. Mistrust inhibits cooperation in the social sphere beyond *guanxi*. Several questions flow from this. Although the present system has been immensely successful to date, how much of that success rests on taking up the slack available in, for example, large amounts of low-cost labor, deep reserves of instinctive family-based entrepreneurship, and acquired technology? Although the system remains successful at the present level of complexity, will it be able to handle the great increase in complexity due to arrive at the other side of the middle-income trap? Can the total system sustain the political stress of devolving influence beyond direct state control, and if so how?

3.8 The role of innovativeness

Innovativeness is one of the twin instincts (with cooperativeness) that are hard-wired into the human frame to enable a society to cope with the adaptation needed to survive. Although expressed through individual agency, it has two higher exponents. Organizations need to adapt to change. And so does society itself. Change itself is seemingly inevitable and only partially predictable, and this latter feature adds extra significance to a society's capacity to handle it.

The world now sees certain industrial districts as main focuses of innovativeness, primary among which is Silicon Valley, but with equivalents at different scales around the globe. Despite their locally embedded nature, there is still much to be learnt from their structures about how innovation may be encouraged. In addition is the more diffuse but still significant matter of adventurousness exhibited by business leaders such as entrepreneurs seeking new combinations of things that create new market opportunities.

From studies of innovativeness it is possible to distil certain requirements for success in both process and outcomes (e.g. Hwang and Horowitt 2012, Redding and Drew 2015). The economic unit regardless of ownership must be capable of being scaled up to take advantage of opportunity; creative individuals in it need to be cooperative with it and yet psychologically autonomous and mobile; the latter need to have fair incentive for being creative; information and exchange need to flow freely to enable both learning and collaboration; surrounding systems of regulation should be seen as fair and protective; and assessments of risk in capital allocation should be rational and evidence-based. The practical application of these principles is likely to vary in form between societies, even though the principles are adhered to.

3.9 China's challenge of innovativeness

In recent decades, China's industrial reputation has rested mainly on its mastery of the role of being the world's workshop. Industry of this nature is largely low to middle tech in form, and design usually derives from foreign sources via product specification and imported machine tools. The success of the 'workshop of the world' is based on an entirely rational response to opportunity and it has achieved great innovativeness *in the coordinating process* by bringing together entrepreneurial energy, low-cost skilled labor, access to world markets via collaborative agencies, and technology acquired via alliances of one kind or another. The official encouragement of foreign direct investment on the condition of technology transfer brought in much technique to fill a gap. But the reliance on the private sector, and its extension at scale into 'local corporates,' did not ensure the building of technical or scientific innovative capacity *of an indigenous kind* into Chinese organizations. The implications of this for the wider context are visible in the finding by Welzel and Inglehart (2013) that the strong connection between a society's cool-water heritage and its rate of technological progress changes around 1990 to take account of globalization. In simple terms it became possible and normal to bring in technical innovation from abroad.

This book is devoted to the question of building innovation capacity in China, and contains chapters devoted in detail to that work-in-progress. This chapter will not itself analyze that progress as the question of actual performance remains quite contentious and requires space for careful scrutiny. Instead, I propose to focus on two aspects of innovation seen in terms of a societal capability rather than a set of actions. This capability is not so much a recorded achievement, but rather the context that enhances or suppresses such achievement. It is the quality of being capable of innovation, and hence *innovativeness*. The essence of the argument is that this catalyst normally rests heavily on empowerment, and that China's quality of empowerment, although rising, is unlikely to reach the level adequate to underpin indigenous innovative achievement at global standards. In that case collaboration with external sources of innovation becomes crucial and is now normal in world economic history. I examine the question briefly at two levels: the organization and the societal context.

In a recent study of the organizational qualities needed for innovativeness, McKinsey ran workshops, interviews, and surveys with 2,500 executives in 300 companies globally (de Jong, Marston, and Roth 2015). This might be taken to yield a definition of the state of the innovation art in companies competing globally. Eight essential actions were identified: aspire, choose, discover, evolve, accelerate, scale, extend, and mobilize. I suggest that these actions are all societally embedded, as is most economic action anywhere. *Aspiring* is an attitude of mind that is set within a society's meanings of respect. *Choosing* is an action that rests on criteria of choice and so on definitions of what priorities should be served, a not entirely calculable function. *Discovery* relates to the nature of a society's intellectual and practical curiosity, and the way it is exercised and channeled. *Evolving* relates to 'defensible and scalable profit sources,' which in turn overlaps with the capacity of an organization to handle the natural consequence of scaling up. If you want to hold on to efficiency per unit of input as the firm grows, you have to generate a spirit of willing cooperation and commitment under conditions of predictable control. *Accelerating* will reflect the nature of human senses of urgency as much as surrounding institutional encouragements. *Scale* depends on empowerment if motivation is to keep pace with organizational complexity. *Extending* suggests external networking, in the practice of which Chinese actors express distinct cultural norms. *Mobilizing* human energy calls into question the nature of motivation and of incentive, both culturally embedded.

If we consider the question of innovativeness at the societal level, perhaps the most significant aspect is how science is brought into fruitful connection with the economy. The workings of innovativeness as described above show a world of extreme collaboration across a myriad of institutions and individuals in a complex social web of people all capable of exerting influence. Against that external norm here again the research points to a problem in China of hierarchical control by government. In other countries with high levels of innovativeness there is a rich and fruitful interchange between scientific research and its commercial application. This is usually guided by a great web of intermediate organizations, committees, funding consortia, and liaison bodies, all freely searching advantage. As described for China by J. Arnoldi and J. Y. Zhang (2012), the fusion of research and its application is handicapped. Knowledge generation and knowledge application are de-coupled in a 'dual reality.' Techno-bureaucrats have undue influence via funding control. External scientific judgment is filtered. Nationally mandated programs are given priority, so that alternative fields of inquiry are discouraged.

Three questions on innovativeness now arise as challenges: Can the dependence so far on technical 'borrowing' be displaced by indigenous technical innovativeness? Will this be enough to get China into a new world of much more intense competition? Can it use alliances with outside firms as a means of making the transition? Answers will emerge from the laboratory in due time.

On alliances a rarely discussed feature of China's industrial scene is the interface with outside firms when cultures clash, and this often prevents the innovation. A detailed case of this phenomenon is reported by Angelika Zimmerman and Marc Bollbach (2015), who studied the long-term attempt by a German automotive components manufacturer to introduce 'lean' production into its China plants. They studied two plants, each with about a thousand employees, and concluded that certain cognitive dispositions and behaviors had inhibited the firm's attempt to introduce lean production. The barriers were seen as outcomes of the institutional and cultural context and included poor problem-solving skills, constrained mind-sets, concerns over the protection of 'face' inhibiting the making of suggestions, concern for harmony blocking the search for root causes, and a strong sense of hierarchy blocking upwards communication. They concluded that the failure to transplant this production system, with its substantial assumptions about employee empowerment, indicates a serious challenge faced by China in matching world standards in high-tech and high-productivity manufacturing. Similar reservations about the negative impacts of strong hierarchy on organizational adaptiveness are widespread in the research literature.

3.10 The problem of innovativeness within hierarchy

As John Child (2014, 1727) observed recently in a review of Thomas Diefenbach's (2013) new book on organizational power, 'Hierarchy and its negative consequences is arguably the most pressing social issue of our times.' Of all the issues faced by China in its journey toward the modern, nothing approaches this challenge in magnitude or difficulty, as it lies at the core of China's definition of its civilization. This is a patrimonial state. It has a strong top and a hollow middle, the latter full of highly energetic people but disproportionately lacking in influence.

This long-standing heritage has shaped the world of Chinese organizations in ways that have constrained so far the socio-economic options. I consider the notion of 'initiative' useful here. It means that people can try new things, can express their inventiveness, and are not held back by inhibitions absorbed from their upbringing and/or their current surroundings. It is the active first stage of behavior conducive to innovativeness. Seen simply, China's organizations fall into two camps:

(a) Large scale and (in most cases) inefficient; lacking in commercial initiative at global standards of competitiveness.
(b) Small to medium in scale and full of initiative but unable to reach large scale at global standards of competitiveness and durability.

Organizations that combine high levels of initiative *and* large-scale efficiency, although some certainly exist, are rare in Chinese culture. Even those in the encouraging environments around the South China Sea do not stay intact at the key transition point of owner succession, losing on average 60 percent of their value at that stage, as J. P. Fan (2012) has demonstrated.

The *combining* of initiative and hierarchy is a *sine qua non* of all the advanced economies. If China cannot find a way of doing that, its growth will level off. The key to this lies in making the hierarchy benevolent, in other words to create organizations that employ people in conditions of motivation and empowerment so as to elicit from them their commitment and creativity for the organization's benefit. As Robert Heilbroner (1985) pointed out in his history of capitalism, this invention of a more benevolent form of domination is the secret of capitalism's success. This applies to any of its main forms: Anglo-Saxon, European, Japanese, and now South Korean. Achieving this, as noted by Max Weber (1930), was a matter of learning that the dominant control of economic assets would not produce value under free market conditions unless both employees and customers became parts of the coalition of influences. The market then takes over some of the role of the state in dealing with the growing complexity of action, an assumption built into the new structural economics noted earlier.

Given these flows of influence affecting innovativeness, the replacement of borrowed technology by indigenously invented technology is unlikely to occur, except in rare cases. Scientific originality is likely to be also handicapped by Party control of scientific policy. But that does not close the door. Given the forces of globalization, and the role of the WTO in making China's business environment more conducive to collaboration, it is probable that technology transfer will continue for a long time to come. The probability exists that the urge toward alliances out of rising necessity will be so strong as to counteract the wishes of the state to develop an independent Chinese business system as its primary response to global competition.

3.11 Three questions

This chapter earlier posed three questions designed to open up a critical review of whether China is likely to put together the transformative capacity needed in the modern context it aims to enter. This context is one of exponentially proliferating complexity. Economic history suggests that this momentum is usually handled by more reliance on the logics of competitive market discipline, albeit conditioned by the overlay of moral imperatives brought in by the combination of cultural norms and government regulation. The process works better when the codification and diffusion of information keep pace with the intricacy of decision-making, as the work of Max Boisot clearly demonstrates (Boisot 1995) and especially for China (Boisot, Child, and Redding 2011). The inability of socio-economic systems to handle such complexity can be disastrous as the last global banking crisis showed. The history of totalitarian states does not provide comfort that political centers can handle this challenge at world standards of competitive efficiency.

China knows this and has taken steps to meet the challenge. Two steps in particular may be identified: the releasing from government constraint of small and medium private sector energy in the Deng Xiao Ping reforms, and the devolution of decision power into the regional hubs. Two controversial issues now remain: (1) How long can the center stay in control of the regional hubs through the Party and over what agendas? (2) How long can the civic energy of a potentially strong middle class remain suppressed, or some equivalent to it be made to work? These questions throw light on the core challenge, namely that unless innovativeness and cooperativeness become the agendas of a large group of empowered citizens with property rights, and with freedom to think beyond dogma, the required quality and quantity of adaptiveness will be lacking. The energy of this middle class can only contribute fully if processes of spontaneous self-ordering are accepted as legitimate. In all such arguments it is necessary to be clear that the straight transplanting of institutions from outside is not here assumed or advocated. The real challenge is for Chinese inventiveness to find its distinct functional equivalents, as did Japan. I return now to the questions.

3.12 Can large-scale organization be achieved indigenously at world standards of efficiency by a fusion of hierarchy and innovativeness

The weakness of large-scale organization in China is strongly connected to the relative failure of the state sector to perform competitively. This judgment is strengthened by the fact that the state firms have run for decades with monopoly advantages of access to finance and markets. Nicholas Lardy (2014) reports that between 1996 and 2012 return on assets in the state sector has fluctuated between 1 percent and 4.9 percent. In the private sector it has fluctuated between 11 percent and 13.2 percent. The low levels of state firms' results are obscured by extraordinary returns on assets in several giant monopolistic firms: six-year averages to 2012 of 25 percent in CNOOC; 19 percent in China Mobile; and 14 percent in the tobacco monopoly. Other studies have applied rigorous costings to financial behavior and suggest that given the favorable borrowing arrangements of the state enterprises, many of them, when seen under conditions of true comparison, have been operating at negative rates of return. Similar distortions do not appear to affect most private sector performance data.

Studies of China's large state firms have consistently reported flaws in quality of organizing (Lieberthal and Lieberthal 2003), and three problems are regularly reported: organizing into vertical silos that prevent middle and upper-middle management from taking a full organizational perspective and of achieving efficient coordination; this 'divide and rule' response expresses a top-down decision style that imposes control but stifles upward communication; an organizational climate of conformity and personal anxiety over risk-taking.

In consequence of these features the inhibiting of individual and collective initiative remains predictable in the large state firms, and so innovativeness affecting ways of organizing is likely to be weak.

In the private sector, a number of very strong firms have emerged to large scale to take the market opportunities and to arbitrage foreign technology for opening the China market. Such firms, even though large, have tended to be dependent on a very small dominant coalition, often a single founding visionary. This kind of dependence works well in guaranteeing clarity of vision and in providing requisite surrounding support in a politicized and personalistic context. So too does it allow a firm to take a long-term view, and it permits risk-taking of a nature that would otherwise meet opposition in conditions of widespread ownership or contentious internal company debate. A great strength of these companies is their cohesion around a personal vision. But their great weakness is the difficulty of maintaining that cohesion when the leadership diffracts. Only very few seem to have made the transition to professional management and even fewer to control under investor interest-groups.

The point for our present agenda is the high dependence in even large private firms for initiative on single individuals, and the long-term fragility of that. Nor is it just that such a person carries the main burden of strategic thinking, but that the relationships that secure the firm's stability of cooperation and support are also largely personalistic and difficult to pass on. The point is equally relevant in the small and medium enterprise sector where the same conditions apply.

China's large-scale organizational efficiency in the longer term rests on finding solutions to the fusing of hierarchy and widespread innovativeness, whether in state or private sector enterprise. As already argued, the real test lies in the future. *The Economist* (March 14, 2015, 15) sees the emergence of 'Factory Asia' with China at the center of a regional web of integrated firms in manufacturing for world markets, including China's own. But that arena is open to all firms to enter, and success in that competition will depend more and more on the organizational capacity to harness initiative, rather than simply on low-cost labor.

3.13 Can social capital be built to a point where strangers can be trusted?

If China retains its inherited culture of what Lau Siu Kai (1982) called 'materialistic familism,' then it is likely to stay true to ancient habits and cultural norms. Many observers of the wider societal picture see China as a perpetuated patrimonial autocracy. The strong and deeply penetrating culture leaves China as more of a civilization than a normal state as noted earlier. That makes it much harder to change fundamentally. If so, structures of trust are likely to remain constrained, because to build a powerful form of system trust is to redesign not just institutions but also the culture of paternalism and dependence. This is because spontaneous forms of order such as autonomous professions, a free press, pluralism and debate over beliefs, and autonomy in education, all bring with them the side-effect of undermining traditional order. Without system trust transactions will continue to rest on *guanxi*. Strangers will continue to be dealt with cautiously. The competition for scarce resources will remain intense. Whatever civil society emerges will remain politicized.

One must sympathize with those responsible for order in a state containing a fifth of the world's people. And one must respect the willingness shown in recent years to experiment pragmatically with socio-economic structures. One should also acknowledge the trend of policy toward market discipline and decentralized authority. But at the same time one must see the nature of the task ahead as requiring quite remarkable adventurousness, imagination, and long-term political will.

The barriers to success in this adventure remain largely invisible. As with the cosmos, they lie like dark energy in what seems an empty middle, exerting influence but remaining intangible and unmeasurable, and thus beyond the reach of most analysis. The contention here is that the endemic mistrust outside *guanxi* will handicap China's capacity to keep pace with what will be coming. The coordination of economic action at the scale and intensity necessary will be constrained by forces beyond direct influence or perhaps even awareness.

3.14 Can conformity and order be achieved without resort to fear, so can a more benevolent form of domination evolve?

Having argued that an invisible barrier exists affecting the knitting together of society horizontally, I now turn to another invisible barrier that affects its being knitted together vertically. The barrier is the use of strong control, punishment, conformity, and discipline. These cause people to respond on a continuum from anxiety to fear. The style is legitimated in government reminders that 'eating bitterness' is a sign of good citizenship and a source of respect, as Michael Griffiths and Jesper Zeuthen (2014) have recently described.

The argument here is not that such forces are inherently illegitimate. Any society makes up its own definition of legitimacy, and in China autocracy is part of a Confucian tradition that includes moral responsibility downward in a hierarchy and compliance upward. Instead, the argument being made is that this is a pre-modern form of domination, and that as such it stifles the release of the societal energy and creativity needed to deal with modern levels of complexity in the (a) intricacy, (b) technicality, (c) integration-needs, and (d) competitive response sophistication, practiced in economies at US$40,000 per capita. The game is played at a different level. This level might be achieved by China, but not while retaining the present-day response.

3.15 Conclusion

This chapter has suggested that there are hidden forces in China's social psychology that remain significant shapers of events in the economy. They reflect deep-seated human responses to societal survival in conditions of radical change. They are founded in ancient responses, invisible, and rarely included in policymaking. They serve to condition the quality and quantity available of two of the most crucial capacities needed by any society when it attempts the transition across the middle-income trap from the pre-modern condition of strong patrimonialism to the modern condition of an empowered citizenry holding the principal role in economic progress.

For China, the prospects are affected by the great weight of its traditions and the very strong path dependence of its political heritage. But these constraints are counterbalanced by several positive features. The government is clearly aware of the challenge. It is experimenting with controlled decentralization with great success so far. Entrepreneurship exists in great quantity. The Chinese people exhibit great tolerance and possess deep reserves of talent.

One of the conceivable options is that China does get through the trap on the basis of (a) adequate absorption of external technology via alliance management, (b) further releasing of the pent-up and widely available spirit of entrepreneurship, and (c) the internal dynamism of the huge internal market. It then reaches, let us say, US$20,000 per capita or its equivalent future rate. In other words, it accepts the costs of a muted middle class in exchange for a continuation of a revived and partially updated form of loose-tight corporatism. It then stays true to its state- (or civilization-) led soul. Then the world sees something it can afford to encourage. For China to attempt the $50,000 per capita level would bring the world to an ecological crisis on present understandings of our fate. That world is changing to make possible new structures of a kind not previously envisaged, and especially in the domain of even greater global cooperation between firms. As suggested in a critique of economic history by Adelman (2015), and as Prasenjit Duara (2015) has argued in detail for Asia, Enlightenment modernity holds no monopoly, and its linear narrative and national exclusivism may become destructive. It has obscured the collective heritage of an interactive and polycentric early modern world visible in Asia prior to the colonial period. It is perhaps in this arena that new forms of modern capitalism will evolve on Chinese soil, and on Chinese terms. This may entail the invention of new purposes for economic action.

References

Adelman, J. (2015) 'What caused capitalism? Assessing the roles of the West and the Rest', *Foreign Affairs*, 94,3, 136–144.

Arnoldi, J., and Zhang, J. Y. (2012) 'The dual reality of the Chinese knowledge economy', *International Journal of Chinese Culture and Management*, 3,2, 160–173.

Beinhocker, E. D. (2007) *The Origins of Wealth: Evolution, Complexity and the Radical Re-Making of Economics*. London: Random House.

Bergere, M.-C. (2007) *Capitalisme et capitalistes en Chine: Des origines a nos jours, XIXe-XXIe siecle*. Paris: Perrin.

Boisot, M. (1995) *Information Space*. London: Routledge.

Boisot M., Child, J., and Redding, G. (2011) 'Working the system; toward a theory of cultural and institutional competence', *International Studies in Management and Organization*, 41,1, 62–95.

Child, J. (2014) 'Book review of Diefenbach, *Hierarchy and Organization*', *Organization Studies*, 35-11-1725-1728.

De Jong, M., Marston, N., and Roth, E. (April 2015) 'The eight essentials of innovation', *McKinsey Quarterly*.

Diefenbach, Thomas. (2013) *Hierarchy in Organization: Toward a General Theory of Hierarchical Social Systems*. London: Routledge.

Duara, Prasenjit. (2015) *The Crisis of Global Modernity: Asian Traditions and a Sustainable Future*. Cambridge: Cambridge University Press.

Eichengreen, B., Park, D., and Shin, K. (2011) *When Fast Growing Economies Slow Down; International Evidence and Implications for China*. Working paper 16919. Cambridge, MA: National Bureau of Economic Research.

Eisenstadt, S. N. (1996) *Japanese Civilization*. Chicago: University of Chicago Press.

Fan, J. P. (2012) 'Founder succession and accounting properties', *Contemporary Accounting Research*, 29,1, 283–311.

Griffiths, M. B., and Zeuthen, J. (2014) 'Bittersweet China: new discourses of hardship and social organization', *Journal of Current Chinese Affairs*, 43,4, 143–174.

Heilbroner, R. L. (1985) *The Nature and Logic of Capitalism*. New York: Norton.

Hofstede, G. (1980) *Culture's Consequences: International Differences in Work-Related Values*. London: Sage.

Hwang, V. W., and Horowitt, G. (2012) *The Rainforest: The Secret to Building the Next Silicon Valley*. San Francisco: Regenwald.

Lardy, N. R. (2014) *Markets over Mao: The Rise of Private Business in China*, Washington, DC: Peterson Institute for International Economics.

Lau, S. K. (1982) *Society and Politics in Hong Kong*. Hong Kong: Chinese University Press.

Lawrence, P. R., and Nohria, N. (2002) *Driven: How Human Nature Shapes Our Choices*. San Francisco: Jossey-Bass.

Lieberthal, K., and Lieberthal, G (October 2003). 'The great transition', *Harvard Business Review*, 3–14.

McCloskey, D. (2010) *Bourgeois Dignity: Why Economics Can't Explain the Modern World*. Chicago: Chicago University Press.

McCloskey, D. N. (2006) *The Bourgeois Virtues: Ethics for an Age of Commerce*. Chicago: University of Chicago Press.

Mokyr, J. (2009) *The Enlightened Economy: An Economic History of Britain 1700–1850*. New Haven: Yale University Press.

Murakami, Y. (1984) 'Ie society as a pattern of civilization', *Journal of Japanese Studies*, 10,2, 279–363.

Najita, Tetsuo. (1998) *Tokugawa Political Writings*. Cambridge: Cambridge University Press.

Nakane, Chie. (1971) *Japanese Society*. London: Wiedenfeld and Nicholson.

Pye, Lucian W. (1990) 'China: erratic state, frustrated society', *Foreign Affairs*, 69, 4, 56–74.

Redding, G., and Drew, A. (2015) 'Dealing with the complexity of causes of societal innovativeness: social enabling and disabling mechanisms and the case of China', *Journal of Interdisciplinary Economics*, presented at the workshop 'Diversities of Innovation: the role of government policies for the future economic basis of societies', Friedrich-Schiller-University and Oxford University, Kellogg College. Oxford, February 17–18.

Redding, G., and Witt, M. A. (2007) *The Future of Chinese Capitalism: Choices and Chances.* Oxford: Oxford University Press.

Weber, M. (1930). *The Protestant Ethic and the Spirit of Capitalism.* London: Unwin.

Welzel, C. (2013) *Freedom Rising: Human Empowerment and the Quest for Emancipation.* Cambridge: Cambridge University Press.

Welzel, C. (2014) 'The sources of societal progress: the contribution from the World Values Survey'. HEAD Foundation Advanced Workshop: Towards New Thinking on the Sources of Societal Progress. Singapore, November 6–8.

Welzel, C., and Inglehart, R., (2013) 'Evolution, empowerment and emancipation: how societies ascend the utility ladder of freedom', Working Paper 29/SOC/2013, National Research University, Higher School of Economics, Moscow.

Witt, M. A., and Redding, G. (eds.) (2014) *The Oxford Handbook of Asian Business Systems.* Oxford: Oxford University Press.

Wittfogel, K. A. (1957) *Oriental Despotism: A Comparative View of Total Power.* New Haven: Yale University Press.

World Bank/China State Council. (2013). *China 2030: Building a Modern, Harmonious and Creative Society.* Washington, DC: World Bank.

World Values Survey. (2009) *World Values Survey 2005 Official Data File V. 20090901.* Madrid: World Values Association.

Xu, C. (2011) 'The fundamental institutions of China's reforms and development', *Journal of Economic Literature*, 49,4, 1076–1151.

Zimmerman, A., and Bollbach, M. F. (2015) 'Institutional and cultural barriers to transferring Lean production to China: evidence from a German automotive components manufacturer', *Asian Business and Management*, 14,1, 53–85.

Zucker, L. G. (1986) 'Production of trust: institutional sources of economic structure, 1840–1920', *Research in Organizational Behavior*, Stamford, CT: JAI Press, Vol. 8, 53–111.

4 | The road ahead for China

Implications from South Korean's experience

MICHAEL A. WITT

Complexity economics argues that economies need three ingredients to produce high levels of economic wealth (Beinhocker 2005): physical technologies, defined as "methods and designs for transforming matter, energy, and information from one state into another in pursuit of a goal or goals" (Beinhocker 2005: 244); social technologies, defined as "methods and designs for organizing people in pursuit of a goal or goals" (Beinhocker 2005: 262); and businesses bringing the two types of technologies together to create value.

Historically, China had no problems with physical technology, as is evident in the large number of Chinese inventions, including paper, printing, gunpowder, and the compass. Chinese scholars apparently also had an early understanding of the principles needed to build a steam engine (Needham 1965), whose development led to the Industrial Revolution in the West.

Yet as Joseph Needham noted, China's prowess in physical technology did not lead to an industrial revolution and thus also not to the higher levels of wealth (and power) Western nations began to enjoy from the eighteenth century onward. This suggests historical limitations either with social technologies or with the business landscape needed to harness it. Indeed, the social aspect has played a prominent role in hypotheses seeking to explain this disconnect between knowledge of physical technology in China and its use. Elvin (1972), for instance, argued that abundant low-cost labor made it unprofitable to invest in machines in China, a phenomenon known as "high-level equilibrium trap." Others (Fairbank, Reischauer, and Craig 1965; Jones 1981) suggested that lack of property rights discouraged investment in fixed assets. And Pye (1985) hypothesized that social conservatism used to maintain order in society stifled the application of new inventions.

China today is very different from its former dynastic self. Yet the challenge on its way to advanced industrialized country status bears

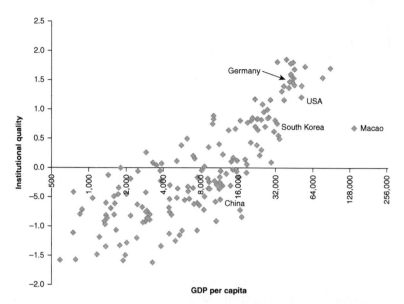

Figure 4.1 Per capita GDP and institutional quality for 166 economies (2013)
   Per capita GDP expressed in purchasing power parity at 2011 prices. Oil-based economies and economies for which the indicators are unavailable omitted.
Sources: World Development Indicators, Worldwide Governance Indicators.

some resemblance with that it has historically faced. While the country has made great strides with respect to physical technologies – even if one takes into account the many issues distorting Chinese patent numbers (Redding and Witt 2009) – and features a vibrant population of businesses keen to take advantage of new opportunities, it remains unclear whether China has developed, or can develop, suitable social technologies that will permit it to evolve into a truly rich society. Institutions are a key aspect of such social technologies (Beinhocker 2005).

   This question is arguably key for the future of China. Among others, it speaks to the puzzle whether it can avoid the middle-income trap. Economists have drawn a causal connection between the quality of institutions – defined as "humanly devised constraints that pattern human interaction" (North 1990) – and economic wealth (North 1990). Figure 4.1 illustrates this relationship by plotting levels of GDP per capita against a crude measure of institutional quality: the average score for each country on the six World Bank Governance Indicators, which are voice and accountability, political stability, government effectiveness, regulatory quality, rule of law, and control of corruption. Countries deriving their wealth mostly from oil are omitted. The estimated location of the middle-income trap is at around USD 15,000–16,000 (Eichengreen, Park, and Shin 2013). The figure suggests a close connection between institutional quality and per capita GDP: we find no poor countries with good institutions, nor rich countries with poor institutions. China, as indicated, finds itself closing in on middle-income trap levels while featuring relatively poor institutional quality. Without further institutional development, it risks getting stuck in the middle-income trap.

The objective of this chapter is to provide a perspective on the institutions – the social technology – that may help, or hinder, China on its way to becoming an advanced industrialized society. It proceeds from the position, anchored in the national business systems literature (Whitley 1999; Hall and Soskice 2001; Witt and Redding 2014b), that there are multiple ways of having good institutions, and thus of becoming rich as a nation. If also draws on this literature to present a model that identifies the key institutions in the functioning of a modern economy.

Using this model, it argues that the Chinese business system today is remarkably similar to that of South Korea[1] around 1980. Like China in 1978, Korea was among the world's poorest nations by per capita GDP[2] at the beginning of its modern economic development in 1961. Like China today, Korea's per capita GDP in 1980 was about 15 percent of that of the United States. And unlike China today, Korea has since joined the ranks of the advanced industrialized nations. Given these parallels and path dependency in the development of institutions over time, the Korean case can thus afford important insights into the possible institutional trajectory of the Chinese economy from here; the challenges it may face, which are likely to be many; and the chances of becoming a truly rich nation, which at present seem modest, despite the potential for further growth noted by Lin (Chapter 2, this volume). The chapter concludes with a set of question for future research growing out of this discussion.

---

[1] For the rest of this chapter, simply "Korea."
[2] At market exchange rates, as reliable purchasing power parity estimates are unavailable for the period.

4.1 National business systems

Assume that the economists are right and good institutions are a prerequisite for national wealth. The question, for China or any other emerging market, then becomes: What do good institutions look like? Typical answers from economists include prescriptions such as the guarantee of property rights or, in line with Figure 4.1, improvements in governance. This tells us very little, however, about the actual institutional structure of the economy.

For insights on this question, we must turn to another field of the social sciences, socio-economics, and more specifically the national business systems literature within it.[3] In line with precedent (Witt and Redding 2013), I subsume under this label both the business systems literature building on Whitley (1992, 1999) and the Varieties of Capitalism literature drawing on Hall and Soskice (2001). A key finding of this literature is that counter to expectations in the 1990s that globalization would lead advanced industrialized economies over time to converge on a single best (Anglo-Saxon) free market structure, institutional differences among these countries are both marked and persistent (e.g., Schmidt 2002; Witt and Redding 2009). There is equifinality in terms of outcomes – economic wealth – built on vastly different foundations.

Take, for instance, the economies of the two leading Western economies, Germany and the United States (Whitley 1999; Hall and Soskice 2001; Witt 2006). The United States features a financial system in which most external funds obtained by firms come directly from the markets. By contrast, German firms rely mostly on banks. The United States has an employment relations system that is characterized, among others, by low levels of unionization paired with relatively high strike activity. Average tenures of employment are around four to five years. By contrast, Germany has strong unions that strike fairly little and average job tenures more than twice those of the United States. Major US firms are usually listed on stock markets with dispersed share ownership. Major German firms are often family-controlled even when listed (e.g., BMW, Henkel, Volkswagen), and those listed firms that are not often engage in mutual ownership through cross-shareholdings. US firms have single boards representing shareholders. German firms

---

[3] I subsume the Varieties of Capitalism literature under this label. For further details, please refer to Witt and Redding (2013).

have two boards, a management board and a supervisory board, with the latter staffed, by law, in equal parts with representatives of shareholders and employees. Networking among firms (as opposed to individuals) in the US pales when compared to the interlocking directorates, cross-shareholdings, officially sanctioned cartels, and joint industry association memberships present in Germany. And US management tends to be top-down, while German management has a strong participatory element through the use of works councils and employee representation on the supervisory boards. In sum, the two countries organize their economic activities in vastly different ways. Importantly, however, they share one feature that may well be decisive for the ability of a nation to become rich: institutionalized trust, in form of well-functioning (though certainly not flawless) governance and, in particular, legal systems (see Redding, Chapter 3, this volume).

Widening the geographic focus, there is agreement in the literature that several types of business systems, or varieties of capitalism, exist among the advanced industrialized countries (though there is disagreement on how many) (Whitley 1999; Hall and Soskice 2001; Schmidt 2002; Amable 2003). Broadly speaking, Germany and Continental Northern European economies as well as Japan are often classified as coordinated market economies (CMEs), while Anglo-Saxon economies are seen as liberal market economies (LMEs). France and Latin European countries are described as mixed or state-led market economies (SMEs). Recent research on Asia further suggests that South Korea and Taiwan form a separate variety of Northeast Asian advanced economies (Witt and Redding 2013). These varieties have, so far, proved fairly stable, though of course they evolve over time. Part of this evolution involves learning from other economies, but even if the intention is to copy institutional structures one to one, the need to fit these grafts into existing institutional structures means that the results often differ in important ways (Streeck 1996). More formally, institutional path dependency constrains business systems in their development, with the consequence that countries with similar institutional structures often follow similar institutional trajectories.

For an informed discussion of the future trajectory of China, then, the question becomes whether we have seen any country with an institutional structure similar to China's join the ranks of the advanced industrialized economies. As already indicated in the introduction, the answer is that we have: South Korea, around 1980. Intuitively, it is not necessarily obvious how the Western-oriented dictatorship that was Korea thirty-five years ago could be structurally similar to present day "socialism with Chinese characteristics." Seeing this similarity requires comparative institutional analysis, which in turn requires a model, or framework, prescribing what institutional aspects of two economies to compare.

I draw here on the perhaps most complete such model, the business systems model by Redding (2005). Figure 4.2 shows a graphical representation of it. Broadly speaking, it argues that components of business systems must be understood and compared at three levels: culture, the institutional environment of firms, and the rules of coordination at the level of the firm. Each of these levels breaks down into three major components. Culture consists of rationale, that is, the objectives of economic activities (e.g., shareholder value maximization) and the accepted tools toward attaining them; identity, which is broadly consistent with Hofstede's individualism vs. collectivism dimension; and authority, which represents hierarchy and thus power distance. The institutional environment of the firm speaks to the rules governing financial capital, human capital, and social capital (seen here as trust, and thus the force that enables financial and human capital to cooperate and generate value). Rules of coordination at the firm level include the areas of ownership patterns and corporate governance, networking across firm boundaries, and coordination inside the firm (such as decision-making modes). Actors such as the state and civil society play a role in shaping these structures, as do external ideational and material forces. Path dependence enters through the role of history in shaping the various components to their present form.

4.2 The business systems of China today and South Korea in 1980

The structure of the business system of present-day China has received extensive analysis in the literature (e.g., Redding and Witt 2006; Redding and Witt 2007, 2009; Witt and Redding 2014a). To save space and avoid redundancy, I will therefore not reiterate the details but summarize in broad terms.

Figure 4.3 shows a simplified business systems analysis of China. It combines salient features of both the state-owned or state-controlled

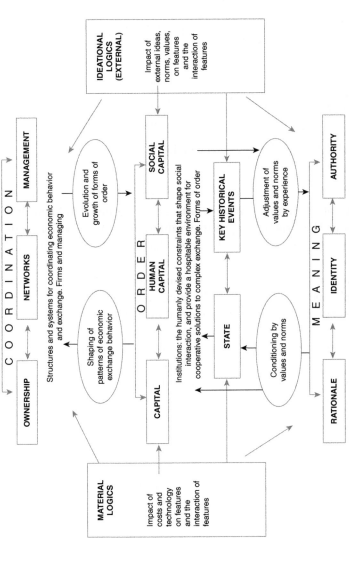

Figure 4.2 Business system model
Source: Witt and Redding, 2009.

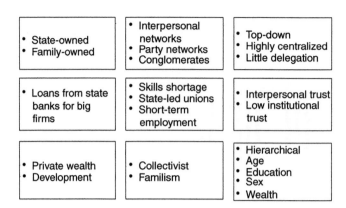

Figure 4.3 A simplified representation of the Chinese business system
Source: Witt and Redding, 2014.

as well as the private sector. At the cultural level, we find a dual rationale of generating private wealth and economic development of the nation. The striving for private wealth is most clearly visible in the private sector, though it is well known that many leaders of the state sector, including leading politicians, have done remarkably well for themselves and their families (cf. Witt and Redding 2014a). The focus on development is stronger in the state sector, even though private entrepreneurs would generally argue that by striving for private wealth, they were contributing to the economic development of the nation. We further find a collectivist identity built on familism. Authority relations are hierarchical. The main determinants of hierarchy are an ironic mix of Confucian criteria (age, education, sex) and the precise kind of material wealth a *junzi* (Confucian gentleman) would have held in disdain.

At the middle level of institutions embedding the firm, China features a bank-led financial system. Most of the commercial loans are provided to the state sector, usually at the behest of state agencies. Capital provided to these firms is obviously patient, in the sense that state companies need not worry about credit lines being withdrawn. In terms of human capital, we find an education system that, so far, has largely failed to match the skills of graduates with those needed by firms, resulting in a skills shortage. Employment tenures for most Chinese employees tend to be fairly short, though workers in the state sector usually still retain their jobs for longer periods of time. Formal organization of labor is achieved through the All China Federation of Trade Unions, which is a branch of the Chinese Communist Party (CCP) and as such represents the interest of the party, not necessarily those of local employees involved in a labor dispute. Social capital (trust) is achieved through personal connections. Institutionalized trust, by contrast, is still missing from the system, not least because the CCP positions itself as above the law.

At the top level, we find a combination of company ownership by the state and families. The latter has been the key driver of economic growth in China over the past decades and by now is estimated to contribute about two-thirds of GDP. In terms of networks, China is permeated by interpersonal, reciprocity-based networks (*guanxi*). Especially in the state sector, we also see the presence of conglomerates (business groups) and pervasive influence of the CCP. Decision-making in firms tends to be strongly top-down, with high levels of centralization and little delegation to employees. Promotions in both the private and state sectors tend to be based on relationships, with the CCP appointing the top leaders of firms in the state sector.

While there are no published formal business systems analyses on Korea in its earlier stages of development, the literature on the Korean developmental state contains sufficient information to effect an analysis at the level of detail needed here (e.g., Amsden 1989; Wade 1990; Kim 1997; Woo-Cumings 1999). The similarities with China are considerable.

At the cultural level, we find a very strong orientation toward economic development of the nation, epitomized in the corporate motto of Samsung at the time: "We do business for the sake of nation-building." The striving for private wealth seems to have been a less conspicuous element of the system, though the leaders of Korean leading firms – large conglomerates known as "*chaebol*" – certainly amassed considerable fortunes during Korean development that are still visible today (cf. Witt 2014). Similar to Chinese society, Korea features familistic collectivism. Society is hierarchical, with strong Confucian influence as a result of the adoption of Neo-Confucianism as state ideology during the Chosun era (1392–1910). The importance of wealth, clearly visible in Korea today, was apparently much less pronounced thirty-five years ago than in China today.

At the middle level, we find very similar arrangements with China's. Korean banks at the time were state-owned and state-run, and their main objective was to funnel capital to the *chaebol* to facilitate economic development. Capital was extremely patient, enabling firm to treat loans as if they were capital and building up high levels of leverage as a result (Witt 2014). In terms of human capital, Korean society likewise suffered from a skills shortage. Employment tended to be very short term, despite the formal promise of lifetime employment given at the time. Independent unions were suppressed, and formal union representation was state controlled through the Federation of Korean Trade Unions. Social capital tended to be based on interpersonal ties. As a result of the absence of the rule of law at the time, institutionalized trust was low (a fact that found visible expression in high levels of corruption in most areas of Korean politics and increasing protest activities against the government during the 1980s and 1990s).

At the top level, Korea around the 1980s featured a combination of state-owned firms, such as utilities companies or the Pohang Steel Corporation, and the family-owned *chaebol*. Families had limited control over their conglomerates, as state planners determined parameters such as expected levels of exports or what industries to enter next. As in China, networking involved high levels of interpersonal connections, such as school ties, and the building of conglomerates, the *chaebol*. Unlike China, party-based networks seem to have been absent in Korea at the time. In terms of management, we also find highly centralized, top-down decision-making with limited delegation – to the point that Korean management was described as "worse than in the military" (Whitley 1999: 146). At least in the *chaebol*, advancement to higher management levels tended to be based on relationships.

While the above analyses obviously gloss over the finer details, it is clear that there are considerable structural similarities between the business systems of Korea in the 1980s and China today. In fact, of the key characteristics of the Chinese business system as summarized in Figure 4.3, we would only need to strike "party networks" from Figure 4.3 and deemphasize the role of wealth in rationale and authority to obtain the broad outlines of the Korean business system around 1980.

4.3 The Korean trajectory since 1980

As noted earlier, the constraining influence of path dependency implies that countries with similar institutional structures are likely to follow

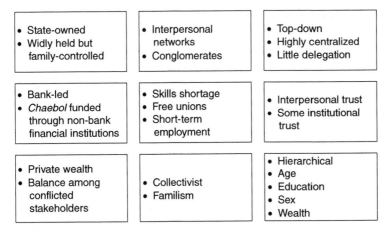

Figure 4.4 A simplified presentation of the Korean business system
Source: Witt, 2014.

similar institutional trajectories over time. Given the similarities between China today and Korea thirty-five years ago, the evolution of Korea since might afford us a glimpse of the future of China, including its ability to transcend the wall of institutions threatening to keep it at middle-income levels.

4.3.1 Changes

The Korean business system has undergone considerable transformations since the 1980s (cf. Whitley 1999), and its present shape is well documented (Witt 2014). Figure 4.4 presents a broad summary. In terms of rationale, the striving for private wealth, especially by families controlling the *chaebol*, remains, but the developmental objective has given way to a need to maintain a tenuous and tense balance between *chaebol* families on the one hand and employees and society on the other (Witt and Stahl 2015). Identity and authority have remained mostly unchanged, though the wealth element under authority has become much more accepted.

At the level of institutions embedding firms, major changes have occurred in each box of the model. Financial capital remains patient and relationship-based, but the main source of capital for the *chaebol* is no longer directed lending by state-owned banks. Rather, the *chaebol* now tap non-bank financial institutions, such as insurance companies and securities firms, that they own. As for human capital, state-controlled unions have given way to free unions. General education is now world class, though skills shortages persist because universities have not succeeded in matching the training they provide with the skills requirements of firms. Employment tenures remain fairly short overall – on a par with the United States – but are around ten years for *chaebol* firms. Social capital has seen the emergence of some institutionalized trust, which might have developed further were it not for a constant stream of revelations about corruption in politics and the apparent impunity with which families controlling the *chaebol* break the law.

At the top level, ownership has seen changes in the private sector. The families who founded the *chaebol* usually own only a small proportion of their outstanding stock. However, they still control them, though now with much less interference from the state as in the 1980s. Control is retained through mechanisms such as pyramidal shareholdings and cross-shareholdings, earning Korea a relatively poor score in terms of corporate governance. State-owned firms persist in key sectors. The network box has overall remained largely unchanged, as have the main outlines of management.

It is worth noting that those elements of the system that underwent marked change usually did so within the larger context of a change in political governance in Korea. In 1980, Korea was a highly centralized, authoritarian dictatorship. Democratization, starting in the 1980s, has since transformed it into a full democracy (Economist Intelligence Unit 2014), though it still remains highly centered on the presidency. Along with this process went liberalization of the financial system, which first resulted in the privatization of banks and, later in the context of the Asian Financial Crisis of 1997/8, foreign ownership of major banks. This has weakened, but not eliminated, the capacity of the Korean state to steer the economy through directed lending. It has also pushed the *chaebol*, which are forbidden to own banks, into expanding their ownership of non-bank financial institutions.

The link with democracy is even clearer in human capital. Union protests played a decisive role in the push for democracy in the 1980s, and democracy obviously enables the existence of independent unions. Unionization rates tend to be fairly low at around 10 percent, though for larger firms such as the *chaebol*, they reach an average of about 45 percent, giving unions clout in negotiations. That does not mean that all is well with labor rights in Korea. Despite the presence of unions, the International Trade Union Confederation rates Korea in the same category as China, making them among "the worst countries in the world to work in," with "no guarantee of rights" (International Trade Union Confederation 2014: 15).

Most importantly, however, the transition to democracy is likely to be closely linked to the development of some institutionalized trust. Institutionalized trust is essentially a result of confidence that a system of rules and processes will, by and large, create fair outcomes (cf. Witt and Redding 2013; Li and Redding 2014). Historical accounts of Korea in the 1970s and 1980s suggest that institutionalized trust, to the extent it existed at all, may well have been limited to the core areas of industrial policy (Amsden 1989; Eckert et al. 1990). Here, the fundamental, and enforced, understanding was that *chaebol* families could expect any help necessary to expand their businesses if only they met government-imposed export targets (Amsden 1989). Korea today, by contrast, has an average governance score of 0.75 in the Worldwide Governance Indicator, which places it at the seventy-fifth percentile (higher being better) among the 210 countries rated in the database. Again, the upside potential is yet to be captured: the scores for Germany and the United States are, respectively, 1.47 and 1.21, and top scorer Finland registered 1.85. But it suggests that Korea has made great strides over the past decades.

The implication of these observations for China is that it will be difficult to divorce the question of further economic development from that of democratization, no matter how hard the CCP tries. Figure 4.5 shows a scatter plot of per capita GDP against the Economist Intelligence Unit (EIU) Democracy Index. The parallels with Figure 4.1 are obvious. Democracy and institutional quality seem to be linked. Indeed, the only non-resource-based nation that, for a while, succeeded in resisting this relationship was Singapore. Party functionaries hopeful of emulating the Singapore experience should note, though, that given the urban nature of the Singapore economy, its GDP levels have tended to overstate levels of development relative to nations with rural hinterlands – it is best compared with cities, not countries. And even Singapore has seen an upward trend in the Democracy Index, having reached "flawed democracy" status in 2014 (Economist Intelligence Unit 2014). Barrington Moore (1966) would thus seem to have been right to link bourgeoisie and democracy.

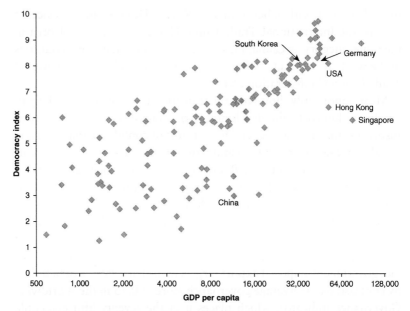

Figure 4.5 Per capita GDP and democracy for 141 economies
Per capita GDP expressed in purchasing power parity at 2011 prices. Oil-based economies and economies for which the indicators are unavailable omitted.
Sources: EIU Democracy Index, World Development Indicators.

Chinese policymakers at this point seem to be trying to sever the link. The most likely outcomes would seem to be either that they fail to prevent democratization, in which case path dependency would suggest a similar trajectory as in Korea, or that they succeed, in which case the evidence in Figure 4.5 would suggest that China would be unlikely to escape the middle-income trap. Put differently, in the next decades, the CCP is likely to be either losing power in a wealthy China, or trying to hold on to power in a stagnant middle-income China.

4.3.2 *Constants*

The changes summarized above coexist with a range of stable elements. First, the importance of family business has endured. This is the case even for large, publicly listed *chaebol* firms. While the families that founded the *chaebol* usually retain only a small proportion of the overall stock of these conglomerates – usually a single-digit percentage – they have managed to retain control, as already discussed. This links to a second constant element, the top-down and centralized nature of decision-making in firms. As before, major decisions are made by the chairman (rarely chairwoman), who is invariably a member of the controlling family. They do not make these decisions without support from numerous staff, but by all accounts, the final decision power still rests with them. Top-down management likewise persists further down the corporate food chain, and delegation levels are among the lowest in Asia, below Indonesia and just ahead of India, Cambodia, and China.

Family control is reinforced by the continued availability of indirect finance. While Korean policymakers had the foresight to prevent the *chaebol* from owning banks, access to non-bank financial institutions continues to provide the *chaebol* with patient capital. One effect is that the *chaebol* can ignore the interests of other shareholders and the corporate governance discount on their share valuations because they do not need the markets to obtain funding.

Likewise, there persists a shortage of usable skills in the labor force, whose causes have not been addressed. As already mentioned, the education system does not succeed in providing students with skills companies need. A report from the Federation of Korean Industries, for instance, suggests that fresh graduates need at least twenty-three months of in-house training to be useful. Only the *chaebol*, and perhaps some foreign firms, have the resources to do this. What complicates matters further is the relatively short employment tenure, meaning that companies investing in their employees will receive little return on their investment. Again, the *chaebol* with employment tenures of around ten years are in a better position. Most Koreans do not work for *chaebol*, however, and the overall result is that Korea has by far the highest level of inactive youth not in employment, education, or training (NEETs) in the OECD. Tertiary education is part of the problem, with about three quarters of Koreans graduating from college, often without economically valuable skills.

These constants mirror the present shape of China, and they provide a sense of likely challenges China will face in the future. One key question will be how to handle highly complex, high value-added products in a top-down environment with limited delegation (cf. Redding and Witt 2007 and Redding, Chapter 3, this volume).

In these structures, the creation of strategy, plans, and overall processes is the prerogative of top leaders. Lower ranks are expected to function within these parameters, subject to key performance indicators used to judge their performance. The result tends to be a silo-structure in which people manage upward and downward but hardly ever connect laterally. Cooperation across functional areas, however, is a key ingredient in handling complexity and thus high value-added products.

One might argue that some Korean firms, such as Samsung, seem to have overcome this challenge. The jury on this point is still out, however. For Samsung, for instance, one question is to what extent success of the firm has been the product of leadership by Lee Kun-hee. Samsung's performance has suffered notably since his heart attack in May 2014, which has prevented him from leading the firm. One might also argue that its success in recent years, much of it built on mobile phones, was the result of a typical fast-follower strategy (cf. Redding and Witt 2007). Striking similarities between Samsung and Apple phones have been widely discussed, and reports have noted that Samsung was following a template it had successfully employed in other product lines before (Eichenwald 2014).

Top-down systems perform well under these circumstances. But Samsung has not been able to coordinate across different areas, for example, by bringing together software, hardware, and cloud-based services, as Apple has. Instead, it remains dependent on external providers such as Google, and vulnerable to firms that can execute the same strategy at even lower cost, such as Xiaomi.

The second large question will be how to build up an education and training system that leaves students with useful skills. There is no doubt that education in China has expanded rapidly (Witt and Redding 2014a). At the same time, more education does not necessarily mean more useful education, as Korea has learned. And China features even shorter employment tenures in the private sector (where most growth has been), which makes it difficult for firms to offer extensive internal training.

4.4 Implications for China and for future research

This chapter proceeded from the position, anchored in the national business systems literature (Whitley 1999; Hall and Soskice 2001; Witt and Redding 2014b), that there are multiple ways of having good institutions, and thus of becoming rich as a nation. If also drew on this literature to present a model that identifies the key institutions in the functioning of a modern economy. Using this model, it argued that the Chinese business system today is remarkably similar to that of South Korea around 1980. Given path dependency in the development of institutions over time, it suggested that the South Korean case can afford important insights into the possible institutional trajectory of the Chinese economy from here; the challenges it may face, which are likely to be many; and the chances of becoming a truly rich nation, which at present seem modest.

The key question for China moving forward is how to improve its quality of governance, and in particular, how to build institutionalized trust.

For scholarly research, the above considerations offer potential for further explorations in at least four areas. First, is it possible to build good institutions, and thus endow a society with social technology needed to get rich, without democratization? In particular, how can one build institutionalized trust without limited government?

For China, this is arguably the key question at this point. Historical precedent suggests an important role for democratization, but the prospect of this occurring in the foreseeable future in China seems, at present, unlikely. It certainly does not seem to be consistent with the intentions of the Xi administration to keep the country under tight CCP control. History is full of unintended consequences, though, and in doing so, he may well help bring about the outcome he is trying to resist (cf. Buckley 2015). But patterns often have exceptions, and these can be highly instructive. It would seem that while we have a good sense of the importance of social capital in the development of nations, much less is still known about how develop it – especially the institutionalized kind.

Second, assuming institutionalized trust, and given equifinality (i.e., the possibility that different combinations of social technologies are equally competitive), what combinations of social technologies may lead to high economic performance? What functional substitutes exist?

The examples of Germany and the United States, discussed earlier, illustrate the motivation for this question. As shown, their economies are structured very differently. At the same time, they both generate roughly comparable levels of per capital wealth. This, at first glance, may not be obvious, with 2013 per capita GDP, at constant 2005 prices and purchasing power parity, at USD 35,724 in Germany and USD

45,665 in the United States (OECD 2015). However, to gain an accurate picture of the performance of the underlying institutional structures, a number of corrections are necessary. For instance, Americans in 2013 on average worked 400 hours longer per year than Germans. Free time has value, and once the opportunity cost of German vacations and shorter working hours is taken into account, GDP levels are approximately the same.

The question for China thus is not how to copy the structures of advanced industrialized nations. Rather, it is how within the constraints of path dependency it can evolve a structure that permits high levels of economic performance. Following the Korean path seems to be the most likely option, but small and possibly conscious changes may have an important impact.

Third, what is the role of regional variations in possibly evolving such functional substitutes? A well-documented characteristic of modern China has been the role of regional experimentation in evolving new information about feasible institutional changes (Xu 2011). These processes may well continue, as the new Shanghai Free-Trade Zone illustrates (even though it very much remains work in progress). Given the linkage of wealth with at least limited government, an intriguing question is whether there is a role for experimentation with political reforms in conjunction with the economic objectives. To the extent the CCP would even consider such an experiment, the key question would be, how can the party at once tie its hands and not interfere with the governance experiment while at the same time remaining ultimately in control? The recent experience of Hong Kong would suggest that the CCP has not found a credible answer.

Fourth, what leeway do micro-level actors – individuals and firms – have to work around institutional misalignments at the systemic level (cf. Witt and Lewin 2007)? To put it differently, how can these actors create a suitable environment for themselves that diverges from the overall systemic institutional structure? For instance, Korean *chaebol* have been able to keep employees for longer periods than usual in Korea, which in turn enabled them to train them with usable skills. Regional experimentation has permitted similar deviations from the norm in China. It would be important to know under what local contingencies firms have managed to address shortcomings of the Chinese business system, and how they have done so. A better understanding of these questions would not only provide valuable insights into the Chinese economy, but also help evolve a better theory on business systems and the local embeddedness of firms in social technologies.

References

Amable, Bruno. 2003. *The Diversity of Modern Capitalism*. Oxford: Oxford University Press.

Amsden, Alice H. 1989. *Asia's Next Giant: South Korea and Late Industrialization*. Oxford: Oxford University Press.

Beinhocker, Eric D. 2005. *The Origin of Wealth: Evolution, Complexity, and the Radical Remaking of Economics*. London: Random House.

Buckley, Chris. 2015. *Q. And A.: David Shambaugh on the Risks to Chinese Communist Rule*. Accessed on March 15, 2015. Available from http://si nosphere.blogs.nytimes.com/2015/03/15/q-and-a-david-shambaugh-on-the-risks-to-chinese-communist-rule/?_r=0.

Eckert, Carter J., Ki-baik Lee, Young Ick Lew, Michael Robinson, and Edward W. Wagner. 1990. *Korea Old and New: A History*. Cambridge, MA: Korea Institute, Harvard University.

Economist Intelligence Unit. 2014. *Democracy Index 2014: Democracy and Its Discontents*. London: Economist Intelligence Unit.

Eichengreen, Barry, Donghyun Park, and Kwanho Shin. 2013. *Growth Slowdowns Redux: New Evidence on the Middle-Income Trap*. Cambridge, MA: National Bureau of Economic Research.

Eichenwald, Kurt. 2014. *The Great Smartphone War*. Accessed on May 20, 2014. Available from www.vanityfair.com/news/business/2014 /06/apple-samsung-smartphone-patent-war.

Elvin, M. 1972. The high level equilibrium trap: the causes of the decline of invention in the traditional Chinese textile industries. In *Economic Organization in Chinese Society*, edited by W. E. Willmott. Stanford, CA: Stanford University Press.

Fairbank, John King, Edwin O. Reischauer, and Alexander M. Craig. 1965. *East Asia: The Modern Transformation*. Boston: Houghton Mifflin.

Hall, Peter A., and David Soskice. 2001. An introduction to varieties of capitalism. In *Varieties of Capitalism: The Institutional Foundations of Comparative Advantage*, edited by P. A. Hall and D. Soskice. Oxford: Oxford University Press.

International Trade Union Confederation. 2014. *ITUC Global Rights Index*. Brussels: ITUC.

Jones, Eric Lionel. 1981. *The European Miracle: Environments, Economies, and Geopolitics in the History of Europe and Asia.* Cambridge: Cambridge University Press.

Kim, Eun Mee. 1997. *Big Business, Strong State: Collusion and Conflict in South Korean Development, 1960–1990.* Albany, NY: State University of New York Press.

Li, Peter Ping, and Gordon Redding. 2014. Social capital in Asia: its dual nature and function. In *The Oxford Handbook of Asian Business Systems*, edited by M. A. Witt and G. Redding. Oxford: Oxford University Press.

Moore, Barrington. 1966. *Social Origins of Dictatorship and Democracy: Lord and Peasant in the Making of the Modern World.* Vol. 268. Boston: Beacon Press.

Needham, Joseph. 1965. *Science and Civilization in China.* Vol. IV: 2. Cambridge: Cambridge University Press.

North, Douglass Cecil. 1990. Institutions, institutional change and economic performance. In *Political Economy of Institutions and Decisions*, edited by J. E. Alt and D. C. North. Cambridge: Cambridge University Press.

OECD. 2015. *OECD.Stat.* Accessed on March 12, 2015. Available from http://stats.oecd.org.

Pye, Lucian W. 1985. *Asian Power and Politics.* Cambridge, MA: Belknap Press.

Redding, Gordon. 2005. The thick description and comparison of societal systems of capitalism. *Journal of International Business Studies* 36 (2):123–155.

Redding, Gordon, and Michael A. Witt. 2006. The "tray of loose sand": a thick description of the state-owned enterprise sector of China seen as a business system. *Asian Business & Management* 5 (1):87–112.

——— 2007. *The Future of Chinese Capitalism: Choices and Chances.* Oxford: Oxford University Press.

——— 2009. China's business system and its future trajectory. *Asia Pacific Journal of Management* 26 (3):381–399.

Schmidt, Vivien A. 2002. *The Futures of European Capitalism.* Oxford: Oxford University Press.

Streeck, Wolfgang. 1996. Lean production in the German automobile industry: a test case for convergence theory. In *National Diversity and Global Capitalism*, edited by S. Berger and R. P. Dore. Ithaca, NY: Cornell University Press.

Wade, Robert. 1990. *Governing the Market: Economic Theory and the Role of Government in East Asian Industrialization*. Princeton, NJ: Princeton University Press.

Whitley, Richard. 1992. *Business Systems in East Asia: Firms, Markets and Societies*. London: Sage Publications.

1999. *Divergent Capitalisms: The Social Structuring and Change of Business Systems*. Oxford: Oxford University Press.

Witt, Michael A. 2006. *Changing Japanese Capitalism: Societal Coordination and Institutional Adjustment*. Cambridge: Cambridge University Press.

2014. South Korea: plutocratic state-led capitalism reconfiguring. In *The Oxford Handbook of Asian Business Systems*, edited by M. A. Witt and G. Redding. Oxford: Oxford University Press.

Witt, Michael A., and Arie Y. Lewin. 2007. Outward foreign direct investment as escape response to home country institutional constraints. *Journal of International Business Studies* 38 (4):579–594.

Witt, Michael A., and Gordon Redding. 2009. Culture, meaning, and institutions: executive rationale in Germany and Japan. *Journal of International Business Studies* 40 (5):859–895.

2013. Asian business systems: institutional comparison, clusters and implications for varieties of capitalism and business systems theory. *Socio-Economic Review* 11 (2):265–300.

2014a. China: authoritarian capitalism. In *The Oxford Handbook of Asian Business Systems*, edited by M. A. Witt and G. Redding. Oxford: Oxford University Press.

eds. 2014b. *The Oxford Handbook of Asian Business Systems*. Oxford: Oxford University Press.

Witt, Michael A., and Günter K. Stahl. 2015. Foundations of responsible leadership: Asian versus Western executive responsibility orientations toward key stakeholders. *Journal of Business Ethics*. Available from http://10.1007/s10551-014-2534-8.

Woo-Cumings, Meredith, ed. 1999. *The Developmental State*. Ithaca, NY: Cornell University Press.

Xu, Chenggang. 2011. The fundamental institutions of China's reforms and development. *Journal of Economic Literature* 49 (4):1076–1151.

5 | Innovation and technological specialization of Chinese industry

KEUN LEE

5.1 Introduction

The middle-income trap (MIT) is a situation in which middle-income countries face a slowdown of growth as they get caught between low-wage manufacturers and high-wage innovators because their wage rates are too high to compete with low-wage exporters and the level of their technological capability is too low to enable them to compete with advanced countries (Lin 2012; Williamson 2012; World Bank 2010 and 2012; Yusuf and Nabeshima 2009). The risk of the MIT is not limited to the selected countries but is relevant to many countries in the world. The China Report by the World Bank (2012) compares the income levels of several countries (compared with that of the United States) in 1960 with those in 2008. This analysis reveals that at least thirty countries have fallen into the MIT. Specifically, income growth is more significantly slowed in upper middle-income countries or in countries with an income level of 20% to 30% of that of the United States.

As China increases its economic growth, reaching around 30% of the per capita income of the United States, it faces the possibility of the so-called middle-income trap, similar to other middle-income developing economies (Lee 2013a). Several countries have attained middle-income status but have subsequently failed to achieve high-income status. Examples from Latin America include Brazil and Argentina, whose growth stalled in the 1980s and 1990s, respectively (Lee and Kim 2009, table 1).

There can be many criteria upon which to judge the possibility of the MIT, and the difficulty is identifying the effective criteria for the assessment. Thus, being agnostic about the causes of the MIT, Aiyar

This chapter is based on a presentation made at the MOR conference held in Hong Kong, early December, 2014, and draws upon Lee and Li (2014) and Lee (2013a). The author thanks comments by the editors of this volume.

et al. (2013) consider as broad a range of factors as possible, such as demographic conditions; institutions; and industry and trade structures, including diversification, physical infrastructure, and macrofinancial developments. They test whether each of these is particularly binding for middle-income countries. On the one hand, the literature finds political institution variables, such as democracy and the rule of law, important for economic growth in general or in low-income countries but insignificant in middle-income countries (Aiyar et al. 2013; Huang, Qin, and Xun 2013; Lee and Kim 2009). On the other hand, physical infrastructure or investment is significant for economic growth in middle-income countries (Aiyar et al. 2013), but China has been investing heavily in this infrastructure and can be considered free from shortage of such. Thus, physical infrastructure would not be an interesting or meaningful criterion to assess the MIT in China.

This study will use innovation as the criterion to assess the possibility of the MIT in China. Innovation is a significant factor for economic growth in middle-income countries and particularly relevant for China, but mixed evidence exists that China has already overcome this constraint or not (Eichengreen, Park, and Shin 2013; Jin and Lee 2013; Lee 2013a; Lee and Kim 2009; Lee et al. 2013; Sylwester 2000). In particular, this study pays attention of the emerging pattern of technological specialization in China, and it addresses the question of whether China is also moving into short-cycle technology-based sectors, which have been the leading sectors of the past catch-up in Korea or Taiwan (Lee 2013a).

The next section discusses further why innovation can be a good criterion to discuss the MIT issue. Then, Sections 5.3 and 5.4 discuss innovation capability and technological specialization of Chinese industry, respectively. Section 5.5 concludes.

5.2 Why innovation as the criterion to assess possibility of the MIT in China

This criterion of innovation is most consistent with the original concern expressed by the term MIT, because numerous studies consider it to occur as middle-income countries get caught between low-wage manufacturers and high-wage innovators because their wage rates are too high to compete with low-wage exporters and their level of technological capability is too low to enable them to compete with advanced countries (Lin 2012; Williamson 2012; World Bank 2010 and 2012; Yusuf and Nabeshima 2009). In other words, the MIT phenomenon is a problem of growth slowdown because of weak innovation.

Also, when countries are divided into income groups, only innovation and higher education matter for upper middle- and high-income countries, whereas political institutions and primary and secondary education matter for low- and lower middle-income countries (Lee and Kim 2009). Eichengreen, Park, and Shin (2013) also find human capital and innovation important, especially tertiary education, for upper middle-income countries. Given that China is already an upper middle-income country, those criteria of higher education and innovation make sense for China.

A World Bank (2005: 11) assessment of the reform decade of the 1990s also observes that growth-oriented actions, such as technological catch-up and the encouragement of risk taking, may be needed for faster accumulation and recognizes technological innovation as one of the most serious bottlenecks of growth in many countries, especially in the middle-income countries of Latin America. Lee and Mathews (2010) also compare the East Asian experience with the elements of the Washington Consensus to argue that the mixed results of the consensus are related to missing or neglected policies, such as technological policies and revolutions in higher education.

R&D-to-GDP ratio is one simple criterion to look at countries' innovation capabilities. Although one might expect a positive correlation between income levels and the R&D–GDP ratio, the ratio suddenly becomes flat among middle-income countries (Lee 2013b), or countries with per capita income between USD 1,000 and USD 10,000. In other words, the ratio does not increase proportionally with per capita income in this group of countries, suggesting that the flat relationship is a root cause of the MIT, as noted in Lee (2013a) by the same graph.

A similar conclusion can be derived by examining the number of US patents filed by countries. In the early 1980s, when the income level of Korea was similar to those of Brazil and Argentina, the number of US patent applications by Koreans was approximately fifty, within the range of other middle-income countries, such as Brazil and Argentina (Lee and Kim 2009; table 1). In the 1980s and 1990s, Korean applications increased rapidly to more than ten times the average of other middle-income countries where incomes remained relatively flat.

In 2000, Korea and Taiwan filed approximately 5,000 US patent applications, whereas other middle- or lower-income countries, including Brazil and Argentina, filed less than 500 per year (Lee and Kim 2009). In other words, the difference between the more successful Asian economies and the less successful Latin American economies (or the reversal of fortune between these two groups of countries) can be explained by the amount of priority given to the enhancement of long-term growth potentials, particularly innovation capability (Lee 2013a; Lee and Kim 2009).

5.3 Innovation capability of China

As stated in the preceding sections, one criterion in assessing the ability of a country to move beyond the MIT is whether the country is sufficiently innovative to achieve a certain level of technological capability backed up by an adequate emphasis on higher or tertiary education. In general, our answer to this question is that China appears to be performing well.

In this regard, literature has already noted several unique features of Chinese industry and firms in building technological capabilities and promoting industrial development. Lee et al. (Lee, Jee, and Eun 2011; Lee et al. 2013) note that unique Chinese features include the following three elements: (1) parallel learning from foreign direct investment (FDI) firms to promote indigenous companies; (2) an emphasis on "forward engineering" (the function of university spin-off firms) in contrast to the reverse engineering of Korea and Taiwan; (3) the acquisition of technology and brands via international mergers and acquisitions. These three elements may be regarded as comprising the Beijing model because they have not been explicitly adopted by Korea and Taiwan (Lee, Jee, and Eun 2011).

Although the above is a qualitative account of China's success in technological learning and upgrading, many quantitative indications are also available as discussed in what follows. First, we can consider the ratio of R&D to GDP, a basic measure of the innovation efforts of a country. Lee (2010) observes that China has strongly been pushing for considerable R&D expenditure and thus surpassed the 1% threshold ratio of R&D to GDP in 2000, earlier than the majority of middle-income countries in Latin America did. The spending of China on R&D as a percentage of GDP, known as R&D intensity, has more than doubled from 0.6% in 1995 to over 1.3% in 2003. This increase has accelerated since the 2000s and is now close to 2.0%. Actually, China is an outlier among middle-income countries with a high ratio of R&D to GDP.

Because of this massive investment in R&D, China has rapidly increased its flow of patents. The average growth rate of domestic invention patenting has increased, from approximately 17% in the earlier period to approximately 49% in the later period (Lee 2010, table 4), with approximately 5,000 patents registered in early 2000 to more than 20,000 in the late 2000s. The number of patent applications abroad (particularly in the United States) has also increased. The number of US patents filed by China reached more than 2,500 in 2010, greater than that of US patents filed by other middle-income countries (less than 300 patents per year) (Table 5.1). In terms of the growth rate of patents, China ranked first in the world in the 2000s, whereas Korea dominated in the 1990s.

Another important comparative criterion is whether China measures up to the three important yardsticks of technological catch-up (Lee and Kim 2010) followed by Japan, Korea, and Taiwan in the past: (a) whether resident patenting catches up with nonresident patenting in a host country, (b) whether regular invention patents catch up with utility model patents (petite patents), and (c) whether corporate patent-ing catches up with individual inventor patenting. Lee (2010) high-lights that all these three patterns of catch-up were observed in China in the mid 2000s. In terms of the number of patent applications in China, the share of domestic inventors outgrew that of foreigners in 2003, with domestic inventors filing more than 50,000 applications. In 2004, the number of regular invention patents exceeded that of utility model patents. In 2007, the number of patent applications by corporations exceeded that of applications by individual inventors, signifying the growing importance of corporate innovation. While these are achieve-ments in terms of domestic patents filed in China, the vast bulk of Chinese USPTO patents are owned by foreign firms, which should be the area China must try to improve.

5.4 Technological specialization in China

As the last but probably the most important indicator of the technolo-gical strength of China, let us turn to technological specialization.

Table 5.1 US patents granted to selected countries (1981–2010)

Country	1981	1985	1990	1995	2000	2005	2008	2009	2010
USA	39,218	39,556	47,391	55,739	85,068	74,637	77,502	82,382	107,792
Japan	8,389	12,746	19,525	21,764	31,295	30,341	33,682	35,501	44,814
Germany	6,304	6,718	7,614	6,600	10,235	9,011	8,914	9,000	12,363
Taiwan	80	174	732	1,620	4,667	5,118	6,339	6,642	8,238
Korea	17	41	225	1,161	3,314	4,352	7,548	8,762	11,671
China	2	1	47	62	119	402	1,225	1,655	2,657
India	6	10	23	37	131	384	634	679	1,098
Brazil	23	30	41	63	98	77	101	103	175
Malaysia	1	3	3	7	42	88	152	158	202

Source: The United States Patent and Trademark Office (USPTO). Table 8.3 of Lee, 2013a.

According to Lee (2013a), technological specialization matters more for countries at the middle-income stage, whereas the traditional trade-based specialization, following the resource-based factor intensity, is relevant from the low- to the middle-income stage.

Technological specialization can be measured by the cycle time of technologies shown by patent portfolio of countries (Lee 2013a). "Cycle time" refers to the speed with which technologies change or become obsolete over time and the speed and frequency at which new technologies emerge (Lee 2013a; Park and Lee 2006). A technology-based sector with short cycle time relies less on existing technologies and can thus leverage the great opportunities brought by new technologies. Lee (2013a) argues that qualified latecomers have great advantages in targeting technological sectors with short cycle time and specializing in these sectors because a short cycle of technologies implies that dominance by the incumbent is often disrupted and that new technologies always present new opportunities. Minimal reliance on existing technologies indicates low entry barriers and high profitability associated with few collisions with the technologies of advanced countries, minimal royalty payments, and even first- or fast-mover advantages or product differentiation (Lee 2013a).[1]

Thus, combined with the new structural economics idea of the "growth identification and facilitation" framework of Lin (Chapter 2 in this volume; 2012), the idea of technological specialization may provide a comprehensive policy framework for economic growth of developing countries. Lin (Chapter 2 in this volume) advises latecomers to closely observe the countries slightly ahead of them, and then to target the mature industries in those countries as their latent comparative advantages. While such recommendations are an effective and practical guide for sectoral targeting for those developing countries, in particular at lower-income stages, this, a more theoretical, argument for technology-based specialization works better for upper middle-income countries. In other words, after a developing country makes some success with inheriting mature sectors from countries above them, it may then be advised also to try to enter sectors based on shorter-cycle technology or even to take the risk of leapfrogging into

---

[1] Of course, other aspects of the technological regime must also be considered; for example, while corporate software is a short-cycle technology, it corresponds to a higher degree of network effects and cumulativeness which make it difficult to enter for latecomer firms.

new or emerging sectors. Of course, the whole process should be a gradual movement into shorter-cycle sectors involving multiple stages. So, the point is that sustained catching-up growth requires not only an entrance into mature industries (which are still new to the latecomers), but also leapfrogging into emerging industries that are new to both the advanced and developing countries.

Technological development in Korea (Lee 2013a) shows the increasing specialization of Korean industries based on short cycle time. The Korean economy began with labor-intensive (long-cycle technology) industries, such as apparel or shoe industries, in the 1960s. The economy then moved toward the short- or medium-cycle sectors of low-end consumer electronics and automobile assemblies in the 1970s and 1980s and then even further to the shorter-cycle sectors of telecommunication equipment (telephone switches) since the late 1980s, and then memory chips, cell phones, and digital TVs in the 1990s. Korean industries have kept moving into shorter-cycle technologies and have thus achieved technological diversification.

Figure 5.1 shows the actual trends in the cycle time of technologies as calculated following US patents jointly held by Korea and Taiwan and those held by China. The numbers in the vertical axis represent the average cycle time of patents held by the economies, defined by Jaffe and Trajtenberg (2002) as the mean backward citation lags, namely, the time difference between the application or grant year of the *citing* patent and that of the *cited* patents. For example, a value of eight on the vertical axis indicates that the average cycle time of patents is eight years, indicating, for instance, that Korea and Taiwan jointly cite eight-year-old patents on average. Since the mid 1980s, both catching-up economies have traveled in a path toward technologies with an increasingly short cycle time. Thus, the average cycle time of the patents held by Korea and Taiwan became shorter, reaching six to seven years by the late 1990s. This duration is two to three years shorter than the average cycle time of the patents held by European G5 countries whose cycle time has ranged from nine to ten years since the late 1980s. Consequently, Korea and Taiwan have a completely different patent portfolio from those of other advanced countries (Lee 2013a). Therefore, we consider the mid 1980s as an important turning point that opened a path for sustained catch-up beyond the middle-income stage. In this period, Taiwan and Korea reached the middle-income level: the per capita GDP of Korea became 25% of that of the United

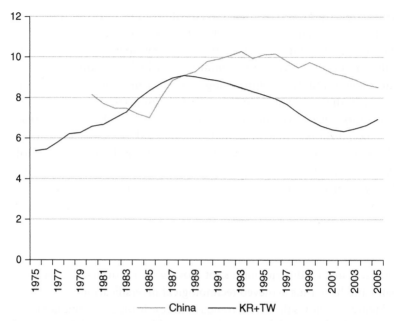

Figure 5.1 Cycle time of technology shown in US patents by China and Korea/
Taiwan
Source: Author's calculation according to method used by Lee, 2013a.

States, and Korea and Taiwan increased their R&D expenditure, with
their R&D–GDP ratio averaging more than 1% annually. Thus, when
these countries decisively began the journey toward more technology-
based growth, the cycle time of their technologies moved in progressively shorter directions, such as various IT products.

However, after they achieved technological catch-up, the next stage
for maturing of specialization should occur. Actually, Figure 5.1 shows
that only in the 2000s, when Korea and Taiwan became more mature
economies, their technologies turned in the opposite direction toward
long cycles. Lee (2013a) explained: "This strategy of technological
specialization in short-cycle technologies during the catching-up period
is a 'detour' because developing countries do not directly and immediately replicate the path and industries of advanced economies that
specialize in long-cycle technologies. Instead, countries that are successful at catching up have moved initially in the opposite direction
progressively   toward   a   sector   with   short-cycle   technologies."

However, as the countries reach the point of technological maturity (as many did in the early 2000s), their success enables them to adopt long-cycle technologies, such as biomedical or pharmaceutical industries.

Therefore, an interesting measure of the prospects of a country beyond the middle-income stage is whether it has reached such a "technological turning point" and has switched from long cycles to short ones along the curve of the cycle time of technologies. Figure 5.1, based on Lee (2013a), shows that China passed such a turning point in the middle to late 1990s, approximately ten to fifteen years later than Korea. The top thirty technologies in the US patents of China (Lee 2013a, table 8.4) are similar to those of Korea and Taiwan from 1980 to 1995. The Chinese hold several patents for semiconductors, information storage, telecommunications, electrical lighting, electrical heating, X-rays, and computer hardware and software. The weighted average cycle time of Chinese technology from 2000 to 2005 was 8.07 years, closer to the Korean/Taiwanese average of 7.69 from 1980 to 1995 than to the Brazilian/Argentinean average of 9.26 in the same period (Lee 2013a).

In sum, the short cycle time of technologies of the US patents held by China and its turning point in the late 1990s can be regarded as additional evidence of the progress of the country in terms of innovation. Jin, Lee, and Kim (2008) and Jin and Lee (2013) also show that the growth engines of China have shifted from FDI, denationalization, and exports to innovation and exports. Cross-province regressions reveal that whereas exports, FDI, and the reduction of the state sector were the important growth engines during the early period, knowledge and innovation have become more important in the recent period and that, among traditional policy variables, shares in exports remain significant, but shares in foreign capital and state ownership have been insignificant to economic growth.

5.5 Concluding remarks

This chapter discusses the possibility of China falling into the so-called MIT in terms of innovation capability, especially its technological specialization into short- or long-cycle sectors. The conclusion is that China has increasingly become innovative and thus differs from other middle-income countries. So, China is not likely to be falling into the MIT at least from the innovation point of view. In terms of technological specialization, China has already passed the "technological turning point" by increasingly moving into short-cycle technology-based sectors. Lee (2013a) shows that China passed such a turning point in the middle to late 1990s, approximately ten to fifteen years later than Korea or Taiwan.

The next issue will be when China will pass the second technological turning point of moving back into the long-cycle technology-based sectors. In the case of smaller economies, like Korea, this second turning point came in the early 2000s. One can expect a giant economy like China to show a more balanced pattern of specialization at an earlier stage or in a shorter period of time after the first turning point. Verification of this conjecture can be done by updating the trend of the average cycle time using the more recent portfolio of the Chinese-held patents. If one can find a new trend that the average cycle time of the Chinese-owned patents are getting longer, for instance, by the increase of patents in biomedical industries, that may be a signal of the arrival of the second turning point of China's technological specialization. There are some signs that this is happening actually, as we are now witnessing the rise of successful companies in diverse fields, including Beijing Genomics Institute (BGI) in biotechnologies. Given that long-cycle sectors may require a longer time to achieve some results, different policy approaches, different from the traditional supply-side-oriented targeting, may be needed. This issue can be a topic for future research.

References

Aiyar, Shekhar, Romain Duval, Damien Puy, Yiqun Wu, Longmei Zhang (2013). *Growth Slowdowns and the Middle-Income Trap*. IMF Working Paper, 71. Washington, DC: IMF.

Eichengreen, Barry, Donghyun Park, Kwanho Shin (2013). *Growth Slowdowns Redux: New Evidence on the Middle-Income Trap*. NBER Working Paper, No. 18673, Issued in January 2013.

Huang, Yiping, Gou Qin, Wang Xun (2013). *Institutions and the Middle-Income Trap: Implications of Cross-Country Experiences for China*. Paper at the International Conference on the Inequality and the Middle-Income Trap in China, hosted by the CCER of Peking University.

Jaffe, Adam B., M. Trajtenberg (2002). *Patents, Citations, and Innovations: A Window on the Knowledge Economy*. Cambridge, MA: MIT Press.

Jin, Furong, Keun Lee (2013). *Growth – Inequality Nexus in China: Lewis and Kuznets Hypotheses*. A paper presented at the International Conference on the Inequality and the Middle-Income Trap in China, hosted by the CCER of Peking University.

Jin, Furong, Keun Lee, Y. Kim (2008). Changing Engines of Growth in China: From Exports, FDI and Marketization to Innovation and Exports. *China and World Economy*, 16 (2): 31–49.

Lee, Keun (2010). Thirty Years of Catch-up in China, Compared with Korea. In Ho-Mao Wu and Yang Yao (eds.), *Reform and Development in China*, pp. 224–242. New York: Routledge.

Lee, Keun (2013a). *Schumpeterian Analysis of Economic Catch-up: Knowledge, Path-Creation, and the Middle-Income Trap*. Cambridge: Cambridge University Press.

Lee, Keun (2013b). Capability Failure and Industrial Policy to Move beyond the Middle-Income Trap: From Trade-based to Technology-based Specialization. In J. Stiglitz and J. Lin (eds.), *Industrial Policy Revolution I*. New York: Palgrave MacMillan.

Lee, Keun, M Jee, J. H. Eun (2011). Assessing China's Economic Catch-Up at the Firm Level and Beyond: Washington Consensus, East Asian Consensus and the Beijing Model. *Industry and Innovation*, 18 (5): 487–507.

Lee, Keun, B. Y. Kim (2009). Both Institutions and Policies Matter but Differently at Different Income Groups of Countries: Determinants of Long Run Economic Growth Revisited. *World Development*, 37 (3): 533–549.

Lee, Keun, B. Y. Kim, Y. Y. Park, E. Sanidas (2013). Big Businesses and Economic Growth Identifying a Binding Constraint for Growth with Country Panel Analysis. *Journal of Comparative Economics*, 41 (2): 561–582.

Lee, Keun, Y. K. Kim (2010). IPR and Technological Catch-Up in Korea. In Hiroyuki Odagiri, Akira Goto, Atsushi Sunami, Richard R Nelson (eds.), *Intellectual Property Rights, Development, and Catch-Up*, pp. 133–162. Oxford: Oxford University Press.

Lee, Keun, Shi Li (2014). Possibility of a Middle Income Trap in China: Assessment in Terms of the Literature on Innovation, Big Business and Inequality. *Frontiers of Economics in China*, 9 (3): 370–397.

Lee, Keun, John Mathews (2010). From the Washington Consensus to the BeST Consensus for World Development. *Asian-Pacific Economic Literature*, 24(1): 86–103.

Lin, Justin Y. (2012). *The Quest for Prosperity: How Developing Economies Can Take Off*. Princeton: Princeton University Press.

Park, Kyoo-ho, Keun Lee (2006). Linking the Technological Regime to the Technologcal Catch-up: Analyzing Korea and Taiwan Using the US Patent Data. *Industrial and Corporate Change*, 15 (4): 715–753.

Sylwester, K. (2000). Income Inequality, Education Expenditures, and Growth. *Journal of Development Economics*, 63 (2): 379–398.

Williamson, John. (2012). *Some Basic Disagreements on Development*. Presentation at High-Level Knowledge Forum on Expanding the Frontiers in Development Policy, hosted by the KDI, held in Seoul.

World Bank (2012). *China 2030: Building a Modern, Harmonious, and Creative High-Income Society*. Washington, DC: The World Bank.

World Bank (2010). *Escaping the Middle-Income-Trap*. In World Bank East Asia Pacific Economic Update 2010, Volume 2: Robust Recovery, Rising Risks. Washington, DC: The World Bank.

World Bank (2005). *Economic Growth in the 1990s: Learning from a Decade of Reform*. Washington, DC: World Bank.

Yusuf, S., K. Nabeshima (2009). *Can Malaysia Escape Middle-Income Trap? A Strategy for Penang*. Policy Research Working Paper 4971. Washington, DC: The World Bank.

6 China's political economy
Prospects for technological innovation-based growth

DOUGLAS B. FULLER

6.1 Introduction

This chapter will investigate China's national innovation system (NIS) while at the same time rejecting many of the assumptions that often accompany that term. As Niosi (2002) noted, just because institutions exist and play a role in a given NIS does not mean that they play the type of productive role often assumed in much of the NIS literature. Indeed, they may themselves be obstacles. Behind the "x-inefficiency" of institutions or even the maintenance of x-efficient institutions is politics (Samuels and Keller 2003). In line with these critiques of NIS, this chapter will examine the political economy behind China's development trajectory both broadly and how these relate to China's technological development trajectory. The main argument is that the very political arrangements that have been so conducive to China's rise to middle-income status present challenges or even outright barriers to China's future technological and economic development.

The chapter will proceed as follows. First, in Section 6.2 the chapter will review what went right for China's development as it moved from being an impoverished country to a middle-income one. Following that, Section 6.3 will examine how some of the key policies that proved beneficial for China's development into a middle-income country have morphed into obstacles to further development. Section 6.4 will examine additional institutional and structural obstacles to China adopting policies to promote the type of technological development arguably necessary for it to become a high-income country. Section 6.5 will examine reasons to remain optimistic about China's developmental prospects. Finally, Section 6.6 will propose two heuristics that scholars should employ when analyzing both China's development and the performance of Chinese firms: the differential cost of capital between different types of Chinese firms and the state's role in shaping markets.

6.2 The pillars of China's past success in achieving middle-income status

China's past success has heavily relied upon labor factors. Massive numbers of underemployed farmers[1] have moved into relatively more productive non-agricultural work, often manufacturing, over the three plus decades of the reform era. This movement out of the countryside has been termed the greatest migration in human history, but more important than where they moved is what they did. From 1978 to 2005, agriculture dropped from employing 70.5 percent of China's total workforce to employing 44.8 percent (Cai, Park and Zhao 2008) even though the population grew by over 250 million people from the start of reforms to 2000 (Wang and Mason 2008). Moreover, the large increase in working-age population relative to consumers (dependents and producers alike) created a demographic dividend that increased growth by 1.28 percent per annum for the 1982–2000 period and 0.28 percent per annum for the 2000–2013 period (Wang and Mason 2008).

Along with the development impetus stemming from moving people from farm to factory and the growth of the working-age population was the tremendous commitment to education by the state and the society that led to an impressive increase in the human capital within the workforce. China's university-educated population rose from 3.8 percent of 18- to 22-year-olds in 1991 to 22 percent in 2006 (Simon and Cao 2009). In 2012, the figure was 27 percent. In terms of total numbers of university students, enrollment in higher education leaped from 1 million in 1980 to 19 million in 2007 (Simon and Cao 2009). While insiders like Peking University professor, Zheng Yefu (2013), and outsiders (cf. Abrami, Kirby and McFarlan 2014) alike have criticized the quality of China's graduates, the increase is nevertheless impressive and other large developing countries, such as India, pale in comparison (Bardhan 2010).

In terms of policy, China made a number of wise choices in years following 1978. First of all, gradualism instead of a rapid and radical

---

[1] Here we are using farmers as a gender-neutral term as many women were and are still involved in agricultural work.

overhaul of the system avoided massive and destabilizing shortfalls in demand over the short term that in turn could have become much larger systemic problems. Gradualism also allowed the government to deal individually with select large problems, such as SOE (state-owned enterprise) reform in the 1990s, without simultaneously confronting a host of other pressing economic issues (Rodrik 2011). While gradualism may have been as much an outcome of politics as a policy choice, it served China well in the initial decades of reform in such areas as dual-track price reform allowing China to grow out of the planned economy rather than disruptively privatizing the state-planned economy in one fell swoop without proper market governance institutions in place (Naughton 1996; Rodrik 2011). Local governments were also given political and fiscal incentives to pursue economic development, and these incentives arguably overcame pressing barriers to development in terms of property rights protection. In other words, these incentives aligned the interests of local governments with business in order to encourage the local state to be a helping instead of a grabbing hand (Qian 2003; Xu 2011). Finally, the state has been able to overcome local protectionism, some of which was a result of the very incentives for local governments mentioned above, and encourage a market in which many sectors exhibit a high degree of market competition (Brandt, Sutton and Rawski 2008).

The key macro-policy has been financial repression. Financial repression is keeping "nominal interest rates lower than would otherwise prevail"[2] and in many cases, including China's, involves lowering the cost of borrowing for select entities (often industrial firms) and an

---

[2] Carmen Reinhardt (2012) cited in Pettis (2013). One commentator asked if the Federal Reserve's successive rounds of quantitative easing constituted financial repression and the answer is that it did not because the implicit assumption behind Reinhardt's statement is the idea that "the interest rates that would otherwise prevail" are in fact determined by the supply of money and demand for money, that is, a market price determined by supply and demand. The Federal Reserve increased the monetary supply, which should affect interest rates by lowering them via increasing supply for a given level of demand, but the key difference with financial repression is that the Federal Reserve did not mandate what the interest rates should be for a given money supply and demand for money. I should note that this chapter does not take an absolute normative stance on financial repression. Financial repression has both its advantages and its pitfalls. The trick is when to use this tool for development and how to wean one's economy from dependence on financial repression before it instigates too much inefficient investment that hurts development more than helps it.

implicit transfer of income from creditors to borrowers (Pettis 2013). Financial repression has played a key role in promoting industrialization in a number of developing countries (McKinnon 1973) including the two most successful developing economies of the post-World War II era, Taiwan and Korea. In China, financial repression has also subsidized industrial producers at the expense of creditors (savers) and China's fast past of industrialization is in part due to this financial repression. A key difference between China's financial repression and that of its East Asian neighbors is that the borrowers in China's case have most often been state firms. State firms as the principal borrowers became a serious problem, as we will see in the next section.

An area vital to innovation in which China has exhibited tremendous progress is R&D spending. The share of GDP devoted to R&D almost tripled from 1995 to reach nearly 2 percent in 2012. Arguably, this rising share can also in part be attributed to financial repression as the government funds most R&D (69 percent of R&D funding), but execution is in the hands of firms (67 percent of funds are spent by firms) (Hout and Ghemawat 2010).

6.3 The turn: how good policies went bad in China

Financial repression, local incentives for local government officials, and gradualism have all turned out to be double-edged swords for China's development. While all helped propel China out of poverty, they have become serious obstacles to further development. This section will examine each in turn and then also briefly discuss demographic changes turning against growth in China.

6.3.1 Financial repression: weapon of massive asset destruction

The problem with China's financial repression is both political and structural. Not only is the state banking system a major mechanism of credit allocation in China, but it is also geared to lend to SOEs. It is widely understood within the system that lending to SOEs is politically safe because the state will cover the bad debts of SOEs as they did in the wake of cleaning up bank balance sheets in the early 2000s. The state banking system has also not built up sufficient capabilities to assess credit risks of private borrowers (Huang 2008; Walter and Howie 2011).

Typically, financial repression runs out of steam in a debt crisis or an extended period of large debt and low growth (Pettis 2013) generated precisely by the subsidized credit being progressively misallocated.[3] In China's case, the deleterious effects of financial repression over time have been magnified because of the very nature of the banking system and its main borrowers. Financial repression has just exacerbated the problems of soft-budget constraints that SOEs face in many places, and it has constrained the development of China's private sector (Huang 2008). Thus, the main borrowers remain inefficient SOEs that engage in asset destruction while the efficient private firms are squeezed out of the formal credit market. The size of the financial repression can be seen through the share of consumption (repressed under financial repression) and investment (encouraged under financial repression). China has experienced an unprecedented low level of consumption as a share of GDP for an economy not in crisis, bottoming out at approximately 34–35 percent of GDP in 2011, and very high investments rates compared to peer countries or even historical examples of countries following financial repression. The average consumption rates for the developing world in recent decades has been 65–70 percent and the global average overall has been 65 percent (Pettis 2013). Taiwan and Korea never reached such low levels of consumption throughout their periods of financial repression.[4] At the same time, from 2006 to 2013 credit increased 87 percent, which far outstripped the massive credit increases in the years leading up to the financial crises in various other countries including the United States and the United Kingdom in the buildup to the Global Financial Crisis.[5]

[3] Pettis (2013: 42) argues the end of financial repression is bad in *every* case, but Taiwan arguably did not even experience a decade of low growth despite pursuing financial repression for decades. However, one must note that Taiwan's financial repression was quite mild compared to its East Asian neighbors (cf. Fields 1997).

[4] Even Yiping Huang et al. (2013: 46–47), who argue that the main estimates for Chinese consumption are too low, demonstrate that since the early 1990s Chinese consumption has been significantly lower than Taiwan and Korea's consumption from the 1960s through 2011.

[5] It is important to note that the high levels of non-performing loans in the United States during the Global Financial Crisis were quickly brought under control and never exceeded 10 percent of GDP. In contrast, China's non-performing loans have most likely exceeded 10 percent of GDP for more than a decade and often

This massive repression of consumption and concomitant subsidization of investment has led to widespread misallocation of credit and asset destruction. The scale of the asset destruction over the last decade is staggering. Pettis and IMF estimates put the yearly transfer of wealth from the savers to the state-linked borrowers at 4–9 percent (Lee, Syed and Liu 2012; Pettis 2013). The anecdotal evidence of misallocation in the form of entire "ghost cities" of uninhabited new infrastructure in places such as Ordos is backed up by Beijing-based Unirule Institute's broader survey of what the state-linked firms have actually done with their cheaply borrowed funds. From 2001 to 2010, the interest rate subsidy accounted for 400–500 percent of SOE profits and direct subsidies and monopoly pricing accounted for another 150 percent (Unirule 2011).[6] Building on estimates by Ferri and Liu (2009), Pettis (2013) argues that the artificially low interest rates explained 500–1,000 percent of SOE profits. In other words, when taking account of the cost of capital, the state-owned sector is destroying assets rather than creating them.

While Premier Zhu Rongji dealt with a previous SOE accumulation of debt in the early 2000s through creating state-backed asset management firms, there are several reasons why this method will not offer such a smooth solution this time around. First, China was saved from this debt burden by very fast growth over the past decade and a half, and almost everyone recognizes growth going forward will be slower than that period. Second, while the asset management companies were supposed to recover some value from this debt that they took off the banks' hands at face value, they in fact were unable to recover much value at all (Walter and Howie 2011). Third, the size of the debt as a share of GDP may be even bigger than that of the early 2000s given the rapid increase in credit since 2006.

---

have been several multiples of that. China's bad debts also far exceeded Korea's bad debt leading upto and directly after the Asian Financial Crisis, and the bad debt still on the books in Japan during the second of its lost decades (Fuller 2013). Comparing Japan's second lost decade to China today is fair because China went through a period of cleaning up the banks' balance sheet through asset management companies taking on the bad debt at face value in the early years of this century and yet more than ten years on China's banks have simply accumulated large amounts of new bad debt.

6   Lardy (2014) critiques in detail Unirule's estimates arguing that they are flawed, but does not directly address those of Ferri and Liu (2009), Lee, Syed and Liu (2012) or Pettis (2013).

All of this indicates even if China completely ends financial repression it is going to do so in a manner that is not dissimilar from other fast-growing economies that pursued financial repression in terms of undergoing relatively slow growth as it deals with its debt burden. Whereas many firms and whole sectors benefited from the "big push industrialization" (Murphy, Shleifer and Vishny 1989) where generally rising industrial investment lifts all industrial sectors with financial repression in full swing, the winding down of financial repression will have the opposite effect. Although financial repression is beginning to unwind with deflation at least turning real interest rates for the state-favored firms positive and interest rate liberalization in principle completed with the October 2015 lifting of the ceiling on deposit rates, it is probably too little too late given the extensive credit misallocation that has already occurred.

6.3.2 Local governments' incentives for development

In addition to the cost of financial repression increasing, previous pro-development incentives for local governments have become problematic to the point of becoming obstacles to future development. Essentially, when China needed to create an environment to encourage investment, aligning local cadre incentives with such investment worked well, but now such incentives misallocate resources and have never actually provided the proper incentives for the hard work of upgrading the industrial activities established by previous rounds of investment. This need for upgrading looms larger and larger as China moves headlong into a possible middle-income trap, and yet the Chinese state has not properly adjusted the incentive mechanisms.

The central and provincial governments have long had hard economic targets, such as investments amounts and local industrial production, as part of the evaluation system for local cadres. In 2007 and 2013, there were central government announcements about reforming this evaluation system away from these hard economic criteria, but there is little evidence that these systems have changed. In addition to the cadre career advancement incentive, land development for revenue purposes has also spurred local governments to seek as much industrial development as possible.

Economic hard targets have been important criteria to judge local cadre performance (Cai and Treisman 2006; Fewsmith 2013; Tsui and

Wang 2004; Yang and Wang 2008). While empirical studies show the overall relationship between prior performance on specific economic criteria and subsequent career advancement to be complicated, there is also a wealth of empirical evidence that local cadres behave in ways that suggest they take these targets seriously. First and foremost, local cadres prioritized these economic targets, especially the targets for industrial investment, as previous research (Whiting 2004; Zhong 2003) and my own research (Fuller 2016) attest. In other words, whether or not meeting these targets eventually helped their careers and missing the targets hurt their careers, interviews and previous research suggests that local officials' perception is that these targets did matter for their careers.[7] Despite the attempted 2007 reforms to lessen the emphasis on these hard economic targets, *zhaoshang yinzi* (attracting investment) remains a priority task for local cadres who still feel under great pressure to garner such industrial investments (Wu 2011; ESJJBD September 17, 2010). Similarly, in the wake of the 2013 reforms, Premier Li Keqiang backpedaled in 2014 by re-emphasizing hard economic targets for local officials and stressing that the growth rate of 7.5 percent was "legally binding" for that year (WSJ June 22, 2014). Other recent reports attest to local officials' continued fixation on *zhaoshang yinzi* (ESJJBD June 27, 2014).

A second incentive to pursue *zhaoshang yinzi* and other hard economic targets is revenue rather than professional advancement. Land is used as collateral for the bank loans needed to build the infrastructure for the zones and, critically, accompanying commercial/residential projects.[8] These commercial/residential projects have been generating revenue in two ways. First, the government does not subsidize the buyers/users[9] of these commercial/residential projects, whereas they

---

[7] Yang and Wang (2008) make the compelling point that the county-level officials act on their career aspirations because they have a chance to be promoted out of the county, but the township officials, who rarely are promoted out of the county, are motivated by a mixture of badgering from the careerist county leaders and the economic interests of the townships in the revenue that land development generates as the bulk of the revenue from this source not sent out of the county is sent down to the township-level.

[8] This ability of local governments to use land as collateral for this development projects was an innovation of the China Development Bank in 1998 presumably as it was eager to provide more loans to local governments for just such activities (NYT February 7, 2014).

[9] Legally speaking, land is not bought and sold in China. Instead, the user rights for fixed periods of time are bought and sold.

do subsidize the costs for industrial investors in the parks in order to attract them in the first place. Second, the commercial activities thus generated are taxed and these business taxes are kept as local revenue rather than shared with the central government whereas the value-added tax (VAT), the primary tax paid by industrial firms, is. Building and expanding industrial zones is an excellent excuse to build these profit-making and tax-generating commercial districts. On top of this, land can be grabbed when the justification is economic development through zone creation and expansion. The compensation given by the local governments to the current users of the land, usually farmers, is generally very low (Su and Tao 2015; Yang and Wang 2008). A 2011 study found that the average compensation given to farmers was US$17,850 whereas the average selling price to commercial developers was US$740,000.[10]

The negative outcomes of these policies have been two-fold. First, the misallocation of resources, particularly land, has accelerated. Not only are the farmers not properly compensated for their land, which is one more way the consumption necessary for moving away from China's investment overdependence is stymied, but Chinese local governments have created an unprecedentedly large amount of industrial land development in recent years. China, which already has an enormous amount of land devoted to industry, also has averaged 40–50 percent of new land development for industry whereas the global average is 10–15 percent (Su and Tao 2015). With declining real estate prices over the last two years due in no small part to too much land development by local governments, local governments dependent on land revenue now find themselves in dire fiscal circumstances.

The incentives also have led to unending development zone "fever" (cf. Zweig 2002) in which local governments create zones and try to become recognized as provincial or national-level zones in order to receive further benefits, including tax breaks. The number of national-level of High-Technology Development Zones (HDTZs) and Economic and Technology Development Zones (ETDZs) has nearly doubled since the beginning of this century with 89 HDTZs and 108 ETDZs established by 2011.[11] In other words, even as the Chinese central

---

[10] The 2011 study was conducted by the Landesa Rural Development Institute, Renmin University, and Michigan State University cited in Fred Magoff (2013).
[11] These figures are from Torch High-Technology Center (2011) and ESJJBD April 18, 2011.

government has recognized the need to move the growth model away from industrial investment, local governments have doubled down on industrial investment.

The other issue is that the local governments are fixated on *zhaoshang yinzi* to the neglect of pursuing any activities to aid upgrading of local activities. My own research across thirteen national-level development zones has found that these zones almost entirely neglect upgrading activities in terms of assigning personnel to cover them and prioritize *zhaoshang yinzi* (Fuller 2016). This stands in sharp contrast to Singapore and Taiwan in their development heydays where officials zeroed in on helping upgrading, and ensuring technology capture from multinationals either through transfer to local firms (Taiwan's primary focus) or the placement of progressively more sophisticated activities locally (Singapore's primary focus).

6.3.3 The political problem of gradualism

While Justin Yifu Lin in his chapter for this volume, Dani Rodrik (2011) and others are correct that gradualism was the correct choice in the past for China in juxtaposition to the shock therapy type of reform that Russia chose, there is an inherent political problem with gradualism as China's economic Cassandra, Wu Jinglian (2011), pointed out years ago. Simply put, gradualism allows those negatively affected to reform to become further entrenched and thus better positioned to oppose reform. To overcome this political problem, reform design must incorporate ways to win over or compensate reform "losers" in ways that are still conducive to further reforms. In essence, China's dual-track pricing was one such policy that worked because often it was the very same SOEs that gained from market prices just as their sales under the plan withered away. Unfortunately, from the beginning of this century, the reform losers (mostly SOEs) and reform winners (mostly private firms) have been two very distinct groups. The long delay in ridding the financial system of systemic bias against private firms has simply further enhanced the political power of SOEs at the same time that it has aligned their interests in opposition to reform. Top party leaders, such as Premier Li Keqiang, have publicly acknowledged a powerful, entrenched opposition to market reforms as a major problem.

One final note on the past positive trends now working against China's model of development concerns demographics. Demographics have become a drag on China's future growth and are projected to depress China's growth by 0.45 percent per annum for the 2013–2050 period (Wang and Mason 2008). Of course, this demographic turn is not all bad as the end of the demographic dividend has caused the labor share of GDP to rise in the last several years and thus has become one vehicle for moving away from China's investment-centric model.

6.4 Institutional and structural obstacles to policies conducive for further development

There are three areas where China is heavily constrained by its institutions and even structural factors, such as geography, that make adopting policies better suited to the transition to a technologically innovative, high-income economy more difficult. The first two obstacles, industrial policy and China's Leninist party-state system, are macro-level ones that cut across the economy as a whole and do not concern simply technologically intensive sectors. Furthermore, they affect central government policies not just the local and regional policies discussed in the previous section about local cadre incentives. The final obstacle, the problems of venture capital in China, relates more narrowly to the issue of encouraging entrepreneurship, especially technology entrepreneurship.

6.4.1 Obstacles to effective industrial policymaking in China

The two economies which successfully moved from low income to high income over the post-World War II period, Taiwan and Korea, both employed industrial policies to encourage movement into new (for them), higher value-added activities. Many other economies have also employed such policies to develop (Amsden 2000; Chang 1994, 2007). Justin Yifu Lin in his chapter and elsewhere has also recognized the need for governments to lower the transaction costs firms face in trying to encourage structural change in the economy that fits with the economy's latent comparative advantage. Many of Lin's suggestions align closely with industrial policy as pursued in successful developers, for example priority access to credit. Beyond Lin's recommendations, it is also important to consider China's industrial policymaking capabilities because even as the amount of financial repression shrinks, the Chinese state appears to be backing the same firms through pursuit of industrial policy. In other words, what was once cheap credit directed via financial repression will now just be cheap credit directed through industrial policy.

The weakness of Lin's recommendations is that they assume that industrial policy can be easily pursued if simple rules are followed, such as using incentives "limited in time and budget allocations" and only entering sectors of economies that have 100–200 percent of the PPP GDP per capita of the economy pursuing the industrial policy. Simply put, these prescriptions ignore the critical issue of the politics that allow state actors the information, capabilities and discipline to carry out such policies. Furthermore, Lin's own prescriptions ignore pertinent facts that muddy the clear prescriptions he has drawn from the development experiences of the high-performing East Asian economies that succeeded in becoming high-income economies. Other than the city-states of Singapore and Hong Kong, these economies did in fact pursue import-substitution industrialization in conjunction with export-oriented industrialization rather than completely eschewing the former. Many of their support policies were also not very well constrained by budget and, even more so, time. Thus, the new structural economics does not offer much more than what Ha-joon Chang, Dani Rodrik and others already have offered in terms of advocating industrial policy. And the new structural economics fails to answer the same critical political question of why some countries empirically have been able to carry out industrial policy effectively whereas others have been equally ambitious in their industrial policy but with disastrous effect (Khan 2000). Or to put it another way, it is not simply that the East Asian success cases were aiming for industries at the 100 percent of their PPP GDP per capita and the economic failures all were aiming far beyond their latent comparative advantage. Looking no further than Malaysia, the economy that mimicked the policies of the East Asian successes most closely but remains in the middle-income trap, suggests that politics determine the efficacy of industrial policy as much as following the prescriptions of new structural economics to the letter.

In the case of China, there are five serious constraints to the effective pursuit of industrial policy: (1) the structure of the state apparatus, (2) the bias of credit allocation toward SOEs and the resulting managerial deficiencies of these firms (3) the information asymmetries due to sheer geographic size and population of China (4) the balance of exports vis-à-vis procurement and (5) corruption. These obstacles are in addition to the incentives for local officials discussed above that discourage local governments from pushing upgrading of local firms and multinationals within their jurisdictions.

There is a large, time-tested stream of scholarship about the fragmented nature of China's state with ferocious battles between horizontal (regional) and vertical lines of authority (the problem is referred to as *tiao tiao kuai kuai* in Chinese, with *tiao* referring to the vertical lines of authority and *kuai* referring to the horizontal/regional authorities) (Schurmann 1968). Priority-setting at the central government level is weak and the *tiao tiao kuai kuai* conflicts further exacerbate this weakness (Lieberthal and Lampton 1992). Local officials enjoy a "soft authority constraint" to interpret government directives as they wish (Lu and Tang 1997).

The second issue is essentially the financial misallocation and lending bias toward SOEs discussed above. Some would go so far as to argue that there is state paternalism on behalf of client SOEs (Moore 2002). While Naughton (2010) argues that the State Asset Supervision and Administration Commission (SASAC) now rewards the central SOEs under its supervision with managerial incentives, others questioned whether this is effective given the larger political aims of the top management teams after their tenure in a given SOE (McGregor 2012) and the power of SASAC over central SOEs, given that the power of appointment resides with the Organization Department of the CCP (Walter and Howie 2011).

Given China's large population and geographic size, the information asymmetries facing industrial policymakers in Beijing are much larger than in the Northeast Asian states that conducted relatively successful industrial policy (Perkins 2001). Nor is it just the sheer size of China that makes the requisite policymaking and coordination difficult. Multinationals have a much larger presence in the Chinese marketplace than they did in the developmental heydays of Korea, Taiwan, and Japan, and this presence makes state coordination of firms more difficult (Naughton 2010).

Fourth, China simply is not as export-dependent as Japan, Korea, and Taiwan were in their developmental heydays, and this presents a major challenge in judging firm performance. Haggard (2004) has argued that these states did not actually have to be very effective at monitoring their firms because they could use the external and hard-to-manipulate metric of exports to judge firm performance. As a continental-sized economy, it is quite natural for China to be less export-dependent, but this fact also means that the Chinese state faces higher informational asymmetries that make judging firm performance difficult. The domination of China's export sector by foreign firms that are not the main targets of China's industrial policy acerbates the information asymmetries working against China's state bureaucrats. On top of these problems, the state's own procurement policies provide incentives for the state-favored firms to focus on the domestic, and especially state-governed, markets that only add to these information problems.

Finally, corruption has exceeded the levels needed to grease the political system in the development success cases of Korea, Taiwan, and Japan (Pei 2008; Perkins 2001; Wedeman 2012). Yimin Lin (2001) sees particularistic networks where officials and private actors trade favors emerging out of the organizational decay of the state as the market economy has advanced. McGregor (2012) argues China's Leninist party-state makes the local party chief a law unto himself resulting in widespread corruption.

6.4.2 The Leninist party-state

The basic Leninist nature of China's party-state governance structure presents serious obstacles to reform. The Chinese party-state on the one hand wants to embark on reforms that allow for a much greater role for private capital in its economy as announced at the Chinese Communist Party's (CCP) Third Plenum of the 18th Central Committee in November 2013. On the other hand, the party-state's Leninist imperative is to remain in control not only of the state apparatus but also of society at large. Thus, China's self-conflicted leadership creates self-conflicted policies. For example, the policy to allow private investment in SOEs aims to use market mechanism to bring efficiency to SOEs, but the policy does not yet offer the opportunity for private capital to take over significant SOEs in sectors the state prioritizes.

More broadly, such reluctance to cede influence to those outside the party suggests that longer term it will be very difficult for the CCP to allow the emergence of an institutionalized market economy of whatever variety. If we consider the types of extant successful advanced capitalism discussed in the varieties of capitalism and comparative capitalism (cf. Hall and Soskice 2001), the CCP is neither on the path to be a mere market referee in the mode of the state in Anglo-American liberal market economies nor is it amenable to allow the emergence of organized and powerful societal interests along the lines of coordinated or organized capitalism seen in much of continental Europe and Japan. The message of the Fourth Plenum of the 18th Central Committee in late 2014 basically emphasized that the purpose of law was to serve the party, and this message indicates the party still does not envision reforms as leading to either of the known successful forms of advanced capitalism. While it is certainly in the realm of possibility that the CCP party-state might create a Leninist form of successful advanced capitalism capable of delivering China to high-income country status, the fact that no economy with such an unconstrained, domineering party-state has been able to do so suggests it is unlikely. This chapter thus disagrees with Witt's analysis arguing that Korea circa 1980 and China are very similar (China's inefficient and dominant state enterprise sector and Leninist party-state structure are two key differences that trump any argument for institutional equivalence between contemporary China and Korea circa 1980 in my mind) while at the same time agreeing with Witt's ultimate verdict that radical change must happen in China's political economy for the country to escape the middle-income trap.

The other issue is even if the leadership of CCP's Leninist party-state was intent on such radical reforms in the vein of Zhao Ziyang, they might very well be constrained by the very legacy of the Leninist party-state. The emphasis on supporting state control over large sections of the economy and, as a consequence, propping up state entities through financial repression, subsidies and monopolies has simply created an enormous array of vested interests against reform within the party-state itself. While a positive interpretation of the ongoing anti-corruption drive would be that its aim is to break the deadlock on reform presented by these vested interests, Premier Li Keqiang's own statement in March 2015 at the party's "double meeting" of the National People's Congress and the Chinese People's Political Consultative Conference bemoaning how anti-reform elements within the party-state have been blocking the implementation of the Third Plenum reform policies underlines just how powerful the anti-reform contingent created by the party-state itself may be.

6.4.3 Weak institutions for funding innovation

China's domestic venture capital industry has resolved its basic legal lacunae. More importantly, changes in China's Partnership Law in 2007 finally effectively distinguished between general and limited partners so the type of general partner-limited partner structures common among venture capital firms elsewhere were finally legal in China. Similarly, changes to the Company Law in 2005 allowed different share classes and these different share classes arguably helped VCs align risk with control rights. Finally, the Ministry of Finance released a circular in 2007 that allowed tax deductions for limited partners in order to encourage venture capital (Zhang et al. 2009).

Unfortunately, the domestic VCs are still not serving as effective funders of technology entrepreneurship. The domestic VCs tend to invest in mature industries and are dominated by state entities. Indeed, the increased amounts of funding provided by state policy, such as the 2007 Guidance Funds, have actually driven down the amount of funds invested in seed and early-stage investments from roughly half in 2006–2009 to 40 percent in recent years (Wang, Zhang and Zhao 2013). In the United States, seed and early-stage investing projects typically constitute more than half of the total projects (Wang, Zhang and Zhao 2013). Thus, at best, much of this funding is taking on the characteristics of private equity investment rather than venture capital investment geared to supporting technological entrepreneurship. Most of these funds have not invested wisely. Lerner (2009) notes that most of the VCs backed by the Chinese state funds have not been successful and just serve to overheat the venture market. Similarly, Fuller (2010) found that very few of the investments (approximately 10 percent) made by domestic VCs were in technology-intensive start-ups as opposed to over a third for foreign VCs. More to the point, data comparing the overall investment in actual venture capital in start-ups as opposed to private equity and other investments shows domestic VCs, including JVs, only contributed 11 percent of the total value with the rest contributed by foreign firms (Zhang et al. 2009).[12]

---

[12] Zhang et al.'s 2009 data from Zero2ipo is clearly for more narrowly defined investment in start-ups given the source and the fact that the amount is a tiny fraction of the "venture capital" investment broadly defined provided by the series of VC annual reports compiled by Wang Yuan and colleagues.

There are two reasons why the relative underperformance of domestic venture capital versus foreign venture capital in promoting technology entrepreneurship is of concern. First, the Chinese state has funneled large and increasing amounts of funds via domestic VCs in order to spur technological entrepreneurship, but these vehicles may not be the correct ones for the mission. Second, the presence of foreign venture capital in China has been a point of political contestation and consequently foreign venture capital remains at regulatory risk of being severely curtailed in China.

A primary reason for the relative lack of technology investments by domestic VC is precisely because these are typically state finance vehicles, often local state ones, with many different missions beyond funding promising start-ups (Fuller 2010; Lerner 2009). And state-financed vehicles loom large in domestic venture capital. In 2006, venture investment sources clearly not linked to the state financial system made up just over 10 percent of the total[13] and in 2012 still made up less than 25 percent of the total (Wang, Zhang and Zhao 2013).

In effect, foreign venture capital has partially substituted for the problems of domestic venture capital in funding China's technology entrepreneurship in China. However, foreign venture capital cannot be an entirely sufficient substitute because there is still regulatory risk involved. In the past, the State Administration of Foreign Exchange (SAFE) and other state organs have made rulings that if implemented would have made it very difficult, even next to impossible, to carry on foreign venture capital activities. With China's closed capital account and other regulations, foreign venture capitalists have generally invested via offshore holding companies that in turn own onshore enterprises.[14] While in past episodes of regulatory threat, local

---

[13] Official SOEs, the government and other public institutions constituted over 37 percent of domestic VC funding in 2006. More importantly, sources connected at least partially to the state, such as banks, security and trust companies, listed companies and other enterprises, comprised 44.7 percent of investment. Banks, security and trust firms are primarily owned by the state. Also, state-owned listed firms while no longer formally designated as SOEs are still functionally state entities. Individuals and foreign investment combined made less than ten percent of the total. An ill-defined category of "others" made up 7.5 percent of total investment (Zhang et al. 2009: 91).

[14] Here I am not talking about the variable interest entity (VIE) structures, which were set up to evade Chinese laws forbidding foreign ownership in certain sectors where foreign investment was forbidden or heavily circumscribed. The legal uncertainty around these structures has basically been resolved with

entrepreneurs and even local government officials have allied with foreign venture capitalists to convince the central government to over-turn or suspend edicts by SAFE and others that threatened the opera-tion of foreign VCs in China, these battles show that the institutional space given foreign VCs to operate is still contested. Future regulations could rapidly narrow or even eliminate this space. With such risks, foreign venture capital is a stopgap, second-best solution to reforming the domestic institutional system.

Other alternatives to venture capital also appear wanting in the Chinese case. China's neighbors, Japan and Korea, have more often than not pursued what is now called intra-preneurship, the funding of new ventures within existing business organizations. With their large conglomerates and especially in the case of Korea, weakly developed external financing, this type of internal entrepreneurship made eminent sense. China has had various schemes to build leading conglomerates, such as the 1997 Large-scale Experimental Enterprise Group Plan of the former State Economic and Trade Commission, but to date, they have not been very successful at least in part because the targets of these policies have generally been SOEs with already accumulated maladies.[15]

6.5 Arguments for optimism about China's future technological development

With all of China's accumulated institutional defects, one could be forgiven in thinking this chapter has an entirely pessimistic outlook

the Chinese state, not unreasonably, declaring them illegal (after all they were set up to evade Chinese laws), but with the significant caveat that VIEs would be tolerated in those situation where the offshore vehicle was controlled by Chinese citizens (the Alibaba rule as some have called it). Foreign VCs did use VIEs in restricted sectors, such as Internet services and education, but not in other sectors where foreign investment was not so severely circumscribed. In the latter sectors, they have had offshore holding companies directly own onshore firms as described in the main text.

[15] One example would be Founder, the Peking University-based conglomerate. After its 1997 designation as one of these state-backed conglomerates, Founder's main IT business began a slow decline and it diversified into an array of sectors where state backing is quite useful including healthcare (leveraging its links with PKU's medical school), real estate, finance, the defense sector and commodities trading (JJGC September 29, 2014). What the conglomerate did not do is invest in internal corporate ventures that could recapture its glory days of the 1980s and early 1990s when the firm had legitimately exciting new Chinese character printing technology (cf. Lu 2000).

for China's prospects for emerging as a high-income innovation-based economy. This section will provide two reasons for optimism.

The two main reasons for optimism are the ongoing institutional borrowing from abroad that has given rise to hybrid firms driving China's technological development (cf. Fuller 2016) and the fundamental strength of China's human capital development. Hybrid firms are China-based enterprises that utilize foreign rather than domestic finance. In effect, these firms are escaping their domestic institutional environment's financial inadequacies by accessing foreign institutions to fund their technological innovation efforts. These firms have been especially effective in high technology sectors and from 2003 to 2009 produced far more of China's lead inventor US utility patents[16] than traditional multinationals or China's domestic firms. Hybrids produced 1,817 such patents compared to 1,214 for MNCs and 409 for domestic firms despite hybrids accounting for only 4. 7–8 percent of R&D spending in China in this period (Fuller 2013). The hybrid firms and foreign venture capital provide a viable if less than ideal fall back option for China's technological entrepreneurship and innovation.

The second reason to be optimistic is China's tremendous record of human capital formation. While many critique the quality of China's ever-increasing number of university graduates, the fact remains that China is educating more people proportionally than ever before, as discussed in Section 6.2. The critiques that China's educational system cannot produce the talent needed for creativity and innovation (Abrami, Kirby and McFarlan 2014; Zhao 2014) have several countervailing facts against them. First, similar types of education exist in and same types of criticism were leveled at Japan, Korea and Taiwan, and yet these three economies all managed to create innovative companies and economies. Indeed, Japan, celebrated for its cool creative culture in the famed "Gross National Cool" article in *Foreign Affairs*, and Korea have become widely recognized not only for their prowess in various areas of industrial innovation but also in culture and creative industries. Second, Shaun Rein (2014) surveying China's promising innovative firms has cogently argued that good companies do not need that many truly creative or innovative people to be successful. Third, it is not just a stereotype that China's education has provided

---

[16] Note these are patents where the lead inventor is based in China.

a very strong foundation for students in mathematics and science as evidenced by the Program for International Student Assessment (PISA) scores from Shanghai.[17] With a large population of science and engineering graduates, China has the raw human capital to become an innovator.

Lest readers think these two points of optimism necessarily trump the institutional weaknesses from the previous sections, a note of caution is in order. Given the increasing negative returns to China's old model of industrial investment-centric development and the politics of trying to overcome the vested interests served by that system, political contestation will determine whether China gets stuck in the middle-income trap or upgrades into wealthy country status. Other countries with increasing human capital have still experienced long periods of suboptimal growth and development and even the stopgap measure of linking to institutions abroad (the hybrid model) is a political act. These links that foster hybrids are now tolerated, but that does not mean the Chinese state will always do so. So it is to political considerations behind various aspects of China's firms and economy that we now turn in considering a new agenda for research.

6.6 Agenda for research: new heuristics for a new approach to studying China

This section will first propose several political economy-informed heuristics that scholars should use in order to better capture both China's technological development as a facet of socioeconomic development and the competitive technological capabilities of Chinese firms. A more nuanced understanding about the political economy of China or, if you will the politics of resource allocation, would shed valuable light on several important topics. The first is the relationship between firm–state relationships and the cost of credit in China. The second is how the state shapes markets. Finally, a third and more minor issue of how to assess patenting by Chinese firms will be discussed. For the first two major heuristics, I will then propose an agenda for future research and policy recommendations for the Chinese state.

---

[17] One might want to dismiss these scores because they are only from Shanghai, but Shanghai's population makes it the same size as a mid-sized European country, such as the Netherlands, and many other regions in China probably would deliver close to Shanghai's results.

The first heuristic is to place Chinese firms in their proper financial context or, in other words, provide a better political economy-informed account of their cost of capital. If one accepts the findings of Yasheng Huang and Michael Pettis among many others concerning the severe bias in lending in China's financial system, then one must accept that certain, principally state-owned, firms have preferential access to credit at very favorable rates. Furthermore, these terms have been so favorable for many years that they account for multiples of the overall profits earned by these firms, that is, these firms by and large are engaged in asset destruction. In stark contrast, the vast majority of private firms still do not have easy and fair access to China's formal financial system (Nee and Opper 2012). With recognition of this financial situation, it is imperative to place firms in their proper financial context in order to judge their performance. For example, an SOE's return on assets (or some other measure of profitability) of 2 percent vis-à-vis private firm's return on assets (or some other measure of profitability) of 2 percent are not equivalent, that is, they suggest very different fundamental performances once the cost of capital for each firm is taken into account.

Recognition of the widely varying cost in capital among Chinese firms in turn suggests further research along the lines of what Yasheng Huang (2008) has already done in trying to resolve the confusion around which firms are actually state-owned and which ones are private. Confusion has reigned in this area because far too much work on Chinese firms and the Chinese economy relies on the formal National Statistical Bureau's categorization of firms. As Huang Yasheng (2008) pointed out, many of the shareholding corporations are controlled by the state despite most often being treated as private or at least non-state-owned. He advocates correctly tracing back the ownership of shareholding firms to see which entities ultimately own a controlling share of the firm. However, Huang does not actually go far enough because he accepts at face value the official definition of foreign-invested enterprises (FIEs) as those firms that have 20 percent foreign ownership. Which entities control FIEs are equally important and in the Chinese context 50 percent rather than 20 percent is a more reasonable threshold for control, at least among non-listed firms. Without such considerations, Huang mistakenly accepts Lenovo as an FIE despite its controlling holding company being majority state-owned until 2010. Thus, the first step in improving the classification of firms' relationships to the state is to carefully trace back their respective ultimate owners.

The second step is to look beyond basic ownership ties (foreign, domestic private, and domestic state) to examine how the state views and treats the firm. While it remains true that the large majority of China's *guojia dui* (national team) of favored firms are state-owned, there are successful private firms that due to their very success have been embraced by the state. Huawei stands out as the prime example. The firm remains under the effective control of Ren Zhengfei and his close associates rather than the state, but the state has identified the firm as one important to support since the mid-to-late 1990s.[18]

While the first step of determining the ultimate controlling owners is relatively easy to do if time-consuming and can be applied to larger data sets if scholars are willing to put in the effort,[19] the second step requires more effort and information of the individual firm so may not be easily applicable to large data sets. Nonetheless, it is important to consider both of these steps in order to have a more accurate picture of the relationship of a firm and its competitors to the Chinese state and thereby have a better approximation of a given firm's cost of capital.

Equally important, only through a more accurate account of the cost of capital can we better judge the efficacy of China's industrial and technological policies. For example, in a much-heralded sector such as wind power, the local firms that have entered this market have by and large been state-owned. While it is already known that these firms have, to put it politely, derivative technology,[20] one must also take into

---

[18]   This author would also argue that Huawei also stands out as the one major state-favored firm that has not succumbed to the capability-eroding "benefits" of cheap credit from the state (Fuller 2016). Tentative explanations for Huawei's enjoying the best of both worlds, enjoying cheap credit while maintaining competitive capabilities, could center on Ren's leadership or the firm's historical trajectory from a firm on the periphery of China's political economy that only later worked its way into the state's favor or Ren's decision early on to hone Huawei's capabilities in international competition (this latter explanation cannot of course then be entirely divorced from Ren's leadership skills).

[19]   On whether scholars are willing to put in this effort, this author remains skeptical given the current easy acceptance of the National Statistical Bureau's categories of firms, but if positivist scholarship is still about working toward closer and closer approximation of reality, then scholars of positivist social science should commit themselves to this hard work.

[20]   A technical consultant, who has been active in this sector in China for over a decade and cannot be dismissed as a China pessimist as he was one of the few who a decade ago argued that China would meet the National Development and

account their cost of capital in evaluating their performance. And this cost of capital may be the answer as to why there has been so little private entry in this sector, which is also an issue worth exploring and evaluating. Is such a sector truly successful and sustainable when private firms appear to have been crowded out of the market?

Similarly, John Child, in Chapter 8, addresses the issue of whether or not China's small and medium-sized enterprises (SMEs) can become innovative. He has correctly pointed out many of the wider social or normative aspects required for successful clusters of SMEs and the areas where China may come up short, such as social trust. However, the heuristic of the cost of capital (an issue Child also acknowledges) points to potentially a much more fundamental barrier to China's SMEs driving technological innovation. While Child himself is much more circumspect, Nee and Opper (2012) emphatically make the claim that private firms via networks are creating a vibrant market economy that will outgrow to displace the current state-dominated economy. However, much of their data simply suggests that private firms make better use of the limited capital to which they have access than state firms do of their copious capital. Such findings do not automatically lead to China's private firms growing out from under the shadow of the state. Instead, these findings beg the question of the relative difference in the amount of credit each group of firms utilizes. If SOEs continue to crowd out private firms from most of the credit market, the organic growing up of a private-firm-led market economy that Nee and Opper envision may never come to pass.

Happily, the policy reforms necessary to rectify the problems of cost of capital discrimination in China have already been proposed by the government in the Third Plenum of the 18th Central Committee held in November 2013. The state clearly recognizes the need to move to a system where the market allocates capital. Unfortunately, thus far not much progress has been made and prominent figures, such as Premier Li Keqiang, have warned of strong vested interests fighting reform. Li warned of this ongoing struggle as recently at the "double meeting" of the National People's Congress and the Chinese People's Political Consultative Conference in March 2015. As a measure of how hard it will be politically for China to wean itself from this established system

Reform Commission's wind power goals, told this author in March 2015 that all the technology of Chinese wind power firms "was either bought or stolen."

of cheap credit, the very same Li Keqiang, in the wake of continuing signs of decelerating growth, was just in the struggling northeast, China's rustbelt, in April 2015 calling for more emphasis on growth and less on anti-corruption, a move widely interpreted as a call to let loose more cheap credit to flow through the established channels. Of course, the most likely result of such new credit creation via the state banking system would be credit flowing predominantly to the same old state-favored firms. In short, the state recognizes the problem and has proposed to rectify it, but the political headwinds against reform are very strong.

The second heuristic needed to better assess China's technological development and the capabilities and performance of Chinese firms is recognition of the role of the state in shaping many markets within China. Too often the metric of success is sales, but the appropriate question in the Chinese case is sales to whom. This heuristic goes hand-in-hand with the previous one as the firms favored with state credit tend to be the ones favored by direct and indirect state procurement. For example, Zeng and Willliamson (2008) have hailed Dawning, the high-performance computing maker, as a significant Chinese innovator despite the firm having sold basically nothing outside of Chinese state procurement. Similarly, at the sectoral level, many have argued for China's success in green technologies (Lewis 2013; Mathews 2014) with evidence from Chinese firms being able to sell successfully into domestic markets that are essentially state procurement as the ultimate buyers remain large state entities, such as the State Grid. The first cut that must be made when judging firm and sectoral success in sales in China is to see if the firms or sector are making significant sales outside of state-controlled channels and, as a second check, sales outside of China.

For future research, scholars must examine the organization of a given sector's marketplace in order to determine how far to take claims of firm- and sector-level success. Such research should go beyond examining public government procurement policies and instead extend to interviews with market participants in order to understand how much state influence there is over the important channels in a given marketplace and the motivations of such state intervention. Furthermore, the changes in the state's role (if any) over time in each given marketplace should be tracked. State procurement about a decade ago was as much as 30 percent of the marketplace for personal computers. Today, it is much less although the state's policies to promote the informatization of the countryside through subsidizing computer purchases have been geared toward supporting domestic PC makers, principally Lenovo (Fuller 2016). In contrast, the market for servers appears to be moving in the opposite direction with growing signs of the government's intention to oust foreign manufacturer's servers from such key networks as banking. Thus for the latter market, the rise in sales of local firms, such as Inspur (Langchao), must not be interpreted as purely due to its enhanced competitiveness vis-à-vis HP and others.

As for public policy recommendations, state procurement does not necessarily have to be abandoned. After all in other cases, state procurement has proven to be an agent for development in many instances outside of China. However, China's state procurement will probably only be effective after China reforms the bias in lending discussed above. Furthermore, the Chinese state needs to employ better metrics to assess firm performance. In line with Haggard's (2004) findings, perhaps China should judge firms by their export performance as this channel cannot be easily manipulated by interference by the Chinese state, particularly after financial reforms.

One final albeit more narrow area in which political considerations must be brought to bear is Chinese patent data. While more and more people now understand that the utility patents within China's patent system are basically unvetted and of very questionable quality, the surge in Chinese inventor patents also has to be understood within its institutional context. The central government and local ones have been offering major financial incentives for patenting, and the explosion in inventor (and utility) patents is the result of these hard targets.[21] Of course, the National Patent Development Strategy for 2011–2020 also calls for a doubling of patent applications filed abroad and offers incentives to support this push. Subsidizing or even paying the full cost for foreign applications certainly lowers the threshold for local firms to file overseas. Hu (2010) recognizes policy inducements as one of the factors behind the surge in foreign patents from China. Given these incentives for domestic and foreign patenting as well as the propensity of

---

[21] The information on the Chinese patent system in this paragraph is drawn from Moga (2012) and Prud'homme (2012).

officials to focus and meet hard targets in China's system, using triadic patents from the EU, Japan and the United States are a better indicator of quality as Prud'homme (2012) cogently argues, especially as they are more expensive to apply for than many other foreign patents. An interesting issue to explore for future research is the different patterns of domestic, international, and international triadic patenting by Chinese firms.

6.7 Conclusion

While China's past developmental success has provided some of the foundations for future growth, especially in the critical area of human capital development, the past is not the entirety of the prologue. Indeed, certain elements of path dependency (the past) may in fact being working against future development. Historical cases of economic development hold certain valuable lessons for development, such as American development in the nineteenth century (the utility of infant industry protection) to more recent examples in China's own region (very active and successful state intervention to boost firm-level capabilities in Taiwan and Korea), but we cannot ignore certain stark differences between China and such historical cases. Foremost among them are China's much larger amounts of financial repression and the targets of that financial repression, state-owned firms. Funneling very large amounts of credit to these generally inefficient state-owned firms has magnified the downside of long-term financial repression in terms of capital misallocation. And this financial favoritism is mirrored in other state actions that skew the market toward politically favored firms. Just as some wealthy Western countries are confronting the problem of too-big-to-fail banks, China now faces the problem of how to unwind this system of finance and favoritism that has become a drag on development, a system which has fostered its own powerful coterie of vested interest within China's party-state itself. The 2013 Third Plenum shows that the CCP leadership itself recognizes both the problem and the solution, but such recognition is not enough. Ultimately, politics will determine whether or not China's party-state is able to transform the financial system and state–business relations enough to grow into a high-income economy.

References

Abrami, R. M., W. C. Kirby and F. W. McFarlan (2014). *Can China Lead?: Reaching the Limits of Power and Growth*. Boston, Harvard Business School Press.

Amsden, A. (2000). *The Rise of the Rest: Challenges to the West from Late-industrializing Economies*. Oxford, Oxford University Press.

Bardhan, P. (2010). *Awakening Giants, Feet of Clay*. Princeton, NJ, Princeton University Press.

Brandt, L., T. G. Rawski and J. Sutton (2008). China's Industrial Development. *China's Great Economic Transformation*. L. Brandt and T. G. Rawski. New York, Cambridge University Press.

Cai, F., A. Park and Y. Zhao (2008). The Chinese Labor Market in the Reform Era. *China's Great Economic Transformation*. L. Brandt and T. G. Rawski. New York, Cambridge University Press.

Cai, H. and D. Treisman (2006). "Did Government Decentralization Cause China's Economic Miracle?" *World Politics* 58: 505–535.

Chang, H. (1994). *The Political Economy of Industrial Policy*. New York, St. Martin's Press.

Chang, H. (2007). *Bad Samaritans: The Myth of Free Trade and the Secret History of Capitalism*. London, Bloomsbury.

Ferri, G. and L.-G. Liu (2009). *Honor Thy Creditors before Thy Shareholders: Are the Profits of Chinese State-Owned Enterprises Real?* Hong Kong, Hong Kong Institute for Monetary Research.

Fewsmith, J. (2013). *The Logic and Limits of Political Reform in China*. New York, Cambridge University Press.

Fields, K. (1997). *Enterprise and the State in Taiwan and Korea*. Ithaca, NY, Cornell University Press.

Fuller, D. B. (2010). "How Law, Politics and Transnational Networks Affect Technology Entrepreneurship: Explaining Divergent Venture Capital Investing Strategies in China." *Asia Pacific Journal of Management* 27(3): 445–459.

Fuller, D. B. (2013). "Building Ladders Out of Chains: China's Hybrid-Led Technological Development in Disaggregated Value Chains." *Journal of Development Studies* 49(4): 547–563.

Fuller, D. B. (2016). *Paper Tigers, Hidden Dragons: Firms and the Political Economy of China's Technological Development*. Oxford: Oxford University Press.

Haggard, S. (2004). "Institutions in East Asian Growth." *Studies in Comparative International Development* 38(4): 53–81.

Hall, Peter A. and David Soskice (2001). An Introduction to Varieties of Capitalism. *Varieties of Capitalism: The Institutional Foundations of Comparative Advantage.* P. A. Hall and D. Soskice. Oxford: Oxford University Press.

Hout, T. M. and P. Ghemawat (December 2010). "China versus the World: Whose Technology is It?" *Harvard Business Review.*

Hu, A. G. (2010). "Propensity to Patent, Competition and China's Foreign Patenting Surge." *Research Policy* 39: 985–993.

Huang, Y. (2008). *Capitalism with Chinese Characteristics: Entrepreneurship and the State.* Cambridge, Cambridge University Press.

Huang, Y., C. Fang, P. Xu and G. Qin (2013). The New Normal of Chinese Development. *China: A New Model for Growth and Development.* R. Garnaut, C. Fang and L. Song. Canberra, ANU E Press.

Khan, M. H. (2000). Rents, Efficiency and Growth. *Rents, Rent-seeking and Economic Development.* M. H. Khan and K. S. Jomo. Cambridge, Cambridge University Press.

Lardy, Nicholas R. (2014). *Markets over Mao: The Rise of Private Business in China.* Washington, DC, Peterson Institute of International Economics.

Lee, I. H., M. Syed and X. Liu (2012). *Is China Over-Investing and Does It Matter?* Washington, DC, International Monetary Fund.

Lerner, J. (2009). *Boulevard of Broken Dreams: Why Public Efforts to Boost Entrpreneurship and Venture Capital Have Failed – And What to Do about It.* Princeton, NJ, Princeton University Press.

Lewis, J. I. (2013). *Green Innovation in China.* New York, Columbia University Press.

Lieberthal, K. and D. M. Lampton (1992). *Bureaucracy, Politics and Decision-Making in Post-Mao China.* Berkeley, University of California Press.

Lin, Y. (2001). *Between Politics and Markets.* New York, Cambridge University Press.

Lu, D. and Z. Tang (1997). *State Intervention and Business in China: The Role of Preferential Policies.* Cheltenham, Edward Elgar.

Lu, Q. (2000). *China's Leap into the Information Age.* Oxford, Oxford University Press.

Magoff, Fred (2013). "Twenty-First-Century Land Grabs: Accumulation by Agricultural Dispossession." *Global Research.* www.globalresearch.ca/twenty-first-century-land-grabs-accumulation-by-agricultural-dispossession/5356768. Accessed July 26, 2014.

Mathews, J. (2014). *Greening of Capitalism: How Asia Is Driving the Next Great Transformation.* Stanford University Press.

McGregor, R. (2012). *The Party: The Secret World of China's Communist Rulers*. New York, Harper Perennial.

McKinnon, R. I. (1973). *Money and Capital in Economic Development*. Washington, DC, Brookings Institution Press.

Moga, T. T. (2012). *China's Utility Model Patent System: Innovation Driver or Deterrent*. Washington, DC, US Chamber of Commerce.

Moore, T. G. (2002). *China in the World Market: Chinese Industry and International Sources of Reform in the Post-Mao Era*. New York, Cambridge University Press.

Murphy, K., A. Shleifer and R. Vishny (1989). "Industrialization and the Big Push." *Journal of Political Economy* **97**(5): 1003–1026.

Naughton, B. (1996). *Growing Out of the Plan: Chinese Economic Reform, 1978–1993*. New York, Cambridge University Press.

Naughton, B. (2010). "China's Distinctive System: Can It Be a Model for Others?" *Journal of Contemporary China* **19**(65): 437–460.

Nee, Victor and Sonja Opper. (2012). *Capitalism from Below: Markets and Institutional Change in China*. Cambridge, MA, Harvard University Press.

Niosi, J. (2002). "National Systems of Innovations Are 'X-Efficient' (and X-Effective). Why Some Are Slow Learners." *Research Policy* **31**: 291–302.

Pei, M. (2008). *China's Trapped Transition: The Limits of Developmental Autocracy*. Cambridge, MA, Harvard University Press.

Perkins, D. (2001). Industrial and Financial Policy in China and Vietnam: A New Model or a Replay of the East Asian Experience? *Rethinking the East Asian Miracle*. J. Stiglitz and S. Yusuf. New York, Oxford University Press.

Pettis, M. (2013). *Avoiding the Fall: China's Economic Restructuring*. Washington, DC, Carnegies Endowment for International Peace.

Prud'homme, D. (2012). *Dulling the Cutting Edge: How Patent-Related Policies and Practices Hamper Innovation in China*. Shanghai, European Chamber of Commerce.

Qian, Y. (2003). How Reform Worked in China. *Search of Prosperity: Analytic Narratives of Growth*. D. Rodrik. Princeton, NJ, Princeton University Press.

Rein, S. (2014). *The End of Copy-Cat China: The Rise of Creativity, Innovation, and Individualism in Asia*. Hoboken, NJ, Wiley.

Rodrik, D. (2011). *The Globalization Paradox*. New York, W.W. Norton.

Samuels, R. J. and W. Keller, Eds. (2003). *Crisis and Innovation: Asian Technology after the Millennium*. New York, Cambridge University Press.

Schurmann, F. (1968). *Ideology and Organization in Communist China*. Berkeley, UC Berkeley.

Simon, Denis F. and Cong Cao (2009). *China's Emerging Technological Edge: Assessing the Role of High-End Talent*. Cambridge, Cambridge University Press.

Su, Fubing and Ran Tao (2015). "The China Model Withering? Institutional Roots of Local Developmentalism." *Urban Studies* 1–21. DOI: 10.1177/ 0042098015593461.

Torch High-Technology Center (2011). *National High-Tech Industrial Zones in China*. Beijing, Ministry of Science and Technology.

Tsui, K. and Y. Wang (2004). "Between Separate Stoves and a Single Menu: Fiscal Decentralization in China." *China Quarterly* 177: 71–90.

Unirule Institute [Tianze Jingji Yanjiusuo] (2011). *The Nature, Performance and Reform of State-Owned Enterprises [Guoyou Qiye de Xingzhi, Biaoxian yu Gaige]*. Beijing, Unirule Institute.

Walter, C. E. and F. J. T. Howie (2011). *Red Capitalism: The Fragile Financial Foundation of China's Extraordinary Rise*. Singapore, John Wiley & Sons.

Wang, F. and A. Mason (2008). The Demographic Factor in China's Economic Transition. *China's Great Economic Transformation*. L. Brandt and T. G. Rawski. New York, Cambridge University Press.

Wang, Y., X. Zhang and M. Zhao (2013). *Zhongguo Chuangye Fengxian Touzi Fazhan Baogao 2013 [Venture Capital Development in China 2013]*. Beijing, Jingji Guanli Chubanshe [Economy and Management Publishing House].

Wedeman, A. (2012). *Double Paradox: Rapid Growth and Rising Corruption in China*. Ithaca, NY, Cornell University Press.

Whiting, S. (2004). The Cadre Evaluation System at the Grass Roots: The Paradox of Party Rule. *Holding China Together: Diversity and National Integration in the Post-Deng Era*. D. Yang and B. Naughton. New York, Cambridge University Press.

Wu, J. (2011). In transforming the development model, it is most important that the government reforms avoid an investment "Great Leap Forward" [转变发展方式政府改革更关键 忌投资'大跃进']. January 19. Renmin Ribao.

Xu, C. (2011). "The Fundamental Institutions of China's Reforms and Development." *Journal of Economic Literature* 49(4): 1076–1151.

Yang, D. Y. and H. K. Wang (2008). "Dilemmas of Local Governance under the Development Zone Fever in China: A Case Study of the Suzhou Region." *Urban Studies* 45(5 & 6): 1037–1054.

Zeng, M. and P. J. Williamson (2008). *Dragons at Your Door: How Chinese Cost Innovation is Disrupting Global Business*. Boston, Harvard Business School Press.

Zhang, C., D. Z. Zeng, W. P. Mako and J. Seward (2009). *Promoting Enterprise-Led Innovation in China*. Washington, DC, The World Bank.

Zhao, Y. (2014). *Who's Afraid of the Big Bad Dragon: Why China Has the Best (and the Worst) Education System in the World*. San Francisco, Jossey-Bass.

Zheng, Y. (2013). *Wu Guo Jiaoyu Bingli [The Pathology of Chinese Education]*. Beijing: Zhongxin Press.

Zhong, Y. (2003). *Local Government and Politics in China*. Armonk, NY, M.E. Sharpe.

Zweig, D. (2002). *Internationalizing China: Domestic Interests and Global Linkages*. Ithaca, NY, Cornell University Press.

Newspaper sources

ESJJBD   *Ershiyi Shiji Jingji Baodao* [The Twenty-First Century Economic Herald]
JJGC   *Jingji Guancha* [The Economic Observer]
NYT   *The New York Times*
WSJ   *The Wall Street Journal*

7 | Transforming China's IP system to stimulate innovation

MENITA LIU CHENG AND CAN HUANG

7.1 Introduction

China has entered the era of science and technology (S&T) in which innovation plays a crucial role in driving economic growth. After historical debates on the national innovation system (NIS), a general consensus has been reached that NIS success can be attributed to the "right" combination of institutional, developmental, and technological conditions (Krumm and Kharas 2004), which determine a country's national technological absorptive capacity (Freeman 1995). The NIS gives various actors, such as universities, industries, and government institutions (Etzkowitz and Leydesdorff 2000), the opportunity to interact, create, and disseminate knowledge across levels (i.e., national, regional, and sectoral) for S&T development (Etzkowitz 2001; Etzkowitz and Leydesdorff 2000; Freeman 1987, 1989, 1995; Lundvall 1992; Nelson 1993). To enhance national absorptive capacity and encourage innovation, governments must adopt a delicate balance of technology policies and incentives to promote successful S&T interaction and knowledge diffusion (Fuller 2015; Krumm and Kharas 2004) and sustain gradual technological catch-up from imitation to innovation.

From the 1980s to the 1990s, Japan, Korea, and Taiwan successfully made this transition (Freeman 1987; Hu and Mathews 2008; Kim 1997; Krumm and Kharas 2004; OECD 1997) in a process similar to the one that China is currently experiencing. Technological catch-up is characterized by an initial period of lax intellectual property rights (IPR) policies and strong incentives to promote the importation of foreign technologies (i.e., by imitation, reverse-engineering, or incremental improvements) and to generate positive technological spillover. Over time, through learning by doing, countries gain greater technological expertise, which contributes to the strengthening and upgrading of their national technological absorptive ability to innovate. As the system gains sophistication, the government needs to tighten technology policies to facilitate a smooth transition from a system focused on quantity to one focused on quality. The adoption of tighter policies pushes domestic firms to become more competitive and, thus, strengthen the nation's technological capacity for innovation.

China began this process in the 1980s, after Deng Xiaoping's 1978 implementation of the Open Door policy, which began with the establishment of an IPR legal framework to integrate China's economy into the world economy and allow foreign direct investment (FDI). To facilitate global integration, China instituted an IPR system modeled after the advanced Western countries' IPR regimes at the time, with adaptations for its social, economic, political, and industrial development context. As a result, China's IPR legal framework became uniquely Chinese, with a dual-track administrative and judicial system, divided into multiple layers of IPR jurisdictional governance at central and local government levels, and spanning different industries under the administration of various government ministries. Although China's IPR legal framework has been in place for thirty years, the effectiveness of its implementation and enforcement has come into question because it is incomplete. The Chinese government is aware of these problems and is making efforts aimed at improving matters quickly and comprehensively by 2020.

7.2 A flawed policy system at the cost of patent quality

China's recent history of S&T progress can be attributed to Deng Xiaoping's campaign to strengthen S&T research in the country as a key to modernization and building the economy. In 1978, nine months before announcing the Open Door policy, Deng addressed a national S&T conference and stressed that "without modern science and technology, it is not possible to build modern agriculture, modern industry, and modern national defense. Without rapid development of science and technology, it is impossible to have rapid development of the national economy" (*People's Daily* 2006). As a result, a series of S&T policy reforms and technology programs were implemented to establish basic and applied research as the central pillars for building a modern and powerful country.

The next major S&T revival campaign was announced in 2005, when, on the occasion of the Chinese Academy of Science's fiftieth anniversary, President Hu Jintao stressed the importance of achieving China's S&T self-sufficiency by "walking the road of indigenous innovation with Chinese characteristics" (*China News* 2005). In February 2006, Hu officially unveiled China's medium- to long-range plans (State Council 2006), which would serve as blueprints to limiting reliance on foreign technology and enabling S&T self-sufficiency by 2020. As part of this strategy, in 2008, China launched the National Intellectual Property Rights Strategy Outline (NIPSO), whose objective was to improve and strengthen China's IP system (SIPO 2014a; State Council 2008a). NIPSO had short- and long-term IP expectations. The short-term objectives called for an increase in IP volume (i.e., the quantity of annual domestic invention patent applications made and granted, Chinese applications filed abroad, world-famous domestic brands, high-quality varieties of plants, high-level integrated circuitry designs). The long-term objectives entailed significant improvements to China's overall IPR environment (i.e., legal IPR environment, market IPR proficiency, public IPR awareness, and indigenous IP quality and quantity). To meet NIPSO's objectives (State Council 2015b), China must maintain an annual growth rate of patents of 19 percent per year, which is two percentage points below the rate it has maintained since 1995.

7.2.1 System of incentives to spur patent applications

Because of its high S&T expectations, China faces tremendous pressure to increase the quality and quantity of innovation. Patents have often been used as an indicator of technological innovation and performance (Griliches 1990). As seen in Figure 7.1, the implementation of NIPSO and related IPR policies to date has contributed to an increase in patent volume. These policies have included a series of incentives to encourage patent applications, comprising subsidies, remuneration, and preferential tax treatment, as follows:

- **Patent subsidies:** Financial subsidies to promote patenting activity are available for funding patent applications, examinations, licensing, and other related costs for invention patents, utility model patents, design patents, and international patents (Wen and Zhu 2007). The subsidies program began in 1999, when Shanghai became the first to launch a program of this kind, and it subsequently spread across the rest of the country (HIPB 2007; Li 2012). Each province establishes its own subsidy limits on approved items based on local economic needs (BJIP 2014; CDIP 2013; SIPA 2012; TJIP 2014).

- **Patent remuneration:** Outstanding inventors and workers are eligible to receive rewards for industrial patent application projects, patent model enterprises, and so on, in a program administered by local and provincial governments (SIPO 2009; *Xinhua News* 2012). The awards not only provide financial support but also give inventors commercial recognition and government legitimacy.
- **Preferential tax treatment:** The Enterprise Tax Law, which took effect in 2008, included tax breaks for new and high-technology enterprises. Applicants able to prove indigenous IP ownership of core technology are eligible to have their income taxed at a rate of 15 percent and to receive deductions for value-added tax paid as well if certain requirements are met (MOST 2008).

Patenting is thus encouraged through the availability of many different financial incentives, can be engaged in at little or no cost, and opens the door to other attractive benefits (i.e., government brand recognition, public image improvement, operating costs reduction, technology

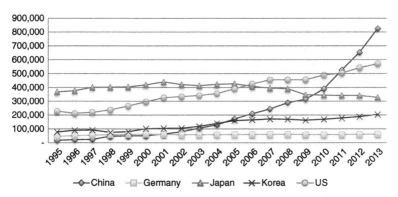

Figure 7.1 Invention patent applications for country office statistics (1995–2013)
Source: World Intellectual Property Organization (WIPO 2015).

licensing, and cross-licensing opportunities). Entities can leverage the use of these incentives to improve business opportunities in the market, and, thus, there is an incentive to patent even if only to obtain various benefits. Among the other nonfinancial benefits are social and professional advancement, in terms of access to scarce government resources, career promotion, and *hukou* (household registration) in desirable locations for state-affiliated entities working in the public sector (*Economist* 2010).

7.2.2 Misalignment between performance and incentives system

The majority of domestic entities suffer from technological limitations, which have hindered their ability to produce technology (Wang 2010). Numerous examples and statistics attest to their limited level of technological proficiency (Li 2012; Liu, Liu, and Huang 2014; Lu 2008; State Council 2015a; Wu 2009). The tremendous pressure to innovate has resulted in potentially inflated statistics and an excess number of patents of questionable quality. Hence, the first problem that China faces is a system of misaligned performance and incentives, which reward patent quantity over quality (*People's Daily* 2014a; Sun 2014).

To meet the demands of this pressure, some entities have taken advantage of the ease of filing and obtaining utility model patents (UMPs) and design patents. Some applicants have attempted to file patents for copycat or repetitive technologies of little value, simply because of the lack of rigor during the UMP and design patent application review process (Fuller 2015; Moga 2012). After patents are granted, patent owners cease annual patent maintenance after they have received the benefits from government incentives (Cao 2014; Cao, Lei and Wright 2014; Moga 2012). The resulting junk or fake patents (Liu, Liu, and Huang 2014) make little or no contribution, were created in the absence of market demand, and lack practical commercial applications and value (Fu, Jiang, and Ma 2010). These patents not only harm the reputation of China's patent system but are harmful to Chinese innovation (Wen and Zhu 2009). First, junk patents inhibit innovation by incurring high costs, raising barriers to patents, and preventing other entities from innovating (Sun 2014). Second, junk patents disrupt healthy market competition and force competitors to pass on the associated costs of IP to end users. Third, junk patents waste public IPR investment and resources aimed at improving patent administration and enforcement (Liu, Liu, and Huang 2014; Wen 2008; Wen and Zhu 2007, 2009).

Unfortunately, it is not possible to ascertain the actual number of legitimate patents and assess their real contribution to China's knowledge economy. In 2005, official statements estimated that junk patents accounted for 50–80 percent of patents granted (CBIN 2005). Because no new statistics on junk patents have been released, one can only assume that the inherent problem persists at a similar rate (Sun 2014). An alternative statistic to approximate the volume of junk patents is the length of time for which patents granted are annually renewed. Annual maintenance fees are accurate indicators of the patent's commercial viability (Liu, Liu, and Huang 2014; Qiao and Wen 2009). According to a 2007 study, on average Chinese firms maintain an invention patent application for 4.09 years, while foreign firms do so for 6.05 years (Qiao and Wen 2009). According to a 2010 study, only 17.9 percent of Chinese firms maintained invention patents for more than seven years (Fu, Jiang, and Ma 2010). The length of patent maintenance time is an indication that either patents lack inherent value due to a lack of industrial applications or firms lack the ability to exploit technologies for commercial and industrial practical applications (Qiao and Wen 2009). In those situations, continued annual patent maintenance expenditures are not warranted (Cao 2014; Huang 2012; Wen and Zhu 2009; Zhang and Chen 2012).

7.2.3 Self-serving behavior and government IPR financial system abuses

A second problem that China faces is a growing trend in which unscrupulous patent applicants abuse China's patent incentives system. Although innovation incentives were initially created to encourage patenting activity (Li 2012; Wen and Zhu 2007, 2009), low requirements and access thresholds have permitted abuses of the system. As a result, even entities that are self-sufficient and do not depend on the incentive benefits from the patent system to survive have flooded the system with low-quality junk patents in order to access those benefits (Liu, Liu, and Huang 2014; Wen and Zhu 2009). This is also one of the reasons that many patents granted are not maintained, especially in the case where applicants file patents for the extraction of government subsidies and later see no reason to pay for maintenance (Fu, Jiang and Ma 2010; Wen 2008).

7.2.4 Reward and punishment imbalances

The third problem is that, at the national level, an imbalance exists between rewards and punishment for transgressions, such that the incentives for patenting are greater than the punishments for IP infringement. On the one hand, the government offers rewards in terms of generous incentives to promote national innovation and patenting activities (Fuller 2015) and because the drivers of innovation are incentives, rather than the rewards from a market system, there is ample motivation for bad actors to take advantage.

On the other hand, punishment for patent infringement is weak. In fact, national statistics indicate that the average compensation for infringement cases is CNY 80,000 (less than USD 13,000) for patents, CNY 70,000 (less than USD 11,500) for trademarks, and CNY 15,000 (less than USD 2,500) for copyrights, which are very low compared with compensation in developed countries (*People's Daily* 2015). These amounts are so low that they are not even sufficient to cover the costs of lengthy legal proceedings, much less compensate IP owners for technological or financial losses due to infringement. The government is currently working on legislation to increase compensation and punitive damage thresholds and decrease the costs of legal action (MOD 2015; State Council 2015a; Supreme Court 2015; *Xinhua News* 2015). Moreover, China's IP legal framework lacks uniformity (*People's Daily* 2015), and despite the establishment of specialized IP courts in Beijing, Shanghai, and Guangzhou, the lack of uniformity affects the legitimacy of the system and introduces disparities in court rulings across geographic regions.

7.3 The current state of patenting activity and technology transfer at Chinese universities

Universities are critical centers of innovation and thus play an integral part in the NIS in China as elsewhere (Hu and Mathews 2008; Li 2012). They are tasked with cultivating national human capital (Hu and Mathews 2008; Wang 2015; Xue 2006) and incubating new technology firms (MOE 2015). But in spite of China's booming economy and market demand for university-developed technology (Graff 2007), university researchers are ill equipped to judge the technologies' market potential (Rosenberg and Nelson 1994) not only because of market inexperience and information asymmetry but also because of the absence of an integrated system connecting R&D planning, production, and marketing generally found within companies to ensure technology application and commercialization success (Rosenberg and Nelson 1994). At the university level, existing policy flaws and the incomplete state of China's IP incentives, policy, and protection systems (*People's Daily* 2015) are among many contributing factors to the low rates of university technology transfer.

At this point, it will be helpful to explain the current state of university R&D investment, performance, and technology transfer in China. As shown in Table 7.1, in 2013, China's gross national expenditure on R&D (GERD) topped USD 191.1 billion. Chinese universities, research institutes, and industries were allocated 7.2 percent, 15.0 percent, and 76.6 percent of this expenditure, respectively. Chinese university GERD funding comes from three main sources: government, industry, and the technology market, as shown in Table 7.2.

Chinese universities contribute about 70 percent of total national basic research (Wang 2015). From 2009 to 2013, universities allocated on average 33 percent, 53 percent, and 14 percent of their GERD funding to basic, applied, and experimental research, respectively (MOST 2010–2013; NBS 2015a). In the same period, university R&D personnel accounted for approximately 11 percent of China's R&D personnel, with 43 percent, 50 percent, and 7 percent of personnel dedicated to basic, applied, and experimental research, respectively (MOST 2008–2013, 2010–2013; NBS 2015a, 2015b).

In 2012, the volume of university invention patents licensed was 43.6 percent of the national total although it accounted for less than 3 percent of total national invention patents granted. Moreover, the volume of university technology transfer contracts (i.e., technology R&D, technology transfer, technology consulting, and technology services) accounted for 20.5 percent of the national total, but its value was 4.6 percent of the national total (see Tables 7.3 and 7.4) (MOST 2008–2013).

Table 7.1 China's gross national expenditure on R&D (GERD) and Government S&T Appropriation Fund Statistics (2004–2013)

Indicators	2004	2005	2006	2007	2008	2009	2010	2011	2012	2013
Gross expenditure on R&D (CNY 100 million)	1,966.3	2,450.0	3,003.1	3,710.2	4,616.0	5,802.1	7,062.6	8,687.0	10,298.4	11,846.6
GERD/GDP (%)	1.2	1.3	1.4	1.4	1.5	1.7	1.8	1.8	2.0	2.1
Government S&T appropriation (CNY 100 million)	1,095.3	1,334.9	1,688.5	2,113.5	2,611.0	3,276.8	4,196.7	4,797.0	5,600.1	6,184.9
Gov. S&T expenditure/total expenditure (%)	3.8	3.9	4.2	4.3	4.2	4.3	4.7	4.4	4.5	4.4

Sources: MOST China Science & Technology Statistics Data Book (MOST 2010–2013), NBS GDP Report (NBS 2014a, 2014b), and China News Report (China News 2014).

Table 7.2 Sources of university gross national expenditure on R&D (GERD) (2009–2013) (in CNY 100 million and percent)

Funding source	2009 Value	%	2010 Value	%	2011 Value	%	2012 Value	%	2013 Value	%
Industry	171.7	36.7	198.5	33.2	242.9	35.3	260.5	33.4	289.3	33.8
Government	262.2	56.0	358.8	60.1	405.1	58.8	474.1	60.7	516.9	60.3
Other	34.3	7.3	39.9	6.7	40.8	5.9	46	5.9	50.5	5.9
Total university GERD	468.2		597.3		688.8		780.6		856.7	

Sources: MOST China Science & Technology Statistics Data Book (MOST 2010–2013) and NBS Basic Statistics for Higher Education S&T Activities (NBS 2014a, 2015a; China News 2014).

Table 7.3 *Volume of university technology transfers (2003–2013)*

| | Invention patents licensed | | Technology transfer contracts | | | | | |
| | Ministry of Science and Technology | | Ministry of Science and Technology & Innofund | | Ministry of Education | | | |
Year	Volume (10,000 patents)	% National	Volume (10,000 items)	% National	% State-owned contracts	% Foreign-owned contracts	% Private contracts	% Other contracts
2003	0.2	50.6	3.8	14.2	27.5	6.7	27.5	19.0
2004	0.3	63.3	3.9	14.8	42.2	4.1	41.8	11.9
2005	0.4	60.2	4.2	15.8	N.A.	N.A.	N.A.	N.A.
2006	0.6	59.3	1.8	8.9	41.1	4.5	39.2	15.2
2007	0.8	55.6	2.7	12.2	41.4	5.5	44.0	9.1
2008	1.0	53.6	2.9	13.0	39.1	5.2	44.9	10.9
2009	1.4	51.5	3.2	14.9	33.1	4.5	51.7	10.7
2010	1.9	44.1	4.2	18.3	30.7	6.0	52.6	10.7
2011	2.5	47.2	5.0	19.4	33.3	4.9	51.3	10.5
2012	3.4	43.6	5.8	20.5	34.3	4.6	51.9	9.2
2013	N.A.	N.A.	6.4	21.8	N.A.	N.A.	N.A.	N.A.

Sources: Innofund Annual Report on Statistics of China Technology Market (Innofund 2004–2014), SIPO Patent Statistics Summary Report (SIPO 2012a), MOST S&T Statistical Reports (MOST 2008–2013), and MOE DOST Statistical Reports (DOST 2007–2013).

Table 7.4 *Value of university technology transfers (2003–2013)*

	Ministry of Science and Technology & Innofund				Ministry of Education			
Year	Total revenue (CNY 100 million)	% National	Avg. revenue per contract (CNY 100 million)	% National	% State-owned contracts	% Foreign-owned contracts	% Private contracts	% Other contracts
2003	106.7	9.8	28.1	70.2	36.7	7.0	19.4	25.2
2004	116.6	8.7	29.7	59.5	52.6	5.7	31.5	10.3
2005	122.6	7.9	29.2	50.3	N.A.	N.A.	N.A.	N.A.
2006	65.0	3.6	35.3	40.1	49.6	5.7	30.9	13.7
2007	100.0	4.5	37.1	37.1	51.1	5.8	33.7	9.4
2008	116.6	4.4	39.6	33.8	42.2	4.5	38.6	14.7
2009	132.6	4.4	41.5	29.2	35.1	4.9	50.0	10.1
2010	196.7	5.0	46.8	27.5	33.1	7.1	48.0	11.8
2011	248.8	5.2	50.0	27.0	34.1	6.0	45.9	14.0
2012	294.0	4.6	50.7	22.2	38.4	5.2	45.6	10.8
2013	329.5	4.4	51.2	20.2	N.A.	N.A.	N.A.	N.A.

Sources: Innofund Annual Report on Statistics of China Technology Market (Innofund 2004–2014), SIPO Patent Statistics Summary Report (SIPO 2012a), MOST S&T Statistical Reports (MOST 2008–2013), and MOE DOST Statistical Reports (DOST 2007–2013).

7.3.1 Technology transfer and IP policy constraints

Today, in spite of significant investment in R&D, Chinese universities' patent technology transfer rates remain low, ranging from 2 percent (*People's Daily* 2015) to 5 percent (MOE 2015) annually. The national rate is 10 percent (NBD 2014), but the government expects universities to transfer technology at a rate of 80 percent (Zhao 2015), an evidently unreasonable expectation.

Besides technology maturity gaps between universities' basic R&D research and industry's commercial applications, one of the main reasons for such a low technology transfer rate is a flawed and incomplete IP system, which suffers from shortcomings involving incentives, ownership and decision-making authority, protection, policy impediments, and distribution of profits.

The first issue relates to a *lack of incentives for university patenting and technology transfer*. At the national level, the number of patents and amount of income generated from technology transfer have become important criteria set by the Ministry of Education (MOE) to evaluate universities' innovation performance (Tang 2006). Although technology transfer is specifically addressed in the "Law on Promoting the Transformation of Scientific and Technological Achievements" (see below), it has not yet been incorporated into the university's performance evaluation system (MOE 2015). Due to the pressure to patent, university researchers often face dilemmas over the best method of IP since not all technology can be patented and the use of other methods may not count toward annual performance tallies (Li 2015). For university researchers, it is critical to meet performance targets to secure access to research funding, career advancement opportunities, awards, and recognition. Mainly to meet patent performance objectives, university researchers do not thoroughly take into account issues related to technology commercialization, infringement, and utilization (Li 2015) in technology development, which has resulted in embryonic technology or contributed to an abundance of junk patents (MOE 2015). Despite the large volume of university patents, university researchers are not able to fully invest and pursue technology transfer on their own because of time and resource constraints (MOE 2015; Zhao 2015). At present, the universities lack an institutional support system to facilitate, support, and promote technology transfer unlike universities in the West (MOE 2015).

The second issue relates to *IP ownership and decision-making authority over patents and technology transfer*. Prior to 1993, regulatory policy in China did not address IP ownership of state-funded research, and, thus, IP ownership was undefined (Lin 2011). Since then, three main policies have emerged to guide, standardize, protect, and facilitate Chinese universities' technology transfer practices and sales:

- **The S&T Progress Law:** In 1993, China implemented its own version of the Bayh-Dole Act, known as the S&T Progress Law (NPC 2007), for the purpose of granting Chinese universities commercialization rights over government-funded technologies and IP. In 2007, China amended the law to clarify ownership rights and added restrictions (Guan, Yam and Mok 2005).
- **The "Law on Promoting the Transformation of Scientific and Technological Achievements":** In 1996, this law was passed with the goal of promoting, guiding, and standardizing state-funded IP technology transfer at universities and research institutions (MOST 2015; NBD 2014). In 2013, various ministries jointly revised the law and produced a "Draft" that, when approved, will give universities greater autonomy in making technology transfer decisions over the transfer, licensing, investment, pricing, and transaction of technological achievements and simplify the bureaucratic process (Liaoning Province 2015; MOST 2015; NBD 2014; SCIO 2015).
- **State Assets Transfer Interim Measures Order No. 3:** This law was passed in 2003 and jointly led by the State-Owned Assets Supervision and Administration Commission (SASAC) and the Ministry of Commerce to regulate and standardize technology transfers of state assets under SASAC's purview (State Council 2003).

These laws jointly define the parameters of ownership by assigning the role that each actor plays in university S&T technology transfer and commercialization (see box). After they are ratified, universities will enjoy greater autonomy over technology transfer and the bureaucratic process to fulfill institutional requirements will be simpler.

> **Role of various agencies in university S&T technology transfer and commercialization**
>
> - *SASAC* is responsible for the supervision and management of state-owned assets and the drafting of relevant laws and regulations for the management of state-assets (SASAC n.d.). Under the State Assets Transfer Interim Measures Order No. 3, now in effect, SASAC is tasked with approving the sale and transfer of state assets on request from the university (State Council 2003). Without SASAC's approval, universities may not proceed with technology commercialization. If any violations are incurred, the university and its researchers may be subject to criminal liability (State Council 2008b).
> - *Universities* are the sole owners of the technology or IP, considered "state assets" (NPC 2007; SIWU 2013).
> - *Technology transfer offices (TTO)* or R&D Management Departments (RDMD) are responsible for the management of university-owned IP (Li 2015; SIWU 2013; ZJU 2005), coordination of R&D collaborations with stakeholders (i.e., other universities and regional governments) (Xue 2009), and reporting annual university innovation and technology transfer performance to the government (MOST 2015).
> - *University researchers* (i.e., professors, postdocs, PhDs) are the inventors tasked with the management, operation, and updating of the technology (ZJU 2005). Researchers are responsible for reporting their technological achievements to the school and transferring them over to the TTO or RDMD for IP management. After this happens, the TTO or RDMD working jointly with the researchers makes the decisions about the IP with respect to technology transfer, ownership, and profit distribution (MOE 2015).

The third issue concerns the *legal risks associated with the transfer or sale of university-owned IP*. According to the current policy, universities are permitted to transfer or sell IP only after a lengthy and complicated bureaucratic approval process by SASAC, the absence of which constitutes a violation of the law. Having the state determine the permitted use of IP, coupled with this lengthy approval process, undermines the timely pursuit and effectiveness of technology transfer/sale (NBD 2014). Any attempts to pursue technology transfer or sale without prior SASAC approval may constitute a violation of the law, which under Article 75 of the "State Assets Law" the parties responsible "... shall be subject to criminal liability if the violation constitutes a crime"

(State Council 2008b). Having the state determine the permissive use of IP coupled with a lengthy and complicated approval process has undermined the timely pursuit and effectiveness of technology transfer/sale (NBD 2014).

To illustrate the complexity of the process, university researchers must secure approval by the school, the TTOs, or RDMDs, or the university (in the case of major inventions) in order to conduct technology transfers (ZJU 2005). After approval has been granted at the university level, the TTO or RDMD submits a technology transfer request to the local and central government SASAC for approval (SIWU 2013; State Council 2008b). The university must have the technology appraised by a qualified agency (State Council 2008b). Ultimately, if the transaction is approved by SASAC, it must take place at a designated public exchange open to public bidding (State Council 2008b). In practice, universities and researchers are highly concerned about this requirement, which reveals new inventions and proprietary technology to the public even prior to industry application or commercialization (Zhao 2015). If the bidding price for the technology is significantly lower than the appraised price (lower than 90 percent of appraised value), SASAC has a right to cancel the transaction and prevent the technology from being transferred (State Council 2008b). Moreover, in view of the current pace of China's technology development, by the time the transfer transaction is finalized, it is possible that the technology may have already become outdated. Even if no complications arise, the entire SASAC approval process can take two years, if not longer.

In 2013, Chinese leadership began a legal ratification process to simplify university technology transfer by granting universities (IP owners) and their researchers (IP inventors) greater autonomy to make decisions over the sale and transfer of state assets (MOST 2015; NBD 2014). Once the final "Draft for Comments" is approved before the end of 2015, universities will only be required to publicize approved technology transfer transactions without having to obtain approval from SASAC.

The fourth issue relates to *policy impediments to university researchers' entrepreneurial start-ups and eventual public listing.* University researchers are encouraged by university policy to leave their current teaching and research positions and pursue start-ups to assist in technology transfer (MOE 2015). Researchers with entrepreneurial aspirations must first obtain approval from their school and by the local and central government SASACs (SIWU 2013). After approval is granted, researchers are required to file approval documentation with the university's TTO or RDMD and are guaranteed their position and salary for up to three years (MOE 2015). Thus, university researchers are confronted with conflicting job demands, which ultimately affect the quality of education and training at universities (MOE 2015).

Although the pursuit of entrepreneurial start-ups has been a successful strategy in developed countries, China lacks a comprehensive institutional support mechanism to foster start-up success and growth (*People's Daily* 2015). Recently, China clarified its position in support of public listings for start-ups as long as the ventures meet state requirements (MOD 2015; State Council 2015a). Start-up owners must seek local and central SASAC approval for public listing of their firm. If the technology transfer venture is approved by SASAC then the start-up owners must submit a request for listing it with the China Securities Regulatory Commission (CSRC) and follow listing protocol if the listing quota has not yet been met. But, in general, the complicated and lengthy process of approval for the transfer of state assets makes the likelihood of listing remote. The lack of alternatives and improbability of becoming publicly listed can affect the value of a start-up, which leads to inaccurate and lower valuation of the IP.

The final issue relates to the *distribution of profits from university-owned IP in the context of technology transfer*. Until recently, profit distribution at universities has not been standardized because of a lack of overarching national policies. In 2015, the government announced that profit generated from technology transfer will belong to the researchers' university and be included in the university's budget for R&D and technology transfer (MOD 2015; NBD 2014; State Council 2015a). In addition, contributors to IP technology will be rewarded for the successful technology transfer and will receive no less than 50 percent of the profit (MOD 2015). Furthermore, the Legislative Affairs Office of the State Council (SCLAO 2015) stipulated the calculation method for service invention remuneration using annual operating profit (5 percent for invention patents and a new variety of plants and 3 percent for others) or annual sales (within the IP's period of validity, 0.5 percent for invention patents and a new variety of plants, and 0.3 percent for others) to estimate a monthly or annual award disbursement capped at 50 percent of the IP's accumulated operating profit.

7.4 The effectiveness of the utility model patent protection system

China's utility model patent (UMP) system has been the subject of controversy since the Patent Law came into effect in 1985. UMPs were originally intended to promote and protect incremental invention activities at small and medium-size enterprises by offering applicants fast-track IPR protection, at the same level of protection afforded to invention and design patents (SIPO 2012b, 2013).

7.4.1 China's patenting activity and current UMP development status

China is first in the world in terms of the number of applications for invention patents, ahead of the United States, Japan, Korea, and Germany since 2011 (WIPO 2015) (see Figure 7.1). In 2013, the volume of China's patent applications alone comprised 32 percent of the world total and was growing 26 percent year-on-year from 2012 to 2013. Moreover, the volume of applications and patents granted for UMPs remained at an annual growth rate of 21 percent from 2012 to 2013, despite negative annual growth in the number of invention (–4 percent) and design (–12 percent) patents granted. Driven by the volume of UMPs, the total number of applications and patents granted grew by 16 percent (2,377,061) and 5 percent (1,313,000), respectively, in 2013 (see Figure 7.2), according to the NSB; of these, UMPs

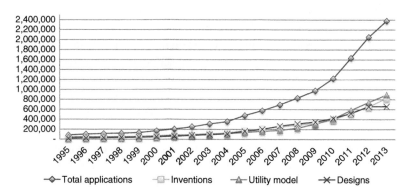

Figure 7.2 Volume of patent applications (1995–2013)
Source: China National Bureau of Statistics (NBS 2015c, 2015d).

accounted for 38 percent and 53 percent, respectively. In 2013, the volume of UMP applications and patents granted reached 892,362 and 692,845, respectively, well above the volume of invention patents by 67,226 and 485,157 and design patents by 232,799 and 280,378 items. Based on these trends, continued UMP growth is expected, especially if the same level of UMP policy execution or patent examination rigor is maintained in the course of fulfilling China's 2014–2020 IPR objectives (State Council 2015b).

7.4.2 *China's UMP patent system and potential system abuses*

As previously mentioned, the Patent Law gives UMPs the same level of protection in terms of scope, validity, and enforcement as the more technically complex, inventive, and innovative invention patents. By equating the level of protection for UMPs and invention patents, the system undermines the original intention of promoting true inventiveness and innovativeness on its own. The system encourages inventors to apply for patents that are of significantly lower technical quality and take advantage of the UMP patenting system, which offers a less rigorous examination process, lower patenting fees, and shorter approval time, yet is equally difficult to invalidate (Moga 2012). Areas in which UMPs are open to abuse include:

- **Level of technical complexity:** UMPs and invention patents differ in terms of the level of technical complexity of the technology being patented, with invention patents covering the scope of new products and processes and UMPs covering the scope of new product shapes and structures alone or in combination more narrowly (SIPO 2008). In spite of UMPs' narrower technical scope, in some cases, broader technical uses beyond the defined scope successfully granted have been documented (Moga 2012). This creates opportunities for applicants to file broad-scope UMPs and gain first-to-market advantages (i.e., increase profits and limit market competition).
- **Examination process:** UMPs consist of a less rigorous patent examination process, which has permitted plagiarized or repetitive UMP applications with little or no technical value to go undetected by the system, a problem that has been acknowledged by the government (SIPO 2013).

- **Patent filing fees:** UMP costs in China are lower than those for invention patents, which not only encourages applicants, even those with limited financial resources, to submit applications but also makes it relatively inexpensive to file more applications for junk patents.
- **Time for approval:** The UMPs' approval time ranges from seven months to a year after an application is filed, much faster than for invention patent applications.

7.4.3 Challenging the validity of a UMP patent

China's Patent Law allows for the validity of registered patents to be challenged by submitting a request to the Patent Reexamination Board (PRB) of the State Intellectual Property Office (SIPO). Invalidating a UMP is difficult because of low invention criteria requirements, and a great deal of time and money must be spent in finding sufficient references to invalidate each claim in it (Moga 2012). Those who raise such challenges must also consider the risks associated with a successful outcome and the possibility of out-of-court financial settlements to avoid costly and lengthy litigation (Moga 2012). On average, invalidation requests take up to two years to resolve and can be expensive, especially relative to how rapid and inexpensive it is to apply for and obtain UMPs. Based on invalidation data from the PRB, the volume of UMP cases is more than double the caseload of invention patents (see Table 7.5). Invalidation requests are made for less than 1 percent of total patents granted.

The rate of invalidation is the same for both UMPs and invention patents (see Table 7.6), counter to the expectation of higher rates for UMPs because examination errors should become more apparent after a second look. In addition, UMPs are not more likely to be invalidated if an infringement case goes to court, rather than being settled (Cao 2013; Cao, Lei, and Wright 2014).

PRB data show a 9 percent jump in the volume of UMPs entirely invalidated in 2008 compared to 2007 (see Table 7.7). This increase can be attributed to the government's increased efforts at upholding IPR protection and coincides with the release of China's National IPR Strategy and revision of the Patent Law.

The reality is that there's a major trade-off between pre-granting examination and post-granting reexamination as the proportion of invalidation requests accounts for less than 1 percent of total patents granted, and

Table 7.5 Statistics on patent invalidation (2008–2013)

Year	Invalidation requests received				Invalidation requests resolved			
	Total	Invention (%)	Utility model (%)	Design (%)	Total	Invention (%)	Utility model (%)	Design (%)
2008	2,038	17.4	48.5	34.1	2,727	15.5	50.6	33.8
2009	2,247	19.8	49.0	31.2	2,310	19.7	46.7	33.6
2010	2,411	21.1	47.6	31.3	1,946	19.9	50.6	29.5
2011	2,749	20.6	48.1	30.9	2,567	21.6	48.5	29.9
2012	2,941	20.5	44.8	34.7	2,599	20.0	47.1	32.9
2013	2,930	20.6	47.6	31.8	2,313	19.2	47.9	32.9

Source: SIPO Annual Reports (SIPO 2008–2013).

Table 7.6 *Statistics on patent invalidation cases and resolution (2008–2011)*

Year	Total resolved	Maintained (%)	Partial invalidation (%)	Entire invalidation (%)
Invention				
2008	309	35	24	41
2009	336	35	24	41
2010	261	30	25	45
2011	381	33	20	47
Utility				
2008	1,045	37	18	45
2009	861	35	17	48
2010	727	33	16	50
2011	990	34	14	51
Design				
2008	655	44	0	56
2009	588	41	0	59
2010	401	38	0	62
2011	559	45	0	55

Source: SIPO Patent Reexamination Board UMP Invalidation Data (Furr and Palla 2012).

which may not warrant the higher costs and increased labor requirements that would be needed to conduct thorough patent examination on every patent application. Hence from a cost analysis perspective, although not ideal, post-granting reexamination proceeding is most efficient in resolving the growing number of invalidation cases requested per year (please refer to Figure 7.3).

7.4.4 Reasons for low foreign UMP activity in China

The advantages of UMPs in China have been particularly attractive to enterprises with limited financial means. In spite of these benefits,

Table 7.7 *Utility model patent statistics on patent invalidation cases and distribution of outcomes (2000–2013)*

Year	Requests	Resolved*	Maintained		Partial invalidation		Entire invalidation	
			No.	%	No.	%	No.	%
2000	622	917	403	44	92	10	270	29
2001	605	865	335	39	103	12	272	31
2002	756	684	194	28	77	11	225	33
2003	834	701	201	29	71	10	213	30
2004	828	623	153	25	58	9	228	37
2005	924	743	223	30	71	10	232	31
2006	1,136	980	250	26	113	12	332	34
2007	1,006	1,113	336	30	142	13	399	36
2008	988	1,381	383	37	189	18	473	45
2009	1,102	1,078	300	35	145	17	416	48
2010	1,147	984	243	33	119	16	365	50
2011	1,323	1,245	341	34	142	14	507	51
2012	1,318	1,224	N.A.	N.A.	N.A.	N.A.	N.A.	N.A.
2013	1,394	1,107	N.A.	N.A.	N.A.	N.A.	N.A.	N.A.

Source: SIPO Patent Reexamination Board UMP Invalidation Data (Furr and Palla 2012; Moga 2012; SIPO 2008–2013) (*The volume of "Resolved" cases also accounts for cases that have been "Withdrawn or Other" by the applicant).

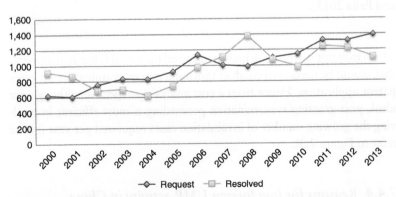

Figure 7.3 Case volume of utility model patents examined by China's patent reexamination board (2000–2013)
Source: SIPO Patent Reexamination Board UMP Invalidation Case Volume (Furr and Palla 2012; SIPO 2008–2013).

foreign firms have filed considerably fewer UMP applications than domestic firms. Domestic firms account for 99 percent of total UMP applications and patents granted per year since 1995, while that of foreign firms is 1 percent (NBS 2015c, 2015d).

This low level has a number of explanations, according to a 2012 study by the US Chamber of Commerce (Moga 2012), which can be divided into three groups as perceived UMP system weaknesses, technology patent suitability, and behavioral preferences.

- **Perceived UMP system weaknesses.** The UMP system has weaknesses that may affect the degree of protection for UMPs. First, because of questions regarding effectiveness and value, foreign-trained attorneys lack familiarity with and look with suspicion at the use of second-tier patents to protect valuable technological investments. These concerns are valid because UMPs are not widely used internationally. Second, from the perspective of financial investment, foreign firms weigh the opportunity costs of IPR protection between UMPs and invention patents. Investment in invention patents, although more costly and time consuming, offers a stronger level of protection and has measurable value across international jurisdictions. Hence, UMPs do not show sufficient cost efficiency due to the risks associated with weaker protection.
- **Technology and patent suitability.** A mismatch exists between technology protection needs and the type of protection offered. First, because of the more narrowly defined technological scope for UMPs, protection for them is not "one size fits all" for all technologies or industries. Highly complex technologies have product shapes and structures that require more protection than is offered. Second, because of the technology product development life cycle and market life span, some technologies require longer protection than the ten years offered for UMPs. In some cases, due to the level of complexity of the technology, foreign firms have long R&D, production, or time-to-market life cycles, which require a longer time horizon for product launch. Thus, in these cases, firms can afford to wait and have the flexibility to choose invention patents over UMPs. But when technologies are expected to have a long market life span, UMP's length of protection is simply insufficient to meet corporate needs.
- **Differences in behavioral preferences.** Individual corporate patenting preferences and behavioral conditioning may cause firms to

refrain from UMP activity. First, domestic and foreign firms differ in terms of their patenting behavior: whereas foreign firms prefer to file inventions, designs, and UMPs in this order of priority, Chinese firms file in the opposite order (Moga 2012). This difference is directly linked to the firm's technological capacity (Cao 2014) and level of complexity of the technology per se. Second, because of individual company preferences, foreign companies prefer not to accumulate patents of questionable value as they may confront enforcement difficulties down the road. Third, because of significant time investments during R&D and product development, firms are motivated to invest in strong patents that provide a prolonged market life span and a continuous revenue stream (Cao 2013).

7.5 Conclusion

China is entering an era in which innovation plays a central role in promoting economic growth and stability. To support these economic goals, the state is under tremendous pressure to implement comprehensive improvements in policies to strengthen its IPR system and protect technological achievements. Doing so will require full implementation of the NIPSO and related IP promotion policies to address systematic institutional weaknesses, outline parameters for guiding S&T development, and allow market forces to steer the direction of China's technological innovation. The purpose of this chapter has been to provide an in-depth examination of existing IP policies and their inherent constraints to address core issues, provide insights, and make suggestions for improving the effectiveness of China's IP policies.

The first section of this chapter addressed incentives as one of the main factors behind the abundance of junk patents, in a system that invites abuse. The root of the problem is the fact that patenting activities are being motivated by incentives rather than market demand, which has led to the burgeoning of patents without useful applications or market potential. The incentives system has been effective in generating a great volume of IP, and it has been useful in shortening the time period needed for the country to become familiar with IPR. But rampant abuses of the system have occurred because access to the incentives has a low threshold.

From a policy perspective, China is trying to realign the performance and incentives system so that market forces will become the main driver of technology development and curb junk patenting (MOD 2015; *People's Daily* 2015; State Council 2015a). From a development perspective, the ubiquity of junk patents is the result of a learning process since China's IPR experience is relatively short and dates back only thirty years. Every country with an advanced IPR system, such as Japan, Korea, and Taiwan in the 1980s through the 1990s (Freeman 1987; Hu and Mathews 2008, 2009; Kim 1997), has gone through the same development process, from imitation to innovation, and has had its government employ industrial development policies to steer the economy into high value-added activity (Fuller 2015). The only difference in the case of China is that the scale of junk invention patents has become more apparent because of the country's massive size and the high volume of patents. Although junk invention patents seem to have flooded the market and heightened stakeholder concerns, these patents in themselves are harmless, as they do not hold any value and do not affect healthy market competition.

To transform China's IP system to stimulate innovation, we argue that first, China must realign its incentives system to foster the pursuit of high value-added technology activities without sacrificing existing performance benchmarks. Second, China must raise the thresholds to access incentives (*People's Daily* 2014a, 2014b) and increase patent examination stringency (Moga 2012) to deter abuse of the system and ensure patent quality. Third, to deter patent infringement, China must standardize and raise compensation and punitive damages in proportion to the severity of the infringement and loss of profits. Finally, the utility of the patent incentives system needs to be reassessed and eventually phased out after the limits to its usefulness have been reached.

The second section of this chapter addressed existing policy constraints affecting universities' patenting activities and technology transfer. Policy weaknesses and the lack of institutional support are the main reasons for the low rates of university technology transfer. To address these problems, the government is currently working on the ratification of new IP innovation policies to simplify and streamline the process of technology transfer. Both the government and universities have a responsibility to develop and implement actionable policies in support of technology transfer. At the national level, the swift approval and implementation of the Law on Promoting the Transformation of Scientific and Technological

Achievements will remove substantial institutional barriers and simplify the bureaucratic process by granting universities decision-making autonomy. Universities will have to amend internal policies in accordance with national laws and motivate researchers to engage in technology transfer – for instance, per recommendation of IP experts in academia, by including technology transfer as a key performance indicator, eradicating conflicting job demands, implementing profit distribution and technology remuneration policies, improving institutional support to facilitate technology transfer and incubate start-ups, and allocating sufficient funding for researchers' development, transfer, protection, maintenance, and updating of valuable IP (MOE 2015).

In practical terms, greater freedom is the key to promoting university innovation and technology transfer. As part of this, the government needs to amend the State Assets Law so that the pursuit of technology transfer is not subject to a lengthy and complicated process of approval. Moreover, universities need to standardize and swiftly implement consistent profit distribution policies.

The last section of this chapter addressed the ineffectiveness of the UMP system and its impact on the level of foreign UMP patenting. Industry's patenting activity is defined by a combination of firm-level factors, such as IP protection system effectiveness, technology and patent choice suitability, and innate behavioral characteristics. Therefore, low foreign UMP patenting rates cannot be attributed solely to a general assessment of perceived system ineffectiveness as companies make careful assessments of technological needs, weighing them against the various methods of IP protection. Since the implementation of the NIPSO in 2008, China has been working to establish a more robust patent supervision mechanism, ensure patent application quality, and strengthen the monitoring, examination, and handling of low-quality patent applications (SIPO 2014b; State Council 2015b). From an IP system perspective, UMPs have been an effective tool, which has helped inventors to patent small incremental inventions at low cost in a short time. Based on the experience of Japan and Korea, China might not need to abolish the UMP system; rather, China should make continuous efforts in increasing the rigor of its IPR policy and improve its IPR institutional system. It is expected that China will experience a decline in the annual volume of UMP applications.

By increasing incentive threshold and application requirements, China will curb junk patenting behavior, increase domestic technological capacity for innovation, resolve existing UMP system flaws affecting technology quality, and bypass the middle-income trap, following in the footsteps of Japan and Korea (JPO 2014; KIPO 2013).

Acknowledgement

"Can Huang is grateful for the financial support of the National Natural Science Foundation of China Grant No. 71402161."

References

BJIP (Beijing Intellectual Property Bureau). 2014. Beijing shi zhishi chanquan ju Beijing shi caizheng ju guanyu yinfa "Beijing shi zhuanli zizhu jin guanli banfa" de tongzhi [Beijing State Intellectual Property Bureau, Beijing Bureau of Finance Regarding the Publication "Beijing City Patent Subsidy Financial Administrative Law" Notification]. October 20. Available at www.bjipo.gov.cn/zwxx/zwgg/201410/t20141020_32950.html.

Cao, S. 2013. Faster but shorter versus longer but slower patent protection: Which do firms prefer? Innovation Seminar, University of California Berkeley College of Engineering, Fung Institute for Engineering Leadership, www.funginstitute.berkeley.edu/sites/default/files/Long%20 UM%20IP%20SWC%2020130808_0.pdf.

Cao, S. 2014. Speed of patent protection, rate of technology obsolescence and optimal patent strategy: Evidence from innovation patented in U.S., China, and several other countries. Environment and Resource Economics Seminar, Department of Agricultural and Resource Economics, University of California Berkeley, http://are.berkeley.edu/fiel ds/erep/seminar/f2014/siwei_cao_patents.pdf.

Cao, S., Lei, Z., and Wright, B. 2014. Speed vs. length of patent protection: Evidence from innovations patented in U.S. and China. Job Market paper, Department of Agricultural and Resource Economics, University of California Berkeley, https://are.berkeley.edu/sites/default/files/job-candidates/paper/SiweiCao_JMP121014.pdf.

CBIN (China Business Information Network). 2005. Woguo chuxian shenqing zhuanli rechao lese zhuanli bizhong gaoda 50% [China experiences a boom in patent applications with a 50% proportion of junk patents]. *China Business Information Network News*, November 16. Available at www.ecchn.com/20061116ecnews3847511.html.

CDIP (Chengdu Intellectual Property). 2013. Chengdu shi zhuanli zizhu guanli banfa (2013 nian) [Chengdu Patent Subsidy Administrative Law (2013)]. Available at www.cdip.gov.cn/ReadNews.asp?NewsID=11735/.

China News. 2005. Hu Jintao zhuxi jiu tigao Zhongguo keji zizhu chuangxin nengli ti san yaoqiu [President Hu Jintao puts forth three requirements to improve China's technological indigenous innovation capability]. June 3. Available at www.chinanews.com.cn/news/2005/2005-06-03/26/582433.shtml.

China News. 2014. 2013 nian guojia caizheng keji zhichu wei 6184.9 yi bi shang nian zeng 10.4% [2013 China government S&T appropriation reaches CNY 618.49 billion: A year-on-year increase of 10.4%]. October 30. Available at www.chinanews.com/gn/2014/10-30/6734769.shtml.

DOST (Department of Science and Technology, Ministry of Education). 2007–13. Gaodeng xuexiao keji tongji ziliao huibian [Higher education science and technology statistics compilation]. Available at www.dost.moe.edu.cn/dostmoe/.

Economist. 2010. Patents, yes; ideas, maybe. *The Economist*, October 14. Available at www.economist.com/node/17257940/.

Etzkowitz, H. 2001. The second academic revolution and the rise of entrepreneurial science. *Technology and Society Magazine, IEEE*, 20, 18–29.

Etzkowitz, H., and Leydesdorff, L. 2000. The dynamics of innovation: From national systems and "Mode 2" to a Triple Helix of university–industry–government relations. *Research Policy*, 29, 109–123.

Freeman, C. 1987. *Technology Policy and Economic Performance: Lessons from Japan*. London: Pinter.

Freeman, C. 1989. *Technology Policy and Economic Performance*. London: Pinter.

Freeman, C. 1995. The "national system of innovation" in historical perspective. *Cambridge Journal of Economics*, 19, 5–24.

Fu, Y., Jiang, X., and Ma, Q. 2010. Zhongguo chuantong wenhua dui guonei zhuanli chan chu zhiliang de yingxiang fenxi [An analysis of the influence traditional Chinese culture has on domestic patent output quality]. *Keji guanli yanjiu*, 16, 252–256.

Fuller, D. 2015. China's political economy and prospect for technological innovation-based growth. In *Building Innovation Capacity in China: An Agenda for Averting the Middle Income Trap*, ed. A. Lewin, J. P. Murmann, and M. Kenney. Cambridge: Cambridge University Press.

Furr, R. B., and Palla, S. W. 2012. *Invalidity Rate Study: China*. San Antonio, TX: Intellectual Property Organization.

Graff, G. D. 2007. Echoes of Bayh-Dole? A survey of IP and technology transfer policies in emerging and developing economies. In *Intellectual Property Management in Health and Agricultural Innovation: A Handbook of Best Practices, Volumes 1 and 2*, ed. A. Krattiger, R. Mahoney, L. Nelsen, J. Thomson, A. Bennett, K. Satyanarayana, C. Fernandez, and S. Kowalski. Oxford: MIHR, and Davis, CA: PIPRA, 169–195.

Griliches, Z. 1990. Patent statistics as economic indicators: A survey. *Journal of Economic Literature*, 28, 1661–1707.

Guan, J. C., Yam, R. C., and Mok, C. K. 2005. Collaboration between industry and research institutes/universities on industrial innovation in Beijing, China. *Technology Analysis & Strategic Management*, 17, 339–353.

HIPB (Hubei Intellectual Property Bureau). 2007. Hubei sheng 2007 niandu shouquan zhuanli butie di yi pi da 120 wan [Hubei first round of annual patent subsidies reaches 1,200,000]. September 6. Available at www.hbi po.gov.cn/show/6212.

Hu, M.-C., and Mathews, J. A. 2008. China's national innovative capacity. *Research Policy*, 37, 1465–1479.

Hu, M.-C., and Mathews, J. A. 2009. Estimating the innovation effects of university-industry-government linkages: The case of Taiwan. *eContent Management*, 15 (2), 138–154.

Huang, C. 2012. Estimates of the value of patent rights in China. United Nations University – Maastricht Economic and Social Research and Training Centre on Innovation and Technology, 48.

Innofund. 2004–2014. Quanguo jishu shichang tongji niandu baogao [Annual report on statistics of China technology market]. China's Ministry of Science and Technology Development and Planning Division and Chinese Technology Market Promotion Administration Center. Available at www.innofund.gov.cn/jssc/tjnb/.

JPO (Japan Patent Office). 2014. *Japan Patent Office Annual Report 2014*. Tokyo. Available at www.jpo.go.jp/shiryou_e/toushin_e/kenkyukai_e/pdf/annual_report2014/part1.pdf.

Kim, L. 1997. *Imitation to Innovation: The Dynamics of Korea's Technological Learning*. Boston: Harvard Business School Press.

KIPO (Korean Intellectual Property Office). 2013. *Statistics: Applications*. Daejeon. Available at www.kipo.go.kr/upload/en/download/Applications.xls.

Krumm, K. L. and Kharas, H. J. 2004. *East Asia Integrates: A Trade Policy Agenda for Shared Growth*. Washington, DC: The World Bank and Oxford University Press. Available at https://openknowledge.world

bank.org/bitstream/handle/10986/15038/280410PAPER0East0Asia0Int
egrates.pdf?sequence=1/.

Li, X. 2012. Behind the recent surge of Chinese patenting: An institutional
view. *Research Policy*, 41, 236–249.

Li, Y. 2015. Gaoxiao zhishi chanquan guanli kunjing yu chulu: Yi Zhejiang daxue
wei li [University IP management predicaments and the road ahead: The case
of Zhejiang University]. International Symposium on Intellectual Property
Management at Universities and Research Institutes, Zhejiang University
Research Institute for Intellectual Property Management, Zhejiang, China.

Liaoning Province. 2015. Guanyu jiakuai cujin keji chengguo zhuanhua de
ruogan yijian liao ke fa [2015] 1 hao [Notification on the views regarding
the publication of accelerating the promotion of science and technology
achievement technology transfer. Liaoning Science Law (2015) no. 1].
Liaoning Province S&T Information. January 19. Available at www.lnin
fo.gov.cn/uploadfile/2015/0130/20150130105102221.pdf.

Lin, M. 2011. China Bayh-Dole Act: A framework fundamental to achieving
the economic potential of China's national patent development strategy
(2011–2020). In *Spring 2011 Eye on China Newsletter*, Foley & Lardner
LLP. April 22. Available at www.foley.com/intelligence/detail.aspx?
int=8043.

Liu, K., Liu, C., and Huang, J. 2014. IPR in China: Market-oriented innovation
or policy-induced rent-seeking? Workshop on the Actual Role of IPRs in
Technological and Business Innovation, School of Law, Singapore
Management University, Singapore.

Lu, W. 2008. Woguo de zhishi chanquan fazhan jinru zhanlue zhuanxing qi
[China's intellectual property rights development entering a strategic
transformation period]. *Juece zixun tongxun*, 1, 45–49.

Lundvall, B.-A. 1992. *National Innovation System: Towards a Theory of
Innovation and Interactive Learning*. London: Pinter.

MOD (Ministry of Defense). 2015. Zhonggong zhongyang guowuyuan
guanyu shenhua tizhi jizhi gaige jiakuai shishi chuangxin qudong fazhan
zhanlue de ruogan yijian [CCP Central Committee and the State Council
view on deepening institutional mechanism reform and accelerate the
implementation of an innovation driven development strategy].
Available at www.mod.gov.cn/xwph/2015-03/24/content_4576385.htm.

MOE (Ministry of Education). 2015. Jianquan zhishi, jishu, guanli, jineng deng
you yaosu shichang jueding baochou jizhi de diaoyan baogao jiaoyu bu keji
si keti zu 2015 nian 4 yue [Building a comprehensive knowledge, technology,
management, capability, and other market elements to determine
remuneration research report by the Ministry of Education S&T Division

Task Force April 2015]. Science and Technology Division Task Force. March 28. Available at http://cqt.njtech.edu.cn/artcle_view.asp?id=17171.

Moga, T. 2012. *China's Utility Model Patent System: Innovation Driver or Deterrent?* Washington, DC: US Chamber of Commerce Asia. Available at www.uschamber.com/sites/default/files/legacy/international/files/0209 39_ChinaUtilityModel_2013Revised_FIN%20%281%29.pdf.

MOST (Ministry of Science and Technology). 2008. Guanyu yinfa "gaoxin jishu qiye rending guanli banfa" de tongzhi [Regarding the publication of high technology enterprises' recognition administrative law notification]. Available at www.most.gov.cn/fggw/zfwj/zfwj2008/200804/t20080428 _61006.htm.

MOST. 2008–2013. *Keji tongji baogao [S&T Statistical Report]*. Development and Planning Division.

MOST. 2010–2013. *Zhongguo keji tongji shuju [China science & Technology Statistics Data Book]*. Available at www.sts.org.cn/sjkl/kjtjdt/.

MOST. 2015. Cujin keji chengguo zhuanhua fa xiuzheng an (cao'an) tiaowen [Law on promoting the transformation of scientific and technological achievements (draft)]. Available at www.most.gov.cn/tztg/201503/t2015 0305_118402.htm.

NBD (*Daily Economic News*). 2014. Guowuyuan tongguo "cujin keji chengguo zhuanhua fa xiuzheng an (cao'an)" [State Council approves "law on promoting the transformation of scientific and technological achievements (draft)"]. November 20. Available at www.nbd.com.cn/arti cles/2014-11-20/877210.html.

NBS (National Bureau of Statistics). 2014a. 2013 nian quanguo keji jingfei touru tongji gongbao [2013 China S&T expenditure investment statistical report]. Available at www.stats.gov.cn/tjsj/tjgb/rdpcgb/qgkjjftrtjgb/2014 10/t20141023_628330.html.

NBS. 2014b. Tongji ju: 2013 nian woguo GDP zeng su 7.7% [NBS: China's 2013 GDP grew by 7.7%]. Available at http://finance.sina.com.cn/china/ hgjj/20140224/093418308381.shtml.

NBS. 2015a. Basic statistics on higher education for S&T activities. Available at http://data.stats.gov.cn/english/easyquery.htm?cn=C01/.

NBS. 2015b. Basic statistics on S&T activities. Available at http://data.stats .gov.cn/english/easyquery.htm?cn=C01/.

NBS. 2015c. Three kinds of applications for patents accepted. Available at http://data.stats.gov.cn/english/easyquery.htm?cn=C01/.

NBS. 2015d. Three kinds of patents granted. Available at http://data.stats.gov .cn/english/easyquery.htm?cn=C01/.

Nelson, R. 1993. *National Innovation Systems: A Comparative Analysis.* New York: Oxford University Press.

NPC (National People's Congress). 2007. Law of the People's Republic of China on progress of science and technology. Standing Committee. Available at www.npc.gov.cn/englishnpc/Law/2009-02/20/con tent_1471617.htm.

OECD (Organization for Economic Cooperation and Development). 1997. National Innovation Systems. Available at www.oecd.org/science/inno/2 101733.pdf.

People's Daily. 2006. 1978 nian 3 yue 18 ri dengxiaoping zai quanguo kexue dahui kaimu shi shang de jianghua [Deng Xiaoping's opening remarks during the National Science and Technology Conference March 18, 1978]. January 5. Available at http://scitech.people.com.cn/GB/25509/5 6813/57267/57268/4001431.html.

People's Daily. 2014a. Daibiao chenxuedong: Kaohe zhuanli shuliang yi chu "lese zhuanli" [Representative Chen Xuedong: Using patent volume to evaluate performance leads to "junk patents"]. March 7. Available at http://ip.people.com.cn/n/2014/0307/c136655-24561817.html.

People's Daily. 2014b. Lianghui ti'an: Tiaozheng zhuanli feiyong bili dali ezhi lese zhuanli [NPC and Chinese People's Political Consultative Conference proposal: The adjustment of patent fees ratio to vigorously curb junk patents]. March 7. Available at http://scitech.people.com.cn/n/2014/030 7/c1007-24557877.html.

People's Daily. 2015. Zhuanli qinquan shiji peichang e pingjun 8 wan zhuanjia jianyi tigao jin'e [Patent infringement actual compensation averages RMB 80,000: experts recommend raising the amount]. February 6. Available at http://ip.people.com.cn/n/2015/0206/c136655-26519125.html.

Qiao, Y., and Wen, J. 2009. Guonei wai faming zhuanli weichi zhuangkuang bijiao yanjiu [A comparative study of maintenance status of domestic and foreign invention patents]. *Kexue xue yu kexue jishu guanli,* 6, 29–32.

Rosenberg, N., and Nelson, R. R. 1994. American universities and technical advance in industry. *Research Policy,* 23, 323–348.

SASAC. n.d. State-Owned Assets Supervision and Administration Commission of the State Council (SASAC) main functions. Available at http://en.sasac .gov.cn/n1408028/n1408521/index.html.

SCIO (State Council Information Office). 2015. Liaoning sheng "guanyu jiakuai cujin keji chengguo zhuanhua de ruogan yijian" xinwen fabu hui [News press release of Liaoning province views regarding the accelerated promotion of science and technology achievement technology transfer].

Available at www.scio.gov.cn/xwfbh/gssxwfbh/fbh/Document/1396282/1396282.htm.

SCLAO (Legislative Affairs Office of the State Council). 2015. Guowuyuan fazhi bangongshi guanyu "zhiwu faming tiaoli cao'an (song shen gao)" gongkai zhengqiu yijian tongzhi [Legislative Affairs Office of the State Council notice regarding "work invention bill (draft for approval)" open for comments]. Available at www.chinalaw.gov.cn/article/xwzx/tpxw/201504/20150400398828.shtml.

SIPA (Shanghai Intellectual Property Administration). 2012. Shanghai shi zhuanli zizhu banfa (2012 nian xiuding) [Shanghai patent subsidy law (2012 revision)]. Available at www.sipa.gov.cn/gb/zscq/node2/node23/userobject1ai9494.html.

SIPO (State Intellectual Property Office). 2008. Patent Law of the People's Republic of China. Available at http://english.sipo.gov.cn/laws/lawsregulations/201101/t20110119_566244.html.

SIPO. 2008–2013. SIPO annual reports. Available at http://english.sipo.gov.cn/laws/annualreports/.

SIPO. 2009. Beijing shi faming zhuanli jiangli banfa [Beijing invention patent remuneration law]. Available at www.sipo.gov.cn/twzb/bjfmzlj/bjzl/200904/t20090420_454649.html.

SIPO. 2012a. 2012 zhuanli tongji jianbao [2012 patent statistics summary report]. Available at www.sipo.gov.cn/ghfzs/zltjjb/201310/P020131025653662902318.pdf.

SIPO. 2012b. Zhongguo shiyong xinxing zhuanli zhidu fazhan zhuangkuang (quanwen) [China's utility model patent system development]. Available at www.gov.cn/gzdt/2012-12/21/content_2295766.htm.

SIPO. 2013. Development of China's utility model patent system. Available at http://english.sipo.gov.cn/news/official/201301/t20130105_782325.html.

SIPO. 2014a. "Guojia zhishi chanquan zhanlue gangyao" banbu shishi 6 zhounian ["China national intellectual property rights strategy outline," six-year implementation]. Available at www.nipso.cn/zhuanti/zl6/.

SIPO. 2014b. The promotion plan for the implementation of the national intellectual property strategy in 2014. Available at http://english.sipo.gov.cn/laws/developing/201405/t20140505_944778.html.

SIWU (Suzhou Institute of Wuhan University). 2013. Wuhan University science and technology transfer, licensing, and industrialization regulations. Available at www.pxto.com.cn/JiGou/dt-show.asp?Resource_ID=169566&ID=63a302d2d6598b61/.

State Council. 2003. Guowuyuan guoyou zichan jiandu guanli weiyuanhui zhonghua renmin gongheguo caizheng bu di 3 haoling qiye guoyou chanquan zhuanrang guanli zhanxing banfa [State-Owned Assets Supervision and Administration Commission and the Ministry of Commerce Order no. 3: Interim measures for the transfer of state-owned property]. Available at www.gov.cn/gongbao/content/2004/con tent_62922.htm.

State Council. 2006. Guojia zhong chang qi kexue he jishu fazhan guihua gangyao (2006–2020 nian) [China medium and long-range science and technology development plan, 2006–2020]. Available at www.gov.cn/jr zg/2006-02/09/content_183787.htm.

State Council. 2008a. "Guojia zhishi chanquan zhanlue gangyao" quanwen ["China national intellectual property rights strategy" outline]. Available at www.nipso.cn/onews.asp?id=9592/.

State Council. 2008b. Zhonghua renmin gongheguo zhuxi ling di wu hao zhonghua renmin gongheguo qiye guoyou zichan fa [Order of the President of the People's Republic of China no. 5 Law of the People's Republic of China on the state-owned assets of enterprises]. Available at www.gov.cn/flfg/2008-10/28/content_1134207.htm.

State Council. 2015a. Full transcript of policy briefing of the State Council on March 27, 2015. Available at http://english.gov.cn/news/policy_brief ings/2015/03/27/content_281475078591808.htm.

State Council. 2015b. Guowuyuan bangong ting guanyu zhuanfa zhishi chanquan ju deng danwei shenru shishi guojia zhishi chanquan zhanlue xingdong jihua (2014–2020 nian) de tongzhi guo ban fa (2014) 64 hao [State Council general office notification regarding the forwarding to the state intellectual property office and other units the in-depth implementation of the national IPR strategy action plan (2014–2020) State Council Law (2014) no. 64]. Available at www.gov.cn/zhengce/con tent/2015-01/04/content_9375.htm.

Sun, J. 2014. Lun woguo lese zhuanli wenti [China's junk patents problem]. *Fazhi yu shehui*, 20, 273 and 281.

Supreme Court. 2015. Zuigao renmin fayuan guanyu xiugai "zuigao renmin fayuan guanyu shenli zhuanli jiufen anjian shiyong falu wenti de ruogan guiding" de jueding fa shi [2015] 4 hao [Amendment "Supreme Court regarding patent dispute case hearing provisions and applicable laws" decision judicial interpretation (215) no. 4]. Available at www.court.go v.cn/zixun-xiangqing-13244.html.

Tang, M. 2006. A comparative study on the role of national technology transfer centers in different Chinese universities. GLOBELICS (Global

Network for Economics of Learning, Innovation, and Competence Building Systems), Thiruvananthapuram, India.

TJIP (Tianjin Intellectual Property). 2014. Guanyu 2014 nian tianjin shi zhuanli zizhu lingqu de tongzhi [Regarding 2014 Tianjin patent subsidy pickup notice]. Available at www.tjipo.gov.cn/xwdt/tztg/201405/t20140 526_65322.html.

Wang, H. 2015. University's IP institute to aid tech transfer. *China Daily*, March 25. Available at www.chinadaily.com.cn/m/cip/2015-03/25/con tent_19908289.htm.

Wang, Y. 2010. *China's National Innovation System and Innovation Policy: Promotion of National Innovation Systems in Countries with Special Needs*. United Nations Economic and Social Commission for Asia and the Pacific. Available at http://nis.apctt.org/PDF/CSNWorkshop_Repor t_P2S2_Wang.pdf.

Wen, J. 2008. Zhengfu zizhu zhuanli feiyong yinfa lese zhuanli de chengyin yu duice [Government patent cost subsidies and the raise of junk patents cause and countermeasures]. *Dianzi zhishi chanquan*, 11, 21–25.

Wen, J., and Zhu, X. 2007. Woguo difang zhengfu zizhu zhuanli feiyong zhengce ruogan wenti yanjiu [Research on China's local government subsidies for patent costs implementation questions]. *Gongzuo yanjiu*, 17(102), 23–27.

Wen, J., and Zhu, X. 2009. Zhengfu zizhu zhuanli feiyong dui woguo jishu chuangxin de yingxiang jili yanjiu [Government patent cost subsidies and the mechanism of influence on China's technological innovation]. *Kexue xue yanjiu*, 27(5), 686–691.

WIPO (World Intellectual Property Organization). 2015. WIPO IP statistics data center. Available at http://ipstats.wipo.int/ipstatv2/.

Wu, H. 2009. Zhongguo zhishi chanquan fazhi jianshe de pingjia yu fansi [An evaluation and reflection of China's IPR legal framework establishments]. *Zhongguo faxue*, 1, 51–68.

Xinhua News. 2012. San men: chutai zhuanli jiangli zhengce gao faming chuangzao jiangli 10 wan [Sanmen: Releases of patent remuneration policies introducing invention awards of 100,000]. November 21. Available at www.zj.xinhuanet.com/dfnews/2012-11/21/c_113749526 .htm.

Xinhua News. 2015. Zuigao fa xiugai sifa jieshi mingque zhuanli jiufen anjian peichang shu'e [Supreme Court amends judicial interpretation to clarify patent dispute cases' compensation amount]. January 29. Available at ht tp://news.xinhuanet.com/legal/2015-01/29/c_1114183208.htm.

Xue, L. 2006. Universities in China's national innovation system. United Nations Educational, Scientific, and Cultural Organization's Online Forum on Higher Education, Research, and Knowledge, November 27–30. Available at http://portal.unesco.org/education/en/files/51614/11 634233445XueLan-EN.pdf/XueLan-EN.pdf.

Xue, L. 2009. *Globalization of S&T in China: Current Status and New Policies*. Tsinghua University. March 29. Available at www.oecd.org/sti/sci-tech/42719725.pdf.

Zhang, G., and Chen, X. 2012. The value of invention patents in China: Country origin and technology field differences. *China Economic Review*, 23, 357–370.

Zhao, R. 2015. Zhishi chanquan zhuanhua [Intellectual property transfer]. International Symposium on Intellectual Property Management at Universities and Research Institutes, Zhejiang University Research Institute for Intellectual Property Management, Zhejiang, China.

ZJU (Zhejiang University). 2005. Zhejiang daxue keji chengguo zhishi chanquan guanli banfa [Zhejiang University science and technology achievements IPR management measures]. March 29. Available at www.doe.zju.edu.cn/attachments/2009-11/01-1259202643-39371.doc.

8 | Building the innovation capacity of SMEs in China

JOHN CHILD

8.1 Introduction

Innovation has a highly significant role to play in helping to avert the possibility of a 'middle-income trap' in emerging economies like China. As such economies exhaust the possibilities of maintaining their competitiveness through the reallocation of labor from low-productivity rural employment and through technology catch-up, so their continued growth in per capita income comes to depend on enhancing their competitiveness and productivity through innovation (World Bank, 2013).

On the face of things, China has made substantial progress along the road to becoming an innovation-based economy. While the share of global R&D expenditure accounted for by developed economies has dropped since 2002, China's has risen steadily. Expressed in terms of total R&D expenditure as a percentage of gross domestic product (GDP), China's rate of catching up is even more impressive (SPI, UNU-Merit and AIT, 2014). China has become the most prominent R&D hub in emerging economies, followed some way behind by India. Both countries have also become net exporters of R&D services as their growing R&D competence and status attract more R&D projects (Berger, 2012). Similarly, the number of patent applications coming from China rose from a very low level in 2000 to reach in 2010 around two-thirds of Japan's and half those of the United States' (SPI, UNU-Merit and AIT, 2014).

China ranks relatively high compared to other major emerging economies for its 'innovation' according to the Global Competitiveness Report (World Economic Forum, 2015). In the 2015 results, China ranked 31st out of a total of 140 countries for which data were collected. This rank was higher than that achieved by Brazil, India, Russia, and South Africa. In the 2015 Global Innovation Index, China ranked

189

29th out of 141 countries, the highest rank among emerging economies (Global Innovation Index, 2015). China also attained the 1st rank for high-technology exports. However, despite the country's heavy expenditure on R&D and high patent production, these rankings imply that its real innovation achievement continues to remain a modest one compared to developed countries (Cao, Li, Li, and Liu, 2013).

Part of the problem China faces is that R&D investments in cutting-edge industries, such as aerospace, biotechnology, and energy-efficient automobiles, may take 15–20 years before they can be commercialized and produce returns. On the other hand, some other knowledge-intensive fields such as information and communications technology (ICT) should yield much faster returns. Second, there is concern that much of China's innovation has been imitative and incremental rather than fundamental and that too much emphasis has been placed on quantitative indicators of innovation rather than on its quality. As Cheng and Huang, and Fuller point out in their chapters, the quality of domestically approved patents in China is very mixed. Third, the institutional context for science and technology (S&T) leaves much to be desired: there is poor coordination between key agencies, a weak system of performance evaluation, and political constraints on the free exchange of ideas (Cao et al., 2013).

In China, most innovation is generated by the private sector. The innovation performance of large state-owned enterprises has been disappointing. This turns the spotlight onto the potential of small and medium-sized enterprises (SMEs) to be leaders in higher value-adding, high-technology innovation, as is typical of developed economies. The innovation capacity of China's SMEs is the subject of the present chapter. Its aim is to discuss the potential contribution of SMEs to innovation and the factors which can support and constrain that potential. Four theoretical perspectives serve to categorize these factors. It concludes with policy implications and issues deserving further research. Although the focus of the chapter is on China, it is believed that some of its insights have relevance for innovation in other emerging economies.

8.2 SMEs in China as sources of innovation

SMEs have the potential to contribute significantly to economic development through their generation of innovation, exports, and employment. In most countries, they are important drivers of innovation. Knowledge-based SMEs in developed economies have demonstrated the potential to combine both innovation and exporting success in ways that are mutually supportive (Knight and Cavusgil, 2004).

There are approximately 11.7 million SMEs in China, comprising almost 77 percent of the country's total companies. They contribute 60 percent of GDP, pay half of the nation's tax bill, and provide over 70 percent of new jobs (Xinhua, 2014). Manufacturing industries account for 52.8 percent of these SMEs, followed by the wholesale and retail industries (35.2 percent); construction (4.6 percent); and transportation and storage (2.6 percent). Largely though their own entrepreneurial initiatives, including the forging of supportive network ties and understandings with local governments, SMEs have become an emergent social and economic force in China. They are overwhelmingly privately owned. Their economic success encouraged political elites in central and local government to recognize their growing contribution and consequently to put into place legal and regulatory structures that legitimize private enterprise (Nee and Opper, 2012; 2013).

Collectively, SMEs have become a significant driver of China's science and technology innovation. They generate 65 percent of China's patented inventions and 80 percent of its new product developments, according to China's Ministry of Industry and Information Technology (MIIT). SMEs that engage in innovation tend to have a higher patent output than do equivalent larger Chinese firms. Their output of product or process innovations, while below the EU average, compares favorably with SMEs in the UK and some East European EU members (SPI, UNU-Merit, and AIT, 2014). These achievements indicate that small firms can make an important contribution to innovation in the Chinese economy (Lundin, Sjöholm, Ping, and Qian, 2007).

However, the full realization of that contribution to innovation presents a considerable challenge. In China, most SMEs are not engaged in any fundamental science- and technology-based innovation. They have not so far been particularly successful in translating intellectual capital into innovative products and services. Rather, they have prospered by adapting known technologies to new market opportunities, and in so doing have reaped high rewards for incremental innovation. Many Chinese SMEs are suppliers to large companies or produce rather conventional outputs such as auto parts and packaging. Compared to Germany, USA, and Japan, China has few highly successful SMEs which are leaders in niche markets (MasterCard Worldwide, 2013). While the success of many Chinese SMEs has in the past derived from their ability to produce relatively mature products at low cost, faced now with rising labor costs and competition from lower-cost developing countries, their ability to prosper will depend increasingly on their ability to engage in product innovation (Hofman, Newman, and Deng, 2014).

So, following a long period during which smaller privately owned firms in China were treated as economic second-class citizens, there is today a heightened awareness of their potential contribution to innovation coupled with a recognition that barriers remain to realizing that contribution. While it has become a key component of Chinese government policy to nurture innovative small businesses (Magnier, 2015), SMEs continue to suffer from disadvantages compared to larger state-owned enterprises when it comes to institutional support. The World Bank report on *China 2030* noted that government-backed research institutes producing fundamental breakthroughs do not have strong incentives to work closely with the firms who could put those new technologies to commercial use, and this applies particularly to collaborating with SMEs (World Bank, 2013). Indeed, SMEs are still somewhat of a 'hidden army' in terms of their recognition in official national statistics

8.3 Factors influencing SME innovation and their relevance to China

Factors influencing the level and quality of innovation conducted by SMEs divide into barriers and facilitators. Since, in most instances the presence of the one indicates the absence of the other, barriers and facilitators can be considered together. These factors can be placed into four broad categories, each of which is associated with a different theoretical perspective. The four categories and perspectives are: (1) the resource-based view; (2) the institutional perspective; (3) the network perspective; and (4) the entrepreneurial perspective. I shall summarize each perspective and then discuss how it throws light on the situation in China and to some extent on that in emerging economies as a whole.

8.3.1 *The resource-based view*

The resource-based view of the firm draws attention to the fact that its competitiveness depends on its ability to secure and organize resources in such as way as to maintain an advantage over other rival firms. These resources need to be scarce, valuable, and difficult to copy. Knowledge and technologies unique to a firm provide it with a potential competitive advantage, and intrinsic innovation is clearly one of their key sources. At the same time, such innovation itself depends on the availability to the firm of critical resources including finance, high-quality personnel, and relevant knowledge. SMEs typically command fewer resources than larger firms, and for this reason another essential requirement for their innovation may be the ability to secure technical and marketing knowledge from external academic or business partners in a way that complements their internal capabilities and learning intentions.

Inadequate financial resources are usually singled out as a major barrier to innovation among SMEs, and indeed as a major barrier to their growth and development in general. These include funding for new venture start-up, funding for expenditure on R&D, and the financing of training to improve employee skills. Expenditure on R&D combined with high staff skills is seen to enhance an SME's absorptive capacity whereby it can recognize, digest, and exploit new external knowledge for the purpose of commercially viable innovation (Cohen and Levinthal, 1990). A shortage of trained and creative scientific staff in China, and difficulties in attracting them to work in SMEs, are thought to be inhibiting innovation. They lower the absorptive capacity of Chinese SMEs and limit their ability to secure full benefit from externally purchased technology (Hou and Mohnen, 2012).

The resource-based view overlaps with other perspectives and it can be regarded as a core perspective for predicting the innovation performance of SMEs. It overlaps with the institutional perspective insofar as state organizations affect the provision to SMEs of resources for innovation. In China while there are government schemes to provide risk capital for innovation, other state institutions such as banks have been criticized for inadequate financial provision. Banks have favored lending to state-owned enterprises (SOEs), which is viewed as a less risky proposition. The resource-based view overlaps the network perspective insofar as links to external networks can provide valuable resources of finance (e.g. via venture capitalists), technical knowledge (e.g. via collaboration with foreign firms), access to new markets (e.g. via supplying to MNEs), and encouragement of an orientation toward innovation and sharing of experience (e.g. though close relations with other SMEs situated in local clusters). Finally, the resource-based view overlaps with the entrepreneurial perspective insofar as the availability of financial resources may encourage SME decision-makers to perceive less personal risk attaching to innovation and access to market-relevant information may enhance their perception of the commercial opportunities that innovation could open up.

A particular angle to the resource-based view of SME innovation is provided by the well-researched nexus between SME innovation and entry into global markets through exporting. The phenomenon of 'born-global' knowledge-based SMEs has demonstrated their potential to constructively combine both innovation and exporting. Love and Roper (2013: 6) summarize the benefits of the joint effects of this relationship: 'The joint effects of innovation and exporting lead to economy-wide productivity benefits through a dynamic competition in which innovating and exporting firms gain market share at the expense of others.' Underlying these joint effects is the possibility that the SME innovation-exporting relationship may be mutually reinforcing (Ganatakis and Love, 2011; Esteve-Pérez and Rodríguez, 2013). On the one hand, exporting can encourage innovation through a learning effect stimulated by pressures in the international market to compete through developing new and improved products and processes. Learning through exporting, especially to knowledge-intensive or highly competitive markets, may be an important stimulus for innovation. On the other hand, innovation can provide a basis for successful exporting (Anh, Jones, Nhat, and Chuc, 2009; Palangkaraya, 2013). Firms with new and improved products or processes can enter and compete in new geographical markets. If innovation also expands domestic sales, economies of scale may enhance export competitiveness. The policy implication of the exporting-innovation link is that the encouragement of SME internationalization, through for example export promotion schemes and facilitating SME partnerships with MNEs, should also stimulate SME innovation. Indeed, one could regard internationalization as an innovation for the small firm, and both exporting and product or process innovation can benefit from many of the same enabling factors.

Hofman et al. (2014) conducted a study of factors selected as potential predictors of the level of product innovation among a panel of 43,732 privately owned Chinese manufacturing SMEs from nine two-digit industries.[1] The data related to the years 2005 and 2006. Their measure of product innovation was that employed by China's National Bureau of Statistics, namely the share of total output accounted for by new products in a specific firm. The findings of the study 'suggest that both internal and external resources play an important role in the process of innovation in private Chinese SMEs' (p. 180). Access to finance was a significant predictor of higher product innovation in firms with multiple owners. R&D expenditure was a predictor of higher innovation levels in all cases. 'Human capital' (average wage per employee) and training expenditure were predictors in many cases. Export intensity (proportion of export sales to total sales) was consistently associated with the level of product innovation. In general, the research lent strong support to the resource-based view of influences on product innovation among SMEs.

Much of the thrust of Chinese official policy on encouraging innovating SMEs is towards enhancing the provision of financial resources and incentives. The Innovation Fund for Small Technology-based Firms (InnoFund) is aimed at SMEs focusing on high-tech R&D. It provides subsidized loans to high-tech and new enterprises in which Chinese ownership is more than 50 percent. The government also provides tax incentives to high- and new-tech firms that are located in designated areas such as science parks. The government is still the main provider of finance for innovation in China. Other sources of finance for SME innovation remain under-developed, especially the provision of risk capital. Banks provide loans at better rates to SOEs than to SMEs, and R&D-active SMEs suffer from shortages of credit. However, with government encouragement, the situation is improving, and an increasing proportion of bank loans is going to SMEs.

The government is also coming to appreciate the essential role of venture capital in encouraging indigenous innovation, recognizing that venture capitalists can be active investors providing SMEs with advice and value-adding services. Together with foreign funds, it is a major contributor to VC funding. Angel investment, which in the USA is

---

[1] Their definition of SME was much broader than normal and included firms with up to 2,000 employees.

a significant source of investment for high-growth start-up companies, is a relatively new concept in China, though a promising avenue for funding new innovation-based enterprises. There are, however, some complaints about the bureaucratic hurdles attached to obtaining funds, as well as about insufficient coordination between the various government agencies involved. The *STI China* report provides details of these various financial supports and incentives, as well as comment on their operation (SPI, UNU-Merit, and AIT, 2014: Section 4.2.2). Fuller notes in his chapter that Chinese domestic VCs tend to invest in mature industries and are dominated by state entities. Consequently they are not serving as effective funders of innovation-oriented entrepreneurship.

The importance of human resources to support innovation is also officially recognized in China through various government educational and training schemes. The quality of higher education is reported to have greatly improved and programs have also been introduced to attract Chinese researchers and scientists to return to China from abroad. However, doubts are raised concerning the intellectual freedom of Chinese universities, which is seen as a precondition for such institutions to be sources of innovation (Abrami, Kirby, and McFarlan, 2014). Also, as noted later in this chapter, the way that knowledge workers are managed in many Chinese SMEs may be inhibiting their contribution to knowledge creation and absorption within the firm.

8.3.2 *The institutional perspective*

There are various ways in which institutions can facilitate as well as hinder innovation. The World Bank *China 2030* report mentions some of these when recommending that China 'improve the institutional arrangements needed to encourage broad-based innovation – such as ease of firm entry and exit, increased competition, enforcement of laws protecting intellectual property rights, quality tertiary education, the availability of risk capital for small and medium enterprises, evaluation of government R&D expenditures, and standard setting in government procurement' (p. 35).

Many countries have official programs offering financial support and incentives for innovating smaller firms. The previous section mentioned those operating in China. Governmental agencies can also endeavor to foster links between SMEs and research institutes, and between SMEs themselves, with a view to promoting the exchange of knowledge in support of innovation. One of the World Bank's key recommendations for improving China's innovation performance is a government initiative to build nationwide research networks to mobilize national talent and to link firms with technically more advanced ones, including multinationals. These domestic networks could also link to international R&D networks to promote an interaction of Chinese researchers with counterparts outside the country, so opening up channels for the import of new ideas and technology transfer. The World Bank also recognizes the role of government-sponsored science hubs and high-tech parks in attracting investment by high-tech multinationals which opens up possibilities for smaller Chinese firms to collaborate with MNEs and benefit from open innovation (World Bank, 2013: 35; see also Chapter 9 by Collinson in this volume).

A further institutional encouragement for SMEs to invest in innovation, especially of a fundamental kind, lies in legal provision to protect intellectual property. In the recent past, Chinese SME owner-managers have expressed the fear that investment in innovation would not achieve satisfactory returns because it was difficult to protect. While companies might be able to take their own measures to protect process innovations, this is more difficult in the case of product innovation, which can be subject to re-engineering (Mitussis, 2010). Official efforts have been made at both central and local levels to strengthen IP protection, but enforcement lags behind enactment and innovation theft remains a concern. As Vivek Wadhwa has commented, in China 'entrepreneurs live in fear of having their ideas stolen by larger players and the government' (Wadhwa, 2013). Although its relative position has been improving, China still only ranked halfway up the 2014 Intellectual Property Rights Index – at 47th out of 97 countries (Property Rights Alliance, 2014).

The term 'institutional voids' has come to be used to denote gaps or weaknesses in formal institutional provisions, especially in developing and emerging economies (Puffer, McCarthy, and Boisot, 2010). According to Khanna and Palepu, institutional voids refer to absent or weak specialized intermediaries, regulatory systems, and contract-enforcing mechanisms in the product, labor, and capital markets of emerging economies (Khanna and Palepu, 2010). They are often evident as 'gaps between formal rules and norms, and their enforcement in daily practice' (Rodrigues, 2013: 14). In China, the incomplete enforcement of IP protection is an example of these gaps.

As well as institutional gaps, the institutions that exist and are shaped by government policies can serve to constrain innovation among SMEs. Fuller in his chapter details the institutional factors that in China are rendering the country's transition to a technologically innovative, high-income economy more difficult. Zhu, Wittman, and Peng (2012) report the institutional barriers to innovation identified by the top managers and owners of forty-one Chinese technology-based SMEs mainly in the pharmaceutical, software, and integrated circuitry industries. The institutional constraint on their innovation activities most frequently mentioned (by 67 percent) was unfair competition from large firms (both SOEs and foreign firms) due to preferential treatment by government agencies in areas such as procurement. This is consistent with the findings of several studies that the strong presence of SOEs in China impedes innovation by smaller firms (SPI, UNU-Merit, and AIT, 2014: 75). The negative overall impact on innovation is increased by the fact that SOEs do not as a whole contribute greatly to China's innovation performance. The other reported institutional impediments to innovation, by frequency of mention, were limited access to financing, lack of specific regulations or clear policies at an operational level, excessive taxation, and an insufficient support system.

The World Bank's indicators of 'Ease of Doing Business' concern regulations and other institutional features that affect the ease or difficulty of doing business in each of 189 countries. Indicators of particular relevance to the vigor of SME innovation are ease of starting a business, getting credit, and enforcing contracts. China's overall rank, combining all 10 indicators, was 90th out of 189 in 2015, a relatively low position although representing a modest improvement on the previous year. Its ranking on ease of starting a business was poor (128th), though a considerable improvement on the previous year. Its rankings on getting credit and enforcing contracts were appreciably higher (71st and 35th, respectively). The implication of these data is that the support for innovation provided by China's institutional context remains patchy and is rather less favorable to SMEs than to larger firms.

A study of Egypt indicated that institutional voids can arise from two factors, both of which are likely to be more prevalent in developing and emerging economies (Child and Narooz, 2014). The first factor is an institution's technical inadequacies in providing services and carrying out its formal responsibilities. The second factor concerns ways in which institutional officials may impose informal conditions on their willingness to offer such services. The latter includes informal arrangements that reflect a privileged relationship that firms enjoy with officials, and in most countries it is larger firms that are likely to enjoy such connections. In China this can reflect the intrusion of political ideology insofar as this continues to grant greater legitimacy to SOEs than to private firms. Also within the purview of this second factor are corrupt practices whereby officials are only willing to support firms if side payments or other favors are offered. It is acknowledged by the authorities in China that informal arrangements of this kind have been widespread and that they can distort the implementation of desired policies, including those intended to foster small firm innovation. The potential handicaps on SMEs' innovation performance imposed by institutional voids manifested in IP theft and corruption reflect low trust in the social context within which Chinese SMEs operate and are likely to discourage the open exchange of ideas and information on which innovation thrives. Unless institutional constraints of this kind are reduced, the implementation of official policies to resource SME innovation will be frustrated.

8.3.3 The network perspective

Innovation by SMEs benefits from their ties to external parties or 'networks,' especially in high-tech fields (Baum, Calabrese, and Silverman, 2000; OECD, 2010). Such ties can facilitate innovation through providing capital, technology, market information, and connections to potential customers of new products. If the SMEs are located in emerging economies and their innovation goals are to exploit existing knowledge, they may need to rely heavily on inward technology transfer through collaboration with MNEs. If their goals are to undertake innovation of a more fundamental exploratory nature, upstream network ties with research institutes and downstream ties with key customers are likely to provide the scientific and technical insights on which such innovation feeds (March, 1991). Although fundamental innovations by SMEs are sometimes portrayed as the inspiration of lone entrepreneurs, it is likely that the relevant knowledge on which such entrepreneurs necessarily build will have been gained externally from previous experience in another organization and that the commercialization of the innovations will benefit from previously formed market contacts. Start-up innovative SMEs are often entrepreneurial spin-offs from universities or from larger firms with an established market position.

The network perspective draws attention to the type of knowledge that SMEs secure from external sources. It asks questions such as whether the 'stickiness' of knowledge (especially its degree of tacitness) means that its inward transfer requires close trust-based social ties and interactions as opposed to relying on more formal transactions (Szulanski, 1996). Access to the uncodified and causally ambiguous knowledge that feeds into basic innovation (Boisot, 1998) may require particularly close and localized relationships between researchers within an SME and external knowledge sources such as universities and research institutes, in addition to close teamwork relations within the firm itself (Karlsson, Johanson, Kobayashi, and Stough, 2014). In the case of exploitative innovation, such as adapting existing pro-ducts to new uses and markets, the knowledge inputted is likely to be of a more explicit codified nature and more readily obtainable. In this case, the most critical external network links may be those that assist the commercialization of innovation by introducing new products to markets. These considerations imply that a portfolio of different net-work links is required to support the innovation cycle as a whole, from idea inception to market delivery (Radas and Božić, 2009; Tolstoy and Agndal, 2010).

The forms of networking on which innovating SMEs rely vary according to their field of activity. Evidence of this is provided by the study that Salavisa and her colleagues conducted into forty-six Portuguese young firms (mostly SMEs) in two knowledge-intensive sectors – biotechnology and telecommunications software (Salavisa, Sousa, and Fontes, 2012). The authors point out that knowledge-intensive sectors are not homogeneous with regard to their innovation processes and that this variation influences the architecture of the innovation networks constructed by the firms. The knowledge base of biotech firms is mainly analytical, meaning that their innovation builds on the creation of new knowledge, with scientific knowledge being very important. The outcomes are frequently radical innovations. By contrast, the knowledge base of software firms is primarily syn-thetic, meaning that innovation is mostly based on the application of existing knowledge, though sometimes through novel combinations.

Contrasts were found in the networks typical of the two sectors. For example, the main source of both formal and informal scientific and technical knowledge for the biotech firms was universities and they also often relied on universities for access to laboratory facilities. For the software firms the main source of scientific and technical knowledge was firms from other sectors, especially their telecommunications clients, while other software firms were also important providers of informal knowledge. Biotech firms tended to rely on science and technology parks and financial institutions (such as venture capitalists) for non-technological resources. The software firms had more modest non-technological resource requirements (lower entry barriers) and relied more on other firms for such resources. Awareness that there are sector variations in the networks on which innovating SMEs rely to provide necessary knowledge and other resources has important implications for innovation policy which are discussed later.

A number of studies have indicated the significant contributions that network cooperation can make to product innovation among Chinese SMEs. Nee and Opper (2012) found in two samples of approximately 700 firms each (c. 90 percent of them SMEs) located in the Yangzi Delta region that 'the rise of innovative activities is deeply embedded in social network structures, which facilitate marginal innovations and diffusion of technology through informal collaboration' (p. 225). These firms' innovations were generally incremental in nature relying significantly on imitation and learning by doing. Customers were by far their main source of ideas for this form of innovation, followed by other firms in the same industry, their own employees or R&D units, technical or industry standards, and suppliers. Inputs from customers were particularly important for process, management, and quality control innovations, whereas inputs for product innovations tended to derive more from conferences and trade fairs, industry technical standards, and universities or research institutes. Even though firms tended to enter into formal contracts for R&D collaboration to specify their respective rights and obligations and distribution of future profits, in most cases these legal contracts reinforced trust-based cooperation that was already established between entrepreneurs. Nee and Opper emphasize the learning and developmental opportunities that the accumulation of informal network ties offer over time.

Zeng, Xie, and Tam (2010) point out that the complexity of innovation processes has led to considerable growth in the use of external networks by SMEs. These authors examined the impact of cooperation networks on the product innovation of 137 manufacturing SMEs in Shanghai. They found that inter-firm cooperation, cooperation with intermediary institutions such as technology intermediaries, venture capital organizations, and industry associations, and cooperation with research organizations such as universities all had positive significant relationships with the level of new product innovation. Inter-firm cooperation with customers, suppliers, or competitors had a particularly strong connection with product innovation. On the other hand, linkage and cooperation with government agencies such as information providers did not predict better product innovation performance. Overall, Zeng et al. conclude that vertical and horizontal cooperation with customers, suppliers, and other firms plays a more distinct role in the innovation process of SMEs than does horizontal cooperation with research institutions, universities or colleges, and government agencies.

Network links, such as belonging to innovation networks and having partnerships with potentially knowledge-transferring MNCs, may also be significant enablers through providing access to appropriate sources of new knowledge. Yu, Hao, Ahlstrom, Si, and Liang (2014) studied 134 relatively young Chinese firms in high-tech industries. They found that those firms having a higher ability to manage their network of relationships competently had a superior new product development performance, the more so when they also possessed a high level of technological capability. Xu, Lin, and Lin (2008) found from their study of SMEs in Guangdong Province that the structural characteristics of SME networks themselves, namely their density, reciprocity, and multiplicity, had a positive association with the innovation capabilities of individual member firms. They concluded that the 'innovative capabilities of firms can be enhanced in a business network characterized by frequent and diversified interactions, as well as collaborative interdependencies among network members' (p. 798).

The potential benefits of network ties for SME innovation has drawn attention to the fostering of physical 'clusters' as a policy goal. Research and science parks, for example, have the intention of encouraging close on-going interaction between technology-based SMEs and research organizations, as well as interaction between SMEs themselves. The idea is that clusters can benefit innovation in various ways: by encouraging innovation as a norm, promoting the sharing of knowledge and relevant experience, attracting highly trained staff, and reducing costs through shared support facilities. The OECD (2009, 2010) has reviewed research and conducted case studies on the innovation benefits of clusters. It concludes that they can be effective in promoting local knowledge-sharing and spill-over. This knowledge-sharing is likely to be promoted by the formation of close personal trust-based relationships which a common location in a cluster tends to encourage. By providing an externally visible innovation focus that attracts MNEs, clusters also encourage the development of SME links into the global value chains of larger firms which can provide another source of technology upgrading (see Chapter 9 by Collinson in this volume). Through creating an attractive working environment, clusters can attract highly talented staff and thus enhance human capital. The social capital they create can foster innovation by encouraging the open exchange of information and ideas, which in turn adds to the wider reputation of the cluster. Experience in Silicon Valley shows that its local eco-system encourages the formation and re-formation of new innovative ventures through social networking among technological entrepreneurs, assisted by the availability of common dining, sporting, and other facilities (Saxenian, 1994; Castilla, Hwang, Granovetter, and Granovetter, 2000).

There is, however, some concern that close networks with strong ties may become inward-looking and lose their ability to adapt due to 'lock-in' and path-dependence (Grabher, 1993). The very attractiveness of clusters or other network forms as social units may eventually come to undermine the innovation performance of their member firms by insulating them from external influences and divergent thinking. Cognitive lock-in can emerge through an inward orientation and groupthink. Functional lock-in can develop through local network links that become too-tightly tied and even hierarchical in nature. Political lock-in can come about if a network or cluster becomes institutionalized with rigid rules and norms that may be introduced by non-firm actors such as support agencies and local authorities (Hassink and Shin, 2005). Developing network ties outside a cluster should offset the threat posed by lock-in to a firm's innovativeness by increasing the diversity and novelty of knowledge at its disposal (Larrañeta, Zahra, and Galán, 2012).

Although SMEs located in clusters generally perform better than those located outside them because of networking benefits and better access to markets, a study of industrial clusters in Sub-Saharan Africa raised another concern. This is that the attractiveness of clusters leads to over-crowding, which may inhibit innovation if it reduces financial surpluses because of intense competition and imposes space constraints (Yoshino, 2011).

8.3.4 *The entrepreneurial perspective*

SMEs tend to be characterized by an individualized leadership (Oviatt and McDougall, 1994). The significant role played by individual decision-makers in SMEs means that their personal characteristics, creativity, and mental outlooks are highly likely to affect their level of commitment to innovation and the innovation performance of their firms. Schumpeter (1942) asserted that entrepreneurs are the source of innovation, creating new possibilities and combinations of resources through an inherent compulsion or 'entrepreneurial spirit.' Drucker also saw innovation as the heart of entrepreneurial activity (Drucker, 1985/2011). Entrepreneurs necessarily play a central role in initiating and building the networks that support innovation. The often-used concept of a firm's 'entrepreneurial orientation' includes dimensions such as risk-taking, pro-activeness, competitive aggressiveness, and innovativeness (Lumpkin and Dess, 1996). It expresses the entrepreneurial disposition of its decision-makers that is likely to underpin a firm's commitment to innovation.

The entrepreneurial perspective envisages three sets of features enabling SME leaders to influence the innovativeness of their firms. Sometimes these are grouped together under broad headings such as entrepreneurial competence or innovative capacity. The first set is psychological and focuses on the cognition and personality of the entrepreneur. It is assumed that features such as high personal drive, willingness to take risks, orientation towards novelty, and cognitive ability will predict greater innovation. The second set of factors is more social in nature and includes the entrepreneur's social capital (network connections). National or local cultures are another social factor category which may bear upon the incidence of innovation through the ways that entrepreneurial actions are influenced by values concerning, for example, uncertainty avoidance as well as by the levels of interpersonal trust that characterize different cultures. Also within the social category is the possibility that different forms of firm ownership (e.g. individual versus family) may either encourage or constrain innovation. The third set of factors draws attention to a range of potential behavioral influences on innovation, including the entrepreneur's managerial style and organization.

Certain characteristics of SME leaders fall into more than one of these categories. For instance, length and quality of an entrepreneur's experience is likely both to add to their cognitive appreciation of innovation possibilities and processes and permit a greater accumulation of social capital. One source of beneficial experience that has been found to positively affect innovation in Chinese firms, through spillover effects, is the presence of entrepreneurs returning from abroad (Liu, Lu, Filatotchev, Buck, and Wright, 2010). Cultural values, a social factor, are likely to influence an individual entrepreneur's orientation toward the risks involved in innovation.

Despite widespread acceptance of the interdependence of entrepreneurship and innovation, there is relatively little direct evidence on which aspects of entrepreneurship encourage innovation by firms, or on the mechanisms whereby individual entrepreneurs encourage such innovation (Harms, Reschke, Kraus, and Fink, 2010). One reason for this paucity of evidence probably lies in the assumption that the two terms are virtually synonymous. The studies that have been conducted generally conclude that a strong entrepreneurial orientation is associated with greater innovation. For example, a study of 181 Australian firms (mostly SMEs) found that when combined with a strong market orientation, entrepreneurial orientation predicted greater and more profitable new product innovation (Atuahene-Gima and Ko, 2001). In their study of entrepreneurs from the southeastern USA, Baron and Tang (2011) found that a positive disposition ('affect') on their part was associated with greater creativity which in turn predicted the rate at which their firms produced radically new products. These relationships were stronger in 'dynamic' (rapidly changing) market environments. Research among Chinese firms has also tended to find a positive relationship between entrepreneurial orientation and product innovation performance (e.g. Tang, Chen, and Jin, 2014).

According to the 2014 report of the Global Entrepreneurship Monitor, China scores somewhat above the average of other emerging economies for its rate of new business formation and 'total early-stage entrepreneurial activity' (TEA) (GEM, 2015: Table A3). China's TEA score is 15.5 percent of the adult population, which ranks it 22nd among the 70 participating countries. China's entrepreneurship is concentrated in its private sector, which Nee and Opper (2012) argue has been the main driver both of institutional change towards a capitalist market-based economy and of innovation. Fan and Child illustrate from their case studies how private Chinese entrepreneurs have acted as 'institutional entrepreneurs' (Grace Fan and John Child, A multilevel model of institutional entrepreneurship: Building a new category of firm in China. Unpublished paper 2013).

However, as noted earlier, there is concern that much of China's innovation has been imitative and incremental rather than fundamental in nature. The distinctive form of innovation that many Chinese private firms have shown so far has been exploitative of existing knowledge. They have demonstrated the capacity to respond rapidly to market changes, largely due to organizational innovations such as effective horizontal teamworking and breaking the process of incremental innovation down into a large number of small steps suited to the capabilities of their engineers and technical staff (Williamson and Yin, 2014). These firms have succeeded in creatively combining ordinary resources and conventional knowledge into extraordinary capabilities and achieved enhanced speed and price–value ratios that are well suited to large numbers of mid- and low-income consumers in the Chinese and other emerging markets (Luo and Child, 2015). One of the challenges that China's policy-makers now face is how to move entrepreneurial innovativeness from the incremental level to one that also produces more novel products and services, especially in the relatively new knowledge-intensive sectors of biotechnology, software, and advanced transportation.

There are a number of factors which may constrain the attainment of this objective. Most fundamental is the endemic fear and lack of trust, coupled with a strong disposition toward hierarchy that Redding notes in his chapter as historically embedded features of Chinese society. These characteristics militate against the open sharing of ideas and information and the willingness to permit innovative initiatives to come from multiple sources including lower-level staff. In a revealing interview-based study, Mitussis (2010) concluded that two main features were inhibiting innovation among SMEs located in Zhejiang Province, an area of China particularly known for its entrepreneurial vigor. The first factor was the authoritarian top-down management structures that were typical of the SMEs. Their entrepreneurs were exercising tight control because they were untrusting both of their employees and of the general environment in which there was a high risk of IP theft and sale of customer lists and operating procedures. This tight control discouraged new ideas from below and the empowerment of new product champions. The second inhibiting factor lay in the heavy reliance on informal personal network ties between the leaders of the SMEs. The personal and restricted nature of these ties was also in part a response to a generally low-trust context. On the one hand, such ties facilitated adaptive behavior in highly competitive markets as well as helping firms to secure support from local institutions. On the other hand, their lock-in effects could limit the stimulus to more fundamental innovation coming from ideas originating from a wider range of domains and also requiring networking between the staff of different firms rather than just between their CEOs.

Finally, there is evidence suggesting that certain ownership and governance configurations of Chinese SMEs may inhibit their innovation, such as an absence of external board members (Shapiro, Tang, Wang, and Zhang, 2015) or having multiple and family owners rather than single-owner entrepreneurs (Deng, Hofman, and Newman, 2013). Single-owner entrepreneurs are likely to have a stronger entrepreneurial orientation and to prioritize innovation more than family or dispersed ownership.

8.4 Implications for policy

Breznitz (2007) has detailed how state agencies in Ireland, Israel, and Taiwan adopted contrasting policies to foster innovation in the IT sector through encouraging different patterns of interaction between MNEs and the private sector. Although these policies reflected the countries' traditions and priorities, their diversity nevertheless suggests the presence of a degree of choice in policy initiatives for stimulating SME innovation. A major choice for China, so far as the state policy on innovation is concerned, is between a directive and a non-directive approach. A directive policy selects sectors, regions, and specific categories of innovation as targets for support, whereas a non-directive policy aims to remove constraints on innovation and then lets this develop in an unplanned manner through entrepreneurial initiatives from below. In other words, is the guiding model to be innovation from above or innovation from below (Nee and Opper, 2012)? Although

China's Medium and Long Term Science & Technology (S&T) Development Plan is top-down in that it selects strategic emerging sectors for innovation and sets targets, other recommendations for developing China's innovation capability suggested by independent reports include measures aimed at granting greater freedom and protection for bottom-up initiatives including those by SMEs.

Recommendations to Chinese policy-makers for encouraging SME innovation have tended to emphasize 'hard' tangible factors (MasterCard Worldwide, 2013; World Bank, 2013; SPI, UNU-Merit, and AIT, 2014). Many of these recommendations are economic and financial. It has, for example, been suggested that indigenous innovation be stimulated by encouraging the growth of the domestic market rather than export growth. This, however, could reinforce the prevalence of exploitative technology adaptation rather than encourage the positive stimulus to more fundamental exploratory innovation deriving from competition in global markets. Another major policy recommendation has been to redress the privileged position of SOEs with regard to market power and resource allocation, in view of the generally superior innovation performance of smaller private firms. A third common recommendation is that China's nascent venture capital industry should be encouraged as a source of risk capital for innovating SMEs as well as the mentoring, professional assistance, and market insights that venture capitalists can provide (World Bank, 2013; Williams, 2015). Senior political advisors have also proposed a unification of preferential tax policies to encourage innovating SMEs (CCTV, 2015).

On the institutional side, changes could be made both in formal provisions and in the values that underpin the system. In the former category, it is recognized that more effective IP protection would reduce the risks to SME investment in fundamental innovation. Also an upgrade in the quality of available human capital could come through improvements to tertiary education and the strengthening of technical and vocational skills. Values are more fundamental, politically sensitive, and therefore difficult to change. However, there is no denying that high-quality science-driven innovation ultimately depends on freedom of inquiry and the challenging of authority. The restrictions placed by China's governmental and party organs on divergent thinking and the open communication of ideas therefore pose a serious handicap on its innovation policy. Yet policy recommendations on this issue have been muted, doubtless because of its sensitivity.

On the networking side, there is recognition of the potential benefit for the transfer of advanced knowledge from facilitating collaboration by Chinese SMEs with MNEs as partners in their global supply chains. It is also suggested that university–industry linkages be strengthened so as to provide more effective means for the adaptation and redevelopment of new technologies and products, including those coming from abroad. As Zeng et al. (2010: 191) conclude, 'policy initiatives [to improve the innovation performance of Chinese SMEs] can only be effective when they focus on the need to promote cooperation between SMEs and innovation partners.'

The reform of hard parameters is unlikely to be sufficient if softer ones continue to work against innovation. Less attention has been given to the policy implications of the 'soft' psychological and social factors that appear to be holding back innovation among Chinese SMEs. Insofar as some of these are cultural in origin, they are not amenable to quick fixes. While many SME leaders already appear to have strong entrepreneurial orientations, the extent to which these are directed at high-quality more fundamental innovation, rather than to the speedy adaptation of existing technology, is open to question. In order to enhance the innovation component of Chinese entrepreneurial orientations, a combination of policies to reduce its risk and to increase awareness of the managerial practices which favor innovation seems to be required. The latter would include a better understanding of the benefits for innovation of open communication within the firm. Lower-level staff would have to be encouraged to enrich the firm's knowledge assets through developing external network links, some involving weak ties, as well as through freer internal discussions. How readily developments along these lines could break through China's embedded cultural context of low trust, emphasis on authority, fear of losing face, and reliance on highly personalized network ties remains an open question. It would certainly seem to require a massive training effort, together with incentives for SMEs to participate in this. Since it is widely agreed that the innovation performance of Chinese SMEs can often benefit from closer collaboration with technologically advanced MNEs, the hiring of staff with international business and cultural experience as a concomitant of such collaboration may help to break down these cultural constraints. As Redding points out in his chapter, cultural change comes slowly, especially when the ethos of a country's institutional and political system reinforces existing thinking and practice.

8.5 Questions for further research

Despite the considerable literature on SME innovation, including increasing research in China, many questions remain open for further inquiry. One question is whether or not the situation in China reflects a more general pattern and can be accounted for by existing theories. China is frequently lumped together with other BRICS countries or other 'emerging' economies, but these are far from being homogenous categories.[2] It is possible that the factors inhibiting or stimulating small firm innovation are broadly similar across different countries – inhibiting factors such as the liability of smallness, limited resourcing, and unfavorable access to advanced knowledge, and stimulating factors such as high levels of education and freedom of expression. However, what requires further comparative investigation is the extent to which the particular configuration of such factors in China is unique to that country's economic, political, and social context. There is a need for more contextual analyses examining the influence on the innovation performance of smaller firms of institutions, such as the state, as well as of 'soft' socio-cultural factors.

There are also a number of more specific questions deserving further research that arise from the coverage of this chapter. Innovation itself is a very broad concept and an indiscriminate use of the term can cause important differences to be overlooked. Closer attention needs to be paid to different forms of innovation such as product, service, and process innovation, and whether the innovation is exploratory, exploitative, or a mixture of both. With the rise of media and cultural industries in mind, recognition needs to be given to the fact that innovation can be aesthetic as well as technological. This chapter has referred to evidence that different enabling conditions tend to be operative with different forms of innovation.

It will therefore be instructive to pursue the question: what are the knowledge inputs required for different categories of innovation and what are the sources of such knowledge? In developed economies, knowledge-based SMEs are linked to global knowledge networks, including advanced research institutes and universities, and other suppliers of advanced inputs. In the high-technology and higher value-adding sectors, many SMEs spin-off from these sources. SMEs in

---

[2] The BRICS countries are Brazil, Russia, India, China, and South Africa.

developing or emerging economies like China need to access such networks so as to facilitate an upgrade to high-value-adding activities – to shift from exploitation to exploration. For example, in China's biotech sector this upgrade would involve progressing from contract research to discovery research. The question is how to achieve this. Does China have adequate networks? Does it require that its SMEs go beyond a primary reliance on domestic knowledge networks and instead gain access to global ones?

In asking which network attachments are required to support a more advanced level of innovation by Chinese SMEs, it would be helpful for future investigations to adopt a more differentiated view of the 'network' concept. For this embraces two important but different facets: first, the external actors with whom it may be beneficial for SMEs to relate directly and, second, the structure of the network itself, which will determine both its richness as a potential resource and how an SME's direct links to it can serve as bridges to further sources of support. Studies suggest that crucial network links for innovation include consumers and users; global supply-chain linkages and production networks; development partners especially via the media of open innovation and sub-contracting; and innovation networks both upstream as with biotech and downstream as with software. These links may be direct ones or come into play through links to third parties.

One set of issues deserving further investigation in China concerns the functions performed for innovation by direct network ties and their characteristics (such as weak versus strong ties). Here Mitussis (2010) raises the important question as to what kind of network is likely to facilitate innovation among Chinese SMEs. His research implies that it is the type of networks which are sufficiently open to provide information on new opportunities and new technological knowledge rather than those performing a defensive risk-reducing function. If, however, China remains beset by fear and mistrust it will not be easy to shift SME networks in this direction. A second set of issues concerns how the structures of the networks themselves have an impact on innovation capability. To address both sets of issue, richer qualitative research will be required to take our understanding beyond statistical associations toward understanding the processes that make network links into effective supports for innovation.

Sector contrasts should be given greater attention in future research. Despite the attention that some innovation scholars have given to them in the past (notably Pavitt, 1984), their relevance for innovation patterns among SMEs is only now coming to be appreciated. As noted earlier from contrasts between biotech and software sectors, the type of knowledge necessary to support innovation, as well as non-knowledge resourcing, varies between sectors. This has major implications for the nuances that should be incorporated into policies to support SME innovation. Given the limited indigenous supports in emerging economies, this insight raises questions such as which sectors offer the best opportunities for innovation-based growth in developing economies? What kinds of knowledge assets do they require? Where can such knowledge assets be obtained?

Innovation in some sectors requires a high level of institutional support. For example, many innovating biotech SMEs are spin-offs from universities and research institutes. They have significant requirements for basic research inputs and highly qualified research personnel. As with many other innovating firms, they also rely on the institutional protection of their intellectual property. Moreover, the long lead-times between drug discovery and proof of concept can impose considerable requirements for risk capital. If many developing economies, including China, continue to exhibit 'voids' in their institutional systems, yet also want to encourage high-tech innovation, questions have to be asked about which among these voids are the most important to fill and how might this be achieved.

Overall, posing questions such as these serves to identify fruitful areas for additional research on what constrains innovation by developing country SMEs, China in particular, and what the necessary conditions are for them to become more innovation-based. The underlying theme is that the conditions enabling SME innovation in developed economies deserve examination for their relevance to developing economies and for the policy implications that follow. We already know that innovation thrives better in some contexts rather than others and that defines the basic challenge for China.

References

Abrami, Regina M., Willima C. Kirby and F. Warren McFarlan 2014. Why China can't innovate. *Harvard Business Review*, 92 (3): 107–111.

Anh, Nguyen Ngoc, Nicola Jones, Nguyen Duc Nhat and Nguyen Dinh Chuc 2009. Capitalizing on innovation for exports by the SME sector. *Tech Monitor*, July–August: 43–46.

Atuahene-Gima, Kwaku and Anthony Ko 2001. An empirical investigation of the effect of market orientation and entrepreneurship orientation alignment on product innovation. *Organization Science*, 12 (1): 54–74.

Baron, Robert A. and Jintong Tang 2011. The role of entrepreneurs in firm-level innovation: Joint effects of positive affect, creativity, and environmental dynamism. *Journal of Business Venturing*, 26 (1): 49–60.

Baum, Joel A.C., Tony Calabrese and Brian S. Silverman 2000. Don't go it alone: Alliance network composition and startups performance in Canadian biotechnology. *Strategic Management Journal*, 21 (3): 267–294.

Boisot, Max 1998. *Knowledge Assets: Securing Competitive Advantage in the Information Economy*. Oxford: Oxford University Press.

Breznitz, Dan 2007. *Innovation and the State: Political Choice and Strategies for Growth in Israel, Taiwan and Ireland*. New Haven, CT: Yale University Press.

Cao, Cong, Ning Li, Xia Li and Li Liu 2013. Reforming China's S&T system. *Science*, 341: 460–462.

Castilla, Emilio J., Hokyu Hwang, Ellen Granovetter and Mark Granovetter 2000. Social networks in Silicon Valley. In Chong-Moon Lee, William F. Miller, Marguerite Gong Hancock and Henry S. Rowen (eds.) 2000. *The Silicon Valley Edge: A Habitat for Innovation and Entrepreneurship*. Stanford, CA: Stanford University Press: 218–247.

CCTV 2015. Political advisors propose supporting micro, small firm innovation. February 16, http://english.cntv.cn/2014/11/28/ART I1417137839508794.shtml.

Child, John and Rose Narooz 2014. Networking by internationalizing SMEs in the light of domestic institutional voids: A comparison of Egypt and the UK. Paper presented to the 30th Colloquium of the European Group for Organizational Studies, July.

Cohen, Wesley M. and Daniel A. Levinthal 1990. Absorptive capacity: A new perspective on learning and innovation. *Administrative Science Quarterly*, 35 (1): 128–152.

Deng, Ziliang, Peter S. Hofman and Alexander Newman 2013. Ownership concentration and product innovation in Chinese private SMEs. *Asia Pacific Journal of Management*, 30 (3): 717–734.

Drucker, Peter F. 1985/2011. *Innovation and Entrepreneurship*. London: Routledge.

Esteve-Pérez, Silviano and Diego Rodríguez 2013. The dynamics of exports and R&D in SMEs. *Small Business Economics*, 41(1): 219–240.

Ganotakis, Panagiotis and James H. Love 2011. R&D, product innovation, and exporting: Evidence from UK new technology based firms. *Oxford Economic Papers*, 63 (2): 279–306.

Global Entrepreneurship Monitor (GEM) 2015. *2014 Global Report*. London: Global Entrepreneurship Research Association. www.gemconsortium.org/report, accessed 7 December 2015.

Global Innovation Index 2015. Cornell University, INSEAD and World Intellectual Property Organization. www.wipo.int/edocs/pubdocs/en/wipo_gii_2015.pdf, accessed 7 December 2015.

Grabher, Gernot (ed.). 1993. *The Embedded Firm. On the Socioeconomics of Industrial Networks*. London: Routledge.

Harms, R., C.H. Reschke, S. Kraus and M. Fink 2010. Antecedents to innovation and growth: Analyzing the impact of entrepreneurial orientation and goal-oriented management. *International Journal of Technology Management*, 52 (1/2): 135–152.

Hassink, Robert and Dong-Ho Shin 2005. Guest editorial: The restructuring of old industrial areas in Europe and Asia. *Environment and Planning A*, 37: 571–580.

Hofman, Peter S., Alexander Newman and Ziliang Deng 2014. Determinants of product innovation in Chinese private small and medium-sized enterprises. In Ken Shao and Xiaoqing Feng (eds.) *Innovation and Intellectual Property in China: Strategies, Contexts and Challenges*. Cheltenham: Edward Elgar, 160–185.

Hou, Jun and Pierre Mohnen 2011. Complementarity between in-house R&D and technology purchasing: Evidence from Chinese manufacturing firms. UNU-MERIT Working Paper no. 2011–048. Maastricht Economic and Social Research Institute on Innovation and Technology (UNU-MERIT).

Karlsson, Charlie, Börge Johansson, Kiyoshi Kobayashi and Roger R. Stough (eds.) 2014. *Knowledge, Innovation and Space*. Cheltenham: Elgar.

Khanna, Tarun and Krishna G. Palepu (eds.), 2010. *Winning in Emerging Markets: A Road Map for Strategy and Execution*. Boston, MA: Harvard Business Press.

Knight, G. A. and S. T. Cavusgil 2004. Innovation, organizational capabilities, and the born-global firm. *Journal of International Business Studies*, 35(2): 124–141.

Larrañeta, Bárbara, Shaker A. Zahra and José Luis Galán González 2012. Enriching strategic variety in new ventures through external knowledge. *Journal of Business Venturing*, 27 (4): 401–413.

Liu, Xiaohui, Jiangyong Lu, Igor Filatotchev, Trevor Buck and Mike Wright 2010. Returnee entrepreneurs, knowledge spillovers and innovation in high-tech firms in emerging economies. *Journal of International Business Studies*, 41: 1183–1197.

Love, James H. and Stephen Roper 2013. SME innovation, exporting and growth. ERC White Paper no. 5. Aston and Warwick Business Schools: Enterprise Research Centre, April.

Lumpkin, G.T. and Gregory G. Dess 1996. Clarifying the entrepreneurial orientation construct and linking it to performance. *Academy of Management Review*, 21 (1): 135–172.

Lundin, Nannan, Fredrik Sjöholm, He Ping and Jinchang Qian 2007. The role of small firms in China's technology development. IFN Working Paper No. 695. Research Institute of Industrial Economics, Stockholm.

Luo, Yadong and John Child 2015. A composition-based view of firm growth. *Management and Organization Review*, 11 (3): 379–411.

Magnier, Mark 2015. China's long, slow road to reform. *Wall Street Journal*, 6 March: 1 and 9.

March, James G. 1991. Exploration and exploitation in organizational learning. *Organization Science*, 2 (1): 71–87.

MasterCard Worldwide 2013. *New Wave of Growth in China: Innovation Through Developing SMEs*. http://newsroom.mastercard.com/asia-pacific/files/2014/03/New-Wave-of-Growth-in-China-Innovation-through-Developing-SMEs.pdf, accessed 6 March 2015.

Mitussis, Darryn 2010. SME innovation in Zhejiang, China: Potential constraints to development of widespread innovation. *Journal of Knowledge-Based Innovation in China*, 2 (1): 89–105.

Nee, Victor and Sonja Opper 2012. *Capitalism from Below: Markets and Institutional Change in China*. Cambridge, MA: Harvard University Press.

Nee, Victor and Sonja Opper. 2013. Markets and institutional change in China. Working Paper #68. Cornell University, Center for the Study of Economy & Society, February. www.economyandsociety.org/wp-content/uploads/2013/07/wp68_NeeOpper_InstitutionalChange.pdf, accessed 7 March 2015.

OECD 2009. *Clusters, Entrepreneurship and Innovation*. Paris: OECD.

OECD 2010. *SMEs, Entrepreneurship and Innovation*. Paris: OECD.

Oviatt, Benjamin M. and Patricia P. McDougall 1994. Toward a theory of international new ventures. *Journal of International Business Studies*, 25(1): 45–64.

Palangkaraya, Alfons 2013. *On the Relationship Between Innovation and Export: The Case of Australian SMEs*. Melbourne: Intellectual Property Research Institute of Australia, University of Melbourne, February. www.ipria.org/publications/wp/2013/WP313.pdf.

Pavitt, Keith 1984. Sectoral patterns of technical change: Towards a taxonomy and a theory. *Research Policy*, 13: 343–373.

Property Rights Alliance 2014. *The International Property Rights Index 2014*. Washington, DC. http://internationalpropertyrightsindex.org/countries, accessed 9 March 2015.

Puffer, Sheila M., Daniel J. McCarthy and Max Boisot 2010. Entrepreneurship in Russia and China: The impact of formal institutional voids. *Entrepreneurship Theory and Practice*, 34 (3): 441–467.

Radas, Sonja and Ljiljana Božić 2009. The antecedents of SME innovativeness in an emerging transition economy. *Technovation*, 29 (6–7): 438–450.

Rodrigues, Suzana B. 2013. Understanding the environments of emerging markets: The social costs of institutional voids. Farewell Address, Rotterdam School of Management, Erasmus University Rotterdam, June 13, reference: ERIM:EFA-2013-002-S&E.

Roland Berger 2012. *Innovation – How the Emerging Markets Are Driving the Global Innovation Agenda*. Munich: Roland Berger Strategy Consultants, September. www.rolandberger.com/media/pdf/Roland_Berg er_8_Billion_Emerging_markets_are_driving_the_global_innovation_agen da_20121109.pdf, accessed 6 March 2015.

Salavisa, Isabel, Cristina Sousa and Margarida Fontes 2012. Topologies of innovation networks in knowledge-intensive sectors: Sectoral differences in access to knowledge and complementary assets through formal and informal ties. *Technovation*, 32 (6): 380–399.

Saxenian, AnnaLee 1994. *Regional Advantage: Culture and Competition in Silicon Valley and Route 128*. Cambridge, MA: Harvard University Press.

Schumpeter, Joseph A. 1942. *Capitalism, Socialism and Democracy*. New York: Harper and Row.

Shapiro, Daniel, Yao Tang, Miaojun Wang and Weiying Zhang 2015. The effects of corporate governance on the innovation performance of Chinese SMEs. *Journal of Chinese Economic and Business Studies*. doi: 10.1080/14765284.2015.1090267.

SPI, UNU-Merit and AIT 2014. STI China: Science, technology and innovation performance of China. D9: Final Report. http://eeas.europa.eu/delega

tions/china/documents/eu_china/research_innovation/4_innovation/sti_ china_study_full_report.pdf, accessed 6 March 2015.

Szulanski, Gabriel 1996. Exploring internal stickiness: Impediments to the transfer of best practice within the firm. *Strategic Management Journal*, 17: 27–43.

Tang, Guiyao, Yang Chen and Jiafei Jin 2014. Entrepreneurial orientation and innovation performance: Roles of strategic HRM and technical turbulence. *Asia Pacific Journal of Human Resources*. doi:10.1111/ 1744-7941.12053.

Tolstoy, Daniel and Henrik Agndal 2010. Network resource combinations in the international venturing of small biotech firms. *Technovation*, 30 (1): 24–36.

Xinhua 2014. Cited in 'Experts urge lending innovation for small firms', http:// africa.chinadaily.com.cn/business/2014-07/08/content_17673157.htm, accessed 1 September 2014.

Xu, Zongling, Jiali Lin and Danming Lin. 2008. Networking and innovation in SMEs: Evidence from Guangdong Province, China. *Journal of Small Business and Enterprise Development*, 15 (4): 788–801.

Wadhwa, Vivek 2013. Chinese can innovate – But China can't. *The Economist Debate*, 14 November, www.economist.com/debate/days/view/1041, accessed 13 March 2015.

Williams, Patrick 2015. Can a Chinese state venture capital fund drive innovation? *East Asia Forum*, 14 February, www.eastasiaforum.org/2015/ 02/14/45225/

Williamson, Peter J. and Eden Yin 2014. Accelerated innovation: The new challenge from China. *MIT Sloan Management Review*, Summer: 27–34.

World Bank [and the Development Research Center of the State Council] 2013. *China 2030: Building a Modern, Harmonious, and Creative Society*. Washington, DC: World Bank.

World Economic Forum 2015. http://reports.weforum.org/global- competitiveness-report-2015-2016/competitiveness-rankings/#indicatorI d=GCI.C.12, accessed 7 December 2015.

Xu, Zongling, Jiali Lin and Danming Lin 2008. Networking and innovation in SMEs: Evidence from Guangdong Province, China. *Journal of Small Business and Enterprise Development*, 15 (4): 788–801.

Yoshino, Yuyaka (ed.) 2011. *Industrial Clusters and Micro and Small Enterprises in Africa*. Washington, DC: World Bank.

Yu, Bo, Shengbin Hao, David Ahlstrom, Steven Si and Dapeng Liang, 2014. Entrepreneurial firms' network competence, technological capability, and new product development performance. *Asia Pacific Journal of Management*, 31 (3): 687–704.

Zeng, S.X., X.M. Xie and C.M. Tam 2010. Relationship between cooperation networks and innovation performance of SMEs. *Technovation*, 30 (3): 181–194.

Zhu, Yanmei, Xinhua Wittmann and Mike W. Peng 2012. Institution-based barriers to innovation in SMEs in China. *Asia Pacific Journal of Management*, 29 (4): 1131–1142.

9 | Who benefits when MNEs partner with local enterprises in China?

SIMON C. COLLINSON

9.1 Introduction

Much of the discussion about growth in transition economies focuses on macro-economic analysis and the policy agenda, without a full understanding of the micro-level foundations of growth. Like John Child in his contribution to this volume we focus on the private sector as the engine of innovation. He looks at small and medium-sized enterprises (SMEs) in China while we examine how local firms evolve their capacity to innovate through partnerships with multinational enterprises (MNEs) based in China.

Technology transfer, learning and spillover effects have long been recognized as key channels for enhancing the ability of firms, industry sectors and economies to innovate and compete. Growth and structural change at the macro level are the products of the aggregate effects of interactions at the micro level, taking place within and between firms. However, the macro-level context, discussed here as a national system of innovation (NSI), has a significant influence on micro-level conditions for capability development. So the two co-evolve, sometimes following a positive spiral of continuous improvement in innovative capacity and competitiveness, which is the policymakers' aspiration, and at other times stalling or reversing. Misalignments between the macro-level policy context, the NSI ecosystem and the micro-level conditions for innovation-related capability development adversely affect this positive growth spiral. They are a key factor underlying stalled development and traps, such as the middle-income trap, and need to be better understood.

This sets the agenda for presenting empirical evidence on the nature of innovation capability development in MNE partnerships in China and the effects of government interventions in the micro-level development processes. We examine how different kinds of MNE partnerships lead to particular kinds of asset recombinations and result in innovation-related ownership advantages or firm-specific advantages (FSAs) for the firms involved in the partnership. The evidence comes from a study which compared a variety of inter-organizational partnerships (joint ventures, contracting and supply-chain relationships, etc.) between MNEs and local firms in China (customers, suppliers, competitors, public R&D organizations, etc.). This focused specifically on recombinations of FSAs that gave rise to measurable improvements in the joint innovation capability of the partners. While some partnerships were short-lived, others managed to sustain a balanced and mutually beneficial give-and-take of assets, capabilities and knowledge resulting in better innovation outputs.

The research shows that industry context is extremely important, particularly in terms of the degree to which (and ways in which) government agencies intervene directly or indirectly in these international partnerships and the effects of this intervention. There are a number of lessons for practitioners and policymakers relating to the national system of innovation specifically and patterns of economic development more generally, in China.

In order to connect with the core themes of this book we start by looking at the macro-economic context. To illustrate some key tensions between policy intentions and on-the-ground effects we focus on the Chinese aerospace industry as a particular system of innovation in which MNE interactions with local firms are particularly important and strongly influenced by government agencies at various levels.

9.2 National systems of innovation and the middle-income trap

Studies at the macro-level, analyzing the progress of developing countries, show how they can 'catch up' with advanced or mature economies by following similar paths of development (Dantas and Bell, 2009; Kim, 1997). Similarly, micro-level research examining firm-level capabilities tends to confirm that firms benefit from a latecomer's advantage, to some extent imitating or learning from firms that have already developed strong innovative capabilities and competitive advantages. Both firms and countries follow a development path pioneered by others, avoiding the costly mistakes inherent in experimentation and exploration. They are able to rely more on imitation and the exploitation of innovations in processes, products and services created by others to grow. During this stage of development governments can focus on providing the necessary conditions, including infrastructure (transport, energy, education), institutions (legal and financial) and policies (semi-open trade, selected industry incentives) to complement private investment and promote technological catch-up.

The newly industrializing countries (NICs) in Asia (e.g. Malaysia, Thailand), Latin America (Brazil, Argentina, Peru) and elsewhere (Jordan, Iran) have broadly followed these approaches. But the development paths for these countries are now more complex; as they reach the technology frontier in a number of key industries the most effective development strategies and the role of government are less clear-cut. In fact a relatively small number of NICs have achieved the levels of productivity of advanced economies.

One indication of the failure of an economy to make this transition is the 'middle-income trap' (Kharas, 2009). Growth slows or stalls before the average per capita income reaches advanced country levels. This interrupts the 'virtuous cycle' of economic growth when rising incomes boost consumption levels driving up demand and production which pushes up wage levels. Causes of this trap include the declining relevance of cheap labour and inter-sectoral transfers of labour and capital investments in infrastructure as drivers of economic growth. This is not entirely new as an insight into the economics of emerging economies. There has long been a consensus around the need for economies to make the transition from a reliance on export advantages based on cheap labour and the switch from 'imitation to innovation' (Kim, 1997, among many others before and since). But recent studies (World Bank, 2013) present compelling additional evidence that (1) this is proving to be a major problem for a range of NICs who achieved impressive growth rates and have now 'stalled', having failed to transition to high-income economies (World Bank, 2013, p. 12, Box 0.1), and (2) this presents a very significant challenge for China in the coming years.

According to some analyses there is a stronger need for the market (the invisible hand) to replace government agencies as the guiding (visible) hand to improve competitiveness across emerging economies. This is partly because the selection mechanisms that operate in markets to allocate scarce resources, choose the next dominant technology platform, or support the flourishing of new enterprises in mature markets are seen to be superior to the ability of governments to 'pick winners' or pre-plan growth. However, a counterview has recently been put forward in the form of the 'new structural economics' (Yifu Lin, 2012 and in this book). This argues that more accurate, targeted development strategies coordinated by governments and focusing on areas of natural comparative advantage are more likely to succeed than market mechanisms alone. Several studies present empirical evidence to suggest that intelligent interventions by governments are responsible for 'higher growth, lower economic volatility, and less inequality' in higher-performing developing countries. Measures of total factor productivity and comparative analyses of value chains are central to this evidence. A central argument of this chapter is that intelligent interventions by government require a better understanding of the 'on-the-ground' micro-level effects of interventions on capacity-building than we currently have.

Whether we favour the market or planned interventions by governments, there is a general consensus, presented by the World Bank (2013): "If countries cannot increase productivity through innovation (rather than continuing to rely on foreign technology), they find themselves trapped" (World Bank, 2013, p. 12, Box 0.1). NSI research provides a useful framework for understanding the macro-level challenges faced by countries attempting to make this transition. This approach puts technological 'catch-up' and the accumulation of innovation-related capability at the heart of economic growth at various levels of analysis, from the national (Bell and Pavitt, 1997; Collinson, 2009; Hobday and Rush, 2007; Lall, 1992; Lundvall, 1992, 2007; Nelson, 1993) to the firm level (Birkinshaw, 2000; Cantwell, 1989; Collinson and Wang, 2012; De Meyer, 1992; Dosi et al., 1988).

Innovation studies tend to look at catch-up at any level as a dual challenge of process and product or service innovation. Innovations in firm-level processes and industry-level business models help solve the productivity challenge by improving firm's ability to add value to current products and services in better or cheaper ways. Product or service innovation gives rise to new or improved offerings to the market. Both enhance the competitiveness of firms, industries and nations.

Innovating at the technology frontier therefore requires different capabilities at the firm level and a different NSI. In most developing economies this challenge involves a move away from a reliance on imitating, transferring or reverse-engineering the innovations of others, towards a stronger level of indigenous capability. This challenge varies by industry because (1) the technologies, processes and capabilities on which competitiveness relies differ in terms of the ease of imitation or transfer and (2) the rents gained from exploitation of others' innovation outputs as a 'fast follower' also vary. A successful competitive strategy in some industry contexts may rely on effective and efficient imitation, rather than riskier innovation. Comparing, for example, the progress of China's mobile telecoms sector against its pharmaceuticals industry provides insights into both (1) and (2).

Returning to the above-mentioned virtuous cycle of economic growth, it is important to note that by enhancing the innovation-related capabilities of a nation's workforce we enhance its ability to add value to processes, products and services. This workforce then becomes more 'valuable' and therefore more expensive (to local and foreign employers), underpinning the shift to high-income and higher levels of consumption. This is related to the classic Heckscher-Ohlin trade model. The key point is that both of the elements that drive the positive economic cycle linking consumption and production in all economies stem from the evolution of indigenous innovation-related capabilities. 'Ratcheting up knowledge creation at every level of economic activity' improves the competitiveness of an economy and drives up incomes and consumption.

Finally, reflecting a number of contributions in this book alongside some of the original work of Bruce Kogut, we should note that: "globalization is less and less about national competition around sectoral dominance but about the location of the value-added activities that compose the global commodity chains" (Kogut, 2003). It is important to examine technological 'catch-up' and the accumulation of innovation-related capability in terms of progress 'up' specific value chains, when we consider the evolution of a particular location over time. This equates (in space) to the relocation of specific value-adding activities to places that have evolved relative advantages for adding particular kinds of value in particular kinds of value chains. I share Bruce Kogut's view that an important conduit (arguably the most important conduit) for change across both these dimensions is the multinational firm. This is a theme we will return to below.

9.3 The China context

Much of the above discussion applies to China at its current stage of transition. Fuller analyses are presented elsewhere in this book, but some of the key developments are worth summarizing. We have seen a strong rise in total factor productivity, at 3 percent per year on average for the past decade, alongside the oft-cited growth trends in gross domestic product (GDP), trade and FDI. Rapid structural change including unprecedented public and private investments in infrastructure, utilities, transport and property construction as well as industry assets has taken place alongside high levels of inward investment and substantial technological spillovers. But many segments are approaching the technology frontier, labour costs are rising and inter-sectoral transfers of labour are declining as is the contribution of capital as a growth driver.

The Chinese government is encouraging enterprises to take a leading role as it adopts a facilitating role. The six pillars of the new government strategy reflect this: consolidating China's market foundations; enhancing innovation; promoting green development; ensuring equality of opportunity and social protection for all; strengthening public finances; and achieving mutually beneficial win–win relations between China and the rest of the world.

China's existing NSI presents a number of advantages in relation to this transition. It has finance to invest in its science and technology and R&D infrastructure and we have witnessed an impressive development of private-sector and public-sector (including university-based) R&D capacity. The usual indicators from international papers and citations to patents, licensing and royalty fees and other IPR revenues have risen accordingly. This is underpinned by an exceptional (by developing country standards) education system producing a stream of science and engineering skills, enhanced by large numbers of students returning to China with overseas degrees and experience. China enjoys strong levels of FDI in R&D as well as in manufacturing, which complement internal investments in the innovation ecosystem. A variety of sources of capital, despite inefficient capital markets (a shortage of effective mechanisms for optimizing the allocation of capital) help drive both entrepreneurial start-ups and new business initiatives in larger firms. An entrepreneurial culture, some established regions that are supportive of small firm growth (Guangdong's Pearl River Delta, Zhejiang and Fujian) and some evolving specialist agglomerations.

A strong component of China's NSI is its large and rapidly developing manufacturing sector. Compared to other countries (Japan in the post-war era and the NICs more recently) China has advanced more quickly through the stages of capability development and across a wider range of industry sectors than has ever been witnessed. There is strong empirical evidence showing that trade and FDI more generally promote upgrading (Bloom et al., 2014) and this has been a significant factor for China.

Government has taken a strong, interventionist approach in an attempt to promote specific kinds of technology transfer and spillovers, to benefit local firms. By leveraging its control over the conditions under which foreign firms are allowed to invest, including mandatory joint ventures for foreign entrants in some sectors, the government attempts to target and facilitate certain kinds of capability development above others.

Some studies suggest that different forms of innovation are relevant for different kinds of catch-up (Wang et al., 2014). There is some evidence for this at the firm level, including research by Williamson and Yin (2014) which suggests that the approach taken by some Chinese firms to 'accelerate' the process of innovation, improving the speed with which incremental improvements are made to the basic products and services created by others, is in itself an innovative capability. The creative recombination of processes, practices and capabilities to enable continuous improvement, quickly commercialize new technologies or rapidly respond to changes in market demand are a key to sustained innovation capacity. These are arguably more important than the creative recombination of technologies, components or product features which provide temporary advantage in a particular market segment.

Particular forms of dynamic capabilities developed by some Chinese firms are specifically suited to low-cost, low-income environments, because that is where they have evolved (Williamson and Yin, 2014). These include effective horizontal team working, breaking the process of incremental innovation to smaller, simpler steps to suit less qualified, cheaper and more available engineering and technical staff (Luo and Child, 2015).

Combining these insights with previous analyses of developing economies (Hobday, 2007) suggests that innovation which is based on formal R&D activities, measured by R&D investment and patents, is even less relevant in the China context. Building innovation capacity more often involves operationalizing existing technologies or processes in new contexts, dominated by less adequate infrastructures, poorly developed supply chains, lower costs and lower skills and 'institutional voids' (gaps or weaknesses in formal institutional provisions; see Chapter 8 by John Child in this volume and Puffer et al., 2010). It also involves focusing on lower-cost products and services for low-income consumers, and this could be part of the 'catch-22' which contributes to the middle income trap. Firms naturally evolve innovative and other dynamic capabilities appropriate to their environment. There is a self-reinforcing circularity between demand for and supply of low- (or high-) cost, low- (or high-) quality, unsophisticated (or sophisticated) products and services, creating a degree of lock-in or embeddedness for local firms (Collinson, 2009).

This underpins the need for additional insights into: (1) the sources, channels and mechanisms at the firm level for developing innovative capabilities, as an input into the challenges of developing innovative capacity at the (aggregate) national level; (2) the ways in which these vary by industry; and (3) the influence of various kinds of government intervention at both the firm level and the industry level.

9.4 Recombinant advantages as a source of innovation capability

We shift the emphasis now to examine inter-firm partnerships as a specific source of innovation-related capabilities. This provides a 'deep dive' into one particular channel for local Chinese firms to gain assets, technology, resources and capabilities to enhance their ability to innovate and catch-up. Our study also shows to how various parts of the Chinese government are intervening in specific industry sectors to promote indigenous innovation.

Bruce Kogut (1993, 2003) proposes that "organizing principles diffuse more quickly among firms within a region than between regions and countries". But he also identifies the multinational corporation as the medium by which organizing principles are transferred globally. He suggests that "subsidiaries do more than transfer and adapt to local environments, they become agents of change in the local economy and for the multinational corporation in a form of co-evolution". Here we examine a subset of the processes by which this happens using 'recombinant advantages' to focus our analysis.

The idea of recombinant advantages has its origins in a well-established literature dedicated to understanding how foreign firms play a role in limiting or enhancing 'indigenous technological capabilities' (Cantwell and Janne, 2000; Collinson, 2009; Dosi et al., 1988). Economists have tried to disaggregate the factors that underpin the growth of total factor productivity (TFP) at the macro level. Other approaches focus on the micro level, examining patterns of firm-level learning (Bell, 1984; Bell and Figueiredo, 2012; Berggren et al., 2011). The spectrum from micro level to macro level and quantitative to qualitative is populated with a wide range of studies including knowledge-management perspectives, the resource-based view (RBV), dynamic capabilities approaches, analyses of networks, industrial clusters and global value-chain analysis and studies of foreign direct investment spillovers. More recently the concept of recombining (Verbeke, 2009) or 'bundling' (Hennart, 2009) of complementary assets to improve their performance has been developed further in international business studies to better understand motivations and effects of MNE partnerships more generally.

It is accepted that firms learn to innovate directly or indirectly from each other. By imitating competitors, collaborating with suppliers, following the demands of clients or working in joint ventures with other firms that have complementary assets, resources or capabilities. We know from our study and others that these firms are drawn together partly by this anticipated complementarity. Each has strengths and gaps in their existing portfolio of assets, resources and capabilities which give rise to relative advantages which they can 'trade' in return for assets, resources and capabilities that compensate for their disadvantages.

It is useful to define a number of different kinds of advantages to frame the empirical analysis that follows. FSAs can be defined as 'unique assets, resources and capabilities proprietary to the organization from which it derives competitive advantage'. Although the term can apply to proprietary services, products, processes or technologies sustainable FSAs are based ultimately on the internalization of an asset, such as production knowledge, managerial or marketing capabilities over which the firm has proprietary control. FSAs are thus related to the firm's ability to coordinate the use of the advantage in production,

Table 9.1 *Four types of firm-specific advantage*

Firm-specific advantages (FSAs)	Asset-related	Transaction-related
Non-location-bound advantages can be applied across a variety of country markets and institutional contexts	(1) Brands, services, products, processes, technologies, knowledge and types of IPR which apply in multiple countries	(2) Capabilities for the creation and coordination of efficient internal hierarchies and markets within MNEs that span a complex diversity of locations
Location-bound advantages only apply in specific country contexts	(3) Brands, services, products, processes, technologies, knowledge and types of IPR which apply in only one country context	(4) Locally applicable knowledge, capabilities, relationships which provide advantage only in specific country contexts

marketing, or the customization of services. In international business studies FSAs are contrasted with CSAs (country-specific advantages) which are defined as 'strengths or benefits specific to a country' that result from its geographic location, natural endowments, labour force, competitive environment, culture, government policies, industrial clusters and so on (Collinson and Narula, 2014; Rugman and Collinson, 2012).

We focus here on four categories of FSAs, mapped out in Table 9.1, which reflect accepted concepts in the literature and proved particularly significant in our empirical study; asset-related or transaction-related and location-bound or non-location-bound. Location-bound advantages are related to CSAs in that they only operate or apply in specific country contexts.

Following Collinson and Narula (2014) and predecessors, location-bound, transaction-related advantages include knowledge of institutions and relational capabilities for institutional avoidance, adaptation and/or co-evolution (Cantwell et al., 2010; Santangelo and Meyer, 2011).

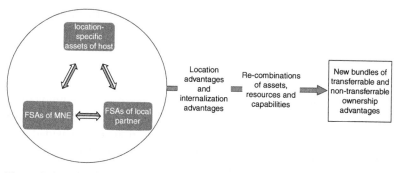

Figure 9.1 Recombinations of location-specific and firm-specific assets leading to new ownership advantages
Source: Collinson and Narula (2014).

Our study examined how recombinations of location-specific and non-location-specific assets and capabilities led to new FSAs for MNEs and their local partners in China, as outlined in Figure 9.1.

Evidence suggests that emerging market firms mainly seek to acquire new FSAs to complement strong CSAs and compensate for weak or non-existent FSAs (Rugman, 2009; Rugman and Doh, 2008). By developing or acquiring FSAs they are able to compete more effectively against local competitors, but more importantly they are able to leverage combinations of CSAs (e.g. cheap labour) and FSAs (e.g. a particular technology) to compete internationally. The 'springboard' theory (Luo and Tung, 2007) and the 'double handspring' adaptation (Williamson et al., 2013) also proposes that MNEs from emerging economies engage in overseas acquisitions to strengthen their international competitiveness.

Local context, including industry specialization; gaps in resources, assets and capabilities; the structures and strategies of local flagship firms; and the role of government, all vary significantly (Collinson, 2013). Because of this heterogeneity it is useful to focus on a specific industry sector as we do below. By applying the above framework we can differentiate between the kinds of innovation-related advantages that Chinese firms are developing with their MNE partners; are they location-bound or do they provide a basis for internationalization (exports and FDI)? This also allows for a more precise understanding of the effects of government interventions and the wider contextual factors which influence specific firm–firm interactions. This in turn may complement, clarify or contradict policy conclusions derived from macro-level analysis alone.

9.5 A study of international partnerships in China

To provide insights into the dynamics of learning and innovation capability development at the firm level we undertook an extensive study of MNE partnerships in China. A questionnaire provided 320 individual company responses from the China-based operations of MNEs (181 US, 88 EU and 51 UK responses). This was complemented by a case-study survey involving 105 semi-structured interviews with managers, engineers, scientists and plant-level personnel based in the home country location of the firm and in China, covering 30 joint projects in 20 MNEs.

In both the questionnaire and the interviews, we attempted to measure improvements in the innovation capabilities of both MNEs and their local partners. At one level this consisted of tracing back from joint outputs (new products, better levels of productivity, etc.) of the partnership to the respective inputs of assets and capabilities from each firm via a process of integration or recombination.

Thirty-four percent of the partnerships captured by our questionnaire were between MNEs and local customers. These were mainly Western suppliers supporting local firms in the manufacturing of products for both export and the local market with both firms sharing production technology and manufacturing expertise. Twenty-four percent of the partnerships were with local suppliers where the MNEs were transferring production technology and creating new distribution channels locally and for export. Supply-chain partnerships therefore dominated the survey responses (58 percent) but a larger amount of joint innovation took place when the MNE partnered with local suppliers, rather than with customers in the role of key supplier. There were thirty partnerships with competitors in the sample, with a stronger focus on joint product development for the local market. Such collaborations focused on sharing marketing, service and manufacturing expertise and know-how, designs and patterns for innovation. Fourteen percent of the responses related to MNE partnerships with public R&D organizations with a focus on support for new product development for the domestic market. The partners shared R&D expertise and local organizations benefitted from education and training as well as income while MNEs gained from low-cost local knowledge.

The kinds of assets and capabilities that were (re)combined within these partnerships included: financial resources; R&D-related expertise; disclosures of know-how, designs and patterns for innovation; new routes/channels to market; marketing or service expertise; access to low-cost labour; access to new suppliers; manufacturing/production expertise and other kinds of management capabilities; knowledge about operating in different business environments. These also map onto the conventional international business studies categories of 'asset-exploiting' and 'asset-augmenting' motivation for FDI. Different partnerships reported a variety of improvements in their combined ability to innovate, including productivity gains (better quality, cost-efficiency, speed-to-market, etc.), improvements in new product development and enhanced market access. Many of these improvements were specific to the China context; however, there was evidence that some local Chinese firms improved their capacity to internationalize through the partnership. Figure 9.2 presents a summary of the findings, showing the main innovation-related benefits for the different types of partnership.

Overall we found that both MNEs and local firms contributed a range of non-location-bound FSAs to the partnership, but the MNEs contributed the greater proportion of these in the form of specific brands, technologies or product and process capabilities relating to firm-level innovation. Both partners also contributed location-bound FSAs, such as knowledge of specific country markets, supplier firms or institutions. But local firms contributed the greater proportion of location-bound FSAs, trading on their local knowledge in return for the above-mentioned non-location-bound FSAs. The findings are presented in aggregate using the following graph showing what MNEs and local firms gained from each other.

Additional empirical findings can be found in Collinson and Narula (2014), alongside a fuller account of the survey and interview-based case studies we compiled. The case studies helped explain the patterns revealed by the questionnaire. They illustrate the complex variety of different kinds of partnerships in different industry contexts which shape different kinds of reciprocity, asset recombination and innovation advantages. This complex variety, including the wide range of government interventions and influences, is hidden to macro-level,

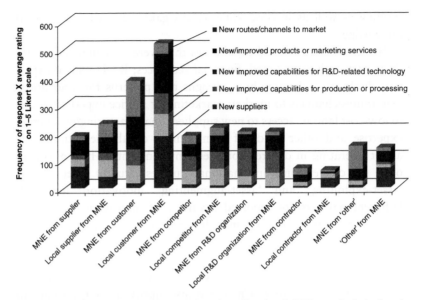

Figure 9.2 The respective innovation benefits for MNEs and their local partners in China

data-driven analyses. Policy lessons based solely on the latter can therefore be imprecise if not plain wrong.

9.6 Multinational partnerships in the Chinese aerospace industry

Four of our thirty partnership projects were studied in two major multinational aerospace firms based in China. These provided excellent insights into the interactions between the firms and the influence of government intervention, at various levels, on the development of indigenous innovation capabilities. The industry context in which the MNEs operated is an important part of the story (for additional background see Boeing and Sandner, 2012).

A senior Western manager, who had been based in China for over twenty years, told us in an interview we held at the firm's regional headquarters in Beijing:

Within the next 15 years there will be three major commercial aerospace corporations; Boeing, Airbus and a Chinese firm. Soon after there may well be two; one of which will be the Chinese firm.

He was emphasizing how serious the Chinese authorities were about developing an indigenous aerospace industry at the time of our study. In fact this has been an explicit goal for several decades, in a context where passenger volumes in China's air transportation industry have grown exceptionally fast. Passenger volumes had been growing at over 10 percent per year, requiring an additional 1,790 aircraft, 49 new airports and 701 airport expansion projects in the 2006–2011 five-year plan.

The Chinese government continues to maintain a strong degree of control over the civil aviation industry. Various agencies aim to improve the reliability and efficiency of the transport infrastructure and promote competitiveness among domestic firms. During our survey the General Administration of Civil Aviation of China (CAAC) was the government agency responsible for the non-military aviation industry. It had rationalized the country's airlines, completing mergers with the 'Big 3' – Air China, China Eastern and China Southern – and some of the smaller airlines.

CAAC was central to the expressed aim of the Chinese government to develop an indigenous 'Made-in-China' aircraft to rival Boeing and Airbus. The government has long been funding this as a prestige project and will continue to do so until it succeeds, but there are question marks over how long it will take and how reliable, safe and therefore saleable the final product will be.

Another senior British executive we interviewed in China described the 'Stairway to Heaven'. Three stages towards local technological maturity in aerospace manufacturing:

Stage (1) 'Made-to-print': local manufacturers follow simple designs for low-end (and later, high-end) manufacturing
Stage (2) Local firms take on responsibility for product modules or 'build-kits', including some re-design and process innovation
Stage (3) Full engineering partnerships with Western firms, with shared design and development, local responsibility for technology, quality, etc., and risk and revenue-sharing (suppliers as shareholders in on-going development processes)

Foreign firms in China, including Airbus and Boeing, Rolls-Royce and General Electric, have been part of this plan. In order to gain access to the growing domestic market they have had to establish partnerships with local Chinese manufacturers. These involve sub-contracting, technology transfer and training with an expressed aim of increasing the local content of aircraft.

AVIC1 (Aviation Industry China) and AVIC2 were responsible for all aerospace manufacturing in China, within the CAAC governance structure. AVIC1 focused on large aircraft and was the main organization charged with developing a complete Chinese-made aircraft. Domestic AVIC1 firms were compelled to follow dual public- and private-sector agendas. As such they could be seen as hybrid organizations rather than pure state-owned enterprises (SOEs) (Collinson and Sun, 2012). Government representatives were fully involved in the JV contracting process and all subsequent procurement, including related technology transfer and local training. However, rather than one unified 'China' interest group there were local rivalries and factions competing with each other to become the lead player, not a simple 'them-and-us' situation vis-à-vis foreign MNEs. As in other industries in China, even those with strong government intervention, a form of 'collaborative competition' drives learning.

We came across one example of this at the local level where the Chairman of the Board of the local joint venture partner was also the town Mayor. This gave rise to a number of benefits and constraints for the MNE relative to other foreign firms. This included preferential treatment through support from the Mayor's office and related government departments. In the most extreme case, this amounted to locking-out a foreign competitor looking to supply components to the Chinese partner through an exclusivity arrangement overseen directly by the Mayor's office. The strategic options open to the Western firm, however, were clearly limited by its partner's power, underpinned by public-sector patronage.

Airbus and Rolls-Royce are useful examples to illustrate the scale of investments in China by Western aerospace firms at the time of our study. Both were involved in a complex range of production joint ventures in aerospace clusters like Xian and Tianjin as a requirement of their investment in China, which provided access to the growing domestic market for civil aircraft. Airbus subcontracted around $60 million per year to five Chinese firms and was expecting this to double over the next five years (by 2014 its industrial turnover in China had reached over $450 million). Components made in China included A320 wing parts, passenger doors and landing gear components. Two major joint ventures were at the centre of Airbus operations in China, in the towns of Xian (Xian Aircraft Corporation with 28,000 employees) and Shenyang (Shenyang Aircraft Corporation with 20,000 employees). Both the local firms were SOEs operating under the AVIC1 umbrella organization.

Rolls-Royce supplied engines to many Chinese airlines and also had a number of key joint ventures, one of which was also in Xian. XR Aerocomponents Ltd (XRA) was a high-tech joint venture with the Xian Aero Engine Company that began in 1997 to cast and machine turbine nozzle guide vanes (NGV) and turbine blades. In 2002, XAE also became an approved classified parts supplier to Rolls-Royce. Other local suppliers included Sichuan ChengFa Aero Science and Technology Ltd (rings, sheet metal and fabrications), Beijing Aero Lever Precision Limited (VSV levers) and Shenyang Liming Aero-Engine Group Corporation (heat shield rings).

Companies like Airbus and Rolls-Royce have transferred manufacturing technology and put in place a range of training programmes to develop the local capabilities at these plants, and among local component suppliers. Rolls-Royce had a joint facility with CAAC in Tianjin, opened in 1997 for the training of technicians, engineers and managers. It had signed six training protocols with CAAC since 1990, including the CAAC Senior Executive Development Programme. While improved productivity was an important goal, the quality and reliability of the components produced here were far more important, given the safety-critical nature of the final product.

One of the joint ventures we examined most closely was dedicated to the local manufacture of wing-boxes, primarily for export to assembly operations in Europe. The local partner provided the premises and plant services in conjunction with local government agencies and the AVIC consortium. It was also responsible for sourcing and managing local suppliers. Both sides of the partnership provided assets in the form of manufacturing equipment and tooling. Factors such as cost, availability, and the need to customise processes to suit local materials and/or supplier capabilities influenced the form of contribution made by the local partner.

Process improvement and innovation at the plant level were measured by a number of indicators. These included output and productivity measures, which showed improvements in scrap yield (how much waste is produced at a plant), for example, and in 'concessions' (buyer's rejection of a component because of minor faults – such as inaccurately cut wing parts) and 'rework' (more substantial returns, accompanied by quality notes as feedback to the supplier). The increased use of quality circles, 'lean' management systems and techniques such as the use of 'visibility boards', which map out operations on the plant floor and monitor process changes, were all used as indicators of improvements in managerial and process-related capabilities. Other advances, such as a move from the use of 2-D to 3-D design drawings, demonstrated engineering, design and product-development innovations. All of which showed how local Chinese managers, engineers and plant-level personnel were learning through their interaction with Western counterparts. In this particular joint-venture operational processes, engineering skills and management capabilities for quality improvement were key asset-related FSAs that the Chinese partner lacked and the foreign MNE provided.

An important form of recombination was the continual adaptation of these processes and techniques to suit local labour, from experienced plant floor supervisors and engineering staff to inexperienced cheap labour. That is to say, capabilities were not so much 'transferred' as adapted and re-shaped in the training or on-the-job learning process to suit the level of local absorptive capacity at every level.

We now know that Chinese suppliers are beginning to have some success as first-tier suppliers to both Airbus and Boeing outside of China. Two suppliers from Tianjin are bidding to supply a new Airbus assembly plant in the USA and Hubei Ali Jiatai Aircraft Equipment Co Ltd, a subsidiary of AVIC, was awarded BFE (buyer furnished equipment) certificate (to supply seats) by The Boeing Co in 2014 (*China Daily USA*, 2014). We can see that these firms have evolved both the range of components they can make and the quality of their output to the point that they are part of the global supply chain for these leading Western firms.

9.7 Discussion

So what are the lessons we have learnt in relation to the challenge faced by China to accelerate knowledge creation and innovation and avoid stalling or hitting the middle-income trap by 2030? In the following discussion, we look at some that are relevant for management practice, but focus mainly on those with relevance for policy.

We do know more about the micro-level conditions that are conducive to certain kinds of recombinations of assets and capabilities for improving the innovation performance of local firms in partnership with MNEs in China. At this level the study provides insights into how firms 'trade' to exploit strengths and compensate for weaknesses. For example, superior technological skills and other FSAs held by MNEs were partly transferred to local partners in return for access to local customers. The data also shows how combinations of all of the four kinds of FSAs shown in Table 9.1 evolved out of various kinds of partnerships to create new FSAs. In our aerospace example, simplified processes were jointly developed to suit the capabilities of plant-level labour and the local supply chain. Similar examples of asset-related FSAs created by a reciprocal pooling of technology and capabilities for locally appropriate innovation were identified. Some of these resulting FSAs applied predominantly in the local Chinese context, providing both firms with additional domestic market advantages. Others were less location-bound, enabling the MNEs to leverage additional FSAs in other markets via existing intra-firm networks and enabling some local firms to internationalize.

9.7.1 Local rules of the game

The MNEs also gained transaction-related location-bound FSAs (Table 9.1) to compensate for their 'liabilities of foreignness', from local Chinese partners. The significance of these can only be fully realized if we understand how different and difficult some aspects of the China context are for foreign firms. Our survey, along with many others, shows how the difficulties faced by foreign firms in China stem from two distinctive sources. First, the anticipated limitations they have to cope with that are similar to those faced in other country markets, such as the lack of engineering and manufacturing skills, gaps in the supply chain, weak intellectual property rights and complex and costly customs procedures. Second, a range of unanticipated complexities and constraints related to widespread ambiguities in the application of laws and regulations in the China context (Collinson et al., 2007). Associated with this, contracting in China tends to be based around relationships and connections (*guanxi*) rather than formal, legal documents. These are the basis of mutual trust-making network 'connections' and institutional positioning more important as the basis for credibility and 'due-diligence' than formal methods of valuation (Kriz and Keating, 2010). These characteristics point to institutional voids, referred to earlier and elsewhere in this book. It not clear, however, that existing definitions of institutional voids quite captures these aspects of our findings.

Both had significant consequences for the activities of these firms and their local partners. But the local 'rules of the game' are (1) influenced by a great deal more than the direct and deliberate interventions of government agencies and (2) a major factor explaining the particular importance of the local partner's knowledge and relationships to the success of the partnership. In simple terms 'good' partners had the connections to overcome obstructive red tape and enable success; 'bad' partners had less or no power, knowledge or institutional leverage to deal with obstructive bureaucrats. These were key factors cited by respondents explaining why some partnerships were successfully sustained, with balanced reciprocity and a measurable improvement in the combined innovation capacity of the partners, while others were short-lived.

Companies in the survey also cited problems with other legacy issues related to joint ventures including: built-in obligations to retain certain individual employees and/or high levels of staffing which undermined efficient operations; long-standing ties to local or (less often) central agency politicians who may have formal roles in the firm, ownership claims or other means of influence; other obligations for payments to specific suppliers, contractors or customers which were economically not justifiable but needed to be honoured to maintain certain kinds of patronage.

The ex ante assessment of the value of other firms' assets and capabilities is difficult in any context, but important when entering into a reciprocal agreement to trade these for mutual gain. Because of the above-mentioned ambiguities, created by both formal and informal government intervention and by the nature of more general rules-of-the-game in China, the transaction-related FSAs of local Chinese firms were particularly difficult for MNEs to assess.

9.7.2 The effects of government interventions

Chinese firms are said to have thrived *because* of the actions of the state and Indian firms have thrived *despite* the actions of the state

(Ramamurti, 2013). This study clearly shows that this statement is rather too general. The motivation for, methods employed and effects of government intervention vary a great deal by industry sector, firm and partnership.

This study illustrates the variety of levels and types of intervention across two broad categories.

(1) Formal, policy-driven at the central, provincial and city or local levels. These include general laws governing business practices (particularly those that govern the activities of foreign firms and partnerships involving foreign firms), industry-specific policies, laws, regulations, tax incentives and so on.
(2) Informal influences of two basic kinds, reflecting the findings discussed above. First, ambiguities surrounding the application of the formal rules and regulations. Their application depends a great deal on context; who is applying them in what circumstances in relation to whom? Second, interventions by public-sector agencies or individuals which were clearly contrary to the formal protocols, including some forms of corruption (discussed below).

One of our MNE respondents explained this in terms of his 'Three Rules for Understanding China':

Rule 1: China is a highly regulated country, in which one needs to learn, understand and follow countless regulations.
Rule 2: China presents a chaotic and unpredictable operating environment in which anything is possible; in fact there are no rules.
Rule 3: Rules 1 and 2 are simultaneously valid.

This is an important backdrop to understand the positive and negative effects of government interventions. We identified a range of positive effects of government action on the development of firm-level innovation capabilities. But there are wide variations depending on the industry context.

Our analysis of the aerospace industry presents a special case, compared to other industries we studied. It illustrates a number of positive effects of government involvement well, with powerful agencies acting as the main gatekeepers limiting access for foreign firms to location-bound assets, capabilities and markets. The cost of gaining access to the rapidly growing commercial aerospace market in China was higher for the MNEs in our study. Access was only legally possible through a series of joint ventures and local partnerships involving a considerable transfer of technology and capabilities for high-quality manufacturing, design and R&D. Government agencies not only built this into initial contracts and monitored progress but they also co-invested in the infrastructure and managed the process of training to improve indigenous capabilities in this industry. These agencies therefore closely stage-managed the co-production of new knowledge and capabilities for locally appropriate product and process innovation.

The AVIC governance structure coordinates a wide variety of policy mechanisms, including:

- foreign ownership regulations including mandatory joint ventures for flagship firms
- import and export quotas and taxes
- joint training, industry standards-setting and R&D investments
- requirements over the growing proportion of locally manufactured content in components and sub-assemblies
- quality and safety legislation
- complementary investment in supply-chain capabilities.

This represents a targeted intervention to develop indigenous industry-specific capabilities, in precisely the fashion advocated by structural economists, to develop, over time, a world-leading aerospace industry in China. The above actions influence parts of the NSI relevant to the aerospace industry alongside firm-level effects that facilitate local innovation. The evidence suggests that it has been successful in that we found a measurable improvement in the level of process innovation (productivity, scrap yield, concessions, etc.) and product innovation (quality, in-built reliability and safety, etc.) achieved in the partnerships through recombination and in local suppliers through learning.

There is of course no benchmark to test this proposition robustly. We cannot tell what would have taken place without any of the above-mentioned government interventions. There were also some negative consequences we identified in the study. It was noted, for example, that small and medium-sized firms (SMEs; both MNEs and local firms) either did not benefit from the formal policies in place (they sometimes did from the informal interventions, if they had the right connections) or were actively discriminated against by the government focus on large firms and SOEs. This finding mirrors those described by John Child in this volume. He presents findings from a broader range of studies citing "institutional constraints on the innovation activities of SMEs due to unfair competition from large firms (both SOEs and foreign firms) due to preferential treatment by government agencies".

At a more general level the uncertainties and ambiguities resulting from the 'local rules of the game' described above had a number of effects on the MNEs we studied. It was clear that this was a key factor influencing many MNEs to invest less in China and/or invest across a more limited range of business functions and activities. The aerospace firms, for example, did not establish global centres of R&D in mainland China because of such uncertainties, including fears about the robustness of IPR regulations. The difficulty of conducting proper due diligence prior to market entry was also a factor mentioned by respondents.

But we would suggest that the most important impact, not of government intervention per se but resulting from the informal influences described above, was to shorten the lifespan of many of the partnerships we studied. They were a destabilizing factor which caused partnerships to end prematurely, curtailing the positive effects of asset and capability recombinations observed most strongly in the more sustained partnerships.

This was observed as a net effect across the survey. However, it is interesting to note that a variety of outcomes, both positive and negative in terms of the development of enhanced innovative capacity, were identified in specific examples of such interventions. The above-mentioned case of the local Mayor also holding the role of Chairman of the Board of the local joint venture partner in the aerospace industry case study provides a concise illustration of this. This was an explicit case of corruption, if we accept the definition put forward by Transparency International, "the abuse of entrusted power for private gain" (www.transparency.org/whoweare/organisation/faqs_on_corruption/2/). At one level it helped local firms by compelling the MNE to transfer more technology and IPR and invest in more local training to local firms in which senior officials had a personal interest (usually part-ownership). But it also had a significant negative effect on the behaviour of the MNE and the sustainability of the partnership.

Overall we would say that the partnerships that managed to maintain reciprocity based on trust, without the self-serving interventions of local policymakers, lasted longer and resulted in a greater degree of joint capability development. To facilitate this requires a continued purge on minor and major corruption in China, alongside greater clarity and predictability in the application of rules and regulations. This requires a broad systemic change in the rules of the game, but not necessarily a reduction in government intervention. Our findings do not support a government that tries to directly pick winners but one that leverages its own power in the market in a wide variety of targeted ways to tip the playing field in favour of accelerated local innovation capability development.

9.7.3 Towards more precise interventions

If we adopt Bruce Kogut's helpful framing (2003), we might view many of the above factors as 'developmental constraints' on the adaptive behaviour of both MNEs and their local partners. Purposeful interventions by governments to develop their economies need to be better-informed by a deeper understanding of the idiosyncratic effects of these developmental constraints. They may be direct or indirect, formal or informal but the sheer variety of contexts which they aim to influence (region, industry, firm, technology, value chain, etc.) makes macro-level, generic, imprecise approaches highly imperfect.

This highlights a number of lessons for governments and for potential areas for future research. In terms of lessons for government one of our central findings is the need for more precise interventions in markets. More specifically, from our study:

- Targeted investments in particular kinds of training to fill skills deficits are needed in order to accelerate local capability development in particular value-chain activities;
- Focusing government support on capital goods equipment, both easing restrictions on specific imports and promoting local development of technology which enables other innovation-related capabilities (precision measurement instruments are an example in aerospace and other kinds of advanced manufacturing);
- A refinement of the benefits and reduction of constraints placed on small firms who make up the major part of local industry supply chains and are hugely adaptive *despite* a biased playing field;

- A continued, but more refined purge on the negative effects of corruption, beyond the generic 'tigers and flies' approach to limit the misallocation of finance and realign incentives structures around capability development. Part of the difficulty is that the mechanisms for intervention (e.g. City or provincial government agencies as the channels of public sector investments) are sometimes the mechanisms for misappropriation;
- Using public-sector procurement (which is a powerful lever in China) to preference certain kinds of local firms in partnership with MNEs, through targeted technology transfer and training.

Further comparative research is clearly needed, given that the approach advocated here is for a more precise and tailored set of government interventions to improve innovation capacity-building. There are clearly costs, as well as benefits, involved in customizing policies and applying them at the local level. These need to be understood far better before dedicating significant effort or resources. Comparisons between industry sectors and within sectors, across different regions and local contexts in China as well as across international locations would help reveal more about how contexts and therefore local economic growth potential varies. These would also reveal how existing government interventions are having different effects across the above dimensions.

This should be done in tandem with the development of better ways of, conceptually and empirically, linking the micro-level foundations of learning, capability-building and innovativeness to the macro-level patterns of industry change and national competitiveness. On the one hand, this means more 'deep dives' tracing macro-level changes in productivity, GDP growth or export competitiveness to specific local contexts where capacity-building is taking place. On the other hand, it means measuring the aggregate effects of many different local interventions in adaptive behaviour which shape how firms interact and learn.

References

Bell, M. (1984) 'Learning and the accumulation of industrial technological capacity in developing countries', in King, K. and Fransman, M. (Eds.), *Technological Capability in the Third World*, London: Macmillan.

Bell, M. and Figueiredo, P.N. (2012) 'Innovation capability building and learning mechanisms in latecomer firms: Recent empirical contributions and implications for research', *Canadian Journal of Development Studies*, 33: 1, 14–40.

Bell, M. and Pavitt, K. (1997) 'Technological accumulation and industrial growth: Contrasts between developed and developing countries', in Archibugi D. and Michie, J. (Eds.), *Technology, Globalisation and Economic Performance*, Cambridge: Cambridge University Press.

Berggren, C., Bergek, A., Bengtsson, L., Saderlund, J. and Hobday, M. (2011) *Knowledge Integration and Innovation: Critical Challenges Facing International Technology-Based Firms*, 2nd Ed., Oxford: Oxford University Press.

Birkinshaw, J. (2000) *Entrepreneurship in the Global Firm*, London: Sage.

Bloom, N. et al. (2014) 'Trapped Factors and China's Impact on Global Growth', CEP Discussion Paper No 1261, http://eprints.lse.ac.uk/60272 /1/dp1261.pdf.

Boeing, P. and Sandner, P. (2012) 'The Innovative Performance of China's National Innovation System', Frankfurt School – Working Paper Series, No. 158.

Cantwell, J.A. (1989) *Technological Innovation and Multinational Corporations*, Oxford: Basil Blackwell.

Cantwell, J.A., Dunning, J.H. and Lundan, S.M. (2010) 'An evolutionary approach to understanding international business activity: The co-evolution of MNEs and the institutional environment', *Journal of International Business Studies*, 41, 567–586.

Cantwell, J.A. and Janne, O. (2000) 'The role of multinational corporations and national states in the globalisation of innovatory capacity: The European perspective', *Technology Analysis and Strategic Management*, 12: 2, 243–262.

China Daily USA (2014) 'Airbus to use Tianjin as delivery hub' by Lu Haoting, 2014-06-17. http://usa.chinadaily.com.cn/epaper/2014-06/17/con tent_17594611.htm.

Collinson, S.C. (2009) 'The MNE as the major global promoter of economic development', in Collinson, S.C. and Morgan, G. (Eds.), *Images of the Multinational Firm*, Ch. 4, 69–92, Oxford: Wiley.

Collinson, S.C. (2013) 'Cross-border M&A by the new multinationals: Different reasons to "go global"', in Williamson, P.J., Ramamurti, R., Fleury, A. and Fleury, M., (Eds.), *The Competitive Advantage of Emerging Market Multinationals*, Cambridge: Cambridge University Press.

Collinson, S.C. and Narula, R. (2014) 'Asset recombination in international partnerships as a source of improved innovation capabilities in China', *The Multinational Business Review*, 22: 4, 394–417.

Collinson, S.C., Sullivan-Taylor, B. and Wang, J.L. (2007) *Adapting to the China Challenge: Lessons from Experienced Multinationals*, London: Advanced Institute of Management (AIM), Executive Briefing.

Collinson, S.C. and Sun, Y. (2012) 'Corporate hybrids and the co-evolution of institutions and enterprise in China', in Pearce, R. (Ed.), *China and the Multinationals: International Business and the Entry of China into the Global Economy*, Cheltenham: Edward Elgar.

Collinson, S.C. and Wang, R. (J.L.) (2012) 'Learning networks and technological capability in multinational enterprise subsidiaries', *Research Policy*, 41: 9, 1501–1518.

Dantas, E. and Bell, M. (2009) 'Latecomer firms and the emergence and development of knowledge networks: The case of Petrobras in Brazil', *Research Policy* 38: 5, 829–844

De Meyer, A. (1992) 'Management of international R&D operations', in Granstrand, O., Hakanson, L., Sjolander, S. (Eds.), *Technology Management and International Business: Internationalisation of R&D and Technology*, Chichester: John Wiley.

Dosi, G. et al. (eds.) (1988) *Technical Change and Economic Theory*, London: Pinter Publishers.

Hennart, J.-F. (2009) 'Down with MNE-centric theories! Market entry and expansion as the bundling of MNE and local assets', *Journal of International Business Studies*, 40: 9, 1432–1454.

Hobday, M. (2007) 'Editor's introduction: The scope of Martin Bell's contribution', *Asian Journal of Technology Innovation*, 15: 2, 1–18.

Hobday, M., and Rush, H. (2007) 'Upgrading the technological capabilities of foreign transnational subsidiaries in developing countries: The case of electronics in Thailand', *Research Policy* 36, 1335–1356.

Kharas, H. (2009) *China's Transition to a High Income Economy: Escaping the Middle Income Trap*, Washington, DC: Brookings Institution.

Kim, L. (1997) *Imitation to Innovation: The Dynamics of Korea's Technological Learning*, Boston: Harvard Business Review Press.

Kogut, B. (1993) *Country Competitiveness: Technology and the Organization of Work*, New York: Oxford University Press.

Kogut, B. (2003) 'From regions and firms to multinational highways', Chapter 10 in Kenney, M. and Florida, R. (Eds.), *Locating Global Advantage: Industry Dynamics in the International Economy*

(Innovation and Technology in the World Economy), Stanford: Stanford University Press.

Kriz, A. and Keating, B. W. (2010) 'Business relationships in china: Lessons about deep trust', *Asia Pacific Business Review*, 16: 3, 299–318.

Lall, S. (1992) 'Technological capabilities and industrialization', *World Development*, 20: 2, 165–186.

Lin, J.Y. (2012) *New Structural Economics*, Washington, DC: World Bank.

Lundvall, B.A. (1992) *National Systems of Innovation: Towards a Theory of Innovation and Interactive Learning*, London: Pinter.

Lundvall, B. Å. (2007) 'National innovation systems – Analytical concept and development tool', *Industry and Innovation*, 14: 1, 95–119.

Luo, Y. and Child, J. (2015) 'A Composition-Based View of Firm Growth', *Management and Organization Review*, 11, 379–411.

Luo, Y. and Tung, R. (2007) 'International expansion of emerging market enterprises: A springboard perspective', *Journal of International Business Studies*, 38: 4, 481–498.

Nelson, R. R. (Ed.) (1993) *National Innovation Systems: A Comparative Study*, New York: Oxford University Press.

Puffer, S.M., McCarthy, D.J. and Boisot, M. (2010) 'Entrepreneurship in Russia and China: The impact of formal institutional voids', *Entrepreneurship Theory and Practice*, 34: 3, 441–467.

Ramamurti, R. (2013) 'The role of international M&A in building the competitive advantage of Indian firms', in Williamson, P.J., Ramamurti, R., Fleury, A. and Fleury, M. (Eds.), *The Competitive Advantage of Emerging Market Multinationals*, Cambridge: Cambridge University Press.

Rugman A.M. (2009) 'Theoretical aspects of MNEs from emerging markets', Chapter 3 in Ramamurti, R. and Singh, J.V. (Eds.), *Emerging Multinationals in Emerging Markets*, Cambridge: Cambridge University Press.

Rugman, A.M. and Collinson, S.C. (2012) *International Business*, 6th Ed., Harlow: FT Pearson/Prentice Hall.

Rugman, A.M. and Doh, J. (2008) *Multinationals and Development*, New Haven, CT: Yale University Press.

Santangelo, G.D. and Meyer, K.E. (2011) 'Extending the internationalization process model: Increases and decreases of MNE commitment in emerging economies', *Journal of International Business Studies*, 42, 894–909.

Verbeke, A. (2009) *International Business Strategy: Rethinking the Foundations of Global Corporate Success*, Cambridge: Cambridge University Press.

Wang, F., Fu, X. and Chen, J. (2014) 'Differential forms of technological change and catch-up: Evidence from China', *International Journal of Technology Management*, 11: 2, 1–25.

Williamson, P.J., Ramamurti, R., Fleury, A. and Fleury, M. (Eds.) (2013) *The Competitive Advantage of Emerging Market Multinationals*, Cambridge: Cambridge University Press.

Williamson, P.J. and Yin, E. (2014) 'Accelerated innovation: The new challenge from China', *MIT Sloan Management Review*, Summer. http://sloanreview.mit.edu.

World Bank and the Development Research Center of the State Council, the People's Republic of China (2013) *China 2030: Building a Modern, Harmonious, and Creative Society*. www.worldbank.org/content/dam/Worldbank/document/China-2030-overview.pdf.

10 Advantages and challenges for Chinese MNEs in global competition

YVES DOZ AND KEELEY WILSON

Globalisation exerts a profound impact on the way multinational firms organise and manage their innovation activities over time. The evolution and transformation from local to regional to globally integrated innovation in developed economies' multinational enterprises (MNEs) has been well researched and articulated in terms of optimal organisational structures, knowledge flows and competence development (e.g., Prahalad & Doz, 1987; Bartlett & Ghoshal, 1989; Cantwell & Janne, 1999; Doz, Santos & Williamson, 2001; Doz & Wilson, 2012; Govindarajan & Trimble, 2012). From the 1990s onwards, the fact that the innovation activities of 'tiger economy' firms developed along a similar trajectory to that taken by their developed MNE counterparts a few decades earlier (in a compressed time frame) reinforced a tacit but well-understood assumption about how firms develop their technological, managerial and organisational capabilities to move from local to global innovation (Mathews & Zander, 2007). However, our observations of leading Chinese firms point to them following a different path towards global innovation, driven by the convergence of a unique set of factors – an enormous and somewhat protected domestic market, lagging home-based resources and rapid internationalisation. In this chapter, we explore both the advantages and challenges facing Chinese firms in relation to upgrading their innovation capabilities to enable them to capture and leverage diverse and dispersed knowledge to build competitive advantage. We begin by outlining why and how Chinese companies are following a different path from that taken by other MNEs and highlight the managerial and organisational implications of this. Based on this exploration we outline a research agenda for better understanding the globalisation of innovation in Chinese firms.

10.1 Global innovation and Chinese firms: challenging conventional wisdom

According to what has become conventional wisdom, uniquely stimulated by their national context, firms first innovate and create new products, components, services or business models specifically designed to serve needs in their home market (Vernon, 1966; Porter, 1990). In the next phase, these home-grown innovations are exported or licensed to foreign markets. Driven by a variety of factors, including cost advantage, responsiveness to local customers, overcoming trade barriers or protecting intellectual property, the innovating firm often invests in overseas manufacturing at this time. As the firm grows, diversifies and needs to access new markets and capabilities, it moves into a third phase in which it adopts a multi-domestic or transnational structure (Bartlett & Ghoshal, 1989) whereby the firm organises its global innovation activities around individual, standalone businesses located in strong local knowledge hubs. While this type of structure brings locally obtained international comparative advantage, it remains a home-centric innovation model, albeit with multiple homes.

A key characteristic of innovation up to this point is that knowledge flows are predominantly unidirectional, from the headquarters or 'lead subsidiaries' of various businesses to subsidiaries (Bartlett & Ghoshal, 1989; Zander & Kogut, 1995). However, as distinct capabilities develop in individual markets (which may involve the growth of knowledge clusters around specific technologies or local ecosystems) and new customer requirements emerge (including low-cost, frugal innovations), some local subsidiaries become experts in specific domains, resulting in the need for a radical overhaul of traditional knowledge flows: Headquarters and lead subsidiaries cease to be the only origin of critical knowledge but instead have to learn from their subsidiaries. At the same time, the adoption of polycentric networks facilitates learning and knowledge transfer across dispersed networks of subsidiaries.

Wider trends have accelerated this evolution of innovation from home-centric control to distributed network. Since the early 2000s, changing demographics, industry convergence, increasing technology complexity, digitalisation, the emergence of new consumer markets and offshore outsourcing – initially of manufacturing and later of engineering and development work – have resulted in a greater dispersion and diversity of the critical knowledge needed for innovation. In this emerging context, the dominant twentieth-century paradigm of 'innovation as science-based original creation' is being replaced by the notion of innovation as bringing together existing knowledge from multiple sources and combining this to create something new. Knowledge integration gains precedence over knowledge creation. This in turn is having a significant impact on the organisation and management of innovation, as neither home- nor host-centric approaches are adequate for integrating knowledge from sources distributed in multiple locations. A globally integrated approach is emerging that transcends firms' boundaries and relies on culture, tools and processes to deliver strong communication, receptivity and collaboration.

In contrast to this well-researched process of the globalisation of innovation in developed economies' MNEs, there is very little understanding of the relatively recent phenomenon of the internationalisation of innovation in Chinese MNEs (Di Minin et al., 2012; Awate et al., 2015). Scholars undertaking research in this field face numerous challenges, ranging from a lack of clarity about the role of national policy in driving individual firm strategies, to the lack of reliable data at the national and firm level, to limited access to research targets willing to open up to outside scrutiny. In spite of these impediments, observing the patterns of globalisation of innovation in pioneer Chinese firms, including BGI, Haier, Huawei, Sany, Lenovo and ZTE amongst others, we have found that these firms are not following the conventional wisdom trajectory from exploiting home-based advantages through to capturing and leveraging host-based advantages. Instead, they are opening a unique path in response to a combination of home market and capability factors.

The first factor differentiating the Chinese approach to globalising innovation is the size and nature of the domestic market. Intense domestic competition coupled with large numbers of demanding middle-market local customers and fast economic growth has led to a rapid cycle, customer-centric model of innovation. Yet China's middle-market consumers do not demand the customisation and advanced technologies so important to developed market consumers but require products and services 'good enough' to meet their needs (Zablit & Chui, 2013). Working with razor-thin margins and fit-for-purpose offerings, Chinese firms have become adept at constantly listening to and learning from customers to discover latent needs and then rapidly developing new goods, services and underlying processes to meet those needs (Veldhoen et al., 2012).

The second factor is the speed at which China is embracing globalisation. At the national policy level this is being driven by the *zou chuqu* or 'go out' policy that from 2000 not only permitted Chinese firms to acquire foreign companies for the first time but encouraged them to expand abroad to acquire assets that would enable them, and China, to move up the value chain. This policy has had a significant impact on the growth of Chinese outbound mergers and acquisitions, which in 2013 was valued at US$68.9 billion. At the firm level, instead of waiting until they are large to internationalise, Chinese MNEs are using international expansion and in particular acquisitions in order to grow (Bonaglia et al., 2007).

In addition to embarking on overseas acquisitions as a platform for growth, ambitious Chinese firms are also undertaking rapid globalisation to advanced markets in order to overcome the third factor marking the Chinese approach to the globalisation of innovation unique – namely, competitive disadvantage from lagging technology, marketing and managerial resources at home (Rui & Yip, 2008; Abrami et al., 2014). Whereas traditionally MNEs evolved into distributing innovative activities after relying exclusively on the superior technologies and capabilities of their home base, Chinese firms often deliberately expand their innovation activities to developed economies to acquire strategic resources and advanced innovation capabilities in order to develop a differentiation advantage (Child & Rodrigues 2005; Deng, 2007) and overcome constraints at home (Luo & Tung, 2007). Take the example of heavy machinery producer Sany. In 2009, it established a $144 million R&D and manufacturing base in Germany. Two years later it announced it would open a new $25 million R&D centre in the United States. In addition to providing the firm with access to world-class technologies, talent, suppliers and standards, Sany explained that they would also benefit by being able to sell products that were 'made in the US' and 'made in Germany' and thus overcome the widely held association, prevalent even in other developing markets, of 'made in China' with inferior quality.

Faced with a large and challenging home market, the speed of internationalisation and home-based competitive disadvantage, Chinese firms are pursuing a different approach to globalising their innovation activities. In contrast to traditional models, it appears that Chinese firms first venture abroad to learn, explore and remedy disadvantages rather than exploit their home-based advantages. Current patterns of foreign acquisitions by Chinese firms show a strong tendency for acquisition targets to be firms with mature technologies and solid brands in the same sector as the acquiring firm. By focusing acquisitions on familiar mature industries and products, where knowledge is likely to be explicit and modular (in well-defined subsystems and components), Chinese firms reduce the burden and risks of learning from their acquisitions. From what we have observed, Chinese firms tend to leave the local management in place – when it acquired German firm Putzmeister, Sany issued the local management team with new five-year contracts, and when they make foreign acquisitions both Huawei and Haier keep local management in place with only light oversight from headquarters. This approach avoids an unfamiliar Chinese management inadvertently destroying value in their acquisition and allows the acquisition sites to 'teach' headquarters about technology, marketing and management.

In addition to accessing technologies and capabilities, once a foreign R&D centre has been acquired or established, Chinese firms place a strong emphasis on learning from local customers in the new markets they enter and this knowledge informs the rest of the value chain, in what is described as reverse capability upgrading (Fu, 2015). This facet of the emerging Chinese innovation globalisation model perhaps most closely exhibits elements of the transnational approach: Rather than integrate the knowledge acquired from local customers with either headquarters or other nodes in their innovation network to create global offerings, the knowledge tends to remain local and is used primarily to improve products and services for the local customer group. Looking at Sany Heavy Industry again, product innovation for its European customers is served from its German operations, while its US subsidiary focuses on innovations for its local markets. The fact that learning remains local points to a lack of capabilities within Chinese firms to successfully innovate using dispersed knowledge sources. While Collinson's chapter (Chapter 9, this book) shows that Chinese firms have been successful at collaborating with Western MNEs, it is worth noting that this has taken place within the familiar context of China and has been based on technology learning and not original innovation.

Despite Zhang and Zhong elsewhere in this volume outlining the barriers Chinese firms face to becoming more innovative, we would suggest that compared with their more established developed country counterparts, large Chinese firms in fact enjoy a number of advantages when setting out to internationalise their innovation activities. They are not constrained by legacies of technology path dependence (Awate et al., 2015) or costly, bloated innovation footprints that are more a reflection of a firm's historical activity than current knowledge requirements. They are capital rich. And, by focusing on strategies that seek out new knowledge from customers in all of their operating markets and technologies and capabilities from developed country subsidiaries, Chinese firms have thus far avoided institutionalising the dominance of the home base, which is a major impediment to integrated global innovation.

Whether the advantages currently favouring leading Chinese firms translate into the flexibility and agility that leads to sustainable competitive advantage depends upon their ability to overcome the inherent challenges in organising and managing an integrated global innovation network. Effective global innovation networks are built on two basic principles: first that each site contributes unique and differentiated knowledge, and second that a high level of knowledge integration between sites is achieved to enable complex (tacit and context-dependent) knowledge to be melded across the global network.

To date, Chinese firms have performed well in terms of innovation when the new knowledge they have accessed and incorporated is closely related to their core knowledge base but have not fared so well when knowledge is more distant (Li-Ying et al., 2014). In fact, John Child explains how Chinese small and medium enterprises (SMEs), a group vital to driving and upgrading innovation in an economy, eschew distant knowledge in favour of imitation and incremental innovation (Chapter 8, this volume). By favouring the acquisition of firms with mature, modular and familiar technologies, Chinese headquarters have been able to learn from their foreign subsidiaries and use this knowledge to improve their offerings at home. However, it is unlikely that this strategy has enabled them to improve their absorptive capacity for integrating more distant, context-dependent and radically different leading-edge knowledge, a capability that helped propel Japanese firms from local to global innovators from the 1980s onwards.

If Chinese firms are to evolve from being deft imitators to skilful innovators and knowledge integrators, they will need to think strategically about optimising their innovation footprints and improving their absorptive capacity by fostering stronger communication and collaboration. Investigating the structures, processes and culture adopted by Chinese firms that enable the headquarters to learn from the periphery, the extent to which knowledge also flows outwards from headquarters to subsidiaries and the mechanisms by which knowledge is assessed and integrated would be a worthwhile area of future research in furthering our understanding of the nascent Chinese model of global innovation. It would also inform how Chinese firms might upgrade their innovation capabilities and ability to leverage globally integrated innovation.

10.2 Optimising innovation footprints

In the first stages of internationalisation, the logics underlying the innovation footprints of many leading Chinese firms have been driven by the need to access technologies and capabilities to overcome their home-based disadvantages as discussed earlier. The extent to which this also applies to state-owned enterprises (SOEs) is unclear as unlike in Korea, where the government's succession of five-year national growth plans were translated directly into chaebol strategies and investments, in China, the link between national policy and SOEs is less transparent. However, as leading Chinese firms outgrow their catch-up strategies and look towards global innovation, they increasingly face the challenge of building and maintaining an innovation footprint that avoids duplication and redundancy and is firmly focused on value creation at every stage of the innovation process.

Each node or site in an innovation network should have a specific purpose and make a unique contribution to the whole. It should complement existing activities and contribute diverse and differentiated knowledge and competencies to the development of new products or services. An example of a Chinese firm that has adopted this type of footprint design in which each site is located to access specific knowledge or tap into a local knowledge eco-system is BGI (formerly Beijing Genomics Institute). Each BGI innovation centre accesses unique complex knowledge that contributes to the group's global capabilities: In Cambridge, Massachusetts, the headquarters of BGI Americas is located in a leading biotech cluster encompassing academic research institutes, pharmaceutical companies and leading research hospitals that BGI partners with. BGI's acquisition of Complete Genomics based in Mountain View, California, gave the group access not only to the design and manufacture of DNA sequencing machines but to the high-tech Silicon Valley cluster. In Davis, California, it partnered with the world's premier agricultural college at the University of California, Davis, to work on the very complicated genomics of plants. In Laos, a fertile agrarian economy, BGI focuses on life sciences, using its genetics database and conventional selective breeding methods to develop better strains of staple foods such as rice, grains and fish critical for the economic development of emerging countries. While Hong Kong is home to the group's global information and logistics centres due to its strong English-language skills, geographical location and unique history as a gateway to China.

The twin pressures of managing costs and the increase in the rate of change (in cycle times, technology development and new market growth) make it essential for innovation footprints to be actively and strategically managed. This point is particularly pertinent for Chinese firms which over the last decade or so have established global footprints mainly via acquisitions of foreign companies with already mature technologies. Disruptive or game-changing innovations in the future are just as likely to come from adjacent industries or new knowledge clusters which can reshape the geographic map of an industry and result in the need for changes in the mandate, management, and internal and external linkages of an existing site.

The world's most innovative firms keep abreast of emerging knowledge hotspots by establishing small 'discovery' innovation units in locations that are the harbingers of change due to unique social or geographic features, accelerated learning environments that support rapid cycle experimentation or regulatory environments that force alternative approaches to be developed (Wilson & Doz, 2011). The purpose of these units is to be in locations that challenge a firm's and industry's orthodoxies and assumptions, thereby forcing them to examine unfamiliar perspectives that may yield new knowledge or knowledge combinations. As Chinese firms seem reluctant to publish or talk about their innovation activities, we can only surmise that with the exception of a few leading firms, including Haier and Huawei, it is unlikely Chinese multinationals are currently designing their innovation footprints and strategies to include discovery units. Yet the speed at which many Chinese firms are developing innovation capabilities would indicate the need for them to start thinking about accessing leading-edge knowledge on a broader front rather than very targeted efforts (such as Huawei recruiting ex-Nokia software developers in Helsinki to build new mobile operating systems). Therefore, research into innovation footprint strategies of Chinese firms would be helpful to corporates and policymakers alike.

There are additional challenges facing developed economy MNEs in the management of their innovation footprints, and the relevance of these for Chinese firms can only be hypothesised about until focused research has been undertaken. First, innovation networks are difficult to co-ordinate and teams in different locations tend to compete rather than collaborate. The barriers to collaboration, including NIH (not invented here) syndrome, NUH (not understood here), fears over potential job losses, language barriers and distrust of people from unfamiliar cultures or competing units, can derail a firm's innovation strategy if not openly addressed. Second, innovation sites can suffer from a 'walled city' syndrome in that they do not have adequate links with the local innovation eco system to add value. Western companies fell victim to this in Japan as they lacked the contextual knowledge as well as contacts to forge meaningful links with Japanese partners and universities and hire the best Japanese engineers. Finally, having a permanent and costly innovation centre in a given location is only necessary when the knowledge being sought is complex, systemic, locally rooted, held in norms, behaviour or cultural assumptions, is highly diffuse and will only be revealed through a process of localised learning. Otherwise, less costly approaches to knowledge access can be sought via flexible temporary learning and foraying expeditions to access technological knowledge embedded in a local context or explicit, codified knowledge can be sought through knowledge intermediaries and open-source solutions.

10.3 Enhancing communication and absorptive capacity

A global innovation footprint has little value without integration across the network. Yet integration does not imply a one size fits all, centrally imposed approach to the management of sites, reporting, incentives, assessment and processes, as individual sites are subject to unique local contexts and can play very different roles in the network.

As different types of knowledge have varying characteristics and degrees of 'stickiness', multiple approaches are necessary to avoid knowledge being imprisoned locally, from systems to share codified knowledge to mechanisms and processes to connect the holders of complex knowledge (e.g., communities of practice, temporary co-location including secondments in dispersed projects and bi-cultural managers bridging contexts). Yet, there are systemic barriers to optimising communication across a dispersed network: People tend to limit communication to other people they know and usually have few incentives to reach out beyond this group; different contexts between locations as well as functions in the value chain are an impediment to communication; transferring complex, context-dependent knowledge from one location to another without losing its meaning is extremely difficult; and without a corporate culture of transparency, collaboration and reciprocity, absorptive capacity will remain low.

Based on current patterns of their innovation globalisation, Chinese MNEs could have a significant advantage over their longer-established competitors with regard to fostering strong communication links across their networks. The headquarters of many developed economy firms are victims of a 'projector mind-set' in which the belief in the supremacy of the home market manifests itself in knowledge being transferred in one direction only, from the headquarters to subsidiaries. In contrast, Chinese MNEs internationalised innovation on the premise of learning from subsidiaries in advanced markets. Whether Chinese firms will be able to extend these knowledge flows beyond the bipartite headquarters–subsidiary relationship to a wider network of connectivity will depend upon them being able to build a culture of reciprocity needed to support the processes, tools and mechanisms for knowledge sharing and make them effective. A few seem to be moving in that direction. Haier, for instance, has product and technology R&D centres outside China that work directly with its software development centre in India.

Given adequate tools and an open collaborative culture in place, sharing explicit, codified knowledge is a relatively straightforward process. Sharing locally rooted, tacit knowledge beyond a co-located sphere, however, is much more of a challenge and perhaps one in which Chinese MNEs have another natural advantage. The success of transferring, absorbing and integrating complex knowledge often relies upon bi-cultural managers – that is, people who have deep and ingrained experience of more than one culture. Their cultural sensitivity and understanding of the subtleties of different cultural cues, norms and behaviours gives them an insight and ability to decontextualise knowledge from one context and transfer it to another. The large diaspora of overseas Chinese and the flow of returnees to China are uniquely positioned to act as bridges within Chinese MNE global networks for sharing and melding diverse and differentiated complex knowledge. Since 2008, a raft of government initiatives to recruit overseas Chinese talent has resulted in an estimated 20,000 high-level overseas Chinese returning to China (Wang, 2013), mostly in the fields of science, technology and higher education. It is estimated that over 70 per cent of directors of key national laboratories and around 80 per cent of academicians in the Chinese Academy of Science (Wang, 2013) were educated outside China. Added to this, ever-greater numbers of Chinese students are studying abroad. Historically over two-thirds of Chinese overseas students settled permanently in the countries they studied in, but in recent years a combination of weak economies in the West and greater opportunities in China has resulted in record numbers of students returning – in 2014 alone 365,000 returned (Zhao & Sun, 2015) – despite increasing resentment towards returnees over the higher salaries they command and favourable access to research grants they enjoy.

10.4 Optimising collaboration

Collaboration is critical for global innovation on two levels: First, intra-firm collaboration across co-specialised, dispersed sites is the only way to access and meld the differentiated knowledge needed to create a pipeline of innovations. Though successful collaboration and co-operation requires more than the effective implementation of knowledge-sharing tools and leveraging bi-cultural managers – it is based on trust and mutual respect. People working in co-located, close-proximity environments share cultural assumptions and behaviours and are cognisant of each other's commitment, ability and integrity. Conversely, geographic and cultural distances are impediments to trust (Doney et al., 1998; Jarvenpaa & Leidner, 1999; Ferrin et al., 2006). Unfortunately, there is a lack of qualitative research into the working relationships between Chinese MNE headquarters and their foreign subsidiaries to offer insight into the extent to which trust has been built and the mechanisms used to achieve this. However, anecdotal evidence from the research experience of colleagues points to discrepancies between senior management interpretations of strategic rationales and goals at Chinese headquarters and their overseas operations, which could signify a lack of trust and inability to collaborate effectively. It would seem that while Chinese MNEs have been very successful in building multi-domestic, transnational-type organisations which rely on co-located innovation at a handful of lead sites, for most the transformation to a globally integrated approach will prove much more difficult as it calls for a fundamental change in the practice of innovation and the organisational culture needed to support this.

The second type of collaboration which has become a more critical aspect of innovation over the last decade is that of co-ideation, co-creation and co-diffusion with external partners – as distinct from co-development with suppliers or joint-venture market access relationships. Increasingly technology complexity and knowledge dispersion across specialisms together with the increased costs and risks of innovation are forcing firms to look outside their organisational boundaries for knowledge and capabilities. Though once again, trust plays a major role in the willingness of firms to enter joint learning alliances. However, a weak, though improving IP protection regime in China (see Cheng and Huang, Chapter 7 in this volume, for more detail), uncertainty about the role of the state in directing the innovation and globalisation strategies of Chinese firms (even private ones) and a recent history of often blatant copying by Chinese firms of technologies and designs belonging to Western and Japanese companies have engendered mistrust between foreign companies and would-be Chinese partners.

Some Chinese firms have been able to transcend the trust barrier by being open, transparent, highly innovative and proving themselves to be good partners. BGI, for example, began life as a participant of the Human Genome Project and a big part of its subsequent business model has been partnering with research institutes, hospitals and pharmaceutical companies around the world. Other Chinese firms have focused on building trust with potential foreign partners by hiring high-profile, credible local management teams, though as few of these 'star' hires

appear to stay long at the Chinese subsidiaries, the degree of trust this
approach builds is questionable.

Chapters by both Redding and Child note that mistrust and strong
hierarchy are engrained features of Chinese society. The resulting cultural reticence to collaborate with people outside one's own *guanxi*
network, combined with weak IP/contract enforcement and poor legal
and judicial systems, seriously impedes Chinese firms' ability to engage
in more open (and increasingly common) forms of innovation.
In addition, Chiu, Liou and Kwan (Chapter 14, this volume) contend
that there is a growing tide of nationalism which may reduce China's
appetite to learn from foreign partners and, we would argue, it could
even impede the ability of Chinese firms to learn from their own
subsidiaries. These cultural and socio-political dimensions raise
a number of critical questions: Given the lack of trust, how do
Chinese firms assess and access knowledge from potential partners?
Are they able to work in innovation-focused strategic partnerships with
foreign firms? And to what extent are Chinese companies accepted by
foreign MNEs as strategic partners? In terms of being potential partners in innovation, do Chinese firms fall victim to preconceptions by
Western companies arising from their experience of Japanese and
Korean firms as superlative strategic learners? How do Chinese firms
identify and build trust with weak foreign companies that are willing to
partner with them, or struggling firms that have some good technical
assets they are willing to share or sell? Once again, we have found a lack
of research and insight into the important questions of how Chinese
MNEs approach innovation alliances with foreign partners and
whether they have the capabilities to collaborate effectively in this
type of partnership.

10.5 A research agenda

The focus of this chapter has been to set out an integrative perspective
on the strategic, organisational and managerial requirements for companies to engage in globally integrated innovation and to analyse the
current situation of Chinese MNEs against this, highlighting the natural advantages these fast-growing companies can leverage and the
particular challenges they face. While the work of many scholars in
the fields of international management, R&D management and organisational behaviour has and continues to provide rich insights and

useful frameworks to help unravel the complexities inherent in managing innovation in multinational firms based in the United States, Europe, Japan and Korea, we have encountered a frustrating lack of research into the phenomena relating to how and why Chinese MNEs are managing the global expansion of their innovation activities. As such, we have drawn together a research agenda which addresses some of the obvious gaps in what should be an important area of research, given the size of China and the rapid growth of Chinese MNEs.

The extent to which Chinese firms expand their innovation activities abroad to counter a lack of capabilities and talent in their home market seems open to debate. On the one hand, Booz and Company estimate that a lack of world-class scientists and engineers in China coupled with poor R&D productivity will leave the country facing an acute shortage of R&D staff by 2020 and this is despite the number of bachelor-degree students in China increasing from less than three million in 2000 to almost twelve million by 2010. According to Huang and Bosler (2014), while the quantity of graduates in China has been on the rise, the quality of the average graduate has declined. However, successful national policies to encourage overseas Chinese working in higher education and particularly science and engineering to return to China over the last decade are leading to improvements in the quality of China's leading institutions, with six making it to the Shanghai Jiao Tong University, Academic Ranking of World Universities global top 200 and three the top 150 by 2014. Though Freeman and Huang (2015) comment that with none in the top 100, China's universities still lag far behind the world's best.

There are serious questions to be addressed in relation to talent acquisition, development and retention that will impact China's future growth: Is China currently producing and likely to produce in the future enough 'world-class' scientists and engineers to meet its innovation growth needs? In a global marketplace for talent, China is currently unable to attract non-Chinese R&D staff. What strategies will have to be employed to overcome this deficit (Korea acutely suffers from the same problem but given different political and cultural contexts, will similar solutions adopted by the chaebol work for China)? What entices overseas Chinese to return and are they really making a disproportionate contribution to China's innovation capability? How are Chinese firms trying to improve innovation productivity at home, given the large numbers of relatively low-cost human resources available? Are Chinese firms able to retain talent in their foreign subsidiaries? And if not, are they able to capture vital innovation knowledge when key staff leave or is it expected that many acquired foreign assets will become less value-adding over time?

Understanding cultural norms and behaviour at the national level is vital for interpreting how firms learn, how they collaborate and how they transfer knowledge. Comparing Chinese culture against the precedents of context-rich Japanese culture and context-poor US culture will be helpful in establishing the processes by which Chinese firms are best suited to learn and collaborate. Firms from context-rich cultures have proven to be better learners in collaborations, by focusing not only on what is explicitly communicated and shared in the collaboration but also on its tacit context, on what was not shared and communicated but might be important. Chinese companies, however, do not benefit from the strong national 'in group' identity that makes Japan, for instance, such a high-context culture. Loyalties in Chinese firms may be more regional, or even confined to family, friends and personal networks, thus undermining a common context.

From what we can observe, when investing abroad, Chinese MNEs seem to favour the acquisition of firms with mature technologies over leading-edge entrepreneurial-type firms. In many ways this is a counter-intuitive move for high-growth firms embarking on large-scale globalisation, as without truly innovative new offerings, processes or business models, they risk losing market share to agile and nimble competitors. We suggest that this behaviour points to a lack of product innovation capabilities at Chinese MNEs: Rather than acquire resources which will make a contribution to their innovation process, Chinese firms are accessing fundamental know-how and competencies relating to a complete product or modular subsystem which they can sell as a standalone entity, in particular when the product is not a priority in their domestic market – Haier, for instance, develops dishwashers in Germany but does not transfer this knowledge to its Chinese operations. We are led to question whether Chinese firms are developing the leading-edge innovation capabilities to compete in high value-added segments. And if so, how are they transferring knowledge and learning within the multi-domestic and transnational organisational structures they have adopted?

The organisational structures that seem to be prevalent in Chinese firms not only raise valid questions about how they learn from their subsidiaries but also how they learn from customers in different locations and whether that knowledge is leveraged more widely across the firm or remains local? In Japanese companies, for example, relationships between foreign R&D centres and Japanese ones have often been fraught with tensions (Asakawa, 2001). Do Chinese firms learn about new markets and technologies via their existing operations, do they set up dedicated listening posts and expeditionary marketing activities or do they hire external consultants and agencies? The issue of organising and managing knowledge flows in Chinese firms is further complicated by a lack of experience in the critical activity of simultaneously combining both Chinese-originating knowledge and overseas-originating knowledge. In contrast, for MNEs from triadic countries, the knowledge flow was typically reversed or became multi-directional over a long period of time, where peripheral knowledge first came to complement home-based knowledge and a gradual process eventually led to recognition of what had once been regarded as peripheral sites becoming critical locations of unique knowledge in the firm's global network. Without this type of gradual evolution, can Chinese firms rapidly build effective innovation footprints and put in place the processes and tools to create the global learning networks needed for innovation?

10.6 Conclusion

In less than two decades, a number of young, ambitious Chinese MNEs have emerged as new global players across a wide range of industries. Unimpeded by costly legacy innovation footprints, cultures of co-location and a tradition of headquarters knowledge projection, these firms are in a strong position to build the right structures, processes and culture in terms of footprint, communication and collaboration and leapfrog many of their longer-established competitors. Building a globally integrated innovation capability from the outset will give them the long-term agility and flexibility to continually anticipate and meet changing customer requirements, access new knowledge and technologies and meld this dispersed knowledge into innovations that are difficult for competitors to copy.

Achieving this will not be without significant additional challenges though: The spectacular growth and internationalisation of many Chinese MNEs has been driven by energetic, determined, savvy owners/founders and whether the next generation of professional managers are able to manage subsequent growth phases quite so successfully remains to be seen. While Chinese firms have been innovative in terms of cost and speed, most are yet to build the capabilities to deliver a pipeline of truly innovative products and services. As innovation inevitably becomes more collaborative and eco-system-based, Chinese firms will have to gain the trust of potential partners around the world that they are genuinely commercial enterprises not tools of the state and that they will not benefit disproportionately from the joint effort. Finally, like Japanese MNEs and Korean chaebols before them, Chinese MNEs will have to build global brands that consumers trust for quality, reliability and innovation.

References

Abrami R M, Kirby W C & McFarlan F W, (2014), 'Why China can't innovate', *Harvard Business Review*, March.

Asakawa K, (2001), 'Organizational tension in international R&D management: The case of Japanese firms', *Research Policy*, Vol. 30, Issue 5, p735–758.

Awate S, Larsen M & Mudambi R, (2015), 'Accessing vs sourcing knowledge: A comparative study of R&D internationalization between emerging and advanced economy firms', *Journal of International Business Studies*, Vol. 46, Issue 1, p63–86.

Bartlett C A & Ghoshal S, (1989), *Managing across Borders: The Transnational Solution*, Harvard Business School Press, Cambridge, MA.

Bonaglia F, Goldstein A & Mathews J, (2007), Accelerated internationalization by emerging markets multinationals: The case of the white goods sector', *Journal of World Business*, Vol. 42, p369–383.

Cantwell J & Janne O, (1999), 'Technological globalisation and innovative centres: The role of corporate technological leadership and locational hierarchy', *Research Policy*, Vol. 28, Issue 2–3, p119–144.

Child J & Rodrigues S B, (2005), The internationalization of Chinese firms: A case for theoretical extension? *Management and Organization Review*, Vol. 1, p381–410.

Deng P, (2007). 'Investing for strategic resources and its rationale: The case of outward FDI from Chinese companies'. *Business Horizons*, Vol. 50, p71–81.

Di Minin A, Zhang J & Gammeltoft P, (2012), 'Chinese foreign direct investment in R&D in Europe: A new model of R&D internationalization?', *European Management Journal*, Vol. 30, Issue 3, p189–203.

Doney P M, Cannon J P & Mullen M R, (1998), 'Understanding the influence of national culture on the development of trust', *Academy of Management Review*, Vol. 23, Issue 3, p601–620.

Doz Y, Santos J & Williamson P, (2001), *From Global to Metanational: How Companies Win in the Knowledge Economy*, Harvard Business School Press, Cambridge, MA.

Doz Y D & Wilson K, (2012), *Managing Global Innovation: Frameworks for Integrating Capabilities Around the World*, Harvard Business Review Press, Cambridge, MA.

Ferrin D L, Dirks K T & Shah P P, (2006), 'Direct and indirect effects of third-party relationships on interpersonal trust', *Journal of Applied Psychology*, Vol. 91, Issue 4, p870–883.

Freeman R B & Huang W, (2015), 'China's "Great Leap Forward" in Science and Engineering', Copyright Elsevier. Available at http://scholar.harvard.e du/freeman/publications/%E2%80%9Cchina%E2%80%99s-great-leap-f orward%E2%80%9D-science-and-engineering%E2%80%9D. accessed June 2015.

Fu X, (2015), *China's Path to Innovation*, Cambridge University Press.

Govindarajan V & Trimble C, (2012), *Reverse Innovation: Create Far from Home, Win Everywhere*, Harvard Business Review Press, Cambridge, MA.

Huang Y & Bosler C, (2014), 'China's burgeoning graduates – Too much of a good thing?', *The National Interest*, 7 January.

Jarvenpaa S L & Leidner D E, (1999), 'Communication and trust in global virtual teams', *Organization Science*, Vol. 10, Issue 6, p791–815.

Li-Ying J, Wang Y & Salomo S (2014), 'An inquiry on dimensions of external technology search and their influence on technological innovations: Evidence from Chinese firms'. *R&D Management*, Vol. 44 Issue 1, p53–74.

Luo Y & Tung R, (2007), 'International expansion of emerging market enterprises: A springboard perspective', *Journal of International Business Studies*, Vol. 38, Issue 4, p481–498.

Mathews J A & Zander I, (2007), 'The international entrepreneurial dynamics of accelerated internationalisation', *Journal of International Business Studies*, Vol. 38, p387–403.

Porter M E, (1990), *The Competitive Advantage of Nations*, Free Press, New York.

Prahalad C K & Doz Y L, (1987), *The Multinational Mission: Balancing Local Demands and Global Vision*, The Free Press, London.

Rui H & Yip G S, (2008), 'Foreign acquisitions by Chinese firms: A strategic intent perspective', *Journal of World Business*, Vol. 43, Issue 2, p213–226.

Veldhoen S, Mansson A, McKern B, Yip G & Kiewiet de Jonge M, (2012), 'Innovation China's next advantage? 2012 China Innovation Survey', *Benelux Chamber of Commerce*, China Europe International Business School (CEIBS), Wenzhou Chamber of Commerce and Booz & Company Joint Report.

Vernon R, (1966), 'International investment and international trade in the product cycle', *The Quarterly Journal of Economics*, Vol. 80, Issue 2, p190–207.

Wang H, (2013), 'China's return migration and its impact on home development', *UN Chronicle*, September, Vol. 1, Issue 3.

Wilson K & Doz Y D, (2011), 'Agile innovation: A footprint balancing distance and immersion', *California Management Review*, Vol. 53, Issue 2, p6–26.

Zablit H & Chui B, (2013), 'The next wave of Chinese cost innovators', *BCG Perspectives*, 23 January.

Zander U & Kogut B, (1995), 'Knowledge and the speed of the transfer and imitation of organizational capabilities: An empirical test', *Organization Science*, Vol. 6, Issue 1, p76–92.

Zhao X & Sun X, (2015), 'Returning graduates face tight domestic job market', *China Daily*, 18 March.

11 Emerging trends in global sourcing of innovation

SILVIA MASSINI, KEREN CASPIN-WAGNER,
AND ELIZA CHILIMONIUK-PRZEZDZIECKA

11.1 Introduction

Over the last decade, employment-on-demand has come to involve not only operational activities (e.g., call centers, standard IT support) but also more strategic and higher value-adding activities and functions, from HR, legal, software development, or marketing and sales to innovation-related services such as research and development (R&D), engineering services, and product design. Two recent trends – firms' disintegration and externalization of innovation processes, and skilled workers offering their services as freelancers in the global online market – are driving the transformation of employment practices and preferences by both employers and employees for technical and knowledge work.

The first trend involves innovation-related activities, traditionally executed within the boundaries of the firm, but increasingly contracted out or handled through various market channel arrangements (Arora *et al.*, 2014; Malone *et al.*, 2003). As early as 1985, large US corporations were reducing, or even eliminating, internal allocations to R&D, while expanding external sourcing of R&D and knowledge (Mowery, 2009). Between 2007 and 2009, 49% of US manufacturing companies that had introduced a new product to the market obtained innovation from an external source using market-based channels such as a license, acquisition, outsource service contract, a joint venture, or cooperative R&D (Arora *et al.*, 2014). A third of innovative companies in EU28 acquired innovation from extramural sources during 2010–2012, with more than half of large firms (+250 employees) using external sources (Eurostat, 2012).

The global sourcing of innovation activities to offshore locations may have been triggered by Western companies' increasing difficulty in recruiting skilled STEM (Science, Technology, Engineering, and

Math) talent domestically. In 2003, the increased H1B-visa immigration quota for skilled labor (Lewin *et al.*, 2009) dropped to 65,000 per year, after having increased to 185,000 in 2000. In Western European countries, the STEM workforce shortage results from both an aging population and dramatically decreased availability of highly skilled engineers. Responding to the increased demand for skilled talent globally, developing countries have offered a broad range of innovation-related services, from routinized support activities to more creative and innovative solutions.

The second related trend involves firms using web-based brokerage platforms to hire talent on demand not only for tasks that support the innovation process but also for those that significantly define the innovation. Larger platforms such as Upwork (formerly Elance and Odesk) and Freelancer.com offer to perform all types of tasks, while niche platforms (e.g., InnoCentive, TopCoder) are used for more complex and specific tasks. These platforms are driving structural changes in the STEM labor market, in the way organizations operate, and in the way knowledge work and innovation are accomplished.

This chapter focuses on these emerging trends in global sourcing of innovation – the disintegration and externalization of innovation processes and the challenges and opportunities for emerging economies such as China and India, and the recent emergence of online knowledge brokers, crowdsourcing, and utilization of STEM talent on demand. The chapter argues that these dynamics evolve to a varied extent in different emerging countries, depending on the degree of initiatives and effectiveness of local institutions and policies in facilitating, stimulating, and supporting the relocation of innovation-related activities from developing countries to their own countries. One example of such institutional evolution is the changing nature of intellectual property rights (IPR) laws in India and China. The chapter outlines challenges and opportunities for emerging countries, including China, as the unbundling of innovation-related activities becomes standard practice.[1]

---

[1] It is worth noting that some leading companies, who may have been among the first organizations to unbundle innovation and product design processes, seem to go back to bundling these activities. For example, Apple brought IC design and various other intellectual tasks in-house; and Google has brought some design tasks in-house from firms like Ideo, the leading product design consulting company.

11.2 Global sourcing of innovation

Offshoring of business services, including innovation, concerns the relocation of business functions, processes, and projects outside the home country; outsourcing is the process of acquiring business functions, processes, and projects previously conducted within the organization from a third-party service provider. Offshoring is about locating activities outside domestic boundaries, and outsourcing is about activities outside the firm's boundary. Offshoring can occur within the firm's boundary, that is, international insourcing, from subsidiaries offshore, or can be outsourced to service providers. It is about "make-or-buy" decisions on a global level. Outsourcing can entail purchasing services within the home country (domestic outsourcing) or from abroad (international outsourcing or offshore outsourcing) (see Table 11.1). Both outsourcing (whether domestic or international) and international insourcing (via fully owned operations abroad) involve a process of disintegration and redesign of business processes and often require reorganizing internal activities.

Global sourcing of innovation involves the reorganization of innovation processes and does not imply transferring entire R&D activities but may entail relocating smaller tasks within those activities, often starting with simpler supporting tasks that can be handled well by technical workers in low-cost countries and, after relevant capabilities, learning, relations, and trust are developed, progressing to more value-adding activities. Examples of the types of innovation-related tasks that firms offshore, from the Offshoring Research Network (ORN) survey where respondents describe in their own words the project they offshored, include design automation, tool design, simulating, drafting and modeling, engineering analysis among engineering services;

Table 11.1 *Sourcing models*

	Insourcing (company-owned)	Outsourcing (vendor)
Domestic	Domestic insourcing	Domestic outsourcing
International/ offshore	Offshore insourcing (fully owned subsidiaries)	Offshore outsourcing

research on new materials and processes, code development, research and development of new technologies as examples of R&D; and prototype design and systems design in product design activities.

Early signs of firms' strategies to source innovation outside their boundaries arose in the late 1970s as a response to the realization that innovation benefits from external sources. However, full externalization of R&D challenges the conventional notion that firms should strategically retain their core competencies (Prahalad and Hamel, 1990), balancing internal R&D efforts (to maintain absorptive capacity [Cohen and Levinthal, 1990]) and external knowledge acquisition. Unlike using external consultants and collaborators, outsourcing of R&D implies full externalization and separation of outsourced activities from internal processes. Additionally, the scale and breadth of recent outsourcing innovation is evidence of a structural change in the way firms organize innovation.

Large multinational enterprises (MNEs) have been conducting innovation activities outside their home countries for a long time, mostly establishing foreign direct investments (FDIs) as fully owned centers for R&D activities. Internationalization of their R&D has increased rapidly in the last two decades (Cantwell and Mudambi, 2005; Gassman and von Zedtwitz, 1999; Howells, 2012; Narula and Zanfei, 2004; von Zedtwitz and Gassman, 2002).

In the 1990s, FDI involving R&D occurred primarily between a small number of highly industrialized countries, in the so-called Triad (the United States, Europe, and Japan). US companies were pioneer investors in R&D facilities abroad and invested first in Europe, then in Japan, and then in the rest of the world (primarily Canada, Australia, and a few Asian countries). European companies invested first in other European countries, then in the United States, then in Japan, and then very limitedly in the rest of the world. Japanese R&D FDI in the United States, Europe, and the rest of the world surged in the early 1980s and significantly increased in these three locations in the late 1980s and 1990s. By 2011, US companies spent close to $73 billion on R&D abroad (in affiliated and unaffiliated locations) – a 150% increase from 2003 (NSF, 2011).

Innovation-related FDI often results when firms seek to exploit firm-specific capabilities in foreign environments. These *asset-exploiting* (Dunning and Narula, 1996) or *home-base-exploiting* (Kuemmerle, 1999) R&D strategies mainly seek to adjust products to a local market, especially when the local demand grows increasingly sophisticated, as in China and other emerging economies. Locating R&D sites near factories supports the transfer of knowledge and prototypes from the firm's home location to actual manufacturing, especially where knowledge in particular technology sectors is accumulating rapidly. In addition, companies may mandate the local business unit to invest in specific new R&D capabilities (Murtha *et al.*, 2001). These *asset-augmenting* (Dunning and Narula, 1996) or *home-base-augmenting* (Cantwell and Mudambi, 2005; Kuemmerle, 1999) R&D activities bring a firm closer to the foreign R&D environment, accessing local knowledge and concurrently developing links with host-country R&D resources to enrich the home knowledge base (Cantwell, 1995; Dunning, 1993; Florida, 1997; Howells, 1990). Traditionally, offshore R&D facilities have offered the potential for knowledge spillovers from and to existing R&D and manufacturing networks, which encompass research universities, publicly funded research institutes, and innovative competitors. Consequently, where to locate R&D offshore activities becomes a highly strategic decision.

In the more recent wave of offshoring innovation, locations are chosen regardless of geographical distance, facilitated by developments in information and communications technology (ICT) and digitization (Dossani and Kenney, 2007) that allow the tapping of talent pools in less developed, lower-cost countries. The rapid advance in ICT enables firms to dis-intermediate and externalize innovation processes through outsourcing and relocation of R&D groups and laboratories overseas (Howells, 1990, 1995). At the same time, the global sourcing of innovation increasingly relies on external providers, through outsourcing contracts. The underlying motives may have also changed. Decisions to source innovation globally are increasingly *replacing* home-based capabilities (Lewin *et al.*, 2009).

The disintegration of R&D processes leads to new geographical configurations of technology development for multinationals, as well as providing new opportunities to small and medium enterprises (SMEs) (Lynn and Salzman, 2009; Massini and Miozzo, 2012). SMEs are able to overcome some of the constraints of limited resources and thus undertake R&D similar to that of larger firms.

According to Eurostat data (see Table 11.2), the percentage of large companies (>=250 employees) cooperating in innovation is much higher than the percentage of SMEs (10–49 and 50–249 employees).

Table 11.2 Cooperation in innovation by enterprise manufacturing sector (average EU28) and company size 2010–2012 (in %)

Firm size by number of employees	Enterprises engaged in any type of cooperation	Enterprises cooperating with other enterprises within the enterprise group	Enterprises engaged in any type of innovation cooperation:				
			with a national partner	with a partner in EU, EFTA, or EU candidates (except a national partner)	with a partner in China or India	with a partner in the US	with a partner in all other countries except in EU, EFTA, or EU candidates, US, China or India
All firms	14.72	32.93	28.75	20.12	3.21	4.94	4.78
10–49	8.1	26.89	22.81	13.57	1.49	2.16	2.80
50–249	18.74	39.04	32.19	26.17	3.08	5.64	5.15
250 and more	41.51	57.93	52.02	47.04	11.76	18.66	16.30

Source: Eurostat (2012). Community Innovation Survey.

In general, it is easier for European companies to engage in innovation collaborations with partners located in other European countries (20.12%) than with those outside the European Union (4.78%). EU companies face greater challenges in collaborating with partners located in countries with less developed institutional environments (such as India and China), compared to other developed countries such as the United States, yet about two-thirds as much innovation cooperation occurs in China and India as in the United States, for all company sizes.

11.2.1 The supply side of global sourcing of innovation

The increasing types of services offered globally by ever-more specialized innovation and knowledge service providers create extensive opportunities for companies of all sizes to consider sourcing such services in low-cost countries.

Service providers are evolving from low-cost providers of commoditized business services to highly competitive businesses providing customized services to heterogeneous industries (Manning *et al.*, 2008). More experienced client firms are seeking more value-adding inputs carried by service providers from emerging countries. At the same time, service providers are bundling services delivered to several clients, benefiting from economies of scale and scope. As shown in Figure 11.1, service providers located in low-cost Asian countries, as well as providers in Europe (Western and Eastern), have grown rapidly between 2007 and 2012, overtaking, in relative terms, providers in North America.

Service providers have been continuously investing in capabilities that give them strong competitive advantage. Chinese providers, in particular, are investing in developing state-of-the-art capabilities, creating centers of excellence and improving efficiency much more aggressively than those in other countries (Offshoring Research Network, *Service Provider Survey 2010–12*).

A more detailed analysis of the locations for sourcing innovation activities – that is R&D, engineering, and product design projects – show that the main destination for all innovation activities is India, followed by China (Figures 11.2–11.4). Other emerging economies, in addition to developed countries, show some specialization on specific innovation activities: (i) Brazil, Russia, and Mexico for R&D; (ii)

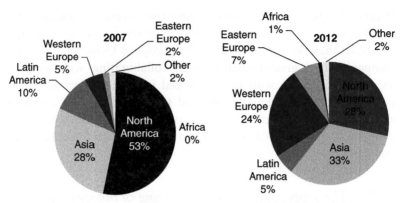

Figure 11.1 Location of service providers, by region, (a) 2007 and (b) 2012
Source: Offshoring Research Network, *Service Provider Surveys 2007–2012*.

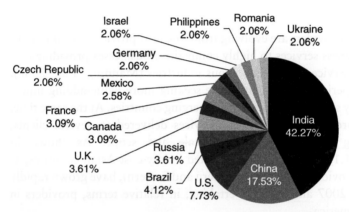

Figure 11.2 Locations of R&D processes (2012) (top 15 locations, % of all locations)
Source: Offshoring Research Network, Service Provider Survey 2012.

Mexico, the Philippines, and Poland for engineering services; (iii) Mexico and Poland for product design.

Comparing innovation projects offshored to India and China, ORN data reveals that while India has maintained its attraction over the last two decades in software development (including application development and maintenance, ADM), China is consistently and increasingly attracting value-adding projects related to R&D, engineering services, and product design (see Figure 11.5).

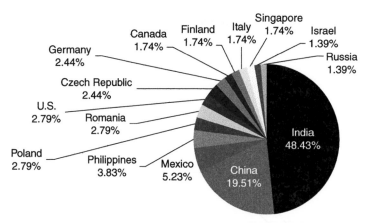

Figure 11.3 Locations of engineering processes (2012) (top 15 locations, % of all locations)
Source: Offshoring Research Network, Service Provider Survey 2012.

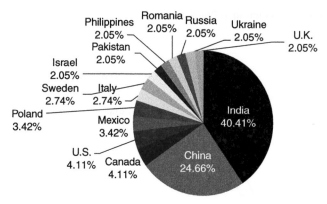

Figure 11.4 Locations of product design (2012) (top 15 locations, % of all locations)
Source: Offshoring Research Network, *Service Provider Survey 2012*.

11.3 Is China overtaking India in global sourcing of innovation?

The phenomenon of offshoring of business services became highly visible as a result of the remarkable success of the IT and software industry in India, associated with the concerns about the Y2K bug at the turn of the millennium. The rapid success in IT was followed by the fast growth of the business services provider industry in India and by

(a)

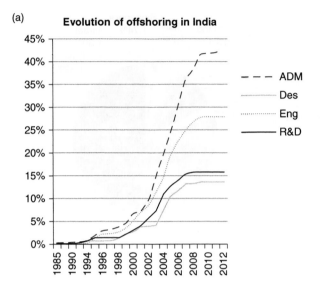

(b)

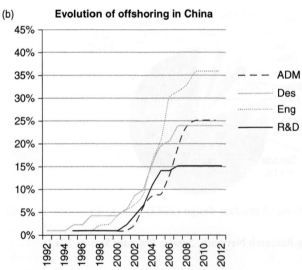

Figure 11.5 Evolution of offshoring processes in (a) India (1985–2012) and (b) China (1992–2012)

Source: Offshoring Research Network, *Service Provider Survey 2012*.

the emergence of large companies such as Infosys, TCS, and Wipro, which have grown into global service providers that compete with top Western companies. The double-digit economic growth experienced by India since 2000 has attracted the attention of analysts, investors, companies, and other emerging economies that aspire to emulate that spectacular growth.

However, in the last few years, India's economic growth and innovation development have not been sustained. India's GDP growth per year dropped from 9.8 in 2007 to 5.0 in 2014 (World Bank Report, 2014). India slipped by fifty-three places in the Global Innovation Index, from 23rd position in 2007 to 76th position in 2014 (Global Innovation Index, 2014). Only a negligible 0.25% of Indian graduate students (across all disciplines) choose to continue with doctoral studies in India, while the completion rate of those who choose to continue with these studies in India is less than 50% (Kurup and Arora, 2010). Despite the 2010 launch of several innovation capacity-building programs under the campaign "Decade of Innovation," no Indian university is in the top 200 research university rankings by Times Higher Education (2014), and only the Indian Institute of Science ranks among the top 151–200 universities in science and among the top 101–150 universities in engineering, with particular strength in chemistry (top 51–75 in 2014) and computer science (top 51–75 in 2013, but 101–150 in 2014). The Indian Statistical Institute only appeared in the top 151–200 in 2013 and in the top 101–150 in 2014 (for computer science). No Indian university appears among the top 200 universities in mathematics (ARWU, 2014). With the exception of the Indian Institute of Science, Indian universities struggle to be world class.

China introduced several initiatives much later than India (see Table 11.3), but quite early in the economic development process, and seemingly more effectively, at least in terms of amount of R&D investments. Initiatives such as 211 Project and 985 Project have invested very heavily to create first-rate universities, improving international visibility of publications in science and technology and ultimately enhancing the knowledge base and absorptive capacity of the country (Zhang *et al.*, 2013). Although more time may be needed before results of national initiatives can be observed fully, the reality is that China has been more aggressive in pushing technological and innovative capabilities.

Table 11.3 *Innovation systems and policies of India and China*

	India	China
Economic/ trade liberalization	Software Export Scheme 1972 Liberalization of import of software 1976, "New Computer Policy" 1984, 1986 import licensing policy for software 1990s full financial liberalization – trade and FDI inflow liberalization (1991) WTO member 1995	Open-door policy 1978 WTO member 2001 Relied on imported technology and FDI, but also high-tech exports (e.g., office machinery, television and radio communication equipment) which represent 30% of total exports in 2005
Science and technology policy	1990s creation of Software Technology Parks by India to develop telecommunication infrastructure and low-cost Internet (National Telecom Policy – 1994)	Aggressive strategic plan since 2006, with the goals of becoming one of world's leading innovation economies; "innovation-oriented society"; developing "indigenous" and "home-grown" innovation (985 projects) Strengthening IP rights legislation and enforcement, despite traditional Confucianism and culture in China against public ownership PRC National Patent Development Strategy 2010 aimed at Chinese government's promotion of indigenous innovation
Education policy	1970s launching of specialized masters level programs at the IITs; proficiency in computer	Expansion of college enrollment since 1999

Table 11.3 (*cont.*)

	India	China
	programming made mandatory for S&T students	Mandatory English education began at grade 3 since 2001
	1980s higher education policy to increase supply of S&T graduates for the 11th Five Year Plan since 2007	
	Customized degrees for foreign companies' needs	
Outsourcing industry policy	Customized degrees for foreign companies' needs	In 2009, twenty-one cities designated as outsourcing hubs[a]
	Development of general infrastructure	

[a]This initiative, which is consistent with Lin's advice on selecting state council identifying industrial policies but letting markets decide survival and success initiative, failed with exception of Dalian, which serves Japanese and Korean companies. The failure is probably due to low English competence, high turnover of staff, and unwillingness of companies to train and upgrade human resources especially investing in ISO compliance (see Chapter 12 this volume by Weidong Xia, Mary Ann Von Glinow, and Yingxia Li).

In terms of STEM talent for global innovation activities, China is leading the group of emerging and developing countries in graduating huge numbers of science and engineering (S&E) students, especially at the bachelor-degree level (1.31 million graduates in 2013). Between 2004 and 2013, China has experienced a rapid compound annual growth rate of about 12% in terms of graduates at both bachelor-degree and post-graduate levels.

As the effect of the spectacular increase in numbers of graduates in S&E, China is in the world-leading position in terms of the number of researchers (see Figure 11.6, where data has been normalized to Spain 2000 = 100).

However, concerns have been raised about the quality of training and education of these graduates. For example, it has been argued that only 10–20% of graduates in China have requisite training and

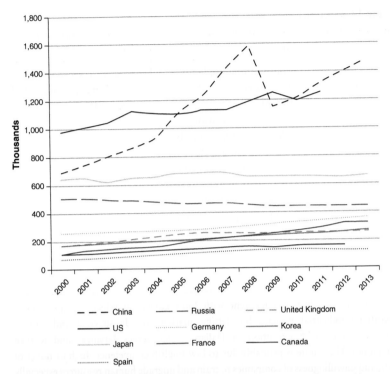

Figure 11.6 Number of researchers in selected countries (2000–2013)
Source: OECD iLibrary; UNESCO.

OECD and UNESCO define "Researchers" as professionals employed by business enterprises as well as research institutes and engaged in the conception or creation of new knowledge, products processes, methods, and systems.

2000–2008: According to OECD iLibrary, data do not correspond exactly to OECD norms. Top 10 in 2013.

background to work for MNEs, because of the overall poor level of English competence and also because the growing domestic economy is absorbing most of those who could be hired (Farrell *et al.*, 2006; Schaaf, 2005).[2] In addition, the best graduates in developing nations prefer Western universities for post-graduate education and often do not return to their home countries, despite national reverse brain-drain

2 While these graduates may not be "global class," they may be sufficiently skilled to upgrade local firm capabilities, and this is also very important in terms of long-run competitiveness.

policies to attract students who receive advanced degrees in STEM disciplines in Western universities (Lewin and Zhong, 2013).

One element that plays an important role in developing indigenous capabilities in an emerging country is the extent and quality of innovation-related activities by foreign companies, which can stimulate the development of innovation= and knowledge-intensive capabilities in the recipient countries. Estimations of global R&D expenditures (in-house as well as purchased from external providers) document a regional shift over the past five years. *Battelle and R&D Magazine* reports that North America (the United States, Canada, Mexico) and Europe have witnessed a decline in the share of global R&D – from 40% in 2009 to 31% in 2014 in North America and from 26% in 2009 to 22% in 2014 in Europe. In the same period, R&D investment in Asia as a share of R&D investment worldwide has increased from 33% to 40%. However, nearly all of this change has been R&D investment in China, which has grown to about 60% of that of the United States (in purchasing power parity, PPP).[3] Contrary to the common belief that emerging countries invest limited resources on innovation and depend on R&D centers from Western companies to develop internal innovation capacity, according to OECD, China has aggressively increased its innovative efforts in recent years, from $55 billion USD in 2005 to $257.8 billion USD in 2013 for total gross domestic expenditures on R&D (GERD), showing a spectacular compound annual growth rate of 20% since 2005. Some estimates even suggest that China's total funding of R&D is expected to surpass that of the United States by 2022. Only a very small amount of the total domestic expenditures on R&D ($2.3 billion USD) comes from foreign sources (see Figures 11.7 and 11.8).

China also shows a clear strategy on increasing its innovative capacity in terms of R&D intensity – R&D expenditures as percentage of GDP. Figure 11.9 presents the changes in R&D intensity from 2003 (1.13%) to 2013, when China spent about 2% of GDP in R&D activities, bringing it to roughly the level of EU15 (average), in particular to the same

[3] Statistics may underestimate the overall investments in R&D, because when a US company sets up a captive R&D center in China, the investment in R&D will not be recorded as R&D funds abroad. The FDI inflow recorded will refer to the main activity of investor; for example, if the company is in fast-moving consumer goods, the inflow will be recorded as FDI in the manufacturing sector (2014 Global R&D Funding Forecast, *Battelle and R&D Magazine*, December 2013).

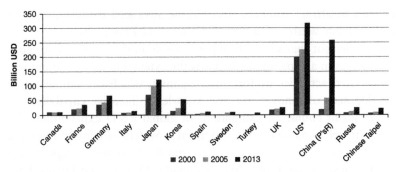

Figure 11.7 Gross domestic expenditure on R&D in total (PPP dollars – current prices)

* Data for 2000, 2005 and 2013.

Definitions: Data includes gross domestic R&D **expenditure by total sectors of performance** (business enterprise, government, higher education, and private non-profit): (i) total source of funds, (ii) funds from foreign business enterprises.

Source: OECD iLibrary.

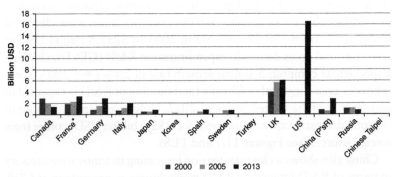

Figure 11.8 Gross domestic expenditure on R&D from foreign business enterprises (PPP dollars – current prices)

* Data for 2000, 2005 and 2013.

Definitions: Data includes gross domestic R&D **expenditure by total sectors of performance** (business enterprise, government, higher education, and private non-profit): (i) total source of funds, (ii) funds from foreign business enterprises.

Source: OECD iLibrary.

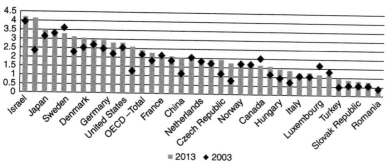

Figure 11.9 R&D intensity (GERD as % GDP) (2003 and 2013)
Source: OECD, iLibrary.

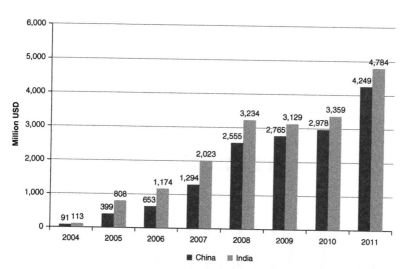

Figure 11.10 Company and other nonfederal funds for industrial R&D performed in China and India by majority-owned US foreign affiliates (in million USD)
Source: NSF.

level as France and the Netherlands. This shows a remarkable increase in R&D intensity, which strengthens China's credibility in becoming a serious actor on the global innovation landscape.

Figure 11.10 reports R&D investments by US companies in India and China over the period 2004–2011 and shows that India has consistently benefited from a higher level of innovation efforts, although the gap has recently been declining. A similar trend is observed for R&D investments by European companies in China, which almost doubled between 2010 and 2012 and are tenfold those of US companies (Eurostat).

Patenting activities, and in particular the number of patents resulting from international cooperation,[4] are considered next. These are other important elements for analyzing the effect of improved IPR laws, the impact of open-door policies, and the extent of engaging with foreign resources to develop indigenous innovative capabilities. In 2013, India was granted 1,878 patents by USPTO (United States Patent and Trademark Ofice) and 182 patents by EPO, far behind China – 5,694 patents by USPTO and 848 patents by EPO.[5]

In terms of engaging with foreign partners for patenting activities, over time the proportion of patents owned by foreign residents in India has been particularly high, with more than 60% of patents belonging to foreigners in the 1990s and 90% in 2010 and 2011. In the same period, China also shows an upward trend in the share of foreign-resident-owned patents, from about 30% in the 1990s, to 50–60% around the turn of the millennium, to about 70% in more recent years (see Figure 11.11). This may be the result of strengthening IP rights

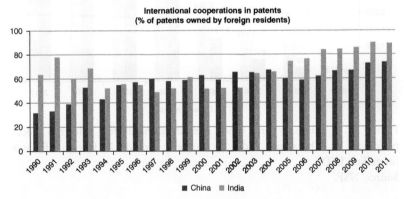

Figure 11.11 Technology creation in China and India: dependence on developed economies
Source: OECD iLibrary; Dataset: International cooperations in patents.

---

[4] For a deeper analysis, see Chapter 7 this volume by Menita Liu Cheng and Can Huang.
[5] Source: OECD, iLibrary, according to applicant country of residence.

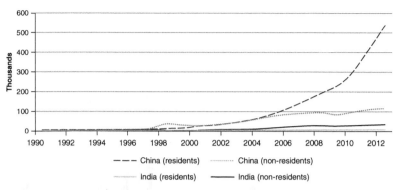

Figure 11.12 Patent applications filed under the Patent Cooperation Treaty by Chinese and Indian residents and non-residents (1990–2012)
Source: World Bank, *World Development Indicators.*

legislation and enforcement, despite traditional Confucianism and culture in China against public ownership, in the last two decades. The question whether India is a global contributor to innovation or has become highly dependent on foreign researchers requires a much deeper analysis that is beyond the scope of this chapter, and possibly more time observations to fully analyze the more recent dynamics. It is likely that foreign-owned patents reflect different patterns in the two countries, since Chinese firms spend far more on R&D than Indian firms. Indian tech firms may also be outsourcers whose patents are assigned to other firms or who do only a small, discrete portion of the overall innovation work and thus they have nothing to patent.

Indeed, patent application data reported in *World Bank Development Indicators* show an indisputable dominance of Chinese residents, compared to India, in innovation and their growing potential in invention for building national advantages on the basis of knowledge and skills (Figure 11.12).

In terms of a country-specific technological specialization, China has recorded a much greater increase in patents than other countries over the period 2003–2013 in a number of technological fields. As Figure 11.13 shows, compared to 2003 when the values of patents for all technologies and all countries are set to 100, China has reached the highest growth in all fields, in particular in ICT, where the number of patent applications has increased by more than sixteen times (from 652 in 2003 to 10,793 in 2011), four times the growth in India (from 150 in

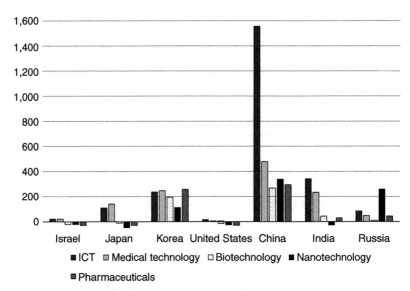

Figure 11.13 Patent applications filed under the Patent Cooperation Treaty by countries in selected technologies – change in 2011 compared to 2003 (2003 = 100)

Note: Country is inventor's country of residence; priority date
Source: OECD iLibrary; Dataset: Patents in technology.

2003 to 662 in 2011). China has clearly surpassed India's capabilities in the sector that made it the place for ICT services in the 2000s.[6]

To conclude, both India and China have enjoyed remarkable success in the emergence of global sourcing of business services, and in particular of innovation processes, experiencing fast economic growth and technological process in the last two decades – India earlier than China, building on the success of the IT and software industry. These phenomena have been possible because of the design and implementation of a number of initiatives aimed at building, improving, and sustaining innovation capabilities, from education to science and technology policies. However, it appears that China has been more strategic in developing capabilities in technological fields where patents are important, allowing Chinese multinational corporations to compete in the global

---

[6] It is worth noting that these data are about patents registered under the Patent Cooperation Treaty, which provides worldwide protection for the duration of their lifetime and should reflect quality of international standards, as well the potential for being copied anywhere in the world.

economy. China has been very aggressive in the volume of domestic investments in science and technology, attracting Western companies to (co-)develop innovation, and developing ambitious plans, such as the National Patent Development Strategy 2010 aimed at promoting indigenous innovation and aspiring to quadruple the quantity of patents by 2020. The enforcement of IPR laws and open-door policies suggests that China is moving in the right direction for becoming a global innovating leader, although it has been argued that the implementation and enforcement of China's IPR legal framework in the last thirty years is still incomplete, without fully effective incentives for researchers to patent inventions with useful applications or market potential, and the need for complementary industrial policy (Fuller, 2015) to enable it to show its effectiveness (Huang and Cheng, 2015).

While Indian outsourcers are still highly competitive, they have not developed their own competencies to expand patentable technologies to compete with China. Indian research institutions do perform at a high level, but they are not able to develop high numbers of top researchers and retain their best ones. As a consequence, India is failing to contribute to leading-edge innovation. In contrast, China appears to be more successful in developing first-rate science and technology universities, improving the international visibility of their publications in science and technology, and encouraging Chinese researchers to stay there or come back. Concerns remain about the effectiveness of English-language education policies in China and the tension between learning how to become a global player in innovation while maintaining Confucianism principles (against public ownership), culture, and values, which make China a distinctive actor in the global economy but may also limit full participation in social science discourse and debate.

11.4 The emergence of online marketplaces for STEM talent on demand: platforms for innovation problem solving and distributed innovation talent

To address the shortage and high cost of domestic talent in Western countries, firms in these countries have begun to experiment with using talent on demand and accessing problem solvers on demand using web-based brokerage platforms, which have become effective mediums for identification and recruitment of qualified and less expensive innovation talents around the world. This recent and very fast-growing phenomenon allows crowdsourcing to discover solutions to carefully specified problems by mobilizing the smallest, remote knowledge pools (Maskell, 2014). Skilled people, often employed by a third party, can assist young single-site firms and facilitate their search for knowledge and solutions through distributed online problem solving. While these platforms – which could be seen as simple search engines – are in their infancy, some large firms (such as P&G, GSK, Microsoft, and Cisco) use them regularly for problem-specific needs and as an alternative to full-time employment.

A firm's previously successful searches for knowledge and solutions sometimes shape its mindset in ways that result in search in wrong directions. And although a firm's previous internal attempts might not have yielded results, its efforts can result in a deeper understanding of the problem at hand, which enables the degree of problem decomposition needed to initiate crowdsourcing. It is difficult at best to communicate the detailed characteristics of a problem to distributed knowledge holders (Maskell, 2014). Often, successful solutions apply knowledge sets that are quite different from those mastered by the prize-awarding firm. Matching solution seekers with problem solution providers is a clear challenge.

The emergence of web-based brokerages is leading to unexpected structural changes in the STEM labor market, with the creation of a virtual and remote but easily accessible contingent employment that forms an online community of specialists, who are growing with a completely new lifestyle. This growing phenomenon is changing the way organizations operate and how knowledge work and innovation are accomplished.

The rapid growth of the online marketplaces for STEM talent is an outcome of multiple drivers, which involve supply-and-demand forces and managerial practices, as well as environmental and institutional forces that co-evolve in influencing firms' adoption of innovative organizational forms and new practices. There are six main drivers and environmental forces.

1. Advances in ICT enabling online collaborations and maturation of intermediate online platforms

Examples include online open-source freelancing techniques that enabled the community of programmers who created Linux and other open-source software applications (e.g., integration of open-source strategies into company product development, such as Google's Android, Redhat, Apache, and MySQL) and companies such as Guru. com, Upwork.com, and Freelancer.com that have pioneered global Internet marketplaces where talent is contracted on demand by project (Malone *et al.*, 2003).

2. A long history in global sourcing
Companies have a long sourcing history first in manufacturing, then in business services (including IT and innovation), and now evolving to online freelancing. Companies are learning and developing unbundling capabilities, and work is becoming more specialized and externalized. This transition and these learned capabilities drive utilization of online marketplaces for STEM talent.

3. The separation of many skilled technologists from organized employment
Many skilled individuals choose to no longer be "employed" in the conventional sense of the term. Rather, they contract with firms who need their services on a project basis (Barley and Kunda, 2004).

4. A skill shortage in the United States
A skill shortage of STEM talent in the United States has driven companies to search for talent globally. As noted earlier, Lewin *et al.* (2009) reported a significant increase in global sourcing of innovation activities to offshore locations in response to the failure by the US Congress in 2003 to renew the expanded H1B immigration quota for skilled labor.

5. The growth of technology start-up companies
Beginning in the late 1990s, a growing number of entrepreneurs and Internet start-up companies pioneered new ways to accelerate the rate of new product development, by employing online freelancers to control costs (often at the urging of venture capitalist backers). Startups are more likely to be born on the web and therefore are more comfortable operating in remote relationships.

6. Savings and labor arbitrage
Companies are actively experimenting with new ways to increase efficiency by re-examining the logic of core employees and implementing

new strict headcount strategies through contingent employment. Also, increased use of contingent labor decreases fringe benefit obligations, allowing firms to hire at lower cost and enjoy labor arbitrage.

The numbers of platforms and their users are increasing rapidly. As of September 2015, 140 online platforms had been designed to intermediate activities in the STEM disciplines. In the case of one platform, for example, in the 18 months between July 2012 and December 2013, the number of jobs and their value doubled, to more than four million jobs (projects), with a total value of $4 billion USD (for all job types, not just STEM) (Elance website, February 2014). Freelancer.com, another large platform, had more than fifteen million registered users (both freelancers and employers) from around the world as of May 2015. Estimates of the economic value of the entire online talent placement industry range between 1.5 and 5 billion USD.

The rapid growth of on-demand employment opens new opportunities for emerging economies. The only requirements are an Internet connection and building an online reputation, backed by online employers' ratings and reviews (similar to Amazon, eBay, and Alibaba). Analysis of Elance data shows that the top ten freelancers' countries are developed countries (the United States, Australia, the United Kingdom, Canada, United Arab Emirates, Singapore, Israel, Germany, the Netherlands, and New Zealand), while 70% of freelancers are located in developing and emerging countries (India, Ukraine, Pakistan, Russia, Philippines, Romania, China) (Elance website, Global Online Employment Report for 2013). Whether this phenomenon will be an engine for growth in developing countries by increasing employment and income, or will inhibit national development by reducing resources for domestic innovation, is yet to be answered.

China is currently a minor player in this global phenomenon. Table 11.4 presents a comparison between India and China using data from one of the largest online platforms (for years 2011–2013). Despite China and India having similar-size populations, India has twenty-three times more registered STEM freelancers than China (2,604,413 and 109,561, respectively). The language barrier may be one explanation for the relatively low representation of Chinese freelancers in the global online marketplace. Other explanations may be higher numbers of STEM talent in India than in China,

Table 11.4 *Use of freelancers in China and India (data of one online marketplace for 2011–2013)*

	India	China
All projects		
Total number of active freelancers	3,696,349	133,544
Total number of employed freelancers	305,919	16,281
% of employed freelancers by country	8%	12%
Number of employers	9,522	921
Number of projects	305,919	16,281
Average USD per project	249	297
Total number of active freelancers as % of country population	0.29%	0.01%
Population (2014)	1,267,401,849	1,393,783,836
STEM projects		
Total number of active freelancers	2,604,413	109,561
Total number of employed freelancers	207,322	13,543
% of employed freelancers by country	8%	12%
Number of employers	9,522	921
Number of projects	207,322	13,543
Average USD per project	265	330
% STEM projects out of total projects by country	70%	82%

Source for population: Worldometers (www.Worldometers.info, September 5, 2015)

and better domestic employment opportunities in China than in India.

The percentage of STEM projects out of total projects is higher for China (82%) than for India (70%), with an average of USD330 per STEM project versus USD265, suggesting that Chinese freelancers work, on average, on higher-value projects that demand higher payment. The percentage of employed freelancers (of total registered freelancers in the country) is higher in China than in India (12% vs 8%, respectively), suggesting online Chinese freelancers cost less than Indian freelancers or have better reputations.

To summarize, the global innovation ecosystem of online marketplaces for talent is a growing opportunity for China to become a source of income as well as a driver for entrepreneurship.

However, language may be a barrier and may require a higher investment in English training to reach international standards. One unique example to overcome the communication barrier is a US-based platform, Freelancer China, which employs Chinese freelancers and provides project governance. More than 200,000 IT experts from China provide online on-demand software developers while keeping complete control over the entire project development process. Nevertheless, losing skilled STEM talent to foreign employers may potentially destroy the investment in talent for developing domestic innovations that would potentially create higher value and benefits for China in the longer term.

11.5 Concluding remarks

The phenomenon of global sourcing of innovation and associated emerging trends require a deep understanding of the complex dynamics that link firm-level strategic decisions of offshoring innovation activities with structural shortage of talent and STEM skills in Western countries. Concurrently, emerging economies are increasingly competing with each other to attract innovation and knowledge-related high value-adding investments, service contracts, and the development of web-based online STEM talent platforms. Five implications and challenges that emerge from these dynamics need further discussion.

1. **Implications for innovation by SMEs:** The growing service provider industry is creating a stronger competition among providers, which results in increased types of services offered and differentiation. Smaller service providers are offering services to SME clients, often neglected by larger service providers. SMEs tend to possess limited resources to invest in overseas operations compared to larger firms, and by sourcing innovation activities globally they can access dispersed talent, augment their internal resources, and increase speed to market. Using online collaboration tools and web-based platforms, SMEs avoid travel expenses and other hidden costs of offshoring. The on-demand online community of STEM talent provides extensive opportunities for SMEs, and indeed companies of all size, to consider sourcing such services in low-cost countries, often exclusively online. Future research should investigate how this new opportunity actually affects the innovativeness of SMEs (e.g., more

innovations, faster time to market, lower costs) and what specific benefits employers realize by using online platforms.

2. **Organizational capabilities challenges:** The disintegration of innovation processes challenges organizational capabilities for managing these processes and balancing internal core activities and external peripheral ones. One main challenge is how to develop effective organizational structures and managerial talent to integrate internal processes for developing knowledge and innovation while using globally distributed talent. In particular, future research should look at what new or adapted organizational structures, processes, and capabilities companies should create to exploit the potential benefits of these changes. How will the disintegration of innovation processes affect challenges of interdependencies fit within organizations? What coordination and integration mechanisms need to be implemented in order to re-combine the discrete and dispersed components of innovation processes and combine them with other organizational processes and functions? What configuration of capabilities (e.g., selection, integration, and coordination capabilities) realizes high value-added outcomes, and how do these capabilities evolve over time?

3. **Innovation capabilities challenges:** Knowledge-intensive service providers are becoming highly specialized in providing advanced customized business services and are eager to be involved in high value-adding tasks for R&D projects. These service providers are mainly located in emerging economies such as India and China, which are determined to become credible players in innovation. On the other hand, the increasing reliance of companies on knowledge developed externally may result in a reduction of their own absorptive capacity and ability to independently develop their own innovations. How can firms continue to develop absorptive capacity if they respond to a shortage of talent by increasingly making use of distributed talent?

4. **IP challenges:** Another issue raised by increased reliance on international co-development of innovation is IP ownership, both at the firm level and at country level. At the firm level, the value of IP assets can be extremely high and central to technology strategies. At the country level, the development and ownership of patents in technologies with high potential for commercialization represent a clear factor of competitive advantage. Therefore, what effective

strategies for IP protection do firms need to develop to overcome risk of IP leakage? How do firms's strategies affect country-level development and ownership of IP? And how do national IP policies affect firms' strategies?

5. **Implications for emerging economies:** In some emerging economies, the high growth rates that resulted from huge capital investments in extractive industries and manufacturing based on labor arbitrage have begun to level off. For example, China is experiencing the end of labor migration from the rural economy as well as the aging of the population. A vital alternative economic growth engine is innovation. An emerging trend in global sourcing of innovation and in on-demand employment (through online marketplaces) is driven by developed economy firms striving to utilize skilled talent everywhere in the world. This raises the question of whether companies in development economies will end up exploiting STEM talent in emerging economies, thus negatively affecting the potential for the economic and technological development of these economies. Alternatively, as a result of international companies' innovation centers, there could be substantial knowledge spillover and transfer of capabilities that stimulate and drive the development of domestic innovation in host countries. In addition, the growth of the online marketplaces for STEM talent could be utilized as an economic engine to help local entrepreneurs test the realization of their ideas fast and at low cost. Further investigation is required to answer the question of whether offshoring and online marketplaces are an engine for growth, or whether they put domestic innovation potential at risk by crowding out skilled STEM talent by companies in developed economies that will retain most of the value from the innovation.

Insights from these questions will help companies and policymakers to identify best practices and develop strategies for innovation.

References

2014 Global R&D Funding Forecast, *Battelle and R&D Magazine*, December 2013.

Arora, A., Cohen, W.M., Walsh, J.P. 2014. The Acquisition and Commercialization of Invention in American Manufacturing: Incidence and Impact, *NBER Working Paper*, No. 20264 Issued in June 2014.

Barley, S.R., Kunda, G. 2004. *Gurus, Hired Guns, and Warm Bodies.* Princeton University Press, Princeton, NJ.

Cantwell, J. 1995. The globalisation of technology: what remains of the product cycle model, *Cambridge Journal of Economics*, 19, pp. 155–174.

Cantwell, J.A., Mudambi, R. 2005. MNE competence-creating subsidiary mandates, *Strategic Management Journal*, 26 (12), pp. 1109–1128.

Cohen, W., Levinthal, D. 1990. Absorptive capacity: a new perspective on learning and innovation, *Administrative Science Quarterly*, 35, pp. 128–152.

Cornell University, INSEAD, and WIPO. 2015. The Global Innovation Index 2015: Effective Innovation Policies for Development, Fontainebleau, Ithaca, and Geneva.

Dossani, R., Kenney, M. 2007. The next wave of globalization: relocating service provision to India. *World Development*, 35 (5), pp. 772–791.

Dunning, J.H. 1993. *Multinational Enterprises and the Global Economy.* Wokingham and Reading, MA: Addison Wesley.

Dunning, J.H., Narula, R. 1996. The investment development path revisited: some emerging issues, in *Foreign Direct Investment and Governments*, ed. J.H. Dunning, R. Narula. London: Routledge, pp. s. 1–41.

Elance.com Elance website – Global Online Employment Report for 2013 (2-24-14).

Farrell, D., McKinsey Global Institute. 2006. *Offshoring: Understanding the Emerging Global Labor Market.* Boston, MA: Harvard Business School Press.

Florida, R. 1997. The globalization of R&D: results of a survey of foreign affiliated R&D laboratories in the USA, *Research Policy*, 26, pp. 85–103.

Fuller, D. 2015. China's political economy and prospect for technological innovation-based growth. Chapter 7 in *Building Innovation Capacity in China: An Agenda for Averting the Middle Income Trap*, ed. A.Y. Lewin, J.P. Murmann, M. Kenney. Cambridge: Cambridge University Press.

Gassmann, O., von Zedtwitz, M. 1999. New concepts and trends in international R&D organization. *Research Policy*, 28, 231–250.

Howells, J. 1990. The location and organisation of research and development: new horizons. *Research Policy*, 19 (2), pp. 133–146.

Howells, J. 1995. Going global: the use of ICT networks in research and development. *Research Policy*, 24 (2), pp. 169–184.

Howells, J. 2012. The geography of knowledge: never so close but never so far apart, *Journal of Economic Geography*, 12 (5), pp. 1003–1020.

Huang, C., Cheng, M.L. 2015. Transforming China's intellectual property system to stimulate innovation. Chapter 8 in *Building Innovation Capacity in China: An Agenda for Averting the Middle Income Trap*, ed. A.Y. Lewin, J.P. Murmann, M. Kenney. Cambridge: Cambridge University Press.

Kuemmerle, W. 1999. The drivers of foreign direct investment into research and development: an empirical investigation, *Journal of International Business Studies*, 30 (1), pp. 1–24.

Kurup, A., Arora, J. 2010. *Trends in Higher Education: Creation and Analysis of a Database of PhDs (NIAS Report No. R1-2010)*. Project Report. NIAS, 2010.

Lewin, A.Y., Massini, S., Peeters, C. 2009. Why are companies offshoring innovation? The emerging global race for talent. *Journal of International Business Studies*, 40 (6), pp. 901–925.

Lewin, A.Y., Zhong, X. 2013. The evolving diaspora of talent: a perspective on trends and implications for sourcing science and engineering work. *Journal of International Management*, 13 (1), pp. 6–13.

Lynn, L., Salzman, H. 2009. The new globalization of engineering: how the offshoring of advanced engineering affects competitiveness and development. *Economics, Management and Financial Markets*, 4 (1), pp. 11–46.

Malone, T.W., Laubacher, R., Scot Morton, M.S. 2003. *Inventing the Organizations of the 21st Century*. Cambridge, MA: The MIT Press.

Manning, S., Massini, S., Lewin, A.Y. 2008. A dynamic perspective on next-generation offshoring: the global sourcing of science and engineering talent. *Academy of Management Perspectives*, 22 (3), pp. 35–54.

Maskell, P. 2014. Accessing remote knowledge – the roles of trade fair, pipelines, crowdsourcing and listening posts, *Journal of Economic Geography*, 14 (5), pp. 883–902.

Massini, S., Miozzo, M. 2012. Outsourcing and offshoring of business services: challenges to theory, management and geography of innovation. *Regional Studies*, 46 (9), pp. 1219–1242.

Mowery, D.C. 2009. Plus ca change: industrial R&D in the "third industrial revolution." *Industrial and Corporate Change*, 18 (1), pp. 1–50.

Murtha, T.P., Lenway, S.A., Hart, J.A. 2001. *Managing New Industry Creation: Global Knowledge Formation and Entrepreneurship in High Technology*. Stanford, CA: Stanford University Press.

Narula R., Zanfei, A. 2004. Globalisation of innovation: the role of multinational enterprises, in *Handbook of Innovation*, ed. Jan Fagerberg, David Mowery, Richard R. Nelson. Oxford University Press.

Prahalad, C.K., Hamel, G. 1990. The core competence of the firm. *Harvard Business Review*, May–June, pp. 79–91.

Schaaf, J. 2005. *Outsourcing to India: Crouching Tiger Set to Pounce*, Deutsche Bank Research. Frankfurt am Main. Germany.

Times Higher Education. 2014. www.timeshighereducation.com/world-university-rankings.

von Zedtwitz, M., Gassmann, O. 2002. Market versus Technology Drive in R&D Internationalization: Four different patterns of managing research and development. Research Policy, 31, 4, 569–588.

Zhang, H., Patton, D., Kenney, M. 2013. Building global-class universities: assessing the impact of the 985 Project. *Research Policy*, 42, pp. 765–775.

Statistical sources

ARWU. 2014. Academic Ranking of World Universities: http://www.shang hairanking.com/ARWU2014.html.

Eurostat. 2012. *Community Innovation Survey.*

National Science Foundation. 2011. *Business R&D and Innovation Survey.*

National Science Foundation, Science and Engineering Indicators. OECD. iLibrary.

Offshoring Research Network, *Service Provider Surveys 2007–2012.*

World Bank, *World Development Indicators.*

World Bank Annual Report, 2014.

UNESCO.

12 | Why is China failing to leapfrog India's IT outsourcing industry?

WEIDONG XIA, MARY ANN VON GLINOW, AND YINGXIA LI

12.1 The evolution of global outsourcing

The emergence and growth of global outsourcing reflects continuous industrial upgrading and the redefinition and relocation of specialized activities along the industrial value chain. Outsourcing gives an enterprise access to the capabilities needed to perform business activities without owning or managing the resources that are required to generate those capabilities. As shown in Table 12.1, in order to provide the context for understanding Chinese institutional factors and their influence on the development path of the Chinese business service outsourcing industry, we illustrate the different types of outsourcing and the evolution of global outsourcing as a by-product of the continuous shift from downstream to upstream activities. The evolution of global outsourcing has two important characteristics.

First, the different stages of outsourcing represent distinct paths and characteristics. Manufacturing outsourcing is very different from business service outsourcing. Within business service outsourcing, there is also a continued shift from downstream information technology outsourcing (ITO) concentrating on IT-related activities, to midstream business process outsourcing (BPO) concentrating on IT-enabled business process activities, to upstream knowledge process outsourcing (KPO) concentrating on IT-enabled knowledge process activities. Even within each of these categories, there is a continuous shift from their respective downstream activities to upstream activities.

Second, shifts from downstream activities to upstream activities require not only the outsourcing vendors to adapt to new process capabilities but also an upgrading of infrastructure from that which supports downstream process capabilities to new infrastructure that

Table 12.1 *Evolution of global outsourcing*

	Manufacturing outsourcing (downstream) from late 1970s	Business service outsourcing (upstream)		Knowledge process outsourcing (KPO) (upstream) from late 2000s
		Information technology outsourcing (ITO) (downstream) from late 1970s	Business process outsourcing (BPO) (midstream) from late 1990s	

Functions outsourced	– Client's well-defined structured manufacturing processes	– Client's well-defined structured IT-related processes
		– Examples of categories:
		  • IT R&D (integrated circuit and electronic circuit R&D, testing platform R&D, e-commerce platform R&D, IT service R&D)
		  • Software development (requirement determination, logical design, physical design, coding, integration, testing, localization, documentation)
		  • Software systems operations and maintenance (business applications/ERP systems)
		  • IT infrastructure operations and maintenance (computers and networks)
			– Client's well-defined IT-enabled data/information-intensive business processes
			– Examples of categories:
			  • Client's internal business processes (e.g., payroll, accounting, human resources)
			  • Client's customer relationship management processes (e.g., call centers, marketing)
			  • Client's supply-chain management processes (e.g., supplier selection, contract management, fulfillment process)
				– IT-enabled knowledge-intensive/creation-based processes
				– Examples of categories:
				  • Research (intellectual property, legal process, research and consulting)
				  • Development (industrial design, engineering design)
				  • R&D services (medical R&D, animation and new media, other product R&D, inspection and testing R&D)

Reasons clients outsource (purposes/drivers)	– Industrial upgrading – Cost reduction – Labor	– Industrial upgrading – Cost reduction – Labor – Efficiency of IT-related activities	– Industrial upgrading – Capability extension (complimented by cost reduction) – Efficiency of IT-enabled virtual business activities	– Industrial upgrading – Transformation/ innovation (complemented by capability extension and cost reduction) – Efficiency of IT-enabled virtual knowledge activities

Table 12.1 (*cont.*)

| | Manufacturing outsourcing (downstream) from late 1970s | Business service outsourcing (upstream) | | |
		Information technology outsourcing (ITO) (downstream) from late 1970s	Business process outsourcing (BPO) (midstream) from late 1990s	Knowledge process outsourcing (KPO) (upstream) from late 2000s
Client approaches to manage outsourcing relationship	Arm's-length transaction-based	Arm's-length transaction-based	Strategic alliance	Collaborative (partnership)
Roles of client and vendor	– Client defines requirements (brain) – Vendor implements (reactive doer)	– Client defines requirements (brain) – Vendor implements (reactive doer)	– Clients defined initial vision/requirements (brain) – Vendor adapts (proactive doers)	– Co-creation/co-evolution/co-innovation – Client (brain) – Vendor (brain)
Vendor's business model	– Economy of scale – Low profit margin	– Economy of scale – Low profit margin	– Capability-based model (economy of scale/economy of scope) – Medium profit margin	– Innovation-based model (economy of scope/knowledge, agility) – High profit margin

supports upstream process capabilities. The upgrading of infrastructure includes not only changing hard infrastructure – such as technology, facilities, communications, and transportation systems – but also transforming soft infrastructure – such as institutions, culture, skills, and processes. The transformation of the soft infrastructure is much more difficult and takes significantly longer than transforming the hard infrastructure.

12.2 China versus India: outsourcing industry development paths and market positions

India has been a top business service outsourcing destination for the last four decades. As China aims at extending its competitive advantage from manufacturing outsourcing to business service outsourcing, leapfrogging India becomes the target for the industry. China and India have both experienced significant national economic reform and growth in the past four decades, with different development paths and market positions. In terms of overall economic development and growth, China has outpaced India. According to the World Bank, in 2013, China's gross domestic product (GDP) ($9.24 trillion) and GDP per capita ($6,560) were about five times and four and a half times India's GDP ($1.875 trillion) and GDP per capita ($1,570) respectively.[1] However, in 2013, India's[2] service outsourcing accounted for about 55% ($86 billion) of the global offshore outsourcing market, whereas China's[3] market share (28%, $45.4 billion) was about half of India's. From 2008 to 2013, China's offshore outsourcing consistently trailed India's by about $40 billion annually. Systemic gaps exist between the two countries with regard to global competitiveness and the market share of their service outsourcing (Asuyama, 2012; Lo and Liu, 2012).

China's difficulties in catching up to India in business service outsourcing are rooted in the systemic differences between the two countries' economic development paths amid massive shifts in global industrial upgrading and the relocation of economic value-chain activities. Between 1949, when the People's Republic of China was founded,

---

[1] World Bank, http://data.worldbank.org.
[2] Source of India data: www.nasscom.org.
[3] Source of China data: China Outsourcing Institute: Report on China Sourcing Development (2014).

and 1978, when its open-door policy regarding economic reform and development was initiated, China focused on a shift from agriculture to industrialization. During the initial period, the country's development aimed at building a traditional, manufacturing-based economy by imitating the Soviet Union's economic development model based on central planning and industrialization. In 1978, China had massive supplies of low-cost labor and undeveloped land but lacked financial resources and advanced technology. By implementing economic reform policies that encouraged foreign direct investment and technology transfer, mostly from Asian countries nearby, China was able to build massive manufacturing infrastructure and capacity, becoming the world's factory, and indeed manufacturing has been the main source of China's GDP growth.

At the same time, starting in the late 1970s, the global outsourcing market grew beyond downstream manufacturing to include upstream business service outsourcing as a result of movement in developed countries up the industrial value chain to higher-value service activities. In contrast to China's initial economic reform and development, which built up manufacturing capacity, India's economic development began with an altogether different value proposition, by taking advantage of opportunities in the emerging business service outsourcing market. India's unique timing and opportunity owed to two factors. First, India had had difficulty in moving labor from agriculture to manufacturing. A large number of management and technology graduates had emerged from the newly established Indian Institutes of Technology (IITs) and Indian Institutes of Management (IIMs). But many of the graduates could not find appropriate employment because of the weak demand for manufacturing talent in the country. Second, in the same period, enterprises in developed countries were struggling with the Y2K crisis due to the low IT capabilities that a majority of global enterprises had. Developed countries such as the United States and the United Kingdom were struggling with their insufficient supply of IT workers and became aware of India's great quantity of underemployed IT professionals, who had English-language proficiency and cultural familiarity with Western countries. So opportunities for IT outsourcing were created by the two sides' complementary needs. Thus India did not follow the same gradual industrial upgrading path as China did, which started with downstream labor-intensive manufacturing outsourcing; rather, it engaged in business service outsourcing to follow the changing global market, and services have become the main source of India's GDP growth, rather than manufacturing, as was the case in China.

The differences in their development paths, particularly the timing of entrance into the different stages of the business service outsourcing value-chain streams, highlight the barriers that China faces in becoming competitive in business service outsourcing, let alone capable of leapfrogging India in it. In essence, China has always been one step behind India in its development of business service outsourcing, and this gap creates a systemic downstream trap for the Chinese business service outsourcing industry. China started to develop policies and national infrastructure for building large-scale manufacturing outsourcing capacity in the late 1970s, but by this time India had already implemented the necessary national policies and infrastructure for building large-scale ITO service outsourcing capacity. When China extended its outsourcing focus from manufacturing to ITO-based business services in the late 1990s, India had already built a mature ITO industry with an established market share in the global market, accounting for a majority share of the United States and Europe, and had already extended its focus from scale-based ITO to developing the ability to deliver high-value-added BPO. So whereas China was trying to use the same mentality and policies to build massive scale-based ITO capacity as it did in manufacturing by using a "low-cost world factory" model, India was building new capabilities based on economies of scope to expand its industry into the business service outsourcing value chain. In the late 2000s, when China was trying to catch up to the BPO market, India had already gained a sizable share of the global BPO market and had increased its upstream value chain to deliver KPO. In addition to its systemic path-dependency barriers caused by its timing of entry and industrial structure, China faces the challenge of overcoming high barriers to entry in a mature business service outsourcing market (Lewin, 2013). Given that English-speaking countries such as the United States and the United Kingdom account for a majority of the demand for global outsourcing, China also faces significant barriers due to the language deficiency of its workforce and significant cultural distance barriers. Higher value-added activities in business service outsourcing require a high level of professionalism and nontechnical skills, and high International Organization for Standardization (ISO) process management maturity – which few

Chinese business service outsourcing companies possess. Additional issues, such as intellectual property rights, and other political and legal challenges also create significant barriers for China in entering the global service outsourcing market. Such entrance barriers are high because, as shown in Table 12.1, as the focus of outsourcing activities extends the value-chain stream from manufacturing, ITO, and BPO to KPO, the relationship between the client and the vendor becomes much more strategic and tightly coupled, and therefore it is much more difficult for a new entrant to break into the market. Thus, China's business service outsourcing industry finds itself in a downstream trap that is much more systemic and difficult to break out of than has been recognized. We argue that this downstream trap is caused largely by the institutional factors that have shaped the structure and development path of business service outsourcing in China. For China to escape this downstream trap, transformational changes must take place in these key institutional factors.

12.3 Institutional barriers in the development of Chinese business service outsourcing

The evolution of Chinese industrial upgrading and its economic development path are deeply influenced by the government's system of central planning and control based on five-year plans. Because of its strong top-down control governance structure, backed by incentive and sanction policies that affect all aspects of the economy in general and each company specifically, this institutional environment plays a critical role that either facilitates or impedes the country's economic and industrial development path. Central to China's institutional policymaking process is a controlled economic experimentalism along with political and ideological pragmatism in the different market environments. As the country's economic development focus extends from a paradigm focusing on manufacturing outsourcing to a new paradigm focusing on business service outsourcing, policies and a policymaking process that worked well in one paradigm may actually become obstacles in a later paradigm. China has undergone three distinct periods of economic restructuring and industrial upgrading since 1949, with a consistent institutional policymaking structure and process.

12.3.1 The first period, 1949–1978: closed-door autocratic economic experimentalism

Between 1949 and 1978, China's economic development was governed purely by top-down central planning. The economic development path during this period was characterized by command-and-control-style policymaking, and the complete political and economic alignment accordingly led to ideological campaigns and economic experiments in a closed-door environment under the control of the government, including the famous "commune economy," "Great Leap Forward" (1958–1960), and "Cultural Revolution" (1966–1976) (Heilmann and Perry, 2011). In contrast to a conventional policy process, in which policy analysis, formulation, and embodiment in legislation precedes implementation, Chinese policy experimentation in this period comprised, first, innovating through implementation and, then, drafting universal laws and regulations (Heilmann, 2008). Policy experimentation was captured in the expression "from point to surface" (Heilmann and Perry, 2011) and started with setting up "experimental points," then constituting "experience models" from "successful cases and experiences," followed by implementing those "experience models" on a larger scale. Typically, special policies were developed according to those experimental points and subsequent implementation of selected "model experience" results (Florini, Lai, and Tan, 2012). The institutional policies and policymaking factors in this closed-door autocratic experimental period made China fall behind the rest of the world, creating significant economic and technological gaps.

12.3.2 The second period, 1978 to early 2000: open-door pluralistic/pragmatic manufacturing-based economic experimentalism

Since 1978, with the implementation of its open-door policy, China has experienced unprecedentedly high economic growth, which has fundamentally changed its role and position in the global economy. China has created a rather unique context in which central planning (with strong regulatory directives as well as financial incentive policies) and the market economy (with market competition and privatization) jointly shape the country's economic growth and the development of various industrial sectors. The country's economic development path since 1978 has been characterized by both experimentalism and pragmatism (Florini, Lai, and Tan, 2012; Heilmann, 2008). The new socialist pragmatism is captured in such famous expressions as "regardless of whether a cat is black or white, as long as it catches mice, it's a good cat" by Deng Xiaoping and "feeling for stones while crossing the river" by Chen Yun.

Although "from point to surface" is still the cornerstone of the country's policy-led experimental economic development approach, the addition of pragmatism to the traditional experimentalism made the post-1978 China economic development path much more multifaceted and contextualized than that of the pre-1978 era. Before 1978, the country's rule-of-man-style policymaking led to nationwide implementation of "model experiences" and "ideological campaigns" without taking into account the diverse social, cultural, and geo-economic environments across the country. In contrast, the post-1978 pragmatism allowed the experimentalism to include a degree of informality and flexibility. The country's policy-led "from point to surface" experimental approach began to acknowledge the great diversity of environments and regional/local variations, as well as dynamic uncertainties involved in adapting to the constantly evolving domestic and global environments. This new method reflected the need for contextualized learning and gave different localities a measure of autonomy when implementing "experience model" policies, to further experiment, negotiate, and implement interpretations and decisions based on local conditions. As a consequence, while government institutions retain ultimate power in policymaking and supervision when using this experimental approach, multiple parallel decision-making and negotiation processes coexist, involving contextualized experimental points and implementation of model-experience policies at different levels of government and across different regions/localities. Therefore, China's economic policymaking and implementation do not form a monolithic process but, rather, a complex pluralistic process involving pragmatic experimentalism characterized by multiple parallel policies and implementation coupled with some informality, which allows a great deal of contextualized interpretation and adaptation in policy implementation (Chen and Ku, 2014; Zhu, 2014).

During its economic reform and rapid growth powered by the development of large-scale manufacturing outsourcing between 1978 and early 2000, these institutional pragmatic experimental policies served

China well. China's industrial policies enabled rapid industrialization and consistent economic growth because these policies facilitated the development of a private sector along the lines of the country's comparative advantages and tapped into the potential of its latecomer advantages (Lin, 2015).

12.3.3 The third period, from early 2000s: institutional barriers for transforming China from manufacturing-based to service-based outsourcing

By the early 2000s, China had established itself as the world's factory. The by-now well-established infrastructure had enabled the country to gain comparative advantages based not only on low labor costs but also on significant financial resources and manufacturing capability. Subsequently, the Chinese government started to push for companies to move up the global industrial value chain to expand services and technology-based exports. As it changed the focus of its policies, the government reduced and reversed government incentives that promoted, protected, and subsidized manufacturing; as a result, a significant number of small to medium-size manufacturing companies closed because of their inability to absorb added costs after losing these incentives. At the same time, policies similar to those used in the previous period to establish the country's manufacturing base were developed to promote, protect, and subsidize the establishment of large-scale services and technology-based exports.

The government's policies regarding business service outsourcing comprise multiple horizontal authorities/agencies and multiple vertical levels from the central to the local governments, with policy interpretation and implementation by different stakeholders in different regions. Thus, a complex and dynamic web of policies has been developed and implemented by different government agencies at various levels as government planning and incentive tools governing different aspects of the business service outsourcing industry. Three major milestone government initiatives have played key roles in shaping the structure and development path of China's outsourcing industry.

The first major initiative, embodied in Policy 18 issued in 2000 by the State Council, was a key turning point in the establishment and growth of IT-based services. China coined the term "informationization" to reflect its desire of using IT to upgrade its industrialization effort. Based on a series of important strategic principles, the State Council issued Policy 18 to declare its focus on "using informationization to lead industrialization, use industrialization to enable informationization" and to place a "high priority on the development of information industry, to vigorously promote the application of information technology, to take a new path to industrialization, to promote national productivity by leaps and bounds." Policy 18 attempted to articulate a vision, a set of guiding principles, and an architectural path for the development of Chinese IT-based services.

The second major initiative, called the "Thousand-Hundred-Ten" project, was initiated in 2006 to implement the State Council's goal articulated in the eleventh five-year plan (2006–2010) to develop a number of bases for national business service outsourcing. To implement this strategic vision, the Ministry of Commerce and the Ministry of Information Industry began to implement the "Thousand-Hundred-Ten" project, whose goal was, within three to five years, to invest more than RMB 100 million to establish 10 bases for service outsourcing, attract 100 of the top 500 global multinational companies to shift some of their outsourced services to China, and found 1,000 internationally qualified Chinese service outsourcing companies. This initiative drove various government ministries and their corresponding provincial and local government branches to actively work together in the development of policies and measures to promote business service outsourcing.

The third major initiative was the designation of twenty-one outsourcing service model cities and the establishment of eighty-four service outsourcing model parks between 2006 and 2010. In 2006, Dalian was the first to be so designated by the Ministry of Commerce and the Ministry of Information Industry, with its established outsourcing service base to Asian countries nearby, particularly Japan and South Korea. The government, at both the national and the local levels, issued many interpretive and implementation policies to provide strong financial support for rapidly establishing and scaling business service outsourcing in China. The central planning approach required all model cities to develop and gain approval for their strategic plans, with growth targets and implementation measures. Table 12.2 illustrates the model cities' goals and their local policies as interpretations and implementation measures over the subsequent three to five years after a city had been designated as a model city.

Table 12.2 Model cities' three- to five-year goals and policies

City	Revenue	Industry size	Workforce, employment	Examples of local opinions and policies	Examples of local incentives
Beijing	RMB 30 billion, 72% of GDP, 70% of labor, 10% annual growth	Attract 500 new companies (150 CMM3 (Capability Maturity Model), 30 CMM5), 1–2 companies with over 10,000 employees; 30–50 companies with more than 1,000 employees	200,000 working in service outsourcing, 50,000 new hires from among university graduates, 50,000 trained, 100,000 new jobs		Special training fund, 15% refund of newly employed university graduate fee, rewards for high-position talents, international authentication fund, rights to self-managed import/ export, 4% subsidy of software exports, CMM certification fund
Tianjin	RMB 30 billion ($1.5 billion in exports)	Attract 1,200 new companies (70 CMM3, 30 CMM5), 1–2 companies with over 10,000 employees; 50 companies with more than 1,000 employees	160,000 working in service outsourcing, 100,000 new hires from among university graduates, training to 120,000 college students, 140,000 new jobs	Opinions on Tianjin Promoting Service Outsourcing Development, Provisional Regulations on Promoting Development of Service Outsourcing in Tianjin Economic Development Zone, Methods on Awarding Investment in Huayuan Industrial Park	

Table 12.2 (*cont.*)

City	Revenue	Industry size	Workforce, employment	Examples of local opinions and policies	Examples of local incentives
				(outside the ring) by Tianjin Hi-tech Industry Park, Preferential Taxation Policies for Development of Software Industry and Integrated Circuit Industry, Notice by the Tianjin Government on Accelerating Development of Software Industry, and Guideline for Development of Service Outsourcing Industry in the Free Trade Zone.	
Shanghai	RMB 120 billion ($1.5 billion in exports)	500 new companies	200,000 working in service outsourcing, 100,000 new hires from among university graduates, training to 50,000 college students, 100,000 new jobs	Notice of the Shanghai Municipal Government's Opinions on Printing and Distributing Several Policies for Encouraging the Development of Outsourcing Industry, Notice on Forwarding and Implementation Opinions of the Circular of the Ministry of Finance, the	

Chongqing	$800 million in service outsourcing exports	10 new top MNCs to outsource services; 20 large and medium-size outsourcing companies with international qualification		State Administration of Taxation and the General Administration of Customs on the Issues Concerning Tax Incentives for the Development of Software and Integrated Circuit Industries. Measures for Certifying and Managing Chongqing's Software and Information Service Outsourcing Enterprises (Trial), Temporary Regulations on Accelerating the Development of Chongqing's Software and Information Service Outsourcing Industry, and Notice of Chongqing Municipal Government on Issuing the Preferential Policies for Inviting Medium and Senior Software Talents, etc.	Maximum of RMB 1 million in incentives to enterprises that passed the Ministry of Commerce's service outsourcing grading and with annual exports of over $500,000
Dalian	RMB 50 billion ($2.8 billion in exports)	4-6 large companies with annual revenue > RMB 1 billion, 50	140,000 working in service outsourcing, 100,000 new hires	Dalian Municipal People's Government's Opinions on Speeding Up the	

Table 12.2 (*cont.*)

City	Revenue	Industry size	Workforce, employment	Examples of local opinions and policies	Examples of local incentives
		well-known Dalian software brands	from among university graduates, training to 50,000 college students, 100,000 new jobs	Development of Software Industry, Stipulations on Introducing Software Talents of Dalian, Opinions on Encouraging the Development of Software Industry, Management of Specially-Allocated Fund for Software Enterprises in Dalian, Stipulations to Protect Individual Information of Dalian Software and Information Service Industry.	
Shenzhen	RMB 180 billion, 27% annual growth; $6 billion software export, 30% annual growth		300,000 working in software outsourcing	Notice on Accelerating the Development of Shenzhen's Service Outsourcing Industry; the Decision on the Optimization of Regional Innovation System for A Fast and Sustainable Development of High and New Technology Industry;	

Guangzhou	2010 service outsourcing revenue should be four times that 2005	8 outsourcing service clusters, 30 MNC service outsourcing companies, 100 companies with international certification (2 companies with more than RMB 1 billion in annual revenue, 2 companies with	60,000 specialized personnel for the service outsourcing industry	Regulations on Providing Further Support for the Development of New and High Technology Industry; Regulations on the Cultivation of Talents in High and New Technology Industry and on the Introduction of Talents; and Measures on the Implementation of "Providing Further Support to the Development of High and New Technology." Opinions on Accelerating the Development of Service Outsourcing in Guangzhou and Administrative Measures for China Outsourcing Base Guangzhou Exemplary Zone; Opinions on Accelerating the Development of Service Industry; Measures of Guangzhou for Certifying	RMB 1 billion to promote ITO/BPO investment, talent introduction/ training, exemplary zone construction, company headquarters development

Table 12.2 (*cont.*)

City	Revenue	Industry size	Workforce, employment	Examples of local opinions and policies	Examples of local incentives
		over 5,000 employees)		High & New-tech Results Transferring Projects, Several Regulations of Guangzhou for Promoting Venture Capital Industry; Regulations of Guangzhou for Encouraging Overseas China's Graduates to Work in Guangzhou; Measures for the Allocation and Management of Guangzhou Science & Technology Fund; Notice on Forwarding the Opinions of Guangzhou Development and Reform Commission on Strongly Promoting Guangzhou's Financial Industry.	
Wuhan	RMB 50 billion ($500 million in exports)	Attract 800 new companies (100 CMM3, 20 CMM5), 2–4	Training of 80,000 college students, 100,000 new jobs	Measures for the Management of Science & Technology Enterprise Hatcher of Wuhan;	Special training fund, 15% refund of newly employed university graduate fee, 50% reimbursement of

companies with over 5,000 employees; 10 companies with more than 1,000 employees

Opinions of the Provincial Government on Accelerating the Development of Software Industry; Opinions of Municipal Government on Further Encouraging the Development of Software Industry and Integrated Circuit Industry; Opinions on the Implementation of Preferential Policies to Accelerate Software Industry Development; Notice of Provincial Government on Issuing Several Policies for Promoting the Development of Software Industry and Integrated Circuit Industry; Notice of the Administrative Office of Municipal Government on Accelerating the Construction and Development of High & New-tech Innovation Service Center.

training fee for pre-occupation training of new employees; RMB100 million each year for qualification certification, international market exploration, personnel training. RMB100,000 reward and additional subsidy for passing software outsourcing certification, preferential land price and lease rental in service park

Table 12.2 (*cont.*)

City	Revenue	Industry size	Workforce, employment	Examples of local opinions and policies	Examples of local incentives
Harbin		A number of large and strong companies and high-end service outsourcing professionals. A large service outsourcing industry park, a service outsourcing training center, and a common software testing platform for service outsourcing companies.			
Chengdu	RMB 80 billion ($500 million in exports), 45% annual growth	Outsourcing enterprises with working staff of over 3,000 and with revenues of over RMB 1 billion	200,000 working in software outsourcing	Chengdu municipal government opinions on the development of outsourcing service; preferential policies for the development of software industry in the hi-tech industry development zone (trial implementation),	RMB 200 million to implement the training plan of outsourcing talent.

Nanjing	RMB 40 billion (RMB 5 billion in export), 40% annual growth	Attract 150 new companies (100 CMM3, 20 CMM5), 3 companies with over 10,000 employees; 20 companies with more than 1,000 employees	200,000 working in service outsourcing, 50,000 new hires from among university graduates	RMB 3 billion for the development of international service outsourcing infrastructure and implementation of preferential policies and awards. The government awards the leading international service outsourcing companies according to performance. Companies that employ over 5,000 people and earn over US$100 million in annual revenues from international service outsourcing will be awarded RMB 10 million. Companies that employ over 2,500 people and earn	policies and opinions on the development of Chengdu's software industry; opinions on the acceleration of the development of outsourcing industry.

Table 12.2 (*cont.*)

City	Revenue	Industry size	Workforce, employment	Examples of local opinions and policies	Examples of local incentives
					over US$50 million in annual revenues from international service outsourcing will be awarded RMB 5 million. Companies that employ over 500 people and earn over US$10 million in annual revenues from international service outsourcing will be awarded RMB 2 million. Companies that earn US$1 million to $10 million in annual revenues from international service outsourcing and grow over 30% will be awarded RMB 0.5–1 million.
Xi'an	RMB 60 billion		300,000 working in service outsourcing		Supporting and preferential policies for outsourcing enterprises, including basic working condition

guarantees, such as network telecommunication, working area allocation; systemized professional service such as HR supply and training, including the loan subsidy, certification subsidy, fund awards needed by the enterprises, so as to further promote the industrial development of Xi'an outsourcing industry.

Jinan	RMB 400 billion ($500 million in exports), 40% annual growth	Attract 150 new companies (6 CMM5), 5 companies with 3,000–5,000 employees; 20 companies with more than 1,000 employees	100,000 working in service outsourcing, 35,000 new hires from among university graduates	Opinions on Promoting the Development of Service Outsourcing Industry; Measures for Certifying Service Outsourcing Enterprises and Training Institutions (Trial); and Temporary Administrative Measures on the Special Fund of Jinan for Service Outsourcing; Opinions of Jinan Government on Strengthening Patent	The subsidy for fresh university graduates and graduates of colleges and secondary schools with no work experience may not exceed 50% of the training fee or RMB 2,000 per person; that for pre-occupation training of new employees may not exceed 60% of the training fee or RMB 3,000 per person. For customized personnel

Table 12.2 (cont.)

City	Revenue	Industry size	Workforce, employment	Examples of local opinions and policies	Examples of local incentives
				Work, Measures of Jinan for Appraising Patents (Temporary).	training, proper subsidies should be provided to service outsourcing enterprises. Incentives are offered at different levels for service outsourcing enterprises in Jinan: RMB 50,000 for enterprises with annual exports between US$1 million and $3 million; RMB 100,000 for enterprises with annual exports between US$3 million and $5 million; RMB 200,000 for enterprises with annual exports between US$5 million and $10 million; and RMB 300,000 for enterprises with annual exports above US$10 million. The incentives are issued in January every year

				according to the actual export value of the previous year as provided by customs statistics. In addition, a service outsourcing contribution award offers RMB 50,000–200,000 as incentives to companies with outstanding contributions to the attraction of service outsourcing businesses.
Hangzhou	$1.924 billion ($1 billion export)	Attract 100 new companies (5 CMM5), 1–2 companies with 10,000 staff	50,000 working in service outsourcing, 50,000 new hires from among university graduates, training for 30,000 college students, 20,000 new jobs	Opinions of the People's Government of Hangzhou Municipality on the Development of Service Outsourcing Industry; Guidance of the People's Government of Hangzhou Municipality on the promotion of brand development; Notice on the Standardization of the Process of Software Enterprise Authentication and Annual Audit; Regulations on the

Table 12.2 (*cont.*)

City	Revenue	Industry size	Workforce, employment	Examples of local opinions and policies	Examples of local incentives
				Management of Specialized Fund on Service Outsourcing in Hangzhou (trial implementation); Regulations on the Establishment of Scientific Innovation Service Platform; Temporary Measures on the Promotion of Financing Guarantee for Innovation-oriented Companies; Opinions of the People's Government of Hangzhou Municipality on the Development and Protection of Intellectual Property Rights and Opinions on the	

| Hefei | RMB 10 billion ($500 million export) | Attract 100 new companies (50 CMM3) | 50,000 working in service outsourcing | Introduction of High-positioning Talents. | Hefei government gives strong financial support by allocating RMB 50 million from its budget to facilitate the development of service outsourcing, with special emphasis on major service outsourcing companies, human resource training, public services, subsidies, and international certification and support funds set up by the ministries of commerce, information industry, science and technology. The government also provides financial support for exports of eligible service outsourcing companies. In addition, it also offers tax incentives and cuts income tax by 15% for the companies that are designated as new |

Table 12.2 (*cont.*)

City	Revenue	Industry size	Workforce, employment	Examples of local opinions and policies	Examples of local incentives
					and high-technology companies by the authorities of science and technology in accordance with national regulations.
Nanchang	2010: RMB 10 billion (8 billion from ITO and 2 billion from BPO); 2015: RMB 40 billion (30 billion from ITO and 10 billion from BPO)		70,000 (in 2010) and 250,000 (in 2015) working in service outsourcing	Preferential policies for service outsourcing companies, such as Policies of the Nanchang Government to Support Development of Service Outsourcing and Methods on Administration of Support Funds for Service Outsourcing Labor Training in Nanchang.	Nanchang will not only allocate from its budget an equivalent amount of capital to the national support fund, but also set up a fund in 2008 to provide financial support to service companies in employment, market development, housing, certification and export. In addition, Nanchang has also promulgated methods on administration of supporting funds for service outsourcing labor training to provide subsidies to companies and training agencies on the

Changsha	RMB 30 billion ($100 million in exports)	Attract 10 top MNCs to outsource services, 20 medium-size to large outsourcing companies pass international qualification certification	100,000 working in service outsourcing	basis of the national standards. To encourage the development of service outsourcing, the Changsha government has set up an ad hoc outsourcing leading group and formulated preferential policies, such as financial policies or tax incentives to promote the development small and medium-size high-tech companies, cartoon animation industry, new materials industry, and university industrial park.
Daqing	RMB 5 billion (in 2010), 15 billion (in 2015)	150 (in 2010) and 300 (in 2015) service outsourcing companies		Daqing will provide the service outsourcing companies with the following incentives: housing rent exemption, subsidies for communications, certification and labor training, preferential loans

Table 12.2 (*cont.*)

City	Revenue	Industry size	Workforce, employment	Examples of local opinions and policies	Examples of local incentives
					and settlement of employees.
Suzhou	RMB 15 billion ($1 billion in exports)	Attract 50 of the world's top 500 companies outsourcing services, 20 of world's top 100 service outsourcing provider companies move to Suzhou park, with 1–2 top 10 ITO/BPO companies	60,000 working in service outsourcing, training 5,000 each year	Tailored Taxation Polices for Technology-based Service Companies in the Suzhou Industrial Parks, Polices on Promoting Development of Technology-based Service Companies in the Suzhou Industrial Parks, Policies on Promoting Development of Service Outsourcing of the Suzhou Industrial Parks, and Policies on Administration of Certification of Technology-based Service Companies in the Suzhou Industrial Parks.	Beginning July 1, 2006, 15% of corporate income tax was cut for domestic and foreign technology-based service companies that have been certified as new and high-technology-based companies. The actual legal payroll of the technology-based service companies that have been certified as new and high-technology-based companies will be deducted before corporate income tax payment. Beginning January 1, 2006, employee education funds, within 2.5% of the total payroll of company in the same year, were deducted from corporate income tax payment for

City					
Wuxi	$3 billion	Attract 20 famous companies to Wuxi; 3,000 service outsourcing enterprises (2,000 software outsourcing, 500 procedure outsourcing, 500 animation outsourcing). 100 companies with over 2,000 employees, 5 with more than 5,000 employees, 1–2 with more than 10,000 employees.	200,000 working in service outsourcing (of which 150,000 will be practical and medium-end employees and 100,000 university graduates)	Three-Year Action Plan to Promote International Service Outsourcing Industry in Wuxi, Opinions on Speeding Up the Development of Service Outsourcing Industry in Wuxi and Opinions on the Development Goal of Service Outsourcing Industry in 2007.	technology-based service companies. Wuxi will give additional funds to enrich the national fund to support the development of service outsourcing. The ratio between local funds and national funds is 1:2. The additional funds are mainly used to support the certification, human resources training, and public platform construction for service outsourcing enterprises.
Xiamen	30% annual growth				

Analyses of the central government's model city initiatives and the corresponding local government's interpretative policies, goals, and implementation measures reveal serious issues that illustrate the systemic barriers caused by the institutional policies and policymaking processes.

First, while the government's intention was to extend the country's economic development focus from manufacturing to services, the overall mind-set and approach underlying government policies are still the same. Using the "from point to surface" experimental policy approach, the government's overall focus has been mainly on investing in the development of physical plant and infrastructure without first considering the structural differences in soft infrastructure, such as mind-set changes, the workforce's lack of foreign-language skills and professionalism, nontechnical skills, companies' lack of maturity in highly standardized processes, protection of intellectual property rights, and systemic problems in the country's education system. The large government investment now made in the 21 model outsourcing cities and a large number of high-tech parks precisely follows the large-scale manufacturing cluster model. The central government not only sets the goals but controls massive resources and incentives, while local governments, at the provincial, city, and district levels, are required to implement the central government's initiatives and policies with their own interpretative policies and financial resources. In essence, the various levels of government became the investors and developers of massive industrial office real-estate space and have had to offer hefty incentives to attract companies to move into those spaces. As a result, instead of focusing on developing a competitive industrial structure and soft infrastructure critical for entering and competing in the global business service outsourcing market, the government policies have led to massive development of land and physical office space. The government policies are also directed at filling and managing those physical spaces by providing large incentives, subsidies, and protective measures so that companies that have grown significantly in size can stay afloat even though they have not been able to grow in terms of real market-based revenues, either locally or globally.

Second, using the same approaches that underlie the five-year plan system, the government's policies reflect ambitious goals that are based solely on the supply side wishful thinking without considering market positioning and feasibility from the demand side.

This approach applies to most of the planning efforts, from the central government's five-year plan to the massive complex web of plans enacted by various horizontal and vertical levels of government, as manifested in the "thousand-hundred-ten" and model city initiatives, as well as the local governments' goals and implementation measures. For example, as shown in Table 12.2, with the exception of Dalian and Shanghai, many model cities established ambitious outsourcing revenue growth goals over a three- to five-year period, without considering demand-side factors, such as the target market and customers, the service outsourcing activities provided, how to enter those markets to establish co-evolutionary business relationships, the changes required in the soft infrastructure, and industrial competitiveness. Dalian had already built its ITO base serving Japan and South Korea because of its geographic proximity, language advantages, and historical cultural similarity to those countries. Shanghai had already built a large-scale financial service outsourcing base. The strategic plans developed by the model cities mostly used population, per capita income, and geopolitical boundaries as the bases for forecasting the growth of revenue. Explicit in the government's initiatives and policies was its position and desire to catch up to India by building up the number and size of companies. The model cities' ambitious workforce and employment growth goals also reflect the government's desire to solve the country's employment problems by founding a large number of service outsourcing companies. As a result of this supply-side policy orientation, the model cities and parks have built up massive capacity, as measured by the number of companies and employees working at them. However, because of the high entry barriers of the service outsourcing market, few companies possess the capabilities and competitiveness that would enable them to successfully enter the global service outsourcing market. Consequently, while China's service outsourcing has caught up to or even surpassed India in terms of the number of companies and employees on paper, China has consistently trailed India in terms of market share and revenue.

Third, because of the government policies' focus on building a large-scale outsourcing industry in a short period, the industry's structure is stuck in downstream outsourcing value-chain activities. The government's policymaking process included little consideration of defining and planning the development of appropriate comparative advantages and industrial structure before building large-scale high-tech parks and massive office space. The 21 model cities are simultaneously expanding the capacity of their service outsourcing companies without differentiating industry and company positions and competitiveness. Resources are wasted, however, as the model cities and parks try to meet the scale growth goals and fill office space in those parks by providing incentives for them to compete against one another in attracting companies and talent from the country's limited pool of qualified managers and professionals. This resulted in high turnover in the industry, which made firms reluctant to invest in meaningful training and employee development programs and further exacerbated challenges in competitiveness that companies face. A few large companies account for the majority of outsourcing contracts and revenue, and even they concentrate on low-value-added technology products/services due to their inability to transition from downstream to upstream service outsourcing (Fan, 2014; Niosi and Tschang, 2009). A majority of these companies are small, with limited comparative resources/capabilities and market competitiveness, and are heavily subsidized and protected by government policies. Without massive incentives and support from so many different government sources, many companies might not even be able to survive.

12.4 Areas for policy development and further research

China cannot build a world-class service outsourcing industry without breaking down the systemic barriers caused by institutional factors. Doing so will require consideration of the relationship between the different stages of the global outsourcing market and the comparative advantages and core capabilities that Chinese service outsourcing companies must possess to be able to compete in the ever-evolving global market. The transition in the basis of the country's economy from manufacturing to service/technology and, finally, to knowledge and innovation requires changes not only in policies that directly promote new industrial sectors and companies but also in the institutional and industrial infrastructure.

Given the complexity and impact of transforming China's institutional factors, building this kind of business service outsourcing will require a significant amount of work to develop the theoretical insights and guidelines for both policymakers and corporate leaders. We propose five critical areas of future research: (1) changing the mind-set;

(2) simplifying the government policymaking and implementation process; (3) redefining comparative advantages; (4) resetting investment priorities; and (5) transforming the industrial structure and enterprise competitiveness.

12.4.1 Changing the mind-set

First, extending the focus of economic development from a low-value-chain stream of manufacturing to a high-value-chain stream of innovation-based services necessitates a change in the mind-set and a recognition that different kinds of policymaking structures and capabilities are needed. During the first stage of economic reform and development, when it was preparing to build a manufacturing base, China recognized its low-cost, high-quality labor comparative advantage and its lack of financial capital and technologies. Thereafter, it created and implemented the pragmatic "from points to surface" experimental policies that enabled different special economic zones to leverage their unique local economic/labor advantages and connections to overseas Chinese to attract foreign direct investment and technology transfer. The development of industrial parks and zones facilitated the emergence of strong manufacturing clusters with incentivized access to resources that directly favored the growth of manufacturing firms (Liu, Weng, Mao, and Huang, 2013). However, the same kind of policymaking cannot be mechanically superimposed on building the country's business service outsourcing and innovation capabilities without recognizing the comparative advantages and competitive capabilities needed at different stages of the global business service outsourcing market. A mind-set shift is needed to move away from manufacturing-based thinking to develop infrastructure, both physical and soft, for the service-based outsourcing industry. Shifting the mind-set is a complex process that will require significant research to clarify which changes are needed, how to implement them, and what to expect from the various stakeholders.

12.4.2 Simplifying the government policymaking and implementation process

Pragmatic experimentalism served China well in its rapid economic development as it built a manufacturing-based economy by overcoming the rigid one-size-fits-all approach inherent in central planning. To some extent, the past four decades in which pragmatism dominated in China's policymaking and implementation have also created a new culture, in which government policy has become so general that all interpretations representing conflicting interests become inherently necessary, possible, and acceptable. Massive resources are wasted because of duplicated and often distorted resource allocation caused by compromises across the convoluted web of stakeholders with opportunistic and conflicting interests. Because the government, represented by both horizontal authorities across different ministries/departments and vertical levels across central, provincial, city, and district levels, is intervening through policies and incentives in all aspects of the business service outsourcing industry and individual firms, exacerbated by the loose pragmatism, the policymaking and implementation process has itself become an undertaking that consumes massive resources and, more importantly, caused industrial and firm development paths to be misaligned. The decision-making process has become a resource-consuming closed loop in which the more the government intervenes, the more complex the policymaking and implementation process becomes, the more pragmatism is needed, and the more government intervention is required to manage the process. There are competing levels of government (vertical inconsistencies and misaligned interests) and sectoral competition among different national institutions (horizontal inconsistencies and misaligned interests) (Van De Kaa, Greenven, and Van Puijenbroek, 2013). Reform is required in the government policymaking and implementation process such that the priorities of government policy are redirected to investment in building the soft infrastructure needed to restructure business service outsourcing.

12.4.3 *Redefining comparative advantages*

Countries need to identify the appropriate comparative advantages in order to upgrade their industrial structure successfully (Lin, 2015). As China shifts from manufacturing-based outsourcing to service-based outsourcing, it must redefine its comparative advantages (and disadvantages). Both China and the global outsourcing market have evolved over the past four decades at a rapid pace. Before China can establish ambitious goals for service outsourcing, it must reconsider the basis of its comparative advantage in the context of the evolving global service outsourcing market rather than relying on its tradition of supply-side capacity building. For example, China has amassed massive financial resources and technology bases, and it has developed a rapidly growing consumer market. The government planning and control system enables China to enjoy high efficiency in planning and implementing large-scale economic reforms, and at the same time entrepreneurship is subject to market-based competition. It has built advanced infrastructure nationwide in transportation, logistics, and communication. However, China no longer has the comparative advantages of low-cost labor and low costs of doing business; living standards have risen, as has the cost of real estate. Therefore, those low costs cannot be used as the basis of a strategy for building a competitive Chinese business service outsourcing industry. One source of comparative advantage for China in Asia is its linguistic and cultural closeness to other Asian countries, particularly Japan and South Korea. In particular, Dalian developed creditable market competitiveness and gained a considerable share of the Japanese and South Korean business service outsourcing markets. For all these reasons, China has great potential to expand into new areas of development, but further research is needed to ensure that its policies are based on an assessment of its comparative advantages that are appropriate to those fields.

12.4.4 Resetting investment priorities

As the outsourcing focus extends from manufacturing to services, process-based knowledge and innovation become essential for meeting the clients' need for complementary capabilities in the upstream value chain. The development of such service process knowledge and innovation requires different sets of resources and capabilities from those needed for manufacturing, and so it also requires intellectual talent and appropriate R&D infrastructure (Abrami, Kirby, and McFarlan, 2014; Fan, 2014). Thus, government policymaking needs to take market demand and competitive forces into consideration. Instead of investing in physical infrastructure, the government should focus on investing in soft infrastructure, which is necessary for building truly competitive service outsourcing in alignment with global market trends. Soft infrastructure includes critical areas such as developing human resource skills, transforming the education system, improving business environments, and enhancing standards for professional certification.

Chinese service outsourcing companies are hindered by their employees' poor English proficiency. In addition, due to the one-child policy and the highly competitive test-driven education system, university graduates do not possess the well-rounded critical thinking skills and experiences that are required for higher value-added business service outsourcing. Bie and Yi (2014) point out that the systemic problems in higher education are not only the result of value paradoxes in the development of mass higher education but also the source of conflict in policymaking and policy implementation. There is a critical gap between what is produced by China's education system and what is needed by a competitive business service outsourcing industry. Such changes require multidimensional transformation and call for long and hard coordinated efforts at all levels of government and across industries.

Although China's physical infrastructure, such as transportation and communication networks, has dramatically improved, the business environment lags behind. One significant challenge that Chinese business service outsourcing faces is clients' perceived risk and high transactional costs associated with a lack of trust in the business and legal environment. The widespread business and government practices related to *guanxi* (personal connections) and bribery have made it very difficult for clients in Western countries to do business with Chinese firms as they must walk a fine line between doing viable business and complying with their legal, ethical, and professional obligations. Those clients also have concerns about the lack of protection of intellectual property rights and uncertainties about cyber and data security. Thus, unless it transforms its business environment, China cannot expect its business service outsourcing companies to compete effectively in the global market.

In contrast to Indian companies, which invest heavily in ongoing professionalization and certification of enterprise process standards, Chinese companies in general are reluctant to invest in professional development because they have a very high level of turnover. There is a general lack of well-established professional certification services as well as enterprise-level management and delivery processes that can meet the certification requirements of accepted international standards.

12.4.5 Transforming industrial structure and company competitiveness

Although both the capacity of the industry and the number of service outsourcing contracts have grown significantly, service outsourcing firms often have low profitability because of inflation, rising labor and real-estate costs, and high transaction costs. Chinese business service outsourcing companies need to transition from low-value-added downstream activities to higher value-added midstream and upstream activities in order to prosper (Lo and Liu, 2012).

As companies move up the value chain, their need for innovation and strategic management and partnership development becomes increasingly important. If government policies continue to incentivize companies to grow only with respect to downstream activities, those companies will have no motivation to innovate and thus will not develop innovation capabilities. Given the low profit margin and rising costs, Chinese companies are also challenged by both survival in the short term and investment in transformation in the long term. Expanding scale blindly may lead to unintended negative consequences, so, rather than aiming for scale in order to stay afloat, Chinese service outsourcing companies should try to grow by seeking new complementary markets.

The Chinese business service outsourcing industry as a whole needs to have more appropriate market diversification and a corresponding competitive portfolio. Currently, there is insufficient differentiation among model cities, model parks, and companies, which engage in widespread imitation and furious competition for the same clients. As a result, even though the capacity of the industry has grown significantly, its overall market competitiveness and revenue-generating capability have not improved. Research is needed to examine appropriate industrial structure and develop a coordinated strategy for the various model cities, model parks, and companies to position themselves with differentiation and complementarity to improve the competitiveness of the overall industry.

Escaping the downstream trap also requires rethinking who the most promising clients are and who the most critical competitors are. The key challenge for Chinese business service outsourcing companies (more than 90% of them are small and medium-size enterprises [SMEs]) is increasing the success rate at identifying and contracting with SME clients in Europe and the United States. Paradoxically, the key challenge that SME clients in Europe and the United States face is in identifying, assessing, and contracting with Chinese business service outsourcing providers. India's factory model is effective for clients in traditional large markets, not for SME client markets, where collaboration and co-creation models are more appropriate. This offers Chinese business service outsourcing companies a rare opportunity to define and develop unique capabilities that will serve emerging European and American SME client markets. Establishing and maintaining excellent customer relationships and creating innovation through offshoring arrangements are the new competitive drivers.

Chinese business service outsourcing companies face some obstacles in entering into and maintaining trust-based long-term client relationships. Most companies tend to pay too much attention to obtaining contracts rather than developing core capabilities through knowledge acquisition. Employees tend to put their own personal interests above the company's interests. Alternative approaches that Chinese companies have been using to enter European and US markets include (1) mergers and acquisitions of overseas companies; (2) sending their own employees overseas to establish branches; and (3) participating in exhibition and trade tours organized by the Chinese government. But the results thus far have not been satisfactory. There is a critical need to understand how to bridge US clients' needs with Chinese offshoring service company capabilities and establish mechanisms to reduce the complex and inefficient intermediary processes.

12.5 Concluding remarks

In the past four decades, China has demonstrated creative adaptation in its economic reforms and development that has allowed its economy to grow rapidly and become dominant. Much of the rapid growth was enabled by government policies that facilitated the accumulation of low-cost, high-quality, labor-intensive manufacturing capabilities assisted by early FDI and technology transfer. However, as China seeks to change the basis of its economy to the provision of services, it must also transition from the policymaking process and focus that were used to build the infrastructure and capability needed for manufacturing to one more in line with services. Its failure to make this transition has created institutional traps that have prevented its business service outsourcing from advancing and from catching up with India. As suggested by Lin (2015), to successfully break out of the low-value industry trap, China must reform and upgrade its soft infrastructure, including institutional, cultural, economic, and educational changes, to support the upgrading of business service outsourcing. In discussing why China cannot innovate, Abrami, Kirby, and McFarlan (2014) say: "The problem, we think, is not the innovation or intellectual capacity of the Chinese people, which is boundless, but the political world in which their schools, universities, and business need to operate, which is very much bounded" (p. 111). Echoing this view, we find that the inability of China's business service outsourcing industry to develop the market competitiveness needed to leapfrog its Indian counterpart is similarly bounded by institutional barriers. We hope that our research will stimulate and promote further debate and research on reforming the Chinese business service outsourcing policymaking process and focus. Until the reforms outlined here are put in place, we see little opportunity for China to leapfrog India in business services. To succeed in this arena, the respective emphases in hard and soft infrastructure in China will need to be greatly reconsidered.

References

Abrami, R.M., Kirby, W.C., and McFarlan, F.W. (2014). Why China can't innovate. *Harvard Business Review*, 92(3), 107–111.

Asuyama, Y. (2012). Skill distribution and comparative advantage: A comparison of China and India. *World Development*, 40(5), 956–969.

Bie, D.R., and Yi, M.C. (2014). The context of higher education development and policy response in China. *Studies in Higher Education*, 39(8), 1499–1510.

Chen, T.J., and Ku, Y.H. (2014). Indigenous innovation vs. *teng-long huanniao*: Policy conflicts in the development of China's flat panel industry. *Industrial and Corporate Change*, 23(6), 1445–1467.

China Outsourcing Institute (2014). *Report on China Outsourcing Development*. Shanghai: Shanghai Jiaotong University Press.

Fan, P. (2014). Innovation in China. *Journal of Economic Surveys*, 28(4), 725–745.

Florini, A., Lai, H., and Tan, Y. (2012). *China Experiments: From Local Innovations to National Reform*. Washington, DC: Brookings Institution Press.

Heilmann, S. (2008). Policy experimentation in China's economic rise. *Studies in Comparative International Development*, 43, 1–26.

Heilmann, S., and Perry, E. (2011). *Mao's Invisible Hand: The Political Foundations of Adaptive Governance in China*. Cambridge, MA: Harvard University Asia Center.

Lewin, A.Y. (2013). *Providers in China and USA: Preliminary Comparison*. Durham, NC: Duke University Outsourcing Research Network Study.

Lin, J.Y. (2015). New structural economics: The third wave of development thinking and the future of the Chinese economy. In *Building Innovation Capacity in China: An Agenda for Averting the Middle Income Trap* (Editors: Arie Lewin), Cambridge University Press.

Liu, R., Weng, Q., Mao, G., and Huang, T. (2013). Industrial cluster, government agency and entrepreneurial development: A case study of Wenzhou City, Zhejiang Province. *Chinese Management Studies*, 7(2), 253–280.

Lo, C.P., and Liu, H.J. (2012). Why India is mainly engaged in offshore service activities, while China is disproportionately engaged in manufacturing? *China Economic Review*, 20, 236–245.

Niosi, J., and Tschang, F.T. (2009). The strategies of Chinese and Indian software multinationals: Implications for internationalization theory. *Industrial and Corporate Change*, 18(2), 269–294.

Van De Kaa, G., Greenven, M., and Van Puijenbroek, G. (2013). Standards battles in China: Opening up the black box of the Chinese government. *Technology Analysis and Strategic Management*, 25(5), 567–581.

Zhu, X. (2014). Mandate versus championship: Vertical government intervention and diffusion of innovation in public services in authoritarian China. *Public Management Review*, 16(1), 117–139.

13 Barriers to organizational creativity in Chinese companies

ZHI-XUE ZHANG AND WEIGUO ZHONG

13.1 Introduction

Since China began its economic reform program in the late 1970s, its economy has experienced rapid growth, with average annual increases in its gross domestic product (GDP) of 9.5% over the past three decades (see Lin 2016, Chapter 2 in this volume). This rapid growth was driven primarily by low-cost labor transferred from agricultural to industrial jobs and massive government investment in infrastructure. As China is exhausting its demographic dividend, which means that the number of labors between the ages of 15 and 59 started to decrease since 2012, the world's second-largest economy is facing serious downward pressure, and the GDP growth rate fell to 7.4% in 2014 – the lowest since 1990. The government has lowered its official growth target for 2015 to around 7%, the lowest annual rate in twenty-five years, and called on everyone to be prepared for this economic slowdown. The term "new normal" has been used to characterize the future Chinese economy as one in which growth will maintain a slower pace, transitioning from its previous rapid rate to one that is more moderate, and it will be increasingly driven more by innovation than by inputs and investment; and the economy's structure over time will continue to improve.

This transition requires Chinese companies to adapt to the new environment and enhance their competitiveness by developing innovative products and updated services. The expanding market economy will force most industries to open up to various types of companies, such as private domestic companies and foreign companies. Unlike in the early years after the initiation of the economic reforms, when

Financial support for this research was provided in part by the National Natural Science Foundation of China under grant number 71372023 to Zhi-Xue Zhang and 71572005 to Weiguo Zhong.

products and services common to many industries were in short supply, many companies now provide competitive products and services in most business sectors – that is, the market has changed from supply-oriented to demand-oriented. Therefore, companies have to compete to gain market share by meeting consumer needs. Customers demand that companies develop differentiated products and services. However, most Chinese companies have enjoyed the benefits of the huge market demand and rapid economic growth in the past three decades, so they have become accustomed to a path to success built on a low-cost strategy. Whether they can develop differentiated products and services through innovation remains to be seen.

How companies can adapt to the rapidly changing environment and escape the development trap is a critical and practical problem. In this chapter, we first reflect on the general growth pattern at Chinese companies and show that most of their development has been driven by high market demand and the rapid pace of overall economic development. Leaders play a particularly critical role in business development and company growth, thus we examine the mind-set of Chinese business leaders and their general business practices over the past three decades. Then, we discuss the multiple barriers to organizational creativity at Chinese companies. Some Chinese enterprises have done well in terms of developing organizational creativity and innovation. We use the cases of Huawei and Tencent to illustrate how these enterprises have evolved. Finally, we discuss some solutions to the problems of Chinese companies with respect to organizational creativity and innovation.

13.2 Growth patterns at Chinese companies

In the past three decades, growth at many Chinese companies has been driven by either the country's huge market or government investment. The first growth pattern is characterized by companies' reaping the benefits from the huge market demand or, as the saying goes, "eating the market." Strong demand from the enormous population has easily fueled explosive growth in many industries.

The second growth pattern at Chinese companies is characterized by taking advantage of government incentives for development or "eating the government." A close connection between business and government officials has been prevalent during the economic transition. Because the promotion of local governors was highly influenced by economic success (Sun, Wright, and Mellahi 2010), local governments were motivated to provide support and resources for companies. According to Zhang and Lin (2014), officials had strong incentives for developing their local economy to increase revenues and to maximize their political accomplishments in the hope of promotion. Government officials in neighboring regions competed in major economic indicators such as the growth rate of local economic development, employment, gross industrial production, and tax revenue. To attract business, they offered support in terms of investing in the construction of infrastructure, making favorable policies for certain industries, and providing financial support or tax breaks for enterprises. Both the central and regional governments are involved in economic activities, which creates close interaction between enterprises and governments. Although the interaction has helped to promote economic development in China (Zhang 2014), it has also inhibited companies from developing their core competence through market competition.

An example of the second type of growth pattern is Suntech, founded by Dr. Zhengrong Shi in 2000 and once a leading firm producing solar photovoltaics (PV) cells in the world. With the continuing strong support from the central and the local governments, Suntech enjoyed huge success in its earlier years and was listed on the New York Stock Exchange (STP, NYSE) in 2005. However, the global financial crisis in 2008 seriously hurt China's exports in PV industry. To deal with the crisis, Suntech should have slowed down its production. However, the local government required it to further expand to create 50,000 additional jobs. Suntech started to decline due to its over-expanded investments, and eventually declared bankruptcy on March 18, 2013. Ironically, Suntech's US counterpart, FirstSolar, has followed a growth pattern of market-oriented innovation. FirstSolar, Inc. used cadmium telluride as a semiconductor to produce panels to compete with the crystalline silicon technology used by companies as Suntech. Cadmium telluride modules are less costly to produce, but are less efficient. FirstSolar developed its core technology and continued to improve the module conversion efficiency. The firm has made much investment in research and development, which enabled its module conversion efficiency to improve more than half a percent every year over the last 10 years. While Suntech and other PV manufactures in China, rapidly expanding their capacity with the support from the government, were in quick decline in 2009, First Solar replaced Suntech to become the largest manufacturer of PV modules in the world.

In sum, while Chinese companies have benefited from having a large market, excellent infrastructure, and low-cost labor for the past three decades, the vast majority of them are not prepared to innovate as they face a more competitive business environment. We find two primary reasons for this phenomenon. First, continuing their opportunity-driven or resource-based business model, companies have generally prioritized an exploitation strategy over an exploration strategy of seeking improvement in their technology, design, and quality. Because customers desire differentiated products and services with superior technology, design, quality, and style, not just those that are just low in cost, many companies are losing their competitive advantage. Second, the reliance on making easy profits has limited companies' motivation for engaging in innovation. Many Chinese companies may not recognize that having a market orientation is the key to surviving competition (Narver and Slater 1990).

13.3 The mind-set of business leaders

Top managers serve as the influence prism at firms, so firms' innovation strategies are related to the values or mind-set of business leaders (Lefebvre, Mason, and Lefebvre 1997). Thus, we discuss the characteristics of Chinese business leaders and their effects on firm innovation strategies and firm innovation. Most leaders of state-owned enterprises (SOEs) have a bureaucratic mind-set because their interests center on advancing their political career over the long term. In contrast, many entrepreneurs, in pursuit of quick profits in the short term and their own career goals, paid little attention to the quality of their products and services and thus were unable to develop innovative products and services. The main reason is that in view of the uncertain social-political environment, they operate on a short-term planning horizon to protect what they have. Both kinds of mind-set have inhibited organizational creativity.

Since the economic reforms were initiated in the late 1970s, the government has introduced various policies and institutional changes to stimulate economic growth, among them greater opportunity for employment that was not reliant on the state and for profit-based incomes. Encouraged by a policy of "allowing some people to get rich first," many people in both rural and urban areas left their jobs at SOEs and opened their own businesses, aiming to earn market-based profits. These businesses mostly involved trading in commodities. Because private property rights were not recognized in either law or practice, people doing business generally lacked a sense of security about their private wealth, and thus they were unable or unwilling to think long term and make long-term plans. Instead, they developed the habit of pursuing quick profits.

When China began its transition from a planned economy to a market economy, it did yet not have many of the necessary rules and regulations. In the face of ambiguous and changing policies in the transition period, entrepreneurs have had to adapt to the complex environment as it evolved and to deal with the problems caused by the inadequacy of institutions. The external environment did not allow them to focus on companies' strategic positioning, product development, and innovation. In the face of an inadequate legal system, government officials had the power to either make judgments on whether a business was legitimate or provide resources and support in the name of fostering local economic development, and private entrepreneurs had to rely on personal connections with officials to either avoid punishment or obtain support. Driven by the belief that "social connection is productivity," Chinese enterprises widely adopted the strategy of strategic networking in order to do business. The more social networks managers had, the better performance their enterprises could deliver (Peng and Luo 2000). Because their firms held a disadvantaged position relative to SOEs, private entrepreneurs paid more attention to social networks (Xin and Pearce 1996). Redding (2016, Chapter 3 in this volume) discusses the handicaps and substantial costs introduced by "dependence on personalism as a prime guarantee of the conduct of others." The payment of political rent to government officials is recognized and even encouraged by the official system (Zhang and Lin 2014). According to a report by the National Statistics Bureau, 66.7% of the enterprises surveyed mentioned that their business was subject to unjustified levies, unjustified charges, and unjustified fines; and 54% indicated they had encountered instances of rent-seeking behavior among local government officials (Zhang and Lin 2014: 104). In this book, both Fuller (2016, Chapter 6 in this volume) and

Lin (2016) talk about the necessity of reducing these kinds of transaction costs. Because they are putting so much energy into developing and maintaining social connections with officials, as well as holding a short-term planning horizon to protect what they have, many entrepreneurs paid insufficient attention to improving their products and services and were unable to understand the needs of customers (Zhang and Lin 2014).

China's market economic system has been characterized as "being multi-ownership-oriented, with the public ownership in the dominance." SOEs are owned by the state through the Assets and Supervision and Administration Commission (SASAC) and by SASACs at the levels of provincial, municipal, and county governments. The SASAC was established as a government agency to represent the interests of the state as a shareholder at the central and local levels (Naughton 2008), whose responsibilities include protecting and increasing state assets, reforming and restructuring SOEs, and harvesting the dividends of state assets from SOEs (Walter 2010). Under the guidance and supervision of SASAC, SOE executives are required to achieve satisfactory financial performance based on which they are rewarded. Moreover, as their appointments and future career paths are determined by the Central Organization Department of the CCP, they are also required to follow the state's policy guidance as government officials do. In fact, some SOE executives do not have the working experience in the context of markets and lack the necessary knowledge and experience for operating enterprises. Although some young managers with market-oriented skills join SOEs (Boisot, Child, and Redding 2011), they usually do not have the motivation of their counterparts in the private enterprises to enhance the SOE's innovation. As innovation implies risk-taking and SASAC requires SOEs to achieve the financial goals, many SOE executives do not have the incentives and courage to invest to innovative activities. As a matter of fact, the performance standards set up for SOEs are not so tight, and SOEs could have allocated resources to do innovations for the sake of long-term development. Furthermore, visionary SOE executives could have relied on political activities such as lobbying, information disclosure, and constituency building to deal with the government, just like Western companies have done to proactively shape the public policy to encourage, protect, and support innovation (Hillman, Keim, and

Schuler 2004; Sawant 2012). However, dominated by the aim for quick return and a risk-aversive mind-set, and imprinted with the gene of following higher up instructions, most SOEs executives have done little in developing companies' technology-based innovation.

In general, Chinese entrepreneurs think about innovation differently from their Western counterparts. Because so many opportunities arose from an institutional void, Chinese business leaders devoted their attention to exploiting these opportunities, rather than to exploring genuine innovation. This conclusion reflects the historical reality that goods, products, and services were extremely scarce before the market reforms were initiated, and the huge but suppressed demand exploded after the reform and opening-up policy were put in place. Firms could be hugely successful just by copying, borrowing, and building on what already existed in other countries, without doing anything innovative. This mind-set has also been reinforced by government policies. Subscribing to the belief that innovation could come from the top down or through central planning, both central and local governments issued many aggressive policies to foster innovation. Thus, "indigenous innovation" was meant to replace the "reform and opening-up" policy as the a priori development strategy. Because business leaders have acquired keen skills at intuiting the intentions of the state, in responding to government policies, their companies select seemingly innovative projects (e.g., utility model patents) that do not involve essential innovation in order to obtain a large amount in government subsidies (Dong, Zhao, and Yuan 2014). This problem is most serious at SOEs, whose executives were promoted after successfully completing political assignments and being officially recognized by government awards.

In sum, business leaders at SOEs strive to meet the output goals set by the state while business leaders at private companies opportunistically extract quick returns from opportunities created by the innovation campaign. Both kinds of mind-set are detrimental for the achievement of essential innovation at Chinese companies.

13.4 Barriers to organizational creativity

Organizational creativity and innovation make a company create something new and fresh. As Thiel (2014) vividly expressed, people who create something new move from zero to one. However, for most Chinese companies, the first step is to move from negative to zero.

Here, we do not mean that zero is the opportunity for radical creativity and innovation but that it is a space for implementing organizational creativity and innovation without constraints. Although most Chinese companies recognize the importance and necessity of innovation, they are still struggling to move forward from negative territory, which has prominent constraints, including multilevel inertia inhibiting the development of innovation-oriented routines, local protectionism and market segmentation, unevenly distributed entrepreneurial energy across regions, an absence of organizational ability in managing innovation, and a shortage of talent with relevant creative skills. Each of these major barriers to organizational creativity at Chinese companies is discussed in turn.

13.4.1 *Inertia inhibiting the development of innovation-oriented routines*

The legacy of a planned economy and the underdeveloped institutional environment have a great impact on Chinese companies' tendency to create relationship-oriented routines rather than market-oriented routines (Peng 2003). Because the belief in the effectiveness of top-down direction over innovation remains, companies ensure their survival and growth by following strategies that are rewarded by the external social-political environment. Although the top-down campaigns (e.g., reform and opening-up policy, indigenous innovation) initiated by the government release a large amount of resources, only companies that comply with the fulfillment of the government's output plan can gain access to them. The government attracts business leaders through the political competition at SOEs and membership in the Chinese Communist Party and participation in the National People's Congress at private companies. For example, the career of a successful official may be enhanced by having an executive position at listed companies (Morck, Yeung, and Zhao 2008) and entrepreneurs at private firms may actively seek political appointments (Li and Liang 2015). All of these help to institutionalize dependence on the government and reliance on social relationships for doing business (Tsui et al. 2004).

This relationship-oriented development strategy can result in the lock-in effect and hinder the creation of innovation-oriented routines. Routines are the building blocks of organizational capabilities, and their systematic generation and modification in response to environmental changes are at the core of firm dynamics (Lewin, Massini, and Peeters 2011: 82). However, the inertia of a planned economy has made Chinese companies develop specific and idiosyncratic organizational knowledge sets and routines for meeting government demands and engaging in social relationships, which are significantly at odds with innovation-oriented routines. It has been well documented that companies with different orientations address the market/customer needs very differently (Kogut and Zander 2000), and managers with a mentality developed in a planned economy have difficulty in changing their thinking and behavior to one that is market oriented (Child and Markoczy 1993; Kriauciunas and Kale 2006). Because innovation-oriented routines are at the metalevel of organizational capabilities, the lack of such routines makes it difficult for Chinese companies to develop internal and external absorptive capacity and the consequent innovation (Lewin et al. 2011).

13.4.2 Local protectionism and market segmentation

The local protectionism and market segmentation in China create barriers to trade and make specialization less beneficial (Bai et al. 2004). Poncet (2005) estimated that transaction costs across provinces in China in 1997 were equivalent to a tariff of 46%. Although some researchers have found that the Chinese market has become more integrated (e.g., Bai et al. 2004; Xu 2002), recent empirical evidence shows that transaction costs across provinces continue to exist and significantly inhibit economic development (Fang 2009; Huang and Wang 2006). The most distinctive characteristic of local protectionism and market segmentation is that economic reform has "resulted in a fragmented internal market with fiefdoms controlled by local officials" (Young 2000). The root of this phenomenon is the cadre evaluation system, which determines the career advancement of local government bureaucrats and drives them to take a short-term perspective.

Although the weight of economic growth performance in the cadre evaluation system has been reduced, the whole system itself has not been fundamentally changed. Indeed, a new rule issued by the State Council clearly states that the cadre evaluation system will incorporate the innovation performance of local governmental officials. Because the political competition has not been ended and the trade barriers across provinces have not been removed, we expect that government officials are likely to continue to use all possible means to compete for promotion, using innovation as just another tool. Therefore, this kind of competition on innovation performance may not benefit the genuine development of organizational creativity and innovation. In other words, because government officials are still taking an important role in pushing the innovation movement, to help them to move up their career ladder, they are more likely to do something that can be evaluated and observed by the upper-level officials but are less likely to put their efforts toward developing an environment or ecosystem that is substantially beneficial for enterprises to engage in innovative activities. Once again, local protectionism and market segmentation will drive government officials to focus on the growth of their respective regions and to withhold innovation resources as leverage to add weight to their competition for positions. Thus, Chinese companies still cannot take full advantage of the nationwide resources for innovation and might have to rely more on the government to gain access to those innovative resources.

13.4.3 Uneven distribution of entrepreneurial spirit across regions

In the contemporary knowledge economy, knowledge is produced in distributed and dispersed communities due to a division of scientific labor (Kogut and Metiu 2001). Having an entrepreneurial spirit is one of the most fundamental factors in organizational creativity and innovation because it can promote the creation of knowledge within each community and initiate and realize the synergies of knowledge across communities (Sawhney and Prandelli 2000). However, the distribution of entrepreneurial spirit in China is quite uneven. Some researchers may simply attribute this to uneven socioeconomic development across regions. By contrast, we believe that China's cultural and historical legacy has had profound effects. First, companies are embedded in different regions with different cultural and historical legacies. For example, Guangdong and Jiangsu are two of the most developed provinces in China and had the highest gross regional product in the first quarter of 2015. As early as the Ming and Qing dynasties (from the 1360s), the Jiangnan area (south of the Yangtze River, Jiangsu province) developed a model of economic development focused on manufacturing, and since the 1840s the Pearl River Delta region (centered in Guangdong province) has relied on a model based on exports. Obviously, the different commercial systems imbue entrepreneurs with different values and energy. Second, different regions have different development trajectories. During the process of reform and opening up, Jiangsu created the Sunan (southern Jiangsu) model, in which township and village enterprises promote regional economic development through manufacturing, whereas Guangdong province relies on an export-oriented economy.

These different historical legacies and development trajectories across regions have made the development of an entrepreneurial spirit uneven at least in two respects: spatial distribution of entrepreneurial spirit and locus of attention within entrepreneurial spirit. First, entrepreneurial spirit is unevenly distributed across regions due to the different factor endowments and the encouragement of some regions to get wealthy first in the reform and opening-up policy. Table 13.1 shows some basic data on the differences in factors related to entrepreneurial spirit across the representative regions.

Entrepreneurial spirit has grown in different regions to different degrees. For example, according to the results of the China Survey System of Entrepreneurs in 2009 (sample size is 5,920 CEOs), when the government changes its role toward marketization, entrepreneurial spirit will increase more among CEOs at companies located in northeastern China (including Heilongjiang, Jilin, and Liaoning provinces) than in other areas. By contrast, when technology changes rapidly, entrepreneurial spirit will increase more among CEOs at companies located in eastern and central China. Moreover, no platform currently exists for those CEOs to engage in dialogue with one another. This isolation makes it difficult for firms to benefit from the synergy that results from conversation and potential collaboration between those operating in different cognitive environments. Companies would become more innovative if such conversations took place.

Second, an emphasis on different dimensions of growth has significant effects on organizational innovation. Entrepreneurs in Jiangsu province emphasize the leveraging of technological potential while entrepreneurs in Guangdong province focus on the leveraging of trading and exporting. Although both kinds of entrepreneurial spirit drive companies to grow, the different locus of attention (manufacturing versus trading/exporting) makes

Table 13.1 Differences in factors related to entrepreneurial spirit across representative regions

Provincial-level jurisdiction	Index of marketization	Reduction of local protection	Legal environment	Intellectual property protection	Usefulness of intermediaries	Regional cultural diversity
China	7.34	7.46	7.91	11.68	5.35	4.39
East	9.49	8.17	12.37	26.07	6.20	3.05
West	5.42	6.40	4.93	3.43	4.31	18.26
Inner Mongolia	6.27	7.87	5.32	1.05	3.27	15.00
Shaanxi	5.65	7.21	5.88	5.74	6.23	1.48
Ningxia	5.94	4.63	4.66	3.53	3.68	19.30
Gansu	4.98	7.23	4.86	1.09	3.60	7.00
Xinjiang	5.12	7.18	4.98	1.78	5.35	26.99
Qinghai	3.25	2.86	3.51	1.16	2.12	21.33
Tibet	0.38	0.10	0.18	1.74	5.17	63.62
Sichuan	7.56	8.54	7.39	10.11	4.96	1.19
Chongqing	8.14	7.94	7.6	10.36	5.13	2.09
Yunnan	6.06	8.46	5.44	1.66	5.92	16.66
Guizhou	5.56	6.46	4.47	1.58	3.89	18.49
Guangxi	6.17	8.36	4.88	1.31	2.36	25.97

Jiangsu	11.54	9.30	18.72	49.01	6.08	0.67
Guangdong	10.42	11.08	13.99	32.68	6.55	3.26
Shanghai	10.96	6.69	19.89	53.04	10.00	1.18

Notes: Eastern areas include Beijing, Tianjin, Hebei, Liaoning, Shanghai, Jiangsu, Zhejiang, Fujian, Shandong, Guangdong, and Hainan; Chongqing and Shanghai are provincial level of municipalities.

Sources: Data on population, GDP per capita, and university education were obtained from National Bureau of Statistics of China, *China Statistical Yearbook* 2011; index of marketization (2009), reduction of government intervention (average index from 1997 to 2009), reduction of local protection (average index from 1997 to 2009), usefulness of industrial association (2008), legal environment (2009), and intellectual property protection (2009) were assessed from indexes developed by the National Economic Research Institute (Fan, Wang, and Zhu 2011); regional cultural diversity was computed as the percentage of ethnic minority population in the total regional population, based on data from the sixth National Census of China, 2010.

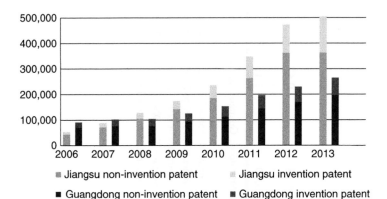

Figure 13.1 Comparisons between Jiangsu and Guangdong on innovation (patent application)

companies different in terms of organizational creativity and innovation, especially in a changing environment. As shown in Figure 13.1, before the financial crisis of 2008, Guangdong had more patents than Jiangsu. However, after 2008, the financial crisis significantly hurt the trading/exporting-oriented economy of Guangdong. Although it remains an empirical question whether financial crisis hurt the innovation development of Guangdong province, we may reasonably infer that the historical legacy of emphasis on manufacturing in entrepreneurial spirit is one of the most important factors enabling Jiangsu to become the most innovative province in China. Lack of innovation focus in the entrepreneurial spirit significantly reduces the motivation of leaders to innovate and thus decreases the innovation efforts of companies (Ahuja, Lampert, and Tandon 2008).

13.4.4 *Lack of organizational capability in managing innovation*

To engage in organizational creativity and innovation, companies must organize to exploit the full competitive potential of their resources (Sirmon, Hitt, and Ireland 2007), and organizational capability in managing innovation becomes particularly relevant (Teece, Pisano, and Shuen 1997). Reflecting how companies transform inputs into outputs using an appropriate organizational structure, management, and compensation policies (Van de Ven and Poole 1995), organizational capability in managing innovation consists of at least three building blocks: structures and systems, resource allocation, and organizational learning and knowledge management tools. Chinese companies have deficiencies in some aspects of organizational capability in varying degrees.

First, organizational structures and systems should be designed to suit the type of innovation (Crossan and Apaydin 2010). However, many Chinese companies originated with a manufacturing model (e.g., original equipment manufacturer), so their organizational structure and systems focus not on innovation but on manufacturing efficiency and they find it difficult to quickly and smoothly switch to an innovation model. In addition, the management and incentive systems rely heavily on interpersonal relationships rather than formalized rules, which may invoke the interpretive scheme of departmental thought worlds and make it difficult to coordinate efforts across departments to realize innovation (Dougherty 1992).

Second, resource allocation reflects whether an organization can efficiently deploy valuable resources for innovation. In an environment of rapid economic growth, Chinese companies do not put their resources into innovation but, rather, allocate slack resources for quick returns. Many companies have conducted unrelated corporate diversification (e.g., entering into real estate) to reap appropriate value quickly (Zhou and Delios 2012). Since the resource allocation is not related to innovation, companies are unable to develop organizational capability in selecting innovative projects, improving resource allocation efficiency, and managing a portfolio of innovation.

Third, innovation depends on organizational learning and knowledge management tools in a systematic way, such as the use of formal idea-generation tools, external linkages with universities and the quality of these linkages, formal information gathering, and customer contact time and frequency (Crossan and Apaydin 2010). Many Chinese companies neither adopt formal knowledge management tools to support the innovation process nor build up R&D platform to organize activities around innovation. Moreover, although some companies may build up a knowledge management system, middle managers may not be motivated to fully exploit the system, for reasons related to the top-down strategy implementation mind-set among business leaders. Organizational innovation can bring radical change to companies, which middle managers might resist for social-emotional reasons and because of their judgments about the legitimacy of those changes (Huy 2011). Middle managers frequently analyze their superiors' statements and actions to look for clues about their motivations, intentions, and capabilities (Huy, Corley, and Kraatz 2014). When middle managers believe that their bosses are deploying them only so that they can compete for promotion, middle managers' attitudes and judgments become negative and will be interlaced with emotional reactions, such that they resist the implementation of innovation activities. As a result, the top-down strategy implementation of organization innovation is doomed to failure.

13.4.5 *Shortage of talent with creativity-relevant skills*

Based on the componential theory of organizational creativity and innovation, three intra-individual components influence organizational creativity (Amabile 1988): domain-relevant skills (expertise, technical skill, and innate talent in the relevant domain of endeavor), creativity-relevant processes (flexible cognitive style, personality traits such as openness to experience, skill in using creative-thinking heuristics, and persistent workstyle), and intrinsic motivation. However, most employees at Chinese companies lack one or more of these components. More specifically, Chinese companies have a shortage of talent with creativity-relevant skills. Chinese education places emphasis on examination rather than scientific exploration, and Chinese culture emphasizes conformity and obedience instead of debating and critical thinking. As a result, Chinese people tend not to perform well on creative tasks compared with their Western counterparts. Niu and Sternberg (2001) found that, in working on collage-making and pencil-drawing, college students from China produced less creative and aesthetic artwork than their US counterparts. All these arguments are consistent with the fact that though Chinese scholars and companies have made substantial progress in publishing scientific papers and filing patents in the past decade, they have produced fewer high-impact research articles and high-quality patents than their US counterparts.

The shortage of talent with creativity-relevant skills might reflect the influence of traditional Chinese culture on employees' cognitive style. Indeed, Cheng (1999) argued that traditional Chinese culture might hinder organizational creativity as defined in the West. Other studies suggest that an individualistic culture is more supportive of the development of creativity than is a collectivistic culture (Morris and Leung 2010). For example, Leung et al. (2014) have found that Chinese employees with a higher tendency to try to save face and maintain interpersonal relations may reduce their behaviors of generation, promotion, and realization of creative ideas. More recently, Wei, Zhang, and Chen (2015) found that two characteristics of Chinese culture, superficial harmony and power distance, inhibit organizational members from speaking up in order to improve performance and correct mistakes. As predicted by componential theory, intra-individual components influence organizational creativity in a multiplicative fashion, and thus a shortage of talents with creativity-relevant skills hurts organizational creativity and innovation.

13.5 Practices aimed at enhancing organizational creativity at Chinese companies

China's technology sector has changed over the past decade. Many enterprises have become leaders in their local market and are striving to promote cutting-edge innovation. Some of them have succeeded in terms of developing innovative products or have even gained competitiveness in the global market. Following are two case studies to illustrate how some Chinese companies deal with the barriers to innovation and develop the organizational capability to engage in innovation: Tencent and Huawei.

13.5.1 Tencent's development of an ecosystem with competitive advantages

China was a walled garden in the Internet world. Popular online brands such as Google, Facebook, and Twitter were all blocked from the Chinese market. Although this walled-garden policy provided a favorable environment for Internet companies in China to flourish, only a small fraction succeeded. Among these players, Tencent, which had a market value of US$206.2 billion as of April 13, 2015, has grown from an imitator to an innovative and successful company. Tencent ranked 8th and 16th among the World's 50 Most Innovative Companies in 2012 and 2013 by *Fast Company*. Starting with QQ, a knockoff of the instant messaging software ICQ, Tencent has expanded its products and services to include a suite of social platforms available to all Internet users. Orchestrating community assets to form an ecosystem was Tencent's most powerful competitive advantage. Its prominent social platforms included QQIM, Qzone, Tencent Weibo, PengYou, WeChat, and online gaming.

Tencent has made great efforts aimed at removing the barriers to innovation and improving its organizational capability to engage in innovation. First, because it was an early private enterprise in Internet applications, Tencent does not suffer from the inertia of routines that can inhibit the development of innovation. From the very beginning, unlike telecommunication companies, which are often entirely or partially state-owned, Tencent and other Chinese Internet companies were privately owned. The government had no incentive for allowing these private companies to flourish and even saw doing so as against its interests. Indeed, Pony Ma, CEO of Tencent, and his partners did not receive any assistance from the Chinese government or its agents during its years of struggle before the company's listing. Therefore, Tencent had full control over its development. Although Tencent did have relationship-oriented routines, it has formed a market-oriented routine. For example, the most important doctrine handed down by the top managers to the frontline employees is "everything centers on customer value." Customers eventually determine the value of products, and Tencent just needs to do whatever it can to satisfy its customers.

Second, Internet connections helped Tencent avoid the difficulties and liabilities caused by local protectionism and market segmentation. On the Internet, Tencent faces almost no constraints with respect to servicing its customers. Officials cannot use Tencent to help them compete for promotion. Moreover, Tencent has built up a very big platform, which can facilitate conversations between managers with different kinds of entrepreneurial spirit across regions. Therefore, Tencent can enjoy the benefits of synergizing complementarities among different kinds of entrepreneurial spirit.

Third, Tencent has developed a unique method of innovation and management of innovation. Tencent has formed a strong culture of product managers. Among the more than 200 division general managers, over 80% were promoted from product managers. The core of a culture of product manager is to keep innovating. Moreover, the firm encourages employees to engage in learning by doing, accelerate the learning process by involving customers, and repeat the process as many times as needed. In addition, Tencent maintains a decentralized R&D structure, and this flat structure allows each R&D employee to explore the possible directions of the product. Then, at the R&D team level, members regularly meet with customers to rapidly test and verify whether the directions fit with the customer value of the products. By doing this, each team serves as a communicator for Tencent with customers. At the division level, managers synergize the efforts across product teams to conduct explorative and exploitive innovation simultaneously.

Finally, Tencent develops talent with creativity-relevant skills internally to keep up with its rapid growth. For example, it has built up a "talent echelon system" to develop talent within each division. In this system, no more than five people are responsible for management in a team, and the rest of the team members must be experts in their field. Tencent has expended a great deal of effort on training and developing employees to become experts in the necessary areas.

In addition to the many innovative products it has developed, such as the online social network QQ, Tencent has also set up open public platforms to attract small enterprises and uses corporate venture capital to support enterprises developing on its open platforms. In 2011, it launched a mobile text and voice messaging communication service, WeChat, which attracted 500 million active users as of the fourth quarter of 2014.

13.5.2 Huawei's development of the organizational capacity for innovation

Huawei, ranked 5th and 18th in the World's 50 Most Innovative Companies by *Fast Company* in 2010 and 2011, has won praise from consumers in the tough competition with many global technology giants and is regarded as the most globally successful company in China. Huawei's business includes telecommunication networks, operations and consulting services, enterprise equipment, and mobile phones. Its products and services have expanded to more than 140 countries and serve 45 of the world's 50 largest telecom operators. As of the end of 2013, 46% of Huawei's 150,000 employees were engaged in research and development (R&D) across 21 R&D institutes around the world. In 2014, it invested US$6.5 billion in R&D, over 13% of its annual revenue.

To remove barriers to innovation and improve its organizational capacity for engaging in innovation, Huawei first developed a strategy based on both relationships and the market early on. For example, to compete with international giants, Huawei established joint ventures with local authorities, which effectively facilitated the penetration of its products into the existing telecom networks. From 2004 to 2014, it has continuously invested more than 10% of sales in R&D, a cumulative total of $30.6 billion over that period. In addition, the first criterion used in evaluating the leadership of managers is skill in dealing with customers, indicating a high level of customer focus. Relationship-oriented routines have helped Huawei gain support from various stakeholders, such as governments, communities, and suppliers, while market-oriented routines have helped Huawei meet customer demands.

Second, to deal with the challenges caused by local protectionism and market segmentation, Huawei initiated a strategy called "surrounding the cities from the countryside," in which Huawei first sold its own PBX switches to hotels and small enterprises in the late 1980s and in 1993 launched its C&C08 program-controlled telephone switch, which was the most powerful switch available in China at the time. By selling the telephone switch in small cities and rural areas and providing quick service for customers, Huawei quickly gained the national market and gained a slice of the mainstream market, dominated by foreign telecom manufacturers. From 2004, Huawei has engaged in a strategy of internationalization by, for example, establishing R&D centers overseas, such as in India, Sweden, the United States, and Australia.

Third, to achieve synergy in entrepreneurial spirit across regions, Huawei has relied mainly on an internal information system and strategic leadership. Each of its divisions and regional subsidiaries are designed to collect local information and identify business opportunities. Then, based on a centralized information system, Huawei can assimilate the information at the firm level. In addition to this formal structural design, Huawei also uses personnel mobility and rotation as an informal mechanism to spark conversations between managers so that they can exchange ideas.

Fourth, Huawei has developed a unique method of innovation and management of innovation. It uses an innovation-follower strategy, by aiming not to create the first product on the market but to refine an existing product to better meet customer demands. From 1998 to 2003, in order to learn from those who were already practiced at innovation, Huawei contracted with IBM for management consulting and thereafter implemented significant transformation of its management and product development structure. In addition, it sought integration between the technology owner and the market owner, by seeking common ground with stakeholders that have market power. Huawei shares the benefits of innovation with these stakeholders in exchange for a part of the market. For example, Huawei and Telekom Research & Development (TM R&D), a wholly owned subsidiary of Telekom Malaysia (TM), launched a joint innovation effort to co-develop customized copper access and 4G for both fixed-line and wireless connectivity in Malaysia. Through this collaboration in the joint lab, both parties shared research facilities and knowledge, and in this way, Huawei was able to decrease its level of R&D investment. Moreover, an internal integration took place such that R&D engineers had to engage in sales and marketing, and salespeople had to participate in R&D. Huawei promotes employees with high performance in the frontline of the market. Every employee needs to experience direct contact with customers. Huawei insists that only frontline employees can fully understand market demands and therefore point the company in the right direction with respect to innovation.

Finally, since the late 1990s, Huawei has aggressively recruited talent, including college graduates from some universities in China and even all those with the same major at some schools. New employees were pushed to work on projects and accumulated their expertise by learning from others. Huawei's organizational creativity and innovation have been fueled to a large degree by this recruiting of talent, providing them with opportunities to work on important projects and rewarding those who succeed in developing products that are desired by customers.

Over the past decade, many practitioners and scholars have tried to understand the secret to Huawei's success. We argue that Huawei does not have any secrets. Although many Chinese companies have reaped the benefit of the huge market, Huawei has made an effort to understand and identify clients' real needs, which were not well addressed by existing service providers and technologies. Beginning in the late 1990s, while most companies in China encouraged their salespeople to use a variety of aggressive sales approaches, Huawei trained its sales staff to help customers understand their needs and then recommend appropriate solutions. To develop the technology-based solutions for customers' problems, the company realized that it needed to invest in the R&D for that development. Thus, it diverged from the pattern of seeking quick profits and failing to invest a reasonable portion of profits in R&D, which, as mentioned above, can hinder organizational creativity.

13.5.3 The keys to success at Tencent and Huawei

The strategies to promote organizational creativity at these two companies are summarized in Table 13.2. One defining common characteristic at both Huawei and Tencent is their market-oriented innovation strategy. They maintain close relations with their customers and respond quickly to requests. Huawei's customer-oriented service strategy makes the firm's products popular with its customers. At Tecent, products are developed based on customer experience and needs, and the emphasis on this is indicated by the fact that Tony Ma, the CEO of Tencent, has also been the chief experience officer. Although these practices are widely used by innovative multinational companies, very few Chinese firms have done so.

13.6 Fostering an entrepreneurial spirit and strengthening management

We now offer some suggestions for Chinese companies in fostering organizational creativity and innovation.

Business practices over the past three decades have shown that private companies are generally more efficient and effective at business operations. Therefore, from the macro perspective, empowering the private sector to play a more prominent role can unlock massive potential for developing innovation. It has been found that entrepreneurial culture, a society's cultural orientation toward entrepreneurship, affects economic performance (Shane 1993) and economic growth (McClelland 1961). Therefore, building a social environment that is favorable to entrepreneurship will be critical, a task in which the government can play an important role, in addition to the policies it has issued in the past two years that seem to indicate new opportunities for private enterprises.

Table 13.2 *Summary of Tencent and Huawei strategies aimed at developing innovation*

Barriers to innovation	Strategy to develop organizational capability and improve innovation	
	Tencent	Huawei
Institutional environment		
Local protectionism and market segmentation	Using Internet and online social network to reap the national market	"Surround the cities from the countryside" International expansion
Different kinds of entrepreneurial spirit	Online communication platform to synergize complementarities	Centralized information system Personnel mobility and rotation
Firm characteristics		
Inertia in routines	Market-oriented routines	Relationship-oriented plus market-oriented routines
Lack of organizational capability	Strong culture of product manager	Innovation-follower strategy
	Flat structure connected with customers	Integration between technology owner and market owner
	Rapid iteration	Promotion of frontline employees
Shortage of talent	Talent echelon system	Aggressively recruiting young talent and giving them the opportunity to develop their expertise

As discussed in the first section, to keep growing in the next decade, private entrepreneurs and business leaders need to change their business strategy from an opportunity-driven and resource-based model to innovation-driven growth. To achieve this objective, business leaders must change their mind-set and fully commit to enhancing organizational creativity. The key to doing this is by fostering an entrepreneurial spirit.

The essence of entrepreneurial spirit is that entrepreneurs are able to both identify market needs and develop innovative products and services to meet customers' needs. Therefore, entrepreneurs need not only to understand the changing market and customers in order to gain customer insights or to find new opportunities but also to obtain the necessary resources to transform insights and opportunities into tangible products and services. Closely scanning the characteristics of the industry, monitoring and noticing changes in it, proactively predicting trends and taking initiative are all crucial and beneficial. Only those who are intrinsically interested in and passionately committed to what they are doing and have grand visions of the changes they intend to make in industry and the market and for customers can accomplish this task. Furthermore, in order to develop products and services to satisfy market demand or customers' needs, companies must have employees who have necessary knowledge, skills, and capability for product development and provide sufficient resources to support their development. However, having qualified employees and abundant resources does not ensure product innovation. Leaders are encouraged to engage in continuous experimentation, to listen to customer feedback, to drive employees to apply their efforts and energies to innovative tasks, and to facilitate an exchange of knowledge and skills among stakeholders. To perform these tasks, leaders must not only develop an organizational culture that is supportive of innovation and build up systems to facilitate organizational learning but also motivate employees to release their creativity. Both entrepreneurship and leadership are vital for organizational creativity and innovation. In particular, whether top management directs enough attention to organizational creativity in formulating the company's strategy is of supreme importance (Ocasio and Joseph 2005). However, many Chinese entrepreneurs developed their mind-set in an opportunity-driven era, and many leaders became accustomed to business models developed in a market that grew rapidly based on suppressed demand, therefore, more business education and training are necessary for them to gain the skills and orientation needed to develop innovative companies.

In addition, business leaders need to drive their organizations to move toward innovation. The mainstream management principles and the common operation practices have proved effective in developing organizational capability. To improve organizational creativity and innovation, firms should take the following steps at a minimum. First, leaders should educate organizational members that an innovation-driven strategy is the only choice for growth. They need to invoke a sense of crisis and urgency to change the mind-set of employees. Second, systematic organizational changes should be made toward fostering innovation, including reconstructing the organizational structure and system around innovation, allocating resources for innovation, building up knowledge-management tools, and developing organizational learning routines across various levels. Third, firms need to provide training on domain knowledge and creativity-relevant skills to help employees express their creativity, which is the basis for organizational innovation.

In sum, the Chinese government has started to liberalize the environment for enterprises to engage in innovation and increase their competitiveness and has launched a "national innovation system" to facilitate entrepreneurship. The inhibiting effects of barriers to innovation are expected to decline over time. Funding and venture capital are available and can provide strong support for entrepreneurs. However, whether enterprises are able to develop their innovative capability depends not only on reforms in organizational structure and incentives but, more importantly, on their determination to change their mind-set, their passion and courage to engage in innovation, their leadership in transforming their organizations, their willingness to develop creative employees, and their persistence in investment in innovation.

References

Ahuja, G., Lampert, C. M., and Tandon, V. 2008. 'Moving beyond Schumpeter: Management research on the determinants of technological innovation.' *Academy of Management Annals* 2(1), 1–98.

Amabile, T. 1988. 'A model of creativity and innovation in organizations.' *Research in Organizational Behavior* 10(1), 123–167.

Bai, C. E., Du, Y., Tao, Z., and Tong, S. Y. 2004. 'Local protectionism and regional specialization: Evidence from China's industries.' *Journal of International Economics* 63(2), 397–417.

Boisot, M., Child, J., and Redding, G. 2011. 'Working the system: Toward a theory of cultural and institutional competence.' *International Studies of Management and Organization* 41(1), 62–95.

Cheng, S. 1999. 'East–West differences in views on creativity: Is Howard Gardener correct? Yes, and no.' *Journal of Creative Behavior* 33(2), 112–125.

Child, J., and Markoczy, L. 1993. 'Host-country managerial behavior and learning in Chinese and Hungarian joint ventures.' *Journal of Management Studies* 30(4), 611–631.

Crossan, M., and Apaydin, M. 2010. 'A multi-dimensional framework of organizational innovation: A systematic review of the literature.' *Journal of Management Studies* 47(6), 1154–1191.

Dong, X., Zhao, J., and Yuan, P. W. 2014. 'Research on innovation efficiency loss of state-owned enterprises.' *China Industrial Economics* 2, 97–108. Guo you qi ye chuang xin xiao lv liu shi yan jiu.

Dougherty, D. 1992. 'Interpretive barriers to successful product innovation in large companies.' *Organization Science* 3(2), 179–202.

Fan, G., Wang, X., and Zhu, H. 2011. *NERI index of Marketization of China's Provinces*. Beijing: Economics Science Press. Zhong guo sheng ji shi chang hua zhi shu.

Fang, J. 2009. 'Market segmentation and the efficiency loss of resource allocation.' *Journal of Finance and Economics* 9, 36–47. Shi chang fen ge he zi yuan pei zhi xiao lv liu shi.

Hillman, A.J., Keim, G.D., and Schuler, D. 2004. 'Corporate political activity: A review and research agenda.' *Journal of Management* 30(6), 837–857.

Huang, Z., and Wang, J. 2006. 'Local protectionism and market fragmentation.' *China Industrial Economics* 2, 60–67. Di fang bao hu he shi chang fen ge.

Huy, Q.N. 2011. 'How middle managers' group-focus emotions and social identities influence strategy implementation.' *Strategic Management Journal* 32(13), 1387–1410.

Huy, Q. N., Corley, K. G., and Kraatz, M. S. 2014. 'From support to mutiny: Shifting legitimacy judgments and emotional reactions impacting the implementation of radical change.' *Academy of Management Journal* 57 (6), 1650–1680.

Kogut, B., and Metiu, A. 2001. 'Open-source software development and distributed innovation.' *Oxford Review of Economic Policy* 17(2), 248–264.

Kogut, B., and Zander, U. 2000. 'Did socialism fail to innovate? A natural experiment of the two Zeiss companies.' *American Sociological Review* 65(2), 169–190.

Kriauciunas, A., and Kale, P. 2006. 'The impact of socialist imprinting and search on resource change: A study of companies in Lithuania.' *Strategic Management Journal* 27(7), 659–679.

Lefebvre, L. A., Mason, R., and Lefebvre, E. 1997. 'The influence prism in SMEs: The power of CEOs' perceptions on technology policy and its organizational impacts.' *Management Science* 43(6), 856–878.

Leung, K., Chen, Z., Zhou, F., and Lim, K. 2014. 'The role of relational orientation as measured by face and renqing in innovative behavior in China: An indigenous analysis.' *Asia Pacific Journal of Management* 31 (1), 105–126.

Lewin, A.Y., Massini, S., and Peeters, C. 2011. 'Microfoundations of internal and external absorptive capacity routines.' *Organization Science* 22(1), 81–98.

Li, X., and Liang, X. 2015. 'A Confucian social model of political appointments among Chinese private entrepreneurs.' *Academy of Management Journal* 58(2), 592–617.

McClelland, D. 1961. *The Achieving Society.* Princeton, NJ: Van Nostrand Reinhold.

Morck, R., Yeung, B., and Zhao, M. 2008. 'Perspectives on China's outward foreign direct investment.' *Journal of International Business Studies* 39(3), 337–350.

Morris, M.W., and Leung, K. 2010. 'Creativity east and west: Perspectives and parallels.' *Management and Organization Review* 6(3), 313–327.

Narver, J., and Slater, S. 1990. 'The effect of a market orientation on business profitability.' *Journal of Marketing* 54(4), 20–35.

National Bureau of Statistics of China. 2011. *China Statistical Yearbook.* Beijing: China Statistics Press.

National Bureau of Statistics. 2011. 'The sixth national census in 2010: Main data bulletin.' www.stats.gov.cn/tjsj/tjgb/rkpcgb/qgrkpcgb/201104/t201 10428_30327.html. Di liu ci ren kou pu cha shu ju gong gao.

Naughton, B. 2008. 'SASAC and rising corporate power in China.' *China Leadership Monitor* 24, 1–9.

Niu, W., and Sternberg, R. 2001. 'Cultural influence of artistic creativity and its evaluation.' *International Journal of Psychology* 36(4), 225–241.

Ocasio, W., and Joseph, J. 2005. 'An attention-based theory of strategy formulation: Linking micro- and macroperspectives in strategy processes.' *Advances in Strategic Management* 22, 39–61.

Peng, M. W. 2003. 'Institutional transitions and strategic choices.' *Academy of Management Review* 28(2), 275–296.

Peng, M.W., and Luo, Y. 2000. 'Managerial ties and firm performance in a transition economy: The nature of a micro-macro link.' *Academy of Management Journal* 43(3), 486–501.

Poncet, S. 2005. 'A fragmented China: Measure and determinants of Chinese domestic market disintegration.' *Review of International Economics* 13(3), 409–430.

Sawant, R. 2012. 'Asset specificity and corporate political activity in regulated industries.' *Academy of Management Review* 37(2), 194–210.

Sawhney, M., and Prandelli, E. 2000. 'Managing distributed innovation in turbulent markets.' *California Management Review* 42(4), 24–54.

Shane, S. 1993. 'Cultural influences on national rates of innovation.' *Journal of Business Venturing* 8(1), 59–73.

Sirmon, D. G., Hitt, M. A., and Ireland, R. D. 2007. 'Managing firm resources in dynamic environments to create value: Looking inside the black box.' *Academy of Management Review* 32(1), 273–292.

Sun, P., Wright, M., and Mellahi, K. 2010. 'Is entrepreneur–politician alliance sustainable during transition? The case of management buyouts in China.' *Management and Organization Review* 6(1), 101–121.

Teece, D., Pisano, G., and Shuen, A. 1997. 'Dynamic capabilities and strategic management.' *Strategic Management Journal* 18(7), 509–533.

Thiel, P. 2014. *Zero to One: Notes on Startups, or How to Build the Future.* New York: Crown.

Tsui, A. S., Schoonhoven, C. B., Meyer, M. W., Lau, C. M., and Milkovich, G. T. 2004. 'Organization and management in the midst of societal transformation.' *Organization Science* 15(2), 133–144.

Van de Ven, A., and Poole, M. 1995. 'Explaining development and change in organizations.' *Academy of Management Review* 20(3), 510–540.

Walter, C. 2010. 'The struggle over ownership: How the reform of state enterprises changed China.' *Copenhagen Journal of Asian Studies* 28(1), 83–108.

Wei, X., Zhang, Z.-X., and Chen, X.-P. 2015. 'I will speak up if my voice is socially desirable: A moderated mediating process of promotive versus prohibitive voice.' *Journal of Applied Psychology* 100(5), 1641–1652.

Xin, K., and Pearce, J. 1996. 'Guanxi: Connections as substitutes for formal institutional support.' *Academy of Management Journal* 39(6), 1641–1658.

Xu, X. 2002. 'Have the Chinese provinces become integrated under reform?' *China Economic Review* 13(2–3), 116–133.

Young, A. 2000. 'The razor's edge: Distortions and incremental reform in the People's Republic of China.' *Quarterly Journal of Economics* 114(4), 1091–1135.

Zhang, J., and Lin, S. 2014. 'Business and government.' In *Understanding Chinese Firms from Multiple Perspectives*, ed. Z.-X. Zhang and J.J. Zhang, 51–79. New York: Springer.

Zhang, Z.-X. 2014. 'The growth path of entrepreneurs.' In *Understanding Chinese Firms from Multiple Perspectives*, ed. Z.-X. Zhang and J.J. Zhang, 81–118. New York: Springer.

Zhou, N., and Delios, A. 2012. 'Diversification and diffusion: A social networks and institutional perspective.' *Asia Pacific Journal of Management* 29(3), 773–798.

14 Institutional and cultural contexts of creativity and innovation in China

CHI-YUE CHIU, SHYHNAN LIOU,
AND LETTY Y.-Y. KWAN

14.1 Introduction

Development of innovation, particularly transformational innovation, is challenging for developing countries. In this chapter, we first review the major drivers of China's rapid economic growth since the late 1970s and argue for the need for technological progress to sustain the country's long-term growth before the country hits the middle-income trap in 2030.

Next, we discuss the institutional and cultural constraints on China's ability to enhance its capability for radical innovations. Based on our analysis of multinational data that cover recent performance of more than 120 economies over a wide spectrum of innovation outputs (including fluency in idea creation, local economic impact, and global absorption rate of new knowledge), we identify several major institutional and cultural factors that may limit abilities of developing countries in general and China specifically to expand the capacity for transformational innovation.

We acknowledge China's proactive attempts to improve the quality of its human capital through projects that aim at enhancing the quality of Chinese universities (e.g., Project 211 and Project 985) and ambitious global talent recruitment schemes (e.g., the Thousand Talents Program). Nonetheless, our analysis challenges the wisdom of relying primarily on human capital improvement and global talent recruitment as the strategy to promote transformational innovation. We also apply our findings to understand the institutional and cultural constraints on China's ability to expand its capacity for transformational innovation and argue for the necessity of creating institutional and cultural environments that protect individual rights, discourage group centrism, and encourage intercultural learning.

Although China has made tremendous progress in economic development since 1978, it is still a developing economy (see Lin, Chapter 2, this volume). Will the Chinese economy be able to continue its growth after 2030 and escape the middle-income trap? Lin (Chapter 2, this volume) thinks it is possible because some Asian economies (e.g., China, Taiwan, Korea) have developed a new paradigm of sustainable economic development (new structural economics) that allows market to be the basic institution for resource allocation, while at the same time retains state control over growth-facilitating structural changes.

However, deeper probing into the sources of China's rapid economic growth casts doubt on the defensibility of an overly optimistic projection of China's future growth (Fuller, Chapter 6, this volume). Importantly, some of the conditions responsible for China's fast growth (e.g., high domestic investment rate, surplus supply of labor) may not be replicable. Before 1978, due to the economic inefficiency inherent in central planning, China was not able to fully exploit its production possibilities. With the transition from a centrally planned economy to an open market economy since 1978, the country's economic efficiency improved, creating higher returns from the existing levels of production inputs, which contribute to 86 percent of Chinese economic growth between 1986 and 1995 (Lau and Park 2007). Although the national saving rate remains very high, the Chinese working-age population has already reached its peak. Lau (2014) estimated that there is still some room for tangible capital-driven economic growth in China in the next two decades. However, the major driver of China's long-term economic growth would be expansion of intangible capital through innovation and technological progress.

If that is indeed the case, it seems timely to examine the factors that would promote or hinder China's capacity for innovation, particularly radical or transformational innovation. The focus of the present chapter is on the possible institutional and cultural constraints that may limit China's ability to expand its capacity for transformational innovation. Before we discuss these constraints, we will first distinguish different types of innovation.

14.2 Types of innovations

Innovation is a multifaceted concept. Innovation researchers (Cornell University, INSEAD, and WIPO 2013) have classified innovation outputs of a country into six types: knowledge creation, knowledge impact, knowledge diffusion, intangible assets, creative goods and services, and online creativity. Knowledge creation refers to the fluency in generating new ideas or applications and is measured by normalized total number of patent applications, utility model applications, and research publications in the country. Knowledge impact refers to the economic and business value generated from innovation and is measured by indicators such as GDP growth rate per knowledge worker and new business density. Knowledge diffusion refers to the extent to which innovations of a country are adopted in other countries and is measured by indicators such as high-tech exports, royalties, and license fees receipts. Intangible creative assets include trademark registrations and ICTs. Creative goods and services include audiovisual and related services, feature films, and other creative goods. Online creativity refers to top-level domains, Wikipedia edits, YouTube videos, and so on.

Performance data are available for over 120 economies in 2013 on all six types of innovation outputs (Cornell University, INSEAD, and WIPO 2013). We used the six types of outputs as input criteria in a cluster analysis and identified four clusters of countries. As illustrated in Figure 14.1, Cluster 1 and Cluster 2 consist of low-income countries. Sample countries in Cluster 1 are Albania, Cambodia, and Kenya, and sample countries in Cluster 2 are Indonesia, Benin, and Mali. Cluster 3 consists of developing and fast-growing countries, including China, India, Russia, Brazil, and Chile. Cluster 4 consists of developed countries like the United States, Singapore, Japan, and Germany.

We are interested in differences in knowledge creation, knowledge impact, and knowledge diffusion among countries because of their differential significance in economic growth. Knowledge creation is a measure of the quantity of new knowledge created in a country; knowledge impact measures the economic value to the country of origin generated by the new products and services in a country; and knowledge diffusion measures the amount of influence the new products and services created in a country have in the global innovation industry.

Performances in these three types of innovation are positively related. For example, countries (e.g., the United States) that produce innovation outputs of high global influence (e.g., Apple computers) tend to produce more new products and services that are of high local

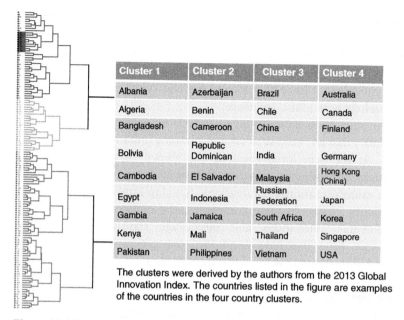

Cluster 1	Cluster 2	Cluster 3	Cluster 4
Albania	Azerbaijan	Brazil	Australia
Algeria	Benin	Chile	Canada
Bangladesh	Cameroon	China	Finland
Bolivia	Republic Dominican	India	Germany
Cambodia	El Salvador	Malaysia	Hong Kong (China)
Egypt	Indonesia	Russian Federation	Japan
Gambia	Jamaica	South Africa	Korea
Kenya	Mali	Thailand	Singapore
Pakistan	Philippines	Vietnam	USA

The clusters were derived by the authors from the 2013 Global Innovation Index. The countries listed in the figure are examples of the countries in the four country clusters.

Figure 14.1 Four country clusters identified by the differences and similarities of six types of innovation outputs

economic value. However, not all new knowledge creations have high local economic impact or global influence, and not all products with high local economic impact have global influence.

For example, in China, the government acknowledges the need for a shift from imitation-driven innovation to transformational innovation in Chinese business. China's Premier Li Keqiang declared at the 2014 World Economic Forum that China is determined to accelerate its growth in science and technology, and R&D spending in China already reaches 42 percent of the US level. Nonetheless, thus far, China has been most successful in different forms of incremental innovation, including cost innovations (changes in product design, production or delivery process, technology or material that will bring down production or delivery costs), process innovations (creation of new processes for producing or delivering an existing product or service), and application innovations (combination of existing products, services, or technologies in a new way to produce a new product). However, China has produced relatively few product innovations that are truly new to the world or high-impact technology with global significance (Yip and McKern 2014). Zhang and Zhong (Chapter 13, this volume) also notes that a popular way Chinese firms use to expand their capacity is through imitating and importing foreign technologies and business models that have high local economic value, instead of creating technology with global influence.

The shift from incremental to radical innovation is not easy for a country that has been successful in pursuing imitation-driven innovation. At the firm level, research has shown that companies with a history of producing incremental innovations are less likely to produce transformational innovations (Dunlap-Hinkler, Kotabe, and Mudambi 2010). In these companies, the established norms favor incremental innovations and discourage transformational ones. Likewise, firms that have dominated one generation of technology often fail to create new breakthroughs in the next generation because the established norms in the company draw attention to incremental improvements of the company's successful products and services (Christensen 2000; see also Zhang and Zhong Chapter 13, this volume).

As shown in Figure 14.2, in all three types of innovation outputs, Cluster 4 countries had the highest performance, whereas Cluster 1 and Cluster 2 countries had the lowest performance. Interestingly, although Cluster 3 countries had higher performance in both knowledge creation and knowledge impact than Cluster 1 and Cluster 2 countries, Cluster 3 countries had the same level of performance in knowledge diffusion as Cluster 1 and Cluster 2 countries. It seems that fast-growing developing countries have begun to catch up with developed countries in knowledge creation and knowledge impact but have made little progress in knowledge diffusion, which often requires transformational innovations.

14.3 The role of human capital and institution support

Two groups of factors that predict the level of innovation performance in a country are human capital and institutional support for innovation (Kwan and Chiu 2015). Human capital refers to an individual's knowledge, skills, expertise, and abilities that allow for changes in action and economic growth (Coleman 1988). A recent OECD multinational study (Organization for Economic Cooperation and Development

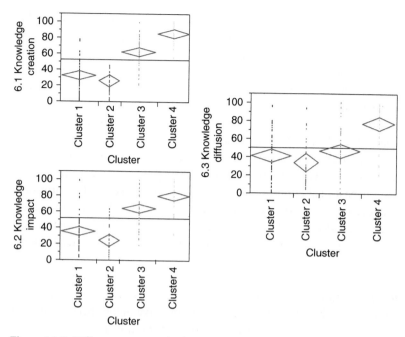

Figure 14.2 Differences among the four clusters of countries in their performance on knowledge creation, knowledge impact, and knowledge diffusion based on GII-2013 data

2013) reveals that in developed countries, business investment in talent management accounts for 20–34 percent of average productivity growth. Another multinational study (Dakhi and de Clercq 2007) found that countries that had higher levels of human capital also had more patents (a measure of knowledge creation) and higher percentages of high-tech export (a measure of knowledge diffusion). Likewise, Bendapudi, Zhan, and Hong (2015) reported in their multinational study that the quality of primary and secondary education in a country, measured through the Program for International Student Assessment (PISA), is positively related to the country's ranking in innovation output. The Global Innovation Index (GII) includes a country-level measure of human capital, comprising indicator variables such as expenditure on education, school life expectancy, assessment in reading, mathematics, and science, pupil–teacher ratio in secondary school, percentage of tertiary enrolment, research and development expenditure, and researcher headcount.

Institutional support includes the legal and political institutions that protect freedom of expression and the innovators' proprietary rights to their intellectual and financial properties (Kwan and Chiu 2015). Institutional support promotes institutional trust, which is defined as an individual's expectation that some organized system will act with predictability and goodwill. Institutional trust in turn facilitates formation of new network ties and knowledge sharing, leading to higher quantity and quality of innovation outputs. Longitudinal data from multiple sources suggest that institutional trust is widespread in societies that were ruled by non-authoritarian political institutions in the distant past (Tabellini 2008). A country-level measure of institutional support for innovation is available from the GII. This measure comprises indicator variables such as political stability, government effectiveness, press freedom, regulatory quality, rule of law, and business freedom.

Using the GII measures of human capital and institutional support for innovation as predictors, Kwan and Chiu (2015) show that countries with higher quality of human capital have higher performance in knowledge creation. Institutional support for innovation does not predict performance in knowledge creation. Thus, it is possible for countries without strong institutional support for innovation to increase their volume of creative outputs through retaining and growing local talents and attracting global talents. In addition, institutional support and human capital have additive effects on knowledge impact. An implication of this finding is that countries with weak institutional support for innovation may still be able to produce products and services that have relatively high local economic value if these countries manage to grow their human capital. This implication is particularly relevant to China given its relatively weak institutional support for innovation (see below).

Finally, for countries to have innovations with global influence, both high-quality human capital and strong institutional support for innovation must be present (see also Child, Chapter 8, this volume). If a fast-growing country has weak institutional support for innovation, investing heavily in the improvement of its education and R&D talents can facilitate knowledge creation and knowledge impact but not knowledge diffusion. Many of the Cluster 3 countries in Figure 14.1 have weak institutional support for innovation. Investment in the quality of human capital may help these countries to catch up with developed countries (Cluster 4 countries) in knowledge creation and knowledge impact but not in knowledge diffusion.

14.4 Institutional constraints on innovation

The preceding analysis underscores the importance of institutional support for enhancing the capacity for transformational innovations with global influence. Several authors in this volume have commented on the institutional constraints on the development of transformational innovations in China. These constraints include inefficient distribution of financial resources, ineffective state interference in the markets (Fuller, Chapter 6, this volume), and insufficient IP protection (Cheng and Huang, Chapter 7, this volume).

State control could be a factor that has contributed to China's fast economic growth in the late 1970s. To jumpstart the transition from a closed centrally planned economy to an open market economy, Russia decisively abolished the mandatory central plan and relied completely on the newly introduced free markets. This "shock therapy" created a rough transition. In contrast, recognizing that the country lacked the supporting institutions in the late 1970s, Chinese policymakers adopted the "Reform without Losers" approach, introducing enterprise autonomy and free market in experimental economic zones while continuing to enforce the existing central plan (Lau 2014). This dual-track approach ensured that the stakeholders who had benefitted from the existing central plan would not suffer loss when market economies were introduced. The success of the dual-track approach requires that the state possesses the authority and power to formulate, revise, and implement economic policies.

Paradoxically, the strategy that has contributed to the smooth economic transition in China may become a liability as the country's income grows. As pointed out by Fuller (Chapter 6, this volume), one negative effect of adopting the dual-track approach is that very large amounts of credits were funneled to inefficient state-owned firms, resulting in capital misallocation. As Fuller puts it, "this financial favoritism is mirrored in other state actions that skew the market towards politically favored firms ... China now faces the problem of how to unwind this system of finance and favoritism that has become a drag on development, a system that has fostered its own powerful coterie of vested interest within China's party-state itself."

What is needed in China is the creation of institutional capital that would support development of transformational innovations. Consistent with this view, the results from a recent multinational study (Aiyar, Duval, Puy, Wu, and Zhang 2013) suggest that institutional factors are the most serious threats to China's economic growth, which may lead China into the middle-income trap. In a recent survey of 280 high-technology firms in China, Gao, Gao, Zhou, and Huang (2015) found that both informal and formal institutional capital have positive effects on radical innovation in China. The effect of formal institutional capital on radical innovation is particularly pronounced in state-owned enterprises and complex markets.

14.4.1 Institutional constraints on human capital

Both institutional support for innovation and human capital are required for a country to develop its capacity for generating innovations with global impact. In the absence of strong institutional support for innovation, investment in human capital may not lead to proportionate increase in transformational innovations.

The Chinese government has played an active role in enhancing the quality of manpower in science and technology through Project 211 and Project 985. Project 211 was implemented in 1995 with the objectives of (a) training high-level professional manpower to support the country's social and economic development and (b) promoting the standards of some key universities and disciplinary areas. Selected universities were given generous central funding to improve their teaching and research infrastructure and laboratory facilities, develop strategic disciplinary areas, and enhance the public service system of higher education (e.g., the library system). Project 985 was initiated to help selected universities to reach world-class level by 2020. Two universities (Peking University and Tsinghua University) were selected in the initial phase of the Project. By 2010, thirty-nine universities were included.

The outcomes of these projects are mixed. In China, global university rankings are widely used to gauge success of the universities. In the 2014 Academic Ranking of World Universities, three mainland Chinese universities were on the list of the world's top 101–150 universities: Peking University, Shanghai Jiaotong University, and Tsinghua University. However, none of the Chinese universities were among the top one hundred universities in the world. An unintended consequence of relying on world university rankings to benchmark performance of universities is that pursuance of excellence in Chinese universities is more imitative than creative, as indicated by the much higher number of imports than exports of educational programs in the country (Li and Chen 2011).

Interestingly, the success of Project 211 and Project 985 was also accompanied by an increase in the number of Chinese students studying abroad. Between 1996 and 2008, the total number of mainland Chinese students studying abroad increased from 20,905 to 179,800 (Gong and Li 2010). China exports more students than it imports, in part because foreign universities are eager to admit best performers from Project 211 and Project 985 universities. Paradoxically, the success of Project 211 and Project 985 has worsened the brain-drain problem in China.

Although Project 211 and Project 985 have helped to raise the international reputation of some Chinese universities and enhance the quality of science and technology manpower in China, Li and Chen (2011) identified two limitations of these projects. First, these projects place lopsided emphasis on attracting star professors with lucrative compensation packages, up-to-date buildings and laboratory equipment, publications, and quick results. Relatively little attention has been given to building institutions and research culture that support transformational research. Second, there is a lack of academic freedom, university autonomy, and institutional support for research in the universities. In fact, the state designates the list of Project 985 institutions and the central government exercises strong regulation over the governance of the universities. State control over universities' internationalization is particularly strict.

Aside from the World-Class Universities Movement, the Chinese government has also launched programs to recruit global talent. An example of these programs is the Thousand Talents Program (TTP) introduced by the Organization Department of the Chinese Communist Party to bring back the Chinese talents who have gone abroad to enhance China's human capital. According to the detailed analysis of the TTP by Zweig and Wang (2013), before the TTP started, the Chinese Academy of Sciences had introduced the One Hundred Talents Program for the same purpose. Overseas Chinese scientists who received the One Hundred Talents Awards were provided generous start-up funds, attractive compensation packages, and leadership roles in research teams. At about the same time, more than one hundred cities established incubators for overseas entrepreneurs in new high-tech zones, offering attractive economic and investment incentives, as well as tax benefits for the returning entrepreneurs. The effectiveness of the One Hundred Talents Program was limited because of the presence of unavoidable distractions from their focal tasks: (1) returnees complained of the large amount of time they needed to spend on cultivating personal relations and (2) returned entrepreneurs running their business in China had to deal with local governments.

The TTP was introduced to attract 2,000 world-class professors to return to the universities in China in four to five years, based on the principles of three *kuan* (permissiveness): being relaxed, tolerant, and lenient. The program targets (1) professors in prestigious foreign universities and research institutes, (2) senior professionals working in famous international companies or financial institutions, and (3) entrepreneurs owning proprietary intellectual property rights or who mastered "core technologies." The returnees were offered attractive settlement allowance, health insurance, and compensation package. Nonetheless, academic returnees lamented that the allocation of grants and awards still depends heavily on personal relations. This analysis led Zweig and Wang (2013) to question whether scientific culture can be changed without institutional transformations, which include establishment of the rule of law, property rights, open and transparent government, lack of corruption, and other attributes of good governance. Consistent with Zweig and Wang's observation, Kenney, Breznitz, and Murphree (2013) also found that in developing countries, business returnee entrepreneurs play a critical role in the development of high-tech industries only after the local entrepreneurs and government have laid the institutional groundwork for innovation.

14.5 Cultural constraints on innovation

14.5.1 *Effect of cultural diversity on creativity and innovation*

The preceding analysis suggests that countries with stronger institutional support for innovation are likely to attract and grow global talents. Across countries, the quality of global talents in a country, measured through the 2013 Global Talent Competitiveness Output Sub-Index (Lanvin and Evans 2013), was strongly correlated with the level of institutional support for innovation measured through the 2013 GII Institution Support Sub-Index ($r = .82$, $N = 101$). This result implies that countries with strong institutional support for innovation are likely to be international hubs of culturally diverse talents. Countries with stronger institutional support for innovation are also likely to attract collaborations from foreign multinational enterprises (MNEs; see Collison, Chapter 9, this volume).

The positive effects of cultural diversity on creativity and innovation have been demonstrated at the individual, firm, and cultural levels. At the individual level, experimental and survey studies (Leung and Chiu 2010; Leung, Maddux, Galinsky, and Chiu 2008) have shown that individuals with more extensive multicultural exposure have higher performance on standardized creativity tests. This is particularly the case when individuals are open to experience (Leung and Chiu 2008) and do not have a strong desire for firm answers in problem-solving (Leung and Chiu 2010). After monocultural individuals had been exposed to ideas and practices in a foreign culture in a controlled experiment, these individuals had higher performance on a creativity task than their counterparts in the control (no foreign culture exposure) condition. In fact, the creative benefits of such brief multicultural exposure lasted for a week (Leung and Chiu 2010). The effect of foreign culture exposure is particularly strong when the ideas of local and foreign cultures are presented side by side (Leung and Chiu 2010). When dissimilar cultures are placed in cognitive juxtaposition, attention is drawn to the differences between cultures (Leung et al. 2008). Awareness of cultural differences would lead individuals to question the validity of the knowledge they acquired in their own culture. Although this experience may evoke unpleasant feelings of cognitive dissonance, it also motivates individuals to resolve apparent differences between cultures and create new knowledge by synthesizing ideas and practices from seemingly dissimilar cultural traditions (Cheng and Leung 2013; Cheng, Leung, and Wu 2011).

At the firm level, Collison (Chapter 9, this volume) has discussed the potential benefits of cross-cultural collaborations between Chinese firms and Western MNEs. Dunlap-Hinkler et al. (2010) classified 1,699 Food and Drug Administration new applications from ninety-eight firms from 1992 to 2002 into incremental innovations and breakthroughs. They found that products that emerged from cross-cultural joint ventures or alliances are particularly likely to be breakthroughs. In China, a survey of 183 high-tech firms has provided evidence that external learning facilitates development of radical innovation (Bao, Chen, and Zhou 2011). At the country level, research shows that cultural diversity has a positive effect on innovation output over and above the contribution of innovation input (Zhan, Bendapudi, and Hong 2015).

14.5.2 Negative effects of group centrism

However, the creative and innovation benefits of cultural diversity have boundaries. First, at the individual level, individuals may react negatively to inflow of foreign culture, worrying that foreign cultural inflow would cause erosion or contamination of the ingroup culture (Chiu, Gries, Torelli, and Cheng 2011; Torelli, Chiu, Tam, Au, and Keh 2011). For example, in China, theoretically the inflow of Han Chinese culture into the Hui-Muslim communities should afford intercultural learning opportunities for both the Hui-Muslims and the Han Chinese. Nonetheless, Hui-Muslims may perceive the inflow of Han Chinese into their communities as a threat to the purity of the Hui-Muslim tradition. In response to this perception, Hui-Muslims may react defensively by resisting intercultural learning and avoiding cultural contacts (Wu, Yang, and Chiu 2014).

At the company level, Collison (Chapter 9, this volume) observed that in China, MNE–local partnerships tend to be relatively short-lived because of a lack of trust and imbalanced reciprocity. At the country level, Zhan et al. (2015) found that although across countries cultural diversity is associated with higher innovation output, this positive association is attenuated in countries with high levels of ethnic polarization.

Thus, it is important to understand when cultural diversity would facilitate creativity and innovation and when it would hinder them. Evidence from multiple sources points to the critical moderation effect of group centrism, defined as the tendencies to (1) view the self as a member of the ingroup, (2) exaggerate the differences between the ingroup and the outgroups, and (3) overestimate the level of homogeneity in a group. Research shows that at the individual level, multicultural experiences do not promote creativity when the individuals have strong ingroup identification (Leung and Chiu 2010). People also tend to reject inflow of foreign culture when they experience an existential need to affirm their ingroup identity (Torelli et al. 2011).

At the firm level, strong ingroup cultural identification has also been linked to rejection of cross-cultural acquisitions, particularly when a foreign MNE acquires an iconic brand of the ingroup culture (Tong, Hui, Kwan, and Peng 2011). At the country level, countries with sharp cultural divides between ethnic groups tend to have lower levels of innovation outputs (Zhan et al. 2015).

14.5.3 Group centrism in China

Group centrism could be an important factor that affects China's capacity for innovation. Research in cross-cultural and cultural psychology has found strong evidence for the relatively strong emphasis on collectivism – the tendency to prioritize group goals over individual goals – in Confucian cultures (Lehman, Chiu, and Schaller 2004). Collectivism is also a core value in Chinese communism. Although the anti-Confucianism movement in the early years of the People's Republic and the rise of market economy since the late 1970s could have weakened the ideological hegemony of Confucian or communist collectivism in China, research shows that the emphasis on collectivist values and practices is still strong in mainland China. For example, the collectivist value of harmony or conflict avoidance within primary and secondary groups is still emphasized in Chinese organizations (Leung, Brew, Zhang, and Zhang 2011). Despite the increase of social, residential, and job mobility in the Chinese labor market, the collectivist practice of building and maintaining strong network ties (*guanxi*) are still important for Chinese individuals to find and secure jobs in the increasingly dynamic labor market (Bian and Ang 1997). The rise of the Chinese economy and the attempt of the Chinese Communist Party to revitalize collectivism through the China Dream campaign have also led to the rise of nationalism and even super-nationalism (the collective imagination of China being a global super-power) in the country. The China Dream campaign was launched to increase China's soft power. It may help to increase the collective pride of the Chinese, reduce the risk of social disintegration resulting from the dominance of unbridled selfish ambitions in the market economies, and confer legitimacy to the ruling regime (see Callahan 2015). Nonetheless, it also has the unintended consequence of adding fuel to group centrism in China. Rise in group centrism also accompanies China's geopolitics and territorial disputes with its neighboring states (He 2007). The rise of group centrism in China could hinder the development of innovation capacity in the country. As noted, multicultural experiences and cultural diversity confer opportunities to inspire new ideas through intercultural learning. However, the strong and growing group centrism in China may orient its citizens to adhere to the Chinese cultural tradition and forgo and even resist opportunities to seek inspirations from foreign cultures.

14.5.4 *Group centrism and team creativity*

Research on team creativity has revealed another potential negative consequence of group centrism on creativity. The heavy emphasis on collectivism in Confucian cultures has led some scholars to question whether individuals who grew up in Confucian cultures can think creatively (Mahbubani 2009). Past research on cross-national differences in creativity and innovation has yielded mixed results (see Chiu and Kwan 2010), with some results showing higher creative performance in more individualist countries (Goncalo and Staw 2006; Niu, Zhang, and Yang 2007), and others showing null effect of cultural individualism on creative performance (Saeki, Fan, and Dusen 2001). For example, Niu et al. (2007) found that individuals from Western cultures (the United States, Europe) outperformed individuals from Asian cultures (e.g., China, Japan) on several creativity tests. However, in a cross-cultural study of performance on the figural test of the Torrance Tests of Creative Thinking, although Americans produced more abstract and elaborate ideas than did the Japanese, the two groups did not differ in the number of ideas generated. Moreover, the ideas generated by the two groups were equally original (Saeki et al. 2001).

One may argue that studies have failed to find significant main effects of individualism on creativity because they compared only a small number of (typically two) cultures on lab tests of creativity. Pronounced effect of cultural individualism on creativity would be found when innovation data from a representative sample of countries and a wide range of innovation outputs are examined. Indeed, this is the case. As mentioned earlier, data from 142 countries on a wide variety of innovation outputs are available from the Global Innovation Output Sub-Index (Cornell University, INSEAD, and WIPO 2013). Using country as the unit of analysis, across countries, after controlling for income of the countries, Innovation Output was positively associated with individualism ($r = .63$, $p < .0001$). These results are consistent with Erez and Nouri's (2010) proposal that individualist cultures are more innovative than collectivist cultures.

Although more individualist countries have more innovative outputs, past studies have failed to find consistent country differences in standardized measures of individual creativity. One reason for this discrepancy is that collectivist values have little impact on individual creativity. Nonetheless, they affect innovation outputs when people work in teams. Research has shown that although originality and usefulness are both important criteria for evaluating the creativity of ideas or products, individualist cultures emphasize originality and collectivist cultures emphasize usefulness more (Erez and Nouri 2010; Morris and Leung 2010). For example, one cross-cultural study (Bechtoldt, De Dreu, Nijstad, and Choi 2010) found that Dutch teams generated more original ideas whereas Korean teams generated more useful ideas when they were (vs. were not) instructed to do their best. These cultural differences are particularly pronounced when teams select ideas for further development and implementation than when individuals generate original ideas in conventional creativity tasks (Li, Kwan, Liou, and Chiu 2013). This is because when a team selects ideas for further development and implementation, its members are likely to take into consideration preferences that are perceived to be normative in the team and/or in the country. Hence, group and cultural norms would have greater impact on idea selection at the team level than on idea generation at the individual level.

Evidence for this idea was found in a study (Liou and Nisbett 2011) that compared the performance of Americans and Taiwan Chinese in a product design task. When instructed to generate new design ideas for a product alone, the ideas generated by the American and Chinese participants were equally original. However, when the participants were assigned to teams and instructed to discuss the ideas generated by the team members and selected some ideas for further development, the ideas selected by American teams were more original than those selected by the Taiwanese teams. In addition, the ideas discarded by the Taiwanese teams were more creative than those discarded by the

American teams. This result shows that American teams are more likely to select the relatively novel ideas for further development, although both Americans and Taiwan Chinese are equally capable of generating original ideas.

14.5.5 Group centrism and integrative research

Solving important and complex problems (e.g., pollution) requires creative synthesis of knowledge and insights from multiple perspectives (interdisciplinary research). It also requires integration of R&D with commercialization of the creative output (transdisciplinary research). Not surprisingly, rapidly growing economies have invested heavily in interdisciplinary and transdisciplinary research. Some countries have set up publicly funded institutes (e.g., A-STAR in Singapore and ITRI in Taiwan) to promote collaborations between disciplines and to bridge R&D and commercialization.

Nonetheless, it is not easy for individuals to traverse multidisciplinary or multifunctional territories. Each discipline is like a culture, with its own knowledge tradition and criteria for evaluating the validity of knowledge (Chiu, Kwan, and Liou 2013). Crossing disciplinary boundaries is like crossing cultural borders. Again, group centrism plays a critical role in the success of multidisciplinary or multifunctional collaboration. Lab experiments show that when asked to solve design problems that require integration of knowledge from multiple disciplines, university students trained in a certain discipline (e.g., engineering, design, business) spontaneously pay more attention to information related to their own discipline than to information related to other disciplines. This is the case particularly for students who believe strongly that each discipline has its distinctive essentialist, immutable characteristics. Students with stronger discipline-centrism also tend to select ideas offered by experts in their own discipline (instead of those from experts in other disciplines) when they create the design (Chiu et al. 2013).

The mission of the Industrial Technology Research Institute (ITRI) is to promote interdisciplinary and transdisciplinary research in Taiwan. In ITRI, thousands of knowledge workers trained in hundreds of different academic disciplines worked together to produce marketable innovations, and conflicts between different disciplinary and functional groups are not uncommon in ITRI. The survey studies we conducted in

ITRI showed that knowledge workers who subscribe to disciplinary centrism (believing that there are pronounced, immutable differences between academic disciplines) tend to report more interpersonal and identity conflicts when they work in interdisciplinary teams. They also tend to report low levels of cooperation in the team and low levels of satisfaction with their job (Chiu et al. 2013).

Evidence from both survey studies in ITRI and process studies of the student innovation teams shows that subscribing to a polyculturalist belief can mitigate the adverse effects of disciplinary centrism on creativity and innovation. Polyculturalism refers to the belief that although there are cultural differences between disciplines, there are also frequent interactions between disciplinary cultures (Morris, Chiu, and Liu 2015). The belief in polyculturalism reduces group centrism and encourages learning from other cultures. Past research shows that when people are motivated to learn from other cultures, their performance in creativity improves after having been exposed to foreign cultures (Maddux, Adam, and Galinski 2010). Data from our ITRI survey also show that knowledge workers who subscribe to polyculturalism tend to report fewer interpersonal and role conflicts when working in interdisciplinary teams. They also tend to have high job satisfaction. When cross-disciplinary student innovation team members share the polyculturalist belief, their teams tend to produce innovative design (Chiu et al. 2013; see also Xia, von Glinow and Lia's discussion on polycontextualism as a paradigm for overcoming institutional barriers facing Chinese IT outsourcing, Chapter 12, this volume).

In summary, the Confucian tradition, communist ideology, the rise of nationalism, and the collective imagination of China becoming a super-nation may have contributed to the prevalence of group centrism at the individual, team, and organization levels in China. The prevalence of group centrism can be an obstacle to enhancing the country's innovation capacity, by discouraging intercultural learning and encouraging adherence to norms that privilege usefulness rather than originality in innovation.

Earlier in this chapter, we reviewed evidence that speaks to the importance of establishing institutional support for innovation, if China wants to expand its capacity for transformational innovation. Nonetheless, the values underlying institutional support for innovation are primarily individualist values (e.g., freedom of expression, protection of individualist proprietary rights). The strong group centrism in

China suggests that aside from political reasons, the value incompatibility of Chinese and innovation cultures may also result in resistance to reforms designed to establish innovation-supporting institutions in China.

Together, our analysis suggests that merely increasing the quality of China's human capital will not be sufficient to promote transformational innovation in China. In fact, without fundamental transformations in China's institutional and cultural environment, given the current institutional and cultural environment, aggressive campaigns to enhance the quality of human capital through world-class university projects or global talent recruitment schemes may not lead to significant breakthroughs in science and technology in China.

14.5.6 Vertical collectivism

Many academic and business returnees in the TTP expect the "lenience" the Program promises to the returnees (Zweig and Wang 2013). However, the reality these returnees need to face is that in China important decisions related to funding and research directions are made by senior academic, government, and party administrators. Returnees may not be used to this top-down decision-making structure in China's academic and business environments.

Cross-cultural psychologists have characterized the type of collectivism practiced in China as vertical collectivism – collectivism that privileges status ranking of groups and individuals within a group (see Chiu and Hong 2006). Vertical collectivism differs from horizontal collectivism, which prioritizes promotion of positive interdependence among group members, who are treated as equals in the group.

Vertical collectivism in China has several important implications for China's effort to enhance its innovation capacity. As mentioned earlier, China has made substantial research investments through programs such as Project 985 and Project 211 to enhance the research capacity of its universities. Together with China's heavy investments in the building of key laboratories and various global talent recruitment schemes introduced by the government and universities, China's research productivity has improved considerably in the past decade, and so has the international recognition of many Chinese universities. Competition for higher university rankings (symbols of institutional status) has been a major driver of innovation in Chinese universities and research institutes. Competing for institutional status is also a strong motivation behind Chinese universities' effort to recruit returnees to the prestigious Thousand Talents Program, because being a host institution of TTP returnees confers status and reputation to the institution (see Zweig and Wang 2013). A downside of inter-institutional competition for status is that universities may place undue emphasis on the metrics of university rankings. Some of these metrics (number of Nobel Prize winners in the university) may have only remote relevance to the knowledge, economic, and social impact of most research activities in the university. Other metrics may direct research effort and resources to trendy research topics that are widely accepted in mainstream international journals, instead of inviting researchers to study theoretically and practically important Chinese phenomena that would significantly advance the frontier of knowledge.

The prevalence of vertical collectivism in China also affects the communication structure in Chinese organizations. For example, in a vertical management, middle managers play two roles. First, decisions are made at the top and passed down to the subordinates through the middle managers. Second, subordinates view their middle manager as their guardian and protector and communicate their expectations to the middle manager. In short, middle management has access to information and expectations from above and below. This type of management structure is common in China, particularly in state-owned enterprises (Menon, Sim, Fu, Chiu, and Hong 2010).

On the one hand, middle managers are in the best position to synthesize information from different levels of management and come up with innovative, integrative solutions to promote organizational growth. On the other hand, middle managers may be overwhelmed by the quantity and complexity of information they need to process and occasionally conflicting expectations from above and below. To manage informational load and complexity, an overwhelmed middle manager may turn to strategies that are widely accepted in the organization to manage information and relationships in the organization, instead of trying to be innovative (Chiu, Morris, Hong, and Menon 2000). The effects of vertical collectivism in Chinese organizations on organizational innovation merit future investigations.

14.6 Conclusions

In this chapter, we argue that China has enjoyed fast economic growth through optimizing its existing tangible capital in the past thirty-five years, and that this approach to economic growth may still be effective in the next two decades. However, China's long-term growth depends on the development of its intangible capital through technological progress and human capital enhancement. Results from analysis of multinational, longitudinal datasets reveal that increased quality of human capital can increase the volume of knowledge creation as well as the local economic impact of innovation in the country. To promote innovations with global influence, countries need to improve on their institutional support for innovation.

We take this perspective to evaluate China's strategies to enhance its innovation capacity. Our analysis shows that China has taken a proactive approach to build up its human capital through its aggressive efforts to raise the standards of its universities and to attract internationally renowned scientists and entrepreneurs who are ethnic Chinese to return to China. Nonetheless, due to historical, political, and cultural reasons, China has been slow in reforming its institutions. We argue that the lack of institutional support for innovation in China will limit the effectiveness of its talent recruitment schemes. We also contend that the strong and rising group centrism that ensues from China's cultural tradition, contemporary political ideology, and rise of nationalism may also hinder China's capacity to learn from foreign cultures and benefit from its cultural diversity. Group centrism also reinforces the cultural tendency to prioritize usefulness and slight originality in innovation, creating a tendency to focus on incremental improvements rather than radical innovations. We close by discussing the potential impact of vertical collectivism, another cultural constraint, on China's innovation capacity-building. This discussion leads to the hypothesis that the vertical management structure in many Chinese organizations may has created cognitive overload in the middle management and hindered organizational innovation.

This analysis leads us to believe that building human capital by itself is not sufficient to help China develop its capacity for transformational innovation. What China also needs are changes in the institutional and cultural environments, at least in the innovation sectors. A radically innovative China needs institutions that support business freedom and freedom of expression, as well as institutions that protect the proprietary rights of the individuals; it also needs a culture that recognizes horizontal individualist values and one that downplays group centrism and supports polyculturalist beliefs.

The idea that innovation and economic growth require institutional and cultural change can be tested in future investigations. First, in China, firms, cities, and regions/provinces differ in their performance in the three types of innovation (knowledge creation, knowledge impact, and knowledge diffusion). It is possible to evaluate the concurrent and predictive associations of performance on different types of innovation and economic growth across cities and regions/provinces. Results from such studies will allow investigators to estimate the differential impacts of different types of innovations on economic development.

Second, quality of human capital and institutional support for innovation also vary across firms, cities, and regions and provinces. Evaluating the degree of association between income growth and measures of the different components of human capital and institutional support across firms, cities, and regions/provinces will allow researchers to test the joint effect of human capital and institutional support on innovation performance. Results from such studies will also allow researchers to identify the specific components of human quality and institutional support that drive innovation. Similar studies can also be carried out to assess the effects of group centrism and vertical collectivism on innovation at firm, city, and province/region levels.

The predictors in the hypothesized relationships can be manipulated in experiments. For example, human capital can be manipulated through the mean level and variability of task-related specific knowledge and skills work team members possess. Institutional support can be manipulated through the quality of informal and formal institutional capital in a work team. Vertical collectivism can be manipulated by introducing intergroup competition. Group centrism can be manipulated by varying the salience of ingroup identity in the team. Accordingly, the causal effects of the manipulated predictors on team performance in innovation tasks can be simulated in experimental studies. For example, to simulate the effect of group centrism and vertical collectivism on innovation in controlled experiments, investigators can instruct teams of varying levels of specific human capital to perform an innovative design task and observe how experimental manipulations of group centrism and vertical collectivism may lower team performance. We are optimistic that results from such studies will advance our knowledge concerning the institutional and cultural constraints on technological progress in China.

References

Aiyar, S., Duval, R., Puy, D., Wu, Y., Zhang L. 2013. 'Growth slowdowns and the middle-income trap.' IMF Working paper 71. Washington, DC.

Bao, Y., Chen, X., Zhou, K. Z. 2011. 'External learning, market dynamics, and radical innovation: Evidence from China's high-tech firms.' *Journal of Business Research*, 65: 1225–1233.

Bechtoldt, M. N., De Dreu, C. K. W., Nijstad, B. A., Choi, H.-S. 2010. 'Motivated information processing, epistemic social tuning, and group creativity.' *Journal of Personality and Social Psychology*, 99: 622–637.

Bendapudi, N., Zhan S., Hong Y.-Y. 2015. 'Quality of education does not always guarantee creative output: The moderating role of cultural values.' Working paper, Nanyang Technological University, Singapore.

Bian, Y., Ang, S. 1997. 'Guanxi networks and job mobility in China and Singapore.' *Social Forces*, 75: 981–1005.

Callahan, W. A. 2015. 'Identity and security in China: The negative soft power of the China dream.' *Politics*, 35: 216–229.

Cheng, C.-y., Leung, A. K.-y. 2013. 'Revisiting the multicultural experience–creativity link: The effects of cultural distance and comparison mindset.' *Social Psychological and Personality Science*, 4: 475–482.

Cheng, C.-y., Leung, A. K.-y., Wu, T. Y. 2011. 'Going beyond the multicultural experience–creativity link: The emotional pathway underlying dual-cultural activation and creativity.' *Journal of Social Issues*, 67: 806–824.

Chiu, C.-y., Gries, P., Torelli, C. J., Cheng, S. Y.-Y. 2011. 'Toward a social psychology of globalization.' *Journal of Social Issues*, 67: 663–676.

Chiu, C.-y., Hong, Y. 2006. *Social Psychology of Culture*. New York: Psychology Press.

Chiu, C.-Y., Kwan, L. Y.-Y. 2010. 'Culture and creativity: A process model.' *Management and Organization Review*, 6: 447–461.

Chiu, C.-y., Kwan, L. Y.-y., Liou, S. 2013. 'Culturally motivated challenges to innovations in integrative research: Theory and solutions.' *Social Issues and Policy Review*, 7: 149–172.

Chiu, C.-y., Morris, M., Hong, Y., Menon, T. 2000. 'Motivated cultural cognition: The impact of implicit cultural theories on dispositional attribution varies as a function of need for closure.' *Journal of Personality and Social Psychology*, 78: 247–259.

Christensen, C. C. 2000. *The Innovator's Dilemma*. New York: Harper Collins.

Coleman, J. S. 1988. 'Social capital in the creation of human capital.' *American Journal of Sociology*, 94: S95–S120.

Cornell University, INSEAD, WIPO. 2013. *The Global Innovation Index 2013: The local dynamics of innovation.* Geneva, Ithaca, and Fontainebleau: Cornell University, INSEAD, and WIPO.

Dakhi, M., de Clercq D. 2007. 'Human capital, social capital, and innovation: A multi-country study.' *Entrepreneurship and Regional Development*, 16: 107–128.

Dunlap-Hinkler, D., Kotabe, M., Mudambi, R. 2010. 'A story of breakthrough versus incremental innovation: Corporate entrepreneurship in the global pharmaceutical industry.' *Strategic Entrepreneurship Journal*, 4: 106–127.

Erez, M., Nouri, R. 2010. 'Creativity in a context: Cultural, social, and work contexts.' *Management and Organization Review*, 6: 351–370.

Gao, Y., Gao, S., Zhou, Y., Huang, K.-F. 2015. 'Picturing firms' institutional capital-based radical innovation under China's institutional voids.' *Journal of Business Research*, 68: 1166–1175.

Goncalo, J. A., Staw, B. M. 2006. 'Individualism-collectivism and group creativity.' *Organizational Behavior and Human Decision Processes*, 100: 96–109.

Gong, F., Li, J. 2010. 'Seeking excellence in the move to a mass system: Institutional responses and changes in Chinese key comprehensive universities.' *Frontiers of Education in China*, 5: 477–506.

He, Y. 2007. 'History, Chinese nationalism and the emerging Sino-Japanese conflict.' *Journal of Contemporary China*, 16: 1–24.

Kenney, M., Breznitz, D., Murphree, M. 2013. 'Coming back home after the sun rises: Returnee entrepreneurs and growth of high tech industries.' *Research Policy*, 42: 391–407.

Kwan, L. Y.-Y., Chiu, C. Y. 2015. 'Country variations in different innovation inputs: The interactive effect of institution support and human capital.' *Journal of Organizational Behavior*, 36: 1050–1070.

Lanvin, B., Evans, P. 2013. *The Global Talent Competitiveness Index 2013*. Singapore: INSEAD.

Lau, L. J. 2014. *What Makes China Grow?* Hong Kong: Institute of Global Economics and Finance, the Chinese University of Hong Kong.

Lau, L. J., Park, J.-S. 2007. 'Sources of East Asian economic growth revisited.' Working paper, Department of Economics, Stanford University, Stanford, CA.

Lehman, D., Chiu, C.-y., Schaller, M. 2004. 'Culture and psychology.' *Annual Review of Psychology*, 55: 689–714.

Leung, A. K.-y., Chiu, C.-y. 2008. 'Interactive effects of multicultural experiences and openness to experience on creativity.' *Creativity Research Journal*, 20: 376–382.

Leung, A. K.-y., Chiu, C.-y. 2010. 'Multicultural experiences, idea receptiveness, and creativity.' *Journal of Cross-Cultural Psychology*, 41: 723–741.

Leung, A. K.-y., Maddux, W. W., Galinsky, A. D., Chiu, C.-y. 2008. 'Multicultural experience enhances creativity: The when and how?' *American Psychologist*, 63: 169–181.

Leung, K., Brew, F. P., Zhang. Z. X., Zhang Y. 2011. 'Harmony and conflict: A cross-cultural investigation in China and Australia.' *Journal of Cross-Cultural Psychology*, 42: 795–816.

Li, C., Kwan, L. Y.-Y., Liou, S., Chiu, C.-y. 2013. 'Culture, group processes and creativity,' in M. Yuki and M. Brewer (eds.), *Culture and Group Processes*. New York: Oxford University Press.

Li, M., Chen, Q. 2011. 'Globalization, internationalization and the world-class university movement: The China experience,' in R. King, S. Marginson and R. Naidoo (eds.), *Handbook on Globalization and Higher Education*. Cheltenham: Edward Elgar.

Liou, S., Nisbett, R. E. 2011. 'Cultural difference in group creativity process.' Paper presented at the annual meeting of the Academy of Management, San Antonio.

Maddux, W. W., Adam, H., Galinsky, A. D. 2010. 'When in Rome ... learn why the Romans do what they do: How multicultural learning experiences enhance creativity.' *Personality and Social Psychology Bulletin*, 36: 731–741.

Mahbubani, K. 2009. *Can Asians Think?* Singapore: Marshall Cavendish.

Menon, T., Sim, J., Fu, J. H.-Y., Chiu, C.-y., Hong, Y.-y. 2010. 'Blazing the trail and trailing the group: Culture and perceptions of the leader's position.' *Organizational Behavior and Human Decision Processes*, 113: 51–61.

Morris, M. W., Chiu, C.-y., Liu, Z. 2015. 'Polycultural psychology.' *Annual Review of Psychology*, 66: 631–659.

Morris, M. W., Leung, K. 2010. 'Creativity east and west: Perspectives and parallels.' *Management and Organization Review*, 6: 313–327.

Niu, W., Zhang, J., Yang, Y. 2007. 'Deductive reasoning and creativity: A cross-cultural study.' *Psychological Reports*, 100: 509–519.

Organization for Economic Cooperation and Development (OECD). 2013. *Supporting Invention in Knowledge Capital, Growth and Innovation.* Paris: OECD.

Saeki, N., Fan, X., Dusen, L. V. 2001. 'A comparative study of creative thinking of American and Japanese college students.' *Journal of Creative Behavior*, 35: 24–36.

Tabellini, G. 2008. 'Institutions and culture.' *Journal of the European Economic Association*, 6: 255–294.

Tong, Y.-y., Hui, P. P.-Z., Kwan, L.Y.-Y., Peng, S. 2011. 'National feelings or rational dealings? The moderating role of procedural priming on perceptions of cross-border acquisitions.' *Journal of Social Issues*, 67: 743–759.

Torelli, C. J., Chiu, C.-y., Tam, K.-P., Au, A. K. C., Keh, H. T. 2011. 'Exclusionary reactions to foreign cultures: Effects of simultaneous exposure to cultures in globalized space.' *Journal of Social Issues*, 67: 716–742.

Wu, Y., Yang, Y., Chiu, C.-y. 2014. 'Responses to religious norm defection: The case of Hui Chinese Muslims not following the halal diet.' *International Journal of Intercultural Relations*, 39: 1–8.

Yip, G., McKern, B. 2014. 'China's many types of innovation.' *Forbes Asia*.

Zhan, S., Bendapudi, N., Hong, Y.-y. 2015. 'Re-examining diversity as a double-edged sword for innovation process.' *Journal of Organizational Behavior*, 36: 1026–1049.

Zweig, D., Wang, H. 2013. 'Can China bring back the best? The Communist Party organizes China's search for talent.' *China Quarterly*, 215: 590–615.

15 Reframing research for cross-cultural management

ROSALIE L. TUNG

15.1 Introduction

Despite the criticisms that have been lodged against Hofstede's cultural dimensions, the influence of his 1980 book *Culture's Consequences: International Differences in Work-related Values* is undeniable. The interest in culture and its consequences – primarily in terms of whether cultural distance (see Kogut & Singh, 1988) can affect organizational functioning across international boundaries – has accounted for the exponential growth in research and publications on culture.

In their content analysis of twenty-four years of publications in the premier international business academic journal the *Journal of International Business Studies* (*JIBS*), Stahl and Tung (2015) found that 21 percent of the papers therein examined the direct or indirect relationships between differences in culture and organizational performance, such as a firm's propensity/disinclination to engage in and the success/failure thereof of collaborative arrangements with partners from other countries, and the transferability of policies and practices from headquarters to culturally distant subsidiary operations abroad.

Cross-cultural research on Asian countries, particularly China, has become popular. The growing importance of Asian economies as a share of world economic growth and the rising number of Westerners who travel to Asian countries to learn more about them have contributed to the surge in research interest on the impact of culture on doing business with Asian countries.

This chapter will first present a quick survey of the evolution of cross-cultural research (or, more appropriately, research across countries) followed by an overview of research on culture, with specific reference to emerging economies, such as China. This cursory survey will reveal that despite progress, the field seems to be plagued by the same issues that confronted researchers several decades ago, primarily the assumption of spatial homogeneity in a given country. The fallacy of this assumption will be highlighted later in a comparison of leadership styles in two highly successful Chinese companies, Alibaba and Huawei. The chapter will then discuss the need to reframe research on cross-cultural management and conclude with some directions for future research, particularly in the context of management of human resources in China from the perspectives of, first, multinationals (MNCs) operating in China and, second, of Chinese companies as they venture abroad in light of China's "Going Global" policy.

15.2 Evolution of cross-cultural research

Research across countries predated Hofstede's seminal work. Tung (1986) identified at least four major theoretical approaches to comparative management studies: first, the socio-economic approach; second, the environmental approach; third, the behavioral approach; and, fourth, the eclectic approach. Each of these approaches is outlined briefly below.

Socio-economic approach.   In their twenty-three-country study of managerial practices, Harbison and Myers (1959) attributed variations to the different stages and pace of economic development across countries. They subscribed to the hypothesis that as countries industrialize, there will be a growing convergence in managerial beliefs. To highlight how the socio-economic environment can impact management practices and policies, there is no better case than that of China. Prior to China's open-door policy in 1977–1978, central planning was the norm. Enterprises received directives from the State and the managers of such enterprises were not responsible for profits and losses because all allocations and revenues were made by and returned to the State. Income equality was emphasized, hence aside from the principle of "moral encouragement," there was little incentive for workers to outperform (Tung, 1981). The absence of market principles and the devastating policies implemented during the Cultural Revolution years (1966–1976) brought the Chinese economy to the brink of collapse after Mao Zedong's death and almost destroyed the Communist Party. With Deng Xiaoping's move to embark on market reforms and open the country to foreign investment, China enjoyed the fastest rate of economic growth in the world for almost three-and-a-half decades that effectively transformed the country into the second (or largest) economy in the world with the most sizable foreign reserves and, in the process, the largest banker to the United States.

The amazing transformations that have taken place in China within a relatively short time span would not have been possible under the socio-economic environment that existed in that country prior to 1977–1978. While cognizant of the important role that changes in the socio-economic environment can play in influencing management practices, the Harbison and Myers model cannot explain for inter-organizational differences in a given country. For example, it cannot explain why not all entrepreneurial start-ups perform as well as Jack Ma's Alibaba. A second limitation associated with the Harbison and Myers model is that it assumes that firms in countries at the same stage of industrialization/economic development will exhibit similar management styles and practices. A cursory review of management practices among OECD countries reveals, of course, that there are marked differences between the United States and Japan, two of the most industrialized economies in the world. In short, by focusing exclusively on broad sociological and economic forces that are far removed from the phenomena under investigation, in isolation of other factors that could also have an influence, the Harbison and Myers paradigm does not lend itself to the formulation nor testing of specific hypotheses that can relate organizational function to select aspects of outcome/performance.

Environmental approach. The Farmer and Richman (1965) model seeks to compensate for the limitations in the Harbison and Myers (1959) approach by including a broader spectrum of variables contained in the external environment (educational, sociological, political and legal, economic), akin to the concept of institutional environment used in the literature today (see Kostova & Zaheer, 1999; Dow & Karunaratna, 2006). Despite the merits associated with inclusion of a more comprehensive set of environmental variables, it still failed to consider forces internal to the organization itself. Theories of foreign direct investment that distinguish between firm-specific advantages (FSAs) from country-specific advantages (CSAs) (see Rugman & Verbeke, 2001, for example) and Jay Barney's (1986) resource-based view (RBV) of the firm take into consideration forces that are internal or specific to an organization within a given country. The focus of these latter theories is on the competitive advantage of firms rather than the competitive advantage of nations.

In short, while the Farmer and Richman model represents an improvement above the Harbison and Myers paradigm, an implicit assumption is made that management is a passive agent that acts in response to environmental constraints. It fails to take into consideration the reality that managers are proactive in manipulating certain environmental variables through the adoption of specific strategies and organizational processes.

Behavioral approaches. Haire, Ghiselli, and Porter (1966) focused on the values, beliefs, attitudes, and perceptions of people to account for variations in group behavior and decision-making as they affect organizational performance. Another behavioral approach is the values dimension model proposed by Hofstede (1980). While an examination of psychological characteristics of people is obviously important, this approach fails to take into consideration broad societal variables. Furthermore, this approach also assumes spatial homogeneity, that is, people within a nation-state are assumed to share the same cultural values.

Eclectic approach. The eclectic paradigm seeks to incorporate variables from different levels: societal, organizational, and individual. Examples of this approach include the Negandhi-Prasad (1975) model and Tung's (1986) systems model of comparative management that used organizational climate as the pivotal construct.

In the Negandhi-Prasad (1975) model, management philosophy and environmental factors were hypothesized to jointly influence management practices in a given organization. Their emphasis on managerial perceptions thus allows for inter-organizational variations in a country; this is more in line with reality. Their model also distinguished between economic and non-economic measures of performance, thus taking into consideration the factors that can be "controlled" by the organization (such as job satisfaction and organizational commitment) vis-à-vis the ones that cannot be controlled (such as the rate of inflation and exchange rate). However, the Negandhi-Prasad model only focused on the unidirectional relationships among variables.

In Tung's (1986) systems model of comparative management, she used organizational climate as the pivotal construct to span different levels of analysis. Organizational climate (OC) refers to "the perceived or experienced qualities of the *total* configural environment" (Litwin & Stringer, 1968:196). Given its holistic nature, OC can encompass variables from the macro environment (national level), meso environment (firm level), and micro (individual) level, and thus conceptually link analysis at these three levels. Because it is a perceptual measure, the use of OC as the critical variable in a systems model of comparative management can allow for and help explain inter-organizational differences across firms within a given country that share the same institutional environment. A paradigm or framework that allows for inter-organizational differences is more consistent with reality as intra-national diversity (i.e., differences within a country) can be as salient as cross-national differences (Tung, 2008a).

Research efforts to develop and/or refine comparative management models more or less ceased with the publication of Hofstede's value dimensions. Since then, the dimensional model has taken hold in cross-cultural research. In other words, the focus of cross-cultural research has shifted from the development of models of comparative management *to* the use of value dimensions as the latter provide a shorthand mechanism for describing a given culture. The introduction of the Kogut-Singh (KS index, in short) further aided this development by making available a ready tool to gauge differences between two or more given societies.

15.3 Why the need to reframe research on cross-cultural management?

In essence, the introduction of Hofstede's dimensions and the KS index has contributed to the popularization of research on culture in the mainstream of IB/IM literature. A dimensional model of cultural differences and indices that gauge cultural distance suffer from major limitations, such as weak explanatory power for the phenomena under investigation (Hakanson & Ambos, 2010). Tung and Verbeke (2010) have referred to these as the four masks that confound cross-cultural studies: first, assumption of "spatial homogeneity within a given nation"; second, cultural distance "systematically engenders negative outcomes"; third, assumption of "homogeneous impact of (national) cultural distance, irrespective of firm characteristics"; and, fourth, questionable practice of "bundling individual distance measures into aggregate indices." Each mask is discussed, particularly in the context of cross-cultural research on China.

15.3.1 Mask 1: "spatial homogeneity within a single nation"

In comparing cross-national (the focus of researchers in international management) with intra-national diversity (the focus of researchers on relational demographics and race relations), Tung (1993) indicated that while there are differences, there are also remarkable similarities in dynamics and processes between these two categories of diversity. In terms of acculturation, Tung (1998) showed that the four-cell typology of acculturation that Berry (1980) developed on the basis of his studies of immigrants in Canada can be fruitfully applied to North American expatriates operating abroad. Using the two dimensions of "attraction to partner's culture" (yes_1, no_1) and "need to preserve one's culture" (yes_2, no_2), Berry identified four possible modes of acculturation by members of the minority culture to that of the mainstream: integration (yes_1, yes_2), assimilation (yes_1, no_2), separation (no_1, yes_2), and marginalization (no_1, no_2). In terms of expatriation success, integration yielded the most positive outcome (Tung, 1998). The same was true for immigrants to Canada (Berry, 1980).

Similarly, Tung (1993) showed that Tannen's (1990) studies of differences in patterns of communication between men and women in the United States (i.e., "genderlect") could be as significant and salient as that between Americans and Japanese. Based on extensive studies that compared the styles and patterns of communication between men and women in the United States, Tannen (1990) found that women tended to be better listeners, to seek harmony, and were more cued to the "silent language." Tung (1993) showed that the stereotypical Japanese exhibited more of the feminine characteristics while the stereotypical American espoused more of the masculine traits identified by Tannen.

The rate of intra-diversity has been exacerbated by several factors: immigration, brain circulation, war for talent, and rising incidence of biracials and biculturals/multiculturals. Each of these factors is explained briefly below.

Immigration. Both the United States and Canada are home to many immigrants from around the world. Tung & Baumann (2009) noted: "In the case of Canada, for example, an estimated 40 percent of residents in major metropolitan areas, such as Toronto and Vancouver, are either immigrants or children of immigrants." Traditionally, the primary source of immigrants to both the United States and Canada was

European countries. More recently, many Chinese have emigrated to the United States and Canada although Hispanics (as a minority group) outnumber the Chinese in the United States.

Brain circulation. In the pre-globalization era, the terms "brain drain" and "brain gain" were commonly used to characterize the outflow (resulting from emigration) and inflow (resulting from immigration) of talent from source to destination countries, respectively. Saxenian (2002) has coined the term "brain circulation" to describe the reality that with globalization, high-demand talent may leave their home countries for periods of time for advanced education and gain international work experience and then re-enter their country of origin (COO) to capitalize on developments and opportunities there. Saxenian (2002) found that a significant percentage of entrepreneurial start-ups in Silicon Valley are by Chinese and Indian immigrants. To take advantage of developments in their COO, many of these immigrant entrepreneurs have established dual beachheads of business in their COO as well as in Silicon Valley. In their study of the information communications technology (ICT) industry in three economies (Taiwan, China, and India), Kenney, Breznitz, and Murphree (2013) found that returnees were important conduits of transfer of technological and managerial know-how from West to East.

This trend of living and working in several countries during one's career is prevalent among the wealthy, especially those from Asia. In a Barclays Bank study of high net worth individuals, they found that 57 percent of respondents have lived in a country other than their own and another 20 percent have resided in "three or more" countries (*The Rise of the Global Citizen?*, 2014). The vast majority of these wealthy individuals prefer to retire in their COO, however. These developments contribute to growing intra-national diversity.

In addition, the practice of deploying ethnic Chinese who have emigrated to other countries to staff their subsidiaries in China is common among many multinationals. The growing willingness of highly qualified individuals to relocate from country to country is consonant with Tung's (1998) finding of boundaryless careers. Furthermore, given the growing importance of the China market, many non-ethnic Chinese with potentials and aspirations for senior management increasingly seek to work in China for a couple of years to gain valuable international experience. These developments, in turn, contribute to the intra-national diversity in China.

War for talent. In 1998, McKinsey coined the term "war for talent" to refer to the reality that both industrialized and emerging markets are often competing for the same pool of human talent (Chambers, Foulon, Handfield-Jones, Hankin, & Michaels, 1998). Decades of inward investment into China combined with the current efforts by Chinese multinationals to invest abroad have translated into an unprecedented demand for human talent. While China is still the most populous country in the world, it faces the paradox of "scarcity among plenty," that is, unemployment or under-employment of the unskilled but insufficient people to fill the positions that require specific competencies (Farrell & Grant, 2005). To this end, China has embarked on medium- and long-range plans to transform its population dividend to "talent dividend" (Wang, 2010). An important component of these plans is to attract highly skilled overseas Chinese to return to their COO.

Given the recency of these governmental plans, it is too early to assess the effectiveness of these programs. Returnees fall into two general categories: those that are government-funded and sponsored and those that are self-funded. Of those in the former category, an estimated 32 percent have returned (Zweig, Chen, & Rosen, 2004). Of those in the second category, roughly 96.1 percent have remained abroad ("More Chinese overseas students return home in 2010," 2011).

The Chinese press refers to overseas Chinese who return as "returnees" while I have coined the term "ex-host country nationals" (EHCNs) (Tung & Lazarova, 2006) to describe them because even though they share the same ethnic background as the people in the receiving country (China in this case), by virtue of their living and working abroad for some period of time, their value systems and terms of employment would be different from those who have continuously resided in China. The return of EHCNs, of course, contributes to intra-national diversity within China.

Biracials and biculturals/multiculturals. An estimated 15 percent of all marriages in the United States are now biracial (Taylor, Wang, Parker, Patten, & Motel, 2012). While offsprings of biracial unions are not necessarily bicultural, the dual heritage of their parents does increase the likelihood that they are more sensitive to differences in behaviors and values of two or more cultural groups. Biracial unions, taken in conjunction with brain circulation, immigration, boundaryless careers, globalization, and the value that companies place on the possession of a global mindset (Tung, 2014a) mean that the number of people who are biculturals/multiculturals will be on the rise.

Collectively, these developments challenge the assumption of spatial homogeneity within a given country. Tung, Worm, and Fang (2008), for example, have found considerable differences in negotiation styles between Chinese in Beijing (the capital city), Shanghai (the commercial hub), Guangzhou (the southernmost Chinese city and close to Hong Kong), and Chengdu (a major city in western China). At the risk of over-generalization, Beijingers tend to be more politically oriented and bureaucratic. Shanghainese are more business-savvy and more focused on the bottom line. Guangzhouers are more entrepreneurial and less concerned about politics and ideology. Chengduers tend to be more traditional. As more recent arrivals to the international business scene, their negotiation styles resemble that of their counterparts on the eastern seaboard a decade or so ago.

Aside from regional differences, there can also be variations across generations. For example, the Chinese born and raised in China after the 1980s possess value systems and attitudes that are different from those born in the pre-1980 era where there was much deprivation and political strife (Egri & Ralston, 2004). Similarly, Tung and Baumann (2009) found that there were more similarities in the attitudes toward money and savings among Chinese from China, Chinese in Canada and Australia, than between the latter two groups vis-a-vis their white counterparts in Canada and Australia. In addition, culture is not static, particularly those in emerging economies where the whole society undergoes seismic changes in virtually all aspects of societal functioning (see Tung, 2008a).

Needless to say, it is more problematic to assume homogeneity among countries in a given region or among countries that share certain philosophical traditions and/or are geographically proximal to each other. In the IB/IM literature, there is a tendency to talk about the Confucian cluster (i.e., countries that are influenced by the teachings of Confucius such as China, Japan and Korea). Nisbitt (2003), for example, asserted that differences between Asians and Westerners stem from human cognition and proceeded to describe such variations. Tung (2014b) referred to this as one of the perils of conducting research on Asia.

15.3.2 Mask 2: cultural distance "systematically engenders negative outcomes"

In their content analysis of publications in *JIBS* between 1989 and 2012, Stahl and Tung (2015:1) found a 17:1 ratio of papers that made negative assumptions (i.e., cultural distance translates into problems/challenges) vis-a-vis those that made positive assumptions. For empirical papers, there was a 15:1 ratio of negative to positive assumptions. This difference suggests that in practice, there are less negative consequences associated with cultural distance. Furthermore, Stahl and Tung (2015) divided the twenty-one years of publications into three time periods and they found that the negative bias decreased over time.

Based on the data at hand, while Stahl and Tung (2015) could not answer the question of whether the results of their content analysis reflect the negative tendency among researchers of cultural distance (i.e., bias) *or* the reality that cross-cultural contacts are fraught with problems and challenges, they did draw attention to two important facts. First, despite the 15:1 ratio of negative to positive assumptions in the empirical papers, 47 percent of the papers actually found a positive/mixed/inconclusive relationship between cultural differences and outcome variables. Second, the results of several meta-analyses suggest that the relationship between cultural differences and performance outcomes are either small or are inconclusive. By and large, the results are contingent on contextual factors (Stahl & Tung, 2015).

In the case of China, given the large KS index between China and many countries in the West, such as the United States, Germany, and France, *if* indeed cultural distance were to lead to misunderstanding and failure, Tung (in press) raised the poignant question of why would so many highly successful multinationals from around the world clamor to enter and/or expand their presence in China?

As Tung (2008a) noted, the assumption that cultural distance or differences pose problems is guided, to a large extent, by the concept of homophily that asserts that people are more comfortable interacting with others who are similar to themselves (Lazarsfeld & Merton, 1954; Ibarra, 1992). If this were true, using the case of Western multinationals in China, only ethnic Chinese could be used to successfully manage host country nationals. There is evidence to the contrary – host country nationals may be more welcoming of managers who are different from themselves (Carr, Rugimbana, Walkom, & Bolitho, 2001; Tung & Lazarova, 2006). In other words, the opposite of homophily, inverse resonance, is at work in some cases.

Taken collectively, these findings suggest that focusing on only one set of factors (in this case, cultural differences) cannot explain for variations in organizational outcomes. In other words, the progress toward understanding cultural characteristics and gauging their differences are necessary *but* insufficient to explain and account for variations in outcome variables.

15.3.3 Mask 3: assumption of "homogeneous impact of cultural distance, irrespective of firm characteristics"

As Rugman and Verbeke (2001) have pointed out, aside from CSAs, it is important to consider FSAs including "subsidiary specific advantages." In China, some FSAs include the ability of multinationals to tap into the knowledge possessed by many members of the vast Chinese diaspora when they seek to enter into the China market and successfully operate there, for example. The Chinese diaspora is the largest in the world and growing – China is now the largest source country of international immigrants (Zhou, 2015). Tung and Chung (2010) have found evidence of the "immigrant effect," that is, firms that are founded/owned by ethnic Chinese or firms that employed ethnic Chinese in key decision-making positions were more likely to enter China via higher commitment modes (i.e., equity investment) vis-à-vis exporting or licensing. This is consistent with Chand and Tung's study (2011) that diasporic members can play the role of boundary spanners to build trust in business transactions between their COO and current country of residence (COR). Many members of the Chinese diaspora have good knowledge and experience in dealing with China and can provide invaluable service to, one, foreign multinationals that seek to enter/operate in China and, second, outward foreign investment from China into their respective COR.

15.3.4 Mask 4: questionable practice of "bundling individual distance measures into aggregate indices"

In light of the mounting criticisms on the limitations of value dimensions and the KS index, a growing number of researchers have now resorted to include institutional distance (Dow & Karunaratna, 2006; Berry,

Guillen, & Zhou, 2010). While the institutional distance indices seek to capture more aspects of the external environment that can affect organizational performance – such as political systems, political risk, protection of intellectual property rights, level of regional integration, and so on – they do not encompass all the factors that should be considered. In other words, "this is not merely a research design issue but goes to the heart of conceptualizing cross-cultural studies: what do IB and management scholars actually try to achieve with their work? Is it establishing more statistically significant relationship versus truly understanding managerial choice and economic performance in a cross-cultural and cross-institutional context?" (Tung & Verbeke, 2010:1270). If the objective is the latter, which it should be, then it appears that no amount of refinement of index development to capture select aspects of the external environment is sufficient. To truly understand managerial behavior and strategies across countries and their relationship to performance, perhaps a return to the effort of developing more comprehensive models of comparative management – an effort that by and large was abandoned – could better serve the interest of IB/IM researchers.

15.4 Directions for future research on cross-cultural management

This chapter has traced the evolution of comparative management models to study similarities and differences in management practices across countries. With the emergence of Hofstede's value dimensions and the KS index for gauging cultural distance, this endeavor to develop comparative management models was sidelined. This explains, in part at least, for the inconsistent findings with regard to the impact of cultural differences on a firm's performance and other outcome variables. Thus, the confusion that surrounded cross-cultural research some four-and-a-half decades ago when Karlene Roberts wrote her classic piece "On looking at an elephant" (1970) still remains. Roberts (1970) ascribed the inconsistent findings to cross-cultural researchers adopting a piecemeal, as opposed to a holistic, approach to understanding differences in management practices. In other words, Roberts criticized the then state of art with regard to comparative management research as resembling the attempts by the six blind men of Hindustan who tried to describe an elephant – depending upon the part of the animal they touched, each had a very different perception and interpretation of an elephant. Roberts' analogy is parallel to Schollhammer's characterization of comparative management theory as a "jungle" (1969) where there is much confusion in the findings depending upon the researcher's angle.

While acknowledging the advances in cross-cultural research made possible by Hofstede's dimensions and institutional indices to compare countries, the challenge that Tung and Verbeke (2010:1270) alluded to, namely that of "truly understanding managerial choice and economic performance in a cross-cultural and cross-institutional context," remains.

To address this challenge, this chapter offers three complementary ways to move the field forward. These include, first, a return to the development of more comprehensive models of comparative management; second, re-conceptualize the construct of cultural differences and distance; and, third, develop contextual cultural intelligence. Each of these is discussed briefly below, particularly in the context of China and other emerging economies.

15.4.1 Development of more comprehensive models of comparative management

The problems associated with using a single factor – whether economic system, socio-cultural differences – to explain for managerial behavior and organizational outcome were outlined earlier in the chapter and will not be repeated here. A systems model of comparative management such as the one proposed by Tung (1986) is an example of a more comprehensive model that takes into consideration the institutional environment and organizational environmental variables (such as industry/sector, strategic mission of the company, strategies pursued by the company, organizational structure) that affect organizational processes. These, in turn, interact with the personal variables of its members (such as age, gender, prior exposure to and experience of other cultures/countries), to yield organizational outcomes (both economic and non-economic measures).

Using the case of China, since virtually all the non-state-owned enterprises were established fairly recently (i.e., in the 1980s and 1990s), the strategies pursued by these companies reflect the personal management philosophies of their owners/founders. Take the case of Huawei, one of the largest manufacturers of telecommunication equipment in the world and founded in 1987 by Ren Zhengfei, a former military technologist with the People's Liberation Army. The strategies that catapulted Huawei from a small startup company to a successful global firm bear the imprimatur of Ren's military background. For example, Ren has adapted successfully some of Mao Zedong's strategies of "using the countryside to encircle and finally capture the cities" and ideological education to train fresh recruits. The former strategy stems from Ren's realization that it would be difficult to first sell to the more developed and sophisticated eastern coastal cities. Instead, he first sold to the less developed provinces in China's hinterland. He adopted essentially the same strategy in entering into foreign markets, particularly Europe. Huawei first entered the lower-end East European markets before venturing into the more developed markets in Western Europe ("Huawei: The long march of the invisible Mr. Ren," 2011). Ren also believed that it was important to use ideological education to instil a "wolf spirit" (adaptive to the surrounding environment, relies on good instinct) among his employees – all new recruits undergo a six-month training company to be inculcated with the company's strong organizational culture that is militaristic in nature. Another trait that reflects his military background is Ren's penchant for privacy – he has never given an interview to any reporter, whether local or foreign.

Contrast Huawei with Alibaba, the e-commerce company co-founded by Jack Ma in 1999. Ma is an English teacher who has no training in engineering nor computer science. By his own admission, Ma has "never written one code, never made one sale to a customer" (Mellor, Chen, & Wu, 2014). He is flamboyant, outgoing and loves to give interviews. In one celebratory gathering for his employees, he even wore a Mohawk-styled platinum blond wig, nose ring, and black lipstick and sang Elton John's "Can you feel the love tonight?" The strategies pursued by Ma, his management style, and the kind of employees attracted to work for Alibaba are very different from those of Huawei. The leadership style and management philosophy of other highly successful Chinese companies, such as Lenovo, Baidu, ZTE, and Tencent, lie somewhere between those of Huawei, on the one hand, and Alibaba, on the other.

Huawei's strategy of first entering the less developed markets before venturing into the industrialized countries stands in stark contrast to Haier's, the largest white goods manufacturer in the world, of "first difficult, then easy." Zhang Ruiman, founder of Haier, asserted that Chinese companies should not be timid in venturing abroad. He used the analogy of sheep and wolves, likening most foreign multinationals in

China to the latter. He urged his Chinese counterparts to pursue a similar strategy – "If we take the position of sheep, we will be devoured ... If we become wolves, we will be capable of competing with our rivals" ("Chinese CEO advises on competition strategies," 2001).

In terms of whether to first enter emerging or developed markets, Xiaomi's strategy parallels that of Huawei's. Xiaomi introduced its first smartphone in August 2011 and has quickly expanded into India, Indonesia, and the Philippines to become the third-largest smartphone distributor in the world.

If the assumption of spatial homogeneity associated with the KS index and variations thereof were to hold, then there would be no difference in organizational culture nor management styles and practices at these highly successful Chinese companies.

While the Chinese companies presented above are all successful and profitable, a question can be raised as to whether they are innovative or not.

Research on a systems approach to comparative management could perhaps also shed light on this important issue of what constitutes creativity and innovation and whether the developments in China thus far constitute innovation. In a way, none of the products manufactured and services provided by the aforementioned Chinese companies constitute cutting-edge technology. There is an ongoing debate in China on this issue and a new term, *shanzhaism*, has been coined to describe the common practice of imitating brands and goods developed elsewhere. *Shanzhai* products were first applied to mobile phones – according to the *Financial Times*, 20 percent of 2G phones sold worldwide are *shanzhai*. Since then, the term *shanzhai* has been used to describe advertisements, product names, and entertainment that mimic those originating elsewhere. In fact, a Peking University Chinese graduate student wrote an editorial under the pseudonym of Steven Zuckerberg entitled, "All of China is a knock-off." His explanation for using a Western pseudonym stems from his belief that opinions made by a foreigner would be taken more seriously by his compatriots (Osnos, 2009).

Kal Raustiala and Chris Sprigman, two law professors from the United States, penned a well-researched book entitled *The Knockoff Economy: How Imitation Sparks Innovation* (2012). Their book documented how pervasive imitation is in many industries, including fashion, cuisine, and football. In their opinion, instead of dampening innovation it may actually encourage it. In the case of fashion, it accelerates obsolescence, thus shortening fashion cycles. When prominent US fashion designer Ralph Lauren was asked by Oprah Winfrey how he has able to remain at the forefront of the fashion industry for over four decades, his retort was: "You copy. Forty-five years of copying; that's why I'm here" (Raustiala & Sprigman, 2014). In the case of cuisine, leading chefs from around the world concur that "truly ground-breaking cooking is necessarily a derivative of what came before" (Raustiala & Sprigman, 2012:190). Even though both Raustiala and Sprigman are lawyers and believe that intellectual property protection is necessary, they conclude with the provocative assertion that imitation has its upside because great innovations are often derived from existing ones. They point to the advantages associated with the growing trend toward open-source operating systems.

Applying this logic to the case of China, *shanzhaism* can help Chinese firms to collapse and leapfrog decades of development elsewhere to enable, and more importantly goad, them to compete worldwide with innovator firms from the more industrialized countries, that is, to behave like wolves rather than sheep. The question still remains as to whether a country can continue to remain competitive in the long term by merely being imitators. While it is impossible to foretell the future, the fact that the Chinese government is cognizant of the important role of creativity and innovations to the long-term sustainability of the country as witnessed by its adoption of a multi-prong approach to, first, invest heavily in research and development, second, upgrade education at all levels, third, continue to send Chinese abroad for advanced education, and, fourth, attract talent from around the world, particularly the large number of highly educated ethnic Chinese overseas, it appears that China may well succeed in this endeavor. In early March 2015, Beijing announced its "internet plus initiative." In response to this, Alibaba and Tencent have quickly embarked on online innovations, such as the provision of supporting services to local governments and business incubators in the country.

It is important to recall that when Japan and South Korea first embarked on their road to technological development, there was also a lot of imitation from abroad. In the case of China, the country has a rich tradition of inventions – gunpowder, paper, the magnetic compass, and bureaucracy, just to name a few. Under the right set of environmental conditions, China produced Zheng He of the Ming dynasty who sailed the high seas. Gavin Menzies, author of *1421: The Year China Discovered America*, asserted that Zheng He had discovered the Americas several decades before Christopher Columbus. Current Chinese President Xi Jinping certainly has the vision, charisma, and determination to spur the revival of China's innovative capabilities that have lain dormant for a few centuries by launching his Silk Road Economic Belt initiative that seeks to link the economic regions from China through Central and South Asia to wind up in Australia. The China-led Asian Infrastructure Investment Bank (AIIB) to fund this initiative has attracted over fifty founding members, including some of the United States' staunchest allies, the United Kingdom and Australia (Tung, in press). Xi's ambitions have extended to China's growing presence in Antartica, literally the end of the world.

The confluence of factors that enable innovation in a country and what constitutes innovation could be examined in a systems model of comparative management. This approach would most probably involve the use of qualitative research, as opposed to quantitative methodological designs popular in our literature, to identify the relevant variables and, more importantly, to understand the complex interrelationships among these variables.

15.4.2 Re-conceptualize the construct of cultural differences and distance

In their recommendations to better understand the role of culture across international boundaries and to redress the conflicting findings on whether cultural differences can yield positive vis-à-vis negative outcomes, Stahl and Tung (2015) have called for the need to re-conceptualize and operationalize the constructs of diversity and cultural distance. For a start, they suggested the adoption of Harrison and Klein's (2007) typology of diversity to re-conceptualize the cultural distance construct through the dimensions of separation, variety, and disparity. Even though Harrison and Klein's typology was intended for use in an intra-national diversity setting (such as multicultural teams that comprise members of different races/ethnic groups within the United States), "separation" can be used to gauge geographic distance and dissimilarities in values and attitudes. "Variety" can be used to analyze the nature and type of cross-cultural interaction under investigation and "disparity" can be applied to examining the interactions between peoples from industrialized vis-à-vis developing economies, and majority versus minority partners. Collectively, these three dimensions can shed more insight on what type of diversity can yield what outcomes and their interactions thereof (Stahl & Tung, 2015).

Applying this to the China context, as noted above, given the large number of Chinese who have studied abroad or at Western-type institutions of higher learning in China, lived and/or worked abroad, or who have worked for foreign-invested enterprises in China, their values and attitudes would be very different from Chinese who have minimal exposure to the aforementioned situations. Hence, the expectations of employees in the former category to work, methods of compensation, leader–member relationships, and performance appraisal would most likely be very different from those in the latter category. Therefore, a one-size-fits-all approach to human resource management even in China will most probably elicit different outcomes from Chinese employees depending on their background and experience.

Furthermore, given the fact that more and more non-Chinese now choose to work in China, this adds to the intra-diversity within China. Their expectations on all aspects of human resource management processes and practices will likely differ from those of the local nationals and EHCNs. In addition, in light of China's "going global" policy, Chinese bosses would have to contend with the attitudes and perceptions of host country nationals abroad. As Leung and Morris (2015) noted, Western employees may be more questioning of their Chinese bosses despite their title and position in the organizational hierarchy.

15.4.3 Develop contextual cultural intelligence

There is a growing body of literature that emphasizes the importance of context, such as polycontextualization (von Glinow, Shapiro, & Brett, 2004), contextual intelligence (Bennis, 2009; Khanna, 2014), and taking the context or situational factors into consideration (Leung, Bhagat, Buchan, Erez, & Gibson, 2005; Tung & Verbeke, 2010; Leung & Morris, 2015). For example, Tung and Verbeke (2010:18) asserted that there is "no direct, generalizable linkage (divorced from a specific situational context) should be expected between cultural distance scores and managerial choice or economic performance."

In many ways, the call for contextual intelligence, or more specifically contextual cultural intelligence, is not new. In the past, these contextual factors were usually referred to as contingencies. There are well-developed contingency theories in the management/international management literature. Fred Fielder's (1967) contingency theory of leadership, for example, has asserted that the most effective leadership style is contingent upon leader–member relations, task structure, and leader position power. Tung (1981) has posited a contingency paradigm for selection and training of expatriates – she argued that the best selection criteria and the most appropriate training programs for those assigned to work in a foreign location depend on, first, the amount of contact required with local nationals to successfully perform the job (such as CEO, marketing manager) and, second, the duration of stay in a foreign country (business travelers vis-à-vis expatriates on a three-year assignment).

To advance our understanding of management styles and practices, efficacy of particular strategies, and organizational performance across countries, it would be useful to identify the contingent/contextual/situational factors that can help address "*how* and *when* it makes a difference" (Leung et al., 2005:368). Similar to the example that Warren Bennis (2012) recounted of Sir Winston Churchill being hit by a car when he was crossing the street in New York in December 1931, it was not a situation where Churchill was stupid nor the driver of the car was careless; rather, Churchill forgot that traffic in the United States keeps to the right, the opposite of that in Great Britain, which he was more accustomed to. In the preceding example, the appropriate question to ask is *not* "why was there a difference"; rather, it should be what were the differences in the context that rendered the occurrence of this accident.

In conclusion, this chapter has highlighted the need to reframe research on cross-cultural management. The directions for future research presented are by no means easy as they call for a departure from the readily available indices that many IB/IM researchers are comfortable with. However, a giant leap in the appropriate direction has to be undertaken in order for practitioners and researchers to fully understand the complexities and nuances of managing across international boundaries and their relationships to performance.

References

Barney, J.B. 1986. Organizational culture: Can it be a source of sustained competitive advantage? *Academy of Management Review*, 11 (3):656–665.

Bennis, W. 2009. *Becoming a Leader*. New York: Basic Books.

Bennis, W. 2012, August 20. Mastering the context. *Bloomberg.com*. www .bloomberg.com/bw/articles/2012-08-20/mastering-the-context. Accessed March 1, 2015.

Berry, H., Guillén, M.F., & Zhou, N. 2010. An institutional approach to cross-national distance. *Journal of International Business Studies*, 41:1460–1480.

Berry, J.W. 1980. Social and cultural change. In Triandis, H.C. and Brislin, R.W. (Eds.), *Handbook of Cross-Cultural Psychology* 5:211–279. Boston: Allyn & Bacon.

Carr, S.C., Rugimbana, R.O., Walkom, E., & Bolitho, F.H. 2001. Selecting expatriates in developing areas: "Country-of-origin" effects in Tanzania? *International Journal of Intercultural Relations*, 25:441–457.

Chambers, E.G., Foulon, M., Handfield-Jones, H., Hankin, S.M., & Michaels, E.G. 1998. The war for talent. *McKinsey Quarterly*, 1–8.

Chand, M., & Tung, R.L. 2011. Diaspora as the boundary-spanners: The role of trust in business facilitation. *Journal of Trust*, 1(1):104–126.

Chinese CEO advises on competition strategies. 2001, October 23. *China Daily*. www.china.org.cn/english/2001/Oct/21056.htm. Accessed May 1, 2015.

Dow, D., & Karunaratna, A. 2006. Developing a multidimensional instrument to measure psychic distance stimuli. *Journal of International Business Studies*, 37(5):578–602.

Egri, C.P., & Ralston, D.A. 2004. Generation cohorts and personal values: A comparison of China and the U.S. *Organization Science*, 15(2):210–220.

Farmer, R.N., & Richman, B.M. 1965. *Comparative Management and Economic Progress*. Homewood, IL: Richard D. Irwin.

Farrell, D., & Grant, A. 2005. *Addressing China's Looming Talent Shortage*. London: McKinsey Global Institute.

Fiedler, F.E. 1967. *A Theory of Leadership Effectiveness*, New York: McGraw-Hill.

Haire, M., Ghiselli, E.E., & Porter, L.W. 1966. *Managerial Thinking: An International Study*. New York: Wiley.

Hakanson, L., & Ambos, B. 2010. The antecedents of psychic distance. *Journal of International Management*, 16(3):195–210.

Harbison, F., & Myers, C.A. 1959. *Management in the Industrial World: An International Analysis.* New York: McGraw-Hill.

Harrison, D.A., & Klein, K.J. 2007. What's the difference? Diversity constructs as separation, variety, or disparity in organizations. *Academy of Management Review*, 32(4):1199–1228.

Hofstede, G. 1980. *Culture's Consequences: International Differences in Work-Related Values.* Beverly Hills, CA: Sage.

Huawei: The long march of the invisible Mr. Ren. 2011, June 2. *The Economist.* www.economist.com/node/18771640. Accessed March 1, 2015.

Ibarra, H. 1992. Homophily and differential returns: Sex differences in network structure and access in an advertising firm. *Administrative Science Quarterly*, 37(3):422–447.

Kenney, M., Breznitz, D., & Murphree, M. 2013. Coming back home after the sun rises: Returnee entrepreneurs and growth of high tech industries. *Research Policy*, 42:391–407.

Khanna, T. 2014. Contextual intelligence. *Harvard Business Review*, September, 59–68.

Kogut, B., & Singh, H. 1988. The effect of national culture on the choice of entry mode. *Journal of International Business Studies*, 19(3):411–432.

Kostova, T., & Zaheer, S. 1999. Organizational legitimacy under conditions of complexity: The case of the multinational enterprise. *Academy of Management Review*, 24(1):64–81.

Lazarsfeld, P., & Merton, R. 1954. Friendship as a social process: A substantive and methodological analysis. In Berger, M. (Ed.), *Freedom and Control in Modern Society*: 18–66. New York: Van Norstand.

Leung, K., Bhagat, R.S., Buchan, N.R., Erez, M., & Gibson, C.B. 2005. Culture and international business: Recent advances and their implications for future research. *Journal of International Business Studies*, 36:357–378.

Leung, K., & Morris, M.W. 2015. Values, schemas, and norms in the culture–behavior nexus: A situated dynamics framework. *Journal of International Business Studies*, 46: 1028–1050.

Litwin, G., & Stringer, R. 1968. *Motivation and Organizational Climate.* Cambridge, MA: Harvard University Press.

Mellor, W., Chen, L.Y., & Wu, Z. 2014, November 9. Ma says Alibaba shareholders should feel love, not no. 3. *Bloomberg.com.* www.bloomberg.com/news/articles/2014-11-09/ma-says-alibaba-shareholders-should-feel-love-not-no-3. Accessed March 1, 2015.

More Chinese overseas students return home in 2010. 2011, March 11. *Xinh uanet.com.* http://news.xinhuanet.com/english2010/china/2011-03/11/c_13773804.htm. Accessed March 15, 2011.

Nisbitt, R. 2003. *The Geography of Thought: How Asians and Westerners Think Differently . . . and Why.* New York: Free Press.

Negandhi, A.R., & Prasad, S.B. 1975. *The Frightening Angels: A Study of U.S. Multinationals in Developing Countries.* Kent, OH: Kent State University Press.

Osnos, E. 2009, March 5. A Chinese pirate unmasks. *New Yorker.* www.newyorker.com/news/evan-osnos/a-chinese-pirate-unmasks. Accessed on May 20, 2015.

The Rise of the Global Citizen? 2014. London: Barclays PLC.

Raustiala, K., & Sprigman, C. 2012. *The Knockoff Economy: How Imitation Sparks Innovation.* New York: Oxford University Press.

Raustiala, K., & Sprigman, C. 2014, September 8. Piracy fuels the fashion industry. *New York Times.* www.nytimes.com/roomfordebate/2014/09/07/who-owns-fashion/piracy-fuels-the-fashion-industry. Accessed September 9, 2014.

Roberts, K.H. 1970. On looking at an elephant: An evaluation of cross-cultural research related to organizations. *Psychological Bulletin,* 74(5):327–350.

Rugman, A., & Verbeke, A. 2001. Subsidiary-specific advantages in multinational enterprises. *Strategic Management Journal,* 22:237–250.

Saxenian, A. 2002. Brain circulation: How high-skill immigration makes everyone better off. *The Brookings Review,* 20(1):28–31.

Schollhammer, H. 1969. The comparative management theory jungle. *Academy of Management Journal,* 12(1):81–97.

Stahl, G.K., & Tung, R.L. 2015. Towards a more balanced treatment of culture in international business studies: The need for positive cross-cultural scholarship. *Journal of International Business Studies,* 46: 391–414.

Tannen, D. 1990. *You Just Don't Understand: Women and Men in Communication.* New York: Harper Collins.

Taylor, P., Wang, W., Parker, K., Passel, J.S., Patten, E., & Motel, S. 2012. *The Rise of Intermarriage.* Washington, DC: Pew Research Center.

Tung, R.L. 1981. Patterns of motivation in Chinese industrial enterprises. *Academy of Management Review,* 6:487–494.

Tung, R.L. 1986. Toward a systems model of comparative management. In Farmer, R.N. (Ed.), *Advances in International Comparative Management,* 2: 233–247. Greenwich, CT: JAI Press Inc.

Tung, R.L. 1993. Managing cross-national and intra-national diversity. *Human Resource Management Journal*, 32(4):461–477.

Tung, R.L. 1998. American expatriates abroad: From neophytes to cosmopolitans. *Journal of World Business*, 33(2):125–144.

Tung, R.L. 2008a. The cross-cultural research imperative: The need to balance cross-national vis-à-vis intra-national diversity. *Journal of International Business Studies*, 39(1):41–46.

Tung, R.L. 2014a. Requisites to and ways of developing a global mind-set: Implications for research on leadership and organizations. *Journal of Leadership & Organizational Studies*, 21(4):229–337.

Tung, R.L. 2014b. Research on Asia: Promise and perils. *Journal of Asia Business Studies*, 8(3):189–192.

Tung, R.L. in press. Opportunities and challenges ahead of China's "New Normal." *Long Range Planning*.

Tung, R.L., & Baumann, C. 2009. Comparing the attitudes toward money, material possessions and savings of overseas Chinese vis-a-vis Chinese in China: Convergence, divergence or cross-vergence, vis-a-vis "one size fits all" human resource management policies and practices. *International Journal of Human Resource Management*, 20:2382–2401.

Tung, R.L., & Chung, H.F.L. 2010. Diaspora and trade facilitation: The case of ethnic Chinese in Australia. *Asia Pacific Journal of Management*, 27 (3):371–392.

Tung, R.L., & Larazova, M.B. 2006. Brain drain versus brain gain: An exploratory study of ex-host country nationals in Central and East Europe. *International Journal of Human Resource Management*, 17 (11):1853–1872.

Tung, R.L., & Verbeke, A. 2010. Beyond Hofstede and GLOBE: Improving the quality of cross-cultural research. *Journal of International Business Studies*, 41(8):1259–1274.

Tung, R.L., Worm, V., & Fang, T. 2008. Sino-Western business negotiations revisited – 30 years after China's open door policy. *Organizational Dynamics*, 37(1):60–74.

Von Glinow, M.A., Shapiro, D.L., & Brett, J.M. 2004. Can we talk, and should we? Managing emotional conflict in multicultural teams. *Academy of Management Review*, 29(4): 578–592.

Wang, H.Y. 2010. *China's National Talent Plan: Key Measures and Objectives*. November 23. Washington, DC: Brookings Institute. www .brookings.edu/research/papers/2010/11/23-china-talent-wang. Accessed January 25, 2011.

Zhou, L. 2015, March 19. More wealthy Chinese set to flood US investor visa scheme: Think tank report. *South China Morning Post.* www.scmp.com/news/china/article/1742325/more-wealthy-chinese-set-flood-us-investor-visa-scheme-think-tank-report?utm_source=edm%26utm_medium=edm%26utm_content=20150320%26utm_campaign=scmp_today. Accessed March 19, 2015.

Zweig, D., Chen, C., & Rosen, S. 2004. Globalization and transnational human capital: Overseas and returnee scholars to China. *The China Quarterly*, 179:735–757.

16 | *China's innovation challenge*
Concluding reflections

ARIE Y. LEWIN, MARTIN KENNEY, AND JOHANN PETER MURMANN

As we hope is the case for the reader, our thinking evolved as we considered, compiled, and edited the chapters. But we kept returning to the two following questions about China's future. First, can China draw upon and outgrow its past, or, as Gordon Redding contends in Chapter 3, will the dead hand of that past limit how much further China can evolve? Second, can China succeed in building a new indigenous economic development model, or will it be "forced" to adopt the basic principles of Western liberal development models that seem to have propelled all the known examples of economic progress? The first chapters frame the basic tension, juxtaposing Justin Yifu Lin's optimistic new structural economic approach to the current situation in China (Chapter 2) against the profoundly pessimistic expectation of stagnation expressed by Gordon Redding (Chapter 3) and Douglas Fuller (Chapter 6). As the editors, we have not settled on either the optimistic or pessimistic perspective, each of which seems equally possible. What we and all the chapter authors agree on is that, over the past five decades, change in China has been strikingly fast and, almost certainly, will continue to be for the next two decades, regardless of the direction taken.

Moving to an innovation-driven economy seems demonstrably necessary for China to move to a higher trajectory of economic growth and attain a high-income economy. Ultimately, an innovation-based economy means nothing less than building a system that can release and harness more of the creative potential of the Chinese people. Researchers have accumulated considerable evidence that there is nothing inherent in the Chinese people that prevents them from being innovative (see Morris and Leung 2010; and Chapter 14 in this volume). The success of Chinese scientists, authors, musicians, businesspeople, and the like in the West also strongly supports this idea.

418

This implies that any barriers to innovation must be related to institutions, organizations, culture, norms, or values, as described in Chapters 13 and 14. Further, it is only at the current stage of development that we should consider whether China can become an innovation-driven economy. Devoting substantial resources, talent, and time to an innovation economy is achievable only when a substantial proportion of a society's population is not consumed with the immediate task of providing for everyday needs. The innovation process itself is one of taking risks, risks that a society largely mired in poverty cannot afford to take, because of the high probability of failure. All our authors agree that China is now at the point where it can – and, indeed, must – enable, encourage, and reward the taking of what might be termed "the innovators' risks."

In many respects, even understanding China today is almost impossible, as it encompasses so many contradictions. This is not surprising. Perhaps no country in history has undergone as rapid and thoroughgoing an industrial and technological change in so short a time. Only fifty years ago, China was an isolated, largely agricultural and backward country characterized by general poverty. It had a relatively straightforward economy that the state fully controlled, using five-year plans. The study of China was confined to a few specialists, and Chinese business inspired little interest. At the time, the possibility that China was capable of innovation was inconceivable.

Things have changed remarkably. Today, as so many of our chapters show, China's political economy has shown a remarkable absorptive capacity for technology created elsewhere and a surprising plasticity and pragmatism in adapting to change. There also can be no question that Chinese engineers, scientists, and managers have a record of invention and innovations, but they are not yet at a sufficient level to make the country an innovation leader. The fundamental question posed in our book – whether China can transition to an innovative economy – has clearly become a vital concern among policymakers and managers in China and globally.

In many ways, Chinese policymakers can only deserve our sympathy, as the situation they face going forward is extraordinarily complex. This complexity will only multiply as the economy grows and becomes further differentiated. Remember that China is home to 1.4 billion people (20% of the global population), with a continent-sized geographic area that hosts production ranging from peasant agriculture to cutting-edge manufacturing using some of the most advanced technologies in the world. Some of the contradictions that China faces are extraordinarily wicked. For example, economists urge China to increase consumption; yet an increase in the consumption of resources in general and fossil fuels in particular by each Chinese to the same level as Americans would exacerbate global climate change. This means that, for the sake of the planet, China and the rest of the countries in the world must find innovative ways to expand their economy without increasing fossil fuel-based energy use. Moreover, China faces many other challenges that demand creative solutions, such as a quickly aging society, a large migrant population, and growing pressure for social welfare and health care. It also needs to decrease administrative and bureaucratic transaction costs and to increase institutional trust as a way to reduce reliance on personal trust, or what Redding in Chapter 3 refers to as the embeddedness of personalism. As China's economy becomes ever more complex, with greater divisions of labor and more feedback loops, central planning and its implementation will be ever so more difficult to manage.

Even innovation, the core topic of this book, is fraught with contradictions. Although it makes society more productive, it can also lead to unemployment. Eric Brynjolfsson and Andrew McAfee (2014), among others, suggest that the advance of electronics and software is leading to a society in which the "machines" will replace human beings for almost all menial tasks. This is not a completely idle threat: The CEO of Foxconn, the Taiwanese electronics product assembler and employer of one million Chinese workers, expects to replace 30% of its workforce with robots by 2020 (Kan 2015). If China is the world's workshop, what will happen when much of the workshop is automated? Chinese would have to find employment in sectors that are not readily automated, just as those in the West have done over the past 200 years. Even in the West many people are concerned that automation will destroy more jobs than it creates. The jury is still out on exactly how this might play out in China or, for that matter, in the rest of the world.

We see looming storm clouds in the form of a debt-saturated economy, growing excess capacity in a number of industries, bouts of "irrational exuberance" in financial markets, a polluted environment, geopolitical tensions, endemic corruption, and a one-party state that often suppresses dissent yet must achieve and maintain social legitimacy among a citizenry that is only partially empowered to address these daunting issues. On the bright side, we see leadership at firms, universities, and, yes, in the government itself that recognizes these challenging issues. Chinese leaders, while constrained by the weight of an entrenched party system and a bureaucracy that wishes to preserve the existing system, are clearly trying to address these challenges (see, e.g., thirteenth Five-Year Plan, 2016–2020, World Bank & Development Research Center of the State Council, P. R. C. 2013). The Chinese population also recognizes these challenges and seems to support the government's effort to tackle them. Even though no one can predict with any certainty which path China will end up taking, we are absolutely certain that the spillover will affect all of us. China is now connected to the rest of the world through massive trade flows, and China has recently showed its aspiration to play the role of a political superpower (see Leonard 2012).

In the years to come, it will become increasingly clear whether the optimistic or the pessimistic outlook on China's ability to develop an innovative economy turns out to be correct. In the process of integrating and finalizing this book, we have come to the conclusion that one succinct and impactful way to gauge Chinese progress is to track a few salient indicators. We suggest that the indicators described below might be helpful in compiling what can be called a "Chinese Innovation Capacity Growth Dashboard."

Effectiveness of the system of intellectual property. Has China adopted policies to create an intellectual property (IP) regime that encourages and rewards innovation by adopting global best practices?

Chapter 7, by Menita Liu Cheng and Can Huang, makes it clear that the Chinese patent office is granting far too many patents for trivial or, in some cases, nonexistent inventions. Government quotas for lower-level jurisdictions and research organizations, combined with subsidies for filing patents, have led countless "junk" patents to be filed and granted. Lax examination procedures create further problems. This state of affairs may, in fact, discourage high-quality inventions that can be commercialized as real innovations.

Effectiveness of R&D resource allocation. Is China adopting global best practices for peer review and competitive allocation of R&D resources?

Although China has made important progress in decreasing automatic R&D allocations and in implementing a more transparent and competitive process for peer review, the government continues to impose central directions, such as the sixteen Mega project initiatives (discussed in Chapter 1). At the same time, continuing efforts at improvement are needed to enable the creation of a flourishing indigenous research environment.

Share of resources flowing to state-owned enterprises.   Is China continuing the gradual privatization of the state-owned enterprises (SOEs)?

The size of the SOE sector continues to vex Chinese authorities. Many SOEs have lost their social, political, and economic value. They are recognized as bureaucratic and inefficient and appear to have difficulty in producing high-quality, innovative products, even though they receive a large fraction of R&D resources. Exposing many of them to more market competition would encourage them to mobilize their considerable assets to become more competitive. The government might want to keep a few SOEs because of their national strategic role but overall the resources going to SOEs need to be reduced.

Ease of starting new firms.   Is China eliminating administrative and extra-administrative obstacles to the formation of new firms?

Recent research has shown that successful Chinese companies allocate disproportionately large time and effort by owners and managers to maintaining relationships with every level of government, primarily because of the embedded practice of "personalism" and because of the widespread practice of exceptionalism (approval of exceptions from existing rules and procedures or promulgating one-time special rules). Indicators to gauge progress toward decreasing administrative obstacles include measures of the time it takes to issue business permits, the number of administrative approvals, the number of rules that have been eliminated, the speed and frequency of adjudicating administrative claims as well as the efficiency of a new, truly independent administrative court that might even sanction government bureaus and individual bureaucrats.

Level of financing for startups and small and medium-size enterprises.   Is China opening access to bank financing and government grants to start technological companies and small and medium-size enterprises (SMEs)?

The flip side of channeling the bulk of Chinese financial resources to SOEs is that startups and SMEs have found it very difficult to obtain financing from banks or other sources (see Chapters 6 and 8). Alibaba's recent establishment of an entity to aggregate household saving and lend it to SMEs is an initiative aimed at overcoming this obstacle. Yet it is still uncertain how far the government will go and what specific mechanisms will be created to ensure that promising technology start-ups and SMEs have access to the financial resources necessary to support innovation.

Share of new-to-world innovations. Are more Chinese firms producing innovative products and business models capable of competing in the global market?

China already possesses very innovative firms, such as Baidu, Huawei, Tencent, and Da-Jiang Innovations (the world's leading civilian drone maker). China also already has a significant venture capital-financed, high-technology sector. An important issue will be whether it can continue to grow and support new innovative firms. Furthermore, to what extent will these firms be able to build products that are not simply knock-offs of products developed elsewhere and whose success is predicated upon the protection they receive from the Chinese government? Finally, many of the venture capital-financed Chinese firms are operating new-to-the-market business models that are not based upon new-to-the-world technology. In the United States, for example, in Silicon Valley, new business model firms continue to emerge, such as Facebook. Similarly, spinoffs based on sophisticated new technologies often developed in university laboratories are a source of new-to-the-world innovations and businesses.

Effective exploitation of foreign R&D assets. Can Chinese firms exploit the foreign R&D assets that they acquire?

As we have seen in Chapter 10, by Yves Doz and Keeley Wilson, Chinese firms have been establishing R&D facilities abroad and increasingly acquiring foreign firms with significant technological assets. One indicator of success in building an innovative country is the ability of firms to absorb, internalize, and integrate the knowledge gained from their foreign assets into their worldwide operations (including domestic operations). A second indictor is the ability to build on this knowledge base to innovate products and technologies beyond incremental improvements.

Chinese share of articles in leading scientific journals. How many Chinese scientific publications are in the top international journals?

As we reported in Chapter 1, Chinese scientific publications have increased dramatically. The improvement in Chinese science and engineering can be judged by the degree to which Chinese scientists and engineers contribute to the global conversation in the sciences through publication in the top international journals and the recognition that their publications receive in terms of citations. With some lag, success should be captured by the upward movement in university research excellence rankings.

Autonomy of Chinese universities.   Will China increase the autonomy of its universities so they can better compete in the global market for science and technology innovation, respond to opportunities and challenges, and better prepare their advanced degree graduates?

Chinese universities are under the direct supervision of the Ministry of Education, provincial governments, or, in the case of the specialized universities, a particular ministry. This bureaucratic control limits their ability to experiment. The obstacles to experimentation mean that, on average, new research opportunities will receive a limited number of responses. Most importantly, it limits the types of knowledge creation competition that can result from opening the higher education system to new universities and winnowing out those that have not changed with the times.

Institutionalized trust.   Can the Chinese government direct attention to, as well as implement, greater transparency and procedural justice, which could lead to an increase in generalized trust?

Innovative ecosystems evolve and expand by enabling trust among strangers, by free flows of information, and by letting innovators disrupt and change the status quo. Such ecosystems may be particularly difficult to achieve in environments where (1) the absence of the rule of law impedes the establishment of trust among "strangers," and (2) conformity, hierarchy, and a lack of questioning are enforced. Fear that questioning might have negative consequences including retaliation has been shown to dampen creativity, which is at the heart of innovation. Changes that enable and nurture institutional trust ultimately may be the most important indicator of whether China can become an innovative country.

Let us end by stressing that we do not presume these are the only indicators one might track or that we have identified all the best ones. We hope that we can stimulate other researchers and policy makers, whether in China or elsewhere, to propose other indicators that would be especially helpful for tracking China's progress in meeting the innovation challenge. Based on the extant literature and the contributions to this book, these indicators strike us as useful in measuring the evolution of the Chinese economy and the strategy China is employing to become an innovative country. Although we cannot predict which path China will take, we certainly hope that it can overcome the enormous challenges that lie ahead and succeed in becoming a high-income country.

References

Brynjolfsson, E., & McAfee, A. 2014. *The Second Machine Age: Work, Progress, and Prosperity in a Time of Brilliant Technologies*. New York: W.W. Norton.

Kan, M. 2015. Foxconn's CEO backpedals on robot takeover at factories. *Computerworld* (June 26, 2015), www.computerworld.com/article/294 1272/emerging-technology/foxconns-ceo-backpedals-on-robot-takeover-at-factories.html.

Leonard, M. (Ed.). 2012. *China 3.0*. European Council on Foreign Relations (ECFR). Available at www.ecfr.eu/publications/summary/china_3.0. Accessed November 27, 2015.

Morris, M.W., & Leung, K. 2010. Creativity East and West: perspectives and parallels. *Management and Organization Review*, 6(3): 313–327.

World Bank & Development Research Center of the State Council, P. R. C. 2013. *China 2030: Building a Modern, Harmonious, and Creative Society*. Washington, DC: World Bank.

Bibliography

"2014 Global R&D Funding Forecast". 2013. *Battelle–R&D Magazine*, December.

Abrami, R. M., Kirby, W. C., and McFarlan, F. W. 2014a. "Why China can't innovate?" *Harvard Business Review* 92(3): 107–111.

2014b. *Can China Lead? Reaching the Limits of Power and Growth*. Boston: Harvard Business School Press.

Adas, M. 1989. *Machines as the Measure of Men: Science, Technology, and Ideologies of Western Dominance*. Ithaca: Cornell University Press.

Adelman, J. 2015. "What caused capitalism? Assessing the roles of the West and the rest." *Foreign Affairs* 94(3): 136–144.

Aghion, P. 2009. "Some thoughts on industrial policy and growth." Working paper 2009–2009. Observatoire français des conjonctures économiques, Sciences Po, Paris.

Aghion, P., David, P. A., and Foray, D. 2009. "Science, technology and innovation for economic growth: Linking policy research and practice in 'STIG Systems.'" *Research Policy* 38(4): 681–693.

Ahuja, G., Lampert, C. M., and Tandon, V. 2008. "Moving beyond Schumpeter: Management research on the determinants of technological innovation." *Academy of Management Annals* 2(1): 1–98.

Aiyar, S., Duval, R., Puy, D., Wu, Y., and Zhang, L. 2013. "Growth slowdowns and the middle-income trap." IMF Working Paper 71. Washington, DC.

Akamatsu, K. 1962. "A historical pattern of economic growth in developing countries." *Journal of Developing Economies* 1(1): 3–25.

Amabile, T. 1988. "A model of creativity and innovation in organizations." *Research in Organizational Behavior* 10(1): 123–167.

Amable, B. 2003. *The Diversity of Modern Capitalism*. Oxford University Press.

Amsden, A. 2000. *The Rise of the Rest: Challenges to the West from Late-Industrializing Economies*. Oxford University Press.

Amsden, A. H. 1989. *Asia's Next Giant: South Korea and Late Industrialization*. Oxford University Press.

Ansari, S. M., Fiss, P. C., and Zajac, E. J. 2010. "Made to fit: How practices vary as they diffuse." *Academy of Management Review* 35(1): 67–92.

Arnoldi, J., and Zhang, J. Y. 2012. "The dual reality of the Chinese knowledge economy." *International Journal of Chinese Culture and Management* 3(2): 160–173.

Arora, A., Cohen, W. M., and Walsh, J. P. 2014. "The acquisition and commercialization of invention in American manufacturing: Incidence and impact." NBER Working Paper, No. 20264.

Asakawa, K. 2001. "Organizational tension in international R&D management: The case of Japanese firms." *Research Policy* 30(5): 735–758.

Ashby, W. R. 1956. *An Introduction to Cybernetics*. London: Chapman and Hall.

Asuyama, Y. 2012. "Skill distribution and comparative advantage: A comparison of China and India." *World Development* 40(5): 956–969.

Awate, S., Larsen, M., and Mudambi, R. 2015. "Accessing vs sourcing knowledge: A comparative study of R&D internationalization between emerging and advanced economy firms." *Journal of International Business Studies* 46(1): 63–86.

Bai, C. E., Du, Y., Tao, Z., and Tong, S. Y. 2004. "Local protectionism and regional specialization: Evidence from China's industries." *Journal of International Economics* 63(2): 397–417.

Bao, Y., Chen, X., and Zhou, K. Z. 2011. "External learning, market dynamics, and radical innovation: Evidence from China's high-tech firms." *Journal of Business Research* 65: 1225–1233.

Bardhan, P. 2010. *Awakening Giants, Feet of Clay*. Princeton University Press.

Barley, S. R., and Kunda, G. 2004. *Gurus, Hired Guns, and Warm Bodies*. Princeton University Press.

Barney, J. B. 1986. "Organizational culture: Can it be a source of sustained competitive advantage?" *Academy of Management Review* 11(3): 656–665.

Barro, R. J. 1974. "Are government bonds net wealth?" *Journal of Political Economy* 82(6): 1095–1117.

Bartlett, C. A., and Ghoshal, S. 1989. *Managing Across Borders: The Transnational Solution*. Boston: Harvard Business School Press.

BBC. 2003. "China puts its first man in space." October 15. Available at http://news.bbc.co.uk/2/hi/asia-pacific/3192330.stm. Accessed July 10, 2015.

Bechtoldt, M. N., De Dreu, C. K. W., Nijstad, B. A., and Choi, H. S. 2010. "Motivated information processing, epistemic social tuning, and group creativity." *Journal of Personality and Social Psychology* 99: 622–637.

Beijing Intellectual Property Bureau. 2014. "Beijing shi zhishi chanquan ju Beijing shi caizheng ju guanyu yinfa 'Beijing shi zhuanli zizhu jin guanli banfa' de tongzhi" [Beijing State Intellectual Property Bureau, Beijing Bureau of Finance Regarding the Publication "Beijing City Patent Subsidy Financial Administrative Law" Notification]. October 20. Available at www.bjipo.gov.cn/zwxx/zwgg/201410/t20141020_32950 .html.

Beinhocker, E. D. 2005. *The Origin of Wealth: Evolution, Complexity, and the Radical Remaking of Economics*. London: Random House.

Bell, M. 1984. "Learning and the accumulation of industrial technological capacity in developing countries." In *Technological Capability in the Third World*, ed. K. King and M. Fransman. London: Macmillan.

Bell, M., and Figueiredo, P. N. 2012. "Innovation capability building and learning mechanisms in latecomer firms: Recent empirical contributions and implications for research." *Canadian Journal of Development Studies* 33(1): 14–40.

Bell, M., and Pavitt, K. 1997. "Technological accumulation and industrial growth: Contrasts between developed and developing countries." In *Technology, Globalisation and Economic Performance*, ed. D. Archibugi and J. Michie. Cambridge University Press.

Bendapudi, N., Zhan, S., and Hong, Y. Y. 2015. "Quality of education does not always guarantee creative output: The moderating role of cultural values." Working paper, Nanyang Technological University, Singapore.

Bennis, W. 2009. *Becoming a Leader*. New York: Basic Books.

2012. "Mastering the context." Bloomberg.com, August 20. Available at www.bloomberg.com/bw/articles/2012-08-20/mastering-the-con text/. Accessed March 1, 2015.

Bergère, M. C. 2007. *Capitalisme et capitalistes en Chine: Des origines à nos jours, XIXe–XXIe siecle*. Paris: Perrin.

Berggren, C., Bergek, A., Bengtsson, L., Saderlund, J., and Hobday, M. 2011. *Knowledge Integration and Innovation: Critical Challenges Facing International Technology-Based Firms*. 2nd ed. Oxford University Press.

Berry, H., Guillén, M. F., and Zhou, N. 2010. "An institutional approach to cross-national distance." *Journal of International Business Studies* 41: 1460–1480.

Berry, J. W. "1980: Social and cultural change." In *Handbook of Cross-Cultural Psychology*, vol. 5, ed. H. C. Triandis and R. W. Brislin, 211–279. Boston: Allyn and Bacon.

Bian, Y., and Ang, S. 1997. "Guanxi networks and job mobility in China and Singapore." *Social Forces* 75: 981–1005.

Bie, D. R., and Yi, M. C. 2014. "The context of higher education development and policy response in China." *Studies in Higher Education* 39(8): 1499–1510.

Birkinshaw, J. 2000. *Entrepreneurship in the Global Firm*. London: Sage

Bloom, N., et al. 2014. "Trapped factors and China's impact on global growth." CEP Discussion Paper 1261. Available at http://eprints.lse.a c.uk/60272/1/dp1261.pdf.

Boeing, P., and Sandner, P. 2012. "The innovative performance of China's National Innovation System." Frankfurt School. Working Paper Series, No. 158.

Boisot, M. 1995. *Information Space*. London: Routledge.

Boisot, M., Child, J., and Redding, G. 2011. "Working the system; toward a theory of cultural and institutional competence." *International Studies in Management and Organization* 41(1): 62–95.

Bonaglia, F., Goldstein, A., and Mathews, J. 2007. "Accelerated internationalization by emerging markets multinationals: The case of the white goods sector." *Journal of World Business* 42: 369–383.

Brandt, L., Rawski, T. G., and Sutton, J. 2008. "China's industrial development." In *China's Great Economic Transformation*, ed. L. Brandt and T. G. Rawski. New York: Cambridge University Press.

Breznitz, D., and Murphree, M. 2011. *Run of the Red Queen: Government, Innovation, Globalization, and Economic Growth in China*. New Haven: Yale University Press.

Brynjolfsson, E., and McAfee, A. 2014. *The Second Machine Age: Work, Progress, and Prosperity in a Time of Brilliant Technologies*. New York: W.W. Norton.

Buckley, C. 2015. "Q. and A.: David Shambaugh on the risks to Chinese communist rule." *New York Times*, Sinosphere blog. Available at http:// sinosphere.blogs.nytimes.com/2015/03/15/q-and-a-david-shambaugh- on-the-risks-to-chinese-communist-rule/?_r=0/. Accessed March 15, 2015.

Bulman, D., Eden, M., and Nguyen, H. 2014. "Transitioning from low- income growth to high-income growth: Is there a middle-income trap?" Policy Research Working Paper 7104. World Bank, Washington, DC.

Cai, F., Park, A., and Zhao, Y. 2008. "The Chinese labor market in the reform era." In *China's Great Economic Transformation*, ed. L. Brandt and T. G. Rawski. New York: Cambridge University Press.

Cai, H., and Treisman, D. 2006. "Did government decentralization cause China's economic miracle?" *World Politics* 58: 505–535.

Callahan, W. A. 2015. "Identity and security in China: The negative soft power of the China dream." *Politics* 35: 216–229.

Cantwell, J. 1995. "The globalisation of technology: What remains of the product cycle model." *Cambridge Journal of Economics* 19: 155–174.

Cantwell, J., Dunning, J. H., and Lundan, S. M. 2010. "An evolutionary approach to understanding international business activity: The co-evolution of MNEs and the institutional environment." *Journal of International Business Studies* 41: 567–586.

Cantwell, J., and Janne, O. 1999. "Technological globalisation and innovative centres: The role of corporate technological leadership and locational hierarchy." *Research Policy* 28(2–3): 119–144.

2000. "The role of multinational corporations and national states in the globalisation of innovatory capacity: The European perspective." *Technology Analysis and Strategic Management* 12(2): 243–262.

Cantwell, J. A. 1989. *Technological Innovation and Multinational Corporations*. Oxford: Basil Blackwell.

Cantwell, J. A., and Mudambi, R. 2005. "MNE competence-creating subsidiary mandates." *Strategic Management Journal* 26(12): 1109–1128.

Cao, S. 2013. "Faster but shorter versus longer but slower patent protection: Which do firms prefer?" Innovation Seminar, University of California Berkeley College of Engineering, Fung Institute for Engineering Leadership. Available at www.funginstitute.berkeley.edu/sites/default/files/Long%20UM%20IP%20SWC%2020130808_0.pdf.

2014. "Speed of patent protection, rate of technology obsolescence and optimal patent strategy: Evidence from innovation patented in U.S., China, and several other countries." Environment and Resource Economics Seminar, Department of Agricultural and Resource Economics, University of California Berkeley. Available at http://are.berkeley.edu/fields/erep/seminar/f2014/siwei_cao_patents.pdf.

Cao, S., Lei, Z., and Wright, B. 2014. "Speed vs. length of patent protection: Evidence from innovations patented in U.S. and China." Job Market paper, Department of Agricultural and Resource Economics, University of California Berkeley. Available at https://are.berkeley.edu/sites/default/files/job-candidates/paper/SiweiCao_JMP121014.pdf.

Caprio, G., and Honohan, P. 2001. *Finance for Growth: Policy Choices in a Volatile World*. New York: World Bank and Oxford University Press.

Cardoso, E., and Helwege, A. 1995. *Latin America's Economy*. Cambridge, MA: MIT Press.

Carr, S. C., Rugimbana, R. O., Walkom, E., and Bolitho, F. H. 2001. "Selecting expatriates in developing areas: 'Country-of-origin' effects in Tanzania?" *International Journal of Intercultural Relations* 25: 441–457.

Chambers, E. G., Foulon, M., Handfield-Jones, H., Hankin, S. M., and Michaels, E. G. 1998. "The war for talent." *McKinsey Quarterly*, 1–8.

Chand, M., and Tung, R. L. 2011. "Diaspora as the boundary-spanners: The role of trust in business facilitation." *Journal of Trust* 1(1): 104–126.

Chang, H. 1994. *The Political Economy of Industrial Policy.* New York: St. Martin's Press.

2007. *Bad Samaritans: The Myth of Free Trade and the Secret History of Capitalism.* London: Bloomsbury.

Chang, H. J. 2003. *Kicking Away the Ladder: Development Strategy in Historical Perspective.* London: Anthem Press.

Chen, A., Patton, D., and Kenney, M. 2015. "Chinese university technology transfer: A literature review and taxonomy." Working paper. University of California, Davis.

Chen, K., and Kenney, M. 2007. "Universities/research institutes and regional innovation systems: The cases of Beijing and Shenzhen." *World Development* 35(6): 1056–1074.

Chen, T. J., and Ku, Y. H. 2014. "Indigenous innovation vs. teng-long huan-niao: Policy conflicts in the development of China's flat panel industry." *Industrial and Corporate Change* 23(6): 1445–1467.

Chen, Y., Li, H., and Zhou, L. A. 2005. "Relative performance evaluation and the turnover of provincial leaders in China." *Economic Letters* 88(3): 421–425.

Chenery, H. B. 1961. "Comparative advantage and development policy." *American Economic Review* 51(1): 18–51.

Cheng, C. Y., and Leung, A. K. Y. 2013. "Revisiting the multicultural experience–creativity link: The effects of cultural distance and comparison mindset." *Social Psychological and Personality Science* 4: 475–482.

Cheng, C. Y., Leung, A. K. Y., and Wu, T. Y. 2011. "Going beyond the multicultural experience–creativity link: The emotional pathway underlying dual-cultural activation and creativity." *Journal of Social Issues* 67: 806–824.

Cheng, S. 1999. "East–West differences in views on creativity: Is Howard Gardener correct? Yes, and no." *Journal of Creative Behavior* 33(2): 112–125.

Chengdu Intellectual Property. 2013. "Chengdu shi zhuanli zizhu guanli banfa (2013 nian)" [Chengdu Patent Subsidy Administrative Law (2013)]. Available at www.cdip.gov.cn/ReadNews.asp?NewsID=11735/.

Child, J. 2014. "Book review of Diefenbach, hierarchy and organization." *Organization Studies* 35(11): 1725–1728.

Child, J., and Markoczy, L. 1993. "Host-country managerial behavior and learning in Chinese and Hungarian joint ventures." *Journal of Management Studies* 30(4): 611–631.

Child, J., and Rodrigues, S. B. 2005. "The internationalization of Chinese firms: A case for theoretical extension?" *Management and Organization Review* 1: 381–410.

China Business Information Network. 2005. "Woguo chuxian shenqing zhuanli rechao lese zhuanli bizhong gaoda 50%" [China experiences a boom in patent applications with a 50% proportion of junk patents]. *China Business Information Network News*. November 16. Available at www.ecchn.com/20061116ecnews3847511.html.

China News. 2005. "Hu Jintao zhuxi jiu tigao Zhongguo keji zizhu chuangxin nengli ti san yaoqiu" [President Hu Jintao puts forth three requirements to improve China's technological indigenous innovation capability]. June 3. Available at www.chinanews.com.cn/news/2005/2 005-06-03/26/582433.shtml.

2014. "2013 nian guojia caizheng keji zhichu wei 6184.9 yi bi shang nian zeng 10.4%" [2013 China government S&T appropriation reaches CNY 618.49 billion: A year-on-year increase of 10.4%]. October 30. Available at www.chinanews.com/gn/2014/10-30/6734769.shtml.

China Outsourcing Institute. 2014. *Report on China Outsourcing Development*. Shanghai: Shanghai Jiaotong University Press.

"Chinese CEO advises on competition strategies." 2001. *China Daily*. October 23. Available at www.china.org.cn/english/2001/Oct/21056.h tm. Accessed May 1, 2015.

Chiu, C. Y., Gries, P., Torelli, C. J., and Cheng, S. Y. Y. 2011. "Toward a social psychology of globalization." *Journal of Social Issues* 67: 663–676.

Chiu, C. Y., and Hong, Y. 2006. *Social Psychology of Culture*. New York: Psychology Press.

Chiu, C. Y., and Kwan, L. Y. Y. 2010. "Culture and creativity: A process model." *Management and Organization Review* 6: 447–461.

Chiu, C. Y., Kwan, L. Y. Y., and Liou, S. 2013. "Culturally motivated challenges to innovations in integrative research: Theory and solutions." *Social Issues and Policy Review* 7: 149–172.

Chiu, C. Y., Morris, M., Hong, Y., and Menon, T. 2000. "Motivated cultural cognition: The impact of implicit cultural theories on dispositional attribution varies as a function of need for closure." *Journal of Personality and Social Psychology* 78: 247–259.

Christensen, C. C. 2000. *The Innovator's Dilemma*. New York: Harper Collins.

Cohen, W., and Levinthal, D. 1990. "Absorptive capacity: A new perspective on learning and innovation." *Administrative Science Quarterly* 35(1): 128–152.

Coleman, J. S. 1988. "Social capital in the creation of human capital." *American Journal of Sociology* 94: S95–S120.

Collinson, S. C. 2009. "The MNE as the major global promoter of economic development." In *Images of the Multinational Firm*, ed. S. C. Collinson and G. Morgan, 69–92. Oxford: Wiley.

2013. "Cross-border M&A by the new multinationals: Different reasons to 'go global.'" In *The Competitive Advantage of Emerging Market Multinationals*, ed. P. J. Williamson, R. Ramamurti, A. Fleury, and M. Fleury. Cambridge University Press.

Collinson, S. C., and Narula, R. 2014. "Asset recombination in international partnerships as a source of improved innovation capabilities in China." *Multinational Business Review* 22(4): 394–417.

Collinson, S. C., Sullivan-Taylor, B., and Wang, J. L. 2007. *Adapting to the China Challenge: Lessons from Experienced Multinationals*. London: Advanced Institute of Management (AIM), Executive Briefing.

Collinson, S. C., and Sun, Y. 2012. "Corporate hybrids and the co-evolution of institutions and enterprise in China." In *China and the Multinationals: International Business and the Entry of China into the Global Economy*, ed. R. Pearce. Cheltenham: Edward Elgar.

Collinson, S. C., and Wang, R. (J. L.). 2012. "Learning networks and technological capability in multinational enterprise subsidiaries." *Research Policy* 41(9): 1501–1518.

Commission on Growth and Development. 2008. *The Growth Report: Strategies for Sustained Growth and Inclusive Development*. Washington, DC: World Bank.

Cornell University, INSEAD, and WIPO. 2013. *The Global Innovation Index 2013: The Local Dynamics of Innovation*. Geneva, Ithaca, and Fontainebleau: Cornell University, INSEAD, and WIPO.

Crescenzi, R., Rodríguez-Pose, A., and Storper, M. 2012. "The territorial dynamics of innovation in China and India." *Journal of Economic Geography* 12(5): 1055–1085.

Crossan, M., and Apaydin, M. 2010. "A multi-dimensional framework of organizational innovation: A systematic review of the literature." *Journal of Management Studies* 47(6): 1154–1191.

Dakhi, M., and de Clercq D. 2007. "Human capital, social capital, and innovation: A multi-country study." *Entrepreneurship and Regional Development* 16: 107–128.

Dantas, E., and Bell, M. 2009. "Latecomer firms and the emergence and development of knowledge networks: The case of Petrobras in Brazil." *Research Policy* 38(5): 829–844.

De Jong, M., Marston, N., and Roth, E. April 2015. "The eight essentials of innovation." *McKinsey Quarterly*, April.

De Meyer, A. 1992. "Management of international R&D operations." In *Technology Management and International Business:*

Internationalisation of R&D and Technology, ed. Granstrand, O., Hakanson, L., Sjolander, S. Chichester: John Wiley.

Deng, P. 2007. "Investing for strategic resources and its rationale: The case of outward FDI from Chinese companies." *Business Horizons* 50: 71–81.

Department of Science and Technology, Ministry of Education. 2007–2013. "Gaodeng xuexiao keji tongji ziliao huibian" [Higher education science and technology statistics compilation]. Available at www.dost.moe.edu.cn/dostmoe/.

Di Minin, A., Zhang, J., and Gammeltoft, P. 2012. "Chinese foreign direct investment in R&D in Europe: A new model of R&D internationalization?" *European Management Journal* 30(3): 189–203.

Diefenbach, T. 2013. *Hierarchy in Organization: Toward a General Theory of Hierarchical Social Systems*. London: Routledge.

Doney, P. M., Cannon, J. P., and Mullen, M. R. 1998. "Understanding the influence of national culture on the development of trust." *Academy of Management Review* 23(3): 601–620.

Dong, X., Zhao, J., and Yuan, P. W. 2014. "Guoyou qiye chuang xinxiao lv liushi yanjiu" [Research on innovation efficiency loss of state-owned enterprises]. *China Industrial Economics* 2: 97–108.

Dosi, G., et al. (eds.). 1988. *Technical Change and Economic Theory*. London: Pinter.

Dossani, R., and Kenney, M. 2007. "The next wave of globalization: Relocating service provision to India." *World Development* 35(5): 772–791.

Dougherty, D. 1992. "Interpretive barriers to successful product innovation in large companies." *Organization Science* 3(2): 179–202.

Dow, D., and Karunaratna, A. 2006. "Developing a multidimensional instrument to measure psychic distance stimuli." *Journal of International Business Studies* 37(5): 578–602.

Doz, Y., Santos, J., and Williamson, P. 2001. *From Global to Metanational: How Companies Win in the Knowledge Economy*. Boston: Harvard Business School Press.

Doz, Y. D., and Wilson, K. 2012. *Managing Global Innovation: Frameworks for Integrating Capabilities around the World*. Boston: Harvard Business Review Press.

Du, Y., Park, A., and Wang, S. 2005. "Migration and rural poverty in China." *Journal of Comparative Economics* 33(4): 688–709.

Duara, P. 2015. *The Crisis of Global Modernity: Asian Traditions and a Sustainable Future*. Cambridge University Press.

Duflo, E. 2004. "Scaling up and evaluation." In *Annual World Bank Conference on Development Economics 2004*, ed. F. Bourguignon and B. Pleskovic. Washington, DC: World Bank.

Dunlap-Hinkler, D., Kotabe, M., and Mudambi, R. 2010. "A story of breakthrough versus incremental innovation: Corporate entrepreneurship in the global pharmaceutical industry." *Strategic Entrepreneurship Journal* 4: 106–127.

Dunning, J. H. 1993. *Multinational Enterprises and the Global Economy.* Wokingham: Addison-Wesley.

Dunning, J. H., and Narula, R. 1996. "The investment development path revisited: Some emerging issues." In *Foreign Direct Investment and Governments,* ed. J. H. Dunning and R. Narula, 1–41. London: Routledge.

Easterly, W. 2001. *The Elusive Quest for Growth: Economists' Adventures and Misadventures in the Tropics.* Cambridge, MA: MIT Press.

Easterly, W., Loayza, N., and Montiel, P. J. 1997. "Has Latin America's post-reform growth been disappointing?" World Bank Policy Research Paper 1708. World Bank, Washington, DC.

Eckert, C. J., Lee, K. B., Lew, Y. I., Robinson, M., and Wagner, E. W. 1990. *Korea Old and New: A History.* Cambridge, MA: Korea Institute, Harvard University.

Economist. 2010. "Patents, yes; ideas, maybe." October 14. Available at www.economist.com/node/17257940/.

2011. "Huawei: The long march of the invisible Mr. Ren." June 2. www.economist.com/node/18771640/. Accessed March 1, 2015.

Economist Intelligence Unit. 2014. *Democracy Index 2014: Democracy and Its Discontents.* London: Economist Intelligence Unit.

Economy, E. C. 2011. *The River Runs Black: The Environmental Challenge to China's Future.* Ithaca: Cornell University Press.

Egri, C. P., and Ralston, D. A. 2004. "Generation cohorts and personal values: A comparison of China and the U.S." *Organization Science* 15(2): 210–220.

Eichengreen, B., Park, D., and Shin, K. 2011. "When fast growing economies slow down; international evidence and implications for China." NBER Working Paper 16919. National Bureau of Economic Research, Cambridge, MA: National Bureau of Economic Research.

2013. "Growth slowdowns redux: New evidence on the middle-income trap." NBER Working Paper 18673. National Bureau of Economic Research, Cambridge, MA.

Eichenwald, K. 2014. "The great smartphone war." *Vanity Fair.* June. Available at www.vanityfair.com/news/business/2014/06/apple-samsung-smartphone-patent-war/. Accessed May 20, 2014.

Eisenstadt, S. N. 1996. *Japanese Civilization.* University of Chicago Press.

Elance.com. 2013. "Global online employment report for 2013."

Elvin, M. 1972. "The high level equilibrium trap: The causes of the decline of invention in the traditional Chinese textile industries." In *Economic*

Organization in Chinese Society, ed. W. E. Willmott. Stanford University Press.

Erez, M., and Nouri, R. 2010. "Creativity in a context: Cultural, social, and work contexts." *Management and Organization Review* 6: 351–370.

Etzkowitz, H. 2001. "The second academic revolution and the rise of entrepreneurial science." *Technology and Society Magazine, IEEE* 20: 18–29.

Etzkowitz, H., and Leydesdorff, L. 2000. "The dynamics of innovation: From national systems and 'Mode 2' to a Triple Helix of university–industry–government relations." *Research Policy* 29: 109–123.

Fairbank, J. K., Reischauer, E. O., and Craig, A. M. 1965. *East Asia: The Modern Transformation*. Boston: Houghton Mifflin.

Fan, G., Wang, X., and Zhu, H. 2011. *Zhongguo shengji shichanghua zhishu [NERI Index of Marketization of China's Provinces]*. Beijing: Economics Science Press.

Fan, J. P. 2012. "Founder succession and accounting properties." *Contemporary Accounting Research* 29(1): 283–311.

Fan, P. 2014. "Innovation in China." *Journal of Economic Surveys* 28(4): 725–745.

Fang, J. 2009. "Shichang fenge he ziyuan peizhi xiaolv liushi" [Market segmentation and the efficiency loss of resource allocation]. *Journal of Finance and Economics* 9: 36–47.

Farmer, R. N. and Richman, B. M. 1965. *Comparative Management and Economic Progress*. Homewood, IL: Richard D. Irwin.

Farrell, D., and Grant, A. 2005. *Addressing China's Looming Talent Shortage*. London: McKinsey Global Institute.

Farrell, D., and McKinsey Global Institute. 2006. *Offshoring: Understanding the Emerging Global Labor Market*. Boston: Harvard Business School Press.

Fast Company. 2013. "The world's top 10 most innovative companies in China." Available at www.fastcompany.com/most-innovative-compa nies/2013/industry/china/.

Ferri, G., and Liu, L. G. 2009. "Honor thy creditors before thy shareholders: Are the profits of Chinese state-owned enterprises real?" Hong Kong Institute for Monetary Research.

Ferrin, D. L., Dirks, K. T., and Shah, P. P. 2006. "Direct and indirect effects of third-party relationships on interpersonal trust." *Journal of Applied Psychology* 91(4): 870–883.

Fewsmith, J. 2013. *The Logic and Limits of Political Reform in China*. New York: Cambridge University Press.

Fiedler, F. E. 1967. *A Theory of Leadership Effectiveness*. New York: McGraw-Hill.

Fields, K. 1997. *Enterprise and the State in Taiwan and Korea.* Ithaca: Cornell University Press.

Florida, R. 1997. "The globalization of R&D: Results of a survey of foreign affiliated R&D laboratories in the USA." *Research Policy* 26: 85–103.

Florini, A., Lai, H., and Tan, Y. 2012. *China Experiments: From Local Innovations to National Reform.* Washington, DC: Brookings Institution Press.

Freeman, C. 1987. *Technology Policy and Economic Performance: Lessons from Japan.* London: Pinter.

1989. *Technology Policy and Economic Performance.* London: Pinter.

1995. "The 'National System of Innovation' in historical perspective." *Cambridge Journal of Economics* 19: 5–24.

Freeman, R. B., and Huang, W. 2015, in press. "China's 'great leap forward' in science and engineering." In *Global Mobility of Research Scientists: The Economics of Who Goes Where and Why.* Elsevier. Available at http://scholar.harvard.edu/files/freeman/files/china_great_leap_forwar d_in_s-and-e_rbf-and-wei-huang_elseviercopyright_ms-for-vol_4-7-15.pd f?m=1428423798/.

Fu, X. 2015. *China's Path to Innovation.* Cambridge University Press.

Fu, Y., Jiang, X., and Ma, Q. 2010. "Zhongguo chuantong wenhua dui guonei zhuanli chan chu zhiliang de yingxiang fenxi" [An analysis of the influence traditional Chinese culture has on domestic patent output quality]. *Keji guanli yanjiu* 16: 252–256.

Fuller, D. B. 2010. "How law, politics and transnational networks affect technology entrepreneurship: Explaining divergent venture capital investing strategies in China." *Asia Pacific Journal of Management* 27(3): 445–459.

2013. "Building ladders out of Chains: China's hybrid-led technological development in disaggregated value chains." *Journal of Development Studies* 49(4): 547–563.

2016. *Paper Tigers, Hidden Dragons: The Political Economy of Technological Development in China.* Oxford: Oxford University Press.

Furr, R. B., and Palla, S. W. 2012. *Invalidity Rate Study: China.* San Antonio, TX: Intellectual Property Organization.

Gao, Y., Gao, S., Zhou, Y., and Huang, K. F. 2015. "Picturing firms: Institutional capital-based radical innovation under China's institutional voids." *Journal of Business Research* 68: 1166–1175.

Gerschenkron, A. 1962. *Economic Backwardness in Historical Perspective: A Book of Essays.* Cambridge, MA: Belknap Press of Harvard University Press.

Goncalo, J. A., and Staw, B. M. 2006. "Individualism-collectivism and group creativity." *Organizational Behavior and Human Decision Processes* 100: 96–109.

Gong, F., and Li, J. 2010. "Seeking excellence in the move to a mass system: Institutional responses and changes in Chinese key comprehensive universities." *Frontiers of Education in China* 5: 477–506.

Govindarajan, V., and Trimble, C. 2012. *Reverse Innovation: Create Far from Home, Win Everywhere.* Boston: Harvard Business Press.

Graff, G. D. 2007. "Echoes of Bayh-Dole? A survey of IP and technology transfer policies in emerging and developing economies." In *Intellectual Property Management in Health and Agricultural Innovation: A Handbook of Best Practices, Volumes 1 and 2,* ed. A. Krattiger, R. Mahoney, L. Nelsen, J. Thomson, A. Bennett, K. Satyanarayana, C. Fernandez, and S. Kowalski, 169–195. Oxford: MIHR; Davis, CA: PIPRA.

Griffiths, M. B., and Zeuthen, J. 2014. "Bittersweet China: New discourses of hardship and social organization." *Journal of Current Chinese Affairs* 43(4): 143–174.

Griliches, Z. 1990. "Patent statistics as economic indicators: A survey." *Journal of Economic Literature* 28: 1661–1707.

Guan, J. C., Yam, R. C., and Mok, C. K. 2005. "Collaboration between industry and research institutes/universities on industrial innovation in Beijing, China." *Technology Analysis and Strategic Management* 17: 339–353.

Guo, G. 2007. "Retrospective economic accountability under authoritarianism: Evidence from China." *Political Research Quarterly* 60: 378–390.

Haggard, S. 2004. "Institutions in East Asian growth." *Studies in Comparative International Development* 38(4): 53–81.

Haire, M., Ghiselli, E. E., and Porter, L. W. 1966. *Managerial Thinking: An International Study.* New York: Wiley.

Hakanson, L., and Ambos, B. 2010. "The antecedents of psychic distance." *Journal of International Management* 16(3): 195–210.

Hall, P. A., and Soskice, D. 2001. "An introduction to varieties of capitalism." In *Varieties of Capitalism: The Institutional Foundations of Comparative Advantage,* ed. P. A. Hall and D. Soskice. Oxford University Press.

Harbison, F., and Myers, C. A. 1959. *Management in the Industrial World: An International Analysis.* New York: McGraw-Hill.

Harrison, A., and Rodríguez-Clare, A. 2010. "Trade, foreign investment, and industrial policy for developing countries." In *Handbook of Economic Growth,* vol. 5, ed. D. Rodrik. Amsterdam: North-Holland.

Harrison, D. A., and Klein, K. J. 2007. "What's the difference? Diversity constructs as separation, variety, or disparity in organizations." *Academy of Management Review* 32(4): 1199–1228.

Hausmann, R., and Rodrik, D. 2003. "Economic development as self-discovery." *Journal of Development Economics*, 72 (December): 603–633.

Hausmann, R., Rodrik, D., and Velasco, A. 2005. "Growth diagnostics." In *The Washington Consensus Reconsidered: Towards a New Global Governance*, ed. J. Stiglitz and N. Serra. Oxford University Press.

Hayhoe, R. 1989. "China's universities and Western academic models." In *From Dependence to Autonomy: The Development of Asian Universities*, ed. G. Philip and V. Selvaratnam, 25–61. Dordrecht: Springer.

He, Y. 2007. "History, Chinese nationalism and the emerging Sino-Japanese conflict." *Journal of Contemporary China* 16: 1–24.

Heilbroner, R. L. 1985. *The Nature and Logic of Capitalism*. New York: Norton.

Heilmann, S. 2008. "Policy experimentation in China's economic rise." *Studies in Comparative International Development* 43: 1–26.

Heilmann, S., and Perry, E. 2011. *Mao's Invisible Hand: The Political Foundations of Adaptive Governance in China*. Cambridge, MA: Harvard University Asia Center.

Hennart, J. F. 2009. "Down with MNE-centric theories! Market entry and expansion as the bundling of MNE and local assets." *Journal of International Business Studies* 40(9): 1432–1454.

Hillman, A. J., Keim, G. D., and Schuler, D. 2004. "Corporate political activity: A review and research agenda." *Journal of Management* 30(6): 837–857.

Hirsch, J. 2015. "Carmakers fret over China's slowing auto market." *Los Angeles Times*, September 2. Available at www.latimes.com/busi ness/autos/la-fi-0902-automakers-china-20150903-story.html. Accessed September 14, 2015.

Hobday, M. 2007. "Editor's introduction: The scope of Martin Bell's contribution." *Asian Journal of Technology Innovation* 15(2): 1–18.

Hobday, M., and Rush, H. 2007. "Upgrading the technological capabilities of foreign transnational subsidiaries in developing countries: The case of electronics in Thailand." *Research Policy* 36: 1335–1356.

Hobson, J. A. 1902. *Imperialism: A Study*. New York: James Pott.

Hofstede, G. 1980. *Culture's Consequences: International Differences in Work-Related Values*. Beverly Hills, CA: Sage.

Hout, T. M., and Ghemawat, P. 2010. "China versus the world: Whose technology is it?" *Harvard Business Review*, December.

Howells, J. 1990. "The location and organisation of research and development: New horizons." *Research Policy* 19(2): 133–146.

1995. "Going global: The use of ICT networks in research and development." *Research Policy* 24(2): 169–184.

2012. "The geography of knowledge: Never so close but never so far apart." *Journal of Economic Geography* 12(5): 1003–1020.

Hu, A. G. 2010. "Propensity to patent, competition and China's foreign patenting surge." *Research Policy* 39: 985–993.

Hu, M. C., and Mathews, J. A. 2008. "China's national innovative capacity." *Research Policy* 37: 1465–1479.

2009. "Estimating the innovation effects of university–industry–government linkages: The case of Taiwan." *eContent Management* 15(2): 138–154.

Huang, C. 2012. *Estimates of the Value of Patent Rights in China*. United Nations University – Maastricht Economic and Social Research and Training Centre on Innovation and Technology, 48.

Huang, Y. 2003. *Selling China: Foreign Direct Investment during the Reform Era*. Cambridge University Press.

2008. *Capitalism with Chinese Characteristics: Entrepreneurship and the State*. Cambridge University Press.

Huang, Y., and Bosler, C. 2014. "China's burgeoning graduates: Too much of a good thing?" *National Interest*, January 7.

Huang, Y., Fang, C., Xu, P., and Qin, G. 2013. "The new normal of Chinese development." In *China: A New Model for Growth and Development*, ed. R. Garnaut, C. Fang, and L. Song. Canberra: ANU E Press.

Huang, Y., Qin, G., and Xun, W. 2013. "Institutions and the middle-income trap: Implications of cross-country experiences for China." Paper presented at the International Conference on Inequality and the Middle-Income Trap in China, CCER of Peking University.

Huang, Z., and Wang, J. 2006. "Difang baohu he shichang fenge" [Local protectionism and market fragmentation]. *China Industrial Economics* 2: 60–67.

Hubei Intellectual Property Bureau. 2007. "Hubei sheng 2007 niandu shouquan zhuanli butie di yi pi da 120 wan" [Hubei first round of annual patent subsidies reaches 1,200,000]. September 6. Available at www.hbipo.gov.cn/show/6212.

Huy, Q. N. 2011. "How middle managers' group-focus emotions and social identities influence strategy implementation." *Strategic Management Journal* 32(13): 1387–1410.

Huy, Q. N., Corley, K. G., and Kraatz, M. S. 2014. "From support to mutiny: Shifting legitimacy judgments and emotional reactions impacting the implementation of radical change." *Academy of Management Journal* 57(6): 1650–1680.

Hwang, V. W., and Horowitt, G. 2012. *The Rainforest: The Secret to Building the Next Silicon Valley.* San Francisco: Regenwald.

Ibarra, H. 1992. "Homophily and differential returns: Sex differences in network structure and access in an advertising firm." *Administrative Science Quarterly* 37(3): 422–447.

Innofund. 2004–2014. "Quanguo jishu shichang tongji niandu baogao" [Annual report on statistics of China technology market]. China's Ministry of Science and Technology Development and Planning Division and Chinese Technology Market Promotion Administration Center. Available at www.innofund.gov.cn/jssc/tjnb/.

International Monetary Fund (IMF). 2014. *World Economic Outlook: Legacies, Clouds, Uncertainties.* Available at www.imf.org/external/pubs/ft/weo/2014/02/.

International Trade Union Confederation. 2014. *ITUC Global Rights Index.* Brussels: ITUC.

Ito, T. 1980. "Disequilibrium growth theory." *Journal of Economic Theory* 23(3): 380–409.

Jaffe, A. B., and Trajtenberg, M. 2002. *Patents, Citations, and Innovations: A Window on the Knowledge Economy.* Cambridge, MA: MIT Press.

Japan Patent Office. 2014. "Japan Patent Office annual report 2014." Tokyo. Available at www.jpo.go.jp/shiryou_e/toushin_e/kenkyukai_e/pdf/annual_report2014/part1.pdf.

Jarvenpaa, S. L., and Leidner, D. E. 1999. "Communication and trust in global virtual teams." *Organization Science* 10(6): 791–815.

Jin, F., and Lee, K. 2013. "Growth–inequality nexus in China: Lewis and Kuznets hypotheses." Paper presented at the International Conference on Inequality and the Middle-Income Trap in China, CCER of Peking University.

Jin, F., Lee, K., and Kim, Y. 2008. "Changing engines of growth in China: From exports, FDI and marketization to innovation and exports." *China and World Economy* 16(2): 31–49.

Jin, X., Patton, D., and Kenney, K. 2015. "Signaling legitimacy to foreign investors: Evidence from Chinese IPOs on U.S. markets." Berkeley Roundtable on the International Economy Working Paper 2015-4. Available at www.brie.berkeley.edu/wp-content/uploads/2015/02/Signalling-Legitimacy-in-Chinese-IPOs-on-the-US-Market1.pdf.

Jones, E. L. 1981. *The European Miracle: Environments, Economies, and Geopolitics in the History of Europe and Asia.* Cambridge University Press.

Ju, J., Lin, J. Y., and Wang, Y. 2015. "Endowment structures, industrial dynamics, and economic growth." *Journal of Monetary Economics* 76: 244–263.

Kan, M. 2015. "Foxconn's CEO backpedals on robot takeover at factories." *Computerworld*, June 26. Available at www.computerworld.com/arti cle/2941272/emerging-technology/foxconns-ceo-backpedals-on-robot-takeover-at-factories.html.

Kenney, M., Breznitz, D., and Murphree, M. 2013. "Coming back home after the sun rises: Returnee entrepreneurs and growth of high tech industries." *Research Policy* 42: 391–407.

Khan, M. H. 2000. "Rents, efficiency and growth." In *Rents, Rent-Seeking and Economic Development*, ed. M. H. Khan and K. S. Jomo. Cambridge University Press.

Khanna, T. 2014. "Contextual intelligence." *Harvard Business Review* (September): 59–68.

Kharas, H. 2009. *China's Transition to a High Income Economy: Escaping the Middle Income Trap*. Washington, DC: Brookings Institution Press.

Kharpal, A. 2015. "Smartphone market is slowing massively … blame China." *CNBC*, August 26. Available at www.cnbc.com/2015/08/26/s martphone-market-is-slowing-massivelyblame-china.html. Accessed September 14, 2015.

Kim, E. M. 1997. *Big Business, Strong State: Collusion and Conflict in South Korean Development, 1960–1990*. Albany, NY: State University of New York Press.

Kim, L. 1997. *Imitation to Innovation: The Dynamics of Korea's Technological Learning*. Boston: Harvard Business Review Press.

Kim, L., and Nelson, R. R. 2000. *Technology, Learning, and Innovation: Experiences of Newly Industrializing Economies*. Cambridge University Press.

Kim, Y. H. 1988. *Higashi ajia kogyoka to sekai shihonshugi [Industrialization of East Asia and World Capitalism]*. Tokyo: Toyo keizai shimpo-sha.

Kogut, B. 1993. *Country Competitiveness: Technology and the Organization of Work*. New York: Oxford University Press.

——— 2003. "From regions and firms to multinational highways." In *Locating Global Advantage: Industry Dynamics in the International Economy*, ed. M. Kenney and R. Florida, chapter 10. Stanford University Press.

Kogut, B., and Metiu, A. 2001. "Open-source software development and distributed innovation." *Oxford Review of Economic Policy* 17(2): 248–264.

Kogut, B., and Singh, H. 1988. "The effect of national culture on the choice of entry mode." *Journal of International Business Studies* 19(3): 411–432.

Kogut, B., and Zander, U. 2000. "Did socialism fail to innovate? A natural experiment of the two Zeiss companies." *American Sociological Review* 65(2): 169–190.

Korean Intellectual Property Office. "2013. Statistics: Applications." Daejeon. Available at www.kipo.go.kr/upload/en/download/Applicati ons.xls.

Kornai, J. 1995. *Highways and Byways: Studies on Reform and Post-Communist Transition*. Cambridge, MA: MIT Press.

Kostova, T., and Zaheer, S. 1999. "Organizational legitimacy under conditions of complexity: The case of the multinational enterprise." *Academy of Management Review* 24(1): 64–81.

Kriauciunas, A., and Kale, P. 2006. "The impact of socialist imprinting and search on resource change: A study of companies in Lithuania." *Strategic Management Journal* 27(7): 659–679.

Kriz, A., and Keating, B. W. 2010. "Business relationships in China: Lessons about deep trust." *Asia Pacific Business Review* 16(3): 299–318.

Krueger, A. 1974. "The political economy of rent-seeking society." *American Economic Review* 64(3): 291–303.

Krueger, A., and Tuncer, B. 1982. "An empirical test of the infant industry argument." *American Economic Review* 72(5): 1142–1152.

Krugman, P. 1979. "A model of innovation, technology transfer, and the world distribution of income." *Journal of Political Economy* 87(2): 253–266.

1993. "Protection in developing countries." In *Policymaking in the Open Economy: Concepts and Case Studies in Economic Performance*, ed. R. Dornbusch. New York: Oxford University Press.

Krumm, K. L., and Kharas, H. J. 2004. *East Asia Integrates: A Trade Policy Agenda for Shared Growth*. Washington, DC: World Bank and Oxford University Press. Available at https://openknowledge.worldbank.org/bit stream/handle/10986/15038/280410PAPER0East0Asia0Integrates.pd f?sequence=1/.

Kuemmerle, W. 1999. "The drivers of foreign direct investment into research and development: An empirical investigation." *Journal of International Business Studies* 30(1): 1–24.

Kurup, A., and Arora, J. 2010. *Trends in Higher Education: Creation and Analysis of a Database of PhDs*. NIAS Report No. R1–2010. Project Report. NIAS, 2010.

Kuznets, S. 1966. *Modern Economic Growth: Rate, Structure and Spread*. New Haven: Yale University Press.

Kwan, L. Y. Y., and Chiu, C. Y. 2015. "Country variations in different innovation inputs: The interactive effect of institution support and human capital." *Journal of Organizational Behavior* 36: 1050–1070.

Lal, D. 1994. *Against Dirigisme: The Case for Unshackling Economic Markets.* San Francisco: International Center for Economic Growth, ICS Press.

Lall, S. 1992. "Technological capabilities and industrialization." *World Development* 20(2): 165–186.

Landau, R., and Rosenberg, N. 1986. *The Positive Sum Strategy: Harnessing Technology for Economic Growth.* Washington, DC: National Academies Press.

Landry, P. F. 2008. *Decentralized Authoritarianism in China: The Communist Party's Control of Local Elites in the Post-Mao Era.* Cambridge University Press.

Lanvin, B., and Evans, P. 2013. *The Global Talent Competitiveness Index 2013.* Singapore: INSEAD.

Lardy, N. R. 2014. *Markets over Mao: The Rise of Private Business in China.* Washington, DC: Peterson Institute for International Economics.

Lau, L. J. 2014. *What Makes China Grow?* Hong Kong: Institute of Global Economics and Finance, the Chinese University of Hong Kong.

Lau, L. J., and Park, J. S. 2007. "Sources of East Asian economic growth revisited." Working paper, Department of Economics, Stanford University, Stanford, CA.

Lau, L. J., Qian, J. Y., and G. Roland. 2000. "Reform without losers: An interpretation of china's dual-track approach to transition." *Journal of Political Economy* 108(1): 120–143.

Lau, S. K. 1982. *Society and Politics in Hong Kong.* Hong Kong: Chinese University Press.

Lawrence, P. R., and Nohria, N. 2002. *Driven: How Human Nature Shapes Our Choices.* San Francisco: Jossey-Bass.

Lazarsfeld, P., and Merton, R. 1954. "Friendship as a social process: A substantive and methodological analysis." In *Freedom and Control in Modern Society,* ed. M. Berger, 18–66. New York: Van Nostrand.

Lee, I. H., Syed, M., and Liu, X. 2012. *Is China over-Investing and Does It Matter?* Washington, DC: International Monetary Fund.

Lee, K. 2010. "Thirty years of catch-up in China, compared with Korea." In *Reform and Development in New Thinking in Industrial Policy China,* ed. H. M. Wu and Y. Yao, 224–242. New York: Routledge.

———. 2013a. *Schumpeterian Analysis of Economic Catch-Up: Knowledge, Path Creation, and the Middle-Income Trap.* Cambridge University Press.

———. 2013b. "Capability failure and industrial policy to move beyond the middle-income trap: From trade-based to technology-based specialization." In *Industrial Policy Revolution,* ed. J. Stiglitz and J. Lin. New York: Palgrave MacMillan.

Lee, K., Jee, M., and Eun, J. H. 2011. "Assessing China's economic catch-up at the firm level and beyond: Washington consensus, East Asian consensus and the Beijing model." *Industry and Innovation* 18(5): 487–507.

Lee, K., and Kim, B. Y. 2009. "Both institutions and policies matter but differently at different income groups of countries: Determinants of long run economic growth revisited." *World Development* 37(3): 533–549.

Lee, K., Kim, B. Y., Park, Y. Y., and Sanidas, E. 2013. "Big businesses and economic growth: Identifying a binding constraint for growth with country panel analysis." *Journal of Comparative Economics* 41(2): 561–582.

Lee, K., and Kim, Y. K. 2010. "IPR and technological catch-up in Korea." In *Intellectual Property Rights, Development, and Catch Up*, ed. H. Odagiri, A. Goto, A. Sunami, and R. R. Nelson, 133–162. Oxford University Press.

Lee, K., and Mathews, J. 2010. "From the Washington consensus to the BeST consensus for world development." *Asian-Pacific Economic Literature* 24(1): 86–103.

Lefebvre, L. A., Mason, R., and Lefebvre, E. 1997. "The influence prism in SMEs: The power of CEOs' perceptions on technology policy and its organizational impacts." *Management Science* 43(6): 856–878.

Lehman, D., Chiu, C. Y., and Schaller, M. 2004. "Culture and psychology." *Annual Review of Psychology* 55: 689–714.

Lenin, V. A. 1916. *Imperialism: The Highest Stage of Capitalism*. Moscow: Progress.

Leonard, M. (ed.). 2012. *China 3.0*. European Council on Foreign Relations (ECFR). Available at www.ecfr.eu/publications/summary/china_3.0/. Accessed November 27, 2015.

Lerner, J. 2009. *Boulevard of Broken Dreams: Why Public Efforts to Boost Entrepreneurship and Venture Capital Have Failed – And What to Do about It*. Princeton University Press.

Leung, A. K. Y., and Chiu, C. Y. 2008. "Interactive effects of multicultural experiences and openness to experience on creativity." *Creativity Research Journal* 20: 376–382.

2010. "Multicultural experiences, idea receptiveness, and creativity." *Journal of Cross-Cultural Psychology* 41: 723–741.

Leung, A. K. Y., Maddux, W. W., Galinsky, A. D., and Chiu, C. Y. 2008. "Multicultural experience enhances creativity: The when and how?" *American Psychologist* 63: 169–181.

Leung, K., Bhagat, R. S., Buchan, N. R., Erez, M., and Gibson, C. B. 2005. "Culture and international business: Recent advances and their implications for future research." *Journal of International Business Studies* 36: 357–378.

Leung, K., Brew, F. P., Zhang Z. X., and Zhang, Y. 2011. "Harmony and conflict: A cross-cultural investigation in China and Australia." *Journal of Cross-Cultural Psychology* 42: 795–816.

Leung, K., Chen, Z., Zhou, F., and Lim, K. 2014. "The role of relational orientation as measured by face and renqing in innovative behavior in China: An indigenous analysis." *Asia Pacific Journal of Management* 31(1): 105–126.

Leung, K., and Morris, M. W. 2015. "Values, schemas, and norms in the culture–behavior nexus: A situated dynamics framework." *Journal of International Business Studies*, 46: 1028–1050.

Lewin, A. Y. 2013. *Providers in China and USA: Preliminary Comparison.* Durham, NC: Duke University Outsourcing Research Network Study.

Lewin, A. Y., Massini, S., and Peeters, C. 2009. "Why are companies offshoring innovation? The emerging global race for talent." *Journal of International Business Studies* 40(6): 901–925.

2011. "Microfoundations of internal and external absorptive capacity routines." *Organization Science* 22(1): 81–98.

Lewin, A. Y., and Zhong, X. 2013. "The evolving diaspora of talent: A perspective on trends and implications for sourcing science and engineering work." *Journal of International Management* 13(1): 6–13.

Lewis, J. I. 2012. *Green Innovation in China.* New York: Columbia University Press.

Li, C., Kwan, L. Y. Y., Liou, S., and Chiu, C. Y. 2013. "Culture, group processes and creativity." In *Culture and Group Processes*, ed. M. Yuki and M. Brewer. New York: Oxford University Press.

Li, H., and L. A. Zhou. 2005. "Political turnover and economic performance: The incentive role of personnel control in China." *Journal of Public Economics* 89: 1743–1762.

Li, K. Q. 2015. "Symposium on science and technology strategy." *Xinhua News Service*, Beijing, China, July 27. Available at http://news.xinhua net.com/english/2015–07/28/c_134455919.htm. Accessed September 14, 2015.

Li, M., and Chen, Q. 2011. "Globalization, internationalization and the world-class university movement: The China experience." In *Handbook on Globalization and Higher Education*, ed. R. King, S. Marginson, and R. Naidoo. Cheltenham: Edward Elgar.

Li, P. P., and Redding, G. 2014. "Social capital in Asia: Its dual nature and function." In *The Oxford Handbook of Asian Business Systems*, ed. M. A. Witt and G. Redding. Oxford University Press.

Li, X. 2012. "Behind the recent surge of Chinese patenting: An institutional view." *Research Policy* 41: 236–249.

Li, X., and Liang, X. 2015. "A Confucian social model of political appointments among Chinese private entrepreneurs." *Academy of Management Journal* 58(2): 592–617.

Li, Y. 2015. "Gaoxiao zhishi chanquan guanli kunjing yu chulu: Yi Zhejiang daxue wei li" [University IP management predicaments and the road ahead: The case of Zhejiang University]. International Symposium on Intellectual Property Management at Universities and Research Institutes, Zhejiang University Research Institute for Intellectual Property Management, Zhejiang, China.

Li-Ying, J., Wang, Y., and Salomo, S. 2014. "An inquiry on dimensions of external technology search and their influence on technological innovations: evidence from Chinese firms." *R&D Management* 44(1): 53–74.

Liaoning Province. 2015. "Guanyu jiakuai cujin keji chengguo zhuanhua de ruogan yijian liao ke fa [2015] 1 hao" [Notification on the views regarding the publication of accelerating the promotion of science and technology achievement technology transfer. Liaoning Science Law (2015) no. 1]. Liaoning Province S&T Information. January 19. Available at www.lninfo.gov.cn/uploadfile/2015/0130/201501301051 02221.pdf.

Lieberthal, K., and Lampton, D. M. 1992. *Bureaucracy, Politics and Decision-Making in Post-Mao China*. Berkeley: University of California Press.

Lieberthal, K., and Lieberthal, G. 2003. "The great transition." *Harvard Business Review* (October): 3–14.

Lin, J. Y. 2009a. "Beyond Keynesianism." *Harvard International Review* 31(2): 14–17.

2009b. *Economic Development and Transition: Thought, Strategy, and Viability*. Cambridge University Press.

2011. "New structural economics: A framework for rethinking economic development." *World Bank Research Observer* 26(2): 193–221.

2012a. *Demystifying the Chinese Economy*. Cambridge University Press.

2012b. *New Structural Economics*. Washington, DC: World Bank.

2012c. *The Quest for Prosperity: How Developing Economies Can Take Off*. Princeton University Press.

2013a. "New structural economics: The third wave of development thinking." *Asia Pacific Economic Literature* 27(2): 1–13.

2013b. *Against the Consensus: Reflections on the Great Recession*. Cambridge University Press.

Lin, J. Y., and Chang, H. 2009. "DPR Debate: Should industrial policy in developing countries conform to comparative advantage or defy it?" *Development Policy Review* 27(5): 483–502.

Lin, J. Y., and Li, F. 2009. "Development strategy, viability, and economic distortions in developing countries." Policy Research Working Paper 4906. World Bank, Washington, DC.

Lin, J. Y., and Monga, C. 2010. "The growth report and new structural economics." Policy Research Working Papers 5336. World Bank, Washington, DC.

——— 2011. "DPR debate: Growth identification and facilitation: The role of the state in the dynamics of structural change." *Development Policy Review* 29(3): 259–310.

Lin, J. Y., and Nugent, J. 1995. "Institutions and economic development." In *Handbook of Development Economics*, vol. 3, ed. T. N. Srinivasan and J. Behrman. Amsterdam: North-Holland.

Lin, J. Y., Sun, X., and Jiang, Y. 2013. "Endowment, industrial structure, and appropriate financial structure: A new structural economics perspective." *Journal of Economic Policy Reform* 16(2): 109–122.

Lin, M. 2011. "China Bayh-Dole Act: A framework fundamental to achieving the economic potential of China's national patent development strategy (2011–2020)." *Spring 2011 Eye on China Newsletter*, Foley and Lardner LLP. April 22. Available at www.foley.com/intelligence/detail.aspx?in t=8043/.

Lin, Y. 2001. *Between Politics and Markets*. Cambridge University Press.

Liou, S., and Nisbett, R. E. 2011. "Cultural difference in group creativity process." Paper presented at the annual meeting of the Academy of Management, San Antonio.

Litwin, G., and Stringer, R. 1968. *Motivation and Organizational Climate*. Cambridge, MA: Harvard University Press.

Liu, K., Liu, C., and Huang, J. 2014. "IPR in China: Market-oriented innovation or policy-induced rent-seeking?" Workshop on the Actual Role of IPRs in Technological and Business Innovation, School of Law, Singapore Management University, Singapore.

Liu, R., Weng, Q., Mao, G., and Huang, T. 2013. "Industrial cluster, government agency and entrepreneurial development: A case study of Wenzhou City, Zhejiang Province." *Chinese Management Studies* 7(2): 253–280.

Liu, X. 2014. "Zhonggong zhongyang guanyu quanmian tuijin yifa zhiguo ruogan zhongda wenti de jueding" [Chinese Communist Party Central Committee decision regarding the comprehensive promotion of the rule of law on a number of major issues]. *Xinhuanet News*, October 28. Available at www.gov.cn/zhengce/20 14-10/28/content_2771946.htm.

Liu, X., and White, S. 2001. "Comparing innovation systems: A framework and application to China's transitional context." *Research Policy* 30(7): 1091–1114.

Lo, C. P., and Liu, H. J. 2012. "Why India is mainly engaged in offshore service activities, while China is disproportionately engaged in manufacturing?" *China Economic Review* 20: 236–245.

Lu, D., and Z. Tang. 1997. *State Intervention and Business in China: The Role of Preferential Policies.* Cheltenham: Edward Elgar.

Lu, H. T. 2014. "Airbus to use Tianjin as delivery hub." *China Daily.* June 17. Available at http://usa.chinadaily.com.cn/epaper/2014–06/17/content_17594611.htm.

Lu, Q. 2000. *China's Leap into the Information Age.* Oxford University Press.

Lu, W. 2008. "Woguo de zhishi chanquan fazhan jinru zhanlue zhuanxing qi" [China's intellectual property rights development entering a strategic transformation period]. *Juece zixun tongxun* 1: 45–49.

Lundvall, B. A. 1992. *National Systems of Innovation: Towards a Theory of Innovation and Interactive Learning.* London: Pinter.

——— 2007. "National innovation systems – Analytical concept and development tool." *Industry and Innovation* 14(1): 95–119.

Luo, Y., and Tung, R. 2007. "International expansion of emerging market enterprises: A springboard perspective." *Journal of International Business Studies* 38(4): 481–498.

Lynn, L., and Salzman, H. 2009. "The new globalization of engineering: How the offshoring of advanced engineering affects competitiveness and development." *Economics, Management and Financial Markets* 4(1): 11–46.

Maddison, A. 2010. "Historical Statistics of the World Economy: 1–2008 AD." Available at www.ggdc.net/maddison/Historical_Statistics/horizontal-file_02-2010.xls.

Maddux, W. W., Adam, H., and Galinsky, A. D. 2010. "When in Rome . . . learn why the Romans do what they do: How multicultural learning experiences enhance creativity." *Personality and Social Psychology Bulletin* 36: 731–741.

Mahbubani, K. 2009. *Can Asians Think?* Singapore: Marshall Cavendish.

Malone, T. W, Laubacher, R., and Scot Morton, M. S. 2003. *Inventing the Organizations of the 21st Century.* Cambridge, MA: MIT Press.

Manning, S., Massini, S., and Lewin, A. Y. 2008. "A dynamic perspective on next-generation offshoring: The global sourcing of science and engineering talent." *Academy of Management Perspectives* 22(3): 35–54.

Maskell, P. 2014. "Accessing remote knowledge – The roles of trade fair, pipelines, crowdsourcing and listening posts." *Journal of Economic Geography* 14(5): 883–902.

Maskin, E., Qian, Y., and Xu, C. 2000. "Incentives, information and organizational form." *Review of Economic Studies* 67: 359–378.

Massini, S., and Miozzo, M. 2012. "Outsourcing and offshoring of business services: Challenges to theory, management and geography of innovation." *Regional Studies* 46(9): 1219–1242.

Mathews, J. 2014. *Greening of Capitalism: How Asia Is Driving the Next Great Transformation.* Stanford University Press.

Mathews, J. A., and Zander, I. 2007. "The international entrepreneurial dynamics of accelerated internationalisation." *Journal of International Business Studies* 38: 387–403.

McClelland, D. 1961. *The Achieving Society.* Princeton, NJ: Van Nostrand Reinhold.

2006. *The Bourgeois Virtues: Ethics for an Age of Commerce.* Chicago: University of Chicago Press.

2010. *Bourgeois Dignity: Why Economics Can't Explain the Modern World.* Chicago: University of Chicago Press.

McGregor, R. 2012. *The Party: The Secret World of China's Communist Rulers.* New York: Harper Perennial.

McKinnon, R. I. 1973. *Money and Capital in Economic Development.* Washington, DC: Brookings Institution Press.

Mellor, W., Chen, L. Y., and Wu, Z. 2014. "Ma says Alibaba shareholders should feel love, not no. 3." Bloomberg.com, November 9. Available at www.bloomberg.com/news/articles/2014-11-09/ma-says-alibaba-share holders-should-feel-love-not-no-3/. Accessed March 1, 2015.

Menon, T., Sim, J., Fu, J. H. Y., Chiu, C. Y., and Hong, Y. Y. 2010. "Blazing the trail and trailing the group: Culture and perceptions of the leader's position." *Organizational Behavior and Human Decision Processes* 113: 51–61.

Ministry of Defense. 2015. "Zhonggong zhongyang guowuyuan guanyu shenhua tizhi jizhi gaige jiakuai shishi chuangxin qudong fazhan zhanlue de ruogan yijian" [CCP Central Committee and the State Council view on deepening institutional mechanism reform and accelerate the implementation of an innovation-driven development strategy]. Available at www.mod.gov.cn/xwph/2015-03/24/con tent_4576385.htm.

Ministry of Education. 2015. "Jianquan zhishi, jishu, guanli, jineng deng you yaosu shichang jueding baochou jizhi de diaoyan baogao jiaoyu bu keji si keti zu 2015 nian 4 yue" [Building a comprehensive knowledge, technology, management, capability, and other market elements to determine remuneration research report by the Ministry of Education S&T Division Task Force April 2015]. Science and Technology Division Task Force. March 28. Available at http://cqt.njtech.edu.cn/artcle_view .asp?id=17171.

Ministry of Science and Technology. 2008. "Guanyu yinfa 'gaoxin jishu qiye rending guanli banfa' de tongzhi" [Regarding the publication of high-technology enterprises' recognition administrative law notification]. Available at www.most.gov.cn/fggw/zfwj/zfwj2008/200804/t2008042 8_61006.htm.

2008–2013. "Keji tongji baogao" [S&T statistical report]. Development and Planning Division.

2010–2013. *Zhongguo keji tongji shuju [China Science and Technology Statistics Data Book]*. Available at www.sts.org.cn/sjkl/kjtjdt/.

2015. "Cujin keji chengguo zhuanhua fa xiuzheng an (cao'an) tiaowen" [Law on promoting the transformation of scientific and technological achievements (Draft)]. Available at www.most.gov.cn/tztg/201503/t20 150305_118402.htm.

Various years. *China Science and Technology Statistics Data Book*. Available at www.sts.org.cn.

Moga, T. 2012. *China's Utility Model Patent System: Innovation Driver or Deterrent?* Washington, DC: US Chamber of Commerce Asia. Available at www.uschamber.com/sites/default/files/legacy/international/files/0209 39_ChinaUtilityModel_2013Revised_FIN%20%281%29.pdf.

Mokyr, J. 2009. *The Enlightened Economy: An Economic History of Britain 1700–1850*. New Haven: Yale University Press.

Moore, B. 1966. *Social Origins of Dictatorship and Democracy: Lord and Peasant in the Making of the Modern World*, vol. 268. Boston: Beacon Press.

Moore, T. G. 2002. *China in the World Market: Chinese Industry and International Sources of Reform in the Post-Mao Era*. Cambridge University Press.

Morck, R., Yeung, B., and Zhao, M. 2008. "Perspectives on China's outward foreign direct investment." *Journal of International Business Studies* 39(3): 337–350.

"More Chinese overseas students return home in 2010. " 2011. Xinhuanet. com, March 11. Available at http://news.xinhuanet.com/english2010/c hina/2011–03/11/c_13773804.htm. Accessed March 15, 2011.

Morris, M. W., Chiu, C. Y., and Liu, Z. 2015. "Polycultural psychology." *Annual Review of Psychology* 66: 631–659.

Morris, M. W., and Leung, K. 2010. "Creativity east and west: Perspectives and parallels." *Management and Organization Review* 6(3): 313–327.

Mowery, D. C. 2009. "Plus ça change: Industrial R&D in the 'third industrial revolution.'" *Industrial and Corporate Change* 18(1): 1–50.

Murakami, Y. 1984. "Ie society as a pattern of civilization." *Journal of Japanese Studies* 10(2): 279–363.

Murphy, K., Shleifer, A., and Vishny, R. 1989. "Industrialization and the big push." *Journal of Political Economy* 97(5): 1003–1026.

Najita, T. 1998. *Tokugawa Political Writings.* Cambridge University Press.

Nakane, C. 1971. *Japanese Society.* London: Wiedenfeld and Nicholson.

Narula, R., and Zanfei, A. 2004. "Globalisation of innovation: The role of multinational enterprises." In *Handbook of Innovation,* ed. J. Fagerberg, D. Mowery, and R. R. Nelson. Oxford University Press.

Narver, J., and Slater, S. 1990. "The effect of a market orientation on business profitability." *Journal of Marketing* 54(4): 20–35.

National Bureau of Statistics. 2011. "Di liu ci ren kou pu cha shu ju gong gao" [The sixth national census in 2010: Main data bulletin]. Available at www.stats.gov.cn/tjsj/tjgb/rkpcgb/qgrkpcgb/201104/t20110428_30327.html.

———. 2014a. "2013 nian quanguo keji jingfei touru tongji gongbao" [2013 China S&T expenditure investment statistical report]. Available at www.stats.gov.cn/tjsj/tjgb/rdpcgb/qgkjjftrtjgb/201410/t20141023_628330.html.

———. 2014b. "Tongji ju: 2013 nian woguo GDP zeng su 7.7%" [NBS: China's 2013 GDP grew by 7.7%]. Available at http://finance.sina.com.cn/china/hgjj/20140224/093418308381.shtml.

———. 2015a. "Basic statistics on higher education for S&T activities." Available at http://data.stats.gov.cn/english/easyquery.htm?cn=C01/.

———. 2015b. "Basic statistics on S&T activities." Available at http://data.stats.gov.cn/english/easyquery.htm?cn=C01/.

———. 2015c. "Three kinds of applications for patents accepted." Available at http://data.stats.gov.cn/english/easyquery.htm?cn=C01/.

———. 2015d. "Three kinds of patents granted." Available at http://data.stats.gov.cn/english/easyquery.htm?cn=C01/.

National Bureau of Statistics of China. 2011. *China Statistical Yearbook.* Beijing: National Bureau of Statistics of China.

National People's Congress. 2007. "Law of the People's Republic of China on progress of science and technology." Standing Committee. Available at www.npc.gov.cn/englishnpc/Law/2009-02/20/content_1471617.htm.

National Science Foundation. 2014. *Science and Engineering Indicators 2014 Digest.* Available at www.nsf.gov/statistics/seind14/index.cfm/digest/stem.htm.

Naughton, B. 1995. *Growing out of the Plan: Chinese Economic Reform, 1978–1993.* Cambridge University Press.

———. 2008. "SASAC and rising corporate power in China." *China Leadership Monitor* 24: 1–9.

2010. "China's distinctive system: Can it be a model for others?" *Journal of Contemporary China* 19(65): 437–460.

NBD. 2014. "Guowuyuan tongguo 'cujin keji chengguo zhuanhua fa xiuzheng an (cao'an)'" [State Council approves "Law on promoting the transformation of scientific and technological achievements (Draft)"]. *Daily Economic News*, November 20. Available at www.nbd.com.cn/articles/2014-11-20/877210.html.

Needham, J. 1954. *Science and Civilization in China,* 7 vols. Cambridge University Press.

Negandhi, A. R., and Prasad, S. B. 1975. *The Frightening Angels: A Study of U.S. Multinationals in Developing Countries.* Kent, OH: Kent State University Press.

Nelson, R. R. (ed.). 1993. *National Innovation Systems: A Comparative Study.* New York: Oxford University Press.

Nelson, R. R., and Romer, P. M. 1996. "Science, economic growth, and public policy." *Challenge* 39(2): 9–21.

Niosi, J. 2002. "National systems of innovations are 'x-efficient' (and x-effective): Why some are slow learners." *Research Policy* 31: 291–302.

Niosi, J., and Tschang, F. T. 2009. "The strategies of Chinese and Indian software multinationals: Implications for internationalization theory." *Industrial and Corporate Change* 18(2): 269–294.

Nisbitt, R. 2003. *The Geography of Thought: How Asians and Westerners Think Differently... and Why.* New York: Free Press.

Niu, W., and Sternberg, R. 2001. "Cultural influence of artistic creativity and its evaluation." *International Journal of Psychology* 36(4): 225–241.

Niu, W., Zhang, J., and Yang, Y. 2007. "Deductive reasoning and creativity: A cross-cultural study." *Psychological Reports* 100: 509–519.

North, D. C. 1990. "Institutions, Institutional Change and Economic Performance." In *Political Economy of Institutions and Decisions,* ed. J. E. Alt and D. C. North. Cambridge University Press.

Ocasio, W., and Joseph, J. 2005. "An attention-based theory of strategy formulation: Linking micro- and macroperspectives in strategy processes." *Advances in Strategic Management* 22: 39–61.

Organization for Economic Cooperation and Development. 1997. "National innovation systems." Available at www.oecd.org/science/inno/2101733.pdf.

2013. *Supporting Invention in Knowledge Capital, Growth and Innovation.* Paris: OECD.

2014. "OECD science, technology and industry outlook 2014." Available at www.keepeek.com/Digital-Asset-Management/oecd/science-and-technology/oecd-science-technology-and-industry-outlook-2014_sti_outlook-2014-en#page1/.

2015. OECD.Stat. Available at http://stats.oecd.org. Accessed March 12, 2015.

Pack, H., and Saggi, K. 2006. "Is there a case for industrial policy? A critical survey." *World Bank Research Observer* 21(2): 267–297.

Pei, M. 2008. *China's Trapped Transition: The Limits of Developmental Autocracy*. Cambridge, MA: Harvard University Press.

Peng, M., and Luo, Y. 2000. "Managerial ties and firm performance in a transition economy: The nature of a micro-macro link." *Academy of Management Journal* 43(3): 486–501.

Peng, M. W. 2003. "Institutional transitions and strategic choices." *Academy of Management Review* 28(2): 275–296.

People's Daily. 2006. "1978 nian 3 yue 18 ri dengxiaoping zai quanguo kexue dahui kaimu shi shang de jianghua" [Deng Xiaoping's opening remarks during the National Science and Technology Conference March 18, 1978]. January 5. Available at http://scitech.people.com.cn/GB/25509/56813/57267/57268/4001431.html.

2014a. "Daibiao chenxuedong: Kaohe zhuanli shuliang yi chu 'lese zhuanli'" [Representative Chen Xuedong: Using patent volume to evaluate performance leads to "junk patents"]. March 7. Available at http://ip.people.com.cn/n/2014/0307/c136655-24561817.html.

2014b. "Lianghui ti'an: Tiaozheng zhuanli feiyong bili dali ezhi lese zhuanli" [NPC and Chinese People's Political Consultative Conference proposal: The adjustment of patent fees ratio to vigorously curb junk patents]. March 7. Available at http://scitech.people.com.cn/n/2014/0307/c1007-24557877.html.

2015. "Zhuanli qinquan shiji peichang e pingjun 8 wan zhuanjia jianyi tigao jin'e" [Patent infringement actual compensation averages RMB 80,000: Experts recommend raising the amount]. February 6. Available at http://ip.people.com.cn/n/2015/0206/c136655-26519125.html.

Perkins, D. 2001. "Industrial and financial policy in China and Vietnam: A new model or a replay of the East Asian experience?" In *Rethinking the East Asian Miracle*, ed. J. Stiglitz and S. Yusuf. Oxford University Press.

Pettis, M. 2013. *Avoiding the Fall: China's Economic Restructuring*. Washington, DC: Carnegie Endowment for International Peace.

Poncet, S. 2005. "A fragmented China: Measure and determinants of Chinese domestic market disintegration." *Review of International Economics* 13(3): 409–430.

Popper, B. 2015. "Apple's second biggest market is now China, not Europe." *The Verge*, April 27. Available at www.theverge.com/2015/4/27/8505063/china-is-now-apples-second-biggest-market/. Accessed September 13, 2015.

Porter, M. E. 1990. *The Competitive Advantage of Nations.* New York: Free Press.

Prahalad, C. K., and Doz, Y. L. 1987. *The Multinational Mission: Balancing Local Demands and Global Vision.* London: Free Press.

Prahalad, C. K., and Hamel, G. 1990. "The core competence of the firm." *Harvard Business Review* (May–June): 79–91.

Prebisch, R. 1950. *The Economic Development of Latin America and Its Principal Problems.* New York: United Nations. Reprinted in *Economic Bulletin for Latin America* 7(1) (1962): 1–22.

Prud'homme, D. 2012. *Dulling the Cutting Edge: How Patent-Related Policies and Practices Hamper Innovation in China.* Shanghai: European Chamber of Commerce.

Puffer, S. M., McCarthy, D. J., and Boisot, M. 2010. "Entrepreneurship in Russia and China: The impact of formal institutional voids." *Entrepreneurship Theory and Practice* 34(3): 441–467.

Pye, L. W. 1985. *Asian Power and Politics.* Cambridge, MA: Belknap Press. 1990. "China: Erratic state, frustrated society." *Foreign Affairs* 69(4): 56–74.

Qian, Y. 2003. "How reform worked in China." In *In Search of Prosperity: Analytic Narratives of Growth,* ed. D. Rodrik. Princeton University Press.

Qiao, Y., and Wen, J. 2009. "Guonei wai faming zhuanli weichi zhuangkuang bijiao yanjiu" [A comparative study of maintenance status of domestic and foreign invention patents]. *Kexue xue yu kexue jishu guanli* 6: 29–32.

Ramamurti, R. 2013. "The role of international M&A in building the competitive advantage of Indian firms." In *The Competitive Advantage of Emerging Market Multinationals,* ed. P. J. Williamson, R. Ramamurti, A. Fleury, and M. Fleury. Cambridge University Press.

Ramamurti, R., and Singh, J. V. (eds.). 2009. *Emerging Multinationals in Emerging Markets.* Cambridge University Press.

Ran, T. 2014. <title?> Presentation at the British embassy, Beijing, March 12.

Raustiala, K., and Sprigman, C. 2012. *The Knockoff Economy: How Imitation Sparks Innovation.* New York: Oxford University Press. 2014. "Piracy fuels the fashion industry." *New York Times,* September 8. Available at www.nytimes.com/roomfordebate/2014/09/07/who-owns-fashion/piracy-fuels-the-fashion-industry. Accessed September 9, 2014.

Redding, G. 2005. "The thick description and comparison of societal systems of capitalism." *Journal of International Business Studies* 36(2): 123–155.

Redding, G., and Drew, A. 2015. "Dealing with the complexity of causes of societal innovativeness: Social enabling and disabling mechanisms and the case of China." *Journal of Interdisciplinary Economics*. Paper presented at the workshop Diversities of Innovation: The Role of Government Policies for the Future Economic Basis of Societies, Friedrich-Schiller-University and Oxford University, Kellogg College. Oxford, February 17–18.

Redding, G., and Witt, M. A. 2006. "The 'tray of loose sand': A thick description of the state-owned enterprise sector of China seen as a business system." *Asian Business and Management* 5(1): 87–112.

2007. *The Future of Chinese Capitalism: Choices and Chances*. Oxford University Press.

2009. "China's business system and its future trajectory." *Asia Pacific Journal of Management* 26(3): 381–399.

Rein, S. 2014. *The End of Copy-Cat China: The Rise of Creativity, Innovation, and Individualism in Asia*. Hoboken, NJ: Wiley.

The Rise of the Global Citizen? 2014. London: Barclays PLC.

Roberts, K. H. 1970. "On looking at an elephant: An evaluation of cross-cultural research related to organizations." *Psychological Bulletin* 74(5): 327–350.

Rodrik, D. 2004. *Industrial Policy for the Twenty-First Century*. Cambridge, MA: Harvard University.

2011. *The Globalization Paradox*. New York: W.W. Norton.

Romer, P. M. 1990. "Endogenous technological change." *Journal of Political Economy* 98(5): S71–S102.

Rosenberg, N., and Nelson, R. R. 1994. "American universities and technical advance in industry." *Research Policy* 23: 323–348.

Rosenstein-Rodan, P. 1943. "Problems of industrialization of Eastern and Southeastern Europe." *Economic Journal* 111(210–211): 202–211.

Rugman, A., and Verbeke, A. 2001. "Subsidiary-specific advantages in multinational enterprises." *Strategic Management Journal* 22: 237–250.

Rugman, A. M. 2009. "Theoretical aspects of MNEs from emerging markets." In *Emerging Multinationals in Emerging Markets*, ed. R. Ramamurti and J. V. Singh, chap. 3. Cambridge University Press.

Rugman, A. M., and Collinson, S. C. 2012. *International Business*, 6th ed. Harlow: FT Pearson/Prentice Hall.

Rugman, A. M., and Doh, J. 2008. *Multinationals and Development*. New Haven: Yale University Press.

Rui, H., and Yip, G. S. 2008. "Foreign acquisitions by Chinese firms: A strategic intent perspective." *Journal of World Business* 43(2): 213–226.

Saeki, N., Fan, X., and Dusen, L. V. 2001. "A comparative study of creative thinking of American and Japanese college students." *Journal of Creative Behavior* 35: 24–36.

Samuels, R. J., and Keller, W. (eds.). 2003. *Crisis and Innovation: Asian Technology after the Millennium.* Cambridge University Press.

Santangelo, G. D. and Meyer, K. E. 2011. "Extending the internationalization process model: Increases and decreases of MNE commitment in emerging economies." *Journal of International Business Studies* 42: 894–909.

Sawant, R. 2012. "Asset specificity and corporate political activity in regulated industries." *Academy of Management Review* 37(2): 194–210.

Sawhney, M., and Prandelli, E. 2000. "Managing distributed innovation in turbulent markets." *California Management Review* 42(4): 24–54.

Saxenian, A. 2002. "Brain circulation: How high-skill immigration makes everyone better off." *Brookings Review* 20(1): 28–31.

Schaaf, J. 2005. *Outsourcing to India: Crouching Tiger Set to Pounce.* Deutsche Bank Research.

Schmidt, V. A. 2002. *The Futures of European Capitalism.* Oxford University Press.

Schollhammer, H. 1969. "The comparative management theory jungle." *Academy of Management Journal* 12(1): 81–97.

Schurmann, F. 1968. *Ideology and Organization in Communist China.* Berkeley: University of California Press.

Shane, S. 1993. "Cultural influences on national rates of innovation." *Journal of Business Venturing* 8(1): 59–73.

Shanghai Intellectual Property Administration. 2012. "Shanghai shi zhuanli zizhu banfa (2012 nian xiuding)" [Shanghai patent subsidy law (2012 revision)]. Available at www.sipa.gov.cn/gb/zscq/node2/node23/userobject1ai9494.html.

Shih, V., Adolph, C., and Liu, M. 2012. "Getting ahead in the Communist Party: Explaining the advancement of Central Committee members in China." *American Political Science Review* 106(1): 166–187.

Sirmon, D. G., Hitt, M. A., and Ireland, R. D. 2007. "Managing firm resources in dynamic environments to create value: Looking inside the black box." *Academy of Management Review* 32(1): 273–292.

Solow, R. M. 1957. "Technical change and the aggregate production function." *Review of Economics and Statistics* 39: 312–320.

Stahl, G. K., and Tung, R. L. 2015. "Towards a more balanced treatment of culture in international business studies: The need for positive cross-cultural scholarship." *Journal of International Business Studies* 46: 391–414.

State Council. 2003. "Guowuyuan guoyou zichan jiandu guanli weiyuanhui zhonghua renmin gongheguo caizheng bu di 3 haoling qiye guoyou chanquan zhuanrang guanli zhanxing banfa" [State-Owned Assets

Supervision and Administration Commission and the Ministry of Commerce Order no. 3: Interim measures for the transfer of state-owned property]. Available at www.gov.cn/gongbao/content/2004/con tent_62922.htm.

2006a. "Guojia zhong chang qi kexue he jishu fazhan guihua gangyao (2006–2020 nian)" [China medium- and long-range science and technology development plan, 2006–2020]. Available at www.gov.cn/jrzg/2006-02/09/content_183787.htm.

2006b. "The national medium- and long-term program for science and technology development: An outline." University of Sydney. Available at http://jpm.li/46/.

2008a. "'Guojia zhishi chanquan zhanlue gangyao' quanwen" ["China national intellectual property rights strategy" outline]. Available at w ww.nipso.cn/onews.asp?id=9592/.

2008b. "Zhonghua renmin gongheguo zhuxi ling di wu hao zhonghua renmin gongheguo qiye guoyou zichan fa" [Order of the President of the People's Republic of China no. 5 Law of the People's Republic of China on the state-owned assets of enterprises]. Available at www.gov.cn/flfg/2008-10/28/content_1134207.htm.

2015a. "Full transcript of policy briefing of the State Council on March 27, 2015." Available at http://english.gov.cn/news/policy_briefings/2015/03/27/content_281475078591808.htm.

2015b. "Guowuyuan bangong ting guanyu zhuanfa zhishi chanquan ju deng danwei shenru shishi guojia zhishi chanquan zhanlue xingdong jihua (2014–2020 nian) de tongzhi guo ban fa (2014) 64 hao" [State Council general office notification regarding the forwarding to the state intellectual property office and other units the in-depth implementation of the national IPR strategy action plan (2014–2020) State Council Law (2014) no. 64]. Available at www.gov.cn/zhengce/content/2015-01/04/content_9375.htm.

State Council Information Office. 2015. "Liaoning sheng 'guanyu jiakuai cujin keji chengguo zhuanhua de ruogan yijian' xinwen fabu hui" [News press release of Liaoning province views regarding the accelerated promotion of science and technology achievement technology transfer]. Available at www.scio.gov.cn/xwfbh/gssxwfbh/fbh/Docume nt/1396282/1396282.htm.

State Council Legislative Affairs Office. 2015. "Guowuyuan fazhi bangongshi guanyu 'zhiwu faming tiaoli cao'an (song shen gao)' gongkai zhengqiu yijian tongzhi" [Legislative Affairs Office of the State Council notice regarding "work invention bill (draft for approval)" open for comments]. Available at www.chinalaw.gov.cn/ar ticle/xwzx/tpxw/201504/20150400398828.shtml.

State Intellectual Property Office. 2008. "Patent Law of the People's Republic of China." Available at http://english.sipo.gov.cn/laws/lawsre gulations/201101/t20110119_566244.html.

——— 2008–2013. "SIPO annual reports." Available at http://english.sipo.gov .cn/laws/annualreports/.

——— 2009. "Beijing shi faming zhuanli jiangli banfa" [Beijing invention patent remuneration law]. Available at www.sipo.gov.cn/twzb/bjfmzlj/bjzl/20 0904/t20090420_454649.html.

——— 2012a. "2012 zhuanli tongji jianbao" [2012 patent statistics summary report]. Available at www.sipo.gov.cn/ghfzs/zltjjb/201310/P02013102 5653662902318.pdf.

——— 2012b. "Zhongguo shiyong xinxing zhuanli zhidu fazhan zhuangkuang (quanwen)" [China's utility model patent system development]. Available at www.gov.cn/gzdt/2012-12/21/content_2295766.htm.

——— 2013. "Development of China's utility model patent system." Available at http://english.sipo.gov.cn/news/official/201301/t20130105_782325 .html.

——— 2014a. "'Guojia zhishi chanquan zhanlue gangyao' banbu shishi 6 zhounian" ["China national intellectual property rights strategy outline," six-year implementation]. Available at www.nipso.cn/zhuanti/zl6/.

——— 2014b. "The promotion plan for the implementation of the national intellectual property strategy in 2014." Available at http://english.sipo .gov.cn/laws/developing/201405/t20140505_944778.html.

State-Owned Assets Supervision and Administration Commission of the State Council. n.d. "State-Owned Assets Supervision and Administration Commission of the State Council (SASAC) main functions." Available at http://en.sasac.gov.cn/n1408028/n1408521/in dex.html.

Streeck, Wolfgang. 1996. "Lean production in the German automobile industry: A test case for convergence theory." In *National Diversity and Global Capitalism*, ed. S. Berger and R. P. Dore. Ithaca: Cornell University Press.

Subramanian, A., and Roy, D. 2003. "Who can explain the Mauritian miracle? Mede, Romer, Sachs, or Rodrik?" In *In Search of Prosperity: Analytic Narratives on Economic Growth*, ed. D. Rodrik. Princeton University Press.

Sun, J. 2014. "Lun woguo lese zhuanli wenti" [China's junk patents problem]. *Fazhi yu shehui* 20: 273 and 281.

Sun, P., Wright, M., and Mellahi, K. 2010. "Is entrepreneur–politician alliance sustainable during transition? The case of management buyouts in China." *Management and Organization Review* 6(1): 101–121.

Supreme Court. 2015. "Zuigao renmin fayuan guanyu xiugai 'zuigao renmin fayuan guanyu shenli zhuanli jiufen anjian shiyong falu wenti de ruogan guiding' de jueding fa shi [2015] 4 hao" [Amendment "Supreme Court regarding patent dispute case hearing provisions and applicable laws" decision judicial interpretation (215) no. 4]. Available at www.court.g ov.cn/zixun-xiangqing-13244.html.

Suzhou Institute of Wuhan University. 2013. "Wuhan University science and technology transfer, licensing, and industrialization regulations." Available at www.pxto.com.cn/JiGou/dt-show.asp?Resource_I D=169566&ID=63a302d2d6598b61/.

Sylwester, K. 2000. "Income inequality, education expenditures, and growth." *Journal of Development Economics* 63: 379–398.

Tabellini, G. 2008. "Institutions and culture." *Journal of the European Economic Association* 6: 255–294.

Tang, M. 2006. "A comparative study on the role of national technology transfer centers in different Chinese universities." GLOBELICS (Global Network for Economics of Learning, Innovation, and Competence Building Systems), Thiruvananthapuram, India.

Tannen, D. 1990. *You Just Don't Understand: Women and Men in Communication.* New York: Harper Collins.

Tao, R., Su, F., Lu, X., and Zhu, Y. 2010. "Jingji zengzhang nenggou dailai jinsheng ma?" [Can economic growth bring about promotion?]. *Guanli shijie* 12(207): 23–36.

Taylor, P., Wang, W., Parker, K., Passel, J. S., Patten, E., and Motel, S. 2012. *The Rise of Intermarriage.* Washington, DC: Pew Research Center.

Teece, D., Pisano, G., and Shuen, A. 1997. "Dynamic capabilities and strategic management." *Strategic Management Journal* 18(7): 509–533.

Thiel, P. 2014. *Zero to One: Notes on Startups, or How to Build the Future.* New York: Crown.

Tianjin Intellectual Property. 2014. "Guanyu 2014 nian tianjin shi zhuanli zizhu lingqu de tongzhi" [Regarding 2014 Tianjin patent subsidy pickup notice]. Available at www.tjipo.gov.cn/xwdt/tztg/201405/t20140526_ 65322.html.

Tianze jingji yanjiusuo [Unirule Institute]. 2011. *Guoyou qiye de xingzhi, biaoxian yu gaige [The Nature, Performance and Reform of State-Owned Enterprises].* Beijing: Unirule Institute.

Tong, Y. Y., Hui, P. P. Z., Kwan, L. Y. Y., and Peng, S. 2011. "National feelings or rational dealings? The moderating role of procedural priming on perceptions of cross-border acquisitions." *Journal of Social Issues* 67: 743–759.

Torch High-Technology Center. 2011. *National High-tech Industrial Zones in China.* Beijing: Ministry of Science and Technology.

Torelli, C. J., Chiu, C. Y., Tam, K. P., Au, A. K. C., and Keh, H. T. 2011. "Exclusionary reactions to foreign cultures: Effects of simultaneous exposure to cultures in globalized space." *Journal of Social Issues* 67: 716–742.

Tsui, A. S., Schoonhoven, C. B., Meyer, M. W., Lau, C. M., and Milkovich, G. T. 2004. "Organization and management in the midst of societal transformation." *Organization Science* 15(2): 133–144.

Tsui, K., and Wang, Y. 2004. "Between separate stoves and a single menu: Fiscal decentralization in China." *China Quarterly* 177: 71–90.

Tung, R. L. 1981. "Patterns of motivation in Chinese industrial enterprises." *Academy of Management Review* 6: 487–494.

1986. "Toward a systems model of comparative management." In *Advances in International Comparative Management*, vol. 2, ed. R. N. Farmer, 233–247. Greenwich, CT: JAI.

1993. "Managing cross-national and intra-national diversity." *Human Resource Management Journal* 32(4): 461–477.

1998. "American expatriates abroad: From neophytes to cosmopolitans." *Journal of World Business* 33(2): 125–144.

2008a. "The cross-cultural research imperative: The need to balance cross-national vis-à-vis intra-national diversity." *Journal of International Business Studies* 39(1): 41–46.

2008b. "Do race and gender matter in international assignments to/from Asia Pacific? An exploratory study of attitudes among Chinese and Korean executives." *Human Resource Management* 47(1): 91–110.

2014a. "Requisites to and ways of developing a global mind-set: Implications for research on leadership and organizations." *Journal of Leadership and Organizational Studies* 21(4): 229–337.

2014b. "Research on Asia: Promise and perils." *Journal of Asia Business Studies* 8(3): 189–192.

in press. "Opportunities and challenges ahead of China's 'New Normal.'" *Long Range Planning*.

Tung, R. L., and Baumann, C. 2009. "Comparing the attitudes toward money, material possessions and savings of overseas Chinese vis-à-vis Chinese in China: Convergence, divergence or cross-vergence, vis-à-vis 'one size fits all' human resource management policies and practices." *International Journal of Human Resource Management* 20: 2382–2401.

Tung, R. L., and Chung, H. F. L. 2010. "Diaspora and trade facilitation: The case of ethnic Chinese in Australia." *Asia Pacific Journal of Management* 27(3): 371–392.

Tung, R. L., and Larazova, M. B. 2006. "Brain drain versus brain gain: An exploratory study of ex-host country nationals in Central and East

Europe." *International Journal of Human Resource Management* 17(11): 1853–1872.

Tung, R. L., and Verbeke, A. 2010. "Beyond Hofstede and GLOBE: Improving the quality of cross-cultural research." *Journal of International Business Studies* 41(8): 1259–1274.

Tung, R. L., Worm, V., and Fang, T. 2008. "Sino-Western business negotiations revisited – 30 years after China's open door policy." *Organizational Dynamics* 37(1): 60–74.

UNCTAD (United Nations Conference on Trade and Development). 2014. *World Investment Report 2014.* Available at http://unctad.org/en/Publ icationsLibrary/wir2014_en.pdf. Accessed August 30, 2015.

United States Patent and Trademark Office (USPTO). Various years. *Calendar Year Patent Statistics.* Available at www.uspto.gov/web/offi ces/ac/ido/oeip/taf/reports.htm.

Van De Kaa, G., Greenven, M., and Van Puijenbroek, G. 2013. "Standards battles in China: Opening up the black box of the Chinese government." *Technology Analysis and Strategic Management* 25(5): 567–581.

Van de Ven, A., and Poole, M. 1995. "Explaining development and change in organizations." *Academy of Management Review* 20(3): 510–540.

Veldhoen, S., Mansson, A., McKern, B., Yip, G., and Kiewiet de Jonge, M. 2012. "Innovation China's next advantage? 2012 China Innovation Survey." Benelux Chamber of Commerce, China Europe International Business School (CEIBS), Wenzhou Chamber of Commerce and Booz and Company Joint Report.

Verbeke, A. 2009. *International Business Strategy: Rethinking the Foundations of Global Corporate Success.* Cambridge University Press.

Vernon, R. 1966. "International investment and international trade in the product cycle." *Quarterly Journal of Economics* 80(2): 190–207.

Von Glinow, M. A., Shapiro, D. L., and Brett, J. M. 2004. "Can we talk, and should we? Managing emotional conflict in multicultural teams." *Academy of Management Review* 29(4): 578–592.

Wade, R. 1990. *Governing the Market: Economic Theory and the Role of Government in East Asian Industrialization.* Princeton University Press.

Wagner, K., Taylor, A., Zablit, H., and Foo, E. 2014. *The Most Innovative Companies 2014: Breaking Through Is Hard to Do.* Boston: Boston Consulting Group.

Walter, C. 2010. "The struggle over ownership: How the reform of state enterprises changed China." *Copenhagen Journal of Asian Studies* 28(1): 83–108.

Walter, C. E., and Howie, F. J. T. 2011. *Red Capitalism: The Fragile Financial Foundation of China's Extraordinary Rise.* Singapore: John Wiley and Sons.

Wang, F., Fu, X., and Chen, J. 2014. "Differential forms of technological change and catch-up: Evidence from China." *International Journal of Technology Management* 11(2): 1–25.

Wang, F., and Mason, A. 2008. "The Demographic Factor in China's Economic Transition." In *China's Great Economic Transformation*, ed. L. Brandt and T. G. Rawski. Cambridge University Press.

Wang, H. 2013. "China's return migration and its impact on home development." *UN Chronicle* 1(3) (September).

2015. "University's IP institute to aid tech transfer." *China Daily*, March 25. Available at www.chinadaily.com.cn/m/cip/2015-03/25/con tent_19908289.htm.

Wang, H. Y. 2010. *China's National Talent Plan: Key Measures and Objectives.* November 23. Washington, DC: Brookings Institute. Available at www.brookings.edu/research/papers/2010/11/23-china-ta lent-wang. Accessed January 25, 2011.

Wang, Y. 2010. "China's national innovation system and innovation policy: Promotion of national innovation systems in countries with special needs." United Nations Economic and Social Commission for Asia and the Pacific. Available at http://nis.apctt.org/PDF/CSNWorkshop_ Report_P2S2_Wang.pdf

Wang, Y., Zhang, X. and Zhao, M. 2013. *Zhongguo chuangye fengxian touzi fazhan baogao 2013 [Venture Capital Development in China 2013].* Beijing: Jingji guanli chubanshe.

Weber, M. 1930. *The Protestant Ethic and the Spirit of Capitalism.* London: Unwin.

Wedeman, A. 2012. *Double Paradox: Rapid Growth and Rising Corruption in China.* Ithaca: Cornell University Press.

Wei, X., Zhang, Z. X., and Chen, X. P. 2015. "I will speak up if my voice is socially desirable: A moderated mediating process of promotive versus prohibitive voice." *Journal of Applied Psychology* 100(5), 1641–1652.

Welzel, C. 2013. *Freedom Rising: Human Empowerment and the Quest for Emancipation.* Cambridge University Press.

Welzel, C., and Inglehart, R., (2013) "Evolution, empowerment and emancipation: how societies ascend the utility ladder of freedom," Working Paper 29/SOC/2013, National Research University, Higher School of Economics, Moscow.

Wen, J. 2008. "Zhengfu zizhu zhuanli feiyong yinfa lese zhuanli de chengyin yu duice" [Government patent cost subsidies and the rise of junk patents cause and countermeasures]. *Dianzi zhishi chanquan* 11: 21–25.

Wen, J., and Zhu, X. 2007. "Woguo difang zhengfu zizhu zhuanli feiyong zhengce ruogan wenti yanjiu" [Research on China's local government subsidies for patent costs implementation questions]. *Gongzuo yanjiu* 17(102): 23–27.

2009. "Zhengfu zizhu zhuanli feiyong dui woguo jishu chuangxin de yingxiang jili yanjiu" [Government patent cost subsidies and the mechanism of influence on China's technological innovation]. *Kexue xue yanjiu* 27(5): 686–691.

Westney, D. E. 1987. *Imitation and Innovation: The Transfer of Western Organizational Patterns in Meiji Japan.* Cambridge: Harvard University Press.

Whiting, S. 2004. "The cadre evaluation system at the grass roots: The paradox of party rule." In *Holding China Together: Diversity and National Integration in the Post-Deng Era,* ed. D. Yang and B. Naughton. Cambridge University Press.

Whitley, R. 1992. *Business Systems in East Asia: Firms, Markets and Societies.* London: Sage.

1999. *Divergent Capitalisms: The Social Structuring and Change of Business Systems.* Oxford University Press.

Williamson, J. 1990. "What Washington means by policy reform." In *Latin American Adjustment: How Much Has Happened?* ed. J. Williamson. Washington, DC: Institute for International Economics.

Williamson, P. J., Ramamurti, R., Fleury, A., and Fleury, M. (eds.). 2013. *The Competitive Advantage of Emerging Market Multinationals.* Cambridge University Press.

Williamson, P. J., and Yin, E. 2014. "Accelerated innovation: The new challenge from China." *MIT Sloan Management Review* (Summer). Available at http://sloanreview.mit.edu.

Wilson, K., and Doz, Y. D. 2011. "Agile innovation: A footprint balancing distance and immersion." *California Management Review* 53(2): 6–26.

Witt, Michael A. 2006. *Changing Japanese Capitalism: Societal Coordination and Institutional Adjustment.* Cambridge University Press.

2014. "South Korea: Plutocratic state-led capitalism reconfiguring." In *The Oxford Handbook of Asian Business Systems,* ed. M. A. Witt and G. Redding. Oxford University Press.

Witt, M. A., and Lewin, A. Y. 2007. "Outward foreign direct investment as escape response to home country institutional constraints." *Journal of International Business Studies* 38(4): 579–594.

Witt, M. A., and Redding, G. 2009. "Culture, meaning, and institutions: Executive rationale in Germany and Japan." *Journal of International Business Studies* 40(5): 859–895.

2013. "Asian business systems: Institutional comparison, clusters and implications for varieties of capitalism and business systems theory." *Socio-Economic Review* 11(2): 265–300.

(eds.). 2014. *The Oxford Handbook of Asian Business Systems*. Oxford University Press.

Witt, M. A., and Stahl, G. K. 2015. "Foundations of responsible leadership: Asian versus Western executive responsibility orientations toward key stakeholders." *Journal of Business Ethics*. DOI:10.1007/s10551-014-2534-8.

Wittfogel, K. A. 1957. *Oriental Despotism: A Comparative View of Total Power*. New Haven: Yale University Press.

Woo-Cumings, M., ed. 1999. *The Developmental State*. Ithaca: Cornell University Press.

World Bank. 2002. *Transition, the First Ten Years: Analysis and Lessons for Eastern Europe and Former Soviet Union*. Washington, DC: World Bank.

——— 2005. *Economic Growth in the 1990s: Learning from a Decade of Reform*. Washington, DC: World Bank.

——— 2010a. "Exploring the middle-income trap." In *World Bank East Asia Pacific Economic Update: Robust Recovery, Rising Risks*, vol. 2. Washington, DC: World Bank.

——— 2010b. "Research for Development: A World Bank Perspective on Future Directions for Research." Policy Research Working Paper 5437. Washington, DC: World Bank.

——— 2015. "GDP growth (annual percent)." Available at http://data.worldbank.org/indicator/NY.GDP.MKTP.KD.ZG/. Accessed September 15, 2015.

World Bank & Development Research Center of the State Council, P. R. C. 2013. *China 2030: Building a Modern, Harmonious, and Creative Society*. Washington, DC: World Bank.

World Intellectual Property Organization. 2015. "WIPO IP statistics data center." Available at http://ipstats.wipo.int/ipstatv2/.

World Values Survey. 2009. *World Values Survey 2005 Official Data File V. 20090901*. Madrid: World Values Association.

Wu, H. 2009. "Zhongguo zhishi chanquan fazhi jianshe de pingjia yu fansi" [An evaluation and reflection of China's IPR legal framework establishments]. *Zhongguo faxue* 1: 51–68.

Wu, J. 2011. 转变发展方式政府改革更关键 忌投资'大跃进 [In transforming the development model, it is most important that the government reforms avoid an investment "Great Leap Forward"]. *Renmin Ribao*, January 19.

Wu, Y., Yang, Y., and Chiu, C. Y. 2014. "Responses to religious norm defection: The case of Hui Chinese Muslims not following the halal diet." *International Journal of Intercultural Relations* 39: 1–8.

Xin, K., and Pearce, J. 1996. "Guanxi: Connections as substitutes for formal institutional support." *Academy of Management Journal* 39(6): 1641–1658.

Xinhua News. 2012. "San men: chutai zhuanli jiangli zhengce gao faming chuangzao jiangli 10 wan" [Sanmen: Releases of patent remuneration policies introducing invention awards of 100,000]. November 21. Available at www.zj.xinhuanet.com/dfnews/2012–11/21/c_1137495 26.htm.

——— 2015. "Zuigao fa xiugai sifa jieshi mingque zhuanli jiufen anjian peichang shu'e" [Supreme Court amends judicial interpretation to clarify patent dispute cases' compensation amount]. January 29. Available at http://news.xinhuanet.com/legal/2015-01/29/c_1114183 208.htm.

Xu, C. 2011. "The fundamental institutions of China's reforms and development." *Journal of Economic Literature* 49(4): 1076–1151.

Xu, X. 2002. "Have the Chinese provinces become integrated under reform?" *China Economic Review* 13(2–3): 116–133.

Xue, L. 2006. "Universities in China's national innovation system." United Nations Educational, Scientific, and Cultural Organization's online Forum on Higher Education, Research, and Knowledge, November 27–30. Available at http://portal.unesco.org/education/en/files/51614/ 11634233445XueLan-EN.pdf/XueLan-EN.pdf.

——— 2009. "Globalization of S&T in China: Current status and new policies." Tsinghua University. March 29. Available at www.oecd.org/sti/sci-tech/ 42719725.pdf.

Yang, D. Y., and H. K. Wang. 2008. "Dilemmas of local governance under the development zone fever in China: A case study of the Suzhou Region." *Urban Studies* 45(5–6): 1037–1054.

Yip, G., and McKern, B. 2014. "China's many types of innovation." *Forbes Asia*.

Young, A. 2000. "The razor's edge: Distortions and incremental reform in the People's Republic of China." *Quarterly Journal of Economics* 114(4): 1091–1135.

Yusuf, S., and Nabeshima, K. 2009. "Can Malaysia escape middle income trap? A strategy for Penang." Policy Research Working Paper 4971. World Bank, Washington, DC.

Zablit, H., and Chui, B. 2013. "The next wave of Chinese cost innovators." *BCG Perspectives*, January 23.

Zander, U., and Kogut, B. 1995. "Knowledge and the speed of the transfer and imitation of organizational capabilities: An empirical test." *Organization Science* 6(1): 76–92.

Zeng, M., and Williamson, P. J. 2008. *Dragons at Your Door: How Chinese Cost Innovation Is Disrupting Global Business*. Boston: Harvard Business School Press.

Zhan, S., Bendapudi, N., and Hong, Y. Y. 2015. "Re-examining diversity as a double-edged sword for innovation process." *Journal of Organizational Behavior* 36: 1026–1049.

Zhang, C., Zeng, D. Z., Mako, W. P., and Seward, J. 2009. *Promoting Enterprise-Led Innovation in China*. Washington, DC: World Bank.

Zhang, G., and Chen, X. 2012. "The value of invention patents in China: Country origin and technology field differences." *China Economic Review* 23: 357–370.

Zhang, H., Patton, D., and Kenney, M. 2013. "Building global-class universities: Assessing the impact of the 985 Project." *Research Policy* 42(3): 765–775.

Zhang, J., and Lin, S. 2014. "Business and government." In *Understanding Chinese Firms from Multiple Perspectives*, ed. Z. X. Zhang and J. J. Zhang, 51–79. New York: Springer.

Zhang, Z. X. 2014. "The growth path of entrepreneurs." In *Understanding Chinese Firms from Multiple Perspectives*, ed. Z. X. Zhang and J. J. Zhang, 81–118. New York: Springer.

Zhao, R. 2015. "Zhishi chanquan zhuanhua" [Intellectual property transfer]. International Symposium on Intellectual Property Management at Universities and Research Institutes, Zhejiang University Research Institute for Intellectual Property Management, Zhejiang, China.

Zhao, X., and Sun, X. 2015. "Returning graduates face tight domestic job market." *China Daily*, March 18.

Zhao, Y. 2014. *Who's Afraid of the Big Bad Dragon: Why China Has the Best (and the Worst) Education System in the World*. San Francisco: Jossey-Bass.

Zhejiang University. 2005. "Zhejiang daxue keji chengguo zhishi chanquan guanli banfa" [Zhejiang University science and technology achievements IPR management measures]. March 29. Available at www.doe.zju.edu.cn/attachments/2009-11/01-1259202643-39371.doc.

Zheng, Y. 2013. *Wu guo jiaoyu bingli [The Pathology of Chinese Education]*. Beijing: Zhongxin Press.

Zhong, Y. 2003. *Local Government and Politics in China*. Armonk, NY: M. E. Sharpe.

Zhou, L. 2015. "More wealthy Chinese set to flood US investor visa scheme: Think tank report." *South China Morning Post*, March 19. Available at www.scmp.com/news/china/article/1742325/more-wealthy-chinese-set-fl ood-us-investor-visa-scheme-think-tank-report?utm_source=edm&ut m_medium=edm&utm_content=20150320&utm_campaign=scmp_to day/. Accessed March 19, 2015.

Zhou, N., and Delios, A. 2012. "Diversification and diffusion: A social networks and institutional perspective." *Asia Pacific Journal of Management* 29(3): 773–798.

Zhu, X. 2014. "Mandate versus championship: Vertical government intervention and diffusion of innovation in public services in authoritarian China." *Public Management Review* 16(1): 117–139.

Zimmerman, A., and M. F. Bollbach. 2015. "Institutional and cultural barriers to transferring lean production to China: Evidence from a German automotive components manufacturer." *Asian Business and Management* 14(1): 53–85.

Zucker, L. G. 1986. "Production of trust: Institutional sources of economic structure, 1840–1920." In *Research in Organizational Behavior*, vol. 8: 53–111. Stamford, CT: JAI Press.

Zweig, D. 2002. *Internationalizing China: Domestic Interests and Global Linkages*. Ithaca: Cornell University Press.

Zweig, D., Chen, C., and Rosen, S. 2004. "Globalization and transnational human capital: Overseas and returnee scholars to China." *China Quarterly* 179: 735–757.

Zweig, D., and Wang, H. 2013. "Can China bring back the best? The Communist Party organizes China's search for talent." *China Quarterly* 215: 590–615.

Index

aerospace industry. *See* Chinese
  aerospace industry
agriculture-abundant countries, 48–49
Airbus, 234–235
Alibaba, 407
anti-corruption campaign, 4–5
Argentina
  MIT in, 108
  patents and, 110–111
asset-augmenting R&D strategy,
  270–271
asset-exploiting R&D strategy,
  270–271
asset-related advantages, 228

behavioral approaches, to cross-
  cultural research, 397
Beijing model, 111
Beinhocker, Eric, 71
benevolent hierarchy, 78–79
BGI, 254–255
biracials and biculturals/multiculturals,
  401–402
brain circulation, 400
Brazil
  MIT in, 108
  patents and, 110–111
business systems
  of China today, 92–95
  Korean changes in, 97–100
  literature, 90
  model, 92
  of 1980 Korea, 95–96

capital. *See also* human capital; social
  capital; venture capital
  accumulation of, 37–38
  research and cost of, 142–144
capitalism
  benevolent hierarchy and, 78–79

Leninist party-state and, 134–135
  varieties of, 90, 91
CCP. *See* Chinese Communist Party
central authority, societal structure and,
  67–68
China
  business systems of, current, 92–95
  concluding reflections on, 418–425
  context and MNEs, 224–226
  cooperation challenge of, 72–74
  global sourcing of innovation and,
    275–287
  group centrism in, 381–382
  India, in global outsourcing industry,
    301–304
  India and online marketplaces,
    290–291
  India compared with, 275–287,
    290–291, 301–304
  innovation capability of, 111–112
  innovation challenge of, 75–77
  innovation systems in, 278–279
  Japan compared with, 69–71
  Korea, studying, and, 102–105
  middle income status success of,
    122–124
  MNEs and, 224–226, 230–232, 239
  new structuralism and, 49–51
  optimistic view of, 6–14
  outsourcing hubs in, 279, 280
  overview of issues related to,
    xvii–xviii
  patenting activities in, 284–285, 286
  per capita income and, 49
  pessimistic view of, 15–18
  R&D intensity in, 281–283
  R&D investment growth in, 281
  R&D investments by US companies
    and, 283–284
  rules of order, 70

China (cont.)
  technological specialization in,
    112–117
  Three Rules for Understanding
    China, 239
  unit of identity in, 69
China Securities Regulatory
  Commission (CSRC), 167–168
Chinese aerospace industry
  Airbus and, 234–235
  context, 232–233
  government control of, 233
  MNEs and, 232–236
  process improvement in, 235–236
  rivalries in, 234
  Rolls-Royce and, 235
  stages to maturity of, 233–234
  wing-boxes and, 235
Chinese Communist Party (CCP). *See
  also* Leninist party-state
  anti-corruption campaign of, 4–5
  Common Program of, 8
Churchill, Winston, 412
civilization pretending to be state, 68
CMEs. *See* coordinated market
  economies
collaboration, MNEs and, 258–260
Common Program, 8
comparative advantage
  factor endowments and, 37
  global outsourcing industry
    redefinition of, 332–333
  identifying latent, 42–43
  industrial policy and, 42–43
  Tencent and, 355–357
  tradable goods industries and,
    43–44
comparative management models
  Alibaba and, 407
  development of comprehensive,
    406–410
  Haier and, 407–408
  Huawei and, 406–407
  shanzhaism and, 408–409
  systems approach to, 408–409
  Xiaomi and, 408
competition
  cooperation and, 71
  digital service economy and, 5
  SOEs and, 80

complexity
  economics, 87
  hierarchy and, 79–80
  societal progress and, 59–60
  strands of, 61–62
  UMP, 170
consumption, financial repression and,
  125
contagion thesis, 73
cool-water hypothesis, 66–67
cooperation
  China's challenge of, 72–74
  competition and, 71
  innovation and, 56–57
  institutions as insurance, 72
  network perspective and, 201–202
  role of, 71–72
  SMEs and, 201–202
  societal progress and, 63–64
  as stabilizing, 59
  trust and, 71–72
coordinated market economies (CMEs),
  91
corruption
  anti-corruption campaign, 4–5
  industrial policymaking and, 134
  pessimistic view and, 16–17
countercyclical policy, 47–48
country-specific advantages (CSAs),
  227–228
creative goods and services, 369–370
creativity
  barriers, organizational, to, 345–355
  entrepreneurial spirit fostering,
    361–362
  group centrism and, 382–384
  Huawei's, 357–360
  inertia inhibiting, 346–347
  knowledge management and,
    353–354
  lack of organizational capability in
    managing, 352–354
  local protectionism inhibiting,
    347–348
  mainstream management principles
    fostering, 362–363
  manufacturing model and, 353
  market segmentation inhibiting,
    347–348
  online, 369–370

overview about, 26–27, 339–340,
345–346
practices enhancing, 355–360
private ownership and, 360
regional distribution of
entrepreneurial spirit and,
348–352
resource allocation and, 353
shortage of talent with skills in,
354–355
suggestions for fostering, 360–363
team, 382–384
Tencent's, 355–357
uneven distribution of
entrepreneurial spirit inhibiting,
348–352
credit
financial repression and, 125–126
industrial policymaking and,
131–132
cross-cultural management
behavioral approaches and, 397
comparative management models
development and, 406–410
conclusions about, 412
cultural differences and distance
reconceptualized, 410–411
cultural distance and, 403–404
cultural intelligence development,
411–412
eclectic approach and, 397–398
environmental approach and,
396–397
evolution of research in, 395–398
future research directions in,
405–412
homogeneous impact of cultural
distance and, 404
individual distance measures and,
404–405
overview about, 28, 394–395
reframing research on, 398–405
socio-economic approach and,
395–396
spatial homogeneity within single
nation and, 399–402
cross-cultural research
behavioral approaches to, 397
eclectic approach to, 397–398
environmental approach to, 396–397

socio-economics approach to,
395–396
CSAs. *See* country-specific advantages
CSRC. *See* China Securities Regulatory
Commission
cultural analysis, 26–28
cultural constraints
cultural diversity and, 378–380
on innovation, 378–387
cultural contexts. *See* institutional and
cultural contexts
cultural distance
homogeneous impact of, 404
negative outcomes and, 403–404
reconceptualized, 410–411
cultural diversity, 378–380
cultural intelligence development,
411–412
Cultural Revolution, education
disrupted by, 8
culture. *See also* cross-cultural management; institutional and cultural
contexts
biracials and biculturals/
multiculturals, 401–402
clashes in, 77
imitation furthered by, 16
Korean, 95
*Culture's Consequences: International
Differences in Work-related Values*
(Hofstede), 394

decentralization
of hierarchy, 79–80
overview about, 19–20
democracy
future prospects for, 103
Korea and, 98–99
MIT and, 5
Deng Xiaoping, 153
liberalization unleashed by, 6–7
S&T and, 153–154
development economics
emergence of, 32
neoliberalism and, 33–34
new structuralism and, 34–35
rethinking, 32–35
structuralism and, 32–33
development incentives. *See* local government development incentives

development zone fever, 129–130
digital service economy
    competition and, 5
    economic growth from, 5–6
discovery units, 255–256
diversity, cultural, 378–380
domestic markets
    MNEs and, 250–251
    optimistic view of, 12–13

East Asian economies, 132
economic restructuring
    first period 1949–1978, 305
    outsourcing service model cities and,
        308–330
    overview of, 304
    Policy 18 and, 307–308
    second period, 1978-early 2000,
        305–307
    third period, early 2000s, 307–330
    Thousand-Hundred-Ten project and,
        308
economic wealth, institutions and,
    88–89
economic zones, special, 45
economics. *See also* development eco-
    nomics; socio-economics
    complexity, 87
    hard targets for, 127–129
    performance and cadre promotion
        link, 127–128
    role of government in crisis of, 47–48
economy
    digital service, 5–6
    diminishing returns in, 4–5
    evolution of, 1–2
    human costs related to, 2–3
    savings rates, 2
    size of, 1–2
education. *See also* knowledge;
    universities
    Cultural Revolution disrupting, 8
    human capital formation and,
        139–140
    Korea and, 101, 102
    MIT and, 110
    optimism about, 139–140
    Project 211 and Project 985 and,
        376–377
    quality of, 279–281

R&D and, 3
SMEs and, 196
EHCNs. *See* ex-host country nationals
Eisenstadt, Shmuel, 69
employment on-demand, 267
Enterprise Tax Law, 155
enterprise-level analysis, 23–24
entrepreneurial mind-sets, 342, 345
entrepreneurial perspective
    individual leadership and, 204
    innovation factors within, 204–205
    resource-based view overlapping
        with, 193–194
    SMEs and, 204–207
    studies conducted related to,
        205–206
entrepreneurial spirit, 348–352,
    361–362
environmental approach, to cross-
    cultural research, 396–397
environmental degradation, pessimistic
    view of, 17–18
ex-host country nationals (EHCNs),
    401
exportation, innovation link with, 194
export-dependency, 133–134
externalities, compensation for, 45–46

factor endowments
    comparative advantage and, 37
    new structuralism and, 36–38
Federal Reserve, financial repression
    and, 123
financial repression
    consumption and, 125
    credit and, 125–126
    end of, 125
    Federal Reserve and, 123
    middle income status achieved via,
        123–124
    overview about, 21–22
    Taiwan and, 125
    weapon of massive asset destruction,
        124–127
financial structure, for developing
    countries, 46–47
firm specific advantages (FSAs)
    defined, 227–228
    four categories of, 228
    MNEs and, 227–229

firms, ease of starting new, 422
FirstSolar, 341–342
Founder, 138
FSAs. *See* firm specific advantages

GDP. *See* gross domestic product
GERD. *See* gross national expenditure
on R&D
Germany
US compared with, 90–91, 103–104
working hours in, 103–104
global outsourcing industry
China versus India in, 301–304
comparative advantages redefinition
in, 332–333
conclusions about, 336–337
evolution of, 298–301
industrial structure and company
competitiveness transformation in,
335–336
institutional barriers in Chinese,
304–330
investment priorities resetting in,
333–334
mindset, changing, in, 331
policy development and, 330–336
policy-making simplification and,
331–332
research, areas for further, 330–336
global sourcing, of innovation
China and India and, 275–287
conclusions about, 292–294
defined, 269–270
employment on-demand, 267
enterprise manufacturing sector and,
271–273
history of, 270, 289
implications and challenges
concerning, 292–294
implications for emerging economies,
294
implications for SMEs innovation,
292–293
in-house innovation sourcing and,
268
innovation capabilities challenges,
293
IP challenges, 293–294
offshoring and outsourcing and,
269–272

online marketplaces for STEM talent,
287–292
organizational capabilities
challenges, 293
overview, 267–268
R&D strategies and, 270–271
SMEs and, 271–273, 292–293
sourcing models and, 269
STEM talent and, 279
supply side of, 273
government. *See also* local government
development incentives
Chinese aerospace industry and, 233
incentives, 340–341
intervention, 38–40, 238–242
MNEs and, 238–243
role in economic crisis, 47–48
S&T appropriation fund statistics, 159
gradualism, 130–131
Great Britain, 42–43
gross domestic product (GDP), 110,
111–112
gross national expenditure on R&D
(GERD)
government S&T appropriation fund
statistics and, 159
university funding sources, 161
group centrism
in China, 381–382
integrative research and, 384–386
negative effects of, 380–381
team creativity and, 382–384
growth patterns
at Chinese companies, 340–342
conclusions about, 342
example of, 341–342
government incentives, 340–341
market demands, 340
guanxi (bonding with strong supportive
norms about reciprocity), 71–72

Haier, 407–408
hierarchy
benevolent, 78–79
complexity and, 79–80
decentralization of, 79–80
initiative and, 78–79
innovativeness fused with, 80–81
innovativeness problem within,
77–79

High Power Distance/Collectivism, 64
high-level equilibrium trap, 87
Hofstede, G., 394
home base-exploiting and augmenting
    R&D strategies, 270–271
Hu Jintao, 154
Huawei, 140–146
    comparative management models
        and, 406–407
    conclusions about, 359–360
    creativity of, 357–360
    information system of, 358
    innovation-follower strategy of,
        358–359
    keys to success at, 360, 361
    overview about, 357–358
    relationship-oriented routines of, 358
    summary of strategies used by, 361
    surrounding cities from countryside
        strategy of, 358
    talent recruiting at, 359
    TM R&D and, 358–359
human capital
    formation, 139–140
    institutional constraints on, 376–378
    role of, 372–375
hybrid firms, technology and, 139

ICT. *See* information and communica-
    tions technology
imitation
    culture furthering, 16
    innovation and, 3–4
    *The Knockoff Economy: How
        Imitation Sparks Innovation*,
        408–409
    shanzhaism, 408–409
immigration, spatial homogeneity and,
    399–400
India
    versus China, in global outsourcing
        industry, 301–304
    China and online marketplaces
        compared with, 290–291
    China compared with, 275–287,
        290–291, 301–304
    fiber optic systems and, 45
    global sourcing of innovation and,
        275–287
    innovation systems in, 278–279

    patenting activities in, 284–285, 286
    R&D investments by US companies
        and, 283–284
    services outsourcing overview and,
        25–26
    university rankings in, 277
individual
    analysis, 26–28
    distance measures, 404–405
    leadership, 81, 204
    Low Power Distance/Individualism,
        64
industrial policy
    comparative advantage and, 42–43
    economic zones and, 45
    failure, reasons for, 41
    growth identification and facilitation
        and, 40–46
    obstacle identification and, 44
    paying attention to successful new
        industries, 45
    pioneering firms compensated for
        externalities, 45–46
    relocation of firms and, 44
    six-step framework for, 43–46
    tradable goods industries and, 43–44
    what's needed for successful, 42–43
industrial policymaking
    constraints to effective, 132–134
    corruption and, 134
    credit and, 131–132
    East Asian economies and, 132
    export-dependency and, 133–134
    information asymmetries and,
        133
    obstacles to effective, 131–134
    SOE finance misallocation and,
        132–135
    structure of the state apparatus and,
        132
industrial revolutions, 60–61
Industrial Technology Research
    Institute (ITRI), 384–385
information and communications
    technology (ICT), 288–289
initiative, hierarchy and, 78–79
innovation. *See also* creativity; global
    sourcing, of innovation; national
    innovation system
    Beijing model of, 111

China's capability of, 111–112
China's challenge of, 75–77
cooperation and, 56–57
cultural constraints on, 378–387
culture clashes and, 77
as destructive, 59
education and, 110
empowerment and, 75–76
entrepreneurial perspective and,
  204–205
exporting link with, 194
factors influencing, 192–207
footprints optimization, 254–256
growth slowdown and, 109–110
handicapped, 26
hierarchy fused with, 80–81
hierarchy problem and, 77–79
history of, 6–7
Huawei and, 358–359
human capital role for, 372–375
imitation and, 3–4
incremental, 206
India's systems of, 278–279
inertia inhibiting routines of,
  346–347
institution support role for, 372–375
institutional barriers to, 198
institutional constraints on, 375–376
*The Knockoff Economy: How
  Imitation Sparks Innovation,*
  408–409
knowledge flows and, 249
Li encouraging, 7–8
Marx and, 4
MIT and, 109–111
MNEs and, 249–256
new structuralism and, 35–36
new-to-world, 423
organizational qualities needed for,
  76
overview about, 25
patents and, 7, 112, 113
quantitative indications of, 111–112
questions surrounding, 77
R&D-GDP ratio and, 110, 111–112
requirements, 74–75
role of, 74–75
routines of, 346–347
SMEs and, 190–207
at societal level, 76–77

societal progress and, 63–64
systems, in China and India, 278–279
technology transfer and, 75, 79
types of, 369–372
unemployment and, 420
vertical collectivism and, 386–387
weak institutions for funding,
  136–138
workshop and, 75
innovation-follower strategy, 358–359
*An Inquiry into the Nature and Causes
  of the Wealth of Nations* (Smith),
  35
institutional and cultural contexts
  conclusions about, 388–390
  cultural constraints on innovation,
    378–387
  cultural diversity, 378–380
  group centrism, in China, 381–382
  group centrism, negative effects of,
    380–381
  human capital, institutional
    constraints on, 376–378
  human capital role and, 372–375
  innovation, institutional constraints
    on, 375–376
  innovation types and, 369–372
  institution support role and, 372–375
  overview, 368–369
  Project 211 and Project 985 and,
    376–377
  TTP and, 377–378
  vertical collectivism and, 386–387
institutional and structural obstacles
  to industrial policymaking, 131–134
  Leninist party-state, 134–135
  middle income status impacted by,
    131–138
  overview, 131
  to policies conductive for further
    development, 131–138
  weak institutions for funding
    innovation, 136–138
institutional perspective
  institutional barriers and, 198
  IP protection and, 197
  networking and, 196–197
  resource-based view overlapping
    with, 193–194
  SMEs and, 196–199

institutional voids, 197
  factors causing, 198–199
insurance, institutions as, 72
intangible assets, 369–370
intellectual property (IP). *See also*
    patents
  conclusions about, 176–179
  effectiveness of system of, 421
  global sourcing of innovation
      challenges for, 293–294
  legal risks and, 166–167
  overview about, 22
  ownership and decision-making
      authority, 165
  pessimistic view regarding, 16
  policy constraints and, 164–168
  profits distribution from university-
      owned, 168
  SMEs and, 197
  technology transfer and, 164–168
  universities and, 165, 166–167,
      168
intellectual property rights (IPR)
  background leading to, 152–153
  conclusions about, 176–179
  financial system abuses, 157–158
  reward and punishment imbalances
      and, 158
  self-serving behavior and, 157–158
interdisciplinary research, 384
invention
  applications, 155
  history of, 6–7
invisible barriers. *See* societal forces,
    invisible
IP. *See* intellectual property
IPR. *See* intellectual property rights
ITRI. *See* Industrial Technology
    Research Institute

Japan
  China compared with, 69–71
  comparative advantage and, 42–43
  decentralization in, 70–71
  human capital formation and,
      139–140
  rules of order and, 70
  Shinto and, 69–70
  unit of identity in, 69
junk patents, 156–157

*The Knockoff Economy: How
    Imitation Sparks Innovation*
    (Raustiala & Sprigman), 408–409
knowledge
  creation, 369–370
  diffusion, 369–370
  from external sources, 200
  flows, 249
  impact, 369–370
  management systems, 353–354
  MNEs and, 253
  SMEs and, 210–211
Korea
  background related to, 87–89
  business system changes, 97–100
  conclusions about, 102–105
  constants, 100–102
  at cultural level, 95
  democratization in, 98–99
  education and, 101, 102
  future research implications,
      102–105
  human capital formation and,
      139–140
  implications for China from
      studying, 102–105
  indirect finance in, 101
  at middle level, 95–96
  1980 business systems of, 95–96
  overview, 20–21, 89
  patents and, 110–111
  Samsung and, 102
  short technology cycles and, 115–117
  since 1980, 96–102
  at top level, 96
  top-down decision making in, 101

labor
  factors, leading to middle income
      status, 122
  migration and, 4–5
land used as collateral, 128–129
Law on Promoting the Transformation
    of Scientific and Technological
    Achievement, 165
leaders, business
  bureaucratic mind-set, 342
  entrepreneurial mind-set, 342, 345
  mind-sets of, 342–345
  risk averse mind-set, 343–344

short-term mind-set, 342–343
social networks mind-set, 343–344
of SOEs, 344–345
leadership, individual, 81, 204
Lee Kun-hee, 102
Leninist party-state
anti-reform elements within, 135
capitalism and, 134–135
institutional and structural obstacles
and, 134–135
self-conflicted policies of, 134
li. See rules of order
Li Keqiang, xvii, 7–8
liberal market economies (LMEs), 91
local government development
incentives
development zone fever and,
129–130
economic performance and cadre
promotion link and, 127–128
hard economic targets and, 127–129
land used as collateral and, 128–129
local cadre performance and,
127–128
middle income status and, 127–130
as obstacles to future development,
127–130
revenue and, 128–129
zhaoshang yinzi and, 128, 130
location bound advantages, 228
Low Power Distance/Individualism, 64

Ma, Jack, 407
Management and Organization Review
(MOR) Research Frontiers
Conference, xvii
market segmentation, 347–348
Marx, Karl, 4
masks
cultural distance, 403–404
homogeneous impact of cultural
distance, 404
individual distance measures, 404–405
spatial homogeneity within single
nation, 399–402
middle income status
China's pillars of, 122–124
conclusions about, 146
financial repression leading to,
123–124

institutional and structural obstacles
impacting, 131–138
labor factors leading to, 122
local government development
incentives and, 127–130
policy choices leading to, 122–123
middle income trap (MIT)
anti-corruption campaign and, 4–5
Brazil and Argentina and, 108
conclusions about, 117–118
criteria for assessing, 108–109
defined, 108
democracy and, 5
education and, 110
growth slowdown and, 109–110
innovation and, 109–111
institutions and, 88–89
NIS and, 122–124, 220–223
overview about, 108
patents and, 110–111
R&D-GDP ratio and, 110, 111–112
societal progress and, 60
technological specialization and,
112–117
migrants
labor and, 4–5
social welfare and, 2–3
migration, 4–5
mind-sets
bureaucratic, 342, 343–345
business leaders, 342–345
entrepreneurial, 342, 345
risk averse, 343–344
short-term, 342–343
social networks, 343–344
of SOEs, 344–345
MIT. *See* middle income trap
mixed or state-led market economies,
91
MNEs. *See* multinational enterprises
model cities
barriers caused by policy in,
328–330
downstream outsourcing value-chain
activities focus in, 329–330
goals and policies, 308–330
outsourcing and, 309–327
point to surface policy approach in,
328
supply side focus in, 328–329

MOR. *See Management and
Organization Review* Research
Frontiers Conference
multinational enterprises (MNEs)
absorptive capacity enhancement in,
256–258
acquisitions of, 24
BGI and, 254–255
challenges facing, 256
China and, 224–226, 230–232, 239
Chinese aerospace industry and,
232–236
collaboration optimization and,
258–260
communication enhancement in,
256–258
competitive disadvantage and, 251
conclusions about, 263–264
conventional wisdom and, 249–254
discovery units and, 255–256
discussion, 236–237
domestic market and, 250–251
FSAs and, 227–229
global innovation and, 249–254
go out policy and, 251
government interventions effects and,
238–242
innovation and, 249–256
innovation footprints optimization
and, 254–256
interventions, towards more precise,
242–243
knowledge and, 253
learning and, 23–24
lessons for governments regarding,
242–243
local rules of game and, 237–238
mature technologies acquisition and,
251–252
NIS and middle income trap and,
220–223
overview about, 23–24, 219–220,
248
recombinant advantages and, 226–230
research agenda related to, 260–263
reverse capability upgrading and, 252
study of partnerships in China,
230–232
Three Rules for Understanding China
and, 239

national business systems literature,
90
national innovation system (NIS)
advantages, 224
China's middle income status success
and, 122–124
manufacturing sector and, 225
middle income trap and, 220–223
overview about, 121–122
STEM and, 152
National Intellectual Property Rights
Strategy Outline (NIPSO), 154
National Patent Development Strategy,
145–146
natural resource-abundant countries,
48–49
neoliberalism, 33–34
network perspective
clusters and, 202–204
cooperation and, 201–202
knowledge from external sources
and, 200
lock-in and, 203
resource-based view overlapping
with, 193–194
SMEs and, 199–204
varying forms of networking and,
200–201
networking
institutional perspective and,
196–197
SMEs and, 196–197
social networks mind-set and,
343–344
varying forms of, 200–201
new structuralism
agriculture and, 48–49
application of, 40–46
China's growth and, 49–51
conclusions about, 51–52
countercyclical policy and, 47–48
developing countries, different
financial structure for, 46–47
development economics and, 34–35
economic zones and, 45
endogeneity and, 38–40
factor endowments and, 36–38
government intervention and, 38–40
government's role in economic crisis,
47–48

growth identification and facilitation, 40–46
hypothesis of, 36–38
industrial policy, six-step framework for, 43–46
industrial policy, what's needed for successful, 42–43
industrial policy failure and, 41
industrial upgrading and, 35–36
innovation and, 35–36
natural resource-abundant countries and, 48–49
obstacle identification and, 44
other issues illuminated by, 46–49
overview about, 18–19
paying attention to successful new industries, 45
pioneering firms compensated for externalities, 45–46
relocation of firms and, 44
Ricardian equivalence trap and, 47–48
technological innovation and, 35–36
tradable goods industries and, 43–44
what is, 35–40
new-to-world innovation, share of, 423
NIPSO. *See* National Intellectual Property Rights Strategy Outline
NIS. *See* national innovation system
non-location bound advantages, 228
North, Douglass, 35–36
Northeast Asian advanced economies, 91

offshoring, 269–272
One Hundred Talents Awards, 377–378
one-child policy, savings rates and, 2
online creativity, 369–370
online marketplaces
China compared with India in, 290–291
drivers of, 288–290
emerging economies and, 290
global sourcing history and, 289
growth of platforms and users of, 290
ICT advances and, 288–289
independent contracting and, 289
skill shortage in US driving, 289
for STEM talent on demand, 287–292

technology start-ups, growth of, and, 289
optimistic view
of China's prospects, 6–14
of domestic markets, 12–13
education and, 139–140
history of invention and, 6–7
overview of, xviii
patents and, 7
of STEM workforce, 13–14
technology and, 138–140
universities, upgrading of, 8–11
of VC funding, 11–12
organizational analysis, 26–28
outsourcing. *See also* global outsourcing industry
China's hubs of, 279, 280
offshoring and, 269–272
service model cities, 309–327
services, 25–26

patents. *See also* utility model patent
conclusions about, 176–179
data research, 145–146
flawed policy and, 153–158
incentives to spur applications, 154–156
increase in, 7, 112, 113
India compared with China regarding, 284–285, 286
innovation and, 7, 112, 113
invention applications for country office statistics, 155
IP ownership and decision-making authority and, 165
junk, 156–157
Korea and, 110–111
lack of incentives for, 164
MIT and, 110–111
National Patent Development Strategy, 145–146
optimistic view and, 7
performance and incentives misalignment, 156–157
preferential tax treatment, 155
remuneration, 155
reward and punishment imbalances and, 158
self-serving behavior and, 157–158
subsidies, 154–155

patents (cont.)
  suitability and technology, 175
  technological catch-up and, 112
  at universities, current state of,
    158–163
  universities producing, 10–11
  volume of, 169
patrimonial autocracy
  benevolence evolving in, 82–83
  building social capital in, 81–82
personalism, 422
  overview about, 27–28
  societal progress and, 62
pessimistic view
  of China's prospects, 15–18
  corruption, 16–17
  environmental degradation, 17–18
  global tensions, 18
  governance challenges, due to size,
    15–16
  IP system and, 16
  overview of, xviii
political analysis, 18–22
private sector, 81
Project 211, 376–377
Project 985, 9, 376–377
protection
  IP, 197
  local protectionism, 347–348
  UMP and, 169–176

R&D . *See* research and development
R&D-GDP ratio, 110, 111–112
recombinant advantages
  MNEs and, 226–230
  origins, 227
reform without losers approach, 375
regional variation, 104
relocation of firms, 44
Ren Zhengfei, 140–146, 406–407
research
  cost of capital, 142–144
  heuristics of, 140–146
  markets shaped by state, 144–145
  patent data, 145–146
  placing firms in proper financial
    context and, 141–142
research and development (R&D). *See
  also* gross national expenditure on
    R&D

education and, 3
exploitation of foreign assets of, 423
increase in, 3, 6
intensity of, 281–283
investment growth in China, 281
investments by US companies,
    283–284
R&D-GDP ratio, 110, 111–112
resource allocation effectiveness and,
    421–422
strategies, 270–271
Tencent and, 356–357
TM R&D and, 358–359
researchers, 167–168
resource allocation
  creativity and, 353
  effectiveness, 421–422
resource-based view
  explained, 193
  exporting-innovation link and, 194
  financial resources and, 193
  innovation predictors study related
    to, 195
  other perspectives overlapping with,
    193–194
  SMEs and, 193–196
reverse capability upgrading, 252
Ricardian equivalence trap, 47–48
Rolls-Royce, 235
routines, innovation-oriented, 346–347
Ruiman, Zhang, 407–408
rules of order, 70

Samsung, 102
SASAC. *See* State-Owned Assets
    Supervision and Administration
    Commission
savings rates, 2
scarcity among plenty paradox, 401
science, technology, engineering, and
    mathematics (STEM)
  global innovation activities and, 279
  NIS and, 152
  online marketplaces for talent in,
    287–292
  optimistic view of, 13–14
  overview about, 25
  recruiting skilled talent in, 267–268
  web-based brokerage platforms and,
    268

workforce, 13–14
science and technology (S&T)
  appropriation fund statistics, 159
  Deng and, 153–154
  Hu and, 154
  NIS and, 152
  role of agencies in university, 166
  S&T Progress Law, 165
sectorial-level analysis, 25–26
self-expression/ secular-rational
    pattern, 64–65
services outsourcing, 25–26
shanzhaism (brand imitation), 408–409
Shinto, 69–70
short technology cycles
  conclusions about, 117–118
  explained, 114
  Korea and, 115–117
  overview about, 21
  software and, 114
  Taiwan and, 115–117
  technological specialization and,
    112–117
silo-structure, 101–102
small and medium-size enterprises
    (SMEs)
  background regarding, 189–190
  clusters and, 202–204
  cooperation and, 201–202
  education and, 196
  entrepreneurial perspective and,
    204–207
  financial resources and, 193
  global sourcing of innovation and,
    271–273, 292–293
  innovation and, 190–207
  institutional barriers and, 198
  institutional perspective and,
    196–199
  IP protection and, 197
  knowledge and, 210–211
  level of financing for, 422–423
  lock-in and, 203
  network concept and, 211
  network perspective and, 199–204
  networking and, 196–197
  overview about, 23
  policies encouraging, 195
  policy implications related to,
    207–209

questions for further research,
    210–212
  resource-based view and, 193–196
  sector contrasts and, 212
  as sources of innovation, 190–192
  varying forms of networking and,
    200–201
  VC and, 195–196
Smith, Adam, 35
social capital, building, 81–82
social welfare, migrants and, 2–3
societal forces, invisible
  barriers to success in, 82
  conclusions about, 83–84
  fear and, 82–83
  overview about, 56–58
societal progress
  autocracy and, 59–60
  complexity and, 59–60
  general problem of, 58–60
  innovativeness and cooperativeness
    and, 63–64
  middle class autonomy and, 63
  MIT and, 60
  outside methods and, 61
  personalism and, 62
  processes associated with, 63–64
  realms of, 58–59
  rules for, 60–64
  traditions and, 60–61
societal structures
  central authority and, 67–68
  civilization pretending to be state, 68
  cool-water hypothesis and, 66–67
  evolutionary shaping of, 64–69
  human drives and, 68–69
  self-expression/ secular-rational
    pattern, 64–65
  survival/traditional pattern, 64–65
  theories of evolution of, 65–69
socio-economics
  analysis, 18–22
  approach to cross-cultural research,
    395–396
SOEs. *See* state-owned enterprises
software, 114
sourcing models, 269
spatial homogeneity
  biracials and biculturals/
    multiculturals and, 401–402

spatial homogeneity (cont.)
  brain circulation and, 400
  immigration and, 399–400
  within single nation, 399–402
  war for talent and, 401
S&T . *See* science and technology
S&T Progress Law, 165
State Assets Transfer Interim Measures
    Order No. 3, 165
State-Owned Assets Supervision and
    Administration Commission
    (SASAC), 165, 166, 344–345
state-owned enterprises (SOEs), 23
  business leaders of, 344–345
  competition and, 80
  finance misallocation and,
    132–135
  flaws, 80–81
  mind-sets of, 344–345
  SASAC and, 344–345
  share of resources flowing to, 422
STEM. *See* science, technology, engi-
    neering, and mathematics
structuralism, 32–33. *See also* new
    structuralism
Suntech, 341–342
supply side
  of global sourcing of innovation, 273
  model cities and, 328–329
surrounding cities from countryside
    strategy, 358
survival/traditional pattern, 64–65

Taiwan
  financial repression and, 125
  human capital formation and,
    139–140
  short technology cycles and, 115–117
technology. *See also* science, technol-
    ogy, engineering, and mathematics;
    science and technology; short
    technology cycles
  acquisition of mature, 251–252
  catch-up, 112
  China's specialization in, 112–117
  growth of start-ups in, 289
  human capital formation and,
    139–140
  hybrid firms and, 139
  ICT, 288–289

ITRI, 384–385
Law on Promoting the
    Transformation of Scientific and
    Technological Achievement, 165
MNEs and, 251–252
new structuralism and, 35–36
optimism about, 138–140
patent suitability and, 175
physical, 87
start-ups, growth of, 289
technology transfer
  conclusions about, 176–179
  innovation and, 75, 79
  IP legal risks and, 166–167
  IP ownership and decision-making
    authority and, 165
  IP policy constraints and, 164–168
  lack of incentives for, 164
  profits distribution from university-
    owned IP and, 168
  role of agencies in S&T, 166
  at universities, 158–163, 164,
    166
  value of university, 163
  volume of university, 159
Telekom Research & Development
    (TM R&D), 358–359
Tencent
  creativity of, 355–357
  keys to success at, 360, 361
  managers of, 356–357
  market-oriented routines of, 356
  open public platforms of, 357
  overview about, 355–356
  R&D and, 356–357
  summary of strategies used by, 361
  synergizing complementarities of,
    356
  talent echelon system of, 357
Thousand Talents Program (TTP),
    377–378
  vertical collectivism and, 386–387
Thousand-Hundred-Ten project, 308
Three Rules for Understanding China,
    239
TM R&D. *See* Telekom Research &
    Development
tradable goods industries, 43–44
transaction-related advantages, 228
transdisciplinary research, 384

trust
building social capital for, 81–82
cooperation and, 71–72
institutionalized, 424
TTP. *See* Thousand Talents Program

UMP. *See* utility model patent
unemployment, 420
United States (US)
Federal Reserve, 123
Germany compared with, 90–91,
103–104
R&D investments by companies in,
283–284
skill shortage in, 289
working hours in, 103–104
universities
academic publications, 10
autonomy of Chinese, 424
GERD funding sources, 161
history related to, 8–10
IP legal risks and, 166–167
IP ownership and decision-making
authority and, 165
lack of incentives for patenting and
technology transfer, 164
optimism and, 8–11
patenting activity, current state of,
158–163
patents and, 10–11
policy impediments to, 167–168
profits distribution from IP, 168
Project 211 and, 376–377
Project 985 and, 9, 376–377
role of agencies in S&T technology
transfer and, 166
technology transfer, current state of,
158–163
upgrading of, 8–11
value of technology transfer at, 163
volume of technology transfers at, 159
US. *See* United States
utility model patent (UMP)
abuses, 170–171
approval times, 171
behavioral preferences differences
and, 175–176

complexity of, 170
conclusions about, 176–178
current development status of,
169–170
examination process, 170
filing fees, 171
invalidated in 2008 compared to
2007, 171
invalidation rates, 171
invalidation requests, 171
low foreign activity reasons,
173–176
perceived system weaknesses, 175
protection system effectiveness,
169–176
technology and patent suitability,
175
validity of, challenging, 171–173

variable interest entity (VIE), 137–138
Varieties of Capitalism literature, 90
venture capital (VC)
alternatives to, 138
foreign, 137–138
laws regarding, 136
optimistic view of, 11–12
SMEs and, 195–196
sources of, 137
weaknesses of, 136–138
vertical collectivism, 386–387
VIE. *See* variable interest entity

war for talent, 401
Washington Consensus
Chile and, 40
lost decades and, 33–34
weapon of massive asset destruction,
124–127
wind power, 142–143
wing-boxes, 235
World Values Surveys, 64–65

Xi Jinping, 4–5
Xiaomi, 408

zhaoshang yinzi (luring investment),
128, 130